TO ASSIST YOU IN EXAMINING –

HUMAN RELATIONS IN MANAGEMENT

Second Edition

By

S. G. Huneryager

I. L. Heckmann

The objective of the book is to present "human relations" as an emerging scientific discipline of study.

A STRUCTURED READINGS BOOK

This textbook provides a unique blending of text material and selected articles. Basic concepts and principles concerning man at work are emphasized. The viewpoints and opinions of the authors are expressed in the text material (see pages 1 to 7) that draws the articles into related segments (see pages 8 to 100). In addition, note on pages 99 and 100 the type of questions provided with each article and with Part I. Your specific attention is drawn to Question 6 on page 100.

A MULTIPURPOSE BOOK

HUMAN RELATIONS IN MANAGEMENT is not merely a readings book. It is specifically designed for many uses on both the undergraduate and graduate level and for executive development programs. It is a valuable contribution to the instructional literature in the field and may be used as:

(1) a basic textbook for the (a) case or lecture course in human relations, (b) advanced personnel management course, and (c) dynamics of organization course

(2) a supplementary text for courses in industrial psychology, industrial sociology, labor problems, business policy relating to personnel, and administration.

HUMAN RELATIONS IN MANAGEMENT

─SECOND EDITION─

S. G. HUNERYAGER

Associate Professor of Management
College of Business Administration
University of Illinois, Chicago Circle

I. L. HECKMANN

Dean and Professor of Management
College of Business Administration
The Creighton University

Published by
SOUTH-WESTERN PUBLISHING COMPANY

Cincinnati
Chicago

New Rochelle, N. Y.

Burlingame, Calif.
Dallas

P16

Library of Congress Catalog Card Number: 67-10071

3 4 5 6 H 3 2 1 0 9

Printed in the United States of America

PREFACE

The second edition of this book represents a substantial revision of our first effort. It includes an expanded number of articles (53) of which 38 are entirely new. Furthermore, 30 of the new articles bear a publication date of 1960 or later, thus indicating our express purposes of combining new and challenging material with some of the more classical and established thinking in the field. The reader familiar with the first edition will also find a significant change in the organization and major content areas of this edition. Two completely new sections—Parts II and IX—have been added, and all other sections have been extensively reoriented and updated to keep them abreast of current developments and research.

Like all fields of knowledge and study in this age of rapid technological development, the seven years which have elapsed since this book was first published have witnessed a truly remarkable advance in our knowledge, skills, and understandings of the complexity of human behavior and organized efforts in working organizations and institutions of all types and sizes. It is our sincere hope that this revision reflects, digests, and effectively integrates as much of this new knowledge as possible for every student and reader. While it is impossible to include all the particular organizational and personal interests of individual readers, we are confident that this edition does span and include the most significant and pertinent topics, issues, and concepts currently being studied, researched, and analyzed with respect to human beings at work in organizations.

We continue to maintain in this edition that "human relations" is an emerging scientific discipline of study. It is quite true that such terms as "organization behavior," "organization theory," "administrative behavior," and "organization pathology," have become very popular terms recently, in many instances taking precedence over the term "human relations." Indeed, the latter term has incurred the disfavor of many students for various and sundry reasons. Such disagreement is healthy disagreement, of course, since it is indicative of the surging impact of the behavioral sciences on managements in all types of organizations. However, our decision to retain the term "human relations," both in the title of the book and in the introductions to each section, falls back upon our stated purpose of summarizing and integrating for present and future managers in all types of organizations the most pertinent and basic knowledge about the behavior, motivations, and interrelationships of the human resources which they must effectively and productively influence, direct, and lead.

We have also increased the scope of this edition. Although the business institution is still the basic organizational frame of reference, more attention is given many other types of organizations and institutions which cope with the same types of human problems as do business firms. We hope that our approach will facilitate the reader's understanding of the nature of the discipline of human relations. And since the practice of any function is correlated with one's knowledge and understanding of the function concerned, we likewise hope that this approach will contribute to an increase in the reader's effectiveness in practicing human relations at work and in his everyday life.

In order to facilitate its purpose, this book is constructed so that it can be used in a number of ways in the academic and business worlds. For example, it can be efficiently used as a basic textbook in human relations and organizational behavior in certain liberal arts, engineering, and business administration courses, or as a supplementary text in a case or problems course in human relations, personnel management, organization theory, administrative behavior, or related courses. We hope that the questions at the end of each article and at the end of each part will be used to strengthen the reader's understanding of human relations and administration. For the business world this book is designed so that it can be effectively used as a basic text or reference book for industrial training courses and management development programs. In addition, the busy executive who does not have time to search out the significant articles in the field will find this book useful for increasing his knowledge and understanding of the complexities of human behavior at work.

We should like to express our gratitude to the many authors and publishers, particularly the American Management Association, who so cooperatively granted permission to reprint the articles used in this book. A note of appreciation is also due to our many friends and colleagues who have contributed comments and criticisms on various topics and ideas expressed throughout the book.

S. G. Huneryager

I. L. Heckmann

CONTENTS

PART III. LEADERSHIP

PART IV. MOTIVATION AND BEHAVIOR

PART V. ORGANIZATION STRUCTURE AND DYNAMICS

PART VI. COMMUNICATION

PART VII. PARTICIPATION AND GROUP DYNAMICS

PART VIII. ORGANIZATIONAL CHANGE

PART IX. HUMAN RELATIONS SKILLS, SENSITIVITY, AND PRODUCTIVITY

PART X. HUMAN RELATIONS IN PERSPECTIVE

PART I. HUMAN RELATIONS AND ADMINISTRATION: AN OVERVIEW

The concept of human relations

When this book was first published, the term "human relations" was the then-current vogue for depicting the complexity of relationships existing between people in working organizations. Because of the maze of connotations given the phrase by many people, however, and especially because of the surging advances of behavioral science knowledge as applied to working organizations, the term is not nearly as popular as it once was. Today some prefer such terms as "organization theory," "administrative behavior," "interpersonal relations," "group dynamics," and so on, for describing the behavior of individuals and groups at work.

As our knowledge of human motivation in the formal, working organization has increased immeasurably in the past five years, new theories and new avenues of inquiry have emerged for the interested student to study and pursue. Wherever and whenever appropriate this revised edition incorporates this new knowledge, theory, and practice into its overall content. Nevertheless, the basic foundation of the entire book still rests upon our original stance—that *human relations is a systematic, developing body of knowledge devoted to explaining the behavior of individuals in the working organization.*

Human relations and the behavioral sciences

As the result of recent developments in the social and behavioral sciences, many new and exciting subjects are contributing to the continued advancement of the human relations discipline. Instead of developing into splinter areas, the behavioral sciences are providing valuable new insights into such topics as decision making, communications, organizational conflict, problems of individual and organizational change and innovation, leadership, and creativity.

Whenever an attempt is made to explain human behavior in any set of circumstances, one encounters a rather formidable task. Obviously there are many diverse phenomena affecting man's reactions to individual situations. Our concern here, however, is the work environment. The study of man, behavior, and the industrial environment overlaps into many of the behavioral science fields. An attempt to explain individual and group behavior necessitates an examination of each of these separate disciplines as a primary step, and then a drawing together or an integration of knowledge must closely follow. This is the interdisciplinary approach to human relations.

What fields of study are drawn upon? Indeed, they are varied and diverse. Human relations is really the application of all the behavioral science disciplines to the management of men. The fields of psychology and social psychology, for example, have given us multitudinous amounts of extremely useful concepts concerning the relation of the individual to his work environment. Testing, job placement, job satisfaction, incentives, and many more subjects have been researched intensively by psychologists, with resulting valuable contributions to the study of man's behavior and its causes.

Although somewhat overlapping with social psychology and anthropology, sociologists have certainly made major contributions with their study of groups, their interrelatedness, and their effects upon group members. One of the newest yet most fruitful branches of sociology has been the work of the group dynamics people. Their concepts of role structures, status, and informal groupings are vital to the efficacy of industrial organizations. The Hawthorne Study was more of a sociological study than anything else. In retrospect, many of our most recent developments in human relations have stemmed from this area.

Political science is another field providing useful information with relation to organization, power struggles between groups and individuals, and the overall administrative process. Semantics, one of our newer disciplines, is greatly aiding the field of communications. Industrial engineering virtually speaks for itself. Physiology is making giant contributions in studying monotony, fatigue, boredom, and job placement. Economics and its many branches, especially labor economics, ranks as one of the foremost disciplines contributing to the theory of industrial human relations. Figure 1 contains a more detailed listing of these various disciplines.

Certainly, all of these and still more have and will continue to make their special contribution to what will someday undoubtedly be a general theory of man and work. Even today teams of researchers composed of scientists from several of these fields are combining in common efforts on a myriad of projects. Thus new frontiers are breached continuously, and efforts in all directions regarding human

FIGURE 1

SUBJECTS CONTRIBUTING TO THE STUDY
OF HUMAN RELATIONS

ANTHROPOLOGY

Cultural dynamics
Organization theory
Status symbols
Ethnic relations

BIOLOGY

Organization theory
Viability
Homeostasis

ECOLOGY AND GEOGRAPHY

Location theory
Nucleation
Environmental adaptation
Dispersion processes
Spatial forces

MATHEMATICS

Information theory
Stochastic processes
Set theory
Descriptive and inductive statistics
Theory of games
Decision making
Probability theory
Linear programming

PHILOSOPHY

Ethical principles
Aesthetic principles
Principles of logic
Principles of semantics

PHYSICS

Gravitation theory

POLITICAL SCIENCE

Administrative law
Administrative theory
Trade regulations and practices
Authoritarianism
Organization theory
Bureaucracy

PSYCHOLOGY

Aptitude analysis
Personality analysis
Scaling techniques
Organization theory
Senses and sensations
Learning theory
Motivational analysis
Perception and sensation
Projective techniques
Rationality

SOCIOLOGY

Interpersonal relations
Morale
Role and status
Class behavioral patterns
Class stimuli
Innovation and change
Organization theory
Primary group behavior
Small group activity
Environmental influences
Public opinion
Sociometry
Formal organization
Social change
Group surveys and testing
Social stratification and values
Social institutions

Source: David L. Huff and Joseph W. McGuire, "The Interdisciplinary Approach to the Study of Business," *University of Washington Business Review*, June, 1960.

behavior and worker motivation are resulting in truly amazing discoveries.

Historical background of the human relations movement in industry

A major difficulty in presenting historical facts is the period of time to choose as a starting point. This difficulty does not escape us here. To pinpoint an exact date, year, or even decade as the beginning of the human relations movement in industry and to trace its path from there on is impossible. Obviously, certain relationships have always existed between employer and employee.

It was not, however, until the latter part of the nineteenth century that much attention was given to the human element in business. Previous to this the era of the corporate mogul held forth, with the principal approach to labor being that of the commodity concept of earlier economists, namely, that workers were something to be bought and sold in the marketplace with only isolated attention being given to them as human beings. Labor unions were struggling for survival, and the humble laborer had to face his pitiful lot of long hours, low wages, and miserable working conditions.

Then, around the turn of the century, Frederick Taylor, along with other lesser known but equally important figures, pioneered the "scientific management" movement. This movement, aimed at systematizing managerial practices and stressing research, standards, and controls in the operation of a business firm, seized industry with a fervor. Indeed, the mass production era had appeared.

Criticism has been levied at Taylor and his contemporaries on the basis that their preachments tended to exploit the worker more than they benefited him. Much was made of the fact that Taylor, in his original efforts, overlooked the social aspects of a man's job and the satisfactions that men must realize in their work. Some claim that scientific management ignored the worker as an integrated personality and was more intent on discipline and control rather than morale. The worker was viewed solely as an individual; little if any recognition was given to the complex social network that comprises any organization of human beings.

But in all fairness to Taylor and his associates in the scientific management movement, it should be pointed out that they did not, as such, overlook the human element in industry. What they did overlook was the relationship of the individual working man to the work group of which he was a part, and it remained for later "pioneers" to demonstrate the tremendous influence these interpersonal relationships have upon industrial productivity and morale.

Not until the decade of the 1920's did the slowly evolving "humanistic" movement take a turn for the better. The major focal point here, as any student of management well knows, was the ever-famous Hawthorne Studies conducted by Elton Mayo and his colleagues.

From this study emerged the first truly objective proof of the positive correlation between productivity and employee participation in the decisions affecting him and his work. In short, Mayo and later colleagues concluded that the factory was a social system in and of itself and that informal groupings in the work situation had a dramatic and vital part to play in the industrial picture. No more was the worker to be viewed solely as a "factor of production"— rather, he had now become a human being, with wants, desires, attitudes, and feelings vitally affecting his productive usefulness. Although much criticism has been levied at the methods used by Mayo and his associates, the conclusions of their study, nevertheless, stand out as a landmark in the ensuing human relations movement.

Other contributing factors in this same time period may be enumerated briefly. This was the era of paternalism and welfare management. Employment departments, later called personnel departments, had been instituted by many companies to cope with employee turnover, trade unionism, problems of selection, and to research new frontiers in employee relations. Oliver Sheldon, writing early in that decade, stressed that the human element had been neglected in industry and that techniques had taken precedence over leadership, understanding, and cooperation. He emphasized the necessity for a professional approach to the human problems of the business environment. Thus, there was dawning awareness on the part of many businessmen of a growing body of thought and knowledge directed towards this human resource.

Interest waned somewhat during the 1930's because of the depression; but with the impetus of resurgent and militant unionism after passage of the Wagner Act, once again business attention was turned towards workers and human resources. World War II and postwar business expansion encouraged what was by that time an exploding movement in industry. Countless numbers of studies to aid the business world were being performed by psychologists, sociologists, anthropologists, and other social scientists. Corporate management had taken on an air of professionalization, and personnel management stood at unprecedented heights. Professional managers, both by force and by choice, recognized the importance of the contributions of social scientists to the direction of men. Slowly but surely, this movement has crystallized into a form now recognizable as a definite body of knowledge. *Today management is explained as being in part a social process—a process of combining techniques with men for the mutual benefit of both.*

The importance of human relations in working organizations

With the growth of the human relations movement, increasing emphasis has been given to the worker as a *whole man*. No longer is he viewed solely as an economic tool but, rather, as a human being who is driven and controlled by diverse elements of society and who has fears, frustrations, expectations, and desires which affect his total makeup. How he performs on his job (his efficiency and productivity) are dependent as much, if not more, on the external aspects surrounding his work place as on the tools and materials he uses.

Therefore, it must be recognized that man as a worker is unique compared to other productive factors. He alone must be *motivated*, not only to do his job but to strive constantly to improve his performance. This, then, remains the cardinal objective of the human relations function: to discover newer and better ways of understanding man and his relation to his work, to motivate him to higher standards of workmanship, and to help as many people as possible to realize their maximum potential.

Studies now show that the typical manager and/or administrator spends anywhere from 50 percent to 75 percent of his time dealing with human problems. Although all managers must be technically competent to perform their jobs, more and more the organization of today requires a manager highly sophisticated in leading and motivating people. Indeed, the success of the manager in his job is heavily dependent upon the success of his subordinates in their work. This dependency relationship means that a manager has to be knowledgeable in the ways of directing and leading others at work.

Complicating this task is the changing nature of our country's labor force. To begin with, today's typical worker is far more educated than his father was, and an educated man is a demanding one. Especially does he demand competence on the part of those for whom he has to work. Furthermore, the basic composition of the labor force is changing. By 1970 almost 50 percent of our labor force will be made up of *professional personnel*—i.e., scientists, engineers, technicians, and administrators. The problems of managing this type of personality are far different than those with which the typical manager is familiar. These are highly creative, freethinking people who are not nearly as dependent upon the organization as are the blue-collar workers and many white-collar workers. They, too, demand a far greater degree of excellence from those who lead and manage them. They represent the new "knowledge worker" of the scientific and space age—dedicated but questioning, committed but freethinking and independent.

Another factor pointing to the need for human expertise on the part of all managers is the sheer complexity of our working organizations of today. General Motors Corporation, for example, has a total wealth equal to the eleventh largest GNP in the world today. Hence, most countries cannot match its wealth. *Ours is rapidly becoming a society dominated by large complex organizations*. It, therefore, becomes readily apparent that the activity of managing and administration in the complex organization is no simple task. It is a very demanding one requiring a great deal of technical and human knowledge.

A corollary of this organizational growth has been the expansion of our knowledge about how to "manage" effectively. So momentous are the decisions made by many of today's managers that they cannot be entrusted to just anyone. No, managers must be systematically *and professionally* trained to ensure their competence in managing. Since managing and administering is so critical in our economic society of today, much attention is being given to the training and development of managers by various groups. In 1965, for example, American industry spent almost $20 billion training employees, with a considerable portion of this amount allocated to management development.

So, the professional manager—highly trained, yet under close scrutiny by all of society, including government, organized labor, employees, stockholders, and the general public—is having to face up to many pressures in our complex work organizations. Noticeable among these pressures is the demand by all parties that he deal more effectively with people, with human resources. For in the final analysis, he must work through, by, and for others. Consequently, professional competence will and does, right now, require a manager dedicated to self-improvement and personal growth, especially with regard to his ability to manage others.

The following articles in this part will further elaborate many of the above ideas. Scott and Knowles, for example, summarize in a very cogent way some basic human relations issues and concepts; Leavitt raises some provocative ideas relative to effective administration and management; Moore examines some foundational aspects of sound human relations; Bernthal summarizes very effectively the contributions of the many behavioral sciences; and McFarland's excellent article discusses three different leadership models as they relate to productivity and organizational growth.

I. MODERN HUMAN RELATIONS IN PERSPECTIVE *

William G. Scott

Human relations incorporates everything or nothing depending on management's point of view. Nearly all management matters would fall into the area of human relations if the mere presence of "the human element" is a criterion for selecting a human relations perspective. Or, human relations would be of no value for management if the field is only a neat batch of slogans and platitudes. Neither of these perspectives, however, is of much significance for management action.

Human relations must be associated with business in a practical and useful way to be important to management action. This article starts with the assumptions of modern human relations and associates them in an over-all model of business activities. This analysis then leads to conclusions regarding management's scope of activities and obligations in its human relations functions.

THE PERSPECTIVE OF HUMAN RELATIONS IN TERMS OF ITS ASSUMPTIONS

It is a matter of record that the assumptions drawn from "the economic man" hypothesis of human motivation and behavior affected management practice in terms of employee relations. In the same way, different assumptions, following the human relations line, also affect management practice. Therefore, it is necessary first to isolate the assumptions of modern human relations in order to understand fully their implications for management action.

The general assumption of human relations

The general assumption states that human relations is an interdisciplinary subject; but what is more, human relations is uniquely greater than the sum of the disciplines which make it up. Further, the benefits which flow from an interdisciplinary approach to understanding the behavior of people qualifies human relations to solve problems of human conflict more adequately.

The whole being greater than its parts is a *Gestalt* or configurationist approach. The study of a painting serves as an example of the meaning of this theory. When one looks at an oil painting from a

---

* From *Personnel Administration*, Vol. 22, No. 6 (November-December, 1959), pp. 9-20, 30. Reprinted with permission.

distance, say of one foot, all that is seen is a mass of paint blobs. But as the viewer moves back from the painting, it assumes a structure, a form, a contour. The configuration which emerges on the canvas is, indeed, more than the sum of the blobs of paint which make it up. Paint and canvas are only the media through which art is expressed.

The configurationist approach, of course, is the central feature of the general assumption stated above. Human relations amalgamates social science disciplines and focuses their theories, data, and methods in combination on human problems. The problem solving virtue of human relations may be expressed in the formula, $2 + 2 = 5$. The extra "1" in the formula comes from the special twist that human relations problem solving gets from utilizing the interdisciplinary method. Human relations, as a result, contributes differently and singularly useful insights into human problems. Human relations attempts to overcome the shortsightedness of specialists working independently on a problem.[1]

Sociology, psychology, and social psychology are the disciplines which make up the backbone of human relations. But this list is expanding through the incorporation of other fields. Anthropology of the cultural and physical varieties is coming into its own in human relations. In communication, semantics and cybernetics are being utilized to understand and to improve the communication processes in organizations. The human relations overtones of the decision-making process are being studied not only by social scientists but also by mathematicians and philosophers. The traditional theories of economics are being reinterpreted in the light of more advanced knowledge in the other social sciences. Even literature in the area of business fiction is being analyzed to gather insights from a heretofore untapped source on the behavior of people in organizational systems.

No attempt has been made to associate the general assumption of human relations to business in particular. This "omission" is intentional because the scope of this assumption applies to the management of many forms of organized endeavors. Hence, the general assumption of human relations is appropriate in government, organized labor, international relations, and the neighborhood garden club.

More than anything, the general assumption is a point of departure. From the standpoint of business management practice, certain action-designed assumptions are especially crucial. These assumptions are not the exclusive property of management in business

---

[1] A statement and criticism of the interdisciplinary assumption may be found in William H. Knowles, *Personnel Management* (New York: American Book Company, 1955), pp. 102-7.

enterprises. They have fallen, however, on the most willing ears in this sphere of organized activity.

The action-designed assumptions

Action-designed assumptions are necessary so that management can cultivate a realistic human relations philosophy, from which operating objectives and policies can be derived. In turn, it is hoped that management practice will reflect these policies and objectives. The eight operating assumptions described, uncritically, below appear to represent a consensus among writers on effective measures to improve and promote successful management of human relations practice.

1. *Good human relations practice is the product of the manager using experience, intuition, and interdisciplinary generalizations to guide him in the action he takes.*[2] This assumption is the essence of the clinical dimension of human relations. It is the most inclusive, with the remaining assumptions being more or less corollaries or tools for implementing good human relations practice.
2. Employee *participation* is often essential to higher productivity and greater human satisfaction. If employees have something to say in affairs that affect their destinies, they will be happier. This assumption has been applied throughout company organization from allowing operative employees a chance to engage in the decision-making process on their jobs,[3] to the development of schemes which promote greater "involvement" of managers in the problems of their company.[4]
3. The *role* assumption stems from the variety of expectations with which an individual is faced at work.[5] Two general categories of roles can be identified. They are the "job-oriented role," and the "informal group-oriented role." In a sociological sense, roles are institutionally determined; for example, the role of the father, the role of the politician, the role of the business executive. The psychologists approach the idea of role in terms of the individual's niche or function in small group interactions. The functional aspect of the concept of role from the standpoint of the executive is linked to the understanding of an individual's behavior as a result of expectation-forces operating on him from many different directions in a business organization.
4. *Communication* has often been referred to as the nervous system of the organization. Anything which impairs the functioning of communication will, as a result, limit organizational effectiveness in terms of the accomplishment of business objectives. The "good communication assumption" is not entirely in the province of human relations.

---

[2] F. S. Roethlisberger, *Management and Morale* (New York: Harper and Brothers, 1941), pp. 138-41.

[3] Lester Coch and John R. P. French, Jr., "Overcoming Resistance to Change," *Human Relations*, 1948, pp. 512-32.

[4] William B. Given, *Bottom-up Management* (New York: Harper and Brothers, 1949).

[5] For a larger treatment of the subject of roles see: Mason Haire's comments in Arthur Kornhauser, Robert Dubin, and Arthur M. Ross (eds.), *Industrial Conflict* (New York: McGraw-Hill Book Company, 1954), pp. 381-82.

It may, in some cases, be a technical or engineering matter relatively immune in the abstract from human manipulation. However, communication is largely a human problem and subject to human foibles. Therefore, the necessity of "good communication" has become the central point of attention for theories and practices designed to unclog communication channels.

5. The next assumption is that *teamwork* is an indispensable element of management practice for organizational survival. Teamwork and cooperation go hand-in-hand; one promotes the other in a situation where employees are mutually striving to obtain the same set of desired consequences.

6. Man is *diversely motivated;* he has a hierarchy of needs which are quite changeable. This assumption is the opposite of the money and motivation, economic incentive notion. Employee work satisfaction, according to this assumption, is not entirely money directed.[6] People derive work satisfactions from job accomplishment, recognition, participation and the like. Very frequently, employee morale and contentment are based not on the paycheck, but on the social and psychological conditions of employment. This assumption questions the very core of the traditional theory of human behavior which presumes economic rationality, and the maximization of monetary rewards by people at work.

7. The seventh assumption is that the plant or office is *a social system.* Viewing the work situation as a complex of variable and interrelated elements is a key feature of modern human relations practice for the executive.[7] The executive must be a relationship expert to deal effectively with the social system in which he is involved.

8. The capstone of the preceding assumptions is the last one which states that *executive skills in human relations practice can be developed.* This assumption, of course, means that the executive's clinical ability can be improved so that he will be equipped to handle concrete human problems successfully. The executive can be trained to be aware, sensitive, and competent to cope with the human problems of the organization. If this assumption is not made, human relations would be merely a rather interesting set of abstractions.

There is always the danger that listings will leave the impression that each item is a discrete, independent unit. This is the farthest from being true in the case of the above assumptions. They are all tied into each other, and together make up a fairly complete picture of the point of view of modern human relations. Figure 1 summarizes the assumptions relating them to the particular social science area which has heavily contributed to their development. This table also

---

[6] For descriptive illustrations of the point see: William H. Whyte, *Money and Motivation* (New York: Harper and Brothers, 1955); see also: Keith Davis, *Human Relations in Business* (New York: McGraw-Hill Book Company, 1957), Chapter 3.

[7] The basic character of this assumption is underscored by the researchers in the classical Hawthorne experiments. See: F. J. Roethlisberger and W. J. Dickson, *Management and the Worker* (Cambridge: Harvard University Press, 1939), Chapter 24.

compares the modern assumptions regarding human behavior to more traditional assumptions.

The general assumption and the action-designed assumptions of human relations have been presented without critical comment. Each assumption could be shown to have shortcomings and inconsistencies. But a detailed criticism of this sort is not within the scope of this paper. However, two rather general criticisms of human relations must be considered next for the sake of perspective.

Modern Human Relations: A Case of Introversion and Shortsightedness?

Introversion

If the assumptions just presented can be considered totally, they add up to guides for action bordered by the rather rigid limits of the day-to-day problems with which the manager must deal. Taken as such, the assumptions are a useful way to view a *certain class of problems*. These problems are those which the manager faces when he turns inward to minimize conflict, to motivate, and to promote cooperation among his subordinates in the organizational social system. According to some writers, this treatment of the plant or office "community" is not adequate for solving conflict problems which arise from larger institutional settings. Sheppard,[8] for one, is severely critical of the failure of the human relations "tight little island" vision to treat the labor organization as a fundamental determinant of industrial harmony.

Sheppard has four indictments of modern human relations which are profitable to summarize.

1. Human relations is a "systematic underestimation . . . of economic and political determinants of industrial peace, either within, or external to, the factory."

2. Human relations restricts the area of observation to the factory, "as if in a vacuum." It does not look beyond the social system of the organization for causes of harmony or conflict.

3. Minimization of conflict by the employer or manager does not come from redistribution of decision-making power or concessions to employee demands, but from the application of social (manipulative) skills. The direction of manipulation is to get employees "to reinterpret their complaints in such a way as to eliminate the company as the object of hostility. . . ."

---

[8] Harold L. Sheppard, "Approaches to Conflict in American Industrial Sociology," *British Journal of Sociology*, December, 1954, pp. 324-41.

FIGURE 1

TRADITIONAL VERSUS HUMAN RELATIONS ASSUMPTIONS CONCERNING HUMAN BEHAVIOR *

TRADITIONAL ASSUMPTIONS	HUMAN RELATIONS ASSUMPTIONS
	1. *From Psychology:* a. Man is diversely motivated. b. Man is not always rational; he often behaves nonlogically in terms of the rewards he seeks from work. c. Man is interdependent and individual behavior must be frequently explained in terms of the social setting at work. d. An executive can be trained in "good" human relations practice.
	2. *From Sociology:* a. The social environment on the job affects and is affected by those in the situation, not only by management. b. The clique or informal organization is a reality, and it affects and is affected by the formal organization. c. Job roles are more complete than job description suggests because of personal and social factors inherent in job functions, but are usually excluded in job analysis techniques. d. The organization must be realistically viewed as a social system composed of numerous interacting parts.
1. People try to satisfy one class of need at work—*the economic need.* 2. There is an automatic sharing of goals in an organization; that is, no conflict exists between individual and organizational objectives—*mutuality of interests.* 3. People try to maximize rewards—*rationality.*	
	3. *From Social Psychology:* a. People are not always anxious to see their objectives in the light of organizational objectives. People have to be influenced. b. Communication channels carry both information relating to the logical-economic functioning of the company *and* the feelings and sentiments of the people who work in the company. c. Participation in the decision-making process has a positive effect on morale and productivity. d. Teamwork is essential for cooperation and sound technical decisions.

weakness →

* Adapted from Leavitt's Comments on Organization Theory in Harold J. Leavitt, *Managerial Psychology* (Chicago: the University of Chicago Press, 1958), pp. 291-303.

4. Thus, industrial relations in the human relations perspective reduces itself "to person-to-person relations, primarily between worker and worker, and worker and supervisor." The main source of conflict is found at this level.[9]

Sheppard's criticism, although mainly centered on human relations neglect of organized labor, has a good deal of universality to it. Human relations could be misleading unless its introverted nature is recognized. For example, the agonies of assimilation of recently migrated racial or national groups into large urban industrial areas could involve numerous conflict situations on the job. These problems are not likely to be solved by the application of human relations skills in the limited sphere of the work environment; job conflicts may be merely symptomatic of reactions to the foreign and frequently antagonistic life in which the migrants find themselves.

Human relations is not a palliative for all human problems. The perspective of modern human relations assumptions in business is not readily adaptable to settle problems of the broader variety just described.

Shortsightedness

Evidence relating to the shortsightedness of human relations assumptions can be assembled from three points. (1) Peter Drucker makes a devastating attack on human relations when he observes that *it lacks adequate focus on work.* Human relations instead places undue emphasis on interpersonal relations and the group. It is not the job, according to Drucker's interpretation of human relations, that determines employee happiness, only the employee's relations to fellow workers. He feels, however, that the functions that poeple perform in an organization are a major determinant of happiness; and that analysis of work and job is the sensible place to begin developing positive motivations for the people who are performing various functions in the organization.[10]

(2) *Modern human relations tends to neglect the economic dimension of work satisfaction.* This shortcoming of human relations is, in part, a result of a number of research studies which have "proven" that the modern employee does not place wages at the top of his need hierarchy. In other words, social and psychological satisfactions have been found to be more important to employees than money.

---

[9] *Ibid.*, p. 326.
[10] Peter Drucker, *The Practice of Management* (New York: Harper and Brothers, 1954), pp. 278-80.

Given the generally high level of personal income these days, coupled with the fact that large numbers of employees have their wages and salaries relatively fixed for fairly long durations, the findings of the primacy of social and psychological needs by research into employees lists of work satisfactions are not very surprising. It would seem natural for individuals to be inclined during periods of wage stability to stress less tangible job satisfactions. This is much like saying, man does not live by bread alone, once he has bread.

For the sake of perspective, economic man should not be buried too deeply. Whyte, in this regard, brings up his "face-value" theory of human behavior.[11] Essentially, this theory is that people often do what they do because of perfectly rational reasons, not because of deep-seated complexes or subconscious motives. Thus, when workers go out on strike, it is because they want more money, and not a Freudian reaction against the father-symbol of authority.

Human relations offers numerous psychological and sociological tools for probing human behavior. But ill-conceived sociological or psychological explanations for conflict or human dissatisfaction may be just as dangerous as assuming that behavior is completely rational in an economic sense. Economic motivation is exceedingly strong, and in many cases, economic explanations are quite appropriate for understanding human behavior.

(3) *The third cause of human relations shortsightedness is the structure of human relations research.* Most of what is known, empirically, about human behavior is a product of human relations research at the operative or, at best, the first level of supervision in the company. Further, most human relations research has been done in the factory or in the military services. The findings of this research, some of which have been translated into generalizations, have been considered appropriate explanations of behavior at higher levels of management. But little research effort has been expended to determine whether or not these generalizations *are* appropriate.

It may certainly be assumed that people usually like to participate, be recognized, and feel a sense of accomplishment no matter what their job happens to be. But these conclusions, obtained from studies of the behavior of operative employees, are not necessarily very useful when a manager seeks to motivate his subordinates who, more often than not, will be other managers. Additionally operative studies are especially lacking for the objective outside observer who wants to learn more about managerial behavior.

---

[11] William H. Whyte, Jr., *The Organization Man* (New York: Simon and Schuster, 1956), p. 40.

In this latter case, embarrassing questions crop up like how do managerial expectations and motivations differ from those of operative employees? How does the manager's view of himself condition the role he plays and the satisfactions he expects from his job? How does the structure and culture of a management group affect the decision they make? What can the data and methodology of political science offer to understanding managerial behavior in large, bureaucratic type organizations?

It is submitted that the shortsighted study of operative employees cannot give satisfactory answers to these questions. Psychology made a vast step forward when psychologists stopped making generalities about people from the study of rats, and started studying people themselves. In much the same way, if human relations seeks generalizations about management, these generalizations should come from the study of management.

The criticisms of introversion and shortsightedness are formidable. But they do not entirely detract from the fundamental soundness of the human relations point of view for management action. Each assumption discussed earlier has, within ethical and pragmatic limits, useful application in the realm of the internal administration of an organization. It is in the setting of the business elements that the perspective of human relations must next be treated.

THE PERSPECTIVE OF HUMAN RELATIONS IN TERMS OF THE BUSINESS ELEMENTS

Management does quite a bit more than "dealing with people" on a personal basis. Fifty years ago this statement would be considered just as simple-minded as it is today. But it has to be made, because the modern emphasis on human relations in literature, college courses, and executive development programs might lead the uncritical and uninitiated to believe that the only thing management does is to try to get along with people.

The purpose of this section is to set out in the form of an uncomplicated model a view of the basic elements which combine an organized enterprise, and then to show those elements in which human relations has a major role. Figure 2 presents diagrammatically the business elements and their relationships. All explanations that follow in this section are based on this figure.

Basic business element [12]

The business elements which comprise the business model are universal to all organized enterprise. The model of the business elements is an effort to place the basic business factors in a logical arrangement. It should be noted at the outset that the right to do business is derived from *organized society* and the purpose of the business is the *satisfaction of human needs*. These two considerations are not part of the business elements, but are actually the beginning and ending points, the reason for being, of the business organization.

Objectives

Objectives are general goals or values sought by the organization. Defined, business objectives are:

1. *Profit*—Pecuniary returns after costs, which are either retained by the company or distributed to owners.
2. *Service*—The obligation which a company has of providing values in a product which the customer has the right to expect, consistent with the price paid.
3. *Social*—General values created by the company in the interest of the public from which no monetary reward is anticipated.
4. *Personal*—The obligation to create an atmosphere conducive to rendering economic, social, and psychological satisfactions to employees.

The objectives of *economy and efficiency* are collateral to the above primary objectives, and relate to the effective operation of the organizations so that the primary objectives can be achieved in an optimum fashion.

Leadership

Objectives are accomplished through leadership which assumes three forms in an organization:

1. *Administrative*—The management of other managers in a line organization. This form of leadership extends from the president down to the first line of supervision.
2. *Staff*—While the staff includes also some elements of line leadership, in this case, staff leadership refers to the effective performance of advisory and facilitative services for the line.
3. *Operative*—The management of employees at the point of the creation of goods or services. This form of leadership is often referred to as first-line supervision.

---

[12] Similar basic business plans have been developed, for example, R. C. Davis, *The Fundamentals of Top Management* (New York: Harper and Brothers, 1951).

FIGURE 2

BASIC BUSINESS ELEMENT CHART *

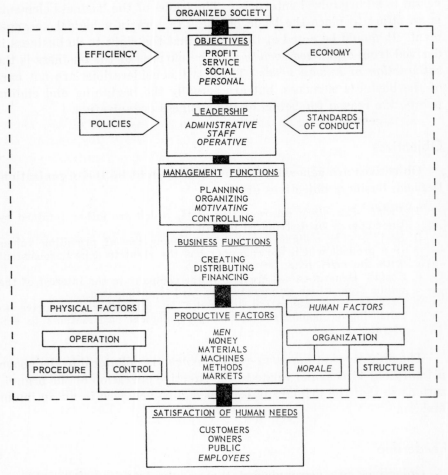

* The figure is adapted from a basic business factor chart developed by the members of the Management Department of Indiana University.

The activities of leaders are circumscribed by organizational policies and standards of conduct—ethics.

Management functions

Management functions give leadership direction. Management functions are a convenient way of describing the activities performed by management in the content of their jobs.

1. *Planning*—considering and establishing related facts in advance to achieve desired results. The essence of planning is the selection of alternatives and standards to set and guide a future course of action.
2. *Organizing*—establishing the proper relationships among work, people, and the work place.
3. *Motivating*—stimulating people to action toward objectives through the application of sanctions (incentives).
4. *Controlling*—insuring that the action taken proceeds according to the previously established plans.

Business functions

Management functions bring life to the functions of a business. The organic business functions are the *creation, distribution, and financing* of a utility. These functions are called organic because they are so vital that the business ceases to exist unless they are performed.

The productive factors

A business creates, distributes, and finances goods and services through the media of management coordination and direction of the productive factors. The physical and human factors, which include men, money, materials, methods, machines, and markets, are merged in a company by organization and operations.

The satisfaction of human needs

The direction which all business activity takes is the satisfaction of the needs of people. It must be noted that the objectives listed as the first element in the business plan coincide with those categories of people interested in the functioning of a business. For example:

Service objective .... Customers
Profit objective .... Owners
Social objective .... Public
Personal objective .... Employees

HUMAN RELATIONS AND THE BUSINESS ELEMENT

The business factors described in the foregoing outline and illustrated in Figure 2 clearly show that an organization is a combination of human and nonhuman elements and processes. The factors which are italicized in Figure 2 are those that most directly involve the application of human skills by management. They are the personal objective, leadership guided by personnel and human relations policies, management function of motivating, and the human segment of the productive factors.

Such matters as general policy making, planning, organizing, and controlling do include consideration of the human factor, of course. The point is that the "nonitalicized" factors in the business plan require more than the use of human skills in order to be accomplished effectively; they require technical skills, overwhelmingly at times.

A case is not being built for a conflict between technical skills and human skills. Quite to the contrary, an executive needs both. The relative degree of importance to him of human skills versus technical skills depends entirely upon what function he performs in the organization. Ideally, the executive should be competent in both skills areas, because the necessity for their use is apparent in practically every part of the business organization. *The skillful executive is one who can blend the human factors with the nonhuman so that the organization can meet its objectives without a loss of dignity among the employees serving it.*

HUMAN RELATIONS AND THE DEVELOPMENT OF THE "WHOLE MAN"

Not long ago at an executive seminar, the conference leader proposed to the men attending that management had the human obligation for developing the whole employee. The argument ran that management's responsibility toward employees did not end with simply the provision of tools, good wages, adequate leisure time, and the proper training to perform jobs. Management must also be concerned with providing the type of environment which would be conducive to extending each employee's scope beyond the narrow confines of the job he was performing. Thus, management had to consider the moral, educational, psychological, and social well-being of the workers. The worker had to be treated as a bio-psycho-spiritual-social organism.

This position was immediately challenged. Some of the conferees wondered if the conference leader had a very realistic view of superior-subordinate relationships. They asked, if it was not sufficient for management to provide good tools and working conditions, decent wages, and enough time to enjoy a higher standard of living. After all, the comments ran, these are the things that American management knows how to do best. Why try to convert managers to combination social workers, psychologists, ministers, and teachers?

The positions of the conference leader and those conferees questioning him were both rather extreme, but they do serve to illustrate a point. Business is a fundamental institution in society; management is the human instrumentality through which the institution is brought to life to serve a socially useful purpose. This purpose is to provide goods and services for the consuming public. The inescapable conclusion is that business still exists to perform an economic function in society.

Management is responsible for seeing that this function is carried out with a certain degree of dispatch. Management may decide that the use of human relations assumptions and tools will facilitate the accomplishment of economic goals; but this decision in no way changes the character or reason for being of the business organization. The introduction of a "human" approach toward the people in a company may simply be a result of a cold, calculated, economic decision on the part of policy makers in the organization.

Naturally, these observations should not be interpreted as generalizations on management motives behind the promotion of good human relations. Indeed, management could stand behind the human relations program as actually the human thing or even the proper spiritual thing to do. *The motive depends on the aspiration.*

The motives underlying human relations practice can be found in any one, or a combination, of three aspirational levels. These aspirational levels are the materialistic productive efficiency, the humanistic, and the theological. These aspirational levels can exist as ends independent of one another. But more likely they are tightly interwoven in an almost infinite number of patterns.

An interpretation of the interrelationships among the aspirational levels could possibly run as follows. A management philosophy which aspires for the materialistic level cannot hope to achieve this goal without recognizing the human dignity of all employees, the humanistic level.

It is just a step from this proposition to the next. Human dignity is firmly rooted in the Judeo-Christian tradition which places great weight on the worth of the individual and the brotherhood of man. Therefore, the theological attitude is that human relations motivated by Christian love has divine approval.

Ordering the aspirational levels

In the traditions of western culture, the aspirational levels for management human relations practice can be arranged hierarchically. The lowest would be the productive efficiency aspiration, and the highest aspiration would be the theological. Few, if any, management practices done in the name of productive efficiency could find justification if the outcome violates human dignity or is opposed to Judeo-Christian doctrine.

Though this observation is somewhat platitudinous, it does bring up the acceptability of management practice if the conditions are reversed. Could management practice done in the name of human dignity or theological doctrine be justifiable if such practice violates the productive efficiency aspirations?

The "automaticity notion"

Few human relations practitioners come to grips with the foregoing question. It is assumed away by the convenient "automaticity notion." This notion assumes that successful accomplishment at one aspirational level will yield desirable outcomes at another. For example, the scientific management pioneers felt that if the productive efficiency aspiration could be attained, the humanistic aspiration could also be attained. Or, the human relationists believed that realizing the humanistic aspiration would go far toward achieving the productive efficiency aspiration. Finally, the theological aspiration satisfies, automatically, the humanistic aspirational level which, in turn, would have positive results on the productive efficiency level.

While this description of the automaticity notion has been oversimplified, the implications of the whole idea are fairly evident. A theory of an automatic relationship among the aspirational levels would tend to distort the picture of the nature of management's function in society. When a conflict of choice occurs (human dignity *or* productive efficiency, Christian principles *or* materialistic expediency) a decision has to be made by management, and management has to accept the consequences of its decision. Heaven is the only place where all aspirational levels are mutually agreeable and consistent. The function of management is to choose goals from an aspirational level which will not always be compatible with alternative goals available in the other aspirational levels. This is the role of decision making.

From all of this, certain concluding observations should be made. The "whole man" approach seems to be asking management to operate on all aspirational levels at the same time. While this demand may be outside the practical limits of human ability, it appears also to be a misdirection of energy when viewed in the light of other management jobs outlined on the Basic Business Element Chart. Our society is specialized, and it is not management's primary function to make other managers and operative employees happy. Fortunately, or unfortunately as the case may be, human relations programs which are supposed to yield employee happiness are only justifiable if the true economic function of the business organization is not impaired.

The curious thing is that some people consider management responsible for the development of the "whole man" in the first place. The argument usually given is that work is a way of life; a man's most important (productive) years are spent on a job. Therefore, management should do what it can to extend an employee's range, to develop him to be a better person.

One wonders how other institutions, which also are supposed to make people better, fit into this picture. Could it be that education and the church, or even the family are so ineffectual that the necessity for human development must fall to management in the business environment? If the answer is positive, then the assumptions of modern human relations should be reconsidered, and the conception of the business organization in terms of its functions should be revolutionized.

QUESTIONS

1. Review the action-designed assumptions underlying human relations theory. Now, do you think these are a workable framework for today's typical manager?
2. Do you agree with the criticisms levied against human relations assumptions? Why or why not? Can you add others?
3. What do you think the proper role is for human relations theory and practice in the modern working organization?
4. What is meant by the "whole man" idea? How does this apply to human relations?
5. How do you think traditional management assumptions and human relations assumptions can best be reconciled?

2. RECENT CONCEPTS IN ADMINISTRATION *

Harold J. Leavitt

My purpose here, which I can not possibly achieve, is to try to organize and summarize recent theoretical developments in administration and organization.

Let me start by saying that I shall use the terms "administration" and "organization" more or less interchangeably; assuming simply that we are all concerned with understanding and perhaps directing the behavior of ongoing groups of people.

We have enough perspective now on the rash of new developments in these areas so that it is feasible to set up some gross categories, and then to describe some examples of novel and stimulating activity within these categories.

My categories are four: The first is the jumping-off place in organizational thinking; i.e., the state of classical organizational theory. This category contains nothing notably new, but it is worth a quick look because it will help us spotlight what *is* new in the "new."

Second, we can look quickly at new descriptive approaches to organization. This category specifically includes the new March and Simon (1959) book; Mason Haire's (1959) use of biological analogies to organizational growth; a series of sociologically-based models like those of Whyte, Sayles, Selznick and others (which I shall not try to run through here) ; and the clinically-based work of Argyris (1957). Many of the sociological models and those of Argyris are not entirely descriptive; they have strong normative elements. These are not so much normative in an analytic sense, however, as in a value sense.

The next category covers analytic-normative studies. For the most part these have their origins in economics and mathematics, with close connection to game theory, and other quantitative and rigorous attacks on decision processes. I shall cite only one example of these, the work of Jacob Marschak (1959).

The fourth and final category is the action-influence category. The question here is not about theoretical developments that show promise of future influence but on currently influential ideas. Names cannot easily be attached to ideas in this realm, but I shall argue that the sophisticated practice of "human relations training" and

* From *Personnel Psychology*, Vol. 13, No. 3 (Autumn, 1960), pp. 287-95. Reprinted with permission.

the impact of "information technology" are the two currently vital and partially conflicting forces on the changing organizational scene.

The jumping-off place

Until relatively recently organization theory meant Taylor and Urwick and ideas like "span of control" and the "exception principle." It seems clear that the impact of these kinds of ideas on the thinking of managers and business school academicians (and they provide a pretty good cue about trends) has lessened. As Simon has pointed out, these early formalizations about administration suffered considerably from—among other things—their hortatory qualities. In retrospect we can isolate at least three other major limitations:

    a. They tended to treat only the physiological attributes of persons, ignoring the complexities of motivation and perception.
    b. They began, usually, with the assumption of a known and fixed organizational task, which can then be differentiated into subparts. They thereby carry a static quality with no provision for organizational search for new tasks, or redefinition of present ones under pressure from a changing environment.
    c. Traditional theory has focused almost exclusively on the individual as the unit of the enterprise, working implicitly toward a goal of functional specialization down to pieces of size one man. Perhaps one reason these early theories missed the major phenomena of individual behavior is precisely because they failed to consider interaction among subparts of organizations.

Recent descriptive models

The freshest ideas about organization and administration belong in this category. There are many of them, semi-independent of one another. They have in common a concern about understanding organizational phenomena and about developing a more adequate underpinning for eventual applications in the real world.

The most important aspect of these descriptive models is that they are descriptive; i.e., impersonal efforts to comprehend, analyze, and predict organizational behavior. They either draw on empirical evidence or permit empirical tests of their propositions and hypotheses.

The March and Simon book is a good example. It is an effort to state a set of interrelated propositions that will account for variation in such diverse intra-organizational phenomena as, for example, intergroup conflict, innovative activities, and compensation.

It draws very heavily upon a dynamic model of individual motivation that includes variables like satisfaction level, search behavior, expected value of reward, and level of aspiration. It offers up some stimulating new concepts, too, differentiating "satisficing" from "optimizing" behavior and points out that the behavior of individuals and organizations is probably more accurately described by the first word than the second. Satisficing means searching for a satisfactory solution to a problem, rather than the optimal one—a process which is far more parsimonious of energy and other costs than optimizing, and a class of behavior which is also far more "sympatico" with dynamic personality theory than with classical economic theorizing.

Perhaps this is enough to give you a flavor of this view of organizational phenomena. It is descriptive-predictive; it is rigorous in that its propositions appear to be empirically testable; and it makes good use of what is known about individual and group behavior.

Let me turn now to another fresh look at organizations. Mason Haire has recently introduced some D'Arcy Thompson-type biological notions into organizational thinking. He cites the square-cube law; i.e., that as the mass of an object is cubed, its surface is only squared; then goes on to show how this surface-volume relationship becomes critical in relation to the biological size of organisms. The giant, in Jack the Giant Killer, were he proportioned like Jack but ten times as big, would include a mass so great as to break his own bones.

Haire's point is that as organisms grow they must change shape, and even create new organs to perform functions not required by another size and shape. He carries the analogy to organizations and then offers data to show similar, and predictable, change phenomena during organizational growth. Using historical data from small companies, he shows consistent relationships between, for example, numbers of people on the "surface" in the organization; i.e., who deal chiefly with the outside environment—receptionists, purchasing agents, salesmen, etc.—and numbers in the inside mass. The work is intriguing, suggestive, and a little worrisome.

Now to consider briefly the most clinically oriented of recent models of organization—the one offered up by Chris Argyris. Argyris' thesis, based largely on observational studies of worker-management relationships, is essentially that organizations are restrictive of individual psychological growth. Argyris argues that people grow from dependence toward independence, from an undifferentiated state to a differentiated one, etc., while some characteristics of large organizations press people back toward dependency, toward nondifferentiation, and toward other "unhealthy," "immature" conditions. Argyris offers prescriptions for cure, but not perfectly precise ones. He seems to offer at least a palliation in the form of organizational changes that will make for greater individual health; e.g., more freedom of decision-making for individual employees, etc.

Argyris' model does not belong entirely in the descriptive category. It lies rather in the limbo between description and prescription. It is concerned with individual mental "health" and the improvement thereof, and, whether intentionally or not, it has a hortatory quality—urging administrators to show greater concern for the mental health of their people.

In one sense Argyris' work seems to me an almost necessary outcome of the last decade's studies of human relations. It draws heavily upon human relations research, and measures almost entirely against criteria of individual and group "maturity." Very little emphasis is placed on other economic or social criteria of organizational effectiveness.

A normative-analytic model

The Marschak view, which is probably unfamiliar to most of you, is based less in psychology than the others I have described, and more in the mathematical economics from which he hails. But it is not psychological nonsense (as some ideas from economics seem to be); it is a good example of the way recent mathematico-economic developments can be focused on administrative processes.

Marschak makes an effort to construct a model of organizational behavior that does not contradict empirical data, and then to show an analytic method for deciding whether one organizational form is better than another.

Let me try to give you just a flavor of the Marschak model. Marschak treats an organization simply as "several persons" who "agree to follow a certain set of *rules* that are supposed to further certain *goals*." This set of rules (Marschak equates them with the sociologists' "roles") *is* the organizational form. Such rules are all concerned with communication: *action* rules about communication outside the organization; *internal communication* rules, which are rules about sending and receiving of messages between members (and which include communication with one's own memory); and *observation* rules which refer to the receipt of messages from outside the organization.

Marschak then specified a simplified problem in which the issue is centralization vs. decentralization; which is to say, whether we build in a rule for intercommunication between subunits or do not. By considering three functions—a payoff function, a probability function, and a factor of the cost of communication—he demonstrates that one can analytically determine (in his little example) the efficiencies of the two alternatives. He argues that such cognitive, analytic methods can be refined for use in real organizations. I would argue further that I see no *fundamental* reason why such methods cannot be integrated into real organizations, made up of real and complicated people.

Action-influence ideas

We can turn now from these efforts to describe or improve upon the behavior of complex organizations. The models we have sketched thus far exist mostly in universities, traveling in circles among academicians via academicians.

But it is appropriate also in this quick review to examine those ideas which are in fact currently having an impact on organizational practice—on the structure of organizations, on the relationships among members of organizations, and on the practices of administrators.

It might be said, first, that classical organization theories are having almost no noticeable *new* impact. Their old impact hangs on, of course; managers still talk about an authority-responsibility balance, about span of control, *et al.* But I have been unable to detect any recent changes in organizational behavior that appear to be consequent to extensions of old organization theory.

However, organizational practice is, I believe, changing under the serious and current influence of two kinds of phenomena, both of which are related to ideas we mentioned earlier. The two are "human relations" and "information technology."

By "human relations" I mean several fairly specific things: first, the techniques of human relations training, out of Lewis and Mayo, and graduated from Bethel; second, the related, business school-taught, business journal-promulgated, and consulting firm-carried-out techniques of "participative" management—techniques which include the use of committees, the encouragement of easy expression of feelings across status levels, etc.

These ideas are having effects, I believe, because they have been converted into technical mechanisms, and it is the technique that makes operational change possible.

These techniques are being adopted partially because they are novel, and we value the novel, but mostly because they offer promise for solving problems of social and self-esteem needs, and problems of interpersonal communication. These kinds of problems seem to have come necessarily to the fore in modern, complex organizations. They have come to the fore, I believe, mostly because some lower order problems have been resolved, and hence are less prominent; because, using Haire's analogy, the enlarged internal mass of most organizations has radically increased the need for better internal mechanisms for processing information.

Whatever the reasons, however, there is abundant evidence (numbers of consulting firms doing such work; the spread of Bethel-like activities into industry; the increasingly "human" views of executives about how to manage) that these ideas are changing industrial organizations, *especially at the middle levels* of the hierarchy.

Dr. Thomas Whisler and I (Leavitt & Whisler, 1958) have elsewhere pointed out the practical conflict between this trend toward human relating middle management and the other major current trend in the technics of management—the intrusion of information technology. Information technology is a label for the amalgam of new mathematical techniques applicable to managerial problems, plus those that are growing up around the computer.

In any case, information technology is moving in on organizations. It is beginning in a very small way to cause quite agonizing reassessments of ideas about decentralization, about where creativity is needed, about what constitutes an executive job, and about the relative merits of human and organizational values. It seems to be leading in many cases to solutions to those same problems of efficient information processing that are very different, perhaps polar, to those offered by human relations techniques.

These two, the techniques of human relations and the techniques of information processing, are the sets of ideas currently finding most widespread application to the practice of management. Right now they seem to me to be causing a mild schizophrenia in organizations. It is my own opinion that the potential, short run power of information technology is, by far, the greater of the two powers; at least as long as the two technologies remain separate from one another. But it is already becoming clear, back at the theoretical level of describing organizations and building organizational models, that the two are inseparably intertwined. The computer is already a tool for psychological and organizational research. Human relaters are already going cognitive, studying with new vigor the processes of conscious thinking and problem solving; studies which will, I am confident, yield a general descriptive theory of organization and administration; a theory which will, in turn, bear practical fruit.

QUESTIONS

1. What does Leavitt feel to be the four major developments in administrative theory in recent years?
2. What is a descriptive organizational model? Prepare an example of one from your own experience.
3. What is the role of human relations in organization development?
4. What is the impact of the organization on individual mental health?
5. Compare the basic ideas of Leavitt with Scott. How do they differ and in what ways are they similar?

3. HUMAN RELATIONS IN INDUSTRY: RESEARCH AND CONCEPTS *

William H. Knowles

The causes of labor unrest and worker dissatisfaction in all their manifestations—from strikes and riots to passive insubordination—are a challenge to man's wit. Reformers of all kinds, revolutionaries, politicians, labor leaders, novelists, social scientists, and personnel managers have suggested ways to bring about labor peace and worker satisfaction. The problem has proved to be complex and stubborn. It remains with us, although it takes on changing forms.

The latest group to attack human problems in industry are specialists in "human relations," who approach industrial relations through the study of small-group behavior, and whom we shall call "human relationists" for want of a better term. They are sociologists, social psychologists, clinical psychologists, psychiatrists, social anthropologists, and, to a lesser extent, political scientists, who study small, informal groups.[1] Many human relationists have entered the field via schools of education, introducing into human relations the ideas of John Dewey and the concepts of progressive education. Only the economist and the historian have been left out of the interdisciplinary team.

A basic tenet of human-relations theory is that primary groups (the family, work crews, union committees, church and lodge groups, bowling clubs, etc.) are fundamental units of society, and that study of them yields a better understanding of the individual, the organization, and society as a whole. Specialists in *industrial* human relations are concerned with the behavior of informal groups at all levels of a business organization. In addition to research in industry, industrial human relationists apply research findings from the study

---

* Reproduced with permission from the *California Management Review*, Vol. 1, No. 1 (Fall, 1958), pp. 87-105. Copyright by the Regents of the University of California.

[1] For definitions of human relations see: A. Paul Hare, Edgar F. Borgatta, and Robert F. Bales (eds.), *Small Groups; Studies in Social Interaction* (New York: Knopf, 1955), pp. 1-9 for a historical view; Mark May, *Toward a Science of Human Behavior: A Survey of the Work of the Institute of Human Relations* (New Haven: Yale University Press, 1950), pp. 4-10 for a definition that places greater emphasis on the biological sciences; E. Wight Bakke and Chris Argyris, *Organizational Structure and Dynamics: A Framework for Theory* (New Haven: Yale Labor and Management Center, 1954), pp. 111-14; Keith Davis, *Human Relations in Business* (New York: McGraw-Hill, 1957), pp. 1-4; N. R. F. Maier, *Principles of Human Relations, Applications to Management* (New York: Wiley, 1952), preface.

of such diverse groups as ladies' sewing circles and army combat terms to work groups within the industrial setting.

EVOLUTION OF TRENDS

Human relations in industry began with the work of Elton Mayo and his associates, and developed from their classic studies at the Hawthorne Plant of the Western Electric Company.[2] Their findings about the informal organization, informal communication, and the informal work group have been reported interminably and their value judgments and philosophical framework have been the subject of a major debate in industrial-relations literature.[3] As the result of this debate, the propositions of the original Mayo group of human relationists at Harvard have been modified. Although individual human-relations specialists vary in their beliefs, in general it may be said that human-relations concepts since Mayo have been modified as follows:[4]

Human relationists no longer hold out the hope of developing an exact science of human behavior and social organization. In the tradition of the scientific managers, the industrial (behaviorist) psychologists and sociologists of the Durkheim positivist school, human-relations specialists in industry once hoped that laws of group behavior and industrial organization could be discovered, making prediction and control possible.[5] If anything, some human-relations specialists now tend to go to the other extreme and proclaim that true understanding of human behavior is subsconscious, subjective, and non-rational rather than intellectual. There tends to be an anti-intellectual, mystical element in present-day human relations.

---

[2] Elton Mayo, *The Social Problems of an Industrial Civilization* (Boston: Harvard University Graduate School of Business Administration, 1945) and *The Human Problems of an Industrial Civilization* (Boston: Harvard University Graduate School of Business Administration, 1946); F. J. Roethlisberger, *Management and Morale* (Cambridge: Harvard University Press, 1941); T. North Whitehead, *The Industrial Worker* (Cambridge: Harvard University Press, 1938).

[3] See William H. Knowles, *Personnel Management: A Human Relations Approach* (New York: American Book Company, 1955), pp. 74-118 for a review of this debate.

[4] Chris Argyris, *The Present State of Research in Human Relations in Industry* (New Haven: Yale Labor and Management Center, 1954); Mason Haire, "Group Dynamics in the Industrial Situation," in *Industrial Conflict*, Arthur Kornhauser, *et al.* (eds.) (New York: McGraw-Hill, 1954), pp. 373-385; William H. Whyte, "Human Relations Theory—A Progress Report," *Harvard Business Review*, Vol. XXXIV (September-October, 1956); Harold L. Wilensky, "Human Relations in the Workplace, An Appraisal of Some Recent Research," in *Research in Industrial Human Relations*, Conrad M. Arensberg, *et al.* (eds.) (New York: Harper, 1957), pp. 25-54.

[5] See Knowles (note 3), pp. 41-43, 61-62, 84, 102-103.

Although Mayo and his group tended to emphasize irrational motives as causes of industrial conflict, human relationists now recognize that such conflict may be a form of rational economic-behavior, and that economic incentives are often a strong motivating force.[6] On the other hand, economists must concede that there are other things in life besides money which men seek to maximize. The study of motivation has proved to be complicated and has yielded little of use to management and union leaders.

The discovery of the informal organization in industry (with its own communications net apparently independent of the formal one), which is sometimes the "real" organization for getting work done, at first led many human-relations experts to deprecate the importance of a conventionally drawn table of organization. They now recognize that the informal organization cannot always adjust itself to production and to the solution of the personal problems of the work force within the structure of the organization. The structure of the formal organization itself may be the actual cause of both production and personnel problems. Dissatisfied with traditional organization theory, specialists in human relations are seeking a reformulation of the principles of organization. Although they have made specific suggestions for the improvement of the formal organization, they have not yet produced a general theory of organization based upon human-relations principles.

Earlier human-relations specialists in industry tended to study the work environment as a closed social system and to ignore such external factors as economic conditions, the community, and the internal politics of the union.[7] Human relationists continue to emphasize the primary social group as fundamental to an understanding of both individuals and society, but they also recognize the importance of economic, political, and social factors. The earlier preoccupation with the work group was related to a philosophy which held that the external environment was essentially cold, hostile, and unfriendly and that the psychic needs of man could be best served in a kind of industrial monastery. Most human relationists today reject this romantic philosophy of "escape from freedom" and argue that the goal of human relations is to develop individuals who can be effective in many groups. Most of today's human relationists are proponents of the open society rather than of industrial feudalism.

---

[6] William H. Whyte, *Money and Motivation* (New York: Harper, 1955).
[7] Abraham J. Siegel, "The Economic Environment in Human Relations Research," in *Research in Industrial Human Relations*, Conrad M. Arensberg, *et al.*, (eds.), (see note 4), pp. 86-99.

Just as human-relations theorists now give greater weight to the formal organization and to the external environment, they also weight more heavily the importance of the individual—his values and his personality—in assessing the behavior of the group. Although psychologists may still be criticized for ignoring the influence of the group on the individual, psychologists-turned-human-relationists have tended to re-emphasize the importance of the individual in shaping the attitudes and values of the group. By placing stress on the social group, some human relationists have supported a philosophy of "togetherness" and the denial of individualism. Once again we are faced with the debate on human nature and the natural order of society. Recent human relationists have reasserted the importance of the individual by stressing the desirability of developing social groups that can be effective without infringing on the individual's right to privacy by tolerating a high degree of nonconformity.

In giving management the role of a benevolent, paternalistic, "natural elite," which understood the true needs of the worker better than the worker did himself, early human-relations literature (in the tradition of pre-World War II management-oriented labor-relations literature) seems basically authoritarian in philosophy.[8] Although this view still lingers, most human-relations specialists have become proponents of industrial democracy as a result of their more recent research in industry. The reasons for this, and the means by which democracy in industry is to be achieved, are a central theme in current industrial human relations and will be taken up later in this paper. Whereas pioneer human relationists were attacked as authoritarians and lackeys of management, the present stress on industrial democracy has caused criticism of another kind: that human relationists are "misty-eyed" idealists whose preoccupation with the rights and dignity of the individual causes them to lose sight of the need for efficiency and profits.

Early human-relations literature was notable for the absence of any extensive discussion of unions and for naiveté as to the unions' function and purpose. The authoritarian philosophical overtones of the Hawthorne studies were anti-union. Today's industrial human relationists understand unionism, recognize the unions' value in industrial relations, and study human-relations problems within the union itself and in union-management relations.[9] More sophisticated

---

[8] For review of authoritarian management philosophy see Knowles (note 3), pp. 149-165.
[9] See articles by Wilbert Moore, pp. 119-130; William H. Whyte, pp. 171-181; Mason Haire, pp. 182-191; and Solomon Barkin, pp. 192-213, all in *Research in Industrial Human Relations*, Arensberg *et al.*, (eds.), (see note 4).

human relationists have no plans for "taming the union," for making the union leaders a second-class nobility in the management elite, nor for establishing an era of unbroken union-management harmony. Just as there is no human-relations organization theory, the exact relationship between human-relations concepts and those of traditional unionism and collective bargaining has not been spelled out, though they do appear to supplement and complement one another.

Elton Mayo spoke of developing human-relations skills in management to resolve problems of industrial unrest, and was attacked for his manipulative approach to employee-employer relations. Present-day human relationists go to the other extreme of being anti-technique. "Manipulation" has become a dirty word. Today, human relationists hold that basic personality changes are necessary to "good human relations" and that simple techniques of getting people to do what they do not want to do are not only morally wrong but ineffective.[10] Manipulation as a continual one-way process may be generally impossible; it does not, however, seem reasonable to say that you cannot sometimes manipulate another person—that is, get him to do what you want him to do.

The Hawthorne and subsequent studies revealed the communications problem of modern industry, and stress was laid upon *channels* of communication, semantic problems, and frames of reference. The inference drawn from the studies was that if individuals could understand one another this would remove the *major cause* of industrial discontent. Latter-day human relationists realize that there are "real" causes for discontent, not arising from mere misunderstanding or lack of information, which are removed neither by channels of communication nor by catharsis. The communications problems raised by early human relationists are not dismissed, but are placed in their proper perspective. The present concern of human relationists in communications is with interpersonal, nonverbal communications invoking subconscious, vaguely-felt emotions.[11] Communications research is currently involved with the phenomena of perception, subception, and empathy in group interaction.

Pioneer human relationists appeared to be unaware that their conclusions from field research carried ethical inferences that did not inevitably follow from the studies. Critics pointed out that alter-

---

[10] William H. Whyte, (see note 4).
[11] S. I. Hayakawa, "Success and Failure in Communications," *Proceedings*, Sixth Western Regional Conference, American Society of Training Directors, San Francisco (October, 1957); Wendell Johnson, "The Fateful Process of Mr. A. Talking to Mr. B.," *Harvard Business Review*, XXXI, 1 (1953), 49-56.

native inferences from the same findings were possible. Human relationists are now more sophisticated and take care to distinguish between findings of fact and value judgments. Initially, human relationists hoped to reduce ethics to a science, and in the process of organizing a scientifically-constructed society, economy, and social group, they expected that all interpersonal relations would be placed on a scientifically ethical basis.

Although present-day human relationists have abandoned the search for an exact science of society and human nature in the sense of prediction and control (as noted previously in this section), the quest for a scientific basis for an ethical society still goes on. Clinical psychologists working with social anthropologists believe that some societies, economies, organizations, and systems of values are conducive to mental illness and that others more in harmony with man's nature produce satisfactory mental health. If mental health can be equated with ethics, there is a scientific basis for recommending some kinds of organizations, values, and leadership styles over others.[12] While many may dispute this line of reasoning, it is refreshing that human relationists are now concerned with the discovery of a suitable industrial environment for mankind rather than continuing the pre-World War II emphasis on "adjusting men to machines."

MAJOR CONCEPTS IN HUMAN RELATIONS

Interrelatedness of personality, primary group, organization, and culture [13]

These concepts are the building blocks of society, and all of them are related to one another. An individual's personality, attitudes, and values are to a large extent shaped by the primary groups to which he belongs or has belonged; but, conversely, primary groups are a reflection of the values, attitudes, and personalities of their members. Most human-relations research has been an examination

---

[12] See Barbara Wooton, *Testament of the Social Sciences* (New York: Norton, 1950); Erich Fromm, *Man For Himself* (New York: Rinehart, 1947). For remarks relating the problem of mental health and culture directly to human relations in industry see Michael Fogarty, *Personality and Group Relations in Industry* (London: Longmans Green, 1956), pp. 23-40.

[13] S. H. Foulkes and E. J. Anthony, *Group Psychotherapy* (London: Pelican, 1957), pp. 40-47; Erich Fromm, *The Sane Society* (New York: Rinehart, 1955); Frederick Herzberg, *et al.*, *Job Attitudes: Review of Research and Opinion* (Pittsburgh, Psychological Service of Pittsburgh, 1957), pp. 19, 229-252; C. G. Jung, *Modern Man in Search of a Soul* (New York: Harcourt Brace, 1933), p. 61; Patrick Mullahy (ed.), *A Study of Interpersonal Relations* (New York: Hermitage Press, 1949), especially articles by Ernest Beaglehole, Harry Stack Sullivan, Talcott Parsons, and Harold Lasswell.

of the relationships between the individual and the group. Research has revealed, for instance, that personality change does take place as one changes membership in groups, that it is easier to change the attitude of the whole group than to change that of an individual member, that an individual gets more of his values from membership in primary groups than he does from the organizations to which these groups belong.

Similarly, the character of groups is in part shaped by the organization and the culture just as the organization is shaped by the culture and the groups. Culture, in turn, is the product of individuals, groups, and organizations. The complexity of these interrelationships explains the difficulty the political reformer has in attempting to bring about change from the top—the corporation president trying out a "new broom," the foreman seeking to change the habits of his crew, or the teacher trying to influence individual behavior.

The human-relations approach to the problems of industry is to assert that some combinations of personalities, groups, organizations, and cultures produce conflict, frustration, and mental illness and that other combinations produce harmony, satisfaction, and mental health. The more neurotic family is likely to produce neurotic children who may be well-adjusted to the neurotic groups and organizations they will join in their neurotic culture. Likewise, healthy individuals, groups, and organizations within healthy cultures interact so as to reinforce each other.

This framework of interrelationships is a very broad generalization. There can be frustrated, overly-aggressive groups and individuals within otherwise healthy organizations, and the opposite may also be true. Moreover, there are many kinds of personality types, groups, organizations, and cultures that are healthy and as many kinds that are unhealthy. Clearly, it is no simple this-or-that relationship. Human relationists have no vision of a static society of placid individuals in passive groups. Organizations, individuals, and groups are dynamic, the direction of their change is largely nonpredictable; but in the process of change the conditions for mental health can be preserved.

Personality problems

Psychologists continue to be perplexed by the infinite variety of personality traits (dimensions) and patterns (syndromes) which seem to defy analysis. Human-relations specialists in industry, however, single out two personality patterns as important to an understanding of the problems of industrial unrest. The first is the authoritarian personality, a personality which tends to be emotionally unstable, to repress facts which are contrary to belief, to be insensitive to the feelings of others, to wrongly estimate the goals of others, and to think of people and of problems in rigid stereotypes. Such a personality type has serious communication difficulties; he has no understanding of his own subconscious feelings, he has difficulty expressing his feelings and in understanding the feelings of others, he tends to judge too soon, and he does not know how to listen to others.[14] Nonauthoritarian, or democratic, personalities have the opposite tendencies.

Human-relations research indicates that the authoritarian personality is common in American industry and a basic cause of much conflict and misunderstanding. Economic issues and power struggles will always be present, but many conflicts which appear on the surface to be economic or to be power struggles are in reality the problems of sick individuals. The treatment of the authoritarian personality would eliminate a major source of industrial unrest and inefficiency. Conversely, no amount of smooth channels of communication or precision in the use of words will help the authoritarian who cannot listen and who thinks in stereotypes.

Another personality syndrome in industrial society that is stressed by human relationists is the *frustration-aggression pattern*.[15] Frustration arises out of the organization of modern industry and urban living in which individuals have casual relationships with many people but have few intimate friends. The result is a lack of "belongingness" to work groups, neighborhood, or even to family. Research indicates widespread frustration arising also from dull, monotonous jobs lacking in creativity and self-expression, from poor supervision, economic insecurity, and emphasis on economic incentives to the exclusion of nonmaterial incentives. The consequence of frustration is aggressive behavior, which only aggravates rather than solves frustration. Carriers of the mental disease of frustration can infect work groups and whole organizations in this manner.

Research suggests that no correlation exists between "normal personality" and work satisfaction or supervisory ability. A general

---

[14] T. W. Adorno, *et al.*, *The Authoritarian Personality* (New York: Harper, 1950); J. A. C. Brown, *The Social Psychology of Industry* (London: Penquin, 1954), pp. 219-276.

[15] Maier (see note 1), pp. 34-36; Ross Stagner, *Psychology of Industrial Conflict* (New York: Wiley, 1956), pp. 155-196; Walter A. Weisskoff, "Industrial Institutions and Personality Structure," *Journal of Social Issues*, VII, 4 (1951), 1-6.

relationship seems to exist, however, between dissatisfaction on the job or lack of supervisory ability and (a) dissatisfaction with things in general, (b) lack of friendliness and identification with social groups, (c) emotional imbalance and lack of understanding of personal psychological needs, (d) poor interpersonal relationships, intolerance of the psychological needs of others, and insensitivity to the communication of those needs, (e) tendency to be unrealistic, arbitrary, and inflexible, and (f) an unhappy home in childhood, with a repetition of the pattern in adulthood.[16]

The work group

The social group is the center of focus of human relations studies in industry.[17] By measuring the roles and status of group members, human-relation specialists study the structure of work groups. By analyzing communication networks, they relate the formal and informal organization of the group to other groups and to the organization as a whole.

One important variable in the behavior of groups and their members is the degree of group cohesiveness, and human relationists are concerned with the causes and implications of cohesive work groups.[18] Another important variable is leadership, which the human relationists consider to be a function of group behavior rather than a characteristic of the individual in the leadership role. A leader can shape a cohesive group, enforce its norms, and change its norms only under certain conditions because he must first gain the acceptance of the group and meet its norms. Human relations, then, studies the nature of leadership and the relation of informal leaders, appointed outside leaders (foremen), elected leaders (shop stewards), multiple leadership, and shared leadership (leaderless groups) to the work group.

Emerging from a multitude of studies the following conclusions appear:

---

[16] Herzberg, et al., (see note 13), pp. 17-20.
[17] Since the group is the center of interest in human-relations studies, there is a vast body of literature on the subject. Some of the standard references are: R. F. Bales, *Interaction Process Analysis: A Method for the Study of Small Groups* (Cambridge: Addison-Wesley, 1950); Dorwin Cartwright and A. Zander (eds.), *Group Dynamics* (Evanston: Row, Peterson, 1953); Leon Festinger, Stanley Schachter, and Kurt Back, *Social Pressures in Informal Groups* (New York: Harper, 1950); Harold Guetzkow (ed.), *Groups, Leadership and Men* (Pittsburgh: Carnegie Press, 1951); George C. Homans, *The Human Group* (New York: Harcourt Brace, 1950); Muzafer Sherif and Carolyn W. Sherif, *Groups in Harmony and Tension* (New York: Harper, 1953); and Herbert Thelen, *Dynamics of Groups at Work* (Chicago: University of Chicago Press, 1954).
[18] Stanley E. Seashore, *Group Cohesiveness in the Industrial Work Group* (Ann Arbor: University of Michigan Survey Research Center, 1954).

1. Informal social groups exist in business and industry. The fact of their existence is important to both management and the worker.

2. Work is a social experience and most workers find satisfaction in membership in social groups. Accordingly, lack of a cohesive work group leads to low morale as expressed in absenteeism, turnover, and malingering.[19]

3. A work group may be cohesive in maintaining low production standards, resisting change, hostility towards supervision and/or other groups, denying membership to newcomers, and demanding strict conformity of its membership. On the other hand, a cohesive work group may have high work standards, accept technological change, be friendly to other groups, cooperate with supervision, and have minimum unwritten codes of conformity for membership.

4. Three factors seem to be important in securing the more desirable kind of cohesive group: leadership of a democratic style rather than an authoritarian or a laissez-faire style,[20] a climate which allows a high degree of participation on the part of the group in decisions affecting its work,[21] and—finally—a type of general organization which permits this kind of group, leadership, and participation in management.

The organization [22]

Not only do business enterprises tend to be dominated by authoritarian personalities, but the management hierarchy by its very nature

[19] Survey Research Center, *The Midwest Study, Report VI, Factors Related to Morale* (Ann Arbor: Michigan Institute for Social Research, 1951).

[20] Thomas Gordon, *Group-Centered Leadership* (Boston: Houghton Mifflin Co., 1955); Carroll L. Shartle, *Executive Performance and Leadership* (New York: Prentice-Hall, 1956); for documentation of research on leadership see Donald A. Laird and Eleanor C. Laird, *The New Psychology for Leadership* (New York: McGraw-Hill, 1956), pp. 22-60, 65-78, 87-94, 113-120, and 175-178.

[21] Brown (see note 14), pp. 186-211; Maier (see note 1), pp. 7-26, 46-49, 93-205; Sherif and Sherif (see note 17), pp. 204-218; Rudolf M. Wittenberg, *The Art of Group Discipline, A Mental Hygiene Approach to Leadership* (New York: Association Press, 1951), pp. 37-100. For documentation of research on democratic group decision-making see Laird and Laird (note 20), pp. 16-17, 83-86, 94-99, 103-108.

[22] Chris Argyris, *Personality and Orgnaization* (New York: Harper, 1957); E. Wight Bakke, *Bonds of Organization, An Appraisal of Corporate Human Relations* (New York: Harper, 1950); Eli Ginsberg and Ewing W. Reilly, *Effecting Change in Large Organizations* (New York: Columbia University Press, 1957); W. G. Scott, *Industrial Leadership and Joint Consultation* (Liverpool: University Press, 1952); Herbert Simon, *Administrative Behavior* (New York: Macmillan, 1957); Fogarty (see note 12), pp. 185-219.

For case studies of organization see Elliott Jacques, *The Changing Culture of a Factory* (New York: Dryden Press, 1952); F. L. W. Richardson, Jr., and Charles R. Walker, *Human Relations in an Expanding Company* (New Haven: Yale Labor and Management Center, 1948).

tends to be authoritarian and the traditional rules of organization contrary to democratic human-relations principles. Consequently, mature individuals with normal personalities are driven away or frustrated by the very character of the business organization. Research indicates that attempts to train supervisors in the democratic style of leadership in order to build effective work teams fail because such a primary group cannot survive in the authoritarian environment of the company as a whole.

The key to industrial peace lies not in "adjusting the worker," in the pre-World War II style, but in adjusting top management. The leadership criteria for good supervision should also be applied to top management, so that an organizational climate will be created in which effective work groups can operate. Corporate organizations following human-relations principles would be decentralized for wide participation in decision-making (because people resist goals that are imposed upon them but become committed to goals set by their group). Their structures would be viewed as interlocking, overlapping groups rather than as pyramids of superior-subordinate relationships between individuals. Accordingly, the traditional problem of delegating authority and responsibility (span of control) would be restated in terms of maintaining communications between groups. And, further, the supervisor's job would be changed from that of giving orders and maintaining quality and quantity standards to that of being spokesman for his group in its relations with other groups and maintaining an effective work team which sets its own goals, solves its own problems, and disciplines its own members.

The culture

Human-relations research reveals that these findings on personality, groups, and organizations are relevant mainly to the culture of the United States, and cannot be applied in wholesale fashion to other cultures. Those raised in authoritarian cultures, with authoritarian families and institutions, do not function effectively in a democratic climate. On the other hand, the United States has a long cultural tradition of democratic values.

Most American institutions, including the home and the public-school system, are democratic; in being authoritarian, business organizations are out of step with the cultural environment. In the past, industry could violate human-relations principles which are in harmony with American culture, so long as not many people were affected and so long as economic coercion was possible; but now, with the growth of industry, more people are affected and full employment and the spread of unionism make economic coercion less workable.[23] Moreover, as William H. Whyte correctly observes, human-relations principles gain much of their impetus from the growth of a middle-management class who are in revolt against the rugged individualists of top management. Finally, industry by its very success in creating wealth has caused men to turn from preoccupation with mere economic survival to a concern with a work environment and way of life which permits a greater degree of self-expression and creativity. (In this connection, human relationists refer to the demand for greater "self-realization.") In brief, our heritage is democratic and there is a general social movement for a more humane, dignified treatment of the individual, and industry is adjusting to this cultural demand.

Human-relations training

Training in human relations has become very popular. Many have relabeled their traditional training programs to capture the popularity of the term. Actually, human-relations training has its own body of theory and teaching method. At the outset, let it be noted that the goal of human-relations training is to bring about the changes in personality, groups, and organizations reviewed in the preceding sections.

Training theory and goals: [24] Training theory in human relations comes from four closely related sources: group dynamics, clinical psychology, progressive education, and the case method as practised by the Harvard Graduate School of Business Administration. A basic proposition is that most, if not all, learning situations take place on an emotional rather than an intellectual level. Accordingly books, lectures, and visual aids that appeal to conscious reason may bring intellectual understanding or even a change in attitude, but will not change *behavior*. Learning by doing means, then, having an emotional experience. From the viewpoint of the clinical psychologist

---

[23] Brown (see note 14), pp. 41-68; Ginsberg and Reilly (see note 22), pp. 18-39; David Riesman, Nathan Glazer, and Reuel Denny, *The Lonely Crowd* (Garden City: Doubleday Anchor, 1956), pp. 32-49, 151-166; Sherif and Sherif (see note 17), pp. 136-156, 159-188; Wittenberg (see note 21), pp. 108-111.

[24] Kenneth D. Benne and Bozidar Muntyah, *Human Relations in Curriculum Change* (New York: Dryden Press, 1951); Gordon (see note 20), pp. 13-45; Laird and Laird (see note 20), pp. 13-15; Maier (see note 1), especially pp. 3-17; Ashley Montagu, *Education and Human Relations* (New York: Grove Press, 1958); Sherif and Sherif (see note 17), pp. 219-229; Thelen (see note 17), pp. 34-91; Irving R. Weschler, Robert Tannenbaum, and John H. Zenger, *Yardsticks for Human Relations Training* (Los Angeles: Institute of Industrial Relations, 1957), pp. 5-11.

the major obstacle to learning is not lack of brain cells but emotional maladjustments which cause the individual to distort, or to close his mind to facts and reality. Accordingly, the learning theory and the theory of therapy for the emotionally disturbed parallel one another.

Although these theories may be challenged as being too inclusive, there is ample evidence that they do apply to problems in human relations. Personality problems prevent individuals from understanding their own difficulties and from being effective in interpersonal relations, and prevent their being sensitive to the needs of others. Lecturing, under these circumstances, increases resistance to change instead of bringing change about. It is no wonder that many executive-development, foreman-training, and salesmanship courses have had little success in actually changing leadership style or sales approach.

Some educational theorists believe that there are subject-matter areas that do not lend themselves to orderly analysis. Any principles that emerge from analytical study are so general as to be of little use to the practitioner in specific situations. Theory only causes the practitioner to be introspective when he should be acting, and a kit of how-to-do-it techniques may be clumsily applied to the specific case.

The goals of human-relationships training programs are:

(a) To gain a better understanding of one's self. To "know one's self" may range from resolving subconscious emotional conflicts to becoming aware of how others react to one's mannerisms.

(b) To broaden and sharpen sensitivity to the feelings of others.

(c) To develop respect for others and to accept individual differences. Reasonable as this may appear, human-relations trainers find that an underlying cause of industrial conflict, often not consciously stated, is conflict between age groups, between male and female, between ethnic groups, or between those with varying physical appearance.

(d) To establish the belief (rejected by authoritarians) that kindness is not a weakness.

(e) To treat all human-relations problems with a clinical approach—to be sympathetic and understanding as if seeking a cure for illness rather than to blame or make accusations as to motives.

From these goals follows a further goal of human-relations training: the overcoming of barriers to interpersonal communication in order to reduce conflict that arises from misunderstanding.

Training techniques: One important training technique in human relations is the unstructured (free-floating) discussion.[25] Group psychotherapists have learned that people with mild emotional difficulties can be helped through group discussion, which avoids the time and expense of psychoanalysis. Although this is not the place to review the theory of group psychotherapy, it should be noted that it has been successful in rehabilitating ex-prisoners of war, alcoholics, the physically handicapped, criminals, and juvenile delinquents. The same theory and techniques apply in sensitivity-training and leadership-development laboratories; group discussion of emotional problems has a therapeutic effect leading to a change in behavior. There is no denying emotional involvement in this learning situation.

A second training technique has resulted from the clinical psychologists' discovery that a patient gains relief, insight, and understanding if allowed to act out situations that seem emotionally disturbing. This therapeutic technique—called "psychodrama"—is applied to industrial situations under the name of role playing.[26] The student is confronted with a variety of typical industrial human-relations problems in which he can play different roles and practice different ways of dealing with the problem. Here again, the student learns no theory or technique, but he becomes more aware of his own style of behavior and its effect on others; he learns to understand others by playing their roles. He learns because he becomes emotionally involved.

Clinical psychologists have provided also a technique of counseling described as permissive, called "nondirective" counseling.[27] The counselor is a sympathetic and understanding listener who mirrors the feelings and thoughts of the patient and responds to his unstated emotions. The patient discovers that he must define his own problem in order to reach a solution by himself. The counselor only offers understanding and encouragement. Again, this is not the place to

[25] Warren Bennis and Herbert A. Shepard, "A Theory of Group Development," *Human Relations*, IX, 4 (1956), 415-435; S. H. Foulkes and E. J. Anthony (see note 13); Gordon (see note 20), pp. 112-272; Marvin A. Klemes and Verne J. Kallejian, "The Group Psychotherapist in Industry: A Preventive Approach," *The International Journal of Group Psychotherapy*, V, 1 (1955), 91-98; National Training Laboratory, *Explorations in Human Relations Training* (Washington, 1953), pp. 9-62; Robert Tannenbaum, Verne Kallejian, and Irving R. Weschler, "Training Managers for Leadership," *Personnel*, XXX (1954), 254-260.

[26] Chris Argyris, *Role Playing in Action* (Ithaca: New York State School of Industrial Relations), Bulletin No. 16 (1951); Davis (see note 1), pp. 210-226; Maier (see note 1), pp. 87-190.

[27] Carl R. Rogers, *Client-Centered Therapy* (Boston: Houghton-Mifflin Co., 1951); Davis (see note 1), pp. 383-402; Maier (see note 1), pp. 38-43; Norman R. F. Maier, Allen R. Solem, and Ayesha A. Maier, *Supervisory and Executive Development, A Manual for Role Playing* (New York: Wiley, 1957).

give a detailed account of the theory, but the technique is of therapeutic value.

Since many problems of employees are of the type that can be handled by counselors, human relationists have recommended that counseling be made a service of the personnel department. This recommendation has not taken hold. Some human relationists recommend also that everyone in the management hierarchy be trained in the techniques of nondirective guidance as a method of dealing with human-relations problems. If every supervisor practiced nondirective counseling, he could overcome subconscious resentment to him as an authority figure, improve communications, and deal with the subconscious personal problems underlying many production problems. In short, training in nondirective guidance is training in a leadership style desirable in democratic work-groups.

The study of cases is a fourth technique used in human-relations training.[28] As the Harvard Business School is deeply committed to the case-study approach for the teaching of skills in business administration, it is not surprising that their human-relations training program places emphasis upon case studies in human relations. Rather than to produce a therapeutic or cathartic effect, the Harvard Business School's objective in human-relations training is to sharpen understanding in an area where there are no general rules and no "right answers" by offering the students "concrete" situations which will permit them to develop a feel for human-relations problems.

CRITIQUE OF HUMAN RELATIONS RESEARCH IN INDUSTRY

Scientific validity

A fundamental objection to the conclusions derived from human-relations research is that they are not supported by adequate scientific evidence.[29] In spite of the bulk of the literature pertaining to human relations in industry, conclusions are based primarily upon four studies: the original Hawthorne study, the Harwood Manufacturing Company study, the Glacier Metal Company study (English), and the comparative studies of the University of Michigan Survey Research Center involving the Prudential Life Insurance Company, the Detroit Edison Company, the Baltimore and Ohio Railroad Com-

---

[28] Kenneth R. Andrews, *The Case Method of Teaching Human Relations and Administration* (Cambridge: Harvard University Press, 1953); Malcolm P. McNair (ed.), *The Case Method at the Harvard Business School* (New York: McGraw-Hill, 1954); F. J. Roethlisberger, *Training for Human Relations* (Cambridge: Harvard University Press, 1954).

[29] See Brown (note 14), pp. 83-95, 276-307.

pany, and the International Harvester Company. Except for the Survey Research Center's studies, the findings may be challenged on the grounds that the company environments selected for study are not typical of industry generally.[30] Human relationists have got a lot of mileage out of four studies. The human relationists deny this charge and point to a growing body of research involving a wide variety of industries and work groups. As classics in the human relations field, these four pioneering studies are most frequently cited, since subsequent studies seem to support the original findings.

Another argument to dispute the scientific validity of human-relations studies relates to the nature of their controlled experiments with small groups. First, the experiments involved school children, college psychology classes, and soldiers. The question may be raised (but not conclusively answered) whether work and management groups are comparable to the experimental groups. Second, do findings based upon temporary, *ad hoc* groups apply to groups that have a continuing relationship with one another? Third, it is pointed out that there is no power relationship in the experimental groups other than the "social power" of personalities, whereas economic power is a real factor in most relationships in industry. Fourth, there is a suspicion that experimental groups are so designed as to prove the hypothesis of the experimentor. (It would be interesting to design an experiment to test the hypothesis that autocratic leaders are more effective than democratic leaders, or that democratic, group decision-making will result in greater resistance to change.) In other words, experiments proving one set of propositions in human relations do not necessarily disprove other sets of apparently opposing propositions. To these criticisms human relationists reply that they do the best they can and will welcome suggestions for better ways of studying small-group behavior.

Finally, some critics question the scientific foundations of human relations on the grounds that much of its theoretical underpinning depends upon findings in clinical psychology, which is concerned primarily with treatment rather than scientific research. Thus its main conclusions are based upon "clinical insight" rather than upon controlled experiments.[31] Laymen are often amazed at the ingenuity of clinical psychologists in interpreting complicated, contradictory facts

---

[30] I am indebted to Daniel Bell for this observation.
[31] H. J. Eysenck, *Uses and Abuses of Psychology* (London: Pelican, 1953), pp. 1-18, 221-241; Foulkes and Anthony (see note 13), p. 196; Calvin S. Hall and Gardner Lindzey, *Theories of Personality* (New York: Wiley, 1957), pp. 1-6, 24-25; Homans (see note 17), pp. 15-46.

so as to create a unified picture and a reasonable, though long, chain of causal relationships. Others join the game by analyzing the psychologist rather than analyzing his analysis—which in turn permits the psychologist to analyze his critics rather than their analyses of his analysis. Clinical psychologists readily admit that they practice no exact science comparable to the physical sciences and charge that those who attempt to do this, like the experimental psychologists, are doomed to failure by the very nature of the problem. Rather than attempting to build an exact science, clinical psychologists try to be scientific in their attitude and in their insights. They are impressed by the consistency of patterns relating personality problems to childhood background, occupation, and group membership. Their accumulation of cases which indicate consistent patterns, while not conclusive, is impressive.

Emphasis on group

A second criticism of human-relations theories is the major theme of William H. Whyte's *The Organization Man*.[32] Human relationists are charged with denying individualism—which is part of our pioneer heritage, political liberties, and laissez-faire tradition—through human-relations training (collectivism in progressive education) and by seeking an environment which exalts the group. The discipline of the boss and of the organization, which can be resisted, is replaced by the discipline of the group which becomes internalized as self-discipline. As a consequence the individual loses his personality in stifling conformity to group norms. The point is well taken against those human relationists who claim that the group is more important than the individual, that the individual's values, attitudes, and personality are mere reflections of those of the group, and that his security, happiness, and status are dependent upon his membership in groups.[33] Such a conclusion from research in group behavior leads to the metaphysical proposition that the individual finds his true self and gains his liberty by completely losing himself in a group.

It is improper to describe the entire human-relations movement as anti-individualist, since other human relationists state the problem

---

[32] William H. Whyte, *The Organization Man* (Garden City: Doubleday Anchor, 1957), pp. 3-154.

[33] For development of the anti-conformity criticism see Clark Kerr and Lloyd Fisher, "Plant Sociology: The Elite and the Aborigines," in *Common Frontiers of the Social Sciences*, Mirra Komarovsky (ed.), (Glencoe, Illinois: Free Press, 1957), pp. 281-309; Riesman, *et al.* (see note 23), pp. 34-48, 161-163, 299-314; David Riesman, *Individualism Reconsidered* (Garden City: Doubleday Anchor, 1956), pp. 12-27. For a particularly bitter attack on anti-individualistic tendencies in human relations see Hans Illing, "C. G. Jung on Present Trends in Group Psychotherapy," *Human Relations*, X, 1 (1957), 77-83.

of group conformity in a different perspective. They point out that for most of human history man has been intimately tied to one single group—the family, which integrated economic, religious, social, political, educational, and recreational activity within a single group. (Social anthropologists observe that primitive peoples do not think of themselves as individuals but identify themselves completely with their group.) Modern society, however, permits membership in a great variety of groups having a variety of norms and values, and permitting a greater variety of personality types. Freedom to be an individual, to select or reject groups and their norms, and to belong to many different groups, is a relatively new experience that humans have yet to master. Instead of returning to primitive society, these human relationists favor the development of mature individuals who can take advantage of the freedom offered by industrial society to achieve self-realization.

To an increasing degree, however, work involves "dealing with people, not things," and decisions are made by committees rather than individuals. Liberal human relationists therefore seek to develop groups that are tolerant of a wide range of personalities and permit a large degree of nonconformity [34]—groups which can cooperate on common problems without first demanding proof of kinship or loyalty oaths.

The nature of conflict

Another criticism, closely related to the conformity issue, is that many human relationists are too preoccupied with the building of group cohesion to reduce conflict and encourage harmony and cooperation.[35] Although it is true that some human relationists equate cooperation with goodness and consider conflict bad and, therefore, conclude that cohesive (harmonious) groups are the best,[36] others hold the more sensible view that only conflict arising from subconscious, nonrational motives and from failure in communications should or can be eliminated. There are enough real, substantive conflicts that groups must resolve. It is normal and healthy for indi-

---

[34] For viewpoints on human relations which respect the individual see Davis (note 1), pp. 57-67; Foulkes and Anthony (note 13), pp. 213-218; and Sherif and Sherif (note 17), p. 38.

[35] For criticism of the human-relations emphasis upon harmony, see Kerr and Fisher (note 33), pp. 300-302; Malcolm McNair, "What Price Human Relations," *Harvard Business Review*, XXXV, 2 (1957), 20-25; William Gomberg, "The Use of Psychology in Industry," *Management Science*, III, 4 (1957), 358-370; Whyte (note 32), pp. 25-35.

[36] For a more balanced view see Sherif and Sherif (note 17), pp. 146-154; Stagner (note 15), pp. 449-514.

viduals and groups to be faced with a reasonable amount of tension from time to time. Life without conflict (challenge)—even if possible—would be intolerable.

The human relationists' emphasis upon harmony and nonlogical causes of conflict has led to the accusation that they ignore the economic, political, and ideological causes of conflict. They are charged with showing sloppy sentimentality when rigorous logic and analytical ability are required. It is said that human relationists, in both controlled experiments and field studies, have neglected the study of power. Sensitive to criticism, human relationists now are including the consideration of power and conflict in their research.[37]

Group decision-making

Human relationists are also criticized for maintaining the superiority of group decision over individual decision. Some critics contend that only individuals can be creative, that group decisions must necessarily be mediocre, that they are time-consuming, and that they are part of the buck-passing, responsibility-shirking trend of the new generation of managers (brought up on group projects in progressive schools). Experimental evidence on the speed and quality of group decisions and brain-storming is conflicting and inconclusive.[38]

There is of course a danger that groups become so imbued with the goal of cohesion and harmony that they hastily reach an agreement without careful examination of facts, alternatives, or consequences. On the other hand, an increasing number of business decisions must be made in committee. Human relationists state that the curse is not the committee system but the inability of people to conduct themselves in committees so as to reach efficient, high-quality decisions. Human-relations research has yielded many practical suggestions for more effective committee operation.[39]

Although some day it may be proved that individual decision is superior to group decision, it has been established that decisions made by the group are more acceptable to the membership.[40] Subordinates resist decisions handed down by superiors simply because they resent authority. People come to understand a problem better if they have a hand in solving it. They become aware of their sub-

---

[37] For criticisms of group decision-making see Whyte (note 32), pp. 63-65.

[38] For a discussion of research on decision-making see Maier (note 1), pp. 254-377; Warren H. Schmidt and Paul C. Buchanan, *Techniques that Produce Teamwork* (New London: Croft, 1954).

[39] For practical suggestions for effective committee operation see Thelen (note 17), pp. 3-33, 284-297; Schmidt and Buchanan (note 38), especially pp. 26-38.

[40] Davis (see note 1), pp. 270-307; Thelen (see note 17), pp. 245-275.

conscious feelings about the problem in the course of discussion. People are more apt to carry out a decision they have participated in making. The group tends to enforce the carrying out of the decision. There are instances where the acceptance of a decision (as in production standards) is more important than the quality of the decision.

The meaning of democracy

Human relationists are criticized for their loose use of the term "democracy" and their tendency to equate nondirective, permissive leadership with democracy.[41] Just as there are times when our national government requires firm, directive leadership, so too in industry. While the emotionally-disturbed patient may need and appreciate nondirective guidance, it does not necessarily follow that normal well-adjusted students, offspring, spouses, or employees will respond enthusiastically to the teacher, parent, husband, or supervisor who serves only as a sounding board for thoughts and feelings. Child psychologists have learned that children worry over the abnormal eunuch-like behavior of parents who conform to the text book ideal of understanding parents. It would seem that supervisors under appropriate conditions may accurately communicate feelings of righteous indignation to enforce the intellectual content of their message. When to express true feelings of emotion and when to bide one's time is a human-relations problem, but has nothing to do with democracy. Some human relationists have equated democracy with "leaderless groups" where rank disappears and all are equal, while others have held that democracy pertains to political democracy (intergroup relations) and is not relevant to small groups. A middle ground would be that collective bargaining and grievance procedure, supplemented by decentralized management down to the work-group level, increases the degree of industrial democracy.[42]

Mysticism

Some human-relations specialists have, in my opinion, a mystical, anti-intellectual bias in their writing that is not supported by research evidence and which detracts from the positive contributions of the

---

[41] Whyte (see note 32), pp. 25-35, 59-61. For an overall discussion of human relations and democracy see F. K. Berrien and Wendell H. Bash, *Human Relations: Comments and Cases* (New York: Harper, 1957), pp. 214-253.

[42] For a balanced view on industrial democracy see Fred H. Blum, *Toward a Democratic Work Process* (New York: Harper, 1953); Maier (note 1), pp. 204-205, 254-301. For a view rejecting democracy in small groups, see Homans (note 17), pp. 419-422, 432-433, 464-467.

movement.[43] Just as clinical and Gestalt psychologists stress the total personality and total environment—saying that the whole cannot be understood by the analysis of component parts—human relationists speak of "the personality of the group" and "the totality of the group situation." Such a view is supported by some experimental evidence, but it does not follow that the group as a mystical body (Herder's romantic *herrenvolk*) is of greater value than the individual members. A group may be something more than the sum of its individual members, but this does not detract from the worth of the individual, nor imply that life is meaningful only through complete identity with a group.[44]

Similarly, some human relationists speak of the "wisdom of the group" not in the sense that two heads are better than one, but in the sense that the group, as an entity, *is* the carrier of a primordial wisdom more trustworthy than the intelligence of individuals.[45] The wisdom of the group is sometimes compared to the "wisdom" of the human body in healing itself without conscious effort and to the "wisdom of nature" which operates best when not thrown into disequilibrium by the purposeful activity of man.[46] The group subconscious is held to be the repository of ancestral wisdom.[47] Some human relationists argue that the "logic of feelings" is greater than the "logic of thought"; that "Seeing is believing, but feelings are the truth." [48] The implication is that conscious, intellectual analysis is "obsessive" and will not lead to right answers and that the subconscious, non-rational, emotional aspects of man should be sharpened and given free rein for creative thought.[49]

---

[43] For a reveiw of the mystical approach which is applicable to mysticism in human relations, see Bertrand Russell, *Mysticism and Logic* (Garden City: Doubleday Anchor, 1957), pp. 1-31. The term "mysticism" is used in this article in the sense used by Russell: 1. The belief in a way of wisdom, sudden, penetrating, coercive, which is contrasted with the slow and fallible study by science. 2. The belief in unity and the refusal to admit opposition or division anywhere. 3. The belief that evil is illusory and all reality is good. Mystics among the human relationists do not seem to follow Russell's other characteristic of mysticism: denial of the reality of time.

[44] For criticisms of mysticism in human relations see David Stafford-Clark, *Psychiatry Today* (London: Penguin, 1953), pp. 134-136, 150-154; Eysenck (note 31), pp. 226-227, 233; Foulkes and Anthony (note 13), pp. 39, 196, 235-255; Clara Thompson, "Anti-Intellectualism and the Individual," *Journal of Social Issues*, XI, 3 (1955), 48-50; Rollo May, "A Psychological Approach to Anti-Intellectualism," *Journal of Social Issues*, XI, 3 (1955), 41-47; Wittenberg (note 21), pp. 5-10.

[45] Abraham Zaleznik, *Worker Satisfaction and Development* (Boston: Harvard University Graduate School of Business Administration, 1956), pp. 130-136.

[46] Homans (see note 17), p. 87.

[47] On the concept of the collective subconscious which has influenced some human relationists, see C. G. Jung, *Two Essays on Analytical Psychology* (New York: Meridian, 1956).

[48] Maier (see note 1), preface and p. 17.

[49] Berrien and Bash (see note 41), pp. 54-69.

In contrast, then, to early human relationists who sought an exact science, some human relationists today would argue that scientific attempts to understand interpersonal relations must fail because the impartial observer cannot become emotionally involved. The emotionally-involved participant, however, has subconscious understanding that he cannot explain because he is too involved to be an analytical observer. The implication is that the development of conscious-level, intellectual ability destroys the more primitive, intuitive powers which are actually a more useful means of reaching decisions on interpersonal relations. Although some human relationists seek to eliminate the "hidden agenda" of emotional undercurrents which obstruct task-oriented group activities, others prefer to trust emotional expression, insights, and feelings as the higher level of reality. The study of group behavior necessarily leads to concern with problems of unspoken communications, the main springs of creativity, and suppressed emotions. Human relationists must deal with these problems, and one can, after all, assert that these forces within groups do not lend themselves to scientific analysis without becoming a mystic.

Evangelism

Those human relationists who are closely allied to the mystics see human relations as a revolutionary movement to save Western civilization from impending doom.[50] The doom theme is an old one, going back to the reaction of the Romantic philosophers to the Industrial Revolution. Durkheim, Mayo, Fromm, and Toynbee further developed the imminent doom thesis. To summarize briefly, the doom thesis holds that modern industrial society is out of tune with the basic needs of human beings. The impersonal, market-oriented economy causes mental illness, creating a market-oriented personality type which, in turn, reinforces both the market orientation and the illness. The tyranny of the impersonal forces of an atomistic free market is more devastating to the individual than the tyranny of the group.

The process through which this occurs is circular: individual freedom leads to competition which in turn leads through rapid technological change to job specialization. Job specialization means the

---

[50] For development of the doom thesis and social neurosis see Berrien and Bash (note 41), pp. 3-21, 254-273; Foulkes and Anthony (note 13), pp. 41-44, 253-254; Homans (note 17), pp. 271, 313-368, 454-468; Jung (note 13), pp. 196-244; Karl Menninger, *Man Against Himself* (New York: Harcourt Brace, 1938); Montagu (see note 24), pp. 26-27, 84-85, 90-96, 122-146; J. L. Moreno, *Sociometry, Experimental Method and the Science of Society* (New York: Beacon House, 1951).

loss of meaningful work—which, because life is no longer meaningful, causes abnormal acquisitiveness of material things. This emphasis on the high standard of living leads ultimately to more competition. Modern industry and urban living destroy primary groups, create uncertainty as to status, and cause psychological insecurity. Proof of this condition is found in the rise in suicides, divorce, alcoholism, mental illness, functionless families, functionless older people, and juvenile delinquents, and in the decline in worker membership in community organizations.

For some human relationists, the solution to this state of affairs lies in human-relations metaphysics. It offers a philosophy which will give meaning to life and to work and will end the evils of acquisitiveness and rootlessness by teaching man how to love his fellow man again. This way of life is that of the cohesive social group, which offers love, security, and purposefulness for the individual. Human relations, in this sense, becomes a revolutionary, evangelical sect whose goal is to remake individuals, groups, organizations, and cultures. Those human relationists who reject the emphasis upon harmony, cohesiveness, and belongingness also reject the doom thesis and feel no need to save the world. While not all human relationists have a revolutionary mission to save the world, few of them deny that there appears to be an interrelationship between labor unrest, social disorganization, modern technology, industrial organization and a highly competitive, materialistic market-oriented economy. Human relationists who are concerned with these variables are not necessarily either romanticists or utopians.

Training

Finally, human-relations training is the subject of much criticism. First, it is said that the training cannot be proved to be of value.[51] This is a difficult objection to cope with, for scientific evaluation is hard and the findings are inconclusive. Some studies suggest that human-relations training has no effect or has negative results, and others indicate that human-relations training yields positive results. However, since no one has demanded a scientific evaluation of the effectiveness of liberal-arts and business-administration curricula, it is not reasonable to ask it of the human-relations curriculum.

---

[51] For discussion of the evaluation of human-relations training see Kenneth Andrews, "Is Management Training Effective?" Part I, *Harvard Business Review*, XXXV (1957), No. 1, pp. 85-94 and No. 2, pp. 63-72; Gordon (note 20), pp. 273-302; Floyd C. Mann, "Studying and Creating: A Means to Understanding Social Organization," in *Research in Industrial Human Relations* (note 4), pp. 146-157; Weschler, *et al.*, (see note 24).

The second criticism of human-relations training parallels the current attack on progressive education's life-adjustment courses.[52] It may be true that the businessman's biggest problems both quantitatively and qualitatively are human-relations problems, but somewhere, someone must have some technical competence. It may be true that administrators must be "specialists in the general," get the "big picture," and must "like people," but the details of running the enterprise cannot be left entirely to the engineers, accountants, and lawyers. Instead of skills in group decision-making, which critics call shirking responsibility, it is suggested that skill in individual judgment and self-confidence be taught. Rather than developing listening ability, critics urge that future executives learn how to present ideas effectively. Human-relations training, which necessarily stresses insight, sensitivity, a feeling for the situation, and the premise that "there are no *right* answers," cannot evaluate student performance. It may be that education is not meant to be painless or to be fun, but to be hard, rigorous work. As in progressive education, perhaps there should be a balance between what are called "hard" content-oriented courses and "soft" human-relations training courses.

The third criticism of human-relations training relates to the mystical and revolutionary evangelism of human relations.[53] It is doubtful whether one should be taught to trust his hunches rather than logical analysis. Individuals and groups may suffer from Calvinistic inhibitions, but it is questionable whether the free reign of feelings in a revival-camp meeting atmosphere is the solution to the problem. When sensitivity becomes sentimentality and self-awareness becomes self-pity, training in human relations is not developing mature individuals. There is a fine line between being conscious of one's motives and reactions, and being so preoccupied with one's self as to become ineffectively self-conscious. Although the revolutionist stresses belongingness as a virtue to be learned in training laboratories, group therapists consider this to be the adolescent stage in group development in which individuals use the group as an emotional crutch. Instead of encouraging this development, some human relationists work toward "group maturity" in which individuals can

---

[52] For points of view on "life adjustment" versus "narrow specialism," see Robert Browne, "Winds of Doctrine," *Adult Education*, III, 2 (1958); McNair (note 28), pp. 25-28; Montagu (note 24), pp. 9-12; Riesman, *Lonely Crowd* (see note 23), pp. 162, 275-336.

[53] For criticisms of the anti-intellectual element in human relations training see Theodore Brumeld, "Anti-Intellectualism in Education," *Journal of Social Issues*, II, 3 (1955), 36-40; Riesman (see note 23), 224-236; Whyte (see note 32), pp. 56, 86-110.

preserve "self" while effectively participating in groups from which they can withdraw to be emotionally independent.[54]

Finally, some critics, raising the question of whether human relations can be or should be taught, argue that the seriously maladjusted need clinical treatment which should not be financed by industry or schools of business administration. For those who would benefit from human-relations training, on the other hand, it is claimed that the course is too brief, that personality change cannot be brought about by a one-semester course or a two-week seminar. To put it briefly, good interpersonal relations are a way of life in which a person must be reared.[55]

In response to these criticisms, human relationists reply that training programs are for normal individuals and that there is experimental evidence that the training, admittedly brief, does improve both on-the-job and marital relations. Human-relations training supplements content-oriented courses and is not intended to replace the established curriculum. Industry and the professional schools in universities include human-relations training as part of the general training program because it is a valuable part of the overall education of the executive, supervisor, administrator, educator, and social worker. Finally, critics of human-relations training cannot escape the fact that traditional teaching methods are not highly effective. Human relationists argue that teachers of subject matter courses will borrow human-relations training methods, as is now being done in business conferences and conventions, to improve the learning process.

EVALUATION

Industrial human relations has two main trends that are so interwoven as to cause confusion and controversy. The first is an evangelical, missionary framework of thinking. Essentially, this is a revolutionary view which sees civilization as on the brink of destruction; those who hold this view believe it to be their duty to save the world. Just as scientific management elevated a few techniques of industrial engineering into a movement aimed at revolutionizing the structure of society, some human relationists have raised the study of primary groups to the level of a utopian ideology. In the scientific-management movement the perfection of tools of measurement yielded natural laws of cooperation which, in turn, led to a technocrat's

---

[54] Foulkes and Anthony (see note 13), pp. 205-210, 227, 242-249.
[55] Gomberg (see note 35), pp. 362-363; McNair (see note 28), pp. 18, 30.

utopia. Human-relations cultists seek cooperation through therapy, "revolution by infiltration" into industry and government via human-relations training courses, and believe that the "withering away" of the state will follow from the decentralizing of authority to leader-less groups.

The cult of human relations, however, is not as modest as psychiatry, whose practitioners admit that the answers to philosophical questions regarding the meaning of life cannot be found in psychiatry. Beyond the treatment of emotional difficulties, the evangelists among the human relationists offer a philosophy of life in mystical union with the group. Where the psychiatrist expects to find a degree of self-sufficiency, tension, conflict, and loneliness in the life of a normal individual, the cultist sees these as defects which create mental illness. From the psychiatric point of view, human-relations training by the cultists may hurt rather than help emotional cripples. It may even be that enthusiastic participation in human-relations alumni clubs is a sign of immaturity rather than a vision of a new era of peace and love—an indication of retarded development rather than of rebirth.

The mystical human relationists draw anti-intellectual conclusions from their interpretation of psychoanalysis. They emphasize the subconscious, the nonrational, the instinctive, and distrust conscious, rational, analytical processes. Moreover, it is the *collective* subconscious that is the source of wisdom, superior decisions, truth, and reality. Science is too objective to discover the truth. Reality is an emotional experience that can be felt but cannot be understood. According to the mystics, rational compartmentalization of knowledge obscures the truth whereas the Gestalt of the group unconscious will discover truth.

The second major trend in the movement puts human relations in its proper perspective. This is the application to industry of concepts and research in the social sciences. In this respect, human relations has made a contribution in providing a general framework for the analysis of industrial relations.

Human relations research has provided us with valuable information about informal groups, organization, leadership, and training. Along with time-and-motion study, this body of information is being applied to the problems of the business enterprise. Human relations has made a contribution by increasing our awareness of the emotional, nonrational, subconscious aspects of interpersonal relations.

These unconscious forces are not limited to those in mental institutions but constitute problems with which all must deal. Furthermore, human-relations studies have made clear that these difficulties are not entirely the consequences of the birth trauma or of rejecting mothers. The nature of the business organization, its leadership, or groups within industry may themselves cause emotional disturbances which are harmful to business as well as to individuals. Finally, the human-relations approach raises questions concerning our industrial, urban culture as a cause of individual, group, and organizational maladjustments. Although mental health is not an exclusive measure of the worth of a culture, it is a fruitful one worthy of further exploration. Followers of this trend within the human-relations movement, instead of wallowing in the nonlogical, would raise subconscious motivation to the conscious level so that irrational conflicts could be eliminated.

As indicated in the first section of this paper, the approach of early human relationists had a management-oriented flavor which was opposed by those labor-relations specialists who saw in collective bargaining a democratic industrial government that both preserved the dignity of the individual and made large-scale business enterprise workable in a political democracy. These same specialists attack as incompatible with individual freedom, collective bargaining, and democracy, that part of the present-day human-relations movement which stresses harmony through conformity.

The other major trend in human relations, however, complements the concept of mature, democratic industrial government. Research evidence supporting greater participation in decision-making by all employees, and favoring a less authoritarian organizational structure and style of supervision, is encouraging to those with a democratic philosophy.

Human relations in industry brings into sharper focus but does not give final answers to questions of industrial democracy, power relationships, conformity, and efficiency. Unless human-relations research comes up with new experiments and fresh ideas there will be no general theory of human relations. As indicated elsewhere in this paper there are gaps in the general theory, which is suggestive rather than conclusive. Current research supports ideas already developed and as such tends to be repetitious. Unless major developments take place, human relations, like scientific management, may be reaching a dead end. In brief, there is one trend in the human-relations movement that, in its extreme form, is a mystical revolutionary cult and may be harmful to both individuals and organizations. Another offers a better understanding of groups and organizations, and, although its framework appears to be limited, it supports viewpoints found in the concept of mature industrial government.

QUESTIONS

1. Summarize the major concepts that Knowles presents as vital to human relations.
2. List and explain the criticisms he makes of human relations.
3. What does Knowles feel the future of industrial human relations to be?
4. What trends have led to the development of human relations theory and practice as we know it today?
5. What were Elton Mayo's contributions to this movement?

4. HUMAN RELATIONS IN ORGANIZATION *

David G. Moore

The human relations approach

The term *human relations* has popularly become identified with the "happiness" school of employee relations—a kind of applied, but somewhat impractical, Christianity which had better be left at Sunday School by men of the secular world. At best, its principles have been regarded as an intimate part of our Judaeo-Christian culture, an essential part of our way of life, and hardly a fit subject for scientific study. The kind of *human relations* with which we are concerned here, however, is something more than the Golden Rule; basically, it is the application of the concepts and research methods of the behavioral sciences to the analysis and understanding of organizational and administrative behavior.

The "human relations" school, which marks its beginnings from the research conducted at Western Electric by that company and at the Harvard Business School in the 'Twenties and 'Thirties, has drawn its major concepts from sociology, social anthropology, and clinical psychology. These concepts have been particularly helpful in understanding dynamic human behavior and problems of human adjustment and change. Since these are important interests also of the administrator, the "human relations" school contributed significantly to management thought. A few of the most useful concepts used in the study of organization from a "human relations" standpoint are discussed below.

Organization as an interacting system

An important first concept to grasp is the notion of "system." The human relations researcher views human behavior, whether at the individual or at the social level, as developing within an interacting framework in which each part influences every other part in a dynamic way. This approach can be seen in Freudian psychology, for example, where personality is viewed as a product of an interacting, highly interdependent system involving the id, the ego, and the superego. It can also be seen in the work of the social anthropologists who study

* David G. Moore, "Human Relations in Organization" in *Concepts and Issues in Administrative Behavior*, Sidney Mailick & Edward H. Van Ness, Eds., © 1962. Reprinted by permission of Prentice-Hall, Inc., Englewood Cliffs, N. J.

societies as interdependent systems involving the technological order, the moral or social order, and the supernatural order. It can be observed somewhat more recently in the research and writings of functional sociologists who seek to understand patterns of human behavior in terms of their function within the larger social framework.

If we view an organization as an interacting system, our insights in general become deeper and sounder. For one thing, we begin to see the social and psychological interpretations that employees at all levels make of events. We become sensitive to the intended versus the unintended consequences of administrative actions. We understand better the intimate relationship existing between the technical and formal aspects of organization and the informal, social system which operates wherever human beings work together. We see the interconnection of events and thus the "reasons" for various patterns of behavior as they emerge out of the processes of change and adjustment characterizing all large-scale organizations.

Viewing an organization as an interacting system is particularly helpful to the administrator since he develops his capacity to seek explanations within broader contexts. He is no longer satisfied with simple, linear explanations of human behavior. He is less prone to blame poor morale, let us say, on first-level supervision, or to attribute inefficiency solely to the influence of labor unions, for instance. The administrator instead acquires the ability to recognize that event *A* is related to a number of other events, both immediate and remote; he learns to view human behavior as part of a context involving many factors of a technical, administrative, social, and psychological nature which are perceived by employees not only at the level of conscious rationality but often at the level of emotions and sentiments.

Beliefs and actions

Any system of human interaction is a product of internalized beliefs and externalized actions. We are using the term *beliefs* to include consciously held values, ideas, and images as well as unconscious and unexpressed sentiments and gut-reactions. Beliefs are expressed in all manmade events—buildings, organizational models, systems of authority, and so on. They are expressed in less obvious ways in gestures, daydreams, and other purely symbolic signs. More than this, they are projected onto events "out there," whether natural or manmade. Thus, man lives in a meaningful world—a world which makes sense to him in terms of signs and symbols which invoke various beliefs and values.

The meaning which men ascribe to the world is not willy-nilly or capricious; it has an underlying logic based upon common human needs, the particular vantage point from which the world is viewed, rules of reason, past beliefs, and, above all, the actual consequences of particular beliefs when they are applied in the existing reality. Men share common needs at the physiological, psychological, and social levels. Of particular importance to the administrator is the common human drive for social identity, sense of worthwhileness, status, and recognition. Even the lowest level in our society say about themselves, "We are the people who are just as good as anybody else!"

A man's perspective depends upon the "social angle" from which he views his world. Social structure is characteristic of any human society. It represents on the one hand the daily activities which are pursued by men as they seek to satisfy their needs. In other words, it is an expression of technological, organizational, and administrative beliefs. In addition, however, social structure expresses the deeper moral order of society, that is, beliefs about man's relationship to man. Social structure in a very real sense precedes the individual. Thus, the individual in any society finds himself occupying particular positions in the social struggle toward which a variety of social as well as technical demands and expectations are directed. As he is caught up within the context of his daily activities, his attention and interests are directed in particular ways. What a man believes, therefore, is at least in part a function of what he does; it makes a big difference whether he is the boss, the employee, the accountant, or the salesman, as we shall see later in this paper.

What is reasonable is what seems logically integrated to the human mind. The human mind, even the primitive mind, strives for logical integration or plausibility. Social beliefs accordingly tend to evolve in an organic, developmental way with the new being integrated with the old, with each new interpretation depending to some extent upon prior premises. The organic, integrated process by which beliefs evolve and take form provides a certain orderliness and a sense of unfolding, even progress, from one generation to the next.

Above all, however, in our dynamic, secular society, the test of the real world is crucial in the development of beliefs. If a particular set of beliefs is unworkable, we strive, however slowly and unwillingly, to change our views.

The human relations researcher has typically been concerned with the interaction of human beliefs and actions. He characteristically has focused attention, first, on the structure of positions and relationships in the organization as these reflect the technological, organizational, and administrative beliefs of managers and employees. He has placed particular emphasis upon the social and moral belief and activity structure of the organization. Second, he has been concerned with the dynamic process of the formation and development of beliefs and consequent actions within the system. Third, he has been interested in the conflict of beliefs which develop within the organization, particularly the divergence of beliefs among administrators and lower-level employees. Finally, he has been concerned with the whole system of beliefs, relationships, and activities as these affect the survival of the organization.

Occupational identification

The importance of position and job demands in human relations in industry can perhaps be well illustrated from our own research in Sears, Roebuck and Company. For a number of years we had the opportunity at Sears of making attitude surveys in many of their retail stores throughout the country. Altogether we surveyed more than 100,000 employees in several hundred operating units. The advantage of this program from a research standpoint was the opportunity it provided to gather comparative data. We were able to go from retail store to retail store listening to the points of view and opinions of employees in similar jobs. It was possible for us to compare the attitudes of big ticket salesmen, service men, or warehouse employees from one operating unit to the next.

One of the most interesting findings of this study was the similarity of the attitudes of employees performing like work. In other words, big ticket salesmen exhibited almost the same pattern of attitudes whether they were located in San Francisco or Dallas. The same was true of other occupational groups. As a consequence, we became exceedingly impressed with the influence of job demands and division of labor on the attitudes of employees and the human relations which developed therefrom. So powerful was this influence, in fact, that we found ourselves discounting personality factors and leadership factors in explaining many aspects of human relations in the work place. It almost appeared that the job and its concomitant factors played more of a part in determining human attitudes and behavior than any other single element.

Now this is not hard to understand when you think about it. Our society offers the individual few opportunities for identification. Ours is a dynamic, changing, mobile society oriented very much to the present and the here-and-now rather than to the past. Traditional institutions geared to a rural society offer few guidelines. There is accordingly a strong tendency for individuals to identify with the job, to develop self-images which are basically occupational images, to view themselves in terms of what they do for a living.

I am a professor, more specifically a sociologist operating in a business school. My name means nothing: Moore is the tenth most popular name in the United States; so is David. I have no community ties. I was born in Connecticut, raised in New York and Chicago, and New York again, went to school in the Midwest. How do I tell people where I'm from? I come from a region, not a place. So, where are my abiding interests? Where is the challenge? What do I sit up nights thinking about? Why, my job of course! I ponder such important considerations, to me at least, as how I can introduce more of the behavioral sciences into a business school curriculum, how I can do a more effective job of writing and describing my ideas, in what areas I can do critical research, how I avoid administrative details, how I can maintain my academic freedom, and so on. In short, I ponder problems created by the kind of job I have.

In pursuing these interests, I offer perhaps some original contributions, but at the same time, I seek support and ideas from likeminded individuals. I feel a sense of kinship with others in similar positions and with similar problems whether I directly associate with them or not. More than this, I find that others in similar positions accept me, and I enjoy the security of having a place and an identity in society. If I am a reasonably aggressive individual, I find myself pushing the interests of my own group and developing very definite ideas regarding who fits in the group and who is opposed to it, who my friends are and who are my enemies. In fact, half the fun of living revolves around the games we play with one another over conflicting occupational interests.

The same process of identification is true of most of the rest of us whether we are managers, professionals, office workers, salesmen, skilled workers, or punch press operators. All of us to a greater or lesser extent find ourselves organized and our lives structured by our work. What we are, what we think about, our problems of adjustment, and our ways of meeting these challenges are inevitably related to the job.

To say simply that we identify or, better still, find our identities in our jobs, does not quite indicate the very intimate relationship existing between job demands and our attitudes and behavior. In order, therefore, to make the point clearer, let us take several examples of occupational groups from industry. We shall begin with the job of the executive. The most important function of the executive in industry is gaining a picture or understanding of the world around him and making decisions about it. He has to set directions and determine among alternative courses of action. This is not easy to do, because the decisions that he makes are not foregone conclusions emerging from the data available like two plus two equals four. First of all, the data available are always fragmentary and incomplete. Second, unforeseen circumstances arising from future events will inevitably occur. As ex-President Truman says: "A school boy's hindsight is always better than a president's foresight." Third, decisions of any importance involve value judgments. Yet, amidst all of this unpredictability, relativity, and fragmentary knowledge, the executive is compelled to make some kind of closure—to reach some kind of conclusion. This at least is the form of challenge which his job presents.

His adjustment is quite understandable, if we know the nature of his decision-making environment. He tries to limit the alternatives presented to him in a variety of ways. For one thing, he strives to measure consequences in terms of concrete, immediate reality. In this connection, one inevitable tool is the idea of cost and efficiency. Another is the strategy of taking short-run profits as opposed to long-run, less certain gains. Another approach which he takes to limit alternative possibilities and reduce the anxiety of ambiguity is to act conservatively and avoid speculation. In other words, contrary to the popular view of the executive, he is not a courageous opportunist, out on the frontier of technological experimentation and product-innovation. He is frequently more concerned with avoiding loss than with taking advantage of every opportunity. Under any circumstances, he limits alternatives by being conservative, by saying "no" more often than he says "yes," by sticking to known situations rather than pursuing speculative will o' the wisps.

Finally—though this by no means exhausts the possibilities—the executive limits ambiguity by developing practical business and management principles. He becomes a man of conviction, a man who operates on the basis of established precepts. This is perhaps one of the most interesting of the adjustments which the business executive typically makes. Over the years, any man in a leadership position tends to develop certain almost philosophical ideas, basic assumptions, and standard formulae which serve as general propositions against which he focuses particular circumstances and from which he deduces syllogistically specific conclusions.

Among the traits most valued in executive circles are moral character, conviction, and courage. The man who has principles and a willingness to act on these principles is esteemed above all others. But the point is that he is a man of conviction by necessity, by the very demands of his occupation. He needs principles much as a die-maker needs tools: as an essential part of his job.

Thus, the executive is a product in part, at least, of the decision-making environment in which he operates. Many other things could be said about him: how, for example, his integrative thinking contrasts with the analytical thinking of his staff, so that frequent conflict occurs between the two. And why does the executive work so hard? Perhaps because he cannot clearly distinguish between what is important and necessary for him to handle and what is unimportant. Therefore, he tries to do everything in chronological order. By doing everything, he avoids the difficulty of having to determine priorities.

Salesmen are another interesting group to analyze from the standpoint of occupational influences. The major challenge or problem of the salesman's job is the anxiety created by the necessity of having to manipulate and control, if possible, the behavior of others. This control must be exercised in a situation where the salesman has no formally established authority over the other person. Therefore, the problem is considerably enhanced and the anxiety is that much greater. In order to reduce his anxiety, the salesman attempts in a variety of ways to screw up his courage. One thing he can do is to inflate his ego and convince himself that he can sell anybody. He cheers himself on just as though he were the football team, the cheer leaders, and the stadium crowd all wrapped up in one person. He's a sucker for any inspirational book or speech. I've seen big ticket salesmen in retailing staging their own rally before store opening, complete with songs, cheers, back-slapping, and boastful predictions about the number of sales which they would make during the day. Sales managers know what it means to build up the motivation of their sales force. Many sales meetings are like oldtime revival meetings. The build-up is terrific. If the sales manager is a real, jumping type of promotional artist, he can develop tremendous motivation. His sales force will literally burst out of the meeting hall, descending on the unsuspecting public like a plague of locusts.

Another way in which the salesman binds his anxieties is to convince himself that the company and its products are the best. He is not manipulating the customer but performing a great service in making his company's product available to the public. Our attitude surveys demonstrate positive attitudes amounting almost to euphoria among salesmen. They score higher than any other group except top levels of management.

Salesmen frequently also maintain their motivation through a "pie-in-the-sky" attitude. Someday they're going to strike it rich, as one executive said, with a product that costs ten cents to make, is sold at a dollar, and is habit-forming. Their appetites are continuously whetted by the occasional "hot" days when everything goes well—when the commissions roll in and they can multiply the day's receipts by 365 and figure they're making $50,000 a year.

Still other anxiety-reducers are the various formulae, some magical, for coping with different customers and diverse sales situations. Salesmen are constantly concerned with problems related to the approach, the sales line, and the final closing. Many companies have worked out the various phases of selling in great detail, giving the sales force elaborate procedures for getting one's foot in the door, holding the customer's attention, and ultimately getting the name on the dotted line. Many salesmen develop a regular catalogue of customer types in order to know how to deal with them—fat ones, lean ones, tall ones, short ones, and so on. Indeed, some become rather expert lay-psychologists.

Thus far, we have been discussing the problems of adjustment which the central objectives of the job create. In addition to these, the job also delineates certain relationships with other occupations. For example, the salesman is related in specific ways to the manufacturing organization, research and engineering, customer service, and shipping. All these other departments can support or hinder the salesman in his work. These other occupational groups have interests too, and they are often in conflict with the aims and objectives of the sales force. One specific area can illustrate this.

The principal aims of the manufacturing organization are stability, standardization, simplicity, and efficiency. The dream of the manufacturing executive is for a stable, enduring, predictable market where the product-demands are relatively unchanging. The sales organization is considerably less concerned with stability, standardization, and order. It recognizes the need for flexibility in order to meet changing customer demands. Thus, to maintain an account, the sales organization may be more than willing to give the customer what he wants. This, it will be observed, is in direct conflict with the interests of manufacturing.

A very high percentage of the human relations problems in any organization are simply honest collisions among occupational groups with diverse, job-created interests.

Not only, then, are the patterns of behavior within occupational groups direct functions of job demands but the human relations oc-

curring among the various groups are, too. The problems of relationship are enhanced by the strong personal identifications which employees make with their own occupations. As previously indicated, a
job is more than a function; to the individual, it is a sense of purpose,
a set of interests, a way of life, a value system, above all a personal
identity.

When you attack my job, you attack me.

When you hinder my work, you thwart my interests.

When you push your own values at my expense, you become my
enemy.

When you fail to understand my interests and values, you are per-
verse, deliberately obstinate, intellectually stupid, and possibly even
morally incompetent.

Status

There is one other set of relationships related to the job which is
exceedingly important to the adjustment of employees and to human
relations generally. Jobs are typically ascribed higher and lower
status in the organization and in the community generally. If the job
is of high status, the incumbent's self-image is most gratifying. If the
job is of low status, the employee may not forsake himself but he
becomes defensive—anxious to prove that he is as good as anybody
else.

Every job, then, creates the additional problem for the employee of
relating himself to those in higher positions and those in lower positions and of maintaining his self-respect amidst this hierarchy. Status
systems occur everywhere but are somewhat more highly developed
in some organizations than in others. They maintain control within
the organization. But they can become dysfunctional if they create
obstacles which block communications, understanding, and cooperation among the various levels. Thus, if employees within an organization become more concerned with the status system than with the job
to be done, much of the purposeful, goal-directed energy of the
organization will be lost.

In summary, then, we can see that the job and the division of labor
within an organization create various demands which provide employees with a way of life, a set of aims, and a perception of themselves in relation to others performing different functions and operating at different levels. In a sense, the occupation gives the employee
an identity—the security of knowing who he is and where he stands.
At the same time, the very security that he gains also narrows his

interests. The more thoroughly identified with the occupation he becomes, the less capable he is of understanding the interests and values
of others. Under these circumstances, it would appear that one of
management's main tasks is to provide the employee with broader
identifications and the opportunity for the development of integrative
interests and values.

Organizational models

Human relations within an organization can be viewed also as a
dynamic process of adjustment between management's simplified and
often limited beliefs about organizational relationships and the actual
beliefs either existing within the broader moral order of our society or
else arising out of the process of adjustment and interaction within
the organization itself. The organizational models held in the minds
of managers and embodied in the functional and hierarchical arrangements, policies, and rules of conduct of the organization are simply
reflections of the beliefs of managers regarding what is right and
proper in organizational relationships. Some of the beliefs which
managers hold are realistic; some in our opinion are very unrealistic.

We should like to contrast two models of organization which are
currently held by American managers. One model might be called,
after Riesman, the inner-directed type; the other, the outer-directed.
We use the term *outer-directed* as opposed to Riesman's *other-directed*
since we wish to call attention to the external orientation of this
model. The essential characteristics of the inner-directed type are as
follows:

A. *Concern with System and Internal Process*

A major characteristic of the inner-directed organization is the constant and abiding concern with the internal processes of the firm. This
is one sense a reflection of the Protestant ethic which holds, among other
things, that if the internalized character of a man is in order, then the
external world and his adjustment to it will take care of itself.

Inner-directed management, if you will, is interested primarily in
developing neat, logical, efficient work systems and procedures. The ideal
model is the machine, an interrelated system, in which all of the parts
work together in the intricate choreography of a well-oiled, well-designed
mechanism.

B. *Inexorable Logic of the System*

In the so-called inner-directed mode of management, it is assumed
that there is one, and only one, best way to get a job done. This "one
best way" is to be sought principally at the tangible level of time emotion
economy, although other elements may enter in. Building an organization represents a gradual but consistent unfolding of the fundamental
and inexorable logic of the "one best system."

C. *Primacy of the System*

Since the system is held to represent the one best way of getting the job done, it is imperative to follow it exactly and permit no deviations. Cooperation and the coordination of human effort is built into the system so that, if each individual performs his part of the total task as it is supposed to be performed, then the total effort will be harmonious, efficient, and unified. The system as a means of insuring coordination and cooperation is thus imposed upon the work force. Indeed, one of the principal tasks of management becomes that of policing the work force at the various levels to insure that the system is being followed.

D. *Centralization of Authority*

The primacy of the system tends to centralize authority. The system cannot be changed willy-nilly, but must be adjusted carefully and in accordance with principles of logic and science. Control and design of the system become management's main tasks. There can be only one system and this must be guaranteed through the highest authority of management.

E. *Multiple Layers of Supervision*

With the need for close control, there is also the need for many layers of supervision, each level supplying pressure to the next lower level. There is also a demand for detailed reports and information regarding each step in the work process and more or less constant control. Problems of coordination are typically solved by the addition of more supervision and a more intricate system of work. The problem of coordination is solved either by more system or by the imposition of more supervision to insure that the system is being followed.

F. *Concern with the Job Within the System*
Rather than Over-All Results

Following the system appears to become more important than overall results to management and employees alike. There is a tendency to become lost within the system and forget what the system was set up to accomplish. The system becomes an end in itself rather than a means to an end.

Under such circumstances, employees tend to identify strongly with their own specialty or function very much in the manner we have previously described. The work system becomes a social system of higher, lower, friends, and enemies in which individual employees or groups of employees push their own interests without regard to over-all accomplishments.

There are many other elements of the extreme form of inner-directed management we have described. These can for the most part be deduced from the characteristics already covered. For example, the primacy of the system means that human beings must adjust to the system rather than vice versa. This is true not only of employees, but also of those who make use of the services of the enterprise.

Another pattern of management which has been developing on the industrial scene is outer-directed management. This pattern is a relatively recent development and is tied very much to the shift from a production economy to a market economy. Its best expression is found in such merchandising organizations as Sears, Roebuck and Company, and the Kroger Company. The market-oriented firm has been roundly criticized in some circles because it appears to lack character. In other words, it has no internal compulsions or needs which it imposes on the external world, but rather attempts to cope with reality as it finds it. It makes adjustments and moves with the times.

The characteristics of outer-directed management in its extreme form would be as follows:

A. *Concern with External Ends and Adjustment*

If inner-directed management is concerned with internal processes, outer-directed management concentrates on the problems of the external world. The business is viewed basically as a problem of relationship among various claimant groups with varying interests which must be integrated and reintegrated in a dynamic, changing world. Attention is concentrated on this external reality, and there is a keen awareness of the kinds of support needed from the various claimant groups for the survival and growth of the enterprise.

B. *Subordination of System to Over-All Results*

The system of work is regarded simply as a means to an end and is not defied as it is in inner-directed organizations. An experimental attitude with regard to managerial and organizational practices develops. There is a willingness to accept diverse and often discordant modes of operation as long as results are achieved. The organization is viewed as an *ad hoc* arrangement which can always be adjusted and changed if need be. There is nothing sacred about it; it is fluid and dynamic.

C. *Decentralization*

The outer-directed organization tends to be more decentralized, since a police force does not have to be maintained to insure that the system is being followed. More than this, there is the acceptance of the idea of decentralized decision-making. The conviction develops that those closest to the scene of action can make certain more appropriate and valid decisions than higher levels of authority.

D. *Overlapping Job Duties and Responsibilities*

The outer-directed organization tends to be sloppy by inner-directed standards. There is frequently a considerable overlapping of job responsibilities and less tendency for employees to stay put within the organization. There is also a willingness and acceptance of the idea of stepping across job lines to get the over-all task accomplished.

E. *Development of Organization vs. Occupational Identification*

The employee at all levels tends to identify more with organizational interests than with occupational aims. By the same token, there is less tendency to type employees in terms of their specialties. There is a greater reliance on whole men as opposed to highly trained automatons or specialists working within the perfect system.

We could elaborate further on the unique characteristics of the outer-directed organization. However, once again additional elements can be deduced from what we have already described.

Now the pattern of human relations which develops within the inner-directed organization, as opposed to the outer-directed, is quite different, as you might expect. We cannot, of course, develop all of these differences here. However, we can touch on a few.

The inner-directed organization with its concentration on internal processes and its deification and imposition of the "one best system" tends to deflect the attention of employees and management from the ultimate ends of the enterprise and to focus their interests on the demands of the job and the problems of adjusting to the system. Human relations in this type of organization tend to be characterized by strong occupational identifications and conflicts among occupational groups. Each occupational group tends to push its own interests and strives to generalize or universalize these interests throughout the organization. There is no over-all ruling principle or measure against which the particular interests of the various occupational groups can be tested. Therefore, power and status become exceedingly important considerations. In extreme cases of occupational conflict, an organization appears to be an arena for struggle among contending occupational groups rather than a coordinated business enterprise. We call such organizations socially neurotic, since they spend more time in internal conflict than in coping with external reality.

In addition to the problems created by occupational identification in the inner-directed organization, there is also the problem of adjusting to narrowly circumscribed activities which often by themselves are meaningless, like a nut on a bolt. Individual activities make little sense separated from the system. Not only is the job meaningless, but the individual who has to identify with the role is equally detached and isolated. He senses this lack of significance and strives to introduce meaning into his life by playing games with management, defending himself in a variety of ways, or else simply by detaching himself mentally from the organization, putting in physical time only.

The inner-directed organization with its authoritarian atmosphere creates tensions in the supervisory areas, too. Supervision is compelled to play the role of a police force, closely controlling activities to insure that the system is being followed. Furthermore, the tall, pyramidal authority structure characterizing the inner-directed organization places a heavy weight of authority on the individual employee. As he looks up in the organization all he can see is bosses—layer upon layer of them.

It is axiomatic in human relations that the more bosses, the more tension.

The inner-directed organization tends to become rigid, lacking the flexibility necessary to cope with a changing external world. This rigidity is due to a considerable extent to occupational identification. Narrowly defined vested interests develop that are resistant to change, particularly to change which threatens the status of the group. The occupational group becomes more concerned with its own survival than with the survival of the organization. Change in the inner-directed organization has to be effected by surgery and is typically traumatic.

One interesting consequence of the inner-directed organization is the lack of trust that frequently develops in the attitudes of management towards employees. In imposing the "one best system" of work, management expects perfect compliance from employees. The likelihood of deviation, when the rules of the game are as tight as this, when there is so little demand for individual expression, and when there is considerable tension in the supervisory area, is very high. Under such circumstances, it is easy for management to develop a somewhat jaundiced view regarding the sense of responsibility of the average employee. Furthermore, narrow occupational interests tend to enhance management's negative impressions. The impression very readily develops that large segments of the work force are concerned only with self-interests and in furthering their own ends. The result in the inner-directed organization is too often more system and more control.

While the so-called outer-directed organization has its problems, they are not the same kind as the inner-directed type. Here, we find less occupational identification and a higher degree of involvement with the over-all aims of the enterprise. The concern of management with external reality tends to permeate the organization. More than this, the organization of jobs tends to place employees, even at the lowest levels, in direct contact with some of the basic tasks of the enterprise in a way which he can understand. The organization is not built from the top down, but inwardly from the over-all tasks which must be accomplished by the enterprise if it is to survive and develop.

With more direct involvement with the external aims of the enterprise, the employee finds his work more meaningful. He is able to share his interests with higher levels of management. Greater reliance can be placed on him so that the pressure of supervision can be reduced. By the same token, status differences and anxieties are lessened and there is less purely defensive behavior within the organization. What conflict does occur within the organization tends to be at the level of ideas rather than at the level of occupational and status interests.

Quite obviously, I have been painting a very favorable picture of the so-called outer-directed organization. I sincerely believe that it is a more effective model than the older pattern, that it not only results in more mature human relations but better results in terms of the aims of the organization, and that it incorporates more completely our present understandings about human nature and social organization. It is not, however, an easy model to apply. It is much easier and, in a way, safer for management to limit the problem of decision-making and reduce the anxiety of ambiguity by concentrating its attention more or less compulsively on means rather than ends, and on internal form rather than external reality.

Reaching out for new ideas, particularly in a dynamic situation, is always more difficult than operating in terms of established routines. Nonetheless, if we are to make real progress in the effective organization of human effort, we must break the shackles of inner-directedness and compulsive organizational rituals and move out into the real world.

QUESTIONS

1. What is the relationship of individual beliefs to individual actions?
2. What were the major conclusions of the attitude studies conducted at Sears, and how do they relate to building a more effective human relations program?
3. Contrast the outer-directed and inner-directed models of organization. Which do you think is more common in business firms today?
4. Illustrate some of the more common problems of the inner-directed model.
5. What is status? Why is it so critical to effective human relations within an organization?

5. CONTRIBUTIONS OF THE BEHAVIORAL SCIENCE APPROACH *

Wilmar F. Bernthal

I. INTRODUCTION

Although our panel chairman has asked us to simulate the blind men describing the elephant, it should be clear that we only temporarily put our blindfolds on, to describe that part of our "elephant" which for the moment is of most intimate concern to us. As each of us focuses on one set of "contributions" to improved management practices, we *do not* mean to imply:

   a. That these are the only or the most significant contributions.
   b. That these contributions are necessarily in conflict with contributions made by the other approaches.
   c. That these contributions have invalidated other, and particularly earlier, contributions to management practice.

Rather, what we imply is that the total subject cannot be viewed objectively without considering the contributions of each part and how these parts are inter-related in the whole. This may be the clue to the apparent difficulty managers experience in trying to apply certain management concepts, theory, and research findings to management practice. A single-track approach to management study or practice often fails to answer the complex problems of the entire system, or causes side-effects in other parts of the system which override the wholesome effects achieved in the subsystem. Placing too great a reliance (or faith) on one approach, to the exclusion of other equally valid approaches, may lead to disillusionment, and often to violent reaction against that approach.

With these reservations in mind, I will dutifully blind myself for the moment to the other relevant approaches, and will review the contributions that the behavioral science approach has made, or can make, to management practice.

II. BEHAVIORAL SCIENCE KNOWLEDGE AND MANAGEMENT PRACTICE

The question of behavioral science contribution to management practice is really twofold. The first part, "What are the behavioral science insights, concepts, research findings, and theories that are

---

* From *Proceedings, Academy of Management Annual Meeting*, 1962, pp. 21-28. Reprinted with permission.

available for *improved understanding* of management?" can be answered by merely pointing out the fantastic development of this field within the last quarter century, and cataloguing the literature and research evolving from it.

The second part of the question, "What contribution has all this made to *improve management practices*?" is more difficult, if not impossible, to answer. One sometimes gets the impression that the behavioral science researcher lives in a world separated from the practicing manager by a wide gulf of interests, goals, values, and personality traits. The amount of idea-transfusion between these two worlds, via consultation, literature, and education, and the extent of actual application to business practice of known ideas, is largely a matter of conjecture which could well become a research subject for members of the Academy of Management.

In this paper, I would like to review the contributions of behavioral science theory and research to management knowledge and then add a few comments on the problem of translating knowledge into management practice.

III. Contribution of Behavioral Science to Management Knowledge

On this panel, we are already segmenting rather artificially four "basic approaches" to improved management practice. Yet each of these approaches, for research purposes, may stem out of further specialized disciplines. Social science specialization has led to separate study of man in his various roles and environments. This segmented study of human behavior sometimes seems to assume that human behavior takes place in a series of watertight compartments, so that the economist can study "economic man," the sociologist "social man," the political scientist "political man," etc. The behavioral science approach to management draws upon all the social sciences, directly or indirectly, and attempts to integrate their insights into a way of thinking about organizational behavior.

The most significant *social science* contributions to management practice undoubtedly have come from economics—the study of man as a consumer, and the development of organizations through which economic needs can be effectively satisfied. The behavioral science approach, however, is usually defined more narrowly to explain man's behavior as a member of producing organizations—individual behavior in a social system designed to achieve productive goals through cooperative effort. The study of history, economics, political science, and anthropology provides insights into the setting in which organizational behavior takes place, while psychology, sociology, social psychology, and applied anthropology provide the more immediate clues to the behavior itself. It is the contributions to management of these last-named areas of social science that I wish to summarize here.

The behavioral science approach to management knowledge also differs from some of the social sciences in terms of its research methodology. While some social scientists, and particularly economists, may analyze human behavior in society by developing logical abstract models incorporating given assumptions about human behavior, behavioral science stresses empirical (real-life) data resulting from controlled observation. Thus, the behavioral sciences can be a rich source of experience which may have immediate relevance to improvement of management practice.

A strict definition of behavioral science would limit our inquiry to research findings. Much of the so-called behavioral science literature for management, however, is interpretive, in that it attempts to translate behavioral science research findings into meaningful concepts for the practicing manager. For purposes of this paper, I will use the term "behavioral science" loosely to incorporate both the basic research and the interpretation.

A. The psychology of individual differences

The early traditional approach to management was based on a sort of "intuitive psychology" which led to emphasis on specialization of work and to economic incentive systems. It said little about man as a social being, although undoubtedly there was some awareness of man's social needs and behavior. However, in an economic context in which man's major purpose in work was to satisfy survival needs, the neglect of the social dimension was not critical. The history of output restriction, even under individual incentive systems, indicates, however, that this intuitive psychology proved inadequate in explaining organizational behavior in a developing economic and social environment.

The psychology of individual differences provides guidelines for matching men and jobs by selecting, testing, developing, and placing personnel so that their potential can best be utilized in organizations. At the same time, it also provides insights into designing machines and jobs to fit the capacities and limitations of the human mind and body. For example, the space age need for design of cockpits and capsules gives "human engineering" new importance as a means for solving problems stemming from the industrial revolution—that of relating man and technology.

Despite individual psychology's continuing contributions to management through selection and placement on the one hand, and through human engineering on the other hand, the emphasis in the behavioral sciences has been in another direction. The behavioral science approach to management has focused not so much on finding abilities as on determining motivations—willingness—of man to work productively. And the emphasis has not been upon man in isolation, but in a social setting. The major contribution of behavioral science is its view of business as a social system. This recognition that organizations are to be viewed as social systems, even if the purpose of the organization is economic, and its technology rational, provides new insights into problems that had been a frustration to managers oriented in a more limited management outlook.

B. Business as a social system

The way of thinking about business as a social system received its major impetus from Chester Barnard in his *The Functions of the Executive* [1] in 1938. At the same time, Elton Mayo and his research group at Harvard came up with notions about informal organization that reinforced the idea that a manager must think about organizations as systems of human relations, rather than purely as related functions or jobs.[2] Business organizations were viewed as cooperative systems having their own culture and subcultures. The approach was that of the anthropologist—to observe objectively the actual behavior of people at work, and to note and analyze these data without introducing assumptions that did not arise from the data.

The conceptual scheme for analyzing organizational behavior in terms of a social system was formalized by George Homans in *The Human Group*,[3] drawing in part upon the earlier work of Eliot Chapple and other anthropologists. In this scheme, the relevant variables are the *activities, interactions,* and *sentiments* that result when technology, economic factors, management and leadership practices, and personal factors are combined in organizations. In this setting, the activities, interactions and sentiments ultimately produce

---

[1] Cambridge, Mass.: Harvard University Press, 1938.
[2] F. J. Roethlisberger and W. J. Dickson, *Management and the Worker* (Cambridge, Mass.: Harvard University Press, 1939). The Hawthorne researchers, in turn, were influenced by the concepts of a social system formulated by Vilfredo Pareto, *The Mind and Society* (New York: Harcourt, Brace and Company, 1935)
[3] New York: Harcourt, Brace and Co., 1950.

the real (or emergent) behavior which determines the organization's productivity, the growth and development of the participants, and their satisfactions or morale.

This conceptual scheme provides a systematic way in which complex behavior patterns in organizations can be analyzed, and through which, hopefully, behavioral consequences of management action can be predicted. Although this scheme is often identified as the Harvard approach, it appears in different variations in many of the behavioral science researches.[4]

C. Variations on a basic theme

Within the broad analytical framework of business as a social system, behavioral scientists have staked out various subthemes for investigation. These differ primarily in the aspect of organizational behavior selected for study, and in the methodology of investigation.

The small group approach. One such variation on the basic theme is the study of leadership, interpersonal relations, communication, and cooperation by controlled studies of small group behavior. This orientation has its roots in the group dynamics of Kurt Lewin, and is illustrated by the work of the Research Center for Group Dynamics at the University of Michigan, and the controlled laboratory studies of small group behavior by Alex Bavelas at Stanford and Robert Bales at Harvard. The case for use of democratic leadership in small groups is developed by Norman R. F. Maier in his *Principles of Human Relations.*[5] Attempts to apply group dynamics concepts to management practice by developing the manager's self-awareness and interpersonal competence are illustrated in the laboratory training (T-Group) of the National Training Laboratories and the sensitivity training of Robert Tannenbaum and his colleagues at the Human Relations Research Group, Institute of Industrial Relations, University of California, Los Angeles.[6]

---

[4] A recent illustration of the Harvard approach is found in Paul Lawrence, *et al., Organizational Behavior and Administration* (Homewood: R. D. Irwin, Inc., 1961). The interactionist approach to analyzing organizational behavior is identified with William H. Whyte in his *Money and Motivation* (New York: Harper and Brothers, 1955) and *Men at Work* (Homewood: R. D. Irwin, Inc., 1962). A recent attempt to translate it into management practice is found in Eliot Chapple and Leonard Sayles, *The Measure of Management* (New York: Macmillan Co., 1961).

[5] New York: John Wiley and Sons, 1952.

[6] The work of this latter group is reported in Robert Tannenbaum, Irving R. Weschler, and Fred Massarik, *Leadership and Organization* (New York: McGraw-Hill Book Co. Inc., 1961). For a study of the effects of sensitivity training upon managerial performance, see Chris Argyris, *Interpersonal Competence and Organizational Effectiveness* (Homewood: R. D. Irwin, Inc., 1962).

The survey research center apporach. The recent book by Rensis Likert, *New Patterns of Management*,[7] summarizes the conclusions of 15 years of research on the relationship of productivity, supervision, and morale by the Survey Research Center of the Institute for Social Research, University of Michigan. The contribution to management practice here is both in terms of the survey research method used to study organizational behavior, and the conclusions drawn from the research. As with other behavioral science research, the publications of the Institute for Social Research, and Likert's book, are loaded with implications for improving managers' leadership attitudes and practices.

The worker and technology approach. One other approach that be-havioral science has taken to improve management practice is to study the relationship of the worker and technology. The studies in the Yale Technology Project concerning the worker and the foreman on the assembly line illustrate research that can help determine the limits of job specialization and standardization in view of the realities of human needs and the social system.[8]

The conflict of individual and organization. A variation on the basic theme which has caused considerable flurry among managers is the McGregor and Argyris thesis of the potential conflict between a healthy human personality and formal organizations administered strictly according to rational principles of organization.[9] Influenced by Freudian psychology, these authors suggest that the dependency relations created by hierarchial authoritarian organizations and en-forced through management direction and control conflict with basic human needs for reasonable independence and self-direction. Insensi-tive managers may force their employees into immature behavior patterns which will prevent the kind of human performance the managers are trying to achieve. McGregor and Argyris thus plead with the manager to check his assumptions about human behavior, and to use with discretion the authority vested in his formal position.

Modern organization theory—the integrative discipline? As new insights are developed into different aspects of human relations within

---

[7] New York: McGraw-Hill Book Company, Inc., 1962.

[8] Charles R. Walker and Robert Guest, *The Man on the Assembly Line* (Cam-bridge: Harvard University Press, 1952), and Charles R. Walker, Robert H. Guest, and A. N. Turner, *The Foreman on the Assembly Line* (Cambridge: Harv-ard University Press, 1956).

[9] Douglas McGregor, *The Human Side of Enterprise* (New York: McGraw-Hill Book Company, Inc., 1960), and Chris Argyris, *Personality and Organizations* (New York: Harper and Brothers, 1957).

the firm, it is only natural that researchers should try to fit these micro-contributions into a macro-framework. Conceivably, this could become the behavioral theory of the firm. Organization theory uses the rigorous methods of economic analysis, but incorporates findings of behavioral science research rather than working with models that assume rational maximizing behavior. In this sense, Chester Barnard laid the foundations for modern organization theory by conceiving of organizations as complex social systems. More recently, the application of research methods from different disciplines to the study of organizations promises to produce new insights for the manager into the relevant variables and their relationships in organizations.[10]

IV. The Step from Management Knowledge to Management Practice

Knowledge is not the only precondition necessary for effective practice or action. Since behavioral science concerns itself with human behavior in its total complexity, the convenient *ceteris paribus* assumption of rationality is hardly applicable. Management is also a form of human behavior, motivated by a complex set of human needs, many of which are nonlogical.

One may hypothesize that the academic researcher in behavioral science has been interested largely in developing knowledge rather than changing management practice. Business and other organizations, on the other hand, have an immediate concern about management practice, and are concerned only secondarily with knowledge. Rather than going through the lengthy and tedious educational process, they tend to look for a short run payoff on training investments. Consequently, they often emphasize skill training, and may become susceptible to shortcuts, fads, gimmicks, or self-defeating devices for changing management behavior.

The missing link in the behavioral science approach, then, seems to be the bridge between knowledge and practice. The barriers to bridging this gap are complex, consisting of rather mysterious psychological and sociological factors that tend to be roadblocks on the "pure rationality route" to organizational effectiveness.

---

[10] See, for example, J. G. March and H. A. Simon, *Organizations* (New York: John Wiley and Sons, 1958) ; Mason Haire (ed.), *Modern Organization Theory* (New York: John Wiley and Sons, 1959) ; Albert H. Rubenstein and Chadwick J. Haberstroh (eds.), *Some Theories of Organization* (Homewood: The Dorsey Press, Inc., and Richard D. Irwin, Inc., 1960) ; Amitai Etzioni, *Complex Organizations* (New York: Holt, Rinehart and Winston, Inc., 1961) ; and Chris Argyris, *Understanding Organizational Behavior* (Homewood: The Dorsey Press, Inc., 1960).

The growing literature on the authoritarian personality is a good illustration of forces within the manager which may constitute impenetrable barriers to improved management action, even though he has full knowledge of alternative approaches to management practices.[11]

Some recent studies of the effectiveness of human relations training also have had a sobering effect on the optimistic assumption that equates knowledge and practice. Both individual personality factors and organizational demands (including the top management values and assumptions) may be real deterrents to translating behavioral science knowledge into practice.[12] This frontier of behavioral science will undoubtedly come in for increased attention in the near future.

Assuming that behavior change depends upon more than knowledge, professors of management and management trainers in industry face an interesting dilemma. It has been demonstrated that training the mind does not necessarily influence practice. Yet to tamper with the personality of the student or manager raises ethical issues about the limits to which one may legitimately invade the privacy of an individual in the interests of organizational effectiveness.

One may visualize a continuum of management training, the goals of which range from simple intellectual experience to complete behavior transformation. On the left extreme of this continuum would be traditional methods of imparting knowledge, with little concern for behavior beyond an *intellectual experience*. These include lecture, guided discussion, and conferences designed to widen the manager's conception horizons. Moving toward greater ego-involvement are various training methods designed to give a *vicarious experience,* such as case study, incident method, role playing, and simulation. Beyond such intellectual and vicarious experiences are attempts to improve management behavior directly by developing greater *self-awareness and social sensitivity* in the manager. These methods are

---

[11] See, for example, Milton Rokeach, *The Open and Closed Mind* (New York: Basic Books, Inc., 1960); T. W. Adorno, *et al., The Authoritarian Personality* (New York: Harper and Brothers, 1951); Chris Argyris, *Personality and Organization* (New York: Harper and Brothers, 1957), pp. 216-18; and, in a more popular vein, Eugene Jennings, "The Authoritarian Cultural Lag in Business," *Journal of the Academy of Management,* August, 1959, and Robert McMurry, "The Case for Benevolent Autocracy," *Harvard Business Review,* January-February, 1958.

[12] Effectiveness of human relations training at the supervisory level was explored in F. J. Roethlisberger, "Training Supervisors in Human Relations," *Harvard Business Review,* September, 1951, and further studied and reported in E. A. Fleishman, E. F. Harris, and H. E. Burtt, *Leadership and Supervision in Industry* (Columbus: Personnel Research Board, The Ohio State University, 1955). For a recent study of the possibility of affecting top management behavior through laboratory training, see Chris Argyris, *Interpersonal Competence and Organizational Effectiveness* (Homewood: R. D. Irwin, Inc., 1962).

directed at the roots of interpersonal competence, and may even aim at personality transformation. It is this area of the management training continuum that forms the battleground on which the limits of the behavioral science approach to improved management practice will be determined.

Current attempts at using laboratory training (T-Group or sensitivity training) among select groups of actual or potential managers already indicate a cautious movement by industry toward influencing management behavior directly. The next logical step in this progression toward internationalizing management training and education could involve limited psychotherapy. Assuming such training is economically feasible, the manager faces difficult ethical questions of whether an organization can legitimately require its managers to submit to sensitivity training or psychotherapy, presumably in the interests of the organization's effectiveness. These questions become even more sticky when one realizes that this progression could lead to psychoanalysis (and perhaps even religious conversion) as means by which managers' personality transformations could be affected. Neither the business firm nor the business school has yet ventured this far in training its personnel for improved management practice.

Both the practical and ethical limits of using behavioral science to transform managers' personalities in the interests of organizational performance need to be explored. The criteria by which these limits are determined need to be made explicit if behavioral science is to assume its legitimate role in the improvement of management practice.

V. Behavioral Science Contributions to Management, in Summary

The contribution of behavioral science to management practice consists primarily of producing new insights rather than new techniques. It has developed or expanded a way of thinking about the role of the manager, the nature of organizations, and the behavior of individuals within organizations. In this sense, the behavioral sciences have contributed significantly to that part of the body of management knowledge concerned with *the manager's leadership role*.

    a. The behavioral sciences have given special attention to a dimension of management that classical management theory assumed or took for granted, namely, the factors in addition to pay that determine the level of motivation and human performance in organizations. They questioned the assumptions about organizational behavior that were implied in early management theory.

b. The behavioral sciences developed the point of view of organizations as complex social systems. In this respect they expanded the conceptual sights of managers from focusing on formal organization as the only relevant perspective of organizational life to dealing with organizational realities in their total complexity.

c. More recently, the behavioral sciences have focused upon the forces in the manager himself, his inadequacies and limitations in developing and maintaining a managerial climate conducive to high human performance. This concern about self-awareness and social sensitivity as a criterion for success may have important repercussions in the selection and development of managers for leadership positions in organizations.

d. Indirectly, the behavioral sciences have confronted management with some difficult questions about the ethical constraints, or limits, the manager faces in using insights into human behavior in the interests of advancing the economic objectives of organizations.

QUESTIONS

1. What has been the general impact of the behavioral sciences on management practices?

2. What was the major contribution of Chester Barnard to modern organization theory?

3. What new training methods are being developed to assist the manager in developing human relations skills? What are some of the difficulties attendant to them?

4. Why should behavioral science be concerned with "forces within the manager"?

5. What is your opinion concerning the value of behavioral science knowledge to managers?

6. ORGANIZATIONAL HEALTH AND COMPANY EFFICIENCY *

Dalton E. McFarland

The concept of organizational health, although merely an analogy, provides useful insights for understanding organizational behavior. These insights are the product of an increasing amount of excellent research on the organizational behavior of executives, supervisors, and rank-and-file workers. By drawing upon some of this research, it is possible to show that business organizations must seek new approaches to problems of organization structure and design if they are to adapt to the changing social, economic, and technological demands confronting them.

The idea of health implies life, growth, and vitality. Viewed in this light, a company is a dynamic system, pulsating with changes that continuously shape the company's evolving character, and hence the attitudes, behavior, and very lives of its employees. A business organization is healthy to the extent that it can thrive in a competitive and often hostile environment.

A healthy organization is both adaptive and innovative, with a high tolerance for internal and external crises, and the ability to forge ahead to new levels of activity. There is a continuous renewal of its vital forces.[1] In the study of organizations renewal and growth are central aspects of the biological analogy. Dubin has examined the linkage systems which make for stability in organizations. He found that stability in individual units and clusters of units in organizations arises from internal work-group bonds, and from mechanisms enabling constituent groups to present a united front to the organization in order to resist changes affecting the group as a whole. Thus he sees the matter of stability both from the standpoint of the system as a whole and from that of its components.[2]

Haire's analysis of organization growth, following a biological model, investigates the interdependence of size, shape, and function in organizations. By empirically studying the histories of a number

* From *Business Topics*, Vol. 13, No. 3 (Summer, 1965), pp. 45-57. Reprinted with permission.
[1] James V. Clark, "What Makes a Healthy Organization?" *California Management Review*, Vol. IV, No. 4 (Summer, 1962), pp. 16-30; Townsend Hoopes, "Creativity: Key to Organizational Renewal," *Business Horizons*, Winter, 1963, pp. 35-42.
[2] Robert Dubin, "Stability of Human Organizations," *Modern Organization Theory*, ed. Mason Haire (New York: John Wiley and Sons, Inc., 1959), pp. 218-71.

of firms, Haire concluded that growth processes characteristic of business firms can be described by relatively simple growth equations of the kind used in population studies and other disciplines, and that general principles underlie this growth. This tentatively confirms the utility of the biological model.[3]

Biological models emphasizing such concepts as growth and stability have important antecedents in the work of economists on the subject of equilibrium. Summarizing this work, McGuire analyzes the writings of Cannon, Boulding, Knauth, and Chamberlain, all of whom have developed theories revolving around the concept of homeostasis, a condition of stability in the bodies of highly developed animals. Cannon, a physiologist, first developed the concept. He also argued that nonphysiological states, such as social, political, and industrial organizations, have evolved mechanisms for preserving their homeostatic condition. Boulding emphasized the homeostatic nature of the firm's balance sheets, reflecting the way in which external pressures cause the disequilibrium to which internal forces in the firm react. Knauth was concerned with the maintenance of trade positions between a firm and other firms in an industry. Chamberlain holds a bargaining theory of the firm which is homeostatic in character. He emphasizes the balances which result from bargains between conflicting interests.[4] All homeostatic theories stress the importance of the stability of the business as a system related to either internal or external forces, or both. The implication in all such theories is that goals or motivating forces other than profit maximization operate either within the entrepreneur, or spring from the environment.[5]

Management theorists have, strangely enough, made little use of equilibrium theory. Chapple and Sayles, in advocating a reassessment of the morale concepts used in business organizations, suggest that

[3] Mason Haire, "Biological Models and Empirical Histories of the Growth of Organizations," *Modern Organization Theory*, ed. Mason Haire (New York: John Wiley and Sons, Inc., 1959), pp. 272-305. Two recent works which directly or indirectly employ an organic or biological point of view in the analysis of management problems are Ralph M. Hower and Charles D. Orth, *Managers and Scientists* (Boston: Division of Research, Harvard Business School, 1963), and David W. Ewing, *The Managerial Mind* (New York: The Free Press of Glencoe, 1964).

[4] Joseph McGuire, *Theories of Business Behavior* (Englewood Cliffs, N. J.: Prentice-Hall, Inc., 1964), pp. 101-108; Walter B. Cannon, *The Wisdom of the Body* (Revised and Enlarged Edition, New York: W. W. Norton and Company, Inc., 1939); Kenneth E. Boulding, *A Reconstruction of Economics* (New York: John Wiley and Sons, Inc., 1950); Oswald Knauth, *Business Practices, Trade Position, and Competition* (New York: Columbia University Press, 1956); Neil W. Chamberlain, *A General Theory of Economic Process* (New York: Harper and Row, 1955); and *The Firm: Micro Economic Planning and Action* (New York: McGraw-Hill Book Company, Inc., 1962).

[5] McGuire, *op. cit.*

morale may be viewed as a measure of organizational health. Basic patterns of activity and interaction and associated personality factors can be viewed as representing a state of equilibrium. This state may be disturbed by stress situations, with equilibrium being restored by various behaviors of the individual experiencing stress. Morale is then defined for an organization as the obtaining of a state of equilibrium in the relations of the constituent individuals.[6]

Organizational health, then, clearly reflects the twin goals of company survival and growth. Survival is a minimum goal, and an important one. But the healthy enterprise pours its energies into a vigorous struggle for progress, if not supremacy, in a competitive environment. Managers use periods of stability to generate the conditions of further growth, and they know how to achieve this growth at costs and risks reasonably commensurate with potential gains.

IMPORTANT DISTINCTIONS

Organizational health should not be confused with company health. Although related, they are not synonymous. Company health is the result of organizational health. Elements such as financial conditions, product acceptance, market position, technological adequacy, and capacity for confronting the impact of economic conditions generally are indicators of company health. Changes in these elements are often the outward manifestations of deep-seated organizational problems. However, there is mutual interaction between these variables and the characteristics of organization, so that causes and effects are difficult to isolate. For example, financial losses apparently caused by changes in consumer tastes, or technological change, may produce symptoms of organizational ill-health as executives struggle to find remedies for the situation. But the financial difficulties might not arise or become so acute, had not organizational difficulties prevented the company from building its resistance to the forces of disintegration.

A company may thus seem to fail because it cannot solve its technical, financial, or economic difficulties. Underlying these manifest problems, however, are latent ones associated with deficient skill in maintaining the conditions of organizational health. A business that does not achieve this health is less able to withstand adverse forces in the economy generally, or the pressures of competitors; nor

---

[6] Eliot D. Chapple and Leonard R. Sayles, *The Measure of Management* (New York: The Macmillan Company, 1961), chap. 9.

can it stem the beginnings of internal decay dormant in every organization. Even a very robust organization can deteriorate under the impact of complex internal and external forces, as in the case of RKO, which, according to one observer, degenerated in five years under Howard Hughes from the nation's fifth biggest motion picture studio into little more than a few bankrupt parcels of real estate. In RKO, neglect and mismanagement "had dissipated its value as a producing unit beyond any hope of recapture; it had become merely a corporate derelict to be salvaged as profitably as possible." [7]

Clearly a company can be in a state of poor organizational health long before the symptoms become apparent. It can outwardly exhibit the earmarks of efficiency, success, and company health at the same time that it is nurturing the seeds of decay. The symptoms lag behind the outward manifestations, often for many years. As in the case of a human being, one's outward appearance can be healthy, but a serious condition, such as tuberculosis, may lurk deceptively within. For example, the anti-trust crisis in the General Electric Company in 1960-61 was preceded by management pressures for profits dating back to the early 1950's, when Ralph Cordiner introduced his plan for decentralization. These pressures continued, while top management failed to keep informed about how recipients of those pressures were reacting.[8] It took General Dynamics almost six years from its decision on jet transports in 1955 to reach the climax of its disastrous $425 million loss by 1961.[9]

Organizational health is thus a critical element supporting the goals of company stability and growth. Because it reflects the environment in which people work, the interrelationships of people, and the human frameworks for managerial decision and action, the question of organizational health is highly relevant to the search for efficiency. Technological bases for efficiency—the methods of marketing, production, and finance—are available equally to all companies: the Monsanto Company, for example, employs essentially the same devices for raising capital that other companies use. But the really significant differences among companies are found in their managerial skills, in the utilization of human resources, and in the productive efficiency that is associated with teamwork, high morale, and high job satisfaction. In modern complex organizations, however, good human relations and good personnel management are not enough. Organization structure has a lot to do with what happens.

---

[7] Richard Austin Smith, *Corporations in Crisis* (New York: Doubleday and Company, 1963), pp. 43-62.
[8] *Ibid.*, pp. 97-138.
[9] *Ibid.*, pp. 63-96.

Efficiency

We must note one more important distinction. Company efficiency and organizational efficiency are not the same. The concept of efficiency itself requires a criterion, and the criteria by which these two concepts are measured are different. Managers regard company efficiency as productive efficiency, or the minimization of unit costs. The aim is low costs per unit of product consistent with the desired level of quality. In contrast, organizational efficiency has fewer specific referents and less objective criteria. Organizational efficiency refers to the way in which the patterns or structures are multipurpose in nature. We expect an organization today to provide channels of communication, systems of delegated authority and command, control networks, service patterns, task accomplishment, status systems, job satisfactions for employees, and the fulfillment of many other human needs.

There is a presumption in most of the management literature that organizational efficiency is a requisite of company efficiency, as well as a presumption that organizational health is a requirement of organizational efficiency. However, this chain of organizational health, organizational efficiency, and company efficiency is a complex one, and research does not yet completely substantiate the validity of these presumptions. But we are confronted with the stark reality of company failures, and with the stubborn fact of widespread job dissatisfaction among the employees of most companies today. A central problem for managers, therefore, is to study and properly diagnose the defects of organizational structures, and to achieve the early detection of potential decay in the interrelationships of people within the organization. Only then can they introduce changes that will increase the payoffs and decrease the human, social, and economic costs of operating the organization.

THREE STRUCTURAL STAGES

Having clarified the concept of organizational health, we can now analyze its relationship to company efficiency. Organization structures evolve through these three recognizable stages: The early pattern of organization is one built around strong leadership by dominant executives. The second stage of development is marked by the emergence of bureaucratic structures and associated patterns of administration. Finally, the firm evolves organizational adaptations to remedy the deficiencies of traditional bureaucratic structures and to equip the company for the future demands almost certain to be made upon it. Here we compare the leadership patterns and some problems of organizational health and company efficiency characteristic of each stage.

Research shows that over the past fifty years, contrary to widespread opinion, there has been substantial innovation and change in the structure and design of organizations. In companies where managers have successfully pursued growth objectives, substantial innovation has been at work in the design and utilization of organization structures as they are adapted to changing needs and conditions. Of special importance are the decisions that affect organizational health—those relating particularly to the design and utilization of the company's organization structure during periods of growth and change.

As companies grow, difficulties of communication, coordination, and control become greater. Technology becomes more complex. Production and distribution shift to a national and international scope. Yet habits, customs, and management philosophies bind the organization to its past. These rigidities inhibit the changes required for survival or further growth. But as changes in technology and other aspects of the enterprise create the need for new ideas in organization structure and design, rigidities must give way. If they do not, the business founders.

If a business successfully evolves a new organizational apparatus in response to changing demands made upon it, it is usually capable of providing for very large expansion. This releases energies devoted to research, experimentation, and exploration for fruitful ways to increase the size and scope of the business. The pace of the company's growth is accelerated both by sales expansion, and by acquisitions and mergers. As a business acquires more and more resources, its earning potential under competent management greatly increases. In businesses undergoing such growth pressures, organizational designs and mechanisms must keep pace with changing needs in the company.

The general characteristics of ongoing organizational change in growing, healthy organizations are shown in summary form in Exhibit I. The first column, Stage 1, describes rudimentary organization structures and leadership patterns characteristic of early, pioneering business enterprises. The second column, Stage 2, summarizes the characteristics of the emerging bureaucratic structures in the period from 1925 onward. The third column presents innovations designed to remedy apparent defects in the design and use of bureaucratic structures. I will now analyze these three stages in substantial detail, describing the intrinsic relationships between organizational health and company efficiency.

I: The great organizers

In the closing decades of the nineteenth century and early decades of the twentieth, emerging business empires reflected the personal inspiration and creative genius of their founders. The spirit of entrepreneurship was widespread; frontier psychology still pervaded the nation; economic opportunity abounded for those willing to adhere to the Protestant ethic, with its adjurations for hard work, thrift, and self-denial. The business enterprises of this period employed plain and simple organizational patterns built around the genius or the whim of a dominant executive. In such businesses, the principal operators were also the principal owners, and they stayed close to the business. They kept the reins under tight control through diligent observation, constant, immediate, and direct contact with the ongoing work, and elaborate order-giving and reporting systems. The leaders around whom such businesses were formed were strong personalities, aggressive and energetic, guided by common sense. Their actions were not entirely untouched by kindness and sympathies of various sorts, but emotions were kept in check, subservient to the problems of production and finance they were trying to solve.

For the enterprise objectives of this period, such methods of administration and management were effective and efficient. Organizations were healthy because they had momentum and strong direction from their leaders. One-man leadership made clear whose decisions were controlling; the source of orders, instructions, or vetoes was known to all employees. Tasks were arranged in groups of related functions, which yielded a logical basis for organizing the work. The top leader was the only coordinating official needed. Such organizations had high capacity for dealing with emergencies and for adapting quickly to changes. No doubt there were many problems not categorized as poor organizational health, but few considered it the company's responsibility to be concerned. Orderly behavior in the company's interest was rationally based, and the expectations for all persons within the organization were kept very clear. Exhibit I details these characteristics.

But "genius management" or "Caesar management," [10] strong-arm control by a single dominant owner-executive, proved inadequate

---

[10] These terms are those of Ernest Dale in his excellent book *The Great Organizers* (New York: McGraw-Hill Book Company, Inc., 1960).

EXHIBIT I

EMERGING LEADERSHIP AND ADMINISTRATIVE PATTERNS IN BUSINESS ENTERPRISES

Stage 1	*Stage 2*	*Stage 3*
CHARISMATIC DOMINATION (LEADERSHIP)	BUREAUCRATIC ORGANIZATION (PROFESSIONAL LEADERSHIP)	TASK-ORIENTED INFORMATION SYSTEMS AND FLUID ORGANIZATIONS
Strong top leader	Organizationally-created leader	Group leadership and decision
Strong owner influence	Indirect owner influence	Indirect owner influence
Non-rational	Highly rational	Highly rational
Hierarchy with informality of roles, positions	Formal roles, offices, and positions; strong hierarchy	Fluid structures; deemphasizes hierarchy
Arbitrary succession in hierarchy	Planned succession; assured careers and merit appointments	Weak hierarchy and more informal offices, positions
Loose functional units	Tight functional units	Task forces, teams, projects, and interfunctional activity
Situation oriented	Institutionally oriented	Systems and computer oriented
Emotional interpersonal relationships	Impersonal relationships	Colleagueship and personal relationships
Unstable; dependent on great leader	Stable and predictable	Stable, but less predictable
Resists specialization and routinization of decisions	Promotes specialization and routinization of decisions	Deemphasizes specialization and routinization of decisions
No organization charts	Strong dependence on charts	Deemphasizes charts
Handles emergencies and new situations well	Less flexible in emergencies and new situations	Slower and more uncertain in emergencies and new situations
Arbitrary reward systems	Planned reward systems	Rewards based on results
No participation in planning or decisions	Controlled participation	Meaningful participation in decisions and planning invited
Strong discipline with arbitrary rules	Strong discipline with fair rules	Deemphasis on rules and discipline
Moderately legalistic	Strongly legalistic	Permissive
Loyalty and conformity to leader	Loyalty and conformity to system and institution	Loyalty and conformity to profession and peer groups

for the later stages of development of these burgeoning firms. To meet new conditions of growth in a competitive free-enterprise economy, one-man domination had to give way to systematic organization and planning, under the leadership of assertive, ambitious, and hard-driving managers capable of creating and applying new concepts of large-scale organizations. The birth of new organizational patterns followed the demand created by growth in size and complexity, and the great organizing geniuses of this early period laid some foundations that have endured to the present day. For example, at the turn of the century the Du Pont Company was foundering near disaster. Alfred I. du Pont and two of his cousins introduced systematic management and organization concepts and saved the company. Twenty years later the Du Pont methods of decentralization and autonomous divisions controlled through centralized policy saved General Motors, then nearly bankrupt under Will Durant. Durant had invented the idea of General Motors, but it was the great organizers—the du Ponts, Alfred P. Sloan, Jr., and others—who made it work.[11]

2: The great bureaucracies

The replacement of "genius" management by the great organizers was, for each business in which it occurred, a critical turning point in its history: the evolution of great bureaucratic structures by which most businesses today operate. The evolution of bureaucratic organization in response to the demands of large-scale objectives is an important achievement in the history of business enterprise.

Some businesses, of course, are more bureaucratic than others, and we should be aware that particular firms would fall on a continuum ranging from somewhat bureaucratic to extremely bureaucratic. No single business is purely bureaucratic or nonbureaucratic. The bureaucratic form is merely an analytical model describing the main characteristics of observable leadership and organizational patterns. Moreover, the term "bureaucracy" is not an epithet, it is a description. It is incorrect to equate this term solely with red tape and other invidious connotations.

The bureaucratic organizational model was first described by Max Weber, a German sociologist writing in the late nineteenth and early twentieth centuries. He studied large governmental organizations,

---

[11] See Ernest Dale, *ibid.*, preface and chapter 2; Alfred D. Chandler, Jr., *Strategy and Structure* (Cambridge: M.I.T. Press, 1962), chapters 2 and 3; Alfred P. Sloan, Jr., *My Years with General Motors* (New York: Doubleday and Company, 1964).

describing complex sets of characteristics that still seem appropriate today in the study and description of large business organizations. However, a second stream of thought reinforced the applicability of bureaucratic concepts: the scientific movement. This was an evolving management philosophy based on characteristics very similar to those of bureaucracy. It stressed the design of pyramidal organizational systems built around efficiency concepts, with the output of organizations as a central aim, and with work measurement, task planning, payment by output, and management efficiency standards predominant.

This conjoining of two important streams of thought found its expression in the academic world, where schools of business administration and schools of industrial engineering developed elaborate courses and a supporting literature. They trained many practitioners —consultants, managers, and teachers—who advocated notions appropriate to the bureaucratic model. Note how the following characteristics of bureaucracy, based on Weber's analysis, are indicative of current philosophies and practices of organization design, leadership, management, and personnel administration:

1. The organizational hierarchy, with chain of command, the concept of unity of command, clear lines of authority.
2. Specialization of tasks and persons within the organization, definite accountability and responsibility.
3. Rationalism, guidance by reason and empirical verification, and accumulation of past experience.
4. Appointment to positions by merit, and a prescribed career system; provision of career training.
5. A formal, impersonal atmosphere.
6. Routinization of procedures, decisions by rules, careful classification of persons, problems, procedures, statuses and rewards, and strict discipline.[12]

Organizational health in a bureaucracy can best be analyzed from two points of view. First, it can be examined for its advantages and disadvantages, and these can be weighed for the purpose of retaining and improving the bureaucratic model. Second, we can raise the question of whether the bureaucratic form can endure at all, or whether it produces so many dysfunctional effects that it will succumb to overwhelming forces of change. If it has reached the upper limits

---

[12] Max Weber, *The Theory of Social and Economic Organization*, translated by A. M. Henderson and Talcott Parsons, ed. Talcott Parsons (New York: Oxford University Press, Inc., 1948). This theory is ably summarized and analyzed in Victor A. Thompson, *Modern Organization* (New York: Alfred A. Knopf, 1960).

to which it can be pushed to yield productivity and desired need satisfactions, or if the costs of achieving its benefits are too great, we may need to find substitute forms or new structural types.

Bureaucratic organization is the most productive arrangement of human effort ever contrived by man. Its superiority, in Weber's view, lies in its capacity to command and utilize technical and scientific knowledge. Its ability to accomplish objective organizational goals has led to phenomenal productivity and the highest standards of living ever achieved by man. In all this the role of the specialist is supreme. More and more persons within organizations are becoming specialists. The bureaucratic form accommodates to the training, utilization, and proper status and economic rewards for the specialist, so that his contribution to goals and sub-goals is rational, predictable, and controllable. If highly efficient productive effort is our main goal, the bureaucratic form is supremely designed for this purpose. It is a highly logical, rational system, self-perpetuating and productive.

But efficiency is not the only demand we make of organizations, and it is in the sphere of human satisfactions that bureaucratic systems fall short. The indictment against bureaucratic models or organization is a growing one, and the criticism centers upon organizational health rather than on bureaucracy's contribution to productivity or company efficiency. It turns out that bureaucratic systems are not particularly consonant with the fulfillment of human needs of their constituent members, or with basic values espoused in our society other than those relating to production, success, and wealth. Their assumptions are not congruent with scientific findings about people. Bureaucratic organizations provide nice ladders of upward mobility by which society at large defines success, and material rewards go to those who can succeed in this kind of system. Yet we suspect the system. We accuse it of creating organization men by valuing blind loyalty and rigid conformity. We doubt its ability to fulfill the psychic, spiritual, self-realizing needs of its members.

On the basis of extensive research, Argyris has advanced an important hypothesis: that organizations based on hierarchical structures and bureaucratic forms of management force their members into states of docility, submissiveness, and dependency that can only lead to severe frustration if the person behaves in a psychologically mature way. Psychological maturity is sacrificed in organizations that rely on strong controls, exact rules, strong discipline, hard-boiled management, production at all costs, pleasing the boss, upward mobility for success, and hierarchical structure, with its political implications. Creativity, innovation, involvement, and human dignity are sacrificed.[13]

Argyris further points out that management may be in danger of mistaking such factors as low absenteeism, low turnover, low grievance rates, and high production for evidences of organizational health, whereas these same results can be obtained by bureaucratic methods of coercion and discipline. In his words,

> Present management thinking about a healthy organization may be oversimplified and at times false. It is not correct to assume that such "products" of the organization as low absenteeism, low grievance rates, and high production are always valid indicators of organizational health. Nor is it safe to take for granted that such criteria are necessarily connected with loyal, ego-involved employees. . . . Management leadership is not the only cause of organization illness. The very nature of organization and of managerial controls (if practiced correctly) makes them equally causal factors. As long as it is necessary to use the pyramid type of organization and to employ managerial controls, employees will tend to experience dependency, subordination, submissiveness, and other indications of psychological immaturity.[14]

Bureaucracies have fought back to correct their defects in the human sphere with impressive lists of personnel administration techniques, and with human relations policies and procedures. Training courses for supervisory personnel and development programs for executives have largely been designed to get more mileage out of the bureaucratic system without fundamentally changing it. Companies have spent millions of dollars on retreading the skills, beliefs, understandings, values, and communications of organization members, without examining their assumptions about people and organizations. These procedures have often been advanced as correctives by consultants and others who are far from being quacks. Human relations activities have been accepted as a matter of faith. The logic is persuasive if one accepts the logics of the bureaucratic system.

We need not, however, oppose good human relations or the training and development of employees. Still, the deeper issue is that we must first ask the purpose of what we do. If we truly have the benefit of organization members in mind as well as the benefit of the organization, we will go beneath the surface far enough to make an examination of the system itself, rather than merely spreading it over with

---

[13] This general hypothesis has been elaborated in numerous publications. See particularly Chris Argyris, *Personality and Organization* (New York: Harper Brothers, 1957); *Interpersonal Competence and Organizational Effectiveness* (Homewood, Ill.: Richard D. Irwin, Inc., 1962); and *Understanding Organizational Behavior* (Homewood, Ill.: Dorsey Press, 1960).

[14] Chris Argyris, "The Organization: What Makes It Healthy?" *Harvard Business Review*, Vol. XXXVI, No. 6 (November-December, 1958), p. 107.

a coating of human relations and personnel administration. As Argyris has pointed out,

> . . . being nice to employees is fine for the company that is coasting along, but it breaks down when there is real pressure for growth, expansion, and efficiency. A company that pictures organizational health as a condition in which the people are all happy will be all right as long as the company is in very sound financial condition and with little prospect of competition. But the philosophy breaks down when management applies pressure for greater goals.[15]

3: Departures from the pattern

Evidence abounds that bureaucratic models are changing, and that bureaucratic structures and concomitant assumptions are undergoing substantial modifications. The character of these changes is still in the realm of prophecy, but the main outlines are becoming clearer. The prime influences are the growing use of computers, changing technologies, the persistent search for productive systems that more closely approach the full range of human needs and satisfactions, and increasingly better research leading to more adequate organization theory.[16]

These changing patterns emerge not only from the failure of bureaucracies to respond to the needs and problems of human beings, but also from deficiencies internal to the bureaucratic concept itself. Eisenstadt, for example, distinguishes three types of equilibrium with respect to bureaucratic concepts.

Autonomy. In the first, a bureaucratic organization maintains its autonomy and distinctiveness, retaining basic structural characteristics that differentiate it from other social groups and enable it to achieve its goals. Holders of legitimate power, such as owners, trustees, or managers, run these organizations.

Bureaucratization. The second possibility extends the bureaucracy's spheres of activities and power, either in its own interest or in those of some of its own elite. It tends to increase the regimentation of different areas of social life, and to some degree to displace its service goals in favor of various power interests. For example,

---

[15] Chris Argyris, "Organization Effectiveness Under Stress," *Harvard Business Review*, Vol. XXXVIII, No. 3 (May-June, 1960), pp. 137-146.

[16] See, for example, Thomas L. and Harold J. Leavitt, "Management in the 1980's," *Harvard Business Review*, Vol. XXXVI, No. 6 (November-December, 1958), pp. 41-48. The writings of Rensis Likert, Robert Kahn, Herbert Simon, Chris Argyris, Warren Bennis, and others are illustrative of this point.

military organizations may impose their will on civilians, or school systems may encroach on parental responsibilities.

Debureaucratization. In case of the third possible outcome, the organization reflects a subversion of the goals and activities of the bureaucracy in the interests of different groups with which it is in close interaction, such as clients and customer. In debureaucratization, the specific characteristics of the bureaucracy (in terms both of its autonomy and its specific rules and goals) are minimized even to the point where functions and activities may be taken over by other groups or organizations. For example, one organization may attempt to divert the rules and operations of a bureaucratic organization so that it functions according to the firm's own values and goals. Bureaucratic organizations are vulnerable to demands that they perform tasks clearly outside their specific scope. These tendencies and possibilities may, in fact, overlap or develop side by side.[17]

DEFICIENCIES

Thompson has also analyzed some of the problems and deficiences of bureaucratic organization structure. The existence of intense specialization of both tasks and persons leads to inordinate problems of coordination and control. Members of such organizations experience serious conflicts in their roles as specialists. They find it difficult to square the needs of the organization as a whole with the particularistic needs of its sub-units. The demands upon the organization produced by specialization are inconsistent with the dictates produced by hierarchical structures.[18]

Thompson also finds that dysfunctional effects result from the bureaucratic model. Some of these effects are similar to those that concern Argyris. Since modern complex businesses are managed by professional salaried managers, rather than owners, corporate earnings are not a direct measure of managerial ability, or of company efficiency. These are affected by several additional factors, among them economic conditions, actions of competitors, and changes in laws. Bureaucratic motivations thus become important in large corporations—important to managers and employees alike.

A manager or an executive is, after all, an employee of a special type, with different status and privileges, but with the same tensions,

---

[17] S. N. Eisenstadt, "Bureaucracy, Bureaucratization, and Debureaucratization," *Administrative Science Quarterly*, Vol. IV, No. 3 (September, 1959), pp. 302-320.
[18] Thompson, *op. cit.*, pp. 81-113.

insecurities, and defense mechanisms as those of any other employee. Some employees seem to be fighting the organization rather than cooperating with it or helping it. They resist its directions and policies. They become pompous and self-important, often preoccupied excessively with rules and regulations for their own sake. Their customary routines become havens of refuge and security. Impersonality and coldness of treatment, both of insiders and outsiders, results.

Most of all, organization members are content to get by with minimum acceptable results, just barely satisfying the organization's requirements. Such behavior patterns may help the individual in his reactions to his experiences and problems within the organization, or in resolving his own personality problems, but they are unplanned by the organization and are of no value in meeting organizational needs and objectives. The insecure, fearful administrator has a strong need to control in order to minimize his fears. The bureaucratic model is peculiarly susceptible to this type of administrator, and the hierarchical structuring tends to strengthen the devices by which he seeks to blunt his fears.[19]

THE IMPLICATIONS OF CHANGE

Some important changing patterns of organization and leadership in business enterprises are emerging. Some of these are indicated in column 3 of Exhibit I. The characteristic trend is toward loosening the structure through the creation of more fluid and informal arrangements. This has the effect of reducing the impact of hierarchy, with its monocratic "one boss for every man" emphasis. Among the devices potentially leading to such results are project management team concepts, and the "results" school of thought in management.

Task forces and project teams can be assembled quickly, and as quickly dissolved. Group members rapidly learn to cooperate and collaborate for common goals, and they share in prompt and adequate rewards. The orientation is toward peer-pleasing rather than boss-pleasing.[20]

In some ways these changes are reminiscent of pre-bureaucratic periods when businesses were run by a single owner-manager, with "great man" concepts. The main strength of the great man was his

---

[19] *Ibid.*
[20] See, for example, Henry E. Dwyer, "Departures from Tradition in Organization Planning," *Personnel,* Vol. XL, No. 4 (July-August, 1963), pp. 18-23.

ability to maintain a fluidity and flexibility of organizational patterns. People were hired to get jobs done; people were far less specialized than they are considered to be today; trouble-shooting, projects, rapidly changing assignments, were the stuff of these early organizations. People were kept off base, guessing about what was to be happening next, and this was thought to be good for them.

Such changes as we have described have grave implications for traditional personnel and management methods associated with the bureaucratic model. Training and development of executives, supervisors, and workers cannot remain the same; systems of reward and punishment must adapt; criteria for selecting new organization members shift from selection to fit specific definable jobs, to the search for talented, creative, innovative people with the capacity to feel secure in more amorphous situations. Perhaps personnel and human-relations concepts of the past twenty years have seemed so inadequate because they have been pitted against intractable problems inherent in bureaucracy itself, rather than because of weaknesses in their logic or techniques.

Such is the challenge before managers today: to wrestle with the problems of organization change and development even if this means discarding the ways of the past. To competent managers, executives, and administrators, such changes will seem like opportunities for development rather than threats to security and status.

QUESTIONS

1. Explain what is meant by the concept of "organizational health."
2. Contrast the three structural growth changes found in the mature organization.
3. What are some of the major characteristics of bureaucracy?
4. What are some of the most important implications for management of the Stage 3 growth model?
5. Which growth model do you think is most prevalent in American industry? Why? Which do you think the typical manager prefers?

GENERAL QUESTIONS ON PART I

1. Explain the principal limitations of the early scientific management movement as it related to the human element.
2. Whose responsibility is it to establish and practice good human relations in a business enterprise?
3. Present your own definition of "human relations." What are some of the principal obstacles impeding agreement on a common definition for this term? How important is a common definition?

4. List and discuss five of the more important theoretical concepts underlying human relations theory?
5. Why is it so important that today's generation of managers be skilled in
   understanding and motivating people at work?
6. How do McFarland's three growth models of organization relate to the
   ideas of both Scott and Leavitt?
7. Should a business firm contain a certain amount of bureaucracy? Are
   governmental agencies more bureaucratic than business firms?
8. What are some criticisms one should direct toward current human relations theory as presented in this section?
9. What is the relationship(s) between: (1) human relations, (2) administrative success, and (3) organization growth and development?
10. In what ways has Part I enhanced your understanding of human relations theory in the working organization?

PART II. THE MANAGER: BACKGROUND, PERSONALITY, AND ROLE

The success of any type of working organization, especially a business firm, is entirely dependent upon its ability to obtain, nurture, and develop managerial talent. One of the factors primarily responsible for the growth and development of our dynamic economy, especially shortly before and after the turn of the twentieth century, was the vital role played by the *entrepreneur* who founded, built, and directed his own business enterprise. Then, as our business organizations grew in size and diversification in the first half of this century, and especially after World War II, the *professional manager* replaced the entrepreneur as the principal agent directing and influencing the continual development of our economic society and its many related institutions. In large part, the increased importance of the managerial role has been a concomitant of the rise of large-scale, complex working organizations. From factory to labor union, from government agency to university, vastness, size, and sheer bureaucratic complexity feature all of these differing yet similar working institutions. Ours is certainly an organizational society.

There are now some signs, however, that more individuals are once again beginning to follow career patterns similar to those of the earlier entrepreneurs. The emergence of the scientific and space era has afforded more and more persons, many of them managers by training and experience, an opportunity to found and build their own firms into large-scale enterprises in a very short time. Rapid technological developments, aiding the development of new industries, are an important stimulant in this direction. Entrepreneurs as such, however, still remain a small ownership elite as compared to the many managers currently at work. And even the entrepreneur must depend upon managers to assist in the directing of his company, once it begins to reach a size requiring more than the governing hand of its founder and/or owner.

So the distinguishing feature of the majority of our large business firms—and other working institutions—remains the professional manager, charged with directing the work of the corporation for many stockholders distantly removed who are often not even familiar with the products marketed by the firm whose stock they own. The manager is thus entrusted with administering the firm, its mission and destiny riding on his ability to compete with managers and executives in other firms and on his ability to effectively utilize the material and human resources at his disposal.

Men who manage have long been the subject of exhaustive and intensive research efforts by those interested in ascertaining the mysteries of managerial success. Why, for example, do some men succeed so remarkably as managers and executives while others, perhaps equally gifted in terms of professional training and intellectual capacities, fail even in similar circumstances? What motivates some men to work long and hard in the hope of becoming successful managers and executives? What personality traits, if any, are common to managers? Even more important, what activities do managers perform in their work which can be isolated and studied to enhance the training and preparation of future managerial talent?

These are crucial questions needing answers. Although there are difficulties of comparison and generalization from organization to organization, there is sufficient evidence via research of managers to permit certain conclusions to be drawn and weighed in some depth.

GENESIS OF THE MANAGER

Before examining some of the major research efforts relative to managerial accession in the firm, it is important to note that many of these studies focus almost exclusively on chief executive officers and/or other top level policy-making officials. The question as to whether or not valid generalizations can be made about managers in general from these data can thus be raised; however, as the same surveys indicate that an increasing number of top managers are arriving at the top via progression through several managerial ranks, data on top managers appear equally applicable and relevant to managers at lower levels.

Social background

W. Lloyd Warner has long studied the careers of big business executives, and his article, contained in this part, summarizes his more recent research findings. Included in his study are career patterns of federal executives along with business executives. His conclusion that there is now increased opportunity for men to advance through the various levels of the organization, as compared to more restricted career mobility in earlier years, is of some significance. A generation and more ago the birth elite, or sons of top managers and owners, tended to dominate the higher ranks of managers and executives. The fortunes of birth and social class thus restricted many men from advancing, vertically speaking, in most business firms. It was a case of "knowing your place in life."

This is not to say that a great number of current executives are not born rather than made; indeed, they are. But the research does show that there is greater opportunity today than ever before for aspiring young men to advance to top-level jobs in the ranks of management. A recent study of 1,000 top officers (presidents, chairmen, and principal vice-presidents) of the 600 largest U. S. corporations by *Scientific American* showed that only 10.5 percent of the current generation of big business executives claimed to be sons of wealthy families, as compared to a 36.1 percent figure in 1950 and 45.6 percent in 1900.[1] Although there are some important qualifications to these statistics, they do reinforce the fact that the increasing professionalization of managers has also enhanced vertical social mobility in managerial selection and advancement.

Educational background

The factor showing up as a decided "must" for all aspiring managers is that of formal education. The *Scientific American* study showed that almost 75 percent of the executives had at least one college degree; and, interestingly, almost all of them had completed some college work. Graduate study and degrees are definitely on the increase, with 35 percent of the executives in this study having obtained at least an M.S. degree. Furthermore, one third of the degrees (bachelor's and master's degrees) were in the science and engineering fields. Supporting the surge for professional education for business leadership is the current statistic showing over 20 percent of all students currently enrolled in colleges and universities to be pursuing degree work in business administration programs.

Warner's research shows 57 percent of the managers studied having college degrees (since this was for 1952, the higher figure in

---

[1] *The Big Business Executive: 1964* (New York: Scientific American, 1964), p. 2.

the *Scientific American* study is more recent and accurate for current managers). The 1959 figures for federal executives showed 81 percent having graduated from college. His study indicates universities attended as well, with some of our larger state universities among the top producers of executive talent today.

Other studies indicate about the same educational patterns for managers. Hence, college training is a critical "must" for aspiring young managers, and increased emphasis is being placed on graduate degrees. The best "educational package" appears to be a bachelor's degree in a technical area, then graduate work in business administration with the M.B.A. degree being stressed.

Functional background

The question of which of the several functional areas of business promises the quickest road to the top is always an interesting one to ask but much more difficult to answer. This is especially true in recent years as traditional departmental lines have been undergoing considerable change. Various studies come up with conflicting opinions here.

Again, *Scientific American* found *technical backgrounds,* as noted earlier, to be very important for career mobility within a company. Yet, other recent studies point to most managers arriving at or near the top via the *general management* route.[2] Mandell's study of 200 top American companies reports that 18.5 percent of the top executives surveyed had a "specialty" of general management. Close on their heels, however, were men with an engineering background (17.5 percent).

Dommermuth also found general management positions being the best springboard to the corporate pinnacle in a study of several hundred corporations over a period of 16 years. In 11 of the 16 years, general management people held more presidencies than men from other functional fields; production men were a close second. Finance was shown to have declined over the years as a source of presidents, whereas marketing has just about held its own. The executive vice-presidency was found to be more and more an important springboard in the past few years. As in other studies, he reported the median age of presidents to be about 50.1 years.

---

[2] *See* Melvin Mandell, "How To Make the Top," *Dun's Review and Modern Industry,* Vol. 78, No. 4 (October, 1961), pp. 46-47; *also,* William P. Dommermuth, *The Road to the Top,* Research Monograph Number 20, Bureau of Business Research, The University of Texas, Austin, Texas, 1965.

The Personality Profile

Is there any such thing as a "managerial personality"? In addition to examining career patterns and personal histories as in the previous section, one of the keys to understanding what underlies managerial success is to study the far more nebulous mental or personality traits (or factors, if you prefer) possessed by successful managers. Admittedly, the process of collecting, classifying, and analyzing these data is not as simple as quantifying factors like age, social background, education, and so on. Prediction of future success based on these data, namely, personality factors, is obviously not nearly as precise. Yet, the manager does function in an environment of stress and ambiguity which decidedly influences and in some part shapes his personality characteristics. To effectively understand organizations and their administrative and managerial processes, one must examine the psychological characteristics of the men who shape both the organization and its processes.

Articles by Ghiselli; Huttner, Levy and Stopol; Wald and Doty; and Henry explore this topic in depth. Ghiselli, for example, concludes that the traits of intelligence, supervisory ability, initiative, self-assurance, and perceived occupational level play a fundamental role in determining managerial success. He places heavy emphasis on the intellectual demands of the managerial job, for, according to him, it is one demanding much creativity and innovation.

Huttner, Levy, and Stopol approach the problem by classification according to occupational groupings of managers, i.e., engineering and R & D executives, sales executives, administrative and accounting executives, and production executives. They further compare differences between more and less effective executives and examine other related issues such as age and company size. Their findings indicate noticeable personality and mental differences between occupational groupings, company size, and age. In general, their work illustrates the importance of a *situational analysis* of managers, as opposed to setting forth any one stereotyped version of *a* successful manager that would fit all firms and/or related organizations.

Wald and Doty did a comprehensive case history study of top executives, and even with a small sample, interesting and informative data were collected. Their test results showed the participants possessed a high level of intelligence, seriousness of purpose, social maturity, firmness and objectiveness with respect to judgment and analytical abilities, frankness coupled with sensitivity to others, understanding and tolerance toward others, and a reasonable degree of emotional stability. Personal drive and ambition stood out as well. Henry's article, long a classic, focuses on the same general factors.

These studies lead to a tentative conclusion that, even with the difficulty in precisely setting forth an "ideal" managerial personality since this will vary among companies and their different management "climates," there are, nevertheless, many common denominators found in the psychological makeup of managers and executives, both over time and in various types of firms. Moreover, as discussed in Ghiselli's article and a subsequent one by Haire, Ghiselli, and Porter reporting their research of managers in many countries, *above all else men who manage do so primarily because of their high need to achieve, to express their inborn and learned talents and to realize (self-fulfillment) their potentials as creative persons*, regardless of specific differences in personalities, values, needs, and attitudes. These psychological "pushes" stand out above things like prestige, security, and wealth. Successful managers and executives are men of exceptional talent, especially with regard to directing the efforts of others.

THE MANAGERIAL ROLE

The concept of "role" has been developed by psychologists to explain how individual behavior is determined in large part by the expectations of others. Although covered in greater detail in Part VII, managers, like everyone else, pattern their behavior in their jobs according to how they think others—including superiors and subordinates, but especially the former—want them to behave.

The concept of managerial role behavior does not deny the uniqueness of personal motivations; but as most of one's behavior is socially determined (that is, determined by our interaction with others in an organized society), managerial behavior is basically determined by the individual manager's reactions to the expectations of other persons with whom he interacts. Hence, how managers *perceive* their roles, and the many factors influencing their perceptions, is very important in understanding their behavior. Managerial role perception is dependent on the individual manager's personal experiences in life and his experiences working as a manager in various organizational settings.

It must also be emphasized that this role behavior is extremely complex, as there is no one single or solitary role that each and every manager engages in. Everyone carries out multiple roles in life and at work, and these naturally vary with the individual. Yet, to develop a realistic and usable concept of the manager and what he does, it is possible and desirable to describe in somewhat general terms the principal components of the managerial role.

Bear in mind, however, that a description of these role components does not imply that all managerial jobs are the same or that all managers approach their jobs in the same way. *Managing is, to a large degree, an individualized activity, dependent upon the man, what he mentally brings to his job, and how he utilizes his talents in the uniqueness of his organizational environment.* He is not like a machine that responds automatically. He remains a distinct individual, albeit coping with similar problems and utilizing many shared and learned skills in common with other managers.

With this in mind, we can now examine some of the "in common" aspects of the managerial role. First, the manager is a *leader.* He cannot function without guiding and directing the work of others. His performance is normally dependent upon how well his subordinates perform. He has to motivate, guide, communicate, influence, counsel and, in general, direct the work of other people to maintain his part or unit of the organizational system at a desired level of production.

Secondly, the manager is a *management process specialist* in that, to perform effectively as a manager, he must be specialized and proficient in such common managerial activities (or functions) as planning, organizing, motivating, controlling, evaluating, investigating, and so on, all of which comprise the management process. These are distinct functions present in all manager jobs, and the proficient manager has to be skilled in all of them. Traditional theories of managing explained the manager's job almost exclusively in terms of these functional skills, but more recent work theory goes beyond the constricting limits of these activities to include other role aspects as well.

Thirdly, the managerial role is that of a *change agent.* With the rapid changes in the modern world of business and in our society, the manager is principally responsible for continually introducing and implementing work system and technological changes within his particular organizational unit. Since the successful implementation of changes is dependent upon human acceptance, he needs to be skilled at securing such acceptance and support. Likewise, change implies *innovation* and *creativity.* The manager should constantly seek new, better, and novel ways of improving organizational performance and minimizing harmful conflict and friction caused by resistance to "the new ways," yet encourage creative conflict and dissatisfaction with the *status quo.* So, he cannot be content with merely sustaining his work domain but must measure up to meeting the challenge of generating growth, improvement, and vitality in the work system and in people.

Fourth, the manager must be *achievement-oriented*. Inherent in the managerial job is accomplishment and attainment of organizational goals as well as personal goals. Business firms and related institutions can only justify their existence in organized society by accomplishing predetermined and distinct purposes. Satisfying all levels of human needs, including those of the general public and the employee group, necessitates managers dedicated to productive results beneficial in an optimum fashion to all concerned. The manager has to be a "doer," an action-oriented individual prone not to hasty, compulsive, plunging behavior but to persistent and steady pursuit of well thought out and conceived personal and group goals, all integrated into the entire company system of goals.

Fifth, the managerial role requires men who are *decision activists*. Note the emphasis is not on decision making but on decision activating. Unfortunately, too many people, including managers, have an erroneous impression that all managers do is to sit back and make "yes" or "no" decisions. Nothing could be farther from the truth, however. Such black or white decisions are not difficult to make, assuming all the necessary information bearing on the decision has been accumulated and weighed and all the people affected by the decision have been appropriately considered and involved in it. The latter points present more problems. Furthermore, making a "final" decision is but the starting point in the decision process. Implementing and carrying out the decision to a successful conclusion, perhaps changing it if necesary, is far more difficult to achieve, but it is the most demanding and difficult of all. In all organizations there are managers who fail (or are failing) ignominiously because they do not perceive the total decision process, often being incapable of envisioning the totality of their decisions over time. These "Edsel" decision makers look more at themselves and their personal benefits rather than at what is good for the organization as a whole.

A decision activist does not concentrate only on a black or white solution to problems or on his own personal image, as few of the former exist and the latter is evidence of a misdirected man. The decision activist first seeks full and complete information through sound, comprehensive research for problem identification, then determines a decision incorporating its potential effects on all parties involved, seeking their involvement and support in actively implementing the decision over time. He is also capable of changing his decisions should conditions change, recognizing that he, too, is fallible as are his subordinates. The decision activist does not decide on a particular course of action because of personal hunch, whim, or fancy, nor does he "delegate" the impossible to others and then pass off failures on the shoulders of "my incompetent subordinates." His decisions (group decisions, we hope) should be based on a realistic appraisal of organizational resources and conditions, present and future, and not on personal benefits to himself or on what he would like to have happen.

Still another aspect of the managerial role is *negotiation*. Managers spend a great deal of their time negotiating with all types of people inside and outside the organization. Some of this negotiation is direct bargaining, such as with unions and suppliers where both parties defend certain rights or prerogatives and a compromise settlement is usually reached.

Other phases of the negotiation role are far more subtle and less understood, however. Personal give-and-take centering around career competition with other managers in the same company is part of life in the working organization. Power plays and jockeying for position highlight this career advancement, and a keen sense of political negotiation is required on the part of the astute manager. This career maze in the corporation, and one's ability to cope with it, can often make or break an aspiring manager. Other forms of negotiating skills are often required to cope with superiors and subordinates making demands which conflict with productive performance on the part of the manager. Hence, many different types of negotiating skills are required as managers devise various strategies to perform in an effective fashion despite many obstacles and/or challenges within the work environment.

Lastly, and critical to good managing, is the need for the manager to perceive the *professional* nature of his role. With our expanding body of knowledge relative to managing, the professional nature of this job is now being recognized. The real "pro" is one dedicated not only to advancing his self-interests and the interests of his employer but also the interests of his profession as well. Professionalization demands recognition of common ethical standards of conduct, knowledge of theory as well as practice ("why's" as much as "what's"), a keen sense of public and social responsibility, emphasis on learning and research to enhance professional growth, and, above all, dedication to continual professional development and growth.

It is not inconceivable that as the professionalization of managers increases managers may "practice" their skills in many business firms and working organizations as doctors do in hospitals. It is also possible that managers may some day have to be licensed to practice as their role in society becomes greater and more demanding.

Professional managers must, therefore, be career oriented and mutually dedicated to the advancement of their profession, their employing firm, and themselves if they are to avoid some of the personal problems discussed by Jennings in his article. Above all, they have to be able to realistically perceive their roles as discussed above, to gain a true notion of self in a demanding and ambiguous environment. All managers grapple with continual uncertainty and risk in their work and have to be constantly adjusting conflicting personal and organizational needs and values. The pressures for career development are great and, as Jennings points out, the ability to adjust to these diverse pressures fundamentally determine individual success or failure as a manager.

7. THE CAREERS OF AMERICAN BUSINESS AND GOVERNMENT EXECUTIVES: A COMPARATIVE ANALYSIS *

W. Lloyd Warner

Introduction: the practical and scientific problems

We people of the United States, animated by equalitarian and aristocratic values and beliefs, both inherent and significant parts of this democracy, have always firmly voiced and attempted to practice equality of opportunity for everyone in our systems of rank. This means in practical terms that every person during his or her career must be able to get a job and during the working lifetime, should abilities and skills permit, advance to higher positions of prestige and power. We believe that men from all economic ranks, those born to low or high position, with the necessary ability, talent, and training, merit the rewards of occupational advancement. Moreover, in our value system not only is this just and right for the individuals involved, but, to make our competitive, economic, and social system work, we believe that in the competition for the most important jobs the best men should win.

Our prevailing fears about ourselves and our society reinforce these more positive feelings about equality of opportunity just stated. Many believe that this condition of equality no longer prevails; large numbers of our population are of the firm opinion that there is less opportunity today than previously for men born to low station to climb to the top. They also are convinced that the social and economic hierarchies of America are growing more rigid, are less open and more closed to the advance of the talented and trained who come from the lower levels of this society. Much of the literature of the social sciences, sociology particularly, especially during the 1930's and 1940's, emphasized the pessimistic side of this important question.

In this chapter I shall report on two extensive researches conducted by my colleagues and myself that were designed to find some of the answers to a number of the more significant questions about this important practical and scientific problem. The men who occupy the highest positions in big business throughout the United States

* From George B. Strother (ed.), *Social Science Approaches to Business Behavior* (Homewood, Ill.: Irwin-Dorsey Press, 1962), pp. 99-123. Reprinted by permission.

were first studied.[1] Those who hold the highest positions of authority in the federal government were then examined.[2] Comparisons were made and conclusions drawn about the amount of movement in each hierarchy. Since the concentrations of power and prestige in business and government include a large proportion of the most powerful and prestigeful positions in the occupational structures of this country, they both provide a factual demonstration of what present reality is and are probable indexes of the general fluidity and rigidity of our society. They help answer questions about the amount of equality of opportunity there is for men of all ranks in the United States.

Before turning to the research results, I shall briefly review the basic questions we asked of our evidence and present the methods and techniques used. We first asked, Who are the big business and big government leaders of America? What kinds of men are they? Do they come from all occupational levels in equal proportions? Are most of these men of big business and high executive authority in the federal government from the elite classes, or do some come in significant proportions from the lower ranks, from the manual workers and white-collar levels and other more modest occupations? Scientifically speaking, the extent to which they are the sons of big businessmen and high government officials is, of course, the extent to which the American society is closed and not open to free competition; it is the degree to which our collectivity is rigid and emphasizes aristocratic principles rather than democratic ones. The extent to which movement takes place from the bottom to the top and from the intermediate levels in these two great hierarchies is a measure of free competition, of a more flexible society, and of a social and occupational system of open statuses.

For those concerned with the political domain and the domestic well-being of the body politic as conceived by Thomas Jefferson and Samuel Adams, we can ask and answer other important questions: Do we have a truly representative government insofar as these federal executives are concerned? Are the men at the very top levels of the federal government representative of the varieties of men and women who compose all walks of life in the American collectivity? Or are they a special group who represent the few (in terms of who they are) and not the many?

---

[1] W. L. Warner and J. C. Abegglen, *Occupational Mobility in American Business and Industry* (Minneapolis: University of Minnesota Press, 1955), and *Big Business Leaders in America* (New York: Harper & Bros., 1955).
[2] W. L. Warner, P. P. Van Riper, N. H. Martin, and O. F. Collins, *The American Federal Executive*, to be published by Yale University Press, 1962.

Comparisons between these studies and earlier ones on these two elites of previous generations, particularly those on big-business leaders,[3] give us reliable answers about trends in the comparative rigidity and fluidity of our occupational structure. Comparisons between the civilian government executives and the big-business leaders yield exact statements about the equality of opportunity in government and business.

Let us briefly define the meanings of business and government executives before we discuss them further. We shall do this operationally. Only big-business leaders who held the highest policy-making positions were selected—those from chairman of the board and owner down only so far as secretary and treasurer. Only the largest corporations among the types of business enterprise, such as manufacturing, mining, finance, transportation, and the like, were chosen. The size of the corporation was defined in terms of the largest share of the gross national product in that category of enterprise. In brief, the big-business leaders were the biggest of their kind in this country.

For government executives, the military leaders ranged from admirals and generals down only to full colonels. For civilians, they ranged from the highest grade level (GS-18 and above) down to GS-14, these being positions of the very highest consequence in the federal government hierarchy. Only civilians are reported on here. Included were executives from the career civil service, those politically appointed, and the foreign service. There were 8,300 business leaders in our sample and approximately 13,000 government leaders. Our sample of each group by various tests proved to be representative and our evidence for each valid. We can, with this brief résumé of the method and purpose of the inquiry, turn to the results of the two studies.

The social and economic origins of the business and government elites

The fundamental question we must first ask is: What were the occupational origins of the men of business and those of government? More precisely put—What were the occupations of their fathers, the economic positions of their families of birth? How many of the two elites came from the wrong side of the tracks? How many were born to high estate or to the more modest intermediate levels between the

---

[3] F. W. Taussig and C. S. Joslyn, *American Business Leaders* (New York: Macmillan Co., 1932).

extremes? To obtain first answers let us turn to Table 1 for the comparative percentages for the executives of big business and government.

The occupational origins of the executives of business and government are broadly alike, yet in many ways they vary rather dramatically. Table 1 lists nine major categories of occupation, running from major executives and owners of large business down the column through professional men, farmers, to unskilled laborers and farm laborers. To the right are the percentages and rank order for the occupations of the fathers of big-business leaders. The next columns list the percentages and rank order for the occupations of the fathers of the civilian federal executives. It will be noticed that about one third (31 per cent) of the fathers of big-business leaders were also major executives or owners; a little more than half that many (18 per cent) were owners of small business; a slightly smaller percentage

TABLE 1

THE OCCUPATIONAL ORIGINS OF BIG-BUSINESS
AND FEDERAL GOVERNMENT EXECUTIVES

	Business Leaders (Per Cent)	Rank order	Federal Executives (Per Cent)	Rank Order
Major executive and owner of large business	31	1	17	2–3
Owner of small business	18	2	14	4–5
Foreman	3	8	5	7
Professional man	14	3	19	1
Clerk or salesman	8	6	9	6
Farmer	9	5	14	4–5
Skilled laborer	10	4	17	2–3
Unskilled laborer	5	7	4	8
Farm laborer	0	9	0	9
Others	2	..	1	..

(14 per cent) were professional men. Business leaders whose fathers were skilled laborers (10 per cent), farmers (9 per cent), and white-collar workers (8 per cent) fill the middle range in the rank order of fathers' occupations; those of the unskilled workers (5 per cent), foremen (3 per cent), and farm laborers (less than half of 1 per cent) were least represented. In general, the sons of men in occupations of higher position and prestige ranked first; those of moderate prestige came next; and the low-ranking occupations, as they are

valued in this society, came in a poor third. For example, there were six times as many sons of higher executives and big-business leaders who themselves were big-business leaders (four times for government) than those who had fathers who were unskilled laborers. This spread in general, as we have seen, is true for both hierarchies.

A somewhat similar arrangement of government executives is revealed in the columns to the right. The more highly placed professions and major executives ranked first and the least-valued occupations last. Yet the differences in the percentages of the two elites, government and business, are important, from the point of view both of scientific inquiry and of their meanings to our society. The sons of the major professions led all others (19 per cent) for government executives. The fathers who were big-business leaders (with 17 per cent) were second. Tied significantly with them were the sons of skilled laborers. They rose to 17 per cent, over their score for business leaders, and therefore ranked second. It will be noted that the sons of farmers rose to 14 per cent from 9 per cent for business leaders.

Given the two spreads of occupational percentage, we can now ask still more significant questions that will tell us more precisely about movement in the society and how the hierarchies of government and business compare in their emphasis on aristocratic and democratic values. The last analysis supplied evidence about the number of men who rose or who had been born to high position. We must now compare these figures with those for the occupations from the whole society, with a hundred and eighty million, to learn in what proportion the various occupations in our society are represented in the two elites. This, of course, will be a simple ratio. What occupations are over- and underrepresented and how much?

An exact measurement can be made by comparing the occupations of the fathers of the business and government leaders with the adult male population at the time these men started their careers. A perfect ratio, statistically speaking, would be 1:1, which means that the same percentage of a given occupation is found among the fathers of business and government leaders as in the general population. For example, if a third of the adult males in our occupational forces were laborers, then, to have an exact representation among government and business leaders, there should be a third of them from the laboring class. If we allow 100 to stand for perfect representation of the proportions between each of the samples and the general population, we can state the fact quite simply. All of this is represented in Table 2, called "What Occupations Get 'Their Share' in Government and Business?"

The nine occupations, beginning with major executives and running down to farm laborers, are found in the center of the table. At the left are the ratios for the business leaders whose fathers belonged to these different occupations. To the right are the fathers of the federal executives. Running laterally through the center of the page is the statement "100 = Neither above nor below their share," meaning that those figures that are above this are overrepresented for particular occupations and those under this line are below what might be expected by chance. We shall first examine the ratios of business leaders and start with the executives who are sons of big-business leaders. Four occupations are over what would be expected by chance among the business leaders. There are 775 sons of major executives or owners of large business for every 100 that would be there by chance. There are 360 for every 100 sons of small businessmen, some 350 sons of professional men, and 133 who had fathers who were foremen.

Among the federal executives, the distribution of ratios is somewhat similar, yet certain significant and important differences are present. The overrepresentation for the men who are sons of big

TABLE 2

WHAT OCCUPATIONS GET "THEIR SHARE" IN GOVERNMENT AND BUSINESS?

Business Leaders Whose Fathers Were:		Federal Executives Whose Fathers Were:	
775	Executive or owner large business	567	Over
360	Owner small business	200	"Their
350	Professional man	475	Share"
133	Foreman	250	
100 = Neither above nor below their share			
80	Clerk or salesman	75	
63	Skilled laborer	113	Under
45	Farmer	88	"Their
16	Unskilled laborer	12	Share"
00	Farm laborer	00	

businessmen drops to 567 for every 100 expected. Sons of professional men rise to 475. Those who are sons of foremen rise to 250, while the sons of owners of small business drop to 200. Down below 100, it will be noted among the big-business leaders that, for every 100 sons of skilled laborers that would be expected, there are but 63, a significant drop below expectancy, whereas for the federal executives there were 113 for every 100, a figure somewhat above expectancy. There are other significant differences among those occupations that are underrepresented between the two elites. For every 100 white-collar men, there are but 80 for businessmen and 75 for those in government. For every 100 farmers, there are but 45 among businessmen, but this figure about doubled with 88 for the government men. However, there are 16 sons of unskilled laborers among the businessmen and only 12 among the executives of the federal government. Broadly stated, the men of government are more representative of the general categories of occupation in our society than are big-business leaders. The overrepresentation tends to be not as great for the more highly placed occupations; on the other hand, the positions that are underrepresented and less valued in prestige tend to be somewhat more highly represented in government than in business. There is, however, the significant variation for the sons of unskilled laborers.

The professions as sources of federal executives

The broad categories of occupation that we have been using are for present purposes; it is impossible here to break them down into smaller, more precise subcategories. However, we can take time briefly to analyze one of the more interesting, that of professional

TABLE 3

THE PROFESSIONS AS SOURCES OF GOVERNMENT AND BUSINESS EXECUTIVES

Profession	Business Leaders	Federal Executives
Lawyer	800	844
Minister	548	667
Engineer	480	477
Doctor	478	595
Other professions	189 *	274

* Includes: teachers, 224; College presidents and professors, 1,417.

men. The professions ranked high both for government and for business as sources of leadership.

The question arises: What professions led all others and what professions were most productive sources of government and federal executives? When one compares the proportions of the various professions between big-business leaders and the civilian federal executives, in many respects they look very much alike (Table 3). The ratios for the sons of lawyers are almost identical. Ministers are second for big-business leaders as for civilian federal executives, but the latter ratio is larger. The proportions for engineers are almost exactly the same—480 for business leaders and 477 for civilian federal executives. Doctors, however, ranked third for civilian federal executives—almost 600 for every 100 that might be expected by chance—and fourth for business—478, or approximately 500 for every 100 expected. The other professions, including teachers and professors, had a proportion of 189 for business leaders and 274 for civilian federal executives. (We did not derive separate ratios for teachers and professors for the business leaders as we did for government executives.)

The sons of professors were present in the civilian federal executive approximately fourteen times more than might be expected, outranking all other professional groups; among all the professions, teachers ranked last. Perhaps, as a point of interest, we might add that comparisons between the civilian federal executives and military leaders bring out a number of rather significant differences among the professions. The sons of lawyers, rather than the sons of professors, outrank all others among military leaders. Their representation is eleven times greater than would be expected from their proportions in the general population. These are followed by the sons of doctors, with nine times more than expected, and by professors, with 750 for every 100 expected. Teachers, for the military as for the civilian, among the professions were last.

Three generations of mobility in business and government

The analysis of the relations between the two generations, fathers and sons, brings out significant and important processes operating in our occupational structure as they are related to the top positions in the two powerful and prestigeful elites. We must now examine the problem from the vantage point of three generations. We can ask and answer the question, Do the two generations tell the complete story, or does the addition of a third generation, the grandparental one, add to our understanding of what occurs in the movement of personnel through the levels of occupation in our society? Because of the limitations of space, we shall present the evidence in summary form to bring out some of the more significant points about the meaning of three generations in the movement of people in and out of high position in business and government.

Without resorting to a long review of percentages and figures, we can briefly summarize the relation of the third generation to the occupational mobility of executives of business and industry. Perhaps the most significant comment that one can make is the tremendous change in proportions from the fathers' to the grandfathers' generations insofar as farmers are involved (see Table 4). For example, over one third of the fathers' fathers of the businessmen were farmers, and an even higher percentage of the government men's grandfathers. Their sons moved to the city, became laborers or white-collar men, or moved into one of the other occupations in sizeable numbers, this being true for all occupations except big business. Many of the laboring group of the third generation tend to move up and to the white-collar class, insofar as the populations of the two hierarchies are concerned. In general, white-collar and the small-business categories are the embarkation points for further mobility.

The government and business elites of today and yesterday: trends of mobility and of equal opportunity

We have now arrived at the place where we can ask and, with approximate accuracy, partly answer the questions, Is mobility increasing or decreasing? Is the American society more open today than yesterday? Or is it becoming more rigid and tending toward closure and inequality?

In 1928 Taussig and Joslyn made their important and authoritative study of American business leaders; to study trends, the research of Warner and Abegglen in 1952 replicated it. It is therefore possible, for the business leaders, to make exact comparisons about the differences or similarities in the amount of mobility between the generation of leaders one generation ago and those of the present day. This is not possible for the government leaders, since no exact studies were made of them at that time or earlier. However, a number were made which do give indications of what has happened among government executives; the results tend to parallel those of

TABLE 4

THREE GENERATIONS OF OCCUPATIONAL MOBILITY

Occupation	Business (Per Cent)		Government (Per Cent)	
	Grandfather	Father	Grandfather	Father
Farmer	35	9	44	15
Laborer	19	15	18	21
Owner of small business	17	18	14	14
Major executive and owner of large business	12	24	6	10
Professional man	10	14	10	19
Minor executive	3	11	4	11
Clerk or salesman	2	8	3	9
Other	2	2	1	1

the business leaders. Before continuing, it must be re-emphasized that the operations of the 1928 study are the same as those for the present-day business leaders. Furthermore, it should be said that the methods used take account of the increase in white-collar, professional, and business classes and the decrease in the percentages of farmers, as well as other changes that have occurred among American occupations from 1928 to 1952. We can now ask, Is there more or less opportunity than formerly?

By using the same methods that were indicated for the previous calculations, we can allow 100 to stand for the perfect proportional representation between the percentages of men coming from the different occupations in 1928 and 1952. We shall again present a table to summarize quickly what is known. Table 5, "Who Got Their Share Yesterday and Today?" displays the ratios for businessmen for the two periods. Those occupations above the lateral line are proportionately above their share, and those below are less than would be expected if chance alone were operating. We shall start from the bottom and move to the top, thus beginning with the laborers. In 1928, only 24 out of every 100 that might be expected were sons of laborers, whereas in 1952 this figure rose to 32 out of every 100. Among farmers the ratios remain practically identical for the two periods, but among white-collar men the ratio moves from 71 to 80. Thus for the less highly ranked occupations there has been a decided increase in the proportion of young men who have come from these more modestly placed occupations in American society. When one inspects the ratios for the two highly placed positions—businessmen and the professions—the exact reverse of what

TABLE 5

WHO GOT THEIR SHARE YESTERDAY AND TODAY?

1928		1952	
	The Businessmen's Fathers Were:		
967	Businessmen	473	Above
433	Professional	350	"Their
			Share"
100 = Neither above nor below their share			
71	White-collar	80	Below
32	Farmers	33	"Their
24	Laborers	32	Share"

occurred in the other occupations is found to be true. For every 100 businessmen that would have been expected, there were 967 in 1928, whereas in 1952 this had dropped to 473. Moreover, the sons of professional men dropped from 433 down to 350. Internal evidence seems to indicate that the sons of those in the higher occupations do not seem to have the same opportunity or the same motivation to go into these occupations as they did a generation ago. On the other hand, it is perfectly clear that the sons of those in the lower occupations more often rise than they did previously.

This analysis of the two principal elites—government and business—seems to indicate that there is a considerable amount of mobility from the bottom to the top; it indicates, of course, that the birth elites are still at an advantage. However, the figures also demonstrate that there is more mobility now than previously. A similar statement for government men, partly based on assumption, can be made. It is based on examination of the kinds of men who previously occupied these positions and from inspections of non-quantifiable material.

We have now reached the point where we can say that, insofar as our two populations permit us to go, there is more mobility now, except for farmers, from all lower levels than previously. And (within the competence of these investigations) clearly the society is more flexible. There is more opportunity for the individuals in business; more men do come from the bottom. Furthermore, fewer sons of the wealthy stay at the top in business than formerly. There is more circulation from the bottom to the top and more movement out of the top than previously. The top statuses (in business) are more open to competition, and the principles of birth, while important and of great significance, do not operate as much as they once did. In brief, the basic values of our society, including that nebulous but all-important belief in the American dream, are more real now and less the stuff of legend and fiction than they were a generation ago. Although we do not have the quantitative evidence for the government leaders of a generation ago, one must hypothecate from available evidence that, in all probability, there is also more mobility and more opportunity in government than previously. The evidence is strongly suggestive that other occupational hierarchies, including some of the professions, are more open than two generations before ours.

The women they marry

Questions must now be asked: Why is this so? What is responsible for this condition, and how is mobility made possible for those born to less highly regarded occupational positions? We must first examine another important part of this problem. The study of occupational succession is usually confined to a comparison of the positions that men previously had with those they occupy at the present time or to a generational analysis of fathers and sons. While these studies are of the utmost importance and necessary, they do not tell us the full story about the openness of a society and the freedom of movement from generation to generation. Particularly, they usually leave out one half of the total population, namely, women and wives. The principal mainstay of any inflexible closed caste system is the control of marriage, the prevention of marriage outside the caste— in brief, endogamy. In any open system of rank the informal rules and the beliefs and values about marriage are such that there is marriage not only at the level of the men marrying but above and below; the marital rules are bimodal. The problem in this society is how much marriage is there at the level of big-business leaders and of the government executives. Do their sons marry at their own levels, or do they marry outside and below? If they marry women only at their own levels, we are indeed approaching a castelike society, even though there is considerable job mobility. If they marry in sufficient proportions outside and below themselves, the indications are strong that the society is far more fluid and open than it is rigid and closed.

Figure 1, "The Wives of the Business and Government Executives," tells much of what we need to know about the attitudes,

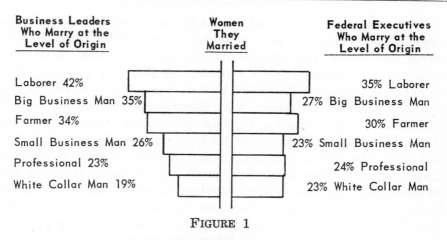

Business Leaders Who Marry at the Level of Origin	Women They Married	Federal Executives Who Marry at the Level of Origin
Laborer 42%		35% Laborer
Big Business Man 35%		27% Big Business Man
Farmer 34%		30% Farmer
Small Business Man 26%		23% Small Business Man
Professional 23%		24% Professional
White Collar Man 19%		23% White Collar Man

FIGURE 1

THE WIVES OF THE
BUSINESS AND GOVERNMENT EXECUTIVES

behavior, and marriage of government and business leaders. Let us briefly indicate what the chart itself means. It will be noticed that at the top left-hand corner one reads "Business Leaders Who Marry at the Level of Origin," meaning their own origin, and at the right is a similar label for federal executives. Between the two is the label "Women They Married." The chart is laid out so that it gives quick understanding of the comparative proportions between the two; it tells what proportions of the executives in each of these two hierarchies of any particular origin marry at their own level. The story is rather eloquent. Of the businessmen who came from laboring origins, 42 per cent married at their own level; 35 per cent of those born to fathers who were big businessmen married women of their own class; some 34 per cent of those whose fathers were farmers married women whose fathers were farmers. The proportions drop down until the white-collar class is reached, where only 19 per cent of the men who were sons of clerks and salesmen married at the level at which they were born. In sum, these figures indicate that the two extremes of the occupational ranks are more likely to marry at their own level of origin. The farmers tend to greater isolation in their marriages as in their mobility; they tend to marry more frequently in their own class than do most other occupational levels and are not conspicuously mobile. These figures also indicate that the white-collar people are most likely to marry on and beyond the level of origin. Space does not permit us to analyze this material here, but tables available show that they marry at all class levels in larger proportions than do men from the other occupations.

A very similar story is told about the marriages of the government leaders. They too tend to marry more outside their level of origin than inside. But the principal difference between the government leaders and the business executives is that they are less likely to marry at their own level than businessmen. For example, 35 per cent of the men whose fathers were laborers married women of that class, whereas 42 per cent of the businessmen did. Only 27 per cent of the men whose fathers were big-business executives married at that level. The government men whose fathers were farmers married daughters of farmers in slightly smaller percentages than did the businessmen. The same is true for those whose fathers were small-business owners, but this is less true for those in the white-collar class. The only exceptions are the fathers who were in the professional and white-collar groups, where the percentages of marriage at their own level for the professions are about the same.

The differences in most cases between the two elites are not very great. However, the marriages of the federal executives tend to be more exogamic than endogamic; they tend, insofar as the number of marriages are concerned, to be more open and flexible and less controlled by the values of status and rank than do those of the businessmen. In both cases, marriage is a product of feelings of rank and status strongly tempered by those of equalitarianism. Many of these figures show that, while many men marry at their own level, many more marry out; and, of those that marry out, some marry above themselves and some below.

Further examination of the details of these marriages show that all categories of occupational origin married into all other levels. However, when the men did marry "out," the farther away the occupations were from their own rank, the smaller the percentage of marriages; and the closer the occupational levels to their own, the greater the proportion of marriages among them.

As a general indicator of how the executives who were sons of laborers married beyond their own levels, it can be said that about the same percentage married the daughters of farmers as they did the owners of small business and white-collar men; a much smaller proportion married the daughters of professional men and big-business leaders. An opposite story is indicated by the marriages at the other extreme, the executives who were the sons of big-business leaders (it will be remembered 65 per cent married outside their own level) : the largest number married the daughters of professional men and the owners of small business; a somewhat smaller percentage married the daughters of white-collar men; and a still smaller percentage married daughters of farmers and laborers.

In sum, the marriages of these two elites show that strong equalitarian principles are operating sufficiently to prevent closure and rigidity in the family system—that powerful system which governs much of the emotional behavior of the members of any society.

Higher education and the mobility of government and business executives

Since we know that there is a significant amount of movement from the bottom and the intermediate occupational levels up to the top levels of big business and big government, these questions once more present themselves: How do these men rise from the lower levels? What equipment do they have? And what are the factors involved that have helped increase mobility in this generation over the previous one? As everyone knows, more and more businessmen equip themselves with college and university training. During the course of this section of our discussion, we shall address ourselves to the basic question of the relation of education to career advancement of big businessmen. We shall first discuss the amount of education obtained by American business leaders and federal executives. We shall briefly indicate the kinds of colleges and give the names of those which trained many of these men. We shall answer these questions: How much education do the business and government leaders get? How many go to college? How many of them come up the hard way, stopping at elementary or high-school grade levels and going to work, to rise by the Horatio Alger route to success? Do the sons of business leaders get the same education as the executives who rise from the working class?

Let us examine how much education the business leaders and government executives obtain during their period of preparation for their careers. Table 6, called "Education: Who Gets It and How Much?" succinctly tells the story. The table is divided into two parts. On the left are the levels of education running from less than high school through to college graduation. Next are two columns of percentages, one giving the percentage of the adult male population who had reached a particular level and the second giving the percentage of business leaders who have that amount of education. To the right are the figures for 1959 (when the federal executive study was done) —the percentage of the U.S. male population of that time who had attained a particular educational level and the percentages of civilian federal executives. Thus comparisons can be made reliably among the several populations. Let us examine the business population first. It will be noted that 57 per cent of all the businessmen had graduated from college, well over half, and that some 19 per cent, another fifth, had gone to college for at least part of the four-year course. In brief, three fourths of all these men had had some college experience, whereas only 13 per cent of the adult males of the United States had

TABLE 6

EDUCATION: WHO GETS IT AND HOW MUCH?

	1952		1959	
Education	U.S. Adult Males (Per Cent)	Business Leaders (Per Cent)	U.S. Adult Males (Per Cent)	Civilian Federal Executives (Per Cent)
Less than high school	55	4	46	0
Some high school	16	9	17	1
High-school graduation ...	16	11	21	4
Some college	6	19	7	14
College graduation	7	57	9	81

this amount of higher education. At the other extreme, 55 per cent of the adult male populations in 1952 had less than high school, whereas but 4 per cent of the businessmen had stopped at this lower level of attainment. The college graduation of businessmen was about eight times more than that of the general population. It might be added that about a third of these men went on to graduate study. All in all, these figures indicate that the contemporary businessman who occupies a very high position (this at a mean age of fifty-four years) tends to be a highly educated man. There are clear indications of the rapid professionalization of this occupation, both by educational attainment and training and through later experience in business.

The statistics for higher education of top government executives are even more extreme. Less than one half of 1 per cent had less than high-school education, whereas 46 per cent of the U.S. adult male population in 1959 belonged in this category. On the other hand, 81 per cent, or more than eight out of ten of these men, had graduated from college, compared with 9 per cent of the U.S. male population. Fourteen per cent had some college, the combined totals reaching the rather astonishing figures of 95 per cent, or more than nine out of ten with college experience. Only 5 per cent had stopped after graduation from high school or with only some high-school experience. These executives are clearly highly educated; time does not permit us to go into the number of M.A.'s, Ph.D.'s, law, and other higher degrees among them, but the proportions are great and highly significant. There obviously is a built-in system of selection operating so that educational attainment is of the utmost importance in contributing to the careers of men in government and to their success in reaching top positions.

Although there has been a general increase in educational attainment in the total population in the country, there has been a still greater increase among business leaders. All groups, those born to each occupational class, show a higher percentage of university graduates today than did the sons of business leaders who were sons of the elite in the 1928 study of Taussig and Joslyn. This, of course, is an astonishing change, for today the sons of men who were workers get more education than those executives a generation ago who were the sons of big-business leaders.

Given the enormous importance of higher education as the principal route to success and as the principal source of attaining the skills necessary for doing the jobs at the top positions in government and business, we must ask, What kinds of university education did they get? What kinds of universities did they attend? For the businessmen, the Ivy League and private schools were the principal sources of educated men, but every variety of university of high or low esteem, sectarian or public school, contributed appreciably to the production of these men. However, one can ask, Did these men who come from other occupational levels attend the same types of universities as those who were born to the business elite and the professions? We shall give only summary answers. At the major Ivy League colleges very few sons of laborers were present. For example, although 16 per cent of the college graduates went to Harvard, Yale, or Princeton, all the fathers of the leaders who went to Harvard were either big-business or professional men. The same is true of Princeton and to a somewhat lesser degree, although not to the same categorical degree, of Yale. The Ivy League colleges, at the time these men were getting their education, tended to produce men who were born to top position. Since such a high proportion of all business leaders was educated, we need to ask, where did the executives who come from the lesser levels go to college? They attended large city and state universities, small sectarian colleges, and many went to technical schools such as M.I.T., Carnegie, and a few to the California Institute of Technology. Their undergraduate work tended to be in the liberal arts and the sciences and graduate training in business administration and law.

The colleges and universities from which the government executives received their higher training are different. We list in rank order the ten most popular institutions of higher learning for business and government in Table 7. It will be noted that several of the colleges where these men received their degrees are located in Washington, D.C., meaning that many received their college education while they were working in government service. Some of them are George Washington, Georgetown, and American University. It will also be noted that a few Ivy League schools, and only one in the strict sense of that term, produced graduates sufficiently to be in the first ten. Perhaps one of the most notable comments on the statistics of the first ten is the number of men who graduated from large state universities, including Minnesota, Wisconsin, California, Ohio State, and Michigan.

We can pursue our inquiry further by asking, "Why is university education becoming the principal route to top executive position? Is it principally because of an advantage gained by use of academic training, resulting in an increase in competence? Or is a college degree merely an advantageous symbol of superiority that acts categorically so that the one who possesses it receives preferential treatment? Do the larger extracurricular experiences of university life, those over and beyond the classroom, play the principal part in the leader's success? In brief, what factors are involved in the obvious success of the university men? [4]

In terms of career pattern, a number of generalizations can be made about college men. They tend to be promoted faster than noncollege men. The college-educated executives reach top positions at an earlier age than do the noncollege men. Most noncollege men obtain more education before they are promoted, indicating the need of education to support their efforts for advancement. Moreover, noncollege men ordinarily serve a longer apprenticeship on the job before they are given the same occupational approval as the college man who possesses a degree when he arrives. During the earlier years of the college man's experiences in big business, the college degree does have some symbolic significance. Moreover, it permits

---

[4] The results of Dr. Robert Scofield's study, which was a continuation of the one on the big-business leaders, are used here. He examined the policy of promotion and inquired into the values and beliefs involved in the recruitment of college men by big-business organizations. The organizations included were selected from those Warner and Abegglen studied.

TABLE 7

THE TOP TEN UNIVERSITIES OF GOVERNMENT AND BUSINESS

Business	No.	Government	No.
Yale	1	George Washington	1
Harvard	2	Harvard	2
Princeton	3	Columbia	3
Cornell	4	University of Chicago	4
University of Pennsylvania	5	University of Minnesota	5
University of Illinois	6	Georgetown	6
Massachusetts Institute of Technology	6	University of Wisconsin	7
University of Michigan	6	University of California (Berkeley)	7
New York University	7	Ohio State	8
University of Minnesota	8	American University	8
Williams College	9	University of Michigan	9
University of California (Berkeley)	8	New York University	10
University of Chicago	10		

better interpersonal relations and social intercourse with the superiors at a level that gives them greater equality with their superiors. However, the final choice for top positions is clearly not dependent on college degrees. At the time when a man reaches the position where he is promoted to the level at which we found him, the question of whether he has or has not a college degree is of little importance. What does matter is how well he performs on the job and the scope of his problem solving, his familiarity with the field, and his behavior as evaluated by the executive standards. It is significant that men who are born to high social status find a college degree important, and some of them necessary; a man who is born to high status often has more questions asked about why he did not get a college degree than one coming from lower occupational background.

The relationship of higher education to career achievement is important, but clearly other factors are operating to increase the use of higher education in business and government.

Why does education—university education—become such an important route to the top? Part of the answer is the massive changes that have occurred in the society which now favor the kind of training that takes place in college; and they are partly due to changes in the structure of business enterprise. There has been a change in the values and beliefs about what kinds of men are best fitted for advancement and what kinds of men are selected in the first place for employment and for future executive positions. The emphasis now tends to be more on the broadly trained man, who, it is believed, can make better decisions in a fluid and emergent society. There has been a change in management ideology about what it is that men should do at the top. Perhaps most important is the increase in size in many of the industrial empires. A large number of them have grown enormously. These are the companies which compete most arduously in the recruitment of college men at their time of graduation or after they have attended schools of business or law or some other institution of advanced education. We can only summarize what is demonstrably true from the research on big-business leaders.

When the big-business organizations were recategorized according to size, running from the very largest down to the smaller ones, we were able to divide them into five levels. The executives of each of these levels were then examined to determine what proportion of them had risen from lower to higher occupational levels. An interesting generalization resulted from this inquiry. The larger the business enterprise, the higher the proportion of men who come from lower levels; the smaller the size of the business enterprise, the smaller the proportion of men from lower levels and the greater proportion born to high position. It seems probable that if our inquiry had taken us to still smaller enterprises—those which would be large, let us say, for smaller cities and towns—the proportions of men born to high position would have increased rather than decreased. In brief, mobility in business for the present day is partly a function of the increasing complexity and the developing hierarchies of large enterprises. Moreover, it seems probable that the educated man is more likely to be equipped to make the decisions necessary in a society that is becoming increasingly complex and be able to deal with the problems that confront executives in high positions who must relate their enterprises successfully to a rapidly changing world. Higher education, which gives a broader view of the world around the person so trained, fits closely with the needs and the broad scope of large business enterprise. As such, it is also the instrument by which the ambitious born to low position can equip themselves to compete for top positions in government and business. It should be added that success breeds success for higher education; for, with an increasing belief and reliance on the ideology of those who select executives for advancement, education is, if not a necessary requirement, then an increasingly advantageous characteristic for candidates for promotion.

We conclude our discussion of the specific problem of occupational mobility in American business and government with a brief comment on the larger problem of interpreting the significance of the results of the two researches in terms of the nature of the present society and in light of some of the contemporary and historical processes. The American society is a fluid, emergent one, with change in the nature of the system. The local communities merge into the larger national collectivity. Large-scale organizations, big government and big business, become increasingly prominent. In this fluid world of change and increasing immensity the managerial group will be drawn increasingly from the educated mobile men who come from the more populous lower occupational levels.

QUESTIONS

1. What similarities between governmental and business executives do you find important in Warner's study?
2. What significant trends in terms of manager development do you see emanating from this article?
3. How important is higher education for today's executive? Should formal educational standards be made mandatory for managerial career advancement in our business firms of today? What problems and/or advantages do you see here?
4. How important is an executive's social background with regard to his career advancement?
5. What does this article tell you about your own future managerial career possibilities?

8. MANAGERIAL TALENT *

Edwin E. Ghiselli

It is, indeed, an honor for me to have been chosen to participate in this series of annual Walter Van Dyke Bingham Memorial Lectures. It permits me publically to express my thanks to a man who many years ago gave me guidance in my professional career, and who stimulated my thinking and encouraged my work in industrial psychology. With all of the recognitions he received, and so well deserved, for his many contributions to his profession and to his country, he always remained a warm and understanding man, ever ready to hear out the ideas of others and to foster their development. So today I do not so much feel that I am delivering a lecture, but rather as though I were again spelling out ideas as I did in the past to Dr. Bingham so that they thereby become clearer in my mind.

The University of Michigan is to be congratulated for having been chosen as the site of this lecture. Again recognition is given to this institution, which because of the high quality and quantity of its research and human product, has played, and increasingly continues to play, so unique and important a role in the history of psychology. Yet it is difficult for me to think of the University as an institution since it is peopled with so many friends and former colleagues. So for this reason, too, I feel I am not giving a discourse but rather that I am again taking advantage of the tolerance and understanding of colleagues to talk about some ideas of mine.

As a representative of her husband's profession, I should like to express our thanks to Mrs. Bingham for her generosity in establishing this series of lectures. Throughout his life Dr. Bingham directed his efforts to fostering the full utilization of human resources. He not only saw the value to society of the assessment of human talents, but also its importance for the self-actualization of the individual. By these lectures devoted to the identification and nurture of human talent, his goals continue to be pursued.

Before World War II industrial psychologists largely concerned themselves with the men and women who labor in the factory or keep the books in the office. But in the past 15 years there has been a great surge of interest in examining the nature of those who in business and industrial establishments direct, administer, and organize—that is, manage. I am not at all sure what has caused this

* From *The American Psychologist*, Vol. 18, No. 10 (October, 1963), pp. 631-642. Reprinted with permission.

shift in interest. I think it not impossible that psychologists have stood in awe of those in high places, viewing managers stereotypically as a category apart from ordinary folk. But now for some reason or another managers are seen as human beings, beings who strive, who bleed, who have feelings, needs, and frustrations, and who differ among themselves in abilities, personality traits, and performance in the same way as do other people. The denizens of Olympus, then, are seen as being of the same stuff as those of Attica.

Psychologists who study management stand accused by critics of the social scene of a score of trespasses, from surreptitiously destroying individuality among managers to trying to raze the very foundation of American business and industry, individual initiative, with precisely the same objective that brought my great grandfather to the California mother lode in 1849—gold. And certainly there is some substance for these critics' adverse comments since there have been a plethora of pseudoscientific discourses about the nature and nurture of managers together with a variety of unvalidated action programs for their selection and training. However, much serious work is being conducted, and while our knowledge and understanding is still small, progress is being made in the development of a solid body of empirically determined facts and in sharper and more exact theory. The best testimony of this is the significant work of the social-industrial psychologists here at the University of Michigan, the effects of which are seen throughout the social sciences and in the business and industrial community.

In recent years a group of us at the Institute of Industrial Relations of the University of California—Mason Haire, Lyman Porter, and myself—have been studying the nature of organizations and the psychological characteristics of managers. The investigations of my colleague, Mason Haire,[1] have shown that as business and industrial organizations grow and develop, it is in the very nature of the case that their integrative and coordinative activities assume greater and greater importance. This is indicated by the fact that the larger an organization becomes the greater is the proportion of individuals in it whose functions are of an administrative rather than of a directly productive sort. With the increasing sizes of our business and industrial establishments, then, there would appear to be a real need for psychologists as well as other social scientists to examine the nature of those who manage, so that these establishments can operate as effective organizations.

---

[1] M. Haire, "Biological Models and Empirical Histories of Growth of Organizations" in M. Haire (ed.), *Modern Organization Theory* (New York: Wiley, 1959), pp. 272-306.

I shall begin my discussion by trying to define the term manager. I fear my definition will not be as tight as one might wish, but perhaps it will suffice to delineate the general realm of occupational activity wherein I wish to examine talent. Then I shall treat briefly with the problem of gauging success in the performance of managerial activities. I believe that success in management must be viewed broadly, and is not yet readily subject to precise and objective measurement. The main body of my presentation will be concerned with an examination of what I believe to be important facets of managerial talent. In this connection I shall present some of my empirical studies of the psychological properties I have termed management traits. Finally, I shall mention briefly some of our findings on the motives and aspirations of managers, since I believe they will cast additional light on the nature of managerial talent.

While management is reasonably distinguishable as a class in the broad spectrum of occupations, it cannot be said that there is any unanimity of opinion on which particular individuals should be included in it. Perhaps a common root to many of the definitions of the term manager is that a manager is any person in an organization who supervises the activities of others. Such a definition not only includes such first line supervisors as industrial foremen, but also leadmen and craftsmen who direct apprentices, neither of whom are considered to be management personnel. Furthermore, there are some individuals whom almost everyone would place in the category of management, such as safety engineers and legal counselors, who may supervise no one but their secretaries. While certainly one element in the decision of whether to classify an individual as a manager, supervision is not the sole criterion.

Another common root in many definitions of management is that which stems from the meaning of the word to manage. Lexigraphically, to manage is to direct, to execute, to carry out, to guide, and to administer, and, interestingly enough, to cope with, to bring about by contriving, and to husband. I am sure that there are many in management who would think that the latter are more descriptive of their activities than are the former. In any event, both arm chair analyses of the job of manager and careful systematic studies of what managers actually do, such as those of Shartle [2] and the Ohio State University group, give support to the use of functions such as these to distinguish the class of managers in the taxonomy of occupations. Certainly the functions of directing, administering, and the

---

[2] C. L. Shartle, *Executive Performance and Leadership* (Englewood Cliffs, N. J.: Prentice-Hall, 1956).

like, do not provide precise criteria for differentiating management positions from those of other sorts, but at least they are guide posts. In general they describe the activities of the persons in the upper portions of the organizational hierarchy.

The personnel of a business or industrial establishment can be roughly classified by level. The individuals at the upper levels are concerned with the overall government of the organization and the formulation of broad plans and policies. Here we find the presidents, vice presidents, and, depending upon the size and nature of the enterprise, those who head major operations or geographical areas. The task of those at the next level is to crystallize the general policies and plans developed at the highest level, formulating them into specific and workable procedures. At this second level are included those who operate divisions or departments in an organization, together with staff personnel who are concerned with specialized activities. The next level are the first line supervisors who are charged with putting into effect the specific procedures prepared at the level above, by the immediate direction of the activities of the line workers. Finally, at the lowest level of the organizational hierarchy are the individuals who directly produce goods and services.

A broad distinction can be drawn between those workers whose activities directly result in the production of goods and services, and those whose activities are of a planful, integrative, and directive character. It is the latter, those in the upper three levels of the organization, who typically are termed management and are distinguished from the producers or line workers. So it is common to speak of three managerial levels, upper management, middle management, and lower management.

If I am to discuss managerial talent, I should, I suppose, be prepared to indicate how a more successful manager can be distinguished from a less successful one. The measurement of job success, the so-called criterion problem, has plagued industrial psychology since its birth. It is not a simple task even with simple jobs, and with management jobs their very complexity makes the problem seem almost insurmountable. The subject has been extensively discussed and empirically examined, but certainly the fundamental issues have not been settled.

Psychologists put great value on precisely quantified and objective appraisals of individuals, appraisals based on concrete and objective measures of each of the various specific aspects of the performance under consideration. While it is obviously true that such appraisals do have many desirable features, I nonetheless believe that there is a case to be made for the purely subjective, global, overall assessments, as are given by one person's opinions or ratings of the performance of another person.

Just because they are expressed in quantified terms, objective measures of performance may erroneously convey the impression that the differences among individuals are great, whereas in fact the differences may be quite small and insignificant. Futhermore, as Likert [3] has pointed out, those aspects of performance which we can measure objectively, often are quite unimportant and irrelevant. The sharpness with which an executive keeps his pencils can be measured with a high degree of reliability but has little bearing on evaluations of his success as a manager. The relevance and importance of the various activities connected with a job are matters apart from their mode of measurement, and, indeed, are purely value judgments. I do not mean to imply that objective measures of managerial behavior are worthless. Quite the contrary. Recent studies of great ingenuity have been most fruitful of ideas, and have given new insights into the nature of managerial functions.[4] Nevertheless I do not believe that at the present time they are sufficiently well worked out and tested, and do not give the types of evaluations required.

Psychologists have examined extensively the subjective evaluations, or judgments, of one person by another, and invariably find them wanting. It has been endlessly demonstrated that one man's assessment of the performance of another is influenced by all manner of irrelevant matters. A foreman's ratings of the job proficiency of his subordinates may be in part determined by whether the men are Giant or Dodger fans, and the ratings of the vice presidents made by the president of a company may be biased by whether they prefer Brand X or Brand Y political party. Furthermore, two individuals seldom agree perfectly in their opinion of a third, and when they do collusion is suspected.

Yet, the fact that subjective appraisals of performance are not entirely based on irrelevant matters, and there is some and often considerable agreement among different assessors, is too often forgotten. Furthermore, as Bingham [5] so clearly pointed out many years ago, subjective appraisals not only permit a meaningful integration of the individual's performance in the various aspects of his job, but

[3] R. Likert, *New Patterns of Management* (New York: McGraw-Hill, 1961).
[4] N. Frederiksen, "Factors in In-Basket Performance," *Psychol. Monogr.*, 1962, 76 (22, Whole No. 541) and R. Tagiuri (ed.), *Research Needs in Executive Selection* (Boston: Harvard University, Graduate School Business Administration, Division Research, 1961).
[5] W. V. Bingham, "Halo, Invalid and Valid," *Journal of Applied Psychology*, Vol. 23 (1939), pp. 221-228.

also permit an evaluation in terms of the demands of the setting in which the job occurs. For the present, then, I prefer subjective evaluations of managerial performance.

I have been cavalierly speaking of management as if it were a single job. This is, of course, quite incorrect. The managerial occupation includes a wide variety of positions and the differences among them are great. Managerial jobs range from those with considerable personal authority and responsibility to those which are purely advisory. Some are completely enmeshed in a fabric of interpersonal relationships, whereas others are as lonely as the job of lighthouse keeper. While some demand a professional background, others require no special training. In the work of Hemphill [6] we have the beginning of an empirically based taxonomy of managerial jobs. But we have so few precise descriptions of managerial jobs and the overlap among them is so great that as a group they appear amorphous. They can be classified into some broad categories such as line and staff, or into functional groups such as production, financial, and sales, but such categories are of the grossest sort.

But I do not see this lack of a clearly defined classification of managerial jobs as a serious problem in the study of managerial talent. It seems to me that one of the characteristics of managers is their movement from one position to another. Furthermore, this movement, often but not always in the form of advancement, is especially characteristic of those of superior talent. There is, then, in a successful manager's career a concatenation of transmigrations among managerial posts which are quite different in character. A person manifests managerial talent not just because he performs well in one given type of position, but because he has the capacity to perform a variety of them well, and the adaptability to change from one activity to another quite different activity.

I have so far tried to make two points, first that it is possible through purely subjective judgment to appraise managerial success, and second that in talking about managerial talent and managerial success we should not just consider an individual's performance on a single job but rather his progress through a series of positions, in other words, his career as a manager.

Over the years I have been called on in one connection or another to assess the managerial talent of a number of men. My appraisals were based entirely on an interview with each man, plus his vita, and very occasionally a conversation with his superior or a colleague.

[6] J. K. Hemphill, *Dimensions of Executive Positions* (Columbus: Ohio State University Press, 1960), Bureau of Business Research Monograph No. 98.

I would like to illustrate my points with four short case descriptions. Two of these men I judged to be of superior managerial talent, and two inferior. The careers of two were entirely in one company and the other two made changes from one establishment to another. All four men were college graduates, having majored either in economics or business administration, and all four were in their middle forties when I saw them. From these four cases I think you will be able to see that it is not at all impossible to gauge the career success of a manager without objective and quantitative measures of his performance.

The first man, after a short and unsuccessful 2 years as a college instructor, took a position in the research and development department of a large organization. After 2 years he became the head of a division in the department, and after 2 more the department chief. His outstanding talents as an analyst brought him to the attention of top management, and with increasing frequency his recommendations were incorporated into the organization's policy. At 35 he became assistant vice president for research and development, and the following year vice president. Here he manifested not only executive ability but also the capacity to influence the board of directors whom top management considered to be far too conservative. The vice president for operations retiring, my man was given his position. The interesting thing is that he was placed in this post purely for storage because he was already marked for the presidency. He had no real feel for operations, and both he and his superiors realized it. By 42 he was executive vice president, and by 45 president. Here we have a career which I believe indisputably is a successful one as a manager.

The second man began his career as a salesman for a small instrument manufacturing company. Because of his aggressiveness as a salesman he was made sales manager, and after 5 more years he was made general manager, and finally president and partner. The company had been experiencing lean times, and it was largely as a result of his efforts, both in promotion and in operations, that it became financially strong. Indeed, its position was so good that a larger company made such a handsome offer the partners could not refuse it. His services then were sought and obtained by a firm of underwriters in a policy making position involving the purchase and reconstruction of small businesses. Again, a career that clearly is a successful one.

The third man began his career with a brokerage house as an analyst. After 8 years he became the head of the bookkeeping division, and by the time he reached his middle thirties he was made supervisor of the office activities. Here he remained until he was 47.

Seeing no further possibility of advancement, and none being promised, he left the company and became a real estate salesman. While, to be sure, in this last job he increased his income, the picture of his career as a manager is quite unimpressive, showing a slow rate of advancement with a final plateau at a lowish level of middle management.

The fourth man began his occupational career with an accounting firm. After some 6 years he was "stolen" by one of the company's clients, to head its accounting division. Later he became the comptroller, but after a few years finding himself unhappy with the responsibility, he quit. He then obtained the position of treasurer with a ferry company in San Francisco, even though the salary was substantially less and he knew it was a dying business. In a couple of years the company dissolved when the ferry route was finally bridged. Out of a job he was back where he began more than 20 years before, seeking employment as an accountant. Here is a career with initial growth and promise, but with a later decline; a career one would not term successful. If his success were measured objectively I suppose the trend would be a quadratic with a negative coefficient. But surely with this, as with the other cases, the subjective assessment is sufficiently precise.

There have been many analyses of the psychological traits important in the performance of managerial functions, together with a substantial number of empirical investigations of the measured traits which distinguish management from line workers, and the measured traits which are related to indices of the success of managers.[7] At the University of California we have tried to obtain some notion of the traits which are of prime importance for managers by comparing the self- and role perceptions of managers at different levels, managers and line workers, and successful and unsuccessful managers.[8] From the constellations of role and self-perceptions which differentiate these various groups, we have endeavored to develop a picture of the significant managerial traits. Material of this sort lends itself to a variety of interpretations, and it is likely others would interpret

[7] W. T. Harrell, *Manager's Performance and Personality* (Cincinnati, Ohio: South-Western Publishing Company, 1961).

[8] E. E. Ghiselli and R. Barthol, "Role Perceptions of Successful and Unsuccessful Supervisors, *Journal of Applied Psychology*, Vol. 40 (1956), pp. 241-244; see also L. W. Porter, "Differential Self-Perceptions of Management Personnel and Line Workers," *Journal of Applied Psychology*, Vol. 42 (1958), pp. 105-108, and his "Self-Perceptions of First-Level Supervisors Compared with Upper-Management Personnel and with Operative Line Workers," *Journal of Applied Psychology*, Vol. 43 (1959), pp. 183-186; L. W. Porter and E. E. Ghiselli, "The Self Perceptions of Top and Middle Management Personnel, *Personnel Psychology*, Vol. 10 (1957), pp. 397-406.

our findings in ways somewhat differently than we have. Nevertheless, we do believe our interpretations have some validity inasmuch as we have been able to demonstrate that certain of these patterns of self-perception are related in important ways to the manner in which task-oriented groups govern themselves.[9]

From these various analyses I have come to the conclusion that important to managerial success are the traits of intelligence, supervisory ability, initiative, self-assurance, and perceived occupational level. I do not mean to imply that success in management is determined solely by these five traits, for certainly there are many others. Nevertheless, it does seem to me that these particular five traits—intelligence, supervisory ability, initiative, self-assurance, and perceived occupational level—play a key role in managerial functions and therefore are major facets of managerial talent. I should, therefore, like to summarize my work on them.[10]

Let me first consider the trait of intelligence. Today we generally accept the proposition that tests of intelligence measure significant psychological properties of the individual. Yet, we do not seem to worry very much any more about what these specific properties are. I suspect there is a certain amount of battle fatigue as a result of the long and indecisive war we psychologists waged among ourselves during the first 4 decades of the century about the nature of intelligence and the validity of tests proclaimed as measuring it. I doubt if there are very many now who consider intelligence as the single all-important ability that Spearman conceived it to be. Rather we tend to think of intelligence tests as measuring a domain of various cognitive abilities more or less related logically if not psychologically. Intelligence we take to be an important determiner of behavior in those situations involving mental power and problem solving, where the individual is called upon to deal with ideas, abstractions, and concepts.

One of the well-popularized results of the first great mass testing of adults, the measurement of the intelligence of soldiers in the

[9] E. E. Ghiselli and T. M. Lodahl, "The Evaluation of Foremen's Performance in Relation to the Internal Characteristics of Their Work Groups," *Personnel Psychology*, Vol. 11 (1958), pp. 179-187, and "Patterns of Managerial Traits and Group Effectiveness, *Journal of Abnormal and Social Psychology*, Vol. 57 (1958), pp. 61-66.

[10] E. E. Ghiselli, "A Scale for the Measurement of Initiative," *Personnel Psychology*, Vol. 8 (1955), pp. 157-64; "Correlates of Initiative," *Personnel Psychology*, Vol. 9 (1956), pp. 311-320; "Occupational Level Measured Through Self Perception," *Personnel Psychology*, Vol. 9 (1956), pp. 169-176; "Traits Differentiating Management Personnel," *Personnel Psychology*, Vol. 12 (1959), pp. 535-544; "Intelligence and Managerial Success," *Psychology Report*, Vol. 12 (1963), p. 898; and "The Validity of Management Traits in Relation to Occupational Level," *Personnel Psychology*, Vol. 16 (1963), pp. 109-113.

American Army in World War I, was the relationship found between level of occupation and intelligence test scores.[11] It was noted that when soldiers were sorted out into groups in terms of their civilian occupations, those in the so-called higher occupations on the average earned higher scores than those in the lower occupations. Since World War I this relationship between level of occupation and intelligence has been demonstrated a number of times. Men in the professions obtain the highest scores, followed in order by those in managerial, supervisory, and clerical jobs, and finally those in the various industrial jobs show average scores in descending order of skilled, semi-skilled, and unskilled workers.

In all of these investigations there is found a substantial amount of variation in scores among individuals in any one occupational group. Thus some factory workers earn higher scores than those earned by some lawyers. Nevertheless, the relationship between level of occupation and measured intelligence is quite substantial.

The intelligence test scores of persons in management positions fall in the higher ranges of the distribution of scores of the general employed population. Furthermore, it appears that by and large those in lower management have the lowest scores and those in upper management the highest ones. There is quite a substantial difference in intelligence between lower and middle management, but the difference between middle and upper management is small. As a matter of fact, lower management and line workers are about the same in measured intelligence. Industrial foremen are about equal to skilled workers, but office supervisors do seem superior to clerical workers. It is probable that among office supervisors are some young people in trainee positions who are slated for higher management positions. The average intelligence test scores of those who hold positions in the upper and middle levels of management is very high, indeed, and is reported to exceed the scores of about 96% of the population.[12] Over the years I have tested several hundred managers at these levels in a variety of different businesses and industries. Interestingly enough their average score, too, happens to fall at the ninety-sixth percentile.

There is a substantial body of evidence which indicates that there is a relationship between level of occupation and the degree to which job success can be predicted by intelligence test scores.[13] As one

[11] W. V. Bingham, *Aptitudes and Aptitude Testing* (New York: Harper, 1937).

[12] Harrell, *op. cit.*

[13] E. E. Ghiselli, "The Measurement of Occupational Aptitude," *University of California Publication of Psychology*, Vol. 8 (1955), pp. 101-216.

moves up the scale of occupations from the unskilled to the upper managerial, one finds not only higher and higher average test scores but also higher and higher correlations between intelligence test scores and job success. Nevertheless, even at the upper two levels of management, the relationship between intelligence test scores and job success is by no means high, and while the reported relationships vary in magnitude from one investigation to another, by and large they are perhaps best described as being moderate.

So one might take the position that the greater the measured amount of intelligence an individual possesses the higher he is likely to rise in the organizational hierarchy, and the greater is the probability he will be a successful manager. But I am not sure that the latter part of this generalization can be accepted without question, at least at the higher levels of test scores. There have been suggestions that at the middle and upper managerial levels there is not a simple one-to-one relationship between intelligence and managerial ability. Rather it would appear that the relationship between intelligence and managerial success may be curvilinear, with not only those managers earning low scores being on the average poorer, but also those earning very high scores.

I have found this to be the case with three groups of managers. The average scores of all of these groups were quite high, as I reported earlier they exceeded the scores of about 96% of the general population. In each group I divided the men into those whose scores fell above this point and those whose scores fell below it. In every group, for the men with the lower scores there was a positive relationship between intelligence and success and for the men with the higher scores the relationship was negative. In other words, for individuals of higher and higher intelligence there is a greater and greater probability they will achieve success as managers until a critical intellectual level is reached. This level is quite high, indeed, but above it individuals with higher and higher scores have less and less chance of being successful managers.

For one of these groups, a group of executives in a financial organization, success was gauged by the higher management of the organization. Without in fact knowing what the scores were, it was the men who earned the highest and the lowest scores whom higher management invited to leave. A second group was comprised of individuals the success of whose managerial careers I appraised. I mentioned earlier the nature of these appraisals and gave some examples. These men were employed in a wide variety of different organizations and held a wide variety of different managerial positions. Yet, the careers of those earning the very highest scores were not as successful as the careers of those who earned somewhat lower scores. The measure of success I used with the third group I think is most interesting and significant. For these men success was gauged solely and entirely in terms of how the individual appraised himself. I asked managers to evaluate their own careers, indicating the degree to which they themselves believed they were successful. These reports were, of course, anonymous. It was both the managers who earned very high and low intelligence test scores who viewed their careers with the greatest misgivings. So there does appear to be some substance to the notion that a curvilinear relationship exists between intelligence and managerial success, with the very very bright, as well as those more poorly endowed, being less likely to be successful than those at intermediate levels.

We have seen that the evidence indicates intelligence to be an important factor in managerial success, and therefore it is one of the facets of managerial talent. Individuals of higher and higher intelligence have greater and greater chances of being successful managers. This relationship holds until a very high level of intelligence is reached, and then there appears to be a brief trend in the opposite direction. Individuals who fall among the top 2 or 3% of the population in intelligence are somewhat less likely to be successful managers than those immediately below them. It is possible that those individuals at the very extreme high levels of capacity to deal with abstract ideas and concepts do not find in managerial activities the intellectual challenge they need.

In recent years, discussions of conditions for effective organizations, particularly those discussions with a so-called human relations orientation, have stressed the importance of leadership. Indeed, the naive student might well suspect that the sole function of management is leadership, with top management leading middle management, middle management leading lower management, and lower management leading line personnel who do all the work. The implication seems to be that if management provided proper leadership, both for itself and for line workers, all organization ills would be cured. While it is unquestionably true that one of the functions of managers is to supervise the activities of those lower in the organization, and that the better supervision management provides the better the organization will function, leadership and the supervision of subordinates is only among the many functions that managers perform.

Still, the life of a business or industrial organization lies in the individuals who people it. If the organization is to function as an effective social entity, its human parts must operate in an integrated fashion. As yet, the most effective integrative machinery our species, Homo so-called sapiens, has been able to develop is an authoritarian hierarchy of individuals, a series of superiors and subordinates, ranging in a business or industrial organization from the president at the top to the line workers at the bottom. Except for the individuals at the top and bottom, each person has two roles, one as the supervised and the other as the supervisor. Each has his activities directed by a superior and in turn directs the activities of subordinates. It is not impossible that in the future social science will provide some quite different type of machinery which more fully utilizes the varieties of human talent and increases individual freedom, creativity, and self-fulfillment. In the meantime, we are stuck with a system wherein ability to supervise the activities of others is a primary matter.

I do not think it appropriate here to enter into a discussion of what constitutes effective supervision. Notions about the nature of good supervision vary widely and are likely to be, if I may say so, contaminated by theoretical notions about leadership, and by social views. It does seem clear that what are good supervisory practices in one situation may be poor in another. For my purposes here I shall simply take good supervision to be that behavior which management, in a given situation, says is good supervision as distinguished from that behavior which management says is poor supervision. In other words, I am again taking ratings, or personal and subjective estimates, as an adequate index of success, in this case as a criterion of supervisory ability. The test I use as a measure of supervisory ability I consider to be a valid measure of this trait since, in widely differing organizations, the scores individuals earn on it are related to the ratings of supervisory ability assigned to them. Therefore, I can perhaps say that by superior supervisory ability I am referring to the effective utilization of whatever supervisory practices are indicated by the particular requirements of the situation.

My findings indicate that there is a relationship between supervisory ability and occupational level just as there is with intelligence and occupational level. As one proceeds up the scale of occupations from line workers through lower and middle management to top management there is a progressive increase in capacity to supervise the activities of others. The difference between lower management and line workers surprisingly enough is small. But there is a considerable superiority of middle management over lower management, and an equally great difference between middle and upper management. In capacity for leadership the higher levels of management are quite superior, and at the top level of management it is outstanding.

As one might expect, with line workers there is little or no relationship between measured capacity for supervision and job performance. But with managers at all organizational levels I find supervisory ability bears quite a substantial relationship to the evaluations of their performance as managers. Indeed, of all of the five traits I have termed management traits, this seems to be of paramount importance. Furthermore, my investigations indicate that supervisory ability is a somewhat more important determiner of success at the upper management levels than it is at the lower levels, though the differences are not great. Ability to direct the activities of others, then, is a significant aspect of managerial talent, and on the average the higher and higher an individual makes his way in the organizational hierarchy the more qualified is he likely to be as a supervisor, and the more important this ability is to his success as a manager.

Many persons in management who possess quite adequate intellectual and social talents and who are highly motivated, nevertheless are sometimes found wanting by their superiors. They do their work carefully, they exercise good judgment, they are zealous, and they are adept at interpersonal relationships. Yet, there is a certain independence and inventiveness which is missing in their performance. Such people are often described as lacking in the quality termed initiative.

At great length managers deplore and bewail the absence of initiative in their subordinates, though they seem less willing to rejoice in its presence. The importance of initiative is stressed at all organizational levels, yet few have addressed it empirically, much less attempted to measure it. Unquestionably initiative is an elusive and vague trait, and is a complex one involving a variety of dimensions of personality. With far less wisdom than I hope is my wont, I have tried both to define and to measure initiative.

It seems to me that initiative has two aspects. One is motivational and involves the beginning of actions, and the other is cognitive and involves the capacity to note and to discover new means of goal achievement. The first aspect involves the ability to act independently and to initiate actions without stimulation and support from others. The second aspect involves the capacity to see courses of action and implementations that are not readily apparent to others. Both aspects have the property of being self-generative. It does not seem to me that initiative implies a capacity to maintain motivation and sustain goal-oriented activity in the face of frustration. Rather a person who possesses initiative is an inaugurator or originator who opens new fields and conceives of novel ways of doing things.

Very likely the test I use to measure initiative is a chancy thing. Even so, I regard it with a certain satisfaction. It is valid in the sense that scores on it are related to superiors' ratings of initiative. But more than that it differentiates those individuals who say they want a job wherein they can use their initiative from those who disclaim any such desire. If I am correct in viewing initiative as being self-generative, then self-reports, such as these reflecting the way an individual proposes to go about things, are of particular importance.

The relationship I find between measured capacity for initiative and age is an interesting one. With line workers there is a progressive decrease in initiative with increasing age, and past the age of 40 initiative shows a sharp and significant drop. On the other hand, with persons in management positions there is a continuous, though small, increase in initiative with age. This suggests the possibility that being in a situation where initiative is not required kills its expression, and being in a job where there are many and continued opportunities to manifest initiative fosters it.

If initiative is an important aspect of managerial talent it should be related to level of occupation; and, indeed, I find this to be the case. Proceeding from line workers through lower and middle management to upper management there is, on the average, an increase in the measured capacity for initiative. Members of upper management appear to be particularly outstanding in this trait. But at all occupational levels there is a wide range of differences among individuals. Even among the laboring groups there is a substantial number of individuals who possess very high levels of capacity for initiative. The supply of people who are outstanding in initiative is substantial. All that is needed is a situation wherein those who possess it can utilize it.

At the upper two levels of management there is a positive relationship between initiative and job performance. The greater the individual's capacity for initiative the more likely he is to be judged as being a good manager. On the other hand, at the lower levels of management and with line jobs, in general I find either no relationship at all between initiative and evaluations of job performance, or a negative relationship. So while initiative might be rewarded at the higher levels of management, at the lower levels it is likely to be punished.

The fourth trait I consider to be an aspect of managerial talent is self-assurance. By self-assurance I mean the extent to which the individual perceives himself to be effective in dealing with the problems which confront him. There are those persons who see themselves as being sound in judgment and able to cope with almost any situation, whereas other people think of themselves as being slow to grasp things, making many mistakes, and being generally inept. The former stand high in self-assurance, and the latter low.

One thinks of the military commander whose utter self-confidence, an almost arrogant self-confidence, permeates his entire troop, reassuring them that all is and will continue to be well, and so impels them to all manner of brave deeds. Undoubtedly the self-assurance of any superior, miltiary or otherwise, often has this sort of effect upon the performance of his subordinates. While certainly self-assurance is often the fool's way, leading him to tread where wiser men will not go, nevertheless it can be the very instrument which enables the individual to deal with his problems and to make decisions about them so that his performance is effective. Because of his confidence in himself he is willing and eager to meet problems head on. Since in many situations any kind of decisive action is better than none at all, the self-confident individual may well achieve the greater success.

Defining self-assurance as I do permits me to demonstrate the validity of my test of the trait in a very simple minded way. With unbounded self-assurance I simply show that my test differentiates people who believe themselves to be effective individuals from those who believe themselves to be ineffective. I have found that my test differentiates those students who see themselves as scholars from those who see themselves as dunces, those workmen who describe themselves as highly skilled from those who describe themselves as being of lesser proficiency, and those managers who openly admit their performance is excellent from those who confess theirs is lacking.

As with the other managerial traits, as one proceeds from the lower occupational levels to the higher ones there is a greater and greater amount of self-assurance manifested by the personnel at those various levels. There is a substantial distinction between lower and middle management, but also between middle and upper management. Highly placed executives are outstanding in the confidence they have in themselves.

With line workers there is no relationship between their measured self-assurance and their job success. At all three managerial levels there is some, but quite modest, relationship. So while I would consider self-assurance a facet of managerial talent, it, together with initiative, seems to be of lesser importance than intelligence, supervisory ability, and perceived occupational level.

I come now to the fifth and last of the traits I have taken to be aspects of managerial talent, the trait I call perceived occupational level. Whether rightly or wrongly, for good or for evil, we order occupations, as I have done here, from the unskilled through the semiskilled, skilled, clerical, sales, and lower management jobs, to the upper management jobs and professions. The average scores earned by these occupational groups on a variety of psychological traits order them in this manner, or approximately so, and the order reflects their social desirability, their snob appeal, in our society. So in our thinking we have crystallized the notion of a scale of occupations, and we place individuals on that scale in terms of the occupational level of the job they now hold, the job they have the ability to hold, the job they aspire to, and the like.

The monumental work of E. K. Strong [14] on occupational interests, work stemming from the early research stimulated by Bingham at the Carnegie Institute of Technology, has, among other things, shown that the patterns of interests of persons at different occupational levels are different. Knowing an individual's interest pattern, then, he can be placed on the scale and be described as having the interests of people in the higher occupations, the middle occupations, or the lower occupations.

Just as individuals differ in their patterns of interests so they also differ in their patterns of self-perceptions. Some persons think of themselves as being honest, cautious, and industrious; others think of themselves as being reliable, inventive, and sociable; and so on. Inasmuch as the patterns of interests of workers at different occupational levels differ, we would expect their self-perceptions also to be different. This I have found to be true. I have developed a test wherein the individual describes himself, and these self-perceptions are different for workers at different occupational levels. So I can locate an individual on the occupational scale by ascertaining the level where workers describe themselves in about the same way as he does.

---

[14] *Vocational Interests of Men and Women* (Stanford, Calif.: Stanford University Press, 1943).

Occupational-level scales based on such matters as interests and self-perceptions generally are considered to measure something akin to level of aspiration. The individual who is placed high on such a scale is regarded as one who wants the responsibility and prestige associated with higher-level jobs, and believes he has the talents required by them. An individual who is placed low on the scale is one who is content with less by way of rewards and status.

By the very nature of my test of perceived occupational level, line workers on the average fall at the lower ranges of the scale and persons holding upper management positions fall at the top, with lower and middle management being intermediately placed. All of the groups are widely differentiated in terms of perceived occupational level, but the largest difference is between lower and middle management. So it would seem that in terms of the way they perceive themselves, line workers and lower management constitute one family, and middle and upper management constitute another family.

I find the same family division in terms of the relationship between perceived occupational level and job proficiency. At the upper two levels of management the relationship between perceived occupational level and job success is positive, and in general at the lower level of management and with line workers it is negative. That is, at the upper levels of management, the more an individual perceives himself in the same way as do those who are in fact high occupationally, the better his performance is judged to be. With lower management and line workers the situation is just the reverse. The more an individual perceives himself in the same way as those who are high occupationally, the poorer his performance is judged to be.

There seems to be adequate justification, then, for considering perceived occupational level as an aspect of managerial talent. Seeing oneself in the same way as those in upper management do would seem to provide the needed stimulation for the individual to perform in ways which insure his moving up the organizational ladder.

I have traced for you my thinking about what I consider to be some of the major facets of managerial talent. Managerial talent has a heavy intellectual component. It perhaps does not represent the very highest levels of abstract thinking, but it does involve the capacity to see and to develop novel solutions to problems. While not synonymous with leadership, managerial talent does manifest itself in the effective direction of others. Finally, managerial talent implies a willingness to depend on oneself coupled with a self-generated impetus to activity and a striving for, and a willingness to accept, the authority and responsibility which goes with high-level positions in organizations. This suggests that the substratum of managerial talent is individuality, and its corollary, the desire for self-realization through creative activity.

Individuality is a term which has very different connotations for different people. Consequently, when one describes a person as being individualistic, some will take him to be a genius and others will take him to be some kind of a nut. If we are to deal with individuality with scientific impartiality we must define it so that the term carries no emotionally loaded meanings. For purposes of examining it empirically, I have defined individuality as the extent to which a person's pattern of traits is unique, that is, the extent to which it is dissimilar from other patterns which are characteristic of many individuals.[15]

Therefore, it is possible to conceive of a dimension of individuality. At the one extreme are those persons whose patterns of traits are very different from those of other people, and at the opposite extreme are persons whose patterns are very much like those of a substantial number of people. Furthermore, we can talk about a person's individuality in a variety of domains of behavior. A person might be very individualistic in his behavior which is job connected, doing things in ways which are novel and different, and at the same time he may be quite nonindividualistic in his social behavior, doing just the things that the large proportion of people do in social intercourse.

With a group of men at the level of middle management, I examined individuality in managerial behavior in relation to job success.[16] My results indicated that the men who displayed the greatest individuality in managerial behavior were in general the ones judged to be the best managers. These findings, of course, are counter to the notion so commonly advanced by social critics today that individuality hinders those who aspire to the higher levels of management. Unquestionably there is some substance to the argument that the way to succeed in business is to conform. Indeed, I can give some supporting instances. But I believe the discussions are clouded by poor definitions of the terms "individuality" and "conformity." Furthermore, I am concerned here with managerial talent and individuality in relation to how the individual does his work, and not to how he behaves with respect to the social milieu of his organization.

---

[15] E. E. Ghiselli, "Individuality As a Factor in the Success of Management Personnel," *Personnel Psychology*, Vol. 13 (1960), pp. 1-10.
[16] *Ibid.*

Haire, Porter, and I are currently engaged in studying the motivations, goals, and attitudes of managers.[17] We have questioned several thousand managers not only in the United States but also in a variety of countries throughout the entire world. Not unexpectedly, we find the effects of cultural differences and that the goals of Japanese and Norwegian managers are not precisely the same, nor are those of Indian and Italian managers. Nevertheless, in one respect we find a high degree of unanimity among managers in all countries and at all levels of management. More than anything else, managers want the opportunity to use their talents to the utmost in their work, to act independently, to realize themselves as individuals. Self-realization and autonomy universally are more important to managers than prestige, social satisfactions, and even security.

So I believe there is some substance for my suggestion that the substratum of managerial talent is individuality and the desire for self-realization through creative activity. It seems to me that this gives flavor and meaning to the picture I drew of the talented manager as one who is well endowed intellectually, gifted with the capacity to direct the efforts of others, self-stimulated to action, confident in his abilities, and striving for a position where he can most fully utilize them.

If it seems I am describing a paragon of all the virtues, let me remind you that I am speaking of talent, which, as Bingham [18] put it, is exceptional ability. There are managers and managers, and not all of them manifest high levels of managerial talent. Indeed, the proportion of those who do may not be large. Those of greater managerial talent do their work well and advance in their organizations, and those of lesser managerial talent perform in a pedestrian manner, leave management for other employment commensurate with their particular abilities, or at retirement terminate their careers at low or intermediate managerial levels. Furthermore, I would point out that persons with the properties I have called managerial talent might well be ill fitted for other kinds of activities. The picture I have drawn of a person with managerial talent very likely does not well describe the scientist, the physician, nor the politician. So I am not describing that rare individual who could equally well be king, prelate, or general. Nevertheless, the individual with managerial talent is a gifted person, and an unusual one. Proper use of

---

[17] M. Haire, E. E. Ghiselli, and L. W. Porter, "Cultural Patterns in the Role of the Manager," *Industrial Relations*, Vol. 2 (1963), pp. 95-117.
[18] W. V. Bingham, *Administrative Ability, Its Discovery and Development*, Pamphlet No. 1 (Washington, D. C.: Society for Personnel Administration, 1939).

his gifts will give him the rewards and satisfactions he needs and deserves, and at the same time will maintain the wheels turning in industry and the goods moving in business for the benefit of society as a whole.

QUESTIONS

1. What does Ghiselli conclude about the relationship of intelligence to managerial success?
2. Do you agree with his observations on the leadership role of the manager? Why or why not?
3. What are the two aspects of initiative he discusses? Explain how they vary and why.
4. Why might blue-collar workers and managers have different perceptions about their work and careers?
5. Do you agree with his five traits needed for managerial success? Can you add any more to this listing?

9. FURTHER LIGHT ON THE EXECUTIVE PERSONALITY *

L. Huttner, S. Levy, E. Rosen, and M. Stopol

A number of hypotheses about the personality characteristics of the "typical" business executive were put forward in an article published in the January/February issue of PERSONNEL.[1] As the article pointed out, these hypotheses were based on informal, though clinical, examination of the data derived from extensive testing of, and interviews with some 250 executives in more than a dozen companies, large and small, and the author emphasized that objective study of the same data was needed to substantiate or refute his impressions.

The data obtained from the quantitative tests administered to this group—mental ability (Thurstone Primary Mental Abilities), achievement (Michigan Vocabulary and Diagnostic Reading), aptitude (Sales Aptitude), and personality (MMPI and Bernreuter) have now been systematically examined. The findings of this extensive research are reported here.[2] In addition to confirming many of the hypotheses advanced in the previous article, they throw some interesting light on the characteristics distinguishing executives of different occupational groups and of greater or lesser effectiveness, as well as on the effects of such variables as age and company size.

It has all along been recognized, of course, that while a composite picture of the average American executive may make interesting reading, its practical value is fairly limited. Every company wants its executives to be better than average; and, when it comes to hiring or promoting one, the problem confronting management is that of assessing how well a particular man will fill a specific position. In other words, the company is looking for a good sales manager, plant superintendent, research and development director, or treasurer, as the case may be. Yet, even to know what makes a "good" sales manager is not really enough. As a matter of practical operating efficiency, the company must also take into account the defects of the man's virtues, lest the very qualities that make him "good" for his particular job turn out a disaster for the organization as a whole.

---

* From *Personnel*, Vol. 36, No. 2 (March-April, 1959), pp. 42-50. Reprinted with permission of the American Management Association. Copyright 1959 by the American Management Association.

[1] E. Rosen, "The Executive Personality," *Personnel*, January-February, 1959, pp. 8-20.

[2] The technical data on which these findings are based will be published elsewhere in the near future.

First, then, do the various occupational groups that make up the management team differ significantly in their traits and characteristics, their good points and bad? If so, how do they differ—and what do these differences imply?

DIFFERENCES AMONG OCCUPATIONAL GROUPS

Our findings indicate that in both large and small companies the differences among the four occupational groups studied are far more frequent than can be attributed to change. Actually, these occupational differences occur with greater frequency in the large companies studied than in the smaller ones. While this may be due in part to the fact that fewer executives from small companies were studied, from our knowledge of the operations of all the companies involved, we believe that the reason lies in the fact that large companies using pre-selection procedures tend to establish more clear-cut occupational sub-groups.

The differences between the occupational groups are most marked in respect to intellectual capacity, education, and professional knowledge. There are also some differences in personality variables, but these do not occur with nearly the same frequency. While it is possible that quite different personality types can gravitate toward the same occupation, whether purely by chance or because a particular opportunity presents itself, we believe that once the data on the more subtle projective tests become available, they will indicate many more significant personality differences among occupations than we have been able to discover with the quantitative test scores studied so far. Even so, the present findings point in a predictable and expected direction:

Engineering and R & D executives

In large companies, where the differences between these men and other occupational groups are most evident, these executives are characterized by great accuracy both in general and specific terms. Their abstract reasoning powers are quite high and they show personality tendencies that are consistent with considerable creativity. On the other hand, they are somewhat inept with verbal material. They are highly skilled in handling spatial concepts and in organizing abstract materials, but are slower in simple routine computations than other executive groups. As might be expected, they are also less familiar with the business end of the company's operations. In general, they are the least dominant of the four groups studied, and are not so well adjusted as are the others. They also show some tendency toward subtle depression and to "keeping their distance" from others; they fit least the stereotype of the business man.

These findings confirm the common-sense view of engineers and R & D executives as intelligent, in the sense of being able to reason in terms of abstractions and spatial concepts, accurate, and somewhat poor communicators. Their relative lack of grasp of the "business angle," coupled with their relatively low dominance, should have important implications for top management. Being less aggressive and less articulate than, for example, sales executives, R & D executives may well fail to make themselves heard or to promote their programs as effectively as other company executives, with the result that R & D activities may receive less attention, and less financial support than they deserve. A recognition of this relative ineptitude of technical personnel should serve as a clue to top management that, instead of relying on the time-tested principle of greasing the wheel which squeaks most, more attention and support should be given to a group which may well have as much to contribute to the company's growth as other more vocal and more demanding members of the management team.

Sales executives

Needless to say, these executives rank high in sales aptitude and intellectually score better on verbal as against nonverbal factors. They are somewhat less accurate than executives in general (i.e., they make more errors). They are highly dominant, sociable, and extroverted, and tend to be generally more people-oriented, more open and relatively more thick-skinned, more optimistic, and more self-assured, than other executive groups. Along with these traits, there is some evidence of self-centeredness and selfishness.

These findings suggest that, in most companies, the sales group will be the most assertive and the most vocal, and that, in promoting this function, its members may tend to take a narrow and somewhat selfish point of view. Such a tendency can be dangerous for the company as a whole and should, therefore, be controlled. Top management should also recognize the dangers of the sales group's tendency to impetuosity (as evidenced in total errors and reasoning errors). Because of their verbal ability and aggressiveness, sales executives may be able to disclaim responsibility for their errors and project them on other groups in the company.

Administrative and accounting executives

As might be expected, this group is quite high on numerical ability, and tends to be more oriented toward tangibles rather than abstractions. These executives have a good theoretical grasp of business, but in general, are rather low in their communication abilities, particularly in their ability to verbalize. Personality-wise they are more constricted, less sociable, and more withdrawn. They show the least signs of original thought or creativity, and are also the least optimistic group, with more frequent indications of overt depression.

These characteristics—in particular the relatively low communication skills and the lack of optimism—suggest that the administrative and accounting executive also presents a problem in balancing the company team. Just as it would seem necessary to discount something of the excessive optimism of the sales executive, so it may be equally necessary to discount the excessive pessimism of the accounting executive; and while it may be advisable to put a brake on the rashness and impetuosity of the sales force, the extreme conservatism of the administrative and accounting group may need bolstering up. (These, of course, are generalizations and it must be remembered that individual differences can run counter to the common occupational trend.)

Production executives

These men are very high on abstract reasoning ability—surprisingly enough, they actually rank higher in this respect than the engineering and R & D group. They also rank highest in their ability to deal with numbers. Production executives seem to be very much oriented toward the concrete; they are bright and make few errors. Personality-wise, they tend to be optimistic, but at the same time are markedly subject to fluctuating moods—a tendency that makes them somewhat similar to engineering and R & D executives. Here again, an awareness of this tendency should make it easier for top management to understand and deal with the production group.

Thus far, we have outlined the characteristics of the average executive in four occupational groups. But, as we noted earlier, it is the better-than-average executive whom most companies are looking for. What characteristics distinguish the more effective from the less effective executive in each group?

Differences Between More and Less Effective Executives

Here, of course, we run up against the question, what is our criterion of effectiveness? After careful consideration, we finally decided to use the amount an executive's salary had increased over a fixed period of time—a ratio that seemed to us to be the most significant and uniform one that we could obtain. It must be admitted, however, that this criterion is somewhat contaminated by the fact that salaries are not determined by individual competence alone.[3] Actually, we think that had the criterion been purer, our findings would have been even more conclusive and that we would have been able to identify even more differences between the more and less effective people than we did.

It should be added that the following comparisons are based on our sample of executives in the large companies—our sample in the smaller companies was too limited to draw any conclusions on this score.

In general, our findings indicate that more effective executives tend to be more intelligent, less error prone, and more knowledgable than less effective ones. Personality-wise, they have more drive, enthusiasm, and are more what business men call a "doer." While these traits might be labeled aggressiveness, this is not aggressiveness of a personal kind, but rather channelized and controlled by acceptance of the prevailing standards of business conduct. The more effective executives also seem to be generally less anxious, more optimistic, and more trusting than their less effective colleagues and are able to maintain a high degree of enthusiasm.

To a considerable extent, also, effectiveness appears to be a matter of a man's possessing not only more than his share of the positive characteristics and traits of his occupational group but also fewer of its weaknesses. At all events, he seems to manifest these to a less marked degree.

Engineering and R & D executives

The more effective members of this group are somewhat better informed both in a professional and business sense. Personality-wise, they are less prone to anxiety and depression, and their interests are more like those of business men.

---

[3] A word would seem to be necessary at this point about the effect of age on salary. Extensive analysis too complicated to outline here brought us to the conclusion that both age and salary ratios genuinely and separately correlated with the test variables.

Sales executives

A number of characteristics distinguish the more from the less effective executives in this group. The more effective sales executives tend to be somewhat more intelligent, score rather higher in reasoning ability, and are somewhat better communicators both orally and in writing. They also read faster. Personality-wise, they are a little more outgoing and more dominant than the general run of sales executives. Significantly, they are much less anxiety prone and generally more stable: they do not easily become upset by ordinary day-to-day emergencies. In this respect, we might call them on the whole more mentally healthy, in the conventional sense of the phrase.

Administrative and accounting executives

The more effective members of this group manifest the same intellectual pattern as the more effective sales executives. They are generally brighter and much better communicators than their less effective colleagues—also less rigid and better able to operate outside the narrow scope of their professional competence. Personality-wise, they tend to be more optimistic and they have a somewhat greater awareness of and ability to conform to the social demands of their business life. They also seem to be less introverted than the less successful members of this group.

Production executives

It is difficult to make any comparisons for this group. There seem to be no specific intellectual differences between its more effective and less effective members and the personality variables are inconclusive.

THE EFFECTS OF AGE

Other research conducted on various age groups has demonstrated a small but significant lessening of intellectual powers with age, particularly where rapidity is an important factor. Our analysis also shows, clearly and consistently, that there is some diminution of intellectual powers with age, especially as regards abstract reasoning ability, the ability to organize abstractions, and reading speed.

We may generalize that, personality-wise, middle age brings with it a dampening of extroversion and dominance and a slight, but significant, increase in pessimism, anxiety, and related defense mechanisms. It is rather difficult to assess whether these personality manifestations are a function of the executive's job or whether they are related to psychological problems in his private life.

Engineering and R & D executives

Among the older members of this group we find a small but positive increase in knowledge of human relations as well as a small but nevertheless positive increase in the ability to communicate. This would seem to suggest that these executives have, over the years, managed to pick up some of the attitudes and skills of the other business men with whom they have associated. There is evidence of a small diminution in their abstract reasoning ability. Personality-wise, the older engineering and R & D executives tend to be more conforming and less idiosyncratic—a fact which suggests that they may be also somewhat less creative. On the positive side, they tend to be somewhat less socially distant and, thus, may interact more effectively with other executives in the company. (This seems to go along with their improvement in communications skills and their improved knowledge of human relations.) The common tendency toward increased worry and pessimism in people approaching middle age is also evident among these executives.

Sales executives

A small but positive increase in error scores characterizes the older members of this group. They also show a small diminution in their powers of abstract reasoning, as well as of organizing abstractions, along with a small decrease in reading speed and general intellectual efficiency. Personality-wise, the older sales executives tend to be somewhat less extroverted than the younger ones, but they remain highly optimistic and, in fact, may even exceed their younger colleagues in this respect. Not only do they remain somewhat thick-skinned, but they also seem to have developed a number of defenses against getting hurt in difficult and unpleasant situations.

Administrative and accounting executives

This group shows no particular changes in intellectual powers with age. (It will be remembered, however, that these executives anyway rank somewhat below the other groups in the ability to reason in abstraction.) Personality-wise, the administrative or accounting executive tends to become more introverted and generally even more conforming, both in business as well as personal matters, with the passage of time. The older executives in this group seem to have developed an almost pollyanna-like attitude toward their problems—a defense mechanism, of course, against overt anxiety.

Production executives

A lessening of abstract reasoning powers and in the ability to organize abstractions is also characteristic of the older members of this group. Personality-wise, they are less dominant than their younger colleagues, and more defensive, in the sense that they tend to project more. They are also somewhat more anxious—a tendency that may possibly manifest itself in psychosomatic symptoms.

EFFECTS OF COMPANY SIZE

Are there any differences between executives in large and small companies? The answer is definitely *yes*. For all occupational groups combined, one-third of all the measurable dimensions showed differences between large and small company executives statistically significant enough to make it highly unlikely that they were merely chance variations.

Ignoring specific occupations for the moment, over-all it appears that the executives of large companies using systematic selection procedures differ from the executives of smaller companies that do not use such procedures in the following ways:

1. The executives of larger companies generally have more extensive and better knowledge of their fields of specialization. This is evidenced by the extent of their technical vocabularies.
2. The executives of larger companies generally have greater mental ability than do those in smaller companies. However, administrative and accounting executives in small companies are somewhat higher on their reasoning and word fluency ability than their counterparts in large organizations.
3. There are specific personality differences between executives in large and in small companies. These differences and their direction are discussed below.

Engineering and R & D executives

The men in the large companies have greater technical knowledge, are much brighter on all the intellectual variables measured, are more creative, and are better communicators. Personality-wise, they are somewhat less defensive than those in smaller companies. Interestingly enough, along with these differences, they also seem to be somewhat more prone to personality deviations. This is not to say that they are more neurotic, but rather that they do not fit the stereotype of the "typical executive" to the same extent as the smaller company R & D or engineering manager. They are specialists in large companies to an even greater extent than they are in small companies.

Production executives

Here again it appears that production executives in larger companies are generally more intelligent, and particularly higher in their ability to reason abstractly than those in smaller companies. They also tend to be more fluent and better communicators, besides being generally more knowledgable in the technical sense and having a better understanding of human relations. Further, they are more energetic, more extroverted, and have a higher self-regard.

Sales executives

Those in large companies score significantly higher in terms of intelligence, knowledgability, and social polish than their small company counterparts. They also seem to be much more energetic and more optimistic in general than sales executives in small companies.

Administrative and accounting executives

As has been pointed out, executives in this group in large companies seem to be less effective in some respects than those in smaller ones. They are generally lower in their abstract reasoning ability, in their word fluency, and in their ability to communicate. They also seem to be much less extroverted. However, it should be noted that these findings are somewhat tentative because of the relatively small size of our sample of administrative and accounting executives in small companies. The data would seem to indicate either that the smaller companies push the brighter, yet less mentally healthy men, into administration or accounting or that they attract such people into their service. The second possibility seems to be the more likely of the two. There are, after all, relatively few positions in this field in a smaller concern, and such positions as exist are relatively close to the top. A big company, on the other hand, will have a large accounting and administrative staff, with several rungs on the managerial ladder to climb. It seems probable, therefore, that the brighter men in this field gravitate toward the smaller company, with its greater opportunities for getting to the top of the ladder.

Perhaps it would be as well at this point to reiterate that these differences are "generally true." It must not be imagined that they necessarily apply in all cases. Nevertheless, the odds are that in any one company the picture will be similar to that outlined here.

What are the implications of this study in general? First, it may be said that the findings reported here uphold the contention that a man's effectiveness in a given executive position *can* be predicted from test scores, coupled with such biographical information as age; and second, that large companies appear to have a distinct edge over their smaller competitors as regards the caliber of their management team. Is this because the brighter and more knowledgable managers naturally gravitate toward larger concerns—or are they there as a result of the systematic selection procedures employed by the large company as a matter of course? Either way, it would seem that smaller companies need to ask themselves whether they are doing all they can to attract good men, and whether their present methods of screening candidates are adequate for the intense competition under which business operates today.

QUESTIONS

1. What might account for the personality differences between executives in large and small companies found by these authors?
2. What were the principal differences found between more versus less effective executives? Do you agree with how they determined "more versus less" effectiveness?
3. Do you think the testing measures used in this study can truly measure the "executive personality?" Why or why not?
4. How would you compare the findings of this study to Ghiselli's ideas?
5. What were the major findings relative to the functional backgrounds of the executives studied?

10. THE TOP EXECUTIVE
—A FIRSTHAND PROFILE *

Robert M. Wald and Roy A. Doty

The relationship between personal characteristics and occupational success is one of the most significant, yet least developed, areas of psychology. In recent years, management has been increasingly aware of the need for developing future executives, and a great many executive development plans have been devised—almost none of them, however, founded on a clearly formulated and systematically established psychological basis.

The question is, are there any dimensions of successful top management that can be identified and measured? Or, more specifically, how do successful executives become what they are? Where do they come from? What kinds of education do they have? Did someone push them ahead, or was their advancement hard fought for? What are their particular abilities, interests, and personality characteristics?

This article is based on a "depth" study of the backgrounds and present characteristics of a group of highly successful corporation officers, and is designed to answer just such questions. The findings indicate that there is in fact a definite pattern of background and personality making for executive competence, and so should help to fill some of the gap of knowledge on this point and serve as the basis for more effective management-development programs.

The trouble with present techniques of executive selection and development—and there are many that have become popular—is that they are backed up by very little research data as to what qualities are desirable in executive candidates. A candidate may be tested, interviewed, and checked until the contents of his personnel file are overflowing. Still the problem remains: What of all this information is truly relevant to executive competence?

THE KEYS TO SUCCESS

Most attempts to discover the keys to executive success appear to fall short for two basic reasons: (a) they are narrow in their approach, and (b) they study people employed below the true top policy-making level.

---

* From *Harvard Business Review*, Vol. 32, No. 4 (1954), pp. 45-54. Reprinted with permission.

Case-history approach

In an attempt to overcome the first limitation a case-history approach was used as the basis for our research. The "whole" executive, past and present, was studied in relation to his work situation by three techniques:

1. A comprehensive, 140-item questionnaire covering home and family background, education, work experience, social development, health and recreation, and present home and family adjustment. (The purpose was to discover the experiences which led to the man's present adjustment.)
2. Three paper-and-pencil tests of intellectual ability, interests, and personality characteristics. (We wanted to appraise as closely as possible the individual's particular psychological make-up.)
3. An interview of two to four hours. (This was to verify and supplement the results of the questionnaires and tests.)

Because these three techniques explore both personal and situational dynamics, the results when integrated indicate how the executive grew into his particular situation, how he developed in that situation, and the personal traits which contributed to his growth and development.

Rigorous criteria

The second shortcoming of previous investigations—selecting other than top-level executives for study—was overcome by adhering to five rigorous criteria. Before including a man we decided that he must:

1. Be serving as an officer in an organization established for at least five years which has, during that time, maintained more than $5,000,000 of business each year;
2. Have served in such a position or positions for at least three years;
3. Be in large measure responsible for planning and coordinating company policy;
4. Have received an annual salary of not less than $20,000 for the last three years;
5. Have been educated in American schools predominantly.

In order to obtain the cooperation of such executives, we decided to approach them through associates and friends. Several executives interested in the study drew up a list of possible participants whose cooperation they were willing to request. The men suggested were then checked against the criteria for inclusion; and the companies represented were analyzed to see whether they constituted a cross section of business and industrial enterprise. In the end 33 executives representing 29 different organizations completed the materials of the study.

Of the 33 men, 20 were associated with manufacturing concerns and the other 13 with nonmanufacturing or commercial enterprises. Positionwise, 17 were board chairmen or presidents, 13 were vice presidents, and 3 were secretary-treasurers. Their ages ranged from 38 to 69, with a median of 53 years. Most of the companies represented were above the mark of $25-million annual volume of business, with many in the $100-million or more category.

A study of only 33 cases may appear insignificant at first glance; yet, when the caliber of the men included and the techniques used to obtain information about them are considered, the group is in fact relatively large. [The identities of the men have been withheld, according to the terms under which they participated in the study, but the Editors have been allowed to examine the list and can attest to the fact that it represents an unusually successful group of top-level executives, employed by well-known companies in a wide variety of industries.]

The data obtained by the study have been analyzed both qualitatively and quantitatively, and compared wherever possible with similar data pertaining to general or standard populations. The meaningful findings may be considered most easily as (a) executives' backgrounds, based on information obtained from the questionnaires and the interviews, and (b) executives' personal characteristics, representing the psychological test results.

Executives' Backgrounds

To understand what circumstances led up to the executives' present adjustment, their family backgrounds, educational experiences, vocational backgrounds, social development, health, and so on, were explored by means of the questionnaire and the interview.

Early family life

The executive questionnaire covered the area of home and family background by asking questions which have turned up time and again on application blanks and personal-data sheets. There is general agreement on the nature, if not the relative importance, of the early determinants of personal development, such as nationality, socio-economic status, and relations within the family. So the following facts may be significant:

1. With the exception of two who immigrated to this company as children, all of the group were born in the United States or its territories.
2. Sixteen or almost half of the participants were reared in cities of 100,000 or more population. Six more were brought up in towns ranging in size from 10,000 to 100,000, and two more in suburbs of large cities.
3. As for the national backgrounds of the parents, 75% of the group had two American-born parents, 10% had one foreign-born parent, and 15% had two foreign-born parents.
4. The group members came from families whose incomes were either average or above average in their communities. Only four of the men studied reported that their parents' incomes were below average; in all these cases the fathers had died while the participants were children.
5. The parents' educational backgrounds were definitely above average. The general educational level in the United States in 1910 (a year in which the typical participant was still a member of the family group) was somewhere between the sixth and eighth grades. The average educational level completed by the parents of the participants was between the eleventh and twelfth grades, with about two-thirds graduating from high school. The parents of only two had completed less than the eighth grade.
6. Somewhat more than half of the fathers were engaged in professional or managerial occupations, whereas only 11% of the total labor force was in this type of work during the same period.
7. The great majority of the group came from homes in which the family relationship was harmonious, and in which the youngsters felt a high degree of "belonging." The parents of only one participant were divorced.

Several conclusions, some of them negative, some positive, can be drawn from this material. There is no indication that the successful executive of today fits the traditional picture of the immigrant or first-generation American boy struggling to rise above his humble beginnings, or the country boy striking out on his own in the big city. Rather there is a suggestion, at least, that being brought up within the cultural environment of a metropolis is more conducive to executive development than early years spent in small towns or rural areas. Further, there is fairly strong evidence that a good, solid, upper-middle-class home, with happy family relationships, is the best start tomorrow's executive can have. Particularly significant is the thought that the influence of professional and management attitudes long before entering the world of work apparently helps to prepare a person for an executive position.

Education

The group members themselves were generally well educated. The average level of formal education was slightly above third-year college. Specifically, 22 of the participants, or 67%, were graduated from college—a very high figure considering that only about ¼ of 1% of the total population of this country was even *enrolled* in college 30 years ago when most of the participants were attending college. And of the 11 participants who did not receive academic degrees, all but 2 took business and accounting courses in business college, trade schools, correspondence schools, or the evening divisions of universities.

Significantly, age apparently made no difference. Those in their 50's and 60's had enjoyed as good educations as those in their 40's.

High school. Several findings stand out as noteworthy among the academic experiences of the group members in high school:

1. The average grade was high—in the neighborhood of "B+" for the 29 high school graduates.
2. The subjects in which most of the group performed best and which they liked best were mathematics and history, followed by English and science.
3. Mathematics was mentioned as the most helpful subject in rising to and succeeding in an executive position; English followed close behind.

College. There is much controversy over the question whether a potential executive should specialize in business administration, engineering, or some other "technical" field in college, or whether he should devote his efforts primarily to the liberal arts. Of the 22 college graduates studied, 4 were graduated from schools of commerce, 4 pursued engineering courses of various types, and as many as 14 received their degrees in the liberal arts. And while 7 of the 14 awarded A.B. degrees did major in a subject related to business, i.e., economics, they of course were required to do a definite proportion of their work in the humanities, arts, and sciences. It follows that a predominant majority of the college-trained group received a general and varied educational experience.

Other more specific findings with regard to the academic phase of college life were:

1. The grade average received by the 22 college graduates approximated "B."
2. The undergraduate majors most frequently elected were, in descending order, commerce and economics (one-third of the executives), English, engineering, and political science.
3. The college subjects in which the group members performed best and in which they had the greatest interest were economics and English; mathematics, history, and political science were runners-up.
4. The college subjects which were felt to have been most helpful in

subsequent vocational pursuits were (a) English, (b) economics, (c) accounting, and (d) political science.

5. Five of the group members were awarded postgraduate degrees in the field of law.

Extracurricular activity. In view of the fact that it has become very common for employers to interpret evidences of leadership in school as indications of future leadership in business, it is significant that these individuals now in top-level business and industrial positions participated to a great extent in extracurricular activities and held numerous offices at high school and college:

1. Of the 29 who completed high school, 86% participated in at least one activity during those four years, and 65% in two or more.
2. Of the 22 who went on to college, 95% entered into one extra-curricular activity there, and 73% engaged in two or more.
3. The most popular activities among the high school group were of the athletic and literary variety. Along with social fraternities, these activities were most popular among the college group also.
4. As for positions held, 11 members of the high school group were elected to positions in student government (5 were presidents of their classes at one time or another); 5 edited the school newspaper, magazine, or yearbook; and 9 were elected officers of various school clubs.
5. Of the collegians, 7 were elected officers of their fraternity chapters (4 as presidents); 6 were elected to student government offices; 2 were editors of one of their college's major publications; and 4 were elected officers of various clubs.

All this evidence concerning education indicates that the main group from which potential executives emerge can be spotted during the formative years.

Work experience

The problem of how the executives advanced through the ranks to top-level management positions was central to the entire research.

From the environmental standpoint, it was found that the majority of the group members felt that their advancement was not entirely due to some superior's "discovering" their talents and pushing them ahead or to hard work, but rather to a combination of both. The following comment is typical:

It's impossible for me to say whether I was promoted entirely because of my performance or whether someone pushed me ahead. I feel it was some of both. One person or another had to be responsible for giving me increased opportunities, and I had to be able to capitalize on them once they were offered. I should say that my present job is the result of both of these factors in equal measure.

The few participants who admitted "sponsoring" as the primary reason for their advancement were executives of business enterprises controlled largely by members of their families. There were also some group members who felt that their positions were due to hard work only, as illustrated by this remark:

> Shortly after I started to work, the great depression hit with full force. Employees were being let go right and left, and I had to work hard to be allowed to stay. Hours meant nothing. When the depression was over, I was conditioned to keep on working much harder than was necessary. Nobody did or needed to push me. I wasn't a "fair-haired boy," but the company rewarded my ambition and my work—ambition and hard work were the major ingredients of whatever success I've enjoyed.

Analysis of the employment histories of the executives showed five common "avenues of progress": (a) sales, (b) long and varied service, (c) family influence, (d) accounting, and (e) law—in the order of their frequency.

Sales. The avenue of advancement via sales tends to be from salesman to sales manager to sales vice president and thence to president. Consider, for example, the president of a company manufacturing electrical appliances:

> Before the electric iron had come into its own, this man was hired as a salesman of this product. The idea struck him that the electric companies wanted to sell electricity just as badly as he wanted to sell irons; so he made a deal with an electric company whereby he offered every one of its employees—meter readers, service men, clerks, and officers alike—75 cents for every iron they sold during a two-week period. The result was that the supply could not keep pace with the demand, and the appliance company was forced to expand its operations. This plan was then introduced all over the country, and it was only a matter of time before its originator was sales manager and then sales vice president.

Long and varied service. This way leads through a minimum of 20 years with a single company and through many types of position. Normally, a man is made an officer of the company as the result of his superior over-all knowledge of the business's operations and objectives.

Family influence. Advancement along this avenue is largely dependent on being a member of the family-ownership group of a company. For instance, the executive vice president of one of the country's largest pharmaceutical houses was the son of its former president; and when the father died, the son inherited a large block of the corporation's stock.

It should be emphasized that this approach is not always as easy as it looks. There is evidence in the comments of the executives involved that their positions were dependent on satisfying the board of directors as to their competence. And there were no marked test-score differences to indicate that these individuals were any less able than the other participants in the study.

Accounting. The clearest example of this avenue is provided by the head of a public utility company. This man successfully carried through the reorganization of a smaller company, and then straightened out the accounting difficulties encountered when it merged with another company. Later, the management of a larger public utility, seeking a financial vice president, knew exactly where to go. The next step was to the presidency.

Law. Business, today, is complex to the degree that every large corporation must employ a legal counsel for the purpose of checking on the proper procedures to be followed in implementing new ideas and plans. One of the participants was hired as full-time legal counsel for a large organization, and was awarded the presidency after winning a number of extremely important cases for the company over a period of years.

Job attitudes

Various questions asked on the questionnaire and during the interview provided information and insight into the vocational attitudes of the group members. In general, it was found that all but one of the group felt that they had always been more interested in their work than had most of the other individuals with whom they associated in business. And given a free choice 85% of them would have selected positions similar to their current ones.

Asked why they worked so hard when they did not have to in order to earn a decent living, the executives usually answered either that they derived a sense of accomplishment from their efforts or that they enjoyed their work more than anything else they did. Two of the remarks were:

1. I work hard because I enjoy accomplishing whatever will contribute to the progress of our company. Planning effectively and then placing the plans in operation are the factors that make business stimulating in all of its associations.

2. When I come home from the office in the evening, my son likes me to play ball with him; and I do. But while it's a game for him, it's work for me. My job is my game, and I'm happiest when I'm at it.

The participants derived much of their job satisfaction from the growth and development of their companies. To accomplish this, it was necessary for them to surround themselves with capable people, to acquire the respect of their associates, to develop team spirit, and to handle adequately the myriad problems concerned with policy making. Basic needs—for self-respect, for the respect of others, and for security—undoubtedly underlie this urge to accomplish; and the group members exhibited each of these needs to a degree much greater than average.

This is ample evidence that the participants had all greatly identified themselves with their companies. Rather than merely selling their services for a certain number of hours each week, they were highly motivated toward, and they received their greatest satisfactions from, the increased importance of their organizations in the total economy.

What aspects of the executive position did the group members like best? Almost half of the members were very much interested in day-to-day dealings with people—in human relations—as typified by the comments of two manufacturing executives:

1. The major task of any executive is to get work done by other people. A shop is not comprised primarily of machines, but is made up of workers who need inspiration and leadership. Somehow, you've got to win your employees over to your point of view and make them *want* to work hard. The days of *forcing* people to do anything are over.

2. The executive's job does not center around the technicalities of operation—these are handled by specialists that the executive hires. Rather, the executive must attend to the generalities of human relations. The question is one of how we can make our employees feel that what they do has an effect on all of us. I don't believe that employee benefits such as recreation programs and adequate retirement pensions are the whole answer. It's more than that. I don't quite know how to phrase it, but it's the feeling tone that permeates the company; and management is largely responsible for creating it.

More information about the participants' interest in human relations comes from their replies regarding their attitudes toward subordinates. It was found that 87% were at least moderately concerned over what subordinates thought and said about them, and 51% were deeply concerned. The entire group felt that their subordinates should be well or very well acquainted with them on the job. And all but one of the participants believed that employee morale and efficiency were closely related.

As for more specific job content, one out of four expressed a liking for the analytical work involved in making decisions on problems in their particular work areas. The managerial aspects and planning phases of their activities were mentioned to about the same degree.

Factors in advancement

A majority of the group members stated that skill in human relations was most important in their own advancement. Important qualities in this connection were the ability to get along with people, social poise, consideration of others, and tact in personal dealings.

Next in importance—mentioned by nine executives—was the capacity to analyze facts and to understand and correctly solve problems.

Seven participants indicated that supervisory ability, the ability to organize not only their own time and work but also the work of others, helped them greatly at the management level. Ability to delegate responsibility, ability to create enthusiasm for a given task, and ability to evaluate the performance of others were mentioned as facets of this characteristic.

A high degree of personal ambition and a desire to improve the over-all value of their organization were believed by six of the group to be important in gaining business recognition. One man put it this way:

> When a novice in business, I was always ambitious to do my work beyond criticism. Later, my aim was to do more than the job required so that I would realize a promotion. Now that I have the top job in the company, I have transferred all of my ambitions over to establishing an even more far-reaching business.

Other qualities mentioned as particularly helpful to advancement were knowledge and skills acquired through educational experiences (five men), willingness and ability to work hard (five), loyalty or the placing of the job before all else (three), and imagination to see ahead and to plan effectively (three).

Advice to aspirants. The principal characteristics which the executives looked for in young men aspiring to top-management positions were, in the main, similar to those previously mentioned as contributing to the executives' own advancement. There was, however, a significant difference of emphasis.

For example, as many as 85% of the participants commented that they would consider no person for a top-level position unless, through his past performance, he had exhibited an extremely high degree of interest in the work of the entire company as well as in his own particular job. This quality, which implies a high degree of identification with the company, was often stressed as being much more important than intelligence or any technical know-how. The following comment is illustrative:

> I'm sure that the man who doesn't enjoy the type of work done by his particular company should not be made an executive in that company. Men are just boys grown tall—they have to like what they are doing to do it well. To be considered for a top spot, you've not only got to like your work; you've got to love it!

The characteristic which these executives put first in their own list of success factors was second—though a close second—in their advice to aspirants: the ability to get along well with others, or skill in human relations. And, though not mentioned as often as skill in human relations as such, interest in the welfare and happiness of associates and of people in general was held by more than half of the participants to be vital to the potential executive.

Social development

The ability to get along well with others, on which the group members placed such great importance, shows up in their social development to a remarkable degree. The great majority had participated in community and social groups and affairs from childhood on—from Boy Scout troops, through high school social activities, on to country clubs and civic organizations. (Fraternal groups like the Elks, Lions, and Moose were definitely the least popular.)

The executives studied felt by and large that they had a good many lasting friendships, stemming from each of the periods in their lives, and also that these friendships were important to them.

The group members were found also to possess high moral and religious standards. Every one of them was brought up with church training; over two-thirds were continuing as active members of established churches; and over nine-tenths expressed belief in a supreme being and in the concept of religion as a positive force essential to properly conducted business and world affairs.

Although business kept them from spending a great deal of time with their families, the group members were vitally interested in and close to their wives and children. Less than 15% had ever been separated from their wives or had previously been divorced. Without exception, their homes and families constituted a great source of satisfaction to them. Many said that they were looking forward to retirement primarily so that they could enter more into family activities.

Physical condition

In view of the deluge of recent newspaper and magazine articles describing the executive as a person ravaged by ulcers, kidney stones, colitis, and the need for rest cures, the findings in regard to executive health are especially interesting. These top-level executives treated the stresses and strains arising from their business dealings as something natural to be taken in their stride, and claimed to enjoy good health on the whole. More specifically:

1. Over 85% of the group reported that they possessed good or excellent health during childhood and adolescence, and as young workers.
2. Good or excellent present health was reported by 79%.
3. Only 33% reported ever having a physical ailment caused by worry or nervousness, e.g., ulcer, spastic stomach, etc.
4. Over 90% reported being not at all or only slightly worried about their own health.

To summarize at this point, the questionnaire and interview findings indicate that the successful executive is a healthy, well-rounded individual personifying the characteristics most highly regarded in our present business culture. He simply possesses those characteristics to an unusually high degree rather than exhibiting any marked peculiarities or special attitudes.

EXECUTIVES' PERSONAL MAKE-UP

In order to obtain as objective a measure as possible of the psychological characteristics of top-level executives, we used:

1. A problem-solving ability test—the *Wonderlic Personnel Test* (Form A);

2. A personality test—the *Adams-Lepley Personal Audit* (Form SS);

3. An interest inventory—the *Kuder Preference Record* (Vocational, Form BB).

EXHIBIT I indicates the mean (or average) percentile scores obtained when the three tests were analyzed and compared with large numbers of general employees. Tests of this kind are not

EXHIBIT I

INTELLECTUAL ABILITY, PERSONALITY CHARACTERISTICS, AND INTERESTS OF 33 TOP-LEVEL EXECUTIVES

(Mean percentile scores)

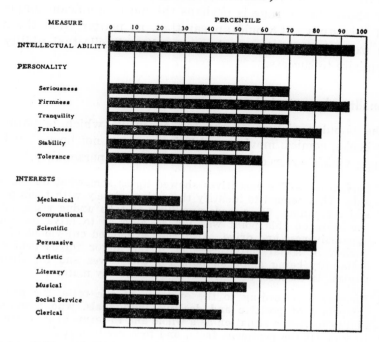

infallible when used alone, but their results can supplement our more subjective evaluations based on the questionnaires and interviews. To the extent that the results are consistent with our other findings or extend them along the same lines, they add weight and firmness to our conclusions.

Intellectual ability

For the most part, the executives studied had superior mental ability; that is, they had the ability to solve complex and abstract problems with speed and accuracy, to adapt to new situations quickly and easily, and to plan effectively. That the group as a whole ranked above 96 percent of a general population of business and industrial workers, and indeed that all but two of the individual executives were above 86 percent, bears this out forcibly.

The group members were also compared in terms of intellectual ability with workers of similar age and educational attainment, and in every instance the executives scored considerably higher than the other employees.

It is logical to expect that executives would tend to be more intelligent than most other workers; but that they evidence mental ability so far above the average is perhaps the most significant single finding of this study. It would appear that, no matter what the nature of an executive's background, outstanding intellectual ability is a prerequisite to success.

Personality characteristics

The popular picture of the top executive which is painted by many books, comics, movies, and TV plays was not borne out by our findings, which covered six different facets of personality.

1. *Seriousness*—The executives showed up as somewhat on the serious side. They tended to identify themselves closely with their positions and companies. They were unwilling to take undue risks, although the score on this point was not so high as to leave no room for aggressiveness and drive. Also, they evidenced enjoyment of a wide variety of social activities—one of the major forces behind their sociability being ambition both for themselves and for their companies. In essence, the executives were socially mature.

2. *Firmness*—According to the evidence of the tests, the group was comprised of positive and decisive individuals, who possessed the ability to view a situation as a whole and in terms of its components, to sort out the pertinent facts, and to come to a realistic conclusion about a problem. This is an obvious requisite for executive competence, but the interesting point is not just that they had the ability to make decisions *soundly* but also that they could make decisions *quickly* and *easily*. They were skilled in concentration and evaluation, and had the capacity to make spontaneous and intuitive judgments.

3. *Tranquility*—The participants, as a group, appeared to be neither excessively irritable nor excessively tranquil. They were adequately sensitive to things out of order, and when sufficiently provoked could be expected to display their annoyance in a definite though controlled manner.

4. *Frankness*—The executives were found to be frank, sincere, and honest in their interpersonal dealings. They were not naive and abrupt but evidenced a favorable amount of tact and diplomacy. Essentially, they possessed skill in human relations, and exhibited basic self-understanding.

5. *Stability*—The group members showed up as average in emotional stability and self-confidence. That they did not appear to be more self-possessed might be explained in several ways: (a) there is some evidence that the executives were motivated to success by a need for

accomplishment and a fear of failure; (b) the executive position, by its very nature, is conducive to anxiety; and (c) most of the executives studied were rather advanced in terms of years and could be expected to feel that they were unable to perform as efficiently as they once could.[1]

6. *Tolerance*—The tests showed that the participants maintained high standards for their own performance and that of others. In general they would not be imposed on, nor would they excessively impose their attitudes and beliefs on subordinates. They were able to see problems from the other person's point of view, but generally they did not allow sentiment to interfere with critical judgment.

Range of interests

The interest of the executive group that registered highest was in dealing with people to enlist their cooperation in the implementation of new projects, plans, and ideas, and in the written and spoken word as media of communicating the ideas. The participants demonstrated the next highest interest in work involving the use of numbers. They were concerned with such matters as the cost of operating a production line, the number of units of the product sold, the amount of return on investments, the profit margins, and so on.

The group members exhibited interest in the average range in artistic and creative work, musical activities, routine office work, and scientific pursuits. In general, they were found to possess a below-average interest in working with machines and tools and in performing work designed to assist other persons with their individual problems. (The below-average score in the latter area does not necessarily mean that the executives were not interested in activities contributing to the welfare of others. In combination with the high persuasive score and information obtained from the questionnaire and interview, it appears to indicate, rather, that their interest was more in managing worthy causes than in helping individuals directly.)

Although all the psychological test results assist in describing the personal make-up of the typical top-level executive, several of them are particularly useful because of the degree to which they show the successful leader surpassing general business and industrial workers in certain crucial characteristics—e.g., mental ability, firmness of thinking, honesty and objectivity, persuasive-aggressive interest, and concern with communicative activities. Over-all, it may be said that the test results confirm our picture of the top-level

---

[1] See Robert N. McMurry, "The Executive Neurosis," *Harvard Business Review* (November-December 1952), p. 33.

executive as a very intelligent individual, who exhibits the ability to deal with problems and people effectively, and who is particularly interested in gaining respect and acceptance for himself and his ideas.

Conclusion

The following general conclusions are supported by the findings of the questionnaires and interviews and by the test results. They are descriptive of the typical top-level executive in terms of where he came from, the nature of his psychological equipment, and, in general, how he has developed:

1. The successful or likely-to-be-successful executive has experienced a happy home life in his earlier years, conducive to the development of security and self-confidence.

2. He is extremely interested in and feels very much attached to his present family unit.

3. The educational level completed by the typical executive is far above the average of the general population.

4. He takes full advantage of varied educational opportunities.

5. He is an active participant in and leader of social organizations during childhood and through his career as a worker.

6. He is interested in religion as a force toward developing high moral and ethical standards.

7. He has experienced and continues to experience good health.

8. He is interested in people—particularly in selling them on the idea of fundamental cooperation. He is interested in the written and spoken word as a means of communicating his ideas. He is not preoccupied with the technical phases of his work, but rather with promoting harmonious human relationships.

9. He possesses very superior mental and analytical ability.

10. He is serious and conscientious in his approach to work. He is willing to take risks only after full consideration of the available facts.

11. He is forceful and intense, actively seeking new work to be done and new methods of doing it.

12. He is objective in facing his personal problems, frank and straightforward in his dealings with people, and spontaneous in his interpersonal relationships.

13. He is ambitious and able to identify his ambitions with those of his company to an outstanding degree.

The implications for the selection and development of executives in the conclusions presented are noteworthy. The characteristics mentioned are found in the individual executive with a high degree of consistency, and with respect to most of them the executives show a significant deviation from people in general. In other words, these characteristics are both identifiable and measurable. There are three very important applications of these findings to business management:

1. A competent person using the comprehensive case-history approach applied in this study should be able to select personnel for executive positions with a high degree of accuracy.

2. Using these same techniques, it appears possible to identify younger employees who have the capacity to become executives in the future.

3. Also, since some of the main interests and attitudes leading to success can be influenced by training and experience, it should be possible to develop these men for leadership more effectively.

Obviously, no one characteristic should ever be considered as determining an individual's chance for success as an executive. Also, of course, there are unique requirements for any particular job which would have to be taken into consideration in evaluating a candidate's suitability for it. Nevertheless, the extent to which the characteristics of an executive candidate approximate (or can be developed to approximate) the total pattern *is* significant.

If there is one broad implication to be drawn from this study, it is that an executive to be successful must feel himself an integral part of his organization and be vitally interested in the people around him. The executives studied were found to have recognized the importance of the human element and to have identified themselves with their various activities at every turn of the road—from early life on. Hence, the man who can identify himself with his company to the degree that his greatest motivation and satisfaction stem from increased business development, and who has appropriate qualifications otherwise, will be a good bet for executive training.

QUESTIONS

1. Do you think a "happy home life" is necessary for executive success? Why or why not? What are some of the qualifications raised by this question?

2. Many researchers feel the typical business leader plays two major roles: one on Sunday in church and one six days a week at work—and the two are not compatible. What would Wald and Doty say about this?

3. How can this study aid in identifying potential management talent?

4. How would you summarize the major findings of this study? Do you agree with them?

5. Compare the top executives described in this study to college professors and teachers. Do you see any similarities and/or differences? What are they?

11. THE BUSINESS EXECUTIVE: THE PSYCHODYNAMICS OF A SOCIAL ROLE *

William E. Henry

Modern business executives have in common many personality characteristics, which are a reflection partly of the socially stereotyped conception of the businessman and partly of some underlying similarities of personality structure. The successful executive represents a crystallization of many of the attitudes and values generally accepted by middle-class American society. Acquisitiveness and achievement, self-directedness and independent thought, are in this group counterbalanced by uncertainty, constant activity, the continual fear of losing ground, and the inability to be introspectively casual.

The business executive is a central figure in the economic and social life of the United States. His direction of business enterprise and his participation in informal social groupings give him a significant place in community life. In both its economic and its social aspects the role of the business executive is sociologically a highly visible one. It has clearly definable limits and characteristics known to the general public. These characteristics indicate the function of the business executive in the social structure, define the behavior expected of the individual executive, and serve as a guide to the selection of the novice.

Social pressure plus the constant demands of the business organization of which he is a part direct the behavior of the executive into the mold appropriate to the defined role. "Success" is the name applied to the whole-hearted adoption of the role. The individual behaves in the manner dictated by the society, and society rewards the individual with "success" if his behavior conforms to the role. It would punish him with "failure" should he deviate from it.

Participation in this role, however, is not a thing apart from the personality of the individual. It is not a game that the person is playing; it is the way of behaving and thinking that he knows best, that he finds rewarding, and in which he believes. Thus the role as socially defined has its counterpart in the personality structure. To some extent, too, the personality structure is reshaped to be in harmony with the social role. The extent to which such reshaping of

* Reprinted from "The Business Executive: The Psychodynamics of a Social Role," *American Journal of Sociology*, Vol. 54, 1949, pp. 286-291, by W. E. Henry by permission of The University of Chicago Press. Copyright 1949 by The University of Chicago Press.

the adult personality is possible, however, seems limited. An initial selection process occurs which reduces the amount of time involved in teaching the appropriate behavior. Persons whose personality structure is most readily adaptable to this particular role tend to be selected, whereas those whose personality is not already partially akin are rejected.

This [section] describes the personality communalities of a group of successful business executives. The research upon which it is based explored the general importance of personality structure in the selection of executive personnel. Many aptitude tests have been employed in industry to decrease the risk involved in the hiring of untried personnel and to assist in their placement. These tests have been far less effective in the selection of high-level executive personnel than in the selection of clerical and other non-administrating persons. Many business executives have found that persons of unquestioned high intelligence often turn out to be ineffective when placed in positions of increased responsibility. The reasons for their failure lie in their social relationships. No really effective means has yet been found to clarify and predict this area of executive functioning. It is to this problem that our research [1] is directed.

From the research it became clear that the "successful" [2] business executives studied had many personality characteristics in common.

---

[1] The research undertaken will be described in its entirety in a subsequent report. In summary it involved the study of over one hundred business executives in various types of business houses. The techniques employed were the Thematic Apperception Test, a short undirected interview, and a projective analysis of a number of traditional personality tests. The validity of our analyses, which were done "blind," rested upon the coincidence of identical conclusions from separately analyzed instruments, upon surveys of past job performance, and upon the anecdotal summary of present job behavior by the executive's superiors and associates. The writer wishes to express his thanks to these executives; to Dr. Burleigh Gardner, of Social Research, Inc., under whose auspices the study was made; and to Carson McGuire, Robert F. Peck, Norman Martin, and Harriet Bruce Moore, of the University of Chicago, for their assistance in the collection and analysis of data and the clarification of conclusions.

[2] Success and failure as here used refer to the combined societal and business definitions. All our "successful" executives have a history of continuous promotion, are thought to be still "promotable" within the organization, are now in positions of major administrative responsibilty, and are earning salaries within the upper ranges of current business salaries. Men in lower supervisory positions; men who are considered "failures" in executive positions; and men in clerical and laboring jobs show clear deviations from this pattern. This suggests, of course, that this pattern is specific for the successful business executive and that it serves to differentiate him from other groupings in industry.
The majority of the executives come from distributive (rather than manufacturing) businesses of moderately loose organizational structure in which cooperation and team work are valued and in which relative independence of action is stressed within the framework of a clearly defined overall company policy. In organizations in which far greater rigidity of structure is present or in which outstanding independence of action is required, it is possible that there will be significant variations from the personality pattern presented here. We are currently extending our data in these directions.

(It was equally clear that an absence of these characteristics was coincident with "failure" within the organization.) This personality constellation might be thought of as the minimal requirement of "success" within our present business system and as the psycho-dynamic motivation of persons in this occupation. Individual unique-ness in personality was clearly present; but, despite these unique aspects, all executives had in common this personality pattern.

Achievement desires

Successful executives show high drive and achievement desire. They conceive of themselves as hard-working and achieving persons who must accomplish in order to be happy. The areas in which they do their work are clearly different, but each feels this drive for accomplishment. This should be distinguished from a type of pseudo-achievement drive in which the glory of the end product alone is stressed. The person with this latter type of drive, seldom found in the successful executives, looks to the future in terms of the glory it will provide him and of the projects that he will have completed—as opposed to the achievement drive of the successful executive, which looks more toward the sheer accomplishment of the work itself. The successful business leader gets much satisfaction from doing rather than from merely contemplating the completed product. To some extent this is the difference between the dreamer and the doer. It is not that the successful executives do not have an over-all goal in mind or that they do not derive satisfaction from the contemplation of future ease or that they do not gain pleasure from prestige. Far more real to them, however, is the continual stimulation that derives from the pleasure of immediate accomplishment.

Mobility drive

All successful executives have strong mobility drives. They feel the necessity of moving continually upward and of accumulating the rewards of increased accomplishment. For some the sense of success-ful mobility comes through the achievement of competence on the job. These men struggle for increased responsibility and derive a strong feeling of satisfaction from the completion of a task. Finished work and newly gained competence provide them with their sense of continued mobility.

A second group relies more upon the social prestige of increased status in their home communities or within the organizational hierarchy. Competence in work is of value and at times crucial. But the satisfactions of the second group come from the social reputation, not from the personal feeling that necessary work has been well done. Both types of mobility drive are highly motivating. The zeal and energy put into the job is equal in both instances. The distinction appears in the kinds of work which the men find interesting. For the first group the primary factor is the nature of the work itself—is it challenging, is it necessary, is it interesting? For the second group the crucial factor is its relation to their goals of status mobility— is it a step in the direction of increased prestige, is it appropriate to their present position, what would other people think of them if they did it?

The idea of authority

The successful executive posits authority as a controlling but helpful relationship to superiors. He looks to his superiors as persons of more advanced training and experience, whom he can consult on special problems and who issue to him certain guiding directives. He does not see the authorities in his environment as destructive or prohibiting forces.

Those executives who view authority as a prohibiting and destructive force have difficulty relating themselves to superiors and resent their authority over them. They are either unable to work smoothly with superiors or indirectly and unconsciously do things to obstruct the work of their bosses or to assert their independence unnecessarily.

It is of interest that to these men the dominant crystallization of attitudes about authority is toward superiors and toward subordinates, rather than toward self. This implies that most crucial in their concept of authority is the view of being a part of a wider and more final authority system. In contrast, a few executives of the "self-made," driving-type characteristic of the past of business enterprise maintain a specific concept of authority with regard to self. They are the men who almost always forge their own frontiers, who are unable to operate within anyone else's framework, and to whom co-operation and team work are foreign concepts. To these men the ultimate authority is in themselves, and their image does not include the surrounding area of shared or delegated power.

Organization and its implications

While executives who are successful vary considerably in their intelligence-test ratings, all of them have a high degree of ability to organize unstructured situations and to see the implications of their organization. This implies that they have the ability to take several seemingly isolated events or facts and to see relationships that exist between them. Further, they are interested in looking into the future and are concerned with predicting the outcome of their decisions and actions.

This ability to organize often results in a forced organization, however. Even though some situations arise with which they feel unfamiliar and are unable to cope, they still force an organization upon it. Thus they bring it into the sphere of familiarity. This tendency operates partially as a mold, as a pattern into which new or unfamiliar experiences are fit. This means, of course, that there is a strong tendency to rely upon techniques that they know will work and to resist situations which do not readily fit this mold.

Decisiveness

Decisiveness is a further trait of this group. This does not imply the popular idea of the executive making quick and final decisions in rapid-fire succession, although this seems to be true of some of the executives. More crucial, however, is an ability to come to a decision among several alternative courses of action—whether it be done on the spot or after detailed consideration. Very seldom does this ability fail. While less competent and well-organized individuals may become flustered and operate inefficiently in certain spots, most of these men force their way to a conclusion. Nothing is too difficult for them to tackle and at least try to solve. When poorly directed and not modified by proper judgment, this attitude may be more a handicap than a help. That is to say, this trait remains in operation and results in a decision-making action regardless of the reasonableness of the decision or its reality in terms of related facts. The loss of this trait (usually found only in cases in which some more profound personality change has also occurred) is one of the most disastrous for the executive: his superiors become apprehensive about him. This suggests an interesting relationship to the total executive constellation. The role demands conviction and certainty. Whenever a junior executive loses this quality of decisiveness, he seems to pass out of the socially defined role. The weakening of other aspects of the ideal executive constellation can be readily reintegrated into the total constellation. The questioning of the individual's certainty and decisiveness, however, results in a weakening of the entire constellation and tends to be punished by superiors.

Strong self-structure

One way of differentiating between people is in the relative strength or weakness of their notions of self-identity, their self-structure. Some persons lack definiteness and are easily influenced by outside pressures. Some, such as these executives, are firm and well-defined in their sense of self-identity. They know what they are and what they want and have well-developed techniques for getting what they want. The things they want and the techniques for getting them are, of course, quite different for each individual, but this strength and firmness is a common and necessary characteristic. It is, of course, true that too great a sense of self-identity leads to rigidity and inflexibility; and, while some of these executives could genuinely be accused of this, in general they maintain considerable flexibility and adaptability within the framework of their desires and within the often rather narrow possibilities of their own business organization.

Activity and aggression

The executive is essentially an active, striving, aggressive person. His underlying motivations are active and aggressive—not necessarily is he aggressive and hostile overtly in his dealings with other people. This activity and aggressiveness are always well channeled into work or struggles for status and prestige—which implies a constant need to keep moving, to do something, to be active. This does not mean that they are always in bodily movement and moving physically from place to place (though this is often true) but rather that they are mentally and emotionally alert and active. This constant motivator unfortunately cannot be shut off. It may be part of the reason why so many executives find themselves unable to take vacations at leisure or to stop worrying about already solved problems.

Apprehension and the fear of failure

If one is continually active and always trying to solve problems and arrive at decisions, any inability to do so successfully may well result in feelings of frustration. This seems to be true of the executives. In spite of their firmness of character and their drive to activity, they also harbor a rather pervasive feeling that they may not really succeed and be able to do the things they want to do. It is not implied that this sense of frustration comes only from their immediate business experience. It seems far more likely to be a feeling of long standing within them and to be only accentuated and reinforced by their present business experience.

This sense of the perpetually unattained is an integral part of this constellation and is part of its dilemma. It means that there is always some place to go, but no defined point at which to stop. The executive is "self-propelled" and needs to keep moving always and to see another goal ever ahead, which also suggests that cessation of mobility and of struggling for new achievements will be accompanied by an inversion of this constant energy. The person whose mobility is blocked, either by his own limitations, or those of the social system, finds this energy diverted into other channels. Psychosomatic symptoms, the enlargement of interpersonal dissatisfactions, and the development of rationalized compulsive and/or paranoid-like defenses may reflect the redirection of this potent energy demand.

Strong reality orientation

Successful executives are strongly oriented to immediate realities and their implications. They are directly interested in the practical, the immediate, and the direct. This is, of course, generally good for the immediate business situation, though the executive with an over-developed sense of reality may cease to be a man of vision; for a man of vision must get above reality to plan and even dream about future possibilities. In addition, a too strong sense of reality, when the realities are not in tune with ambitions, may well lead to a conviction that reality is frustrating and unpleasant. This happens to many executives who find progress and promotion too slow for their drives. The result is often a restlessness rather than an activity, a fidgetiness rather than a well-channeled aggression, and a lack of ease that may well disrupt many of their usual interpersonal relations.

The nature of their interpersonal relations

In general the mobile and successful executive looks to his superiors with a feeling of personal attachment and tends to identify himself with them. His superior represents for him a symbol of his own achievement and desires, and he tends to identify himself with these traits in those who have achieved more. He is very responsive to his superiors—the nature of this responsiveness, of course, depends on his other feelings, his idea of authority, and the extent to which he feels frustrated.

On the other hand, he looks to his subordinates in a detached and impersonal way, seeing them as "doers of work" rather than as people. He treats them impersonally, with no real feeling of being akin to them or of having deep interest in them as persons. It is as though he viewed his subordinates as representatives of things he has left behind, both factually and emotionally. Still uncertain of his next forward step, he cannot afford to become personally identified or emotionally involved with the past. The only direction of his emotional energy that is real to him is upward and toward the symbols of that upward interest, his superiors.

This does not mean that he is cold and that he treats all subordinates casually. In fact he tends to be generally sympathetic with many of them. This element of sympathy with subordinates is most apparent when the subordinate shows personality traits that are most like those of the superior. Thus the superior is able to take pride in certain successful young persons without at the same time feeling an equal interest in all subordinates.

The attitude toward his own parents

In a sense the successful executive is a "man who has left home." He feels and acts as though he were on his own, as though his emotional ties and obligations to his parents were severed. It seems to be most crucial that he has not retained resentment of his parents, but has rather simply broken their emotional hold on him and been left psychologically free to make his own decisions. We have found those who have not broken this tie to be either too dependent upon their superiors in the work situation or to be resentful of their supervision (depending, of course, upon whether they are still bound to their parents or are still actively fighting against them).

In general we find the relationship to the mother to have been the most clearly broken tie. The tie to the father remains positive in the sense that he views the father as a helpful but not restraining figure. Those men who still feel a strong emotional tie to the mother have systematically had difficulty in the business situation. This residual emotional tie seems contradictory to the necessary attitude of activity, progress, and channeled aggression. The tie to the father, however, must remain positive—as the emotional counterpart of the admired and more successful male figure. Without this image, struggle for success seems difficult.

The nature of dependency feelings and concentration upon self

A special problem in differentiating the type of general successful executive is the nature of his dependency feelings. It was pointed out above that the dependency upon the mother-image must be eliminated. For those executives who work within the framework of a large organization in which co-operation and group-and-company loyalty are necessities, there must remain feelings of dependency upon the father-image and a need to operate within an established framework. This does not mean that the activity-aggression need cannot operate or that the individual is not decisive and self-directional. It means only that he is so within the framework of an already established set of over-all goals. For most executives this over-all framework provides a needed guidance and allows them to concentrate upon their achievement and work demands with only minimal concern for the policy-making of the entire organization. For those executives who prefer complete independence and who are unable to work within a framework established by somebody else, the element of narcissism is much higher and their feelings of loyalty are only to themselves rather than to a father-image or its impersonal counterpart in company policy. These feelings differentiate the executives who can co-operate with others and who can promote the over-all policy of a company from those who must be the whole show themselves. Clearly there are situations in which the person highly concentrated upon self and with little feeling of dependency loyalty is of great value. But he should be distinguished in advance and be placed in only situations in which these traits are useful.

The successful executive represents a crystallization of many of the attitudes and values generally accepted by middle-class American society. The value of accumulation and achievement, of self-directedness and independent thought and their rewards in prestige and status and property, are found in this group. But they also pay the price of holding these values and of profiting from them. Uncertainty, constant activity, the continual fear of losing ground, the inability to be introspectively leisurely, the ever present fear of failure, and the artificial limitations put upon their emotionalized interpersonal relations—these are some of the costs of this role.

QUESTIONS

1. What is mobility drive?
2. What is achievement motivation? What does it have to do with executive success?
3. Do you see any conflicts between feelings of dependency and reality orientation? If so, what are they?
4. Why does the successful executive tend to identify with his superiors? What are the leadership implications involved here?
5. What is the executive role as set forth by Henry? How does it compare to previous articles?

12. CULTURAL PATTERNS IN THE ROLE OF THE MANAGER *

Mason Haire, Edwin E. Ghiselli
and Lyman W. Porter

We have a good many impressionistic reports of national managerial stereotypes, ranging from scholarly summaries through journalistic descriptions to tourist-anthropological anecdotes. Hardly a traveller finishes a whirlwind tour or a scholar a three-day conference at Salzburg or Copenhagen but what he is ready—even eager —to describe the way European managers think. Useful though these insights have been, we also need strictly comparable data—responses to the same questions asked of samples of managers in a number of countries. That was the task of this study: to find an empirical answer to the question of similarities and differences in managers' attitude.[1] In these days of rapid change in international trade patterns and increased proximity of countries, it is not necessary to emphasize the importance of a further understanding of managers' viewpoints, and if they exist, of national differences in such viewpoints. As a first approach, a questionnaire, asking identical questions, was administered to a sample of managers in each of a number of countries.

Carefully collected objective data offer great advantages, although they are less immediately satisfying than global intuitive impressions. But something must be sacrificed for rigor. In asking identical questions in all countries, one is limited to the questions that apply to all countries. It is difficult to frame a question about pricing, wage-setting, or accounting practices that will apply equally well in the United States, Spain, and Denmark. One is forced back, for questions that are relevant to all, to fundamental issues that are common to all, rather than techniques and practices. For this reason, and also because of the investigators' professional interests, the present study focused on three phases of management thinking: (1) views on leadership and how one gets work done well and efficiently, (2) the way in which the role and practices of the manager are seen by managers themselves, and (3) the satisfactions a manager wants and gets from his job.

* From *Industrial Relations*, Vol. 2, No. 2 (February, 1963), pp. 95-117. Reprinted with permission.

[1] This study is part of the research program of the Institute of Industrial Relations at the University of California (Berkeley) and was supported by a grant from the Ford Foundation.

Before we go on to deal with results, a word must be said about two big problems in this kind of research. Sampling is one of them. The other is omnipresent in cross-cultural research. The thinking of managers is part of the culture itself. The instrument that asks them to express their thinking is, thus, both a part of the culture and the way we study the culture. Each of these points presents real difficulties for a cross-cultural study of management.

About 3,500 responses were collected from managers in 14 countries. We aimed at a minimum of about 200 from each country, and, in general, we roughly fulfilled the goal. The sample for each country is not strictly representative of the total management population of each country. However, the samples are representative of rather large groups. Care was taken to sample different kinds of industries, geographical areas, levels of management, and the like. It seems unlikely that the discerned differences among managers in different countries are ascribable to sampling error. With all its limitations, the present sample is probably an adequate first approximation. To have been deterred by the difficulties of sampling would have meant accepting the counsel of despair. These data will add to the growing body of demographic descriptions of management which will eventually lead us to an ideal description.

Another real difficulty arises in translating a questionnaire of this type. Each item must be translated so it is not only literally correct but also carries the same impression. The first translations were made here by a translator native to the country involved. They were then independently translated back to English, as a check, by a second native. Finally, they were checked in the countries for which they were intended by social scientists and businessmen. The process is arduous and tedious and seems to have been fairly successful.

Incidentally, a good deal comes out of the job of translating itself. For example, *leader* does not translate well except in Scandinavian languages. Even before *Duce* and *Fuehrer* became loaded with special connotations, the word fit poorly in continental European languages. The word "manager" with its roots in the Latin *manus*, hand, means one who handles, but in the Romance languages its use is virtually restricted to the rider's management of a horse—a connotation of simple guidance and unilateral control that would probably be unacceptable in industry. Many managerial terms are so specifically American in origin that they have been adopted unchanged in various languages. Finally, many psychological concepts—such as the need for esteem—are so closely tied to what esteem means in the culture that it is difficult to separate the thing measured from the means of measurement. These problems all restricted the things that could be asked about and occasionally involved undesirable circumlocutions.

The present report is a preliminary one in two senses. In the first place, it deals with only 11 countries out of the 14 studied and only about 2,800 managers out of the final total. In the second place, it reports the first analyses of the data. Because the full analysis of the data will not be completed for some time, however, it seemed worthwhile to prepare this preliminary report.

In general, the results will be reported in three parts: the section of the questionnaire devoted to leadership first, cognitive patterns and the cultural role of the manager second, and, finally, satisfactions of managers.

Leadership

The first section of the questionnaire consisted of eight statements to which managers were invited to respond by checking a point on a five-point scale from "agree strongly" to "disagree strongly." The items were chosen on the basis of a logical pattern and an attempt was made to cover a fair portion of the gamut of managerial attitudes on leadership. The description of attitudes of this sort as running from "democratic to autocratic forms of leadership" is too hackneyed and overloaded with meaning to be of great value, but this description is similar to many. To put it in the frame of international studies of management, the ends of the scale resemble the points Harbison and Myers describe as "dictatorial or authoritarian" on the one hand and "democratic or participative" on the other.[2] The significance of the scale will become clearer as the results are indicated.

There are two ways one can look at these data: in terms of the substantive meaning of the items and the responses, and in terms of the way the countries group together. Taking up the first point, the eight items concerned with leadership were grouped into four logical categories. These categories were designed to represent concepts in the developing human-relations idea of a manager as a manager of people. They are as follows:

A. The belief in the individual's innate capacity for initiative and leadership.
B. The belief in sharing information and objectives.
C. The belief in participative management.
D. The belief in internal control (essentially self-control of the individual flowing from the job and from understanding and commitment) rather than external control (punishment, reward, promotion).

---

[2] F. Harbison and C. Myers, *Management in the Industrial World* (New York: McGraw-Hill, 1960).

In logical terms, the first category seems to be an absolutely essential first step to the other three. The basic reason for adopting shared objectives, participation, and internal control is the contention that individuals have a capacity for initiative and leadership that is untapped by a formal unilateral command form of organization. The logical precedence of category A and its character as a building block for the others makes the results particularly striking. The outstanding first finding is that there is universally more acceptance of what might be called higher order concepts of management than there is of the basic conviction that the individual has initiative and leadership capacity (see Figure 1).[3] By "higher order" concepts, we mean those identified in categories B, C, and D. These (a) logically follow after category A, and (b) deal with management *practices*. No matter how we group the data, this finding stands out. In each country, in each group of countries, in all the countries taken together, the responses to the first category are different from any of the other categories or from all three taken together. The difference is large and compelling.

What can this mean? Presumably, unless one believes in untapped capacity for leadership in subordinates, a classical unilateral directive management is best. Here we find a lack of basic confidence in others and at the same time a leaning toward participative group-centered management. It is at least possible that this result is the effect of the partial digestion of 15 years of exhortation by the group-oriented consultants and professors of management. These ideas—at the level of management practices—have become common currency among management groups and in executive development programs and training courses. The data suggest that the ideas dealing with management practice have been persuasive, while the basic conviction about the nature of people remains unchanged. To the extent that this is true, and to the extent that the attitudes expressed in category A do indeed underlie sophisticated management practices, this is an unfortunate state of affairs. It is a little like building the techniques and practices of a Jeffersonian democracy on a basic belief in the divine right of kings.

This finding illustrates a sampling problem in all such studies. It is possible that those who are inclined to cooperate are also those who have been impressed by modern (human-relations?) management concepts. To the extent that this is true, it probably accentuates the

---

[3] The position of a country on a scale represents the median score of all the managers in that category. In some cases items have been reversed to fit a single scale. The numerical values are unimportant here.

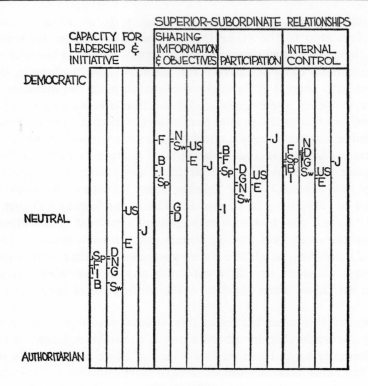

FIGURE 1

AVERAGE VALUES ON ATTITUDES TOWARD LEADERSHIP *

* The following key applies to Figures 1 through 7: B—Belgium, D—Denmark, E—England, F—France, G—Germany, I—Italy, J—Japan, N—Norway, Sp—Spain, Sw—Sweden, US—United States.

commitment to the higher-order management practices represented in categories B, C, and D. However, even though this response-bias may exist, the fact remains that a large body of managers in each country—and presumably the most advanced—hold the views which have been described.

Among these last three categories of belief there is less difference in level of response. As can be seen from Figure 1, attitudes of managers in all the countries cluster near the same value on all three scales. The belief in participation is perhaps a little weaker than in sharing information and internal control, but the difference is small in comparison with the gap between category A and all the others.

One can look at the data in Figure 1 and be impressed by the relatively narrow range of differences among all 11 countries. They all cluster low on category A and roughly together on B, C, and D. Before considering the differences, the similarity is important to notice. In these areas of attitude there are not large, insuperable differences in beliefs about leadership among the countries. We are accustomed to some large differences in prevailing myths about these countries: the icy-eyed Prussian, the fiery, aloof Don, the equalitarianism of the shopkeeper of France and England, Sweden's Middle Way, and the like. At least in their expressed conviction, however, these cleavages do not appear sharply. Managers' views on how to manage people are somewhat similar.

Turning to the differences among countries, Figure 1 again shows the picture.[4] Are there groups of countries? How do they cluster? One way to seek an answer is to observe the way countries shift positions from one part of the chart to another. For example, England and the U. S. seem to shift as a pair. On each of the four scales they tend to be positioned—with respect to all the others—in much the same way. They usually are fairly close in scores, although that may be less useful as a sign of grouping than their tendency to move together relative to all the others. Japan does not fit neatly with any group of countries. It moves by itself. On the four scales, it moves with England and the U. S. twice, with European countries once, and by itself once. It probably must stand alone on the basis of these data. The four continental European countries with a strong Latin background—France, Spain, Belgium, and Italy—move together rather tightly and can probably be usefully distinguished from the Northern European-Scandinavian group of Norway, Sweden, Denmark, and Germany. This gives us four clusters of countries: the Anglo-Saxon pair, Japan, Continental (Latin) Europe, and Northern (Teutonic) Europe.

The difference between the U. S. and all others is largest in category A. U. S. managers express the belief that all men are created equal more strongly than any of the others. Presumably managers think that they themselves have the capacity for leadership and initiative; U. S. managers feel, more than others, that the average person has the same capacities also. On the other categories the U. S. does not stand out from the group in the same way. Our textbooks and lectures may have exported a new concept of management which rests on a concept of man that is less accepted abroad.

---

[4] In Figure 1, the countries are divided into four groups. These are the groups that seemed to stand out through all the data. The separation illustrated here is not designed to create clusters, but to make it easier for the reader to see the groups as a whole.

Are the clusters ethnic or industrial? The answer seems to be largely ethnic. Norway and Sweden, industrially rather different, are very close together on the basis of these data. Denmark, though somewhat more agricultural than Sweden, tends to move closely with its Scandinavian neighbor. Germany, similar industrially to France, is close to the continental countries whenever the three Scandinavian countries are, but when it differs, it tends to swing with its Teutonic neighbors. France, Spain, Belgium, and Italy, a diverse package as far as industrialization is concerned, tend to swing together. England and the United States stand together, and Japan stands alone.

As far as the logical relationship among the categories is concerned, one might reason as follows. First comes the belief that most people have (untapped) capacities for initiative and leadership. If this idea is accepted, the manager might share information and objectives with them. Subsequently, and to a somewhat less extent, subordinates might be invited to participate in decisions. Finally, and to a still lesser extent, measures of self-control might be increasingly decentralized. Thus, the logical order of categories might follow their listing here, with a progressive embodiment in management practice of the basic belief in the individual. We have already pointed out that this relationship does not prevail, since attitudinal support for higher-order concepts of management (categories B, C, D) far outstrips the basic belief in the individual. How does the order work out, considering only the three categories of management practices? Is the logical pattern followed? Not often. Managers in England and the U. S. show more tendency to favor sharing information than eliciting participation or encouraging internal control. This at least approaches the logical model. In other clusters of countries the situation tends to be reversed. The commitment to internalized control tends to be greater than the willingness to share information or invite participation.

What can this mean? On the surface it appears impossible. How can an individual find direction and evaluation of himself in the work process if information and objectives are not shared? If we accept his self-direction, why stop short of participative management? In general, why is the psychological pattern different from the logical? It is perhaps easier to understand the variation in attitudes toward sharing information and objectives if we think in cultural terms and in terms of corporate tradition. In England and the U. S. there is a tradition of knowing and debating national issues and of full and frank disclosure of corporate financial data that differs from the rest of the countries taken as a whole. One can see why managers tend to share more in the Anglo-Saxon countries.

With respect to the category on participation, the three major clusters of countries are substantially the same. Japan favors participation somewhat more. No clue is immediately available to explain this deviation. This leaves only the fourth category. Managers in countries other than the U. S. and England tend to believe more strongly that one finds reward and direction in the work. For the most part, managers in the other countries also believe in this more strongly than they do in either participation or sharing information. It may well be that this belief in work-centered reward and direction arises from the craft and guild tradition, perhaps stronger elsewhere than in the Anglo-Saxon countries. In any case, two things seem clear: first, the patterns of management beliefs about leadership do not follow any simple logical pattern, and second, the pattern is more or less explicable in terms of cultural traditions in the countries. Management beliefs seem shaped more by such traditions than by degree or kind of industrialization.

How do these data compare with the findings of other major comparative studies of management, for example, that of Harbison and Myers? Without being contentious, let us lift a group of relevant statements from their section on Comparisons among Countries.

1. In general, France and Italy have been characterized by a large number of small enterprises, looked on by the family as a source of personal security and conducted in an atmosphere of widespread absence of trust.
2. The British social system, although much more flexible than it was fifty years ago, still carries over a strong feeling of the virtue of "aristocratic" values and gives a high mark to the "right" background in a man. In this respect it may be less egalitarian than that of the Swedes, although in Sweden the business elite is still drawn predominantly from a small group.
3. Japan, among the advanced industrial countries, appears to have retained many of the precapitalistic features of an earlier period and has managed to harness many supposedly "feudal" values to the service of its economic development.
4. The German social system has also had a strong authoritarian element, but this has been modified to some extent by the early development of organizations outside of the dominant classes and the need, in a political democracy, for the elite groups to make concessions of various sorts in order to maintain their power.[5]

These views are not exactly mirrored in our data. The absence of trust in Italy is perhaps apparent in the comparative reluctance to share information and allow participation, but France ranks considerably higher on both of these scales. Our data suggest that English managers are slightly less egalitarian than those in Sweden

[5] Harbison and Myers, *op. cit.*, pp. 123-24.

in terms of sharing information and looking for internal control among subordinates. However, in England there is a greater degree of commitment to the basic capacities of man and to participation. The Japanese fit in fairly well with the U. S. and England on everything but participation; here they are more democratic. Finally, the German authoritarianism appears, but is almost exactly matched in Denmark, and fits the same general pattern of the non-Anglo-Saxon countries. The data presented here provided a more differentiated picture, and this perhaps accounts for some of the variations in findings.

Harbison and Myers go on to say:

> 5. The process of industrialization tends, other things being equal, to limit managerial authority, both as a consequence of its direct effects on the industrial system and of its indirect effects on society as a whole. Directly, the increasing complexity and interdependence of many tasks make it necessary to elicit the cooperation of subordinates; the much larger size of establishment makes it necessary to increase the number of people in key managerial posts and makes it much more difficult to recruit them entirely from a narrow group, such as the family. Indirectly, the broadening of educational opportunities, the assumption of welfare responsibilities by governments or independent institutions, and the growth of rival organizations (such as labor unions), place checks on the power of management and prompt it to seek accommodation rather than arbitrary power.
> 6. In none of the less developed countries except Israel did we find "constitutional" management of the type prevalent in Sweden, England, or the United States.
> 7. Authoritarian and paternalistic practices are also common in France and Italy, despite the presence of labor movements. Centralization of control is characteristic in the French firm, as it is in the Italian or the Indian firm, for example. Despite the advanced stage of industrialization, the same pattern of authoritarian and paternalistic management seems to prevail in Japan—largely because of the social structure which, in prewar Japan at least, emphasized the unquestioning loyalty of subordinates to their superiors, as in the Japanese family.[6]

As has been suggested, the shift from unilateral command to a more participative management does not so neatly follow stages of industrialization in our data. One might roughly identify England, Sweden, Germany, and the U. S. as the most highly industrialized of our group. Perhaps France, Belgium, and Japan would fall in a second group, and Italy, Spain, Norway, and Denmark would be classified as countries still in stages of growing industrialization. Our data on managerial control do not follow such a classification of industrialization (or any other simple one). As has been suggested, we seem forced

---

[6] *Ibid.*, pp. 125-27.

to turn to cultural traditions to understand managerial beliefs about power and authority.

The argument based on the stage of industrialization has been prevalent for a long time, and this is perhaps true because most of the relevant studies have been done by scholars with a background in economics. The kinds of questions we ask here are determined partly by our base in other social sciences. It is, therefore, not surprising that we find other-than-economic indicators useful in distinguishing the clusters of countries.

Years ago psychologists began to argue with economists about the "economic man" concept as a tool for explaining the motivation of the individual at work. In some senses, the "stage of industrialization" argument is a more sophisticated and more complex form of the same phenomenon. One tries to see, for example, management's view of authority as a function of the level of technological and economic development. The attitude is treated as a dependent variable flowing from independent variables arising from the nature of the business activity. Another possibility—not entirely an exclusive alternative, but partly an enlarging complement—is the view that management's attitude about control is part of a broad web of values and beliefs determined by and part of a stream of cultural traditions outside the business—assumptions about man, political organization, human rights, and the like. The form of the organization, then, determined partly independently of the business, is imposed on a particular level of industrialization, which, in turn, is determined partly independently of the broad noneconomic cultural tradition.

When we view, for example, beliefs about control as part of a philosophy of management, it is not so surprising that we need to consider both economic and cultural traditions. We must have room for both the Protestant Ethic and scientific management in our casual texture. The appeal to "the conscience of the King" influences management's (and the public's) view of control as does the Industrial Revolution. Among our clusters there is a strong cleavage between the generally Roman Catholic countries and the Protestant North. It is not surprising that there are broad determinants of managerial philosophies, values, and the concept of man.

Are the Common Market countries similar on the basis of these data? No more so than the cultural-geographical grouping would indicate. It is possible that they were more different four years ago and will be more similar four years from now, but today they look like separate nations with common cultural streams, rather than a United States of Europe. One is tempted to ask, "Is England one of the leading Scandinavian countries?" Its isolation from the continent, its leadership in the Outer Seven, and the Anglo-Scandinavian political philosophy suggest the possibility. The answer here is "No." England moves with the U. S. fairly independently of Scandinavia, which tends to move with Germany.

Japan's role in these clusters is interesting. While she stands somewhat alone in this particular family of nations, the difference is not as great as one might expect in a country so recently changed from an absolute monarchy, a cartellized and controlled economy, and a somewhat feudal concentration of capital. Where Japan stands out from the others it is almost uniformly in the direction of a more liberal position. It is perhaps well to remember that the scores represent agreement with statements of belief. There is no way at present to show how closely practice follows expression.

Cognitive patterns in the role of the manager

Another part of the questionnaire attempted to get at the managers' perceptions of the role and practices of the manager. A variety of things depend on these views—what the manager feels is appropriate and inappropriate behavior in his role as manager, what kinds of values will be seen by one considering management as a career, the degree to which he can wholeheartedly invest himself in the role, and the like. In short, such views reflect the whole cultural assessment of the function of managing. To approach this problem, the more experimental and more projective semantic differential technique was used.

The semantic differential method aims, essentially, at discovering and defining a kind of cognitive map. With a group of concepts, it is possible to say how far each is from every other and in what direction. The meaning of the concepts and their psychological dynamics can be inferred from their positions in this kind of constructed mental space. Quantitatively, this is accomplished by asking respondents to rate each concept on a series of scales which remain the same across all concepts. In this case two groups of concepts were used, one dealing with management functions, and one with the superior-subordinate relationship in the culture. For functions, the concepts *to decide, to direct, to persuade, to cooperate,* and *to create* were used, as well as the more negative *to cheat, to reprimand,* and *to make a mistake.* An ordering of these into a cognitive pattern gives us some idea of a nation's view of what a manager does. In addition, hierarchical relationships were compared in three major social institutions: the army, the church, and business.

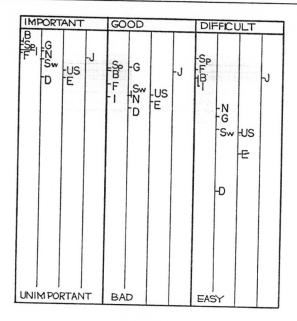

FIGURE 2

SCALED RESPONSES TO THE CONCEPT "TO DIRECT"

The detailed statistical analysis, of the semantic differential is long and complex and will be reported more fully elsewhere. Preliminary results of this analysis are not as illuminating as in the case of the other two methods, but a brief mention is worthwhile because it illustrates further the kind of clustering of countries that occurs. For this brief presentation, four concepts and three scales have been selected. The concepts are *to direct, to persuade, to cooperate,* and *to reprimand.* Each country's responses are shown in Figures 2, 3, 4, and 5 on the scales of importance, goodness, and difficulty.

Taking all the concepts together, *to cooperate* is thought to be the most important. *To direct* is a close second, *to persuade* is next, and finally, *to reprimand* is the least important (of these four) in the manager's repertoire. The same order holds, roughly, for goodness. Cooperation and direction are very, very good, persuasion somewhat less so, and reprimanding the least of all. Difficulty, however, is another story. Directing is the hardest thing to do. Persuading is next hardest. Reprimanding is easier, but cooperating is slightly easier still.

Turning to the way the countries group together, we see essentially the same clusters we saw before. Spain, France, Belgium, and Italy

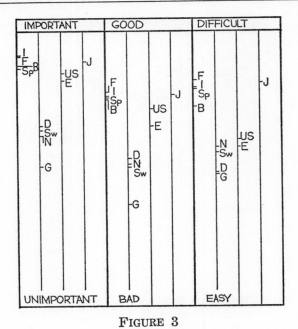

FIGURE 3

SCALED RESPONSES TO THE CONCEPT "TO PERSUADE"

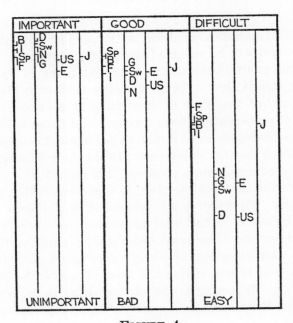

FIGURE 4

SCALED RESPONSES TO THE CONCEPT "TO COOPERATE"

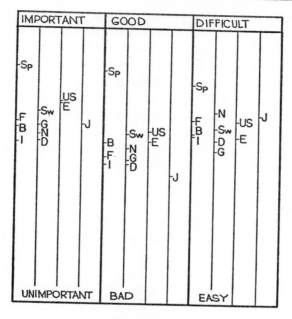

FIGURE 5

SCALED RESPONSES TO THE CONCEPT "TO REPRIMAND"

tend to move together in a tight group. (In one case—which will be discussed later—Spain deviates markedly.) England and the U. S. behave alike, again fairly closely linked. In general, Germany and the three Scandinavian countries vary in a similar pattern. Japan, in these data, could be fitted into the (Latin) continental group of countries.

Spain stands out from all others on the function of reprimanding. It is more important in Spain, it is better, and, somewhat surprisingly, it is more difficult. Spain's isolation on this dimension is heightened by another outstanding feature of these data: there is remarkably close correspondence among managers in all the countries in their perception of these functions. While an occasional country stands out—e.g., Denmark finding direction unusually easy, or Germany finding persuasion relatively unimportant, and not very good—still, in general, they shift together. From cooperating to reprimanding, for instance, they tend to move down on all three scales in a bunch.

The broad implications of these data appear less clearly than in either of the other two sections of the study at this stage of statistical analysis. It is necessary to wait until the analysis is completed to give a good picture of cognitive mapping in these areas. Meanwhile, two points stand out in the preliminary clustering. Firstly, there is remarkable agreement among countries in their perceptions of these functions. They are not scattered widely, but tend to bunch together, indicating a strong common thread in the way people view these things regardless of country. Secondly, within this relatively homogeneous set of responses, clusters of countries are still distinguishable. Such variation as there is tends to preserve small tight subgroups. They are substantially the same ethnic or cultural clusters that appeared in the preceding section.

Motivation and satisfactions

The third section of the study was concerned with the types of satisfactions managers want from their jobs and with the degree to which they feel these different needs are actually being satisfied through their jobs. To obtain information on these points, five types of psychological needs were studied. These needs can be considered as arranged in order from the basic or most prepotent need for security through social, esteem, and autonomy needs to the least prepotent need for self-actualization. This order of needs on the basis of priority or prepotency stems from the theoretical thinking of a number of psychologists and has been used on a wide scale in recent psychological studies of motivation, especially in relation to work. Thus, the results obtained in this study for these different types of needs can be related back to an underlying theoretical foundation.

Before proceeding with a discussion of findings, it is useful to describe briefly the five types of needs. *Security needs* were not defined for the respondent, but were interpreted in a general way as one's feeling of safety and assurance in a particular managerial position. *Social needs* referred to the desire to develop close friendships and the opportunity to give help to other people; thus both ingoing (from others to the person) and outgoing (from the person to others) aspects of needs for social satisfaction were covered in the questionnaire. *Esteem needs* covered both self-esteem and esteem received from other people. *Autonomy needs* referred to the authority connected with the manager's position and the opportunity for independent thought and action. Finally, *self-actualization needs* tapped feelings of self-fulfillment, worthwhile accomplishment, and personal growth.

The specific questions in each of these five need areas asked managers to make three responses: (1) How important is this to me? (2) How much (of the need satisfaction) is there *now* in my position? and (3) How much (of the need satisfaction) should there be in my position? The answers to the first question were used to determine the importance attached to particular needs, that is, what the manager wants to get from his position. To determine degree of fulfillment or satisfaction, or what he feels he *is* getting from his position, the difference between responses to Question 3 and Question 2 was computed for each item for each respondent. Thus, the larger the difference between "should be" and "is now" the greater was the indicated *dis*satisfaction.

Importance of needs

The most striking finding concerning managerial feelings about the importance of different needs is the relative similarity of thinking from country to country with regard to a particular need. That is, for example, those type of needs which are considered most important in one country tend also to be regarded as most important in other countries. Likewise, those needs considered least important in a particular country are usually also thought to be least important by managers in other countries (see Figure 6).

Which needs *were* regarded as the most important? In every country, without exception, needs for self-actualization were deemed most important. French, Japanese, and U. S. managers felt most strongly about these needs, but the differences from country to country were very slight. In other words, not only did self-actualization needs consistently rank above other needs, but they were also given quite consistent ratings of importance by the various groups of managers. This means that, at least at the level of response, managers put primary emphasis on opportunities for growth, for realizing their potential, and for worthwhile accomplishment. The unanimity of this reaction across countries demands attention.

Needs for autonomy were generally regarded as second in importance, although for certain countries they were third rather than second. Managers in Sweden, Germany, and Japan felt slightly more strongly about these needs than managers in the other countries, while Norwegian and Danish managers attached slightly less-than-average importance to autonomy needs. Again, however, as was the case in needs for self-actualization, the differences among the countries in the ratings of importance assigned to these needs were small.

Third in importance among the five types of needs was the need for security. In contrast to the results for self-actualization and

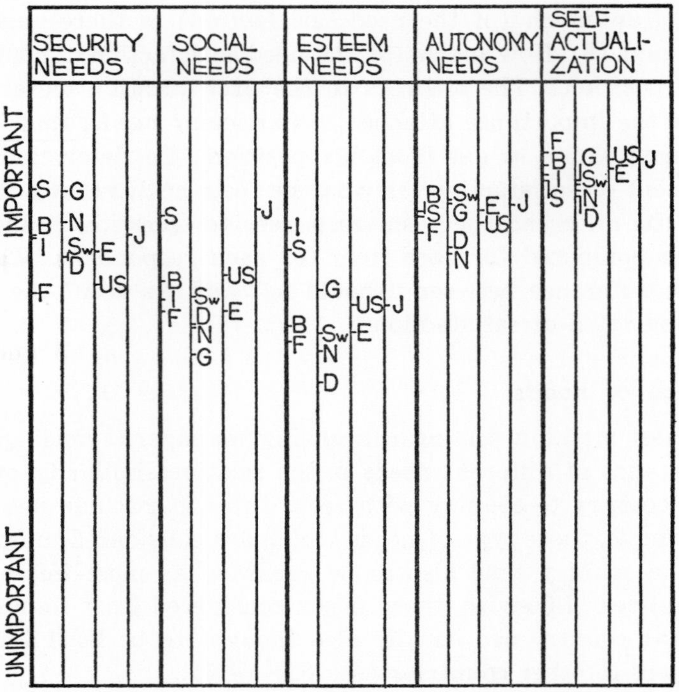

FIGURE 6

AVERAGE VALUES ON THE IMPORTANCE
OF VARIOUS NEEDS

autonomy, however, the countries were more widely spread in the average importance they attached to this need. Managers in Spain and Germany especially regarded it as more important than did those in other countries, while French and American managers gave it less importance than those elsewhere. Its relative ranking among the five types of needs ranged from second to fourth in importance.

Social needs ended up in fourth place in importance for most of the countries, although they ranked third for the United States and Japan and fifth for Germany and Italy. German managers gave this need an especially low value, not only in relation to other needs but also in relation to managers in other countries. The social needs were similar to security needs in producing some degree of spread among countries.

Finally, needs for esteem were regarded as least important in all of the countries except Italy, where they were regarded as next in importance after self-actualization, and Germany, where they were rated fourth rather than fifth in importance. Needs for esteem thus were like security and social needs in producing some variation in ratings among countries. The Italian managers gave them a much higher rating than did managers in any other country; on the other hand, Danish managers gave them a particularly low rating.

As pointed out earlier, the most impressive finding in connection with the importance attached to different needs was the relative similarity in the way quite different countries and cultures felt about them. A Spanish manager is not very different from a German manager or each from an English or Japanese manager in the ratings they give to the importance of each need. This similarity, of course, is not complete. Especially for security, social, and esteem needs there was some degree of variation from country to country. But even for these the variation usually was not great except for an isolated case or two. And, for autonomy and self-actualization the similarity was very close. One should note especially that the similarities were greatest for the two needs, self-actualization and autonomy, which were regarded as most important. This suggests that managers feel most strongly about the needs that bring the closest agreement in the value assigned to them. Esteem and social needs produced the least agreement among countries and were thought of as least important.

The over-all similarity among managers in different countries in their evaluations of the importance of needs may indicate that what people want from their jobs is relatively unaffected by the cultural environment in which they operate. At least this seems to be true of managers. Whether it is also true of other groups of employees cannot be determined, of course, from our data. Managers, and perhaps all people, seem to be alike in terms of what they regard as important needs to fulfill in their work situations.

The satisfaction of needs

The findings for need fulfillment or satisfaction are in contrast with those previously reported for the importance attached to various needs. Although managers tend to be alike from country to country in what they *want* from their jobs, they tend to be quite different in what they *think they are getting* from their jobs. Both the absolute ratings of satisfaction for a particular need vary from country to country, and so also do the relative rankings of one or another need in comparison to all other needs. That is, the mean satisfaction for a given need, say esteem, may be high for country A and low for country B, but also country A may regard this need as the most satisfied of the five needs, whereas country B regards it as about third in satisfaction.

Because the absolute and relative satisfaction of most of the five needs varies considerably from one country to another, it is not possible to give any meaningful over-all ranking of the needs in terms of the degree to which they are satisfied. The greatest similarity among countries is with regard to satisfaction of the need for self-actualization (see Figure 7). In all countries except Japan, it is considered as the *least* satisfied of all of the five needs. (The results for Japan show a peculiar pattern similar to no other country in that all needs, self-actualization included, are regarded as equally satisfied.) Although the need for self-actualization produces the greatest dissatisfaction in almost all countries, the dissatisfaction is greatest in Italy, Spain, France, and the U. S. On the other hand, managers in Japan, especially, and in the Scandinavian countries, to some extent, are not as dissatisfied on self-actualization as most of the other countries.

Needs for autonomy are seen as the second greatest producers of lack of need fulfillment in most of the countries. Managers in Spain, France, and Italy indicate somewhat greater dissatisfaction in this area than do those in other countries, while Scandinavian and Japanese managers again indicate slightly less-than-average dissatisfaction.

Needs for esteem rank as the third most unsatisfied needs in some countries, the fourth in others, and the fifth or least dissatisfied in still others. Social and security needs show an even wider variation, ranking in each case from second most dissatisfied in some countries to the most satisfied need in other countries.

Just as in the two major preceding sections of this paper, probably the most meaningful analyses of the data for perceived satisfaction or fulfillment can be made if the various countries are grouped by patterns or profiles of satisfactions for the five types of needs rather than if each need is considered separately. If this grouping is carried out, four fairly clear groups of countries emerge. First are the four countries of mid/southern continental Europe: Spain, Italy, France, and Belgium. The second group includes Germany and the three Scandinavian countries. The third cluster includes the two English-speaking countries, England and the United States. Japan stands by itself, its pattern being completely different from that of the United States or any European country.

The mid/southern continental European group of countries has one outstanding feature in its pattern of satisfactions, and that is

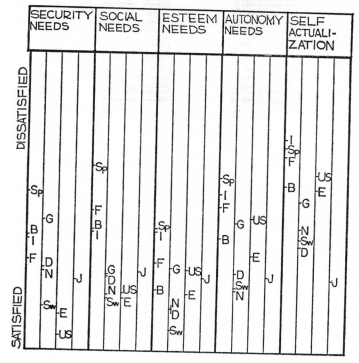

FIGURE 7

DEGREE OF SATISFACTION IN VARIOUS NEEDS

the fact that considering all needs taken together, managers from these countries are more *dis*satisfied than those from any other countries or groups of countries. For four of the five need areas, self-actualization, autonomy, esteem, and social, the managers from these four countries indicate more dissatisfaction than each of the other groups of countries. Only in the security area is dissatisfaction in three of these countries exceeded, and that only slightly, by Germany. Thus, even in the security need area average dissatisfaction in this group of countries is comparatively high. The nation with the most dissatisfied managers by far within this first grouping of mid/southern continental European countries is Spain. Following in order are Italy, France, and Belgium. This group of four countries feels most dissatisfied with self-actualization needs, as do all of the other groups except Japan. Next in order of dissatisfaction for this group are autonomy and social needs. The fact that social needs are almost tied for second in terms of relative dissatisfaction (among the five needs) for this group is noteworthy, for this is a higher relative dissatisfaction for these needs than is the case with any of the other three groups of countries. Security and esteem needs are placed fourth and fifth in dissatisfaction by managers from these four countries.

Germany, in this section of the study, could in some ways be grouped with the preceding four countries of mid/southern continental Europe and in other ways with the group of three Scandinavian countries. Germany is somewhat similar to its four more southern European partners in having a relatively high over-all level of dissatisfaction, and is, in fact, closely related to Belgium in this respect. However, in the profile pattern of ranking of the five needs in terms of dissatisfaction Germany seems more similar to its neighbors to the north. Like the Scandinavian countries, it tends to feel relatively well satisfied in esteem and social need areas and relatively less well satisfied on security needs. Security needs for German managers, in fact, are as unsatisfied as autonomy needs.

Scandinavian managers are clearly "satisfied" managers, at least in terms of their own perceptions of their situations. They are most satisfied of any of the groups of countries on autonomy and, particularly, esteem needs. For the other three need areas—self-actualization, social, and security—they are the most satisfied among the continental European countries. Considering all five needs, the Scandinavian managers are definitely more satisfied than managers from the most southern European countries, Spain and Italy. The Scandinavian managers, like the German managers, feel that security needs are no better satisfied in their jobs than autonomy needs. Thus, among the five types of needs, dissatisfaction in the need for security ranks relatively higher for the Scandinavian countries than for the U. S., England, and the mid/southern continental countries.

The two English-speaking countries have a somewhat different pattern of satisfactions from any of the European countries. For the most prepotent needs, security and social needs, the U. S. and English managers are more satisfied than those in any other cluster of countries (including Japan). For esteem and autonomy needs, the English-speaking managers are more satisfied than German managers and those in most other continental European countries, but less satisfied than the Scandinavian managers. For self-actualization needs the managers from America and England again report more fulfillment—though not very much more—than the four mid/southern continental countries, but less fulfillment than German or Scandinavian managers. The pattern of satisfactions for the two English-speaking countries might be summarized best by noting that the satisfactions decrease exactly in the order in which the five needs are theorized to decrease in priority or prepotency. That is, the managers from these countries report the greatest satisfaction for the most prepotent need of security, less satisfaction for esteem and autonomy, and finally the least satisfaction for the least prepotent need, self-actualization.

Japan presents a picture of the "inscrutable East" as far as its pattern of satisfactions is concerned. Quite unlike that of any other country, the Japanese pattern shows an equal degree of satisfaction among the five types of needs. Japanese managers feel just as satisfied (or dissatisfied) about self-actualization needs as they do about esteem, security, or any other types of needs. This uniformity of response from one type of need to another was not approached in any other country, is therefore a truly unique response pattern, and is the reason that Japan has been grouped in a category of countries by itself. In terms of amount of satisfaction indicated by the Japanese managers compared to the amount shown by managers from other countries, the Japanese are considerably more satisfied than any other group of countries on needs for self-actualization. On needs for autonomy they are about equal with the Scandinavian countries in having the most satisfaction. For esteem, social, and security needs, Japan is about average in expressed satisfaction. Over-all, then, Japanese managers report generally high need fulfillment.

The findings with regard to the patterns of satisfactions among different groups of countries are relatively easy to describe. However, when one moves from description to interpretation, the task becomes more difficult. For example, there is the very clear-cut finding that managers in the northern European countries, especially the Scandinavian countries, are more satisfied than those in the southern European countries, especially Spain and Italy. (There is, in fact, almost a perfect correlation between the over-all degree of satisfaction and the median latitude of European countries.) Does this mean that geography or climate somehow influences how much satisfaction managers think they are deriving from their jobs? Can latitude determine attitude? This seems unlikely. Degree of industrialization is somewhat correlated with the north-south geographical axis in Europe, yet it would be difficult to say that this variable is necessarily highly correlated with the satisfaction findings. The lowest group in satisfaction includes, for instance, France and Belgium, highly industrialized, and Spain and Italy. The high group includes the three Scandinavian countries, very different from one another in degree of industrialization.

The answer seems to lie more in social-cultural factors, especially in terms of the role of the manager in occupational status hierarchies and the role of business in the day-to-day affairs of each country. Business organizations are probably more highly respected institutions in the Scandinavian countries and England, and managers who reach middle or top management levels can derive greater feelings of security, social, and esteem satisfactions. Explanations of greater satisfactions in the areas of autonomy and self-actualization, though, do not fit even this theory very well. Perhaps the reason these two needs are so much better satisfied in the northern Teutonic countries lies in the way in which business firms are organized. Middle and top managers in these countries may be given more freedom and more authority to make decisions unhampered by other parts of their organizations or by governmental regulations. This greater autonomy could in turn lead to increased opportunities for self-development and self-fulfillment, that is, to increased self-actualization satisfaction.

One interesting aspect of the findings on satisfaction was the fact that the theoretical classification of the five types of needs according to their priority or prepotency exactly fit the pattern of results for the United States and England, but not for any other group of countries.

It has often been suggested that basic needs—such as for security—are a necessary first step to others. As they are satisfied, and as the assurance grows that they will continue to be satisfied, the others become possible. An hierarchical necessity has been imputed to this ordering of needs. In these data, it appears only in the Anglo-American countries. This suggests, perhaps, that the theoretical formulation is especially relevant to the cultural conditions existing in these two English-speaking countries. It also may suggest that industrial and business firms in these two countries have succeeded in satisfying basic needs first and are currently in a position where employees, at least managerial employees, are directing their efforts increasingly to each higher step on the scale of need prepotency. In other countries than these two, past conditions in business organizations may not have led to such a systematic, step-by-step fulfillment of needs from the most basic to the least basic. In essence, then, this part of the findings for need satisfaction indicates either that the theory of prepotency of needs is particularly well adapted to organizational behavior in the U. S. and England, or that industrial firms in these countries have created conditions that fit the theory.

It is important to relate the findings for perceived satisfaction of needs to the results reported earlier in this section concerning managers' perceptions of the importance of needs. Needs which are considered most important by managers, regardless of country, tend to be those needs which are least satisfied in virtually all of the countries studied. This finding should suggest that it is particularly necessary for those who have ultimate responsibility for running a firm to pay special attention to incentives in these areas if they are concerned with managerial motivations. In the event of marked deficits in need satisfaction of the kind reported here, incentives probably must be geared to the deficiencies that are experienced. Where the sense of lack of satisfaction is more uniform, policy regarding incentives would presumably be based on the reported importance of various needs.

There is a fairly uniform agreement from country to country about which needs are regarded as most important and which are least important. But, when the question turns to "how well satisfied are these various needs?" the findings differ considerably from country to country.

The discrepancy between importance and satisfaction of needs raises a crucial question. These data indicate remarkable similarity in estimates of importance and wide variations in degree of satisfaction. This fact seems to go immediately to the question of whether managerial motives of the kind we have been discussing are general characteristics of people or products of the situation. The homogeneity of importance across a variety of cultures suggests strongly that the needs arise from the nature of people. Their satisfaction varies with situations. There is little evidence here to suggest that the basic motivational equipment with which the manager approaches his job varies from country to country. What does vary is what he finds there.

Summary

This is a preliminary report of data. More exhaustive analysis will appear later. Meanwhile, some general findings emerge:

1. One cannot help but be struck by the consistent groupings of countries through all three parts of the study. Not only is the grouping consistent, but it tends to follow ethnic lines rather than level of industrialization.

2. The pattern of uniformity and diversity in the data is also striking. It seems possible to identify variables which are enduring and relatively culture-free characteristics of people and other variables which are more situationally determined. This is outstanding in the uniformity of importance of needs and the great difference in their satisfaction. It also appears in the uniform swings on attitudes toward leadership while preserving national differences and in the similar grouping on the semantic differential.

3. Managers in all the countries studied could profitably examine these data. They might ask themselves if this is the way they see it, if this is the way they want it, and what the differences may mean to their countries' economies.

QUESTIONS

1. What values do you see in comparing foreign managers to American managers?
2. What similarities between all ethnic managers do you see in this study?
3. What relationships were found between authoritative, control-oriented managers and social structure?
4. What significant differences showed up between foreign and American managers?
5. How do you account for the interesting findings relative to the basic needs of the various managers surveyed?

13. MENTAL FAILURE: EXECUTIVE CRISIS *

Eugene Emerson Jennings

We are about to enter the mind of the business executive. The executive who will be analyzed has a particular problem: he is undergoing a career crisis, feeling his whole career is in jeopardy. He may not know exactly how his career crisis came about. His attempts to resolve his crisis have failed. In his desperation he finally turns to a professional counsellor for help.

What does an executive who is caught up in the entanglements of business life look like? What causes him to rise to the top only to lose his emotional footing? And if mastery of his career crisis is delayed sufficiently, what kinds of problems are thereby created? How does an executive successfully resolve his crisis and restore harmony with his corporate environment? In short, why do executives crack up, and how are they put back together again?

My counseling of executives in a career crisis has provided insight into the kinds of pressures that bombard members of the business world. These forces are not unique. Rather, some executives have a built-in capacity to handle these pressures better than others. The pressures of corporate existence are basically three. The first set of pressures come from superiors who have the power to give and withhold rewards of all kinds. Then there are the pressures that come from the goals and objectives of the organization as felt in the executive's particular job. Lastly, there are the pressures that come from within the executive himself. These pressures come from his definition of who he is and what he wants to become. These three sets of pressures are always present in varying degrees, even before a career crisis strikes. But when it strikes, they become super active; and if mastery is delayed, they will eventually clog the whole mind, driving out other pressures or giving them a secondary prominence. What emerges from an extended career crisis is a triangle of pressures interlocked in a way that suggests wholeness. This is the corporate triangle.

Life in the corporate triangle is a convenient way to express the activity of the mind caught up with the pressures of a career crisis. The mental life of this executive pivots on this triad of pressures.

* From *Management of Personnel Quarterly*, Vol. 4, No. 2 (Summer, 1965), pp. 7-17. Reprinted with permission.

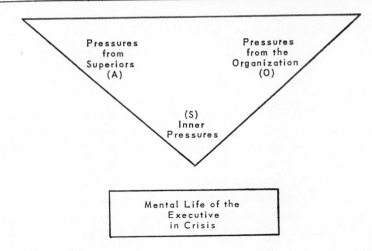

AGENTS OF CRISIS

When a mental crisis develops, executives of the highest public stature may react in elementary ways, much the same as ordinary people. Their defenses may be no less neurotic, their solutions no less imaginative. Their normal thinking and activity patterns may become overly relied upon at a time when change may be required. Or they may resort to radical solutions that would normally be alien to their acquired identities. They are apt to have unmanageable definitions of their problem and an exhausted supply of solutions. Some have severely damaged the most important quality of success and health notions of self, securely rooted in confidence. As the clinician knows, those who doubt themselves tend to doubt the whole world. In panic and desperation the executives come seeking professional help, but even this they do ambivalently. Guilt and shame prevent an easy access to their private inner worlds. Once penetration has been made, this inner world is far less confusing than the size and complexity of their corporations would suggest. It has always been exciting for me to notice that the men who manage our vast corporations have reduced the workings of the corporate system to a very few elementary notions. To be sure, there is a lot more to running a business, but in a career crisis certain boundaries are attached to the administrative process that perhaps do not arise in a normal administrative situation.

Instead of becoming generalized to include other phases of his life style, the executive's career crisis, at least initially, does for most the very opposite. The executive begins to shore up the problem and settle upon a few possible useful tools. After all, his main concern is to become mobile again, to become or stay meaningfully attached to the administrative process. To an executive, the worst anxiety is the feeling of becoming separated from the central concerns of the firm. Separation anxiety haunts the executive who has as his central value the active control of the administrative apparatus of the corporation.

Separation, however, is seldom abrupt and discrete. In the large corporation the gradual removal of an executive from the central administrative process is seldom perceived at the point of initiation. This is the terror of it all. He feels he is not really pulling his weight; the tempo is moving against him, but he is not sure. A number of business practices have developed in recent times to cushion the "inhumanity" of arbitrary punishment or discharge. He may be "kicked upstairs," "by-passed," gradually frozen out, disenfranchised, or placed on a dusty corporate shelf with problems that never need to be solved. When he has finally confirmed the tragic proportions of the situation, it is almost too late to institute strategic changes. All he knows is that he has done something wrong, and somebody in a position of authority has directly or indirectly sanctioned his gradual removal for "reasons," many of which are unknown to him or which are too threatening to be consciously entertained for long periods of time.

An executive in a career crisis tends to focus on problems of authority and goal achievement activities of the corporation. These factors are, in turn, evaluated in terms of the kind of person the executive believes he is and would like to become. His notions of self are intermingled with his notions of what the president or chairman of the board expects of him and what the corporate goals actually require of him. Few career crises may be understood without ascertaining these notions of authority, organization, and self. The executive in a career crisis comes prepared to focus decisively upon these few notions and charge them with both highly causal and productive values.

Notions of authority

As we enter the managerial mind, we at once see that these notions carry several levels of meaning. One set of meanings may be called conventional. Conventional notions of authority, organization, and self spring essentially from the society at large. Each society evolves certain generalized attitudes and beliefs about authority and what an authority figure should or should not do. Our culture defines certain roles as authority bearing, and persons filling these positions are viewed as authorities. There are roles of authority designated in all of our basic institutions. The role of a superior in any one of these institutions carries certain conventional or well accepted meanings. Although there are only a few studies on this subject, they generally demonstrate that authority is the right to order the behavior of others.[1] In a study of school children's perceptions of labor and management, the boss was perceived as one who gave orders and the worker as one who did what he was told to do.[2] Superiors are generally considered to have the right to expect obedience and loyalty from subordinates. It is commonly assumed that these conventional notions of authority are acquired from birth onward. The main agent for transmitting these notions are parents and parental figures. These notions become internalized early in the growth process and become basic instruments for making one's way through the world. From one standpoint, life is a maze of authority figures who must be properly perceived and sufficiently accommodated in order to acheive a productive life. By the time the individual arrives at the door of the employment office of the business firm, he has already acquired vast experiences with authority and authority figures. These experiences have become condensed into brief, simple, often unconscious meanings that allow proper identification with the authority system. To be sure, some youths have inadequate notions of authority that prohibit assimilating with the authority system of the corporation. However, the vast majority of our youth have notions of authority that allow satisfactory relationships to superior individuals.

A study of 30, 40, and 50 year olds in management echelons in business shows that the younger generation has an amazingly simple orientation to its immediate world. They see the business world as demanding accomplishment and achievement. They are convinced that assertively following the leads provided them will result in success. "Their interest in their own inner feelings—their emotions, personal desires, and wishes—is negligible. They consult the expectations, the policy, the precedent, not themselves."[3] It is apparent that at this point they come prepared to do what is required of them and to look to their superiors for guidance and help.

---

[1] See W. B. Miller, "Two Concepts of Authority," *The American Anthropologist*, April, 1955.

[2] See M. Haire, F. Morrison, "School Children's Perception of Labor and Management," *Journal of Social Psychology*, 1957, 46, pp. 179-197.

[3] W. E. Henry, "Conflict, Age and the Executive," *Business Topics*, Michigan State University, Spring, 1961, pp. 15-24.

In another study the top executive is pictured as being able to inhibit his aggressive feelings toward authority because of his high opinion of their function and character.[4] This notion of authority as positive and necessary appears in some studies to be related to executive mobility. A study of 473 executives from fourteen firms shows that the successful executive's idea of authority is that it does not hamper, inhibit, or constrain him; he accepts it without resentment. "He looks to his superiors as persons of greater training and experience whom he can consult on problems and who issue guiding directives to him which he accepts without prejudice." This is a most necessary attitude since it controls his relations to superiors. "Executives who view their superiors as prohibiting forces have trouble working within an organization. Unconsciously, they resent superiors, or do things to obstruct the work of their bosses, or, finally they may assert their independence unnecessarily." [5]

Two examples of unproductive notions of authority are provided by Burleigh Gardner. A young man was accepted for a junior executive training position. He had fine qualifications, good college training, excellent appearance and poise, and agile mental abilities. The psychological analysis detected only one potential source of real difficulty—his concept of authority. He saw his associates as competitive persons whom he must outwit. He had no clear-cut image of superiors as guiding or directing figures. Hence, it was predicted that he would soon get into difficulty with his associates and superiors. For about two weeks none of these symptoms appeared. Then, his associates began to complain to their department head that this man was being overly critical and cutting in on their work. Soon after, the young man became increasingly difficult to direct; he became more resistant to suggestions about his work. Finally, the company was forced to release him.

Another example by Gardner concerns a middle-aged man who had been with one company for about two years and requested a transfer to another department. He had been placed in several positions in various departments of the company. In each of these he had done reasonably good work, and there had been no outstanding complaints about him. His name had come up for promotion several times, but somehow he never was promoted. He was tested when he had requested another transfer, and the test analyses—made before any of the above history was known—showed him to be a man of

[4] E. Rosen, "The Executive Personality," *Personnel*, January-February, 1959, pp. 10-20.

[5] Burleigh B. Gardner, "What Makes Successful and Unsuccessful Executives." *Advanced Management*, September, 1948, pp. 116-125.

good, though not outstanding abilities, and intellectually able to cope with most intermediate level positions. His concept of authority, however, placed him at the top; unconsciously he felt himself to be better than most of his superiors. When this finding was presented to the man's superiors, they were able to substantiate it completely. They cited instance after instance in which the man acted as if he were doing the company a favor by working there. Gardner concludes that the subordinate's idea of authority made it difficult for him to take orders and operate successfully within the organization.

It is apparent from these two case studies by Gardner that the notion of authority as inhering in the self of the executive is unproductive. The dominant notion of authority among successful executives involves activities and people in the milieu outside the self. The successful executive feels a part of a wider, more final authority system from which he gains a large measure of his opportunity to act. In contrast, the self-made man has the notion that authority originates with himself, which precludes assimilating with the larger authority structure. Henry, who has done extensive research on executive personality, remarks, "It is of interest that the dominant crystallization of attitudes about authority is toward superior and subordinate, rather than towards self." [6]

In a study of over 8,000 executives, W. Lloyd Warner found that, "Perhaps one of the most significant personality characteristics of the successful corporation executive is his conception of authority; that is of crucial importance to interpret properly the actions of an executive at a top level position.[7] What happens when youth enter the business world with notions that authority and authority figures are threatening and prohibiting? One possible answer is provided by a study of 500 businessmen who started their own firms after World War II.[8] Their notions of authority are that it is essentially restrictive, relentless, and rejecting. Their pattern of activity upon leaving school is to run into authority figures, clash, leave, and find another job, only to become once again rebelliously involved in another authority system. Obviously, their notion of authority as restrictive largely accounts for establishing their own enterprise which gives substance to the notion that they are their own boss. In managing their firms they are explicit, overt autocrats in contrast to executives

[6] W. E. Henry, "The Business Executive, Psychoanalysis of a Social Role," *American Journal of Sociology*, January, 1949, pp. 186-291.
[7] W. L. Warner and J. Abegglen, *Big Business Leaders in America* (New York: Harper & Bros., 1960).
[8] D. G. Moore, O. F. Collins, D. Unwalla, *Enterprising Men*, Bureau of Business, Michigan State University, 1964.

who live within an established structure and who are essentially multicratic or flexible in their administrative styles.[9]

In the corporation world bosses are the prime givers. The whole process of the distribution of satisfaction, power, and achievement opportunities is governed by authority figures. It rests largely with them whether the expectations of each member of the corporation are destined to have reasonable fulfillment. In the modern corporation the key to probably the most potent of all executive needs, the improvement and defense of one's self image, lies with the "boss set." It is these very relationships that occupy the center of the stage of much psychological difficulty.

An executive, whether president or manager, never completely separates his psyche from authority influence. The promising young executive's identity is always being influenced by the passage through layers of authority. He not only emulates his superiors at times, but adopts their view and opinions as his own. This is aided by some superiors who identify themselves with the subordinate to some extent and try to make themselves more assimilable by taking over some of the subordinate's values, beliefs, and standards. In reverse, some subordinates are authority resistant. They view superiors as a class of people who are necessary, but basically useless, reactionary, depriving, or perhaps threatening.

In sum, the typical executive views authority figures as controlling and helpful rather than destructive and prohibiting, has the ability to attract the attention of these older, better trained men, and to learn rapidly from them for considerable advantage. This notion of authority seems to be common to our society, particularly the middle classes. While this trust pattern seems certainly true for many people, particularly executives, others have a distinct mistrust pattern toward superior authorities. Forthcoming evidence will show that many in the lower classes do not have this positive but reserved attitude toward authority. The entire careers of some executives show the difficulty of maintaining their upward relationships well. This mistrust is often times translated into a desire to manipulate and take advantage of their superiors. In some cases they, too, can learn readily from their superiors and readily terminate relationships with superiors that are detrimental. Executive development is the process whereby the individual brings his notion of self and his superiors into a meaningful, unified relationship within the goal achieving activities of the corporation.[10]

---

[9] E. E. Jennings, *The Executive*, Harper & Row, 1962.
[10] See W. R. Dill, T. L. Hilton, W. R. Reitman, *The New Managers* (Englewood Cliffs, N. J.: Prentice-Hall, 1962).

Notions of organization

This latter phrase suggests that notions of authority are highly tied to notions of organization. The notion of authority that the successful executive has involves a sense of belonging to a larger order or system of power and prerogative. Obviously, an elementary notion of authority includes the right to order certain kinds of behavior, not just any or all varieties. There are bounds to authority, and a major boundary is supplied by the explicit and implicit purposes for which the authority system is established. Thus, a boss is expected to authorize behavior that is organizationally directed and relevant. In fact, his main task is to show the relevance of his commands to the goals and purposes of the organization. This act is commonly referred to as rational authority. Irrational authority is where the boss expects commands to be obeyed without his showing their clear, convincing relationship to corporate objectives and welfare.

What constitutes the conventional notion of organization in its most elementary form seems to be interconnectedness. Our society is highly equipped today to teach children that the universe is orderly and intricately tied together. In this sense, organization essentially means that everything is or in some way can be interrelated. This notion of organization allows individuals to relate to each other and to place a high value upon the products of interaction.

The research of Piaget with children is particularly instructive here. The infant's point of view is that he is the center of the world. Seeing the baby joyfully watching the movements of his feet gives the distinct impression of the joy felt by commanding the world. "When the baby takes delight in movements situated in the outside world, such as the movements of the ribbons of its cradle, he must feel an immediate bond between these movements and his delight in them." [11] At this stage of infancy, everything participates in the nature of, and can influence, everything else. Activity becomes possible because what the baby does has its counterpart in responses from others and things. The infant grows into childhood with the confidence that events cause other events to happen, that the world is not without sequence, that there is an essential amenability to human and physical manipulation. Because of this sequential aspect of events, the child can become an event himself and thereby participate in the affairs of the world much the same as these affairs impinge upon him. Because every act is seen to have a potential

---

[11] Jean Piaget, *The Child's Conceptions of the World* (Paterson, N. J.: Littlefield, Adams & Company, 1960), p. 153.

consequence, the child can order his behavior around anticipated consequences. Goal-directed behavior gradually replaces random behavior. He increasingly organizes his behavior by setting goals and determining their efficient achievement. Others are later seen as capable of entering into this organizational process, and the child's activities become expanded to include the goals and activities of others. He achieves the capacity and skill to play the games of others and, later in life, to work for their goals as though they were his own. From early infancy the child becomes gradually organization-prone. All of which is predicated on this primitive belief that all things are in a way connected or may be connected by the insertion of a human act of will.

In short, through the agency of the home, the child learns the elementary process of transaction, which involves giving and receiving, making demands upon others, and submitting to other's demands. The notion of taking a role and assuming a position within a group serves to provide the youth a capacity to perform highly specialized jobs and tasks as well as to become properly equipped for them in adulthood. When the young man appears at the employment office, he is prepared to perform limited roles and to seek great satisfaction in their proper achievement.

Essentially, his notion that things must be organized around particular ends allows him to identify with the ends and goals of the enterprise as they are represented to him at his station or position. These more immediate ends or goals become the means whereby the promising young manager learns to bring things together and perform elementary administrative tasks. The notion of an essential interconnectedness among events and things and the affirmative desire to organize makes practical an identification with the corporation as a goal-achieving activity. Through sustained work performance and upward advancement, the goals of the firm take on more precise meaning. Continually adjusting one's behavior to the demands of efficient organization as measured by the achievement of corporate goals produces a positive affirmation of the corporation itself. The executive and the corporation eventually come to be emotional counterparts.

Referring to the study of 30, 40, and 50 year olds, we observed that the younger man seeks to associate himself with the formal goals of the organization as they are defined at his level.[12] In the studies of successful executives, the dominant crystallization of the

---

[12] W. E. Henry, "Conflict, Age and the Executive," *op cit.*, p. 18.

attitude toward organization was the need to take seemingly isolated events or failures and see relationships that may tie them together. Gardner reports, "The ability to bring order out of chaos is another characteristic of successful executives. . . . In short, they can organize efficiently." [13] What is not said is the obvious. To look for relationships betwen things and events essentially calls for an underlying notion that there is an essentially possible interconnectedness. This notion of an essential interconnectedness allows operating within vast complicated systems without losing faith that who one is, one's identity, is important, and does count. It allows at the executive level a capacity to hold together the parts of a highly changing organization, and with confidence he can restructure the parts when this is called for by the goal-achieving requirements.

This notion of organization as an essential quality of human and physical events allows for the direction of vast amounts of energy in narrow purposeful channels that otherwise might be dissipated. Warner shows that the successful executive works with facts, is direct in his approach to problems, does not get involved in such issues as irrelevant details, organizes his thinking, is markedly crisp and decisive, makes up his mind, and follows through to a solid and definite conclusion.[14] Furthermore, the successful executive is so oriented toward the idea of an essentially possible interconnectedness among things and events that he often over organizes his environment and himself. Henry reports:

> This ability to organize often results in a forced organization, however. Even though some situations arise with which they feel unfamiliar and are unable to cope, they still force an organization upon it. Thus, they bring it into the sphere of familiarity. This tendency operates partially as a mold, as a pattern into which new or unfamiliar experiences are fit.[15]

Henry concludes that the executive has a strong tendency to rely upon techniques that will work and to resist situations which do not readily fit this mold. All of which shows how strongly the executive is prepared to identify emotionally with organization and the goals of the corporation.

The intricate interconnectedness of the big industrial corporation requires vast amounts of faith in the basic benevolence of organization. In 1935 Theodore Quinn, vice president of General Electric Company and Gerard Swope's self-chosen successor, resigned while

---

[13] Gardner, *op. cit.*, p. 117.
[14] Warner and Abegglen, *op. cit.*, p. 69.
[15] W. E. Henry, "The Business Executive," *op. cit.*, p. 287.

still in his early forties. His explanation, "I began to realize that I was serving no socially worthwhile purpose in helping a giant to become even bigger." [16] In his book, *Giant Business*, he levels his charge against the monster corporations that have the unilateral power to let others live by tolerance only. He paints a gloomy picture of thousands of small subcontractors and distributors existing in a state of peonage to big business, fearful that at any time they be cut off and annihilated. He indicts the big organization for what it has done to individuals inside. He contrasts the great self-reliance and ambition of the young man of his own generation with the stunted or idealized notions of self among the young men entering the vast bureaucracy of big business today. He compares the warmth of human association found in the small business corporation wherein corporate goals are felt to be close to performance and achievement. There is, he maintains, utter inhumanity of man toward man when the corporate goals and organization are involved. "The absorption of human lives in industrial centralization, and in the techniques of less responsible mass movements, belittles the individual. The loss of conscience, mutual respect, consideration, and wholesome humanity becomes greater than any possible gain." To Quinn, what large scale organization leaves out is an essential personal interrelatedness that comes from "living out one's life in the company of people who really know each other, deep down, and who, living in one community usually face together social discipline, integration and maturity."

Many successful corporation executives will take issue with Quinn's notions of the pathology of big business organization. Individuals will see that he can act within the huge interstices that occasion big, complex organizations. Unlike Quinn, the typical executive feels that he can become a significant event in a complex of forces that are anchored around goal-achievement and organization. Besides, several studies show that the tendency to feel inadequate and to throw oneself upon the mercy of the organization is found as much or more in the small company. Porter made a study of comparative behavior of executives in small and large firms and reported that large companies produce more favorable management attitudes, greater challenges, and less conforming behavior than do smaller companies.[17] Although this study is not adequate, what seems clear is that an individual without the capacity to seek out the silent

---

[16] Theodore S. Quinn, *Giant Business* (New York: Citadel Press, 1950); and *Unconscious Public Enemies* (New York: Citadel Press, 1956).

[17] L. W. Porter, "Where Is the Organization Man," *Harvard Business Review* (November-December, 1963), pp. 53-61.

opportunities that exist about him, whether he is in large or small grouping, will become threatened by the demands of organization. This capacity seemingly hinges upon the internalization of the belief that organization is basically helpful for the purposes of self realization. Without this conventional faith, organizations large or small may become threatening.

Notions of self

Successful executives typically know who they are, where they are going, and how to get there. These notions of self greatly facilitate organized life. Because the individual feels able to exert some control over his destiny, he is capable of voluntarily entering into organized life and making responsible decisions for others. Our society provides some generally accepted notions of the kind of person one would become. Once again research is neither clear nor adequate. But it is largely believed that conventional notions of self refer to individuals who can act upon cues derived largely from within. The American stereotype of an individual is particularly relevant. He is one who has his feet solidly placed on the ground, knowing what he wants and looking forward to achieving it. It is of interest to note that almost all concepts of mental health value largely the notion that an individual should be able to stand on his own feet without making undue demands and impositions on others.[18] However, the notion of independence suggests an inner freedom that allows the possibility of choice and decision. Basic to this well accepted American stereotype is the prior idea that each human being is a unique and separate self. Maintenance and advancement of this uniqueness is the process of self-realization.

The conventional notion of self is simply a person who is capable of maintaining and achieving his essential uniqueness or individuality. Registering this essential individuality through activities of work and play becomes the implementation of this conventional notion. From this viewpoint life is a continual process of developing and realizing notions of individuality. Self-realization implies the capacity to register in activities the resources that stem from one's basic individuality.

Men at the top typically have strong notions of self. They are firm and well defined in their sense of self identity. For example, the executive may view himself as basically a judge. Clarence

---

[18] M. Jahoda, *Current Concepts of Positive Mental Health* (New York: Basic Books, 1938), p. 80.

Francis, former chairman of General Foods Corporation, has said, "Today, most managements, in fact, operate as trustees in recognition of the claims of employees, investors, consumers, and government. The task is to keep those forces in balance and to see that each gets a fair share of industry's rewards." In contrast, Robert S. McNamara, Secretary of Defense, has said, "I see my position here as being that of a leader, not a judge. I'm here to originate and stimulate new ideas and programs, not just to referee arguments and harmonize interests." Both of these executives used divergent views of themselves as career guidelines. Both notions of self center around problems of authority and goal organizing.

The Warner study shows that successful executives "know what they are and what they want and have developed techniques for getting what they want." Of course, how each gets what he wants may be different, but this strength and firmness is a common and necessary characteristic. Henry remarks that too great a firmness of self identity leads to rigidity and to inflexibility. "And while some of these executives could genuinely be accused of this, in general they maintain considerable flexibility and adaptability within the framework of their desires and within the often rather narrow possibilities of their own organization.[19]

The executive's view of himself is his most crucial tool of developing and maintaining a productive and satisfying administrative career. When threatened, his career may suffer a partial or complete setback. The search for an adequate executive identity is a central value, and when this search is restricted and limited, such as under conditions of acute threat, the executive's upward mobility is hindered, if not jeopardized. To regain feelings of upward mobility, the executive must once again conduct this search with the resources available to him. He must tap openly and productively the broad range of personality resources at a time when these very resources are being severely restricted and limited. Too few people are equipped to draw back from a conflicting situation and gain distance at such a time. Yet, it must be done somehow and to some degree if one is not to be continually overwhelmed at each point of crisis. Few human beings welcome career crises. We may speculate that few executives arrive at the top without several crises that shake their emotional foundations. At such times a very important event happens. Essentially, a threat to the executive's feeling of who he is and

---

[19] W. E. Henry, The Business Executive," *op. cit.*, p. 286.

how capably he can perform requires stepping out of one's own identity and scrutinizing it. In therapy situations the executive is encouraged to do more formally and objectively what he might otherwise have to do by himself. He is asked to examine whether what he thinks he is and what he believes he is capable of becoming is at all realistic or desirable. He takes himself as an object. This act does two things. It forces through a clearer, more precise identity or picture of himself in his capacity or role of executive. It allows him to evaluate this portrait. Interestingly enough, he will evaluate partially this identity in terms of what his authority and corporate demands and wishes suggest, and his self evaluation in light of his own personal needs and expectations. Eventually, all three must become realistically represented and a career strategy devised to lead to an eventual accommodation or balance. The end process provides a better, more reliable definition of what constitutes for that particular person the executive role. In short, although a career crisis is not openly received, it turns out to be inevitable for many at some time, and the extent to which it is resolved provides insight into how better to behave as an executive.

BASES OF THE CRISES

Since the successful executive's notions of self are highly consistent with notions of authority, the successful executive postulates authority as controlling and helpful. He identifies with the authority system and gains from this association his own notions of what constitutes proper and improper authority. Numerous studies show that middle management members identify themselves by the qualities they ascribe to their superiors.[20] These qualities serve as guides for the development of increasingly sophisticated administrative skills. The self identity of the executive emerges also as a product of a positive association and affirmation of the organization. The Rosen study shows that, "He reacts sharply and at once to its gains or losses, not primarily because he sees in the company's gain a potential advantage for himself, but rather because its gains are his gains." [21] The author has clinical experience to offer in support of this point. When the corporation achieves success, the executive enjoys satisfaction. Failure causes genuine worry regardless of how his own position is affected.

---

[20] L. W. Porter and E. E. Ghiselli, "The Self Perceptions of Top and Middle Management Personnel," *Personnel Psychology*, Vol. 10, 1960, pp. 397-406.
[21] Rosen, *op cit.*, pp. 10-20.

On top of all this, the successful executive is also an autonomous person. To be autonomous, first, means the capacity to find a productive role. This necessarily means fitting into a network of human organization. It also necessarily means submitting to the requirements of the authority system. The notion of freedom is forged within this matrix of notions of self, organization, and authority. The autonomous person has the capacity to conform to certain essentials of organization and of authority out of self choice. Thus, Reisman defines the autonomous person as one who is capable of conforming to the behavioral norms of his society—a capacity the anomic usually lacks.[22] Warner refers to the autonomous executive as one who: (1) can apply the rules of society himself, by his own decisions, (2) knows and can act on what is right and wrong, and (3) is intellectually capable of making the discriminations that are necessary in a fluid society to operate in positions that are often ambiguous. The autonomous individual is capable of making decisions from within rather than being completely dependent upon the influence of forces coming from without. Warner studies show that the typical successful executive has an autonomous self.[23] From his standpoint, notions of self that evidence autonomy stem largely from learning how to establish relations with systems of authority and corporate goal achievement that provide opportunity to achieve personalized goals and values.

The need for autonomy, however, is no guarantee of mobility and success. Warner cites a case of an executive, Evans, who moved nearly to the top of his corporation. Evans is a man who must, to accomplish his administrative goals, feel that he is free of other phases. He requires a specific goal and will work most effectively when he feels he can concentrate absolutely all his attention, thought, and efforts on that goal. Rules and people, morals and affection, are constricting and dangerous. "They are both tempting and weakening, and serve to prevent the independence and freedom for his situation that Evans requires." Evans has a good deal of difficulty in maintaining the high degree of autonomy he needs to feel comfortable. "His approach to other men is hesitant, and he feels uncertain of himself in relation to them. He mistrusts other men, feels they are thinking ahead of him and using him rather than his being in a dominant position. This causes him considerable dis-ease, and in

---

[22] D. Reisman, N. Glazer, R. Denny, *The Lonely Crowd* (New York: Doubleday, Anchor, 1953).

[23] W. L. Warner, *The Corporation in the Emergent American Society* (New York: Harper & Bros., 1962).

defense he seeks to establish his own individuality distinct from them." [24] All of which makes his relations with others unpleasant, overbearing, and aggressive, and this seemingly tough, able, independent executive becomes increasingly isolated from others. Eventually, he is given a position which allows him autonomy, but which is peripheral to the central administrative process of the firm.

Evan's case illustrates that the search and need for autonomy may create administrative isolation. We also notice how Evan's notions of self have become idealized to prevent easy relationships to significant others in the executive group. Few escape the contempt and superiority stemming from his idealized notions of self. Warner concludes that this kind of executive is seldom seen at the top. In short, notions of self also spring from within the executive as an active bearer of skills and potentials of achievement. All executives have private notions of what they are and would like to become which are brought to bear upon their performance of the administrative tasks. The successful executive has the capacity to express his self-defined needs and desires within the framework granted by the authority system to achieve self-realization. This capacity to achieve self-realization within the corporate framework provides the necessary changes that assure survival and growth. Men who are only what the corporate system requires and who take their cues solely from without are not capable of making the necessary changes that ensure corporate growth and success. In contrast, successful executives have typically strong self identities.

Faulty notions of authority, organization and self

We have seen preliminary evidence that the successful executive has a positive affirmation of the role of authority, of the goals of the corporation, and of the self as an active bearer of productive powers. The corporate triangle is essentially a set of basic notions that evolve from active participation in the administrative role. Other ingredients undoubtedly exist to enhance administrative effectiveness. But the notions represented by the AOS (authority-organization-self) frame of mind are irreducible minimums of corporate life. Leave any one of them out, and the psychological world of the executive becomes unintelligible. The trilogy of notions may be evoked by the simplest act of interrogation. Merely ask an anxious executive about his administrative responsibility, and his remarks will throw up impressions of himself, boss, and corporation.

---

[24] Warner and Abegglen, *op. cit.*, pp. 94-97.

The key factor to understanding the business executive is that the corporate triangle exists within the executive mind. It is a convenient way of referring to the events and happenings that occur within the inner world of the executive. To the individual, reality is what he perceives it to be. He does not act upon what the boss is really like, or his organization, or even himself. Rather, his behavior is based upon what he thinks his boss is like, what he thinks his corporation demands of members, what he thinks he expects of himself. The corporate triangle is not objective, of course, but subjective and wholly individual. However, he may not be cognizant of this difference. Difficulties in performing effectively as an executive are often associated with unproductive and unreal definitions of what the boss is really like or the executive's understanding of what is required to be a good corporation man may be out of proportion to actual requirements. His self image may be out of touch with his basic skills and abilities. It is interesting that these images of self, boss, and organization, that may not entirely correspond with reality, may allow for productive adjustments in the executive's behavior.

Many times in clinical situations the executive may have impressions that are not completely realistic, but allow him to achieve an inner harmony within himself or maintain a harmony with his boss and organization. Generally, however, the ingredients of the corporate triangle are not simply figments of the imagination. They must largely correspond with actual features and characteristics of the objects represented. Executives constantly search out evidence of what they, their superiors, and organizational goals are like. This is called reality testing. When they approach a new superior and new position in the corporation, they sample aspects of each. It is much like one approaches a strange food by tasting a very little of it in order to ascertain whether one wants to eat it in larger quantities. Prior experiences with a variety of foods help the individual to determine the qualities of the experience and to make statements of like and dislike.

As the young manager progresses up the corporate ladder, he constantly tests his views of his new superior, or corporation position with prior experiences. He, then, locates these objects in his own inner world. They take on meaning and value to provide a basis for operating effectively in the new function. By the time he becomes an executive at the higher levels of his organization, he has a well developed ability to detect what the powers to be and the successful achievement of corporate goals require of him. If the images evoked by these requirements of self, superiors, and organization's goals and policies are unbearable or unmanageable, the executive will experience emotional discomfort. The notion of the corporate triangle serves to provide us with a basis for pinpointing emotional problems of executives.

It is this author's view that the executive achieves administrative proficiency by learning to master the strong pressures exerted upon him by his superiors, corporate goals, and self needs and aspirations. We shall show that the pressures emanating from self, boss, and organization are complex and often inconsistent. However, they can be resolved. The promising, developing manager who adjusts to them well stands a good chance of moving higher up the ladder of power and responsibility. Those who do not make the adjustment face the prospect of stagnating in their present jobs, or falling back, or even of exhausting their emotional reserves to the point of complete breakdown.

The executive who experiences a career crisis may have faulty or unproductive notions that directly relate to the corporate triangle. He may feel despondent, inadequate, and insecure because he feels incapable of doing what the boss insists. Or he may feel humiliated, resentful, and lonely because he refuses to make the sacrifices corporate goals and purposes typically require of an executive at his high level. Or he may feel aggressive, destructive, and rebellious because he places a higher value upon his abilities and skills than others about him. Few executives do not have uncomfortable feelings at some times. When they do, they usually reveal one or several of these notions as the sources of the disturbance. Eventually, all notions will emerge as important to diagnosis and therapy. For example, an executive who suffers from an enlarged view of himself reveals in subsequent discussions with the counsellor some kind of emotional reaction to some superior and/or to some corporate value or activity. The executive who initially reveals a strong distrust of his superiors reveals an image of himself and/or his corporation that affects and gives form to his suspicions. Men who find the corporation life impossible reveal feelings toward themselves and their bosses that can not be excluded from their problem.

Few executives lack a well defined picture of themselves in the role of managers. Those who do not are without a psychic center of gravity and are a prey to the conflicting expectations and requirements of corporation life. Likewise, the consequences for a bad self image may be disastrous to the executive and his corporation. This may be illustrated by the recent near tragedy of General Dynamics, the world's biggest manufacturer of weaponry. Shortly after an ill advised venture into jet transports was started by the Convair Division, the board of directors voted to displace the dying founder of General Dynamics, Jay Hopkins, with Frank Pace, an Arkansas lawyer who had been president of West Virginia University, director of the budget and secretary of the Army. Although he had never run a business, he was confronted as chief executive officer with a highly decentralized empire, operated by strong-minded divisional heads. One of the divisions, Convair, hastily developed a jet transport that was erroneously priced below cost and styled without adequate market potential. The consequence of this failure was a 425 million dollar loss. Clearly Pace had not controlled the activities of Convair as a business executive would at the chief executive level. Pace viewed his difficulty as not being trained as a businessman. In fact, he never really viewed himself as a business executive. The question, however, is if he had this view of himself, why did he allow himself to be placed in a position that uniquely required a business executive's point of view and training. Was it because his spectacular career allowed the belief that he could handle almost any situation?

At a distance it is hard to say what may have been the reason for Pace's misplaced trust in himself and others at General Dynamics. We can suspect that improper view of one's self or failure to act upon proper self image enter much into executive failure. Did Roger Blough, chairman of the board of United States Steel, fail to see the possible political repercussions of his across the board price rise due to political naivete? During a press conference set up to explain his actions, he confessed that he knew little about politics. If he was as politically naive as he believes he was, why did he not approach an obviously political decision with more caution and advice? Was it because he did not know he was as politically dull as he appeared to himself after his unfortunate decision? No doubt he now has a different or more complete image of himself as an executive. The acquisition of a useful self image is often times painful.

Clinical experience suggests that changes in self image are based upon a need. One acquires self insight because there is some basic reason to be more aware of what one is. The executive's self image is the distillate of past experiences acquired in the performance of administrative responsibilities. In sum, we penetrate the inner world of the business executive further to see what his personal image is linked to and differentiated from the image of his authority figures, commonly called the bosses. An adult person, such as a top executive, is generally assumed to know his own identity. Nevertheless, his reply to, "Who are you?" is often hedged and qualified by his image of his boss or bosses past or present. The reason is that the executive who emerges at the top has moved up through a maze of bosses. Each is different, but all have in common the power to give and withhold. The acts of bosses often force through different notions of self.

THE PATTERN OBSERVED

The presence of all three notions does not mean that each is *equally* represented in the executive mind. Some executives are preoccupied with what they are and who likes or dislikes them. They may be self-centered and stand in contrast to those authority-centered executives who may be moored to the problem of handling superiors or subordinates. The corporation-centered executive may be overly sensitive to the requirements of organizational life or view with alarm the growing problems of adjusting to bureaucratic tyranny. Whatever is the case, self, authority, or organization-centered, the executive becomes such from a relatively protracted set of experiences. He usually shows a pattern going sometimes as far back as his early entrance into the business world, that involves difficulties with himself, superiors, or organization.

To be sure, not all executives show a pattern. Some seemingly experience no difficulty of an unusual degree until they reach a particular station. If studied at this time, his case could not be justifiably labelled "centered." But suppose for the first time he meets an impossible boss who scares the wits out of him. Perhaps, he handles the situation badly, only to find himself on the outside looking in. He may move to another corporation or get a transfer within, only to discover another difficult boss. After two or three extremely difficult superiors, the executive might begin to feel emotionally involved in problems of power, authority, and prerogative. He may even at times detect a dreadful fear of superiors. With a history of this duration, one could legitimately call his case authority-centered. The same history of difficulty would be equally necessary to label the next case self or organizational-centered.

It is not known how many executives are self, authority or organizational-centered. In fact, these categories were not constructed for purposes of scientific research. They came from clinical or therapeutic situations and are somewhat arbitrary because they seldom lead to successful solutions of executive problems. To say that an executive is authority-centered does little to help him. But by starting with his history of authority difficulty, a basis for bringing other aspects of the executive problem into view is provided. It is at this point that the other figures of the triangle show up. One can not become self-centered by living in a vacuum. People and activities become the basis for idealized images of one's self. Furthermore, people and activities become the agents of therapy. The only way to help an executive who has grandiose notions of self as an administrator is to help him construct a different picture of those around him and to engage in different administrative activities. The authority system and organizational goals and purposes are inextricably involved in this therapy. This is not to say that other factors are not important. However, if the executive's anxiety is anchored in his administrative role, notions of authority, organization, and self are always present and serve as the basic factors of his therapy.

History of the AOS frame

The requirements of the corporate triangle are historically verifiable. In the early, entrepreneurial stage of business activity, the problems of organization, unity, and integrity were minimal. The emotional difficulties of aspirants to the top positions were largely authority-centered. The boss was more crucial to the subordinate than the purposes or goals toward which the corporation was operationally directed. These were totally the boss's concern. Authority was directly and overtly exercised, and the boss set himself up as a model. He tended to believe in a sharp separation between work and pleasure and tended to feel personally threatened by idleness and apathy. One had to love to work, which meant to show high respect and regard for the dictates of the boss. There was high use of punishment or coercion in enforcing this strict relationship of submission and deference to his authority.

In this authority-centered period of American business, the trusted subordinate often adjusted by internalizing the norms, values, and beliefs of his chief boss. He became an extension of his chief in his own conception of himself, while at the same time he performed at an emotional distance from him. The development of a substantially broadened base of corporate activity forced the need for a more cooperative form of executive behavior. Instead of a single authority center, groups and committees, formal and informal, sprung up to give overall direction to the massive concern. Participation brought on an enlarged consciousness of the total base of corporate activity. A high use of indulgence and casualness in dealing with superiors and subordinates proceeded to shrink the emotional distance between superior and subordinates. Communication, reasonableness, and human relations became crucial qualities. The effect was to allow the aspiring executive to become more attached to the ongoing purposes and goals of the corporation. The corporation became emotionally alive in the subordinate executives as an identity which, as such, was useful to them as an instrument of administration. Executives who moved to the top learned to feel an obligation to the goals and purposes of the firm that transcended the personal interests of themselves and their bosses.

The executive today must be as organization-minded as his predecessor was authority-centered.[25] By this is meant that the executive does not think separately of the interests of the stockholder, the employees, and the customers. On the contrary, this new executive thinks of the interests of his corporation, without regard to the special interest of stockholder, workers or customers. It exists as a total psychologized reality. This reality is basically the essential interconnectedness of the many interest groups that press claims upon him. It is this organization or interrelatedness of these claimant interests that give the executive his concept of the corporation. To this concept he attaches his notions of self. The result is that he thinks and acts as if it were his corporation, even if he has no ownership share in it. As Katona shows, when the corporation achieves success, the executive enjoys satisfaction. Deterioration causes genuine worry, regardless of how his own position is affected.[26] It is interesting to speculate that executives today enjoy more autonomy because of the emergence of meaningful identification with corporate goals alongside authority expectations. Executive authority is more rational because it is justified more on the basis of the objective necessities of efficient corporate goal achievements and less on the rights of command.

The development of organization-minded executives does not occur in a vacuum. Someone or group must initiate and reinforce this form of identification. This is where the bosses come in. The executive is not simply a corporation or organization-centered man. Today, he must be very cognizant of the role of personal, unmediated authorities. He must be every bit as cognizant of authority figures as the executive at the turn of the century. Unlike him, the present executive must assume a high identification with the corporation as an entity. In short, the executive's psychic center of gravity pivots around two forms of awareness, authority and organizational. But

[25] See Ernest Dale, *The Great Organizers* (New York: McGraw-Hill, 1960).
[26] See George Katona, *Psychological Analysis of Economic Behavior* (New York: McGraw-Hill, 1951), p. 197.

there is still one more base upon which executive identity develops. It is the expectations that the executive himself levies upon himself, in addition to those placed upon him by the requirements of authority and corporate goal achievement.

Arriving Is Departing

The making of an executive occurs within an array of successful separations and attachments. Movement within the ranks of the corporate hierarchy necessarily involves the capacity to become emotionally attached to authority figures and corporate goals as found in the particular work situation. Movement up requires the capacity to detach from previous managerial activities and attach to new conditions. For an upward aspiring junior executive there is a consistent, inward directing force that guides his upward advances. This inner force allows an easy separation from present activities and productive attachments to new assignments. He welcomes these changes because of the intense desire to achieve. For the upward and mobile, achievement is centered in striving to get closer and closer to the heart of the administrative process. The central values and goals of the firm are represented by the activities of the executive's group. This group is charged with the responsibility of charting the overall and long range direction of the firm and administering these strategies through organization. Success is measured by steady progress toward the central administrative processes symbolized by line and staff people in the executive group. Because the mobile executive has a high need to achieve ever larger and larger administrative challenges, arrestment of this upward mobility is interpreted as threat to the opportunity to realize the potentialities of the self. Anxiety or feelings of inadequacy or incapability are cued off by arrestment of mobility. Clinical evidence gathered from counselling mobile executives shows that the dynamic basis of anxiety is the threat of becoming separated from the central administrative tasks of the firm. Administrative anxiety is also the fear that one can not successfully remove the blocks that have been thrown up to the upward striving manager. Administrative anxiety also occasions the president who has arrived at the top but who feels a growing sense of threat to his remaining there.

Executives who face separation from the central administrative tasks of the firm, and junior executives who incur arrestment of movement toward those central tasks, feel the essential elements of a career crisis. A career crisis is a crisis of self. Invariably it involves a narrowing of awareness to basically include problems of authority, organizational goals and performance, and self. Administrative anxiety is normal to all those who traverse to corporate structures. Whenever one separates and attaches, there is a degree of anxiety. There are three basic points at which anxiety is most likely to occur. The first is the anxiety upon entrance into the firm. Entrance anxiety essentially ensues from having to make a separation from college life and the unstable commitments of early adulthood. The attachment to the firm is generally made in a technical sense. This entrance phase, lasting about five years, places the individual in a formal or informal training program. If he has no technical skill acquired in college, this may be acquired in the entrance phase. The junior executive's attachments are basically those of one who is or becomes technically qualified in accounting, engineering, sales, personnel, or some other functional activity. The second point is movement into the middle ranks essentially which requires dropping behind technical attachments and acquiring managerial attachments. The middle ranks are essentially managerial. Here the technical skill is found in the manager's subordinates. He is required to know how to manage them to accomplish departmental and sectional goals. Accountants, salesmen, engineers, and scientists too often want to keep their technical expertise. They become anxious at making the separations and attachments required of managers.

The third point of anxiety is to meet the requirements of administration as opposed to management. Activity in the middle and upper middle ranks is essentially operating in nature. It is concerned with setting of specific suborganization goals within the confines of overall policy directives from the top. Activity at the top is concerned with developing overall corporate strategy and designing organized structures to achieve goals and purposes of the firm. It concerns appraising and evaluating corporate achievement. Here the operating mind of the manager must be left behind and strategical, evaluative, long range concern of administration must be acquired. Separation from the operating orientation and attachment to the administrative orientation proves difficult for many.[27] Different notions of authority, different orientations toward the corporation, and different images of self are involved in all three of these transitions. The capacity to separate and attach without incurring acute feelings of anxiety is crucial to the making of a corporate executive.[28] The present con-

---

[27] A. D. Chandler, Jr., *Strategy and Structure* (Cambridge, Mass.: Massachusetts Institute of Technology, 1962).
[28] Warner and Abegglen, *op. cit.*, p. 100.

cern of this author is with administrative anxeity. We aren't here concerned with the nature and basis of anxiety producing situations in the big business corporation, and the effects upon the manner in which executives perform their administrative functions. Many problems of these men are unprecedented and novel. They must make decisions about corporate goals that are not clearly related to the traditional needs of business enterprise. They are men with tremendous power without the traditional restraints of business authority. They are men whose activities occur within a small group at the top. This small group has replaced the individual as the practical unit of top administration.

The development of strong notions of self confidence and esteem are today complicated by the lack of traditional authority, the division of complex, externally oriented corporate goals, and the emergence of a corporate oligarchy. For most, anxiety is so common and prevalent that it becomes an unconscious force in their careers. For some, administrative anxiety becomes the eventual cause of breakdown and failure. The costs to the firm of executive failures are unknown. The consequences to society of neurotic behavior leading to poor judgment are equally unknown. It can be assumed that the potential hazards to firms and society are great. In a society highly dependent upon the productive efficiency of huge business corporations, the question of executive anxiety and failure can no longer be secondary to matters traditionally studied as economics. When firms were competitive, executive failure was cancelled out by the market forces, and society was not directly jeopardized. Big business corporations by their very essence make the personalities of the men at the top count in the affairs of national welfare.

Conclusion

In conclusion, this penetration of the mind of an executive in a career crisis points out the need to master the strong pressures inherent in the corporate triangle. These pressures are often complex and inconsistent but they can be resolved. The manager who adjusts well to them stands a good chance of moving higher up the ladder of success. Those who do not make the adjustment face the prospect of stagnating in their present jobs, or falling back, or even of exhausting their emotional resources to a point of complete breakdown. Any one of these results could spin off a terrible career crisis.

QUESTIONS

1. What is the corporate triangle? How does it primarily affect the manager?
2. What is a managerial career crisis? How does a typical manager react to such a crisis?
3. How does the issue of authority affect the executive according to Jennings?
4. What are the self-notions typical of the top executive?
5. How do you compare Jennings' ideas to Ghiselli's and Henry's?

GENERAL QUESTIONS ON PART II

1. List all of the so-called traits necessary for executive success noted in this section. To what extent do they overlap or conflict?
2. Do you think this listing is all-inclusive? Do you agree that it gives a realistic portrayal of today's new breed of managers and executives?
3. Which of the articles in this section do you feel most realistically portrays the business executive? Why?
4. Compare yourself and your personal "makeup" to the managerial image depicted in this section. Do you think you "have what it takes" according to this image? Why or why not?
5. Do you think there is value in studying the executive personality? If so, what values are there to: (a) the business firm and (b) the individual.
6. What differences do you note between the governmental versus the business executive? Would their organizational values be different?
7. Do you see any differences between the entrepreneur and the professional manager?
8. Do you think it important to classify managing as a profession? What would be the advantages? Disadvantages?
9. Some people suggest that managers, especially in large organizations, should be tested and licensed like physicians and lawyers. Do you agree? Why or why not?
10. What is the managerial role?

PART III. LEADERSHIP

Even though the subject of leadership has grown in recent years to the point where it can almost be considered a discipline in itself, it should be noted that our original contention still holds true, namely, that human relations in the context of the business environment is in great part the story of leadership. The reason for this is predicated on the fact that human relations, as a body of knowledge, is concerned with the behavior of industrial man. Because the leader's fundamental responsibility in any form of organization is to get work done through people, and because he can achieve this only by successfully influencing the behavior of the human beings to whom work has been assigned, it follows that the leader must be thoroughly acquainted with the forces and factors that cause and influence human behavior. In other words, he must know and understand the basic principles, concepts, and techniques of human relations. As the format of this book indicates, therefore, leaders, whether they be foremen, supervisors, executives, or what have you, must, in their difficult and complex task of collecting and collating the efforts of others to achieve a common goal, effectively motivate their subordinates by communicating to them, training and developing them, preparing them for changes, counseling them, and so on. For unless they do these things, they cannot possibly hope to accomplish the objectives of the organization. Consequently, it seems clear that the key to effective leadership is human relations.

Although human relations is an integral part of the leadership function, it is not, of course, the only responsibility a leader has or the only knowledge he needs. In fact, there are many things a leader must know and do long before contact with human beings becomes necessary. These "things" include, generally speaking, the basic managerial functions involved in all leadership positions, namely, planning, organizing, coordinating, and controlling work. But to consider these functions here is beyond the scope of this book. The serious student of leadership must, therefore, direct his investigation toward additional fields of knowledge, particularly those of management, psychology, and sociology if he wishes to perceive the totality of the leader's job. What is important to recognize here, however, is that managerial functions such as planning, organizing, coordinating, and controlling all lead to the determination of work that must be performed by human beings. If this were not true, there would be no need for leaders—managers. To be a leader, therefore, requires that one have people to lead. And the purpose of leading these people is to get done work that we have determined must be done. This, as we said before, requires the practice of human relations.

Approaches to Leadership

It is axiomatic that a leader's success in getting work done through others depends to a great degree on his knowledge of the principles, concepts, and techniques of human relations—and his ability to apply that knowledge. Equally evident is the fact that knowledge of the process of leadership per se is critically related to the art of influencing human behavior. That is to say, simply knowing what causes people to behave and how to influence human behavior will not necessarily insure successful leadership. Consequently, to understand the totality of the nature of leadership, it is also necessary to investigate and understand the components and process of the function itself.

Because many of the writings in this section explore the nature of leadership in detail, no attempt will be made here to definitively analyze the many and diverse views of the leadership process. Instead, it is hoped that the following brief review of some of the approaches that have been used to investigate leadership and to explain its nature will help the reader organize and clarify his thoughts as he probes this area further.

Trait aproach

One of the earliest approaches to the study of leadership is called the trait theory. Utilizing an inductive procedure, researchers and writers in this area have attempted to explain leadership on the basis of personality traits and characteristics of successful leaders. Ordway Tead, for example, insists that there are ten qualities that are essential for effective leadership, namely, physical and nervous energy, a sense of purpose and direction, enthusiasm, friendliness and affection, integrity, technical mastery, decisiveness, intelligence, teaching skill, and faith.[1] Chester I. Barnard, on the other hand, lists such factors as physique, skill, technology, perception, knowledge, memory, imagination, determination, persistence, endurance, and courage.[2]

Examination of Tead's and Barnard's lists indicates immediately a basic difficulty with the traitist approach, namely, that seldom, if ever, do any two lists agree on the essential traits and characteristics of effective leadership. The net result is that of confusion, predicated on a foundation of generalities and semantical problems. Because of these difficulties and numerous other considerations, such as size of sample, period of time covered, and so on, it is not surprising to find many other researchers who vehemently disagree with the traitist theory.

Type approach

Another basic attempt to explain the nature of leadership is that of the *leadership-type* approach. Researchers following this route have concluded that there are essentially four types of leaders: (1) the dictatorial leader; (2) the autocratic leader; (3) the democratic leader; and (4) the laissez-faire leader.

Dictatorial leadership, according to this approach, is that type of leadership which gets work done through fear. The dictatorial leader—or negative leader as he is frequently called—holds over the heads of his subordinates the threat of penalties and punishment, such as discharge, demotion, poor ratings that may prevent promotions or wage increases, and so on. The theory is that the followers, in order not to lose the means of satisfying some of their needs and wants, are motivated to do what the leader tells them to do. Although this type of leadership apparently gets results, there is serious doubt that the quantity and the quality of the results achieved can remain high over the long run, particularly in view of the fact that the results obtained are frequently accompanied by the dissatisfaction of those led.

Autocratic leadership is characterized by centralization of authority and decision making in the leader. Although this type of leader tends to emphasize neither negative nor positive leadership, he motivates his subordinates by forcing them to rely upon him for need satisfaction. As such, he takes full authority and responsibility for

---

[1] Ordway Tead, *The Art of Leadership* (New York: McGraw-Hill Book Company, Inc., 1935), p. 83.

[2] Chester I. Barnard, *The Functions of the Executive* (Cambridge, Mass.: Harvard University Press, 1938), p. 260.

the work to be done. He permits no participation in the decision-making process and tolerates no deviations from what he has told his followers to do. This type of leadership also gets results. But it suffers from the serious disadvantage that it can be only as good as the leader is. If the leader is weak and inefficient, the followers will be weak and inefficient.

Democratic leadership, unlike autocratic leadership, is based on decentralization of authority and decision making. This type of leader is characterized by the degree to which he consults with his subordinates on problems, goals, and tasks that face him and the group as a whole. The theory behind this type of leadership is that it encourages the followers to function as a social unit and that it makes full use of the talents and abilities of the members of the group. As a result, the subordinates achieve a greater measure of belonging and recognition, which motivates them to higher levels of efficiency. Although some people do not agree with this, there is, nevertheless, general agreement that democratic leadership offers more promise to industry than any other type of leadership. It suffers, however, from the disadvantage of requiring a better quality of leader.

Laissez-faire leadership, or *free-rein leadership* as it is popularly called, exists when the leader allows the group to establish its own goals and make its own decisions. Usually the only contact the leader has with the group occurs when he provides it with the information it needs to get a job done. As such, he makes little contribution to over all effort. The net result is frequently disorganization or chaos, primarily because this type of leadership permits different individuals to proceed in different directions.

Situational approach

A more recent and generally acceptable approach to the study of leadership is that of the situationalists. According to these advocates, leadership is specific and always relative to the particular situation in which it occurs. Therefore, who becomes the leader or who is the leader of a given group engaging in a particular activity is a function of the total situation, which includes not only the leader and the subordinates and other groups to which the leader is related, but also myriad other human, physical, organizational, and time variables as well. In essence, situationists are more concerned with finding new ways of identifying leaders than they are with developing a theory of leadership.

A basic conclusion of the situationist approach is that the successful leader must be adaptive and flexible. As the situation changes, whether it be from minute to minute or from day to day, so must the leader change his style of leadership. Consequently, at any one point in time he may display certain traits and characteristics and follow the format of a particular type of leadership, whereas at another point in time he may display an entirely different set of traits and follow another type of leadership. If this conclusion is accepted, it does offer some logical explanation for the confusion that exists in and between the traitist and the type approaches. However, much empirical work needs to be done before this conclusion can be validated. And therein lies a problem for the situationists, for in this approach even the measuring instruments that are employed become a part of the situation and thereby influence it.

Other approaches

Although space does not permit a detailed examination of them, there are several other approaches to the study of leadership that should be briefly mentioned here. One of these approaches is to analyze leadership from the viewpoint of the *group* involved. Advocates of this approach maintain that the success of the leader is determined in many ways by his subordinates. Accordingly, these researchers investigate the makeup of groups and the actions and interactions of the members within it. Another approach is that of *organization*. Followers of this approach view leadership as a functional relationship between leader, followers, and organization. Although closely akin to the situationist approach, it is usually concerned, however, only with the structure of leadership.

Even though much confusion and disagreement exists in our present state of knowledge of leadership, there are signs that some day the various approaches to this important function will be combined into highly organized, interdisciplinary research. When this occurs, our understanding of leadership will become clearer than ever before. As a result, industry in particular and mankind in general should benefit immeasurably.

LEADERSHIP STYLE

Before closing this introductory section, it should be pointed out that anyone who is in a supervisory or managerial position should be cognizant of both his style of leadership and the impact of that style on the behavior of others. The reason for this is simple. The leader's efforts to influence the behavior of people, which is his fundamental task, are obviously related to his perception and understanding of the nature and process of leadership. In other words, he will behave as a leader—or develop a leadership style—in accordance with his conception of the leadership role. It follows, therefore, that the more acquainted the leader is with himself, his assumptions and beliefs regarding human behavior, his leadership style, and the relationship of that style to the performance of subordinates, the better able he will be to more effectively influence human behavior. This is particularly clear in view of the fact that any change in one's efforts to influence others must of necessity demand and follow a change in the leader himself. Consequently, if the leader wishes to improve his ability to change the behavior of others, he must first and foremost change his own behavior. And to do this, he must not only be aware of how he behaves as a leader, but also how his behavior affects the performance of others.

Although we have not yet established an objective yardstick that can be used to evaluate leadership performance, it must be recognized that the boundaries of our knowledge of the nature and function of the leader's role do permit some self-assessment of managerial behavior. For example, the rather generally accepted conclusion of the situationalists, namely, that leadership is always relative to the situation and that, consequently, the leader must be able to adapt and adjust to each situation, clearly provides the manager with at least two criteria against which he can compare his own conception and style of leadership. These criteria are, of course, sensitivity (that is, the ability to perceive and understand the needs of human beings and the myriad situations with which the leader is faced every day) and the flexibility to adapt and adjust to each situation so that the style or approach to leadership that is demanded or warranted by the situation can be manifested.

Our knowledge regarding the various types of leadership and the effects of each type on the behavior of subordinates should also serve as benchmarks for self-evaluation. Although such assessment undoubtedly requires a rather high degree of personal sensitivity to begin with, it should not be too difficult for the informed person to honestly and objectively determine if he is predominantly autocratic, dictatorial, laissez-faire, or democratic in nature. If he is willing to admit that he is more one of these than the others, he should also be willing to admit that there is considerable room for improvement in his leadership style. This assumes, of course, that he accepts the fact that the world of work, composed as it is of diverse and complex human situations, usually requires the leader to practice all known types of leadership. In fact, it is entirely possible that he may have to do so at various points of time with each of his subordinates. Armed with such information, however, he should be in a much better position to change his own behavior and, hence, more effectively influence the behavior of others.

Because space does not permit a more thorough analysis of the facets of our knowledge of the nature of leadership—facets that can be used to assess and develop one's own leadership style, the reader is of necessity charged with the responsibility of developing these benchmarks as he pursues his study of this area and of conscientiously measuring himself against them. Although this will admittedly be a difficult task, it is nevertheless a task that must be done, and can only be done, by the individual himself. Unless he is willing to accept and do this, he cannot possibly hope to improve his ability to get work done through others. This undeniable fact is predicated again on the simple truth that an attempt to change the behavior of a subordinate requires and can only follow a change in the behavior of the leader. Knowing one's self, therefore, is an integral and critically important part of the nature and process of leadership.

Although much research and writing have been done on the leadership function, it is surprising to discover how little we actually know about it and how much of what we know is subject to widespread disagreement. It is gratifying to note, however, that in recent years considerable organization and clarity of thought have been achieved in the study of this area. That is not to say, of course, that we have solidified our knowledge of this important process. On the contrary, it is obvious that much work remains to be done—that, in fact, we are only beginning to combine our efforts into highly organized, interdisciplinary research. But, as the articles that follow indicate, the confusion and contradictions are beginning to disappear, and a new discipline is beginning to emerge.

In choosing the following articles, an attempt was made to pick those that will help the reader gain greater insight into the nature of and the complexities of leadership per se and the approaches used to study and explain it. Jennings' article was chosen, therefore, because it is a comprehensive and penetrating analysis of the "anatomy of leadership." Golembiewski's article was selected because it contains a review of research findings and analyzes the difficulties of choosing a leadership style. The article by Bavelas was picked because it is an excellent commentary on the distinction between the idea of leadership as a personal quality and the idea of leadership as an organizational function. Tannenbaum and Schmidt's article was included not only because it is now a classic in its field but also because it definitively develops the requirements of situational leadership. And, last of all, Spotts' article was selected because it contains an excellent analysis of the various approaches to the study of leadership. If the reader will study the content of these articles and integrate, compare, and contrast the information they contain, his understanding of the nature of leadership should become clearer and more useful to him. As a result, his own style of leadership should become more apparent and meaningful, not only in terms of how he behaves as a leader but also in terms of how his behavior affects the behavior of others.

14. THE ANATOMY OF LEADERSHIP *

Eugene Emerson Jennings

We hear often that ours is an age without heroes and that business is without leaders. The towering personalities of the past seem, to some, to have considerably more specific gravity than their successors of today.

This indictment, while containing some truth—more, in fact, than should leave us feeling comfortable—overlooks the rugged individualists still on the business stage; more than a handful of flamboyant entrepreneurs and, throughout the ranks of business, aggressive, assertive individuals who openly or secretly hunger for leadership roles.

Nonetheless, the charge that we have allowed leadership to lapse as a necessary executive art deserves close examination. In too many companies the careful man has replaced the tycoon who was willing, in an earlier time, to take uncommon risks by boldly seizing initiative. Decision-making has become diffused, decentralized and impersonal in many organizations.

Why this has happened is, to some extent, an inevitable result of social and economic change. The unrestrained, owner-managed enterprises of the late 19th and early 20th centuries are no more. Ownership of our largest and even many of our smallest organizations is today dispersed, and direction flows not from an ownership caste but from cadres of professional managers who are responsible to boards of directors, to government regulators, to organized workers and to a fickle consuming public.

But more important than why the climate of leadership has changed is that today's business organization, and tomorrow's, will require a new breed of restless men with imagination—men perhaps not cut from the same cloth as the old titans but nonetheless ready and able to break free of conventional procedure and move into untried fields. The problem, therefore, is: How can business encourage its managers and managerial aspirants to assume a more vigorous leadership role?

Today's approach to leadership

The term "leadership" is indiscriminately applied to such varied activities as playground supervisor, committee chairman, club president, business executive, and politician. Furthermore, research has

* From *Management of Personnel Quarterly*, Vol. 1, No. 1 (Autumn, 1961), pp. 2-9. Reprinted with permission.

produced such a variegated list of traits presumably to describe leadership that, for all practical purposes, it describes nothing. Fifty years of study have failed to produce one personality trait or set of qualities that can be used to discriminate between leaders and non-leaders.

This failure to identify leadership traits in individuals has led us to look elsewhere for the keys to leadership. If a person does not become a leader because he possesses a particular pattern of personality characteristics, maybe he becomes a leader because of something outside of him; that is, the situation determines which men will rise and be chosen to leadership.

The transfer from the personality to the situation has altered our whole approach to leadership. The situational approach appealed to our ideal of democracy, our belief in the impact of the environment on the individual and our need to do something quickly about our shortage of leaders. Because it denied that leaders are born and affirmed that leaders are made, this approach stimulated a deluge of executive training and leadership development programs.

No doubt leaders often need propitious moments to rise. Without such occasions they might remain unknown. In this sense, the situation is indeed influential, but need not be determining. *First*, aggressive action can sometimes overcome a difficult situation. *Second*, initiative often helps determine what the situation actually is. The individual manager can never know the exact situation unless he pits himself vigorously against it. It is in striving to overcome adversity that he finds his full capacity for leadership. This is a fact too often forgotten today.

Admittedly, great events in history are always a marriage between the man and the circumstances, but what is crucial is which predominates. The fact is that the situation holds within it the distinct possibility of several different leaders rising to power. The "right man for the right situation" is a subtle but lethal kind of fatalistic thinking that must not be cultivated if business is to maintain its necessarily dynamic and creative nature.

What leaders do

Where modern measurement fails to define leadership, history offers some suggestions. Plato, for example, conceived his ideal society as having three occupational classes—workers and slaves, guardians, and philosophers. In this society the king would draw up the plans and the philosophers would carry them out with the aid of the civil service and military officers comprising the guardian class. Here we have a specific distinction between leadership and execution. Leadership determines the overall plan and infuses the system with a character and direction that could not come by keeping close to the day-to-day stream of problems.

Hence the leader is a beginner of plans carried out by an executive. Machiavelli, Carlyle, Nietzsche, William James, Woodrow Wilson, John Dewey, Lenin, Franklin D. Roosevelt and Churchill all made similar distinctions. Few who have given thought to this distinction have failed to find merit in it. The leader's role is initiating, beginning. It is born of imagination and a sense of mission. It involves great personal risk.

The executive may bring about changes too, but they are of the type warranted by the situation and appropriate to the organization. He operates more in terms of active needs that can be handled by immediate supervision. Consequently, he does not substantially change the character or direction of his organization.

Although both types are needed, few leaders make good executives and few executives make good leaders. It is the rare man who excels at both.

Who are today's leaders?

If, in today's society, we are replacing dynamic men with efficient men, the next question is: What causes this imbalance? The answer may be provided by a closer look at the qualities of leaders. They are found in the sense of purpose, power and self-confidence. In numerous studies of both contemporary and historical figures, these three qualities stand out as essential to fulfilling the role of leadership. When any one of these qualities is lacking, leadership suffers.

Bureaucracy limits leadership

Men who lead must have vision of real possibilities of the future and must articulate them to the people. This ability to raise one's sights, to get above the struggle, to see beyond triviality, is becoming increasingly rare. We may disparage the men who today see only dimly what tomorrow will clearly need to be done, but there is a condition which subsumes all of us. This condition is one of bureaucratic stagnation. In a society such as ours, there is the strong tendency to develop a civil-service mentality. Our whole society is developing this bureaucratic mind in business, unions, church, school and government.

The individual's role is largely identified by the position he occupies, and these positions, in turn, are systematically integrated to provide the highest degree of coordination and efficiency possible. Public distrust of the bureaucracy is not a reaction against inefficiency, however. The bureaucracy is quite efficient in most cases, due to its emphasis on coordination and efficiency to the exclusion of all other goals. It is a common characteristic of the bureaucratic individual that, while his single-mindedness brings specific events into sharper focus, he is blind to the periphery beyond which lies a different world.

Bureaucratic society assigns each individual his functions, the area of his authority and the standards of proficiency. The worker is harnessed in to ensure the exact performance essential to keep the huge system under control. If any sort of decision is assigned to him or demanded of him, it is duly taken within the limited province of his function without his having to delve to the bottom of things. Duties and regulations laid down to guide him are applied meticulously in such a manner that risk is avoided. There is no semblance of a genuinely creative community of action, let alone sensitive insight into things above and beyond. Initiative is not possible to any great degree or the whole system would fall apart. Risk is eliminated by the sacred adoption of the system's rational rules and regulations, even though they appear irrational to the individual.

Greatness—or efficiency?

In a society becoming heavily bureaucratic, as we are, great men are subordinated to efficient men. The executive type has dethroned the leader. Plato's "achievement" is without its antecedent "beginner." No one person really "begins." Man is enmeshed at all times in an intricate set of relationships that prohibits his seizing the helm and steering a course of his own choosing. Our community "leaders" of today rarely want to shoulder responsibility. They seldom want to decide anything without endorsement. Some committee, group or precedent must be represented in everything they do and upon which they can shift the onus if things go wrong. In the bureaucratic society, the ultimate court of appeal is a previous set of actions that have become a method or system held consecrate because at one time, when things were less complex, it more visibly promoted the general interest. The ends were more within assessment. Upon this method or system, in one of its multifarious forms, accrues the individual's final responsibility. Each individual is a tiny wheel with a fractional share in the decision, but no one effectively decides.

But all of this is consciously realized by many people; many rebel, some silently and some openly. They feel so intimately interlocked in social processes that they do not know how much they rely upon others and their system. Leadership is not a conscious problem to people today because they are not conscious of themselves as leaders. They wonder curiously about what people mean who refer to them as leaders.

The bureaucratic mode of human existence destroys heroic vision. We are today a relatively unpurposeful society. So much is this the concern today that Eisenhower ordered a commission to look into national goals. Luce of Time-Life, Inc., ordered a series of articles on "What Is Our National Purpose?" It is interesting that neither endeavor created much of a national reaction. No great movements for change and reform have emerged. But yet, to speak intelligently today of our national purpose is beyond our ability, so long have we become accustomed to seeing the parts, not the whole, immediate aims rather than long-range goals.

Bureaucracy and the civil-service mentality have contributed in the past to the destruction of the Roman and British empires. They are presently engulfing the individual in America, his ability to see and feel beyond his role or commitment.

Organizations demand conservatism

This lack of heroic vision makes individuals "all too executive." Today all too many executives merely add their dots to a series of dots reflecting the evolving histories of their organizations. Under the ethic of finishing the unfinished task started by his great predecessors, this type of executive receives the advantages and benefits of power-seeking without incurring the risk of the leader's attempt at major innovation. In short, he seeks success and personal advantage but does not have a sense of purpose or historical opportunity.

The illusive and masquerading feature of all of this is that the organization typically continues to get bigger. Someone usually gets credit for the growth partly because giving credit is a strong habit carried over from our heroic past. The mania for bigness is, however, a perfect example of how many executives today fit into the on-going direction and character of their organizations in such a manner that they merely midwife the enterprises through what are

actually predetermined courses. There is no change from the normal
or expected pattern of growth as a consequence of his personal
efforts, but rather only a continued increase in size and complexity
under the illusion of heroic leadership.

It simply is not fair for the executive under these circumstances
to be given the title of a leader since change is really not change
after all.

The power struggle

In other words, power is a disruptive and reformative—a creative
—tool in the care of a leader. The power of one who acts as an
executive is a sustaining and maintaining—a conservative—tool.
Many executives today do not have a strong creative opportunity or
sense of purpose but have the same drive for power as their predecessors. An individual who has a strong drive for power, but who
does not have a strong purpose to which he can attach that drive,
would necessarily appear more power-seeking than he might actually
be. There is, of course, a lot to be said for the argument that his
power drive may tend to increase in the absence of an objective
goal that will give it form and sanction. But in either case, the very
"nakedness" of his power-seeking would seem to prompt him to
inhibit it, which in turn brings on a psychological condition whereby
it becomes even more difficult to develop heroic thrust. If we keep in
mind, then, that the problem of many executives today is that they
must appear to be thrusting and aggressive while at the same time
not appear to be too power-seeking, we have in capsule the essence
of what they are trying to do. In other words, how to extricate themselves from these paradoxical demands is indeed the key to their
success today.

One reason why all too few executives wish to have power to
accomplish great and noble things is that the power struggle involves
considerable personal risk. To remove the risk one must, of course,
make his power permanent. But in making his power permanent the
executive cannot make it apparent, for in doing so he necessarily
makes enemies of both those who are equally driven by the same urge
and those who abhor the evil effects that power brings to both the
organization and the personality of the individual. Implementing the
power drive subtly and silently is a delicate skill that separates the
power elite from the more common contenders. It is extremely difficult to learn the rules of acquiring through subtle means the necessary power with which to control others. It is for this reason that

many executives fail to achieve the power necessary to effect major changes.

We might note that the price of failure is, often more than not, forfeiture of the gains won by the attempt at leadership. This penalty often includes the loss of executive position. So the accepted pattern of many executives has become to gain power and make it permanent by not personally causing or sponsoring major innovations. For them it is safer to use power as a conservative force than as a creative force. Consequently, this kind of executive is not only as interested in gaining power as was his predecessor, but he is today incomparably more skilled in gaining and maintaining his power than in knowing and using his power for creative purposes.

The executive who makes the mistake of emerging into the fierce light of daring leadership is apt to become caught in dilemmas his talents are inadequate for resolving.

Furthermore, a major innovation is something that requires time to work itself out. Even if the program goes on to achieve success in heroic proportions, the executive could be knocked off because of an errant move in the interim. Anyone who takes long chances will find that the averages are against him. This we found to be an axiom of political experience. Major changes set loose unknown forces that gather a momentum of their own and smash through to results unwanted by anyone, including the executive. Consequently, it is far wiser to sponsor many minor changes that only appear to be tests of ability although they must, of course, be beneficial to the organization, and many executives are becoming aware of this fact.

Using group responsibility

One favorite technique of many executives today is to place the responsibility for major changes in the hands of groups and thus shield themselves from the responsibility of complete failure. The idea here is to delegate to the "responsible group" those problems that are of major significance. By this means, the executive assumes more "individual responsibility" for the more numerous minor innovations with the thought that many minor innovations will give heroic stature more easily than one major change, especially one that hazards failure or is cushioned by group responsibility. In effect, the strategy is to become cumulatively heroic through acts that are so integrated as to compound themselves.

It may be argued that this new conservatism is made possible partly by large bureaucratic organizations wherein decisions must be increasingly made by the group method. Since the group is generally more conservative than the individual, the executive naturally becomes less radical and creative. Then too, the increasing use of group meetings, both formal and informal, has forced out into the open the good intentions of the executive. As long as the executive could personally and privately deal with his superiors, subordinates and peers, he did not have to reveal or fear to reveal his intentions toward power. He received ethical justification under the code of enlightened self-interest.

But the convening of a group makes it imperative for the ambitious executive to manifest the most noble intentions simply because a group has a moral quality that is not found in the members taken separately. All good princes today know that in such quasipublic gatherings as conferences, committees and even informal meetings, one must never be anything less than noble and moral and, above all, never appear too eager or overtly ambitious. The revealed ambition of an executive is grossly magnified by the ratio of the number of group members who witness the accidental dropping of his disguise. This means that in group meetings the executive today must hide his apparent need and drive for power by not being radically different, or at least not standing pat on a radical program. He knows that sponsoring a terribly different idea automatically forces him to draw upon the total power resources available to him. This is never done today.

Taking the limited offensive

The third characteristic of a leader is his strong inner will to resist forces that might move him away from his mission or purpose. He must be strong in character and use the full force of his personality. There is a growing tendency today in our society to assume a limited offensive. For many, the mark of the successful individual is that he never uses the full potential of his personality. Of course, no one ever uses the full potential of his personality, but we are concerned here that many an executive uses increasingly less. This lack of self-directedness shows up in his interpersonal relations. He is calm but engaging, argumentative at times but not disagreeable, alert but not too trusting. He approaches people easily but also he is able to move out when he gets involved. The word is "heavy" when he talks about the conversations he seeks to avoid. When caught unavoidably in a "heavy," he has the skill to work problems through to a convenient and acceptable solution, but in those cases his personality is invariably engaged on behalf of calming the disturbances, restoring the equilibrium and thwarting accusations of being "difficult."

In all cases, blows of lethal and total effectiveness must never be swung, even in the form of words. It is far better to succeed a little bit than to destroy the opposition completely, which always brings trouble later because of bitterness and recrimination. Pleasantries can never remove the pain of a grievous offense. This kind of individual believes strictly in a limited offensive with maximum opportunity for numerous engage-disengage sequences that will persuade but not offend. Above all, he must not make apparent his resources as an individual apart from his position, because of the tendency to impute ambition to the individual who shows personal talents that are not directly identified with the accepted norms and practices of his function and position. In other words, there is a tendency to confuse the individual with his formal rank and function in the hierarchy.

No sense of mission

Many individuals generally have no grand design, no mission, no great plan calling for change and progress. It is the true leader who has a grand design, which is reflected by a chain-like sequence of relevant and integrated events that serve as stepping stones. Of course, the grand design may not be easily deciphered until it is completed. Contrariwise, the individual lets each situation dictate to him his special set of techniques and plans of action. He sees no overall strategy except that which reflects the on-going and established interests of the various claimant groups involved in his organization. This allows him maximum flexibility without the personal risks of long-range programs.

It is difficult for the typical individual to have a deep and disturbing sense of mission when he is so specialized and boxed in by bureaucratic formulas that he cannot rise above the trivia to see what is ahead, above and behind. But if he suffers from "administrivia," he more importantly suffers from annihilation of all privacy.

Escape from thinking

Heroic leadership requires not so much a determination to outmaneuver the other fellow, but an ability to anticipate the effects of action now in progress and to devise plans that will be essentially preventive rather than remedial. But who is doing the thinking? Telephone any executive during business hours and you will probably be told that he is "at a meeting," for he spends most of his time "in conference." The executive has a genius for cluttering up his day, and many have somehow managed to persuade themselves that they are too busy to think, to read, to look back and to see into the future. Being busy is more than a national passion, as some believe, and it is more than an excuse—it is a means of escape. The real question concerning the opportunity for leadership is not the time or lack of it that is provided for thought, but the value that is placed on thought. Our society has always been action oriented, but lately what little thought has existed has been largely sacrificed to meetings where thinking is done in haste and geared to specific problems at hand, to say nothing of the power tactics that consume vast amounts of intellectual and emotional energy.

The individual today has a passion for discussion. He may use grave and decisive words, may even adopt divergent attitudes at strategic moments, but never stands his ground, especially for a radical idea or program. The stance that he takes is commonly referred to as "a convenient point of reference," but this reference is subject to shifting. By this means he is able to transfer the discussion to a new plane, insisting upon complete objectivity when it is necessary to ensure avoiding any subjective or emotional involvement. The individual's true home is a kind of superficial intellectualism in which his thoughts appear to have a logical coherence, his word choices are for maximum effect. He oozes with intuitions and hunches, or he reports on the latest research findings from scientific studies of elaborate detail, rigorous methodology and unimpeachable authorship. The use of anonymous authorities is itself an indication of how he has become abstracted from the reality about him.

Executives fight a phantom battle

Now what all of this amounts to is that the power struggle going on within these vast human systems found in business, government, education and union organization is without a fighting front. It is a phantom battle. The clever use of the "littles" of sophistry, the impersonalization of arguments, the resorting to anonymous authorities, and the appeal to the "powers that be" (which somehow always remain nameless), make the development of a purposive life futile. The executive fights among the shadows and the noble myths are subject to momentary change. What appears at first to be a united front becomes later divided against itself, where adversaries join forces and the man on the right or left of the large oval conference table stands ready to pose as a friendly "devil's advocate" or "his majesty's loyal supporter," depending upon what the situation warrants. The attempt to discover the true fighting front and unveil the nameless powers for even a brief moment is to destroy ambiguity and oddly enough to promote general resistance and unrest. Apparently a modern truth today is that to be safe one must never feel secure.

Executives lack creativity

In summary, and in preparation for the challenge and conclusion, the individual is rapidly becoming a kind of powerseeker who appears to be a leader because he is skillful in getting support, popularity and rapport with a minimum of "heavy" involvement. He is trying hard to become skillful at working with people and using resources of committees and decision-making groups. He appears to be a good human relations practitioner or social engineer, but actually considers these human relations principles as means by which he may intelligently and subtly play the power game. But in playing this game he does not cause major innovation.

This is the new rule which makes the power game drastically different from that of his predecessors such as Carnegie and Rockefeller, Senior. Seeking only to fulfill the expectations of others and to live within the established imperatives of his organization, the executive finds it unnecessary to the pursuit of self-interest to champion radically new and great programs and to risk willingly the greater inner resources available to him as a unique individual. What at first glance appears to be a lack of self-direction due to a kind of cunning or strategy turns out, after a second look, to be a result of inner weakness. The executive today is not to be seen as a malicious power-seeker; he is not to be morally castigated. His problem is not completely his fault. He is to be understood as one who lives in a high pressure system in which there are few opportunities available to him whereby he can attach his ambition and desire to succeed to the top to a great and noble purpose. In short, it is not out of choice that the executive wears the face that he does. Unfortunately this feature makes his problem incomparably more difficult.

Although we do not know how many have taken to the anonymity of large-scale organization as their avenue of escape from the responsibilities of leadership, it seems plausible that this picture represents many of the top executives in our major large institutions, including

business and government. We might further believe that as the scale
and complexity of these institutions increase, and the pressures they
necessarily generate become more imperative and inhibiting, even
the strongest-willed executive will find it necessary to operate without
greatly engaging his unique and effective personality. The increasing
pattern of half-hearted attempts at leadership is tending toward
drastic consequences of which the annihilation of the individual's
productive or creative resources is one of the more imminent
possibilities.

What is the ideal leader?

With these possibilities besetting the aspiring leader today, what
are the conditions of ideal? What is an ideal type of leader? Our
superior man is necessarily a "free man," but not free in the sense
that he exists outside of an organizational system. Our ideal is not
a hermit because a hermit is still a prey to the world. While fighting
against his world, a hermit only escapes it in order to continue to
exist as a human being. He thus takes on a kind of sincere falseness
which negates his virtuous intentions. It is simply foolhardy, in a
society as heavily populated and as massively organized as ours is
today, to believe that one can escape physically. And it is unheroic.

The fact that the individual cannot escape places limitations on
Clark Kerr's recommendation for coping with organizational society.
Mr. Kerr rebelled at the current practice of human relations and
recommended that the individual should give himself to many
organizations rather than to one and reserve for himself the aspiration of limitlessness rather than project this quality into the character of organization. This is precisely what the contemporary
person is doing today, but he does not get in return this feeling of
limitlessness.

Only becoming half-involved in any one organization prevents the
individual from realizing his true and full powers within. He cannot
come into meaningful grips with his huge organization unless he
firmly resolves that he is going to play an active, aggressive role in it.
It is only through active participation in molding events with a sense
of direct responsibility for their consequences that one can achieve
the personal strength necessary to live in harmony with the pressures
of the organization without being absorbed by them. And this is
what the executive needs today. Rather than a social ethic with
which to justify and give sanction to the enormous power of the
organization over him, the individual needs a stronger will with

which to put his total productive resources to work for him and his organization.

The concept of our ideal shows us that only through struggle, through meeting directly the harshness and tyranny of the real world, can a man come to his own self. Until then he feels extremely abstracted from the stream of life, and he consumes vast amounts of physical and psychological energy trying to overcome his feelings of powerlessness.

But more importantly, he can never really get the feel of the true character and direction of the organization if he does not become totally involved in it. Without this feeling and grasping kind of intellect, it is difficult to become intimately involved in a creative plan to make over the character or rechart the direction of the enterprise or some part thereof. One can only fall back on the drive for power—the common denominator among the alienated— when he does not have the inspiration to lead and accomplish a great and noble life purpose. But this purpose must of necessity be intimately tied to the character and direction of the organization in which the individual seeks his principal source of livelihood. No amount of leading and accomplishing great and noble purposes in extra-organizational endeavors, as seen in the current rage for charity, community and recreational activities, will overcome the psychological vacuity brought on by the lack of purposeful involvement in an individual's major activity throughout the day. This fad of finding purpose in life outside of the business or government or union organization is a prime example of the modern individual's tendency today to distribute himself among too many organizations.

While the organization balloons to gigantic proportions and the executive comes to find less and less personal involvement in it, he is, so to speak, busily passing the charity hat around in his community to help the needy and the suffering. It is not fanciful to suggest that this extraorganizational effort is the executive's way of escaping from his primary leadership responsibilities. Nor is it disrespectful to suggest that this escape mechanism is a desperate attempt to recapture his lost sense of personal worth.

For some executives, however, the extraorganizational activity is done merely because this is what a successful and well-adjusted executive should do today. In this case he cannot be classed as a leader for he is not really sincere. But we must reaffirm that in many cases the executive becomes an extraorganizational man not because of choice but rather because of a compulsive need to escape from an environment that offers less and less opportunity for personal thrust. The extraorganizational pattern is an important means whereby the executive who has a strong drive for power can more fully satisfy this need. It is not possible to relate this type of activity to virtue because it results from compulsiveness, from inner weakness, rather than from inner strength. That is to say, the executive becomes an extraorganizational man not because he is a superior person whose vast reserve of energy cannot be adequately used by any one organization, but rather because he has a low reserve of energy owing to a lack of both power and opportunity to use whatever productive resources he has within his principal organization.

We now arrive at the heart of the matter. The leader of the future will be that individual with the great mission to overcome the mass feeling of alienation and self-inadequacy. He will recognize that this struggle starts not with his community, nor even with his principal organization, but rather it starts with *himself*. He puts his own house in order; he gradually and diligently develops the necessary values, courage, and self-control whereby he can successfully become identified with, but not absorbed by, his organization. He disciplines himself to wholeness, and from this newly acquired inner strength he dominates the pressures of his organization and leads the people about him. In this way power over others comes to him because he is inwardly a superior person. The emergence of this hero, who is admittedly a rare gift to any organization or society, will by the changes he helps bring about prepare the way for other executives to become better leaders.

There are many executives today who are on "crusades" to restore the uncommon man, bring back the independent spirit, destroy the organization man and revive the Titan's inner-directed conscience. They write books, give speeches, appear in only the most proper public gatherings and social circles, associate with the elites of their choice, buy and in some cases read the best literature, and identify with the most sophisticated authors. If it were not for the fact that they are so noisy and public about this build-up we would actually think of them as somewhat sincere. Contrarily, we cannot help but believe that this eagerness to appear to be something akin to our superior person is really the attempt to assure themselves that they are what they are not.

It follows that only a few will be able to recapture the will to lead. Of course, it never has been absolutely extinct, but the point is that these few promising executives need to be encouraged or they will find that their way back to conspicuous leadership will be too strenuous for them. Some may believe that everything must be done, every available resource must be used to help develop the promising executive into a superior type of person. The danger of this advice is that the appearance of a leader with the hero's sense of historical purpose cannot be well planned and predicted. This, however, makes it all the more imperative that we should do certain things that are within our power to create a conducive atmosphere for the reappearance of the man of exceptional talent.

How today's organizations kill leadership

To this end there are certain specific practices within our society that warrant special criticism at this time. To begin with, the organization today has achieved a life of its own. It goes rambling on seemingly immune to the personal advances of any one executive. It has created a kind of social or impersonal system of leadership which is the product of many individuals acting expertly at their chosen tasks. Then, too, the reduction of competition allows the oligopolistic or monopolistic firm to ramble on without apparent need for the great and personal mastery of the heroic monarch of the past. As Crawford Greenewalt has said, the "responsible group" has replaced the "responsible individual" and the corporation's health and future is that much more assured. This, however, is questionable.

But with the replacement of the responsible individual by the responsible group, the executive is merely given a more concrete and convenient unit whereby he can advance his own individual interests without any more opportunity for heroic leadership. In fact, there is less opportunity for heroic thrust when the responsible group has replaced the responsible individual. The last thing that the executive needs today is to have this additional obstacle placed before him which he must hurdle in his attempt to be aggressive and creative. One does not place another obstacle before an individual who already feels alienated and powerless. Nothing has caused as much arrestment of his leadership opportunity as the responsible-group concept. We have previously suggested that it will make all the more the power artist and that much less the purposeful leader.

There are few features of our society that show less faith in personal, conspicuous leadership than in this growing concept of the responsible group. It may be suggested at this time that the growth in acceptance and use of the responsible group portrays, in dramatic form, our growing loss of faith in conspicuous leadership and our feelings of inadequacy. The group might very well be used to keep the individual informed of what is going on, but he should not be allowed to use it as a chief tool for power-seeking. Executives should

be encouraged to seek power that comes from a superior inner awareness and sensitivity to what the future character and direction of the
firm should be, not power that comes from an ability to manipulate
people and to use social techniques.

The need for inner strength may indicate that the executive
should be protected from groups by having conferences formally
scheduled. At present many committees are called on an informal
basis which often amounts to calling a conference whenever someone
pushes the panic button. Since the panic button is pushed often in an
alienated society, the executive is always in conference. By having
conferences as infrequently as possible, the executive will not be at
the mercy of the panic-button pusher. At least this might be tried
until the promising executive has developed sufficient inner reserve
to restrain from pushing the panic button or jumping mechanically
to the alarm whenever he or some other executive gets into a little
difficulty. He will then have to look within for the resources with
which to work himself out of difficulty—an almost unheard of practice today in many organizations. This too may be too much of a
struggle for him today so that care must be taken that he is not given
too much freedom from the group without an adequate recovery of
his individual resources.

Who will be our leaders?

It is impossible to determine who the future leaders will be. Any
attempt at scientific selection will produce a contemptible arrogance
resulting from a lack of awareness of the limitations of technical
kinds of identification and selection. Attempts to determine exactly
the traits of a leader have resulted in complete failure. In spite of
this we all have a crude but amazingly efficient sensitivity to the
essence of leadership and to the existence of great leaders. We can
recognize them even though their characteristics cannot be scientifically measured. The tendency today is to deny these rare men any
psychological room, let alone social status and organizational prestige.
We have tried to present some of the characteristics by which we
can identify leaders, but these traits were only roughly described
because words can only approximate the emotional quality with which
we identify our heroes. To be sure the actual worship of heroes today
has acquired a grotesque posture as seen in current biographical
literature. But the essential spark is still there in the minds and
hearts of many people and needs only to be rekindled.

In other words, it is not that we cannot recognize our leaders,
but rather that we no longer value them as highly as we once did.

Therefore, scientific tests should definitely be discouraged so that our eminently more superior powers of observation and intuition can once again help us to find and to raise to our highest positions men of rare and exceptional leadership potential. In this way talent and ability will be brought into line with position, all of which will help, but of course not guarantee, a return to heroic leadership.

Recommendations as to how to structure and reorganize for the rebirth of leadership could become so demanding and pervasive that the tendency to rely too heavily upon organization to eliminate the organization man could move us one notch back rather than one notch forward. All suggestions to help bring about a superior man in our organization should be tempered by judicious concern for the extreme fallacy of organizing to return to independence. We must be careful to place our reliance upon the individual to find his way to psychological recovery and not upon the forces inherent in the group and organization.

Time out to think

With this due caution, there is still another recommendation reflected in our concept of the superman. This recommendation concerns the value we place upon thought that is private deliberation resulting from a well-disciplined use of one's intellectual reserves. Each executive who shows promise of heroic leadership should be allowed ample opportunity to think. Perhaps once every five or seven years he should be given a year off with pay so that he can read and study and perhaps even write. When it is possible to organize his time and responsibilities, he should be given time off to think—to get away from his office, and become aware of the broader possibilities found in studying literature, philosophy, art and the social sciences. Under proper and well-conceived circumstances this effort will not be an escape from leadership responsibilities, although this is a distinct danger. However, this program can be effective only with men who are willing and able to make major innovations and assume great responsibility and risks and who will profit from getting out and seeing a broader or higher purpose to which their organizations and they may become devoted. A vigorous emphasis on the value of the thoughtful man will allow a leadership to come forth that will be devoted to great and noble missions not out of compulsive needs but out of choice that comes from inner wisdom.

Of course, finding ways to give the promising executive this opportunity to develop his intellectual resources will require a change in present-day values. The direction and character of the typical business organization will have to be changed since the man of action has heretofore been its standard breed. While we wait for some great innovator to show us the way toward the major innovation, there are some small things we can do ourselves. Most important among these is to reverse our tendency to walk into offices and homes, and back-yards for that matter, because of an overpowering need to have friends and acquaintances. We can afford to be hard on ourselves and others who want not privacy but companionship. A good brother's keeper is one who helps the other person to suffer a little by leaving him alone and unengaged because this will in the long run help him to struggle and perhaps find himself.

The challenge

Human progress occurs to a great extent through the intellectual efforts of its great men. Leadership might well be viewed as thought in command, while action and implementation might be the limitations imposed upon the individual who does not have or cannot use superior intellectual resources. Displacing or eliminating this great resource will assuredly reduce our opportunity and potentiality for change and progress.

In conclusion, ours is a society whose chief characteristic is a lost sense of self-direction as seen in the tendency to escape from leadership responsibility. The challenge is to revive the individual's unique powers of purposive striving and his courage to assume and sustain great risks. To be sure, there are many recommendations that could be made to this end, but because the purpose of this article is to diagnose our problem today, we have highlighted only a few. They include denial of the value of extraorganizational effort, resistance to the responsible-group trend, respect for a man's privacy, faith in men of rare ability and giving highest value to that talent reflected in thought deliberation.

QUESTIONS

1. What is the basic point of Jennings' article? Do you agree?
2. What qualities does Jennings feel are essential to fulfilling the role of leadership?
3. How does bureaucracy limit leadership?
4. Explain Jennings' concept of the ideal leader. How does his view differ from the situational, trait, and type aproaches?
5. Explain what Jennings means by the statement "organizations kill leadership."

15. THREE STYLES OF LEADERSHIP AND THEIR USES *

Robert T. Golembiewski

Managers who have tried to keep track of research and thinking on the subject of leadership may well sympathize with the centipede that was asked how it managed its legs, for this innocent question, the limerick tells us, reduced the unfortunate creature to lying "distracted in a ditch considering how to run."

The question asked in the leadership literature—"How does one lead men?"—is every bit as disconcerting as the one put to the centipede. Nevertheless, the parallel between them is not quite exact. The centipede, until he had to think about it, was only doing what came naturally and doing it well. Leadership in the work situation, however, does not belong to the order of instinctive behavior. Doing what comes naturally in striving for leadership often leaves much to be desired.

Though management has tended to be all too receptive to endorsements for this, that, or the other leadership approach, its interest has sound foundations. In the first place, a considerable body of evidence shows that the productivity of a work unit is affected by the kind of leadership the unit receives. In the second, decisions about what style of leadership to adopt must to some extent be made for the company as a whole rather than being left to the intuitions of individual managers. Still, management's interest has not been satisfied, for the evidence supporting any one leadership style can always be countered, and frequently is, by evidence supporting its precise opposite. The bewildered organization that has tried and abandoned one style after another may well be pardoned for asking, "Where do we go from here?"

Fortunately, it is beginning to look as if a theory based on empirical findings is at last in the making. No one yet knows exactly what its ultimate content will be, but its outlines can now be perceived and—even more important—can be put to use to improve managerial practice.

At this point, it may be useful, therefore, to review the research findings that form the skeleton of this theory and to examine their practical implications. But before doing so, it is necessary to define

* From *Personnel*, Vol. 38, No. 4 (July-August, 1961), pp. 34-45. Copyright 1961 by the American Management Association. Reprinted with permission of the American Management Association.

the term "leadership"—though this in itself is a question that has stirred up endless controversy. For the purposes of this article, however, "leadership" will be taken to mean the consistent ability to influence people in desired ways.

On the classification of leadership styles, fortunately, there is more agreement. Most authorities recognize three basic types: "leader-centered," or "autocratic"; "group-centered," or "democratic"; and "individual-centered," or "free-rein." [1] The supposedly modern view, of course, is that the group-centered style is the most conducive to productivity. By contrast, the traditional view admits only the leader-centered style, regards the group-centered style as a plaything of psychologists, and dismisses the free-rein style as constituting not leadership, but rather its surrender.

Each in Its Place

Supporters of any all-or-nothing view have one thing in common: they will often be surprised to find that the research literature does not consistently support any one leadership style. The reason for this lies not in any failing of the research itself but in the simple fact that there is no "best" style. Indeed, the question "Which kind of leadership should we use?" prevents any useful answer. The question should be, rather, "Which kind of leadership *when?*"

This "when," it is worth pointing out, constitutes an integral part of the question, for every scientific formulation must at some point specify the conditions it covers. Even the well-tested law explaining what happens when objects are dropped holds true only for objects that are heavier than air. If the objects are dropped at certain points in space, moreover, they will "fall up," or float.

This approach provides a partial explanation of the apparent chaos of the research literature. Many studies that seem to contradict each other are simply accounts of leadership phenomena under different conditions. Studies based upon observation of similar conditions, on the other hand, have yielded a pattern of consistent results.

Fortunately, leadership study has now taken on a "situational" approach. The main point of this approach has been well expressed in popular terms by Auren Uris, who advises the would-be leader as follows: "The skill with which you apply the three basic tools of leadership—autocratic, democratic, and free-rein techniques—determines your personal success as a leader." [2]

---

[1] For a typical treatment, see A. Uris, *How to Be a Successful Leader* (New York: McGraw-Hill Book Company, Inc., 1953), pp. 32-39.

[2] *Ibid.*, p. 31.

What, then, are the conditions that should be taken into account in the choice of a leadership style? There are many. Four among them, however—personality, task characteristics, task roles, and group characteristics—are particularly important and have been explored in a number of research studies. A separate examination of each of these conditions should provide some guidelines for translating such advice as Uris' into action.

Personality

As the advocates of group-centered leadership often fail to realize, not all people can function well under the same kind of leadership. There are, for example, many people whose personalities make them unfitted for a group- or individual-centered style.[3] Such a person was Administrator H, described in Harold Lasswell's *Psychopathology and Politics*.[4] A childhood marked by unfortunate sexual experiences and domination by an overbearing, prudish father had left him sharply, though unconsciously, ambivalent toward authority. Consequently, he worked well under supervision but invariably became careless when he was given substantial freedom on the job.

Needless to say, giving free rein to a subordinate like H would bring nothing but trouble, though over the long run his personality might possibly change enough to permit a looser kind of supervision. Studies of "authoritarianism" confirm these common-sense conclusions about how to deal with men like Administrator H. Authoritarians behave in ways that reveal compulsive conformity based upon a view of the world as menacing and unfriendly. Though they are not necessarily people of low intelligence, they think in relatively few channels, from which they cannot be moved. In addition, they seek security through the exercise of authority or, better still, through surrender to some powerful authority figure.

Studying authoritarianism in military groups, Medalia formulated and tested the following two hypotheses: [5]

1. People with strong authoritarian tendencies will be more likely to accept formal military leaders with the conventional traits of the

---

[3] Many personnel men are aware of these personality effects and therefore recruit only from those groups of people whose general social training seems likely to produce the personality characteristics appropriate to the organization's leadership style. Thus some companies seek out rural workers because of their alleged amenability to formal discipline.

[4] *The Political Writings of Harold D. Lasswell* (Glencoe, Ill.: The Free Press, 1951), pp. 127-35.

[5] N. Z. Medalia, "Authoritarianism, Leader Acceptance, and Group Cohesion," *Journal of Abnormal and Social Psychology*, Vol. LI, No. 2 (1955), pp. 207-13.

TABLE 1

RELATION OF AUTHORITARIANISM IN MEMBERS OF A MILITARY GROUP TO ACCEPTANCE OF FORMAL HEADS AND INTENT TO RE-ENLIST

	AUTHORITARIANISM			
LEADER ACCEPTANCE				Difference Between
	High	Medium	Low	High and Low
Above Median	59%	52%	36%	+23
Below Median	41	48	64	—23
Total	100%	100%	100%	
INTENT TO RE-ENLIST				
Yes or Undecided	38%	34%	24%	+14
No	62	66	76	—14
Total	100%	100%	100%	

"good officer" than will people with weak authoritarian tendencies.

2. People with strong authoritarian tendencies will be more likely to re-enlist than will people with weak authoritarian tendencies.

The data that emerged from his study are shown in Table 1. Not only do these findings support both hypotheses but, when one takes into account certain technical factors in the study that tended to obscure any relations, they suggest a very strong relation between personality and leadership style.

The practical advantages of adapting leadership style to personality characteristics seem clear from this study. In the groups analyzed, it could mean a 23 per cent increase in the acceptance of the formal leader by his subordinates and a 14 per cent increase in the intent to re-enlist. These figures indicate the need for developing a valid diagnostic indicator of the leadership style to which an individual will respond best. Comparable changes in a business organization would certainly prove well worth the cost of meshing leadership style and personality factors.

A word of qualification must, however, be inserted here. Most people have wide "response repertoires." That is, they are able to perform the wide range of behaviors required by the various styles of leadership despite their personal preference for a particular style.

This adaptability was demonstrated by Berkowitz in an experiment with a communication network that channeled a great deal of information to some positions and very little to others.[6] Half the subjects were assigned to communication positions in which they would have to act in ways that were not congruent with their personalities: submissive people were placed in central positions, dominant people in peripheral positions. The other half were assigned to the positions appropriate to their personalities. Though the two kinds of subjects at first performed quite differently, Berkowitz found, the "misplaced" subjects generally managed to adjust to the demands of their positions by the last of the three trials in the experiment.

Berkowitz' experiment, however, was brief. The findings of other research projects indicate that if it had continued, the subjects in the first group would ultimately have displayed reactions ranging from dissatisfaction to attempts at sabotaging the work process. Just when it is that such reactions begin to appear will be determined by circumstances and personalities. But when they do hit, they hit hard.

A manager, then, may vary his style of leadership, but he cannot force people to act forever in ways that are uncongenial to their personalities. This imposes a difficult task upon the manager and the organization—ascertaining the behavior preferences of the individual subordinates and then arranging the work so as to allow them to carry out their tasks in the manner they prefer. Unless this is done, the formal head will remain just that, rather than being accepted by his men as their leader.

Task characteristics

The second major condition affecting the usefulness of any given leadership style is the nature of the task to be performed. Though little work has so far been done in classifying tasks, it should be adequate here to note that tasks may be distinguished in terms of (1) the obviousness of the solution to the problem or of the work itself and (2) the amount of cooperation the task requires.

Unfortunately, research to date has for the most part assumed that all tasks are quite complex and require a great deal of interpersonal cooperation. Because socio-emotional factors affect performance most strongly when the task is of this kind, the leader-centered style, which tends to generate emotional flareups, usually shows up poorly under these circumstances, while the group-centered style shows up well.

Many tasks, however, do not have these assumed characteristics. One of Deutsch's experiments illustrates the value of distinguishing

[6] L. Berkowitz, "Personality and Group Position," *Sociometry*, Vol. XIX, No. 4 (1956), pp. 210-22.

between kinds of tasks.[7] The prediction to be tested was that internally cooperative groups would be more effective than internally competitive groups. When groups of both kinds attempted to solve human relations and puzzle problems, it was found, the "cooperative" groups did indeed perform better on a number of measures of effectiveness, including quantitative and qualitative output, member satisfaction with group functioning and output, and amount of aggressive behavior. But on several measures the differences between the two kinds of groups were more marked for the human relations problem than for the puzzle problem. It seems as if the objectively demonstrable nature of the puzzle solution made it difficult for members of the "competitive" groups to block each other in subtle ways. (Certainly, the nature of the task would have made direct blocking seem ridiculous.) The open-endedness of the human relations problem, on the other hand, gave them ample opportunity to run each other ragged.

In terms of leadership style, these data suggest that the leader-centered style is particularly inappropriate to tasks that have more than one possible solution and that require a considerable amount of interpersonal cooperation. More important still, the data seem to leave little room for the leader-centered style even on tasks with just the opposite characteristics, for, as has already been noted, the group-centered style generally proved the more effective not only for the human relations problem but for the puzzle problem as well. In actual business and industrial situations, it should also be pointed out, emotional tensions can affect performance adversely at any number of points in the operation—at far more points than in Deutsch's experimental situation. Moreover, the marked preference most people show for the group-centered style furthers its claim to being the more useful of the two.

This does not mean, however, that the leader-centered style should be rejected out of hand. A situation in which most of the operators are strongly authoritarian and the task is a simple one requiring little cooperation is obviously tailor-made for authoritarian leadership.

THE ROLE OF INTELLIGENCE

Calling a task "simple" of course implies some relation between the task itself and the intelligence of the people who are to perform

---

[7] M. Deutsch, "The Effects of Cooperation and Competition upon Group Process," D. Cartwright and A. Zander (eds.), in *Group Dynamics: Research and Theory* (Evanston, Ill.: Row, Peterson and Company, 1953), pp. 319-53. See especially tables 23.5, 23.7, 23.9, and 23.11.

it. The importance of taking this relation into account in deciding upon a leadership style has been demonstrated by a simple experiment with a game based on "Twenty Questions." [8] As Table 2 indicates, though all the subjects worked on essentially the same task, the "Brights" did their best under a group-centered style, and the "Dulls" under a leader-centered style. The relation was especially marked for the "Dulls," whose problem-solving efficiency was only half as high under group-centered leadership as under authoritarian leadership.

Regulating work assignments by task and personality characteristics may seem like a great deal of bother, but the 100 per cent performance difference for the "Dulls" suggests that the extra bother will more than pay its own way. Indeed, business would most likely

TABLE 2

EFFECTS OF LEADERSHIP STYLE AND MEMBERS' INTELLIGENCE UPON GROUP PERFORMANCE IN "TWENTY QUESTIONS" GAME

MEMBERS' INTELLIGENCE AND LEADERSHIP STYLE		MEASURES OF PERFORMANCE	
		Median No. of Questions Asked Per Problem	Per Cent of Problems Solved
Bright	Group-centered	15.5	100.0
	Leader-centered	18.5	87.5
Dull	Group-centered	31.0	37.5
	Leader-centered	24.5	75.0

find it profitable to subsidize the research necessary for the development of even more precise ways of differentiating people than those now available. The "Brights" in this experiment—to give just one illustration of the value of this greater precision—probably included some authoritarian subjects. (Though low intelligence is frequently accompanied by high authoritarianism, high intelligence is not so frequently accompanied by low authoritarianism.) Excluding the authoritarians from the "Bright" sample would probably have had two effects: the performance of the remaining "Brights" under group-centered conditions would have improved, and that of the "Brights" under leader-centered conditions would have deteriorated. In the industrial situation, both the individual and management could profit from a more comfortable "fit" of employees to their tasks.

[8] A. D. Calvin et al., "The Effect of Intelligence and Social Atmosphere on Group Problem-Solving Behavior," *Journal of Social Psychology*, Vol. XLV, First Half (1957), pp. 61-74.

Task roles

Still another question to be considered in choosing a leadership style is "Who does what?"—that is, "What are the roles of the leaders and followers?" Though the very notion of leadership implies a set of roles different from those of followership, just what functions are covered by each set cannot be rigidly prescribed. Indeed, the distribution of functions is often the product of social consensus, and may vary even among work teams performing the same operation in the same organization.

Roles do, however, fall into three broad categories: roles peculiar to the superior, roles peculiar to the subordinate, and "mixed" roles, whose functions are performed by either or both. The general argument here, by way of preview, is that each of these three classes implies a different leadership style.

Evidence indicates that supervisors who are successful in influencing their subordinates' behavior in the desired directions—that is, supervisors who are leaders—work at sharpening these differences in roles. In a study by Kahn and Katz, supervisors of section gangs on a railroad and supervisors of clerical sections in an insurance company were asked how much of their time was usually spent in supervisory matters, and how much in other matters.[9] Their answers, shown in Table 3, revealed that the supervisors with low-producing sections were two or three times more likely to perform the same duties as their men, or to perform the paperwork aspects of their jobs, than the supervisors with high-producing sections.

These findings can be explained by a little common-sense reasoning: The behavior of the low-producing supervisors reflects either a lack of consensus about roles in their work groups or their own failure to respect an existing consensus. Whatever the case, conflict is likely, and must inevitably result in productivity losses.

Not only should the superior differentiate his functions from those of his subordinates, but he should, of course, perform certain *specific* functions. The amount of planning he does, for example, is directly related to the productivity of his section. Some interesting data on this score were obtained by asking foremen in a tractor factory whether they were able to plan their work ahead as much as they liked.[10] Though their answers, given in Table 4, suggest that the high-producing foremen actually did more planning than the low-producing foremen, it should be noted that the foremen were talking about the

[9] R. L. Kahn and D. Katz, "Leadership Practices in Relation to Productivity and Morale," in Cartwright and Zander, *op. cit.*, p. 615.
[10] *Ibid.*, p. 619.

TABLE 3

TIME SPENT IN SUPERVISING IN RELATION TO SECTION PRODUCTVITY

SECTION PRODUCTIVITY	50% or more of time spent in supervising %	Less than 50% of time spent in supervising %	Not Ascertained %	Total %
Insurance company				
High	75	17	8	100
Low	33	59	8	100
Railroad				
High	55	31	14	100
Low	25	61	14	100

TABLE 4

FOREMEN'S PERCEPTION OF OPPORTUNITY FOR PLANNING IN RELATION TO SECTION PRODUCTIVITY

	FOREMEN'S RESPONSES			
SECTION PRODUCTIVITY [11] %	Can plan ahead as much as needed %	Sometimes have trouble planning far enough ahead %	Can seldom or never plan ahead %	Total %
97-101	37	42	21	100
91-96	51	32	17	100
86-90	29	41	30	100
80-85	29	46	25	100
50-79	14	40	46	100

fulfillment of their planning expectations, not about how much planning they actually did or how much they thought necessary. It seems reasonable to assume that high-producing foremen were more aware of the importance of planning than the others. Thus their less-than-complete satisfaction may reflect high hopes rather than low accomplishment. If this is so, then they must have been even more active in planning their work than the table suggests.

Tables 3 and 4 deal with but two of the three categories of roles outlined above: roles peculiar to the subordinate and roles peculiar to the superior. There is, however, substantial evidence of the harm that superiors do in failing to respect the third category of roles:

---

[11] Productivity is expressed as per cent of standard.

TABLE 5

A PROVISIONAL MODEL OF ROLES AND APPROPRIATE LEADERSHIP STYLES

CATEGORY OF ROLES	TYPICAL FUNCTION	GENERALLY APPROPRIATE LEADERSHIP STYLE
1. Roles peculiar to the superior	Setting general goals	Leader-centered
2. "Mixed" roles	Relocating machines on which individuals have worked for many years	Group-centered
3. Roles peculiar to the subordinate	Deciding how to use a tool	Free-rein

those whose performance is "mixed." The conflict generated by supervisory insensitivity to this third category is, of course, the subject of much of the human relations literature.

But what leadership styles do these three categories demand? As the provisional model in Table 5 shows, it seems likely that the superior's roles are best handled with a leader-centered style, "mixed" roles with a group-centered style, and the subordinate's roles with a free-rein style. This does not, however, mean that the superior should surrender all his power over certain functions. On the contrary, every role assumes a set of guidelines for behavior, and the three leadership styles are merely different techniques for developing and enforcing them. When the guidelines are violated—whatever the leadership style under which they were developed—the supervisor is put into a decisive position.

If, for example, a worker insisted on tightening bolts with his teeth, his fellow workers and his supervisor would undoubtedly be scandalized and would agree that the worker's freedom in deciding how to perform this operation did not extend quite so far as all that. Group pressure—especially in a work unit operating under group-centered leadership—might encourage him to change his ways. But the supervisor would still be on the spot, formally and socially. He would have to supplement this pressure and perhaps take formal action. When violations of the behavioral guidelines are winked at, the supervisor invariably comes off a loser.

The supervisor who would be a leader, then, must have a deft touch. A useful criterion for determining when to step in can be found in the concept of "relevance," that is, in how the issue ranks in terms of its importance to, say, the employees, the organization as a whole, or the boss.

The more relevant an issue is to the group, experimental evidence shows, the more willing the group is to accept a relatively authoritarian way of dealing with it. Thus a leader who is strongly supported by his group may depend primarily on free-rein and group-centered styles, which encourage member involvement. When a relevant issue arises, however, he will exercise substantial influence, and, in fact, the group will expect him to do so. (The leader-centered superior with a work unit of authoritarians will, of course, hold a tight rein on most matters and therefore need not have such a delicate touch. But such situations are rare.)

An issue may, of course, be relevant to the formal organization but not to the group. If, for example, the work unit neglects its responsibilities to the company on the question of the level of production, the superior may have to use a leader-centered style despite the group's reluctance to have him do so. On less relevant matters, however, he would do well to balance it with a group-centered or free-rein style, which would reduce any tension generated by the leader-centered style. The "relevance" concept, in other words, supplements the model in Table 5, for an unanticipated relevant item may appear in any one of the three categories. The handling of such items will in the long run determine whether the formal head continues to function as a leader or loses his control over the group.

Group characteristics

Discussing the relevance of an issue for a work group implies that the group has developed certain common standards *of* its own and *on* its own. This characteristic of groups—the tendency to develop group norms and group goals—may be accompanied by fairly powerful mechanisms for imposing the group's will upon its members and upon the outside world. The group therefore plays a large part in determining the success of the various leadership styles. Group properties have, of course, been examined at length in the social science literature, and this author has sketched their broad implications for organization performance elsewhere.[12]

One aspect worth considering here is the degree to which the group *as a group* accepts its formal head. If the group feels that its supervisor is not fulfilling its needs, it may find itself a more satisfactory leader from within its own ranks. This should not be a matter of indifference to industrial managers, for the emergence of an

---

[12] R. T. Golembiewski, "The Small Group and Public Administration," *Public Administration Review*, Vol. XIX, No. 3 (1959), pp. 149-56.

informal leader who acts as spokesman for a work unit is often associated with low productivity. In the Kahn and Katz study, workers in railroad section gangs were asked, "Is there some one man in the section who speaks up for the men when they want something?" Fewer than one in six respondents in the high-producing sections answered *yes*, while over half the respondents in the low-producing sections did so.[13]

Must the Leader Be Liked?

Such data as these, however, should not be taken as an endorsement of group-centered leadership. All three styles are equal to the task of winning informal acceptance for the formal head, though under different conditions. Moreover, the supervisor is not always well advised to try to raise his informal status to the level of his formal status. He must consider, among other things, the nature of his group's norms, which he will have to respect if he is to gain informal acceptance. If, as is by no means uncommon, the norms favor low output, his attempt to gain high informal status may force him to compromise his formal position.

The dangers of such an attempt are illustrated in a study of aerial bombardment crews by Adams.[14] Each member of each crew was ranked on several measures of status within the crew—formal rank, popularity, reputed flying ability, and so on. When the formal ranks of the members of any crew were quite similar to their ranks on the other measures, Adams found, the crew as a whole did well on "social performance" (harmony, intimacy, and the like). The crews that showed up best in these two respects, however, were not the best in "technical performance" (e.g., bombing accuracy). These findings seem reasonable. The popularity of the formal leaders of these crews was probably based in part upon their respect of a norm opposed to outstanding technical performance. Obviously, it did not make them particularly effective in their formal position. On the contrary, their closeness with their men helped the crews resist the demands of the "outside" organization.

A supervisor inheriting a work unit with a low-output norm faces a difficult task in choosing a style of leadership. If he employs a free-rein style, he will most likely succeed only in supporting the group norm. At the other extreme, the use of a leader-centered style

---

[13] Kahn and Katz, *op. cit.*, p. 616.
[14] S. Adams, "Status Congruency as a Variable in Small Group Performance," *Social Forces*, Vol. XXXII, No. 1 (1953), pp. 16-22.

may well harden the group's resistance to the formal organization. Even if the supervisor succeeds in breaking the group norm, he will most likely arouse antagonisms bound to affect the work process sooner or later.[15] (One major exception must be noted here: Groups of authoritarians, as has already been pointed out, will generally respond well to a leader-centered style. But this offers little practical consolation, given the apparent rarity of such groups.) Finally, it is the group-centered style, paradoxical though it may seem, that offers the best chance of success in changing a low-output norm, and group-centered leadership has actually proved useful in a number of instances. The reason for this seems to be that low output is a means by which the members of a work unit protect themselves against some perceived threat. A group-centered style often acts to make the group members feel less threatened and thus reduces their need for the low-output norm. But this is not inevitable.

In sum, every leadership style stands liable to failure in the attempt to develop and enforce a more acceptable output norm. If none of them works, the supervisor has no choice but to stop being a practicing psychologist and recommend that the unit be broken up.

Concluding Notes

The difficulties of choosing a leadership style, then, are great even if only a single condition is considered. From the two preceding paragraphs alone it should be clear that the question of how to lead any given work group is far more complex than is recognized by any existing generalizations, all of which call for a single leadership style. To compound this complexity, however, the four sets of conditions discussed in this article always appear in combination, so that some elements in a situation may favor one style while some elements favor another.

In fact, our increasing knowledge of the complexity of the question has outmoded the traditional designations of leadership styles. These designations, which suggest exclusive categories, ought to be modified so as to express the ways in which leadership styles continuously change in response to changing situations. The suggestions presented above outline the nature of the necessary changes. Needless to say, though these suggestions are consistent with the available

---

[15] Such a situation is analyzed in R. T. Golembiewski, "O & M and the Small Group," *Public Administration Review*, Vol. XX, No. 4 (1960), pp. 205-12.

research findings, they will need further verification before they can be considered rules for action.

Finally, it must be noted that the foregoing discussion has centered on the question "What are the conditions under which various leadership styles are most useful?" and has, in effect, neglected the question "What *should be* the dominant leadership style?" This neglect should not be taken as indicating that the question of value is unimportant. Rather, it recognizes that in practice the choice of a leadership style implies, and is preceded by, a value choice. In the field of leadership, as in every other, the use of empirical regularities must always be guided by considerations of what ought to be.

QUESTIONS

1. State the conditions that must be taken into account in the choice of a leadership style.
2. What are the practical advantages of adapting leadership style to personality characteristics? What research findings support this?
3. Why is the leader-centered style inappropriate to tasks that have more than one possible solution and that require a considerable amount of interpersonal cooperation?
4. Distinguish the broad categories of roles and explain their implication to leadership styles.
5. What does Golembiewski recommend a supervisor do if none of his leadership styles works? Do you agree? Why?

16. LEADERSHIP: MAN AND FUNCTION *

Alex Bavelas

There is a useful distinction to be made between the idea of leadership as a personal quality and the idea of leadership as an organizational function. The first refers to a special combination of personal characteristics; the second refers to the distribution throughout an organization of decision-making powers. The first leads us to look at the qualities and abilities of individuals; the second leads us to look at the patterns of power and authority in organizations. Both of these ideas or definitions of leadership are useful, but it is important to know which one is being talked about, and to know under what conditions the two must be considered together in order to understand a specific organizational situation.

Early notions about leadership dealt with it almost entirely in terms of personal abilities. Leadership was explicitly associated with special powers. An outstanding leader was credited not only with extensions of the normal abilities possessed by most men but with extraordinary powers such as the ability to read men's minds, to tell the future, to compel obedience hypnotically. These powers were often thought of as gifts from a god, as conditional loans from a devil, or as the result of some accidental supernatural circumstance attending conception, birth, or early childhood. Today, claims of supernatural powers are made more rarely, but they are not entirely unknown. Of course, milder claims—tirelessness, infallibility of intuition, lightning-quick powers of decision—are made in one form or another by many outstandingly successful men. And when they do not make them for themselves, such claims are made for them by others who, for their own reasons, prefer such explanations of success to other more homely ones.

Outright supernatural explanations of leadership have, in recent times, given way to more rational explanations. Leadership is still generally thought of in terms of personal abilities, but now the assumption is made that the abilities in question are the same as those possessed by all normal persons: individuals who become leaders are merely presumed to have them to a greater degree.

For many years, attempts to define these abilities and to measure them failed. This was not only because the early techniques of measurement were primitive and unreliable but for a more important

* From *Administrative Science Quarterly*, Vol. 4, No. 4 (March, 1960), pp. 491-98. Reprinted with permission of author and publisher.

reason. The traits that were defined as important for leadership were often nothing more than purely verbal expressions of what the researcher felt leaders *ought* to be like. Few of the many lists of traits that were developed had very much in common. Typical of the items that frequently appeared on such lists were piety, honesty, courage, perseverance, intelligence, reliability, imagination, industriousness. This way of thinking about leadership is still very common. It persists, not because it is helpful in analyzing and understanding the phenomenon of leadership, but because it expresses a deep and popular wish about what leaders *should* be like.

Modern trait research proceeds in a very different way. Leadership traits are no longer selected arbitrarily. They are, instead, largely derived from the results of tests that are carefully designed, administered, and interpreted. And the techniques of measurement and analysis which are applied to the data that are gathered have been extensively developed and refined. Numerous trait studies have been made of the physical, intellectual, and social characteristics of leaders. On various tests, persons who are leaders tend to be brighter, tend to be better adjusted psychologically, and tend to display better judgment. Studies that have concentrated on the social behavior of leaders show that they "interact" more than nonleaders. They tend to give more information, ask for more information, and to take the lead in summing up or interpreting a situation.

Despite these accomplishments, the trait approach has in recent years been subjected to increasing criticism. A common objection is that the results are obtained by a method that requires an initial separation of people into "leaders" and "nonleaders" or "good leaders" and "not-so-good leaders." The validity of the distinguishing traits that come out of such work, the argument goes, can only be as good as the validity of the preliminary grouping of the persons being studied. All of this leads to the question, "On what basis is the initial separation of subjects made, and how is it justified?"

At first glance, this may appear a trivial and carping question. In fact, however, it is one of the most serious obstacles in the way of all leadership research. It is obviously impossible to define "good leaders" without reference to a system of values. To say that a man is a "good leader" means that his behavior and its consequences are held to be of greater worth than other behaviors and results.

What system of values shall the researcher adopt that is both scientifically acceptable and socially useful in distinguishing good or successful leaders from others? Many attempts have been made to find a suitable criterion, but the results have been generally unsatisfactory—not that it is difficult to find standards which are desirable and inspiring, but that such standards tend to be based, just as the early lists of traits were, on qualities that are difficult or impossible to measure. And often they just do not seem to "work." For example, there have been attempts to distinguish leaders from nonleaders in terms that rest essentially on moral and ethical considerations. It may be a significant commentary on our society that there appears to be no particular correlation between a man's ethics and morals and his power to attract followers.

It has been suggested that many of the philosophical difficulties that attend the definition of "good leader" can be avoided if one accepts the more limited task of defining "good executive." In business and industry, one would like to think, there should be practical, quantitative ways of making the distinction. Many attempts have been made in this direction. Reputation, financial success, hierarchical position, influence, and many other criteria have been tried without much satisfaction. The inadequacies of such standards are obvious to any experienced executive.

There is a second and more interesting objection that has been made to the trait approach. It is based not on the question of the accuracy or the validity of the assumptions that are made but upon the nature of the "traits" themselves. Traits are, after all, statements about personal characteristics. The objection to this is that the degree to which an individual exhibits leadership depends not only on *his characteristics*, but, also, on the *characteristics of the situation* in which he finds himself. For example, a man who shows all the signs of leadership when he acts as the officer of a well-structured authoritarian organization may give no indication of leadership ability in a less-structured democratic situation. A man may become influential in a situation requiring deliberation and planning but show little evidence of leadership if the situation demands immediate action with no opportunity for weighing alternatives or thinking things out. Or, to take still another instance, a man may function effectively and comfortably in a group whose climate is friendly and co-operative but retreat and become ineffective if he perceives the atmosphere as hostile.

The case for the situational approach to leadership derives its strength from this fact: while organizations in general may exhibit broad similarities of structure and function, they also, in particular, show strong elements of uniqueness.

It is a matter of common observation that within any normal industrial organization, providing there has been a sufficient past, there will be found patterns of relationships and interaction that are highly predictable and highly repetitive. Some of these reoccurring situations will be unique to that organization. It is this uniqueness that is referred to when one speaks of the "personality" of a company. This is what a management has in mind when it selects a new member with an eye to how he will "fit in." The argument of the researcher who stresses the situational aspects of leadership is that these unique characteristics of an organization are often crucial in determining which of two equally competent and gifted men will become a "leader," and further that in the very same organization these unique patterns may change significantly at different levels of the hierarchy. The very same "leadership abilities" that helped a man rise to the top may, once he is there, prove a positive detriment.

The status of trait and situational leadership research can be summed up in this way: (1) the broad similarities which hold for a great number of organizations make it possible to say useful things about the kind of person who is likely to become a leader in any of those organizations, and (2) the unique characteristics of a particular organization make it necessary to analyze the situational factors that determine who is likely to become a leader *in one particular organization*. To put it another way, when specific situational patterns are different from organization to organization, one cannot say what personal traits will lead to acknowledged leadership. Instead, one must try to define the leadership functions that must be performed in those situations and regard as leadership those acts which perform them. This point of view suggests that almost any member of a group may become its leader under circumstances that enable him to perform the required functions of leadership and that different persons may contribute in different ways to the leadership of the group.

In these terms we come close to the notion of leadership, not as a personal quality, but as an *organizational function*. Under this concept it is not sensible to ask of an organization "who is the leader?" Rather we ask "how are the leadership functions distributed in this organization?" The distribution may be wide or narrow. It may be so narrow—so many of the leadership functions may be vested in a single person—that he is the leader in the popular sense. But in modern organizations this is becoming more and more rare.

What are these "leadership functions?" Many have been proposed: planning, giving information, evaluating, arbitrating, controlling, rewarding, punishing, and the like. All of these stem from the underlying idea that leadership acts are those which help the group achieve its objectives, or, as it is also put, to satisfy its "needs." In most face-to-face groups, the emergence of a leader can well be accounted for on this basis. That person who can assist or facilitate the group most in reaching a satisfactory state is most likely to be regarded as the leader. If one looks closely at what constitutes assistance or facilitation in this sense, it turns out to be the making of choices or the helping of the group to make choices—"better" choices, of course.

But can the function of leadership be reduced simply to decision making or the facilitation of decision making? The objection can be raised that such a definition is much too wide to be useful. Every action, even every physical movement one makes, is after all "chosen" out of a number of possible alternatives. If when I am at my workbench I pick up a screwdriver in preference to a hammer, I am clearly making a choice; am I, by virtue of that choice, displaying leadership? Something is obviously wrong with a definition of leadership which imputes it to any act that can be shown to have involved a choice. Common sense would argue that customary, habitual, and "unconscious" actions, although they may logically contain elements of choice, should be separated from actions that are subjectively viewed by the person taking them as requiring a decision. Common sense would also argue that questions of choice that can be settled on the basis of complete information should be considered differently from questions of choice in which decisions must be taken in the face of uncertainty. And common sense would argue that some distinction should be made between decisions that, although made on equally uncertain grounds, involve very different orders of risk.

This is, of course, the implicit view of the practicing manager, and although it may contain very knotty problems of logic it is the view that will be taken here. Stated in general terms, the position that will be taken is that organizational leadership consists of *uncertainty reduction*. The actual behavior through which this reduction is accomplished is the making of choices.

We saw above that not all choices are equally difficult or equally important. Some choices are considered unimportant or irrelevant and are ignored, and of course whole areas may be seen as so peripheral to the interests of the organization that they are not perceived as areas of choice at all. Other choices that *must* be made are so well understood that they become habitual and automatic. Some of these are grouped into more or less coherent bundles and given a job name. The employee learns to make them correctly as he becomes skilled in the job. In most job evaluation plans, additional credit is given if the job requires judgment. This is a way of saying that there are choices remaining in the job that cannot be completely taken care of by instructions but must be made by the employee as they come along.

There are other choices which, although they are equally clear and habitual, are of a more general nature and do not apply just to a specific job but apply to all. These are customarily embodied in rules and procedures. Rules and procedures are, in this sense, decisions made in advance of the events to which they are to be applied. Obviously, this is possible and practical only to the extent that the events to which the rules and procedures apply can be foreseen, and the practical limit of their completeness and specificity depends on how these future events can be predicted.

Following this line of analysis, it is theoretically possible to arrange all the logically inherent choices that must be made in operating an industrial organization along scales of increasing uncertainty and importance. At some level in this hierarchy of choices, it is customary for management to draw a line, reserving for itself from that point on the duty and the privilege of making the required decisions.

Precisely where a management draws this line defines its scope. The way in which a management distributes the responsibility for making the set of choices it has thus claimed to itself defines its structure. What organizational leadership *is* and what kinds of acts constitute it are questions that can be answered only within this framework of scope and structure. In these terms leadership consists of the continuous choice-making process that permits the organization as a whole to proceed toward its objectives despite all sorts of internal and external perturbations.

But as every practicing manager knows, problems occasionally arise that are not amenable to the available and customary methods of analysis and solution. Although uncertain about which choice to make, a management may nevertheless have to make a decision. It is in situations of this kind that many of the popular traits attributed to leaders find their justification: quickness of decision, the courage to take risks, coolness under stress, intuition, and, even, luck. There is no doubt that quick, effective, and daring decisions are a highly prized commodity in a crisis, but just as precious a commodity is the art of planning and organizing so that such crises do not occur. The trend of management has been to remove as many of its decisions as possible from the area of hunch and intuition to that of rational calculation. More and more, organizations are choosing to depend less on the peculiar abilities of rare individuals and to depend instead on the orderly processes of research and analysis. The occasions and opportunities for personal leadership in the old sense still exist, but they are becoming increasingly rare and circumscribed.

This new emphasis has not eliminated the role of personal leadership, but it has significantly redefined it. Under normal conditions of operation, leadership in the modern organization consists not so much in the making of decisions personally as it does of maintaining the operational effectiveness of the decision-making systems which comprise the management of the organization. The picture of the leader who keeps his own counsel and in the nick of time pulls the rabbit out of the hat is out of date. The popular stereotype now is the thoughtful executive discussing in committee the information supplied by a staff of experts. In fact it may be that the brilliant innovator, in the role of manager, is rapidly becoming as much an organizational embarrassment as he is an asset.

This trend, reasonable though it may appear on the surface, conceals two serious dangers. First, we may be systematically giving up the opportunity of utilizing the highest expressions of personal leadership in favor of managerial arrangements which, although safer and more reliable, can yield at best only a high level of mediocrity. And second, having committed ourselves to a system that thrives on the ordinary, we may, in the interests of maintaining and improving its efficiency, tend to shun the extraordinary.

It is no accident that daring and innovation wane as an organization grows large and successful. On different levels this appears to have been the history of men, of industries, of nations, and even of societies and cultures. Success leads to "obligations"—not the least of which is the obligation to hold what has been won. Therefore, the energies of a man or administration may be absorbed in simply maintaining vested interests. Similarly, great size requires "system," and system, once established, may easily become an end in itself.

This is a gloomy picture, because it is a picture of decay. It has been claimed, usually with appeals to biological analogies, that this is an inevitable cycle, but this view is, very probably, incorrect. Human organizations are not biological organisms; they are social inventions.

Questions

1. Distinguish early and modern approaches to leadership trait research.
2. What, according to Bavelas, is one of the most serious obstacles to leadership research? How can this obstacle be overcome?
3. Explain the basic objections to the trait aproach to leadership.
4. What is Bavelas' opinion of the situational approach? Do you agree?
5. Briefly explain what Bavelas means by leadership as an organizational function.

17. HOW TO CHOOSE A LEADERSHIP PATTERN *

Robert Tannenbaum
Warren H. Schmidt

❡ *"I put most problems into my group's hands and leave it to them to carry the ball from there. I serve merely as a catalyst, mirroring back the people's thoughts and feelings so that they can better understand them."*

❡ *"It's foolish to make decisions oneself on matters that affect people. I always talk things over with my subordinates, but I make it clear to them that I'm the one who has to have the final say."*

❡ *"Once I have decided on a course of action, I do my best to sell my ideas to my employees."*

❡ *"I'm being paid to lead. If I let a lot of other people make the decisions I should be making, then I'm not worth my salt.*

❡ *"I believe in getting things done. I can't waste time calling meetings. Someone has to call the shots around here, and I think it should be me."*

Each of these statements represents a point of view about "good leadership." Considerable experience, factual data, and theoretical principles could be cited to support each statement, even though they seem to be inconsistent when placed together. Such contradictions point up the dilemma in which the modern manager frequently finds himself.

NEW PROBLEM

The problem of how the modern manager can be "democratic" in his relations with subordinates and at the same time maintain the necessary authority and control in the organization for which he is responsible has come into focus increasingly in recent years.

* From *Harvard Business Review*, Vol. 36, No. 2 (March-April, 1958), pp. 95-101. Reprinted by permission of Robert Tannenbaum, Warren H. Schmidt, and *Harvard Business Review*.

Earlier in the century this problem was not so acutely felt. The successful executive was generally pictured as possessing intelligence, imagination, initiative, the capacity to make rapid (and generally wise) decisions, and the ability to inspire subordinates. People tended to think of the world as being divided into "leaders" and "followers."

New focus

Gradually, however, from the social sciences emerged the concept of "group dynamics" with its focus on *members* of the group rather than solely on the leader. Research efforts of social scientists underscored the importance of employee involvement and participation in decision making. Evidence began to challenge the efficiency of highly directive leadership, and increasing attention was paid to problems of motivation and human relations.

Through training laboratories in group development that sprang up across the country, many of the newer notions of leadership began to exert an impact. These training laboratories were carefully designed to give people a first-hand experience in full participation and decision making. The designated "leaders" deliberately attempted to reduce their own power and to make group members as responsible as possible for setting their own goals and methods within the laboratory experience.

It was perhaps inevitable that some of the people who attended the training laboratories regarded this kind of leadership as being truly "democratic" and went home with the determination to build fully participative decision making into their own organizations. Whenever their bosses made a decision without convening a staff meeting, they tended to perceive this as authoritarian behavior. The true symbol of democratic leadership to some was the meeting—and the less directed from the top, the more democratic it was.

Some of the more enthusiastic alumni of these training laboratories began to get the habit of categorizing leader behavior as "democratic" *or* "authoritarian." The boss who made too many decisions himself was thought of as an authoritarian, and his directive behavior was often attributed solely to his personality.

New need

The net result of the research findings and of the human relations training based upon them has been to call into question the stereotype of an effective leader. Consequently, the modern manager often finds himself in an uncomfortable state of mind.

Often he is not quite sure how to behave; there are times when he is torn between exerting "strong" leadership and "permissive" leadership. Sometimes new knowledge pushes him in one direction ("I should really get the group to help make this decision"), but at the same time his experience pushes him in another direction ("I really understand the problem better than the group and therefore I should make the decision"). He is not sure when a group decision is really appropriate or when holding a staff meeting serves merely as a device for avoiding his own decision-making responsibility.

The purpose of our article is to suggest a framework which managers may find useful in grappling with this dilemma. First we shall look at the different patterns of leadership behavior that the manager can choose from in relating himself to his subordinates. Then we shall turn to some of the questions suggested by this range of patterns. For instance, how important is it for a manager's subordinates to know what type of leadership he is using in a situation? What difference do his long-run objectives make as compared to his immediate objectives?

EXHIBIT 1

CONTINUUM OF LEADERSHIP BEHAVIOR

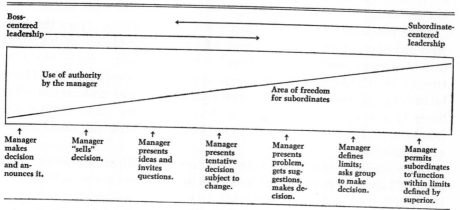

RANGE OF BEHAVIOR

Exhibit I presents the continuum or range of possible leadership behavior available to a manager. Each type of action is related to

the degree of authority used by the boss and to the amount of
freedom available to his subordinates in reaching decisions. The
actions seen on the extreme left characterize the manager who maintains a high degree of control while those seen on the extreme right
characterize the manager who releases a high degree of control.
Neither extreme is absolute; authority and freedom are never without their limitations.

Now let us look more closely at each of the behavior points
occurring along this continuum.

The manager makes the decision and announces it. In this case
the boss identifies a problem, considers alternative solutions, chooses
one of them, and then reports this decision to his subordinates for
implementation. He may or may not give consideration to what he
believes his subordinates will think or feel about his decision; in any
case, he provides no opportunity for them to participate directly in
the decision-making process. Coercion may or may not be used or
implied.

The manager "sells" his decision. Here the manager, as before,
takes responsibility for identifying the problem and arriving at a
decision. However, rather than simply announcing it, he takes the
additional step of persuading his subordinates to accept it. In doing
so, he recognizes the possibility of some resistance among those who
will be faced with the decision, and seeks to reduce this resistance
by indicating, for example, what the employees have to gain from
his decision.

The manager presents his ideas, invites questions. Here the boss
who has arrived at a decision and who seeks acceptance of his ideas
provides an opportunity for his subordinates to get a fuller explanation of his thinking and his intentions. After presenting the ideas,
he invites questions so that his associates can better understand what
he is trying to accomplish. This "give and take" also enables the
manager and the subordinates to explore more fully the implications
of the decision.

The manager presents a tentative decision subject to change. This
kind of behavior permits the subordinates to exert some influence on
the decision. The initiative for identifying and diagnosing the problem remains with the boss. Before meeting with his staff, he has
thought the problem through and arrived at a decision—but only a
tentative one. Before finalizing it, he presents his proposed solution
for the reaction of those who will be affected by it. He says in effect,
"I'd like to hear what you have to say about this plan that I have

developed. I'll appreciate your frank reactions, but will reserve for myself the final decision."

The manager presents the problem, gets suggestions, and then makes his decision. Up to this point the boss has come before the group with a solution of his own. Not so in this case. The subordinates now get the first chance to suggest solutions. The manager's initial role involves identifying the problem. He might, for example, say something of this sort: "We are faced with a number of complaints from newspapers and the general public on our service policy. What is wrong here? What ideas do you have for coming to grips with this problem?"

The function of the group becomes one of increasing the manager's repertory of possible solutions to the problem. The purpose is to capitalize on the knowledge and experience of those who are on the "firing line." From the expanded list of alternatives developed by the manager and his subordinates, the manager then selects the solution that he regards as most promising.[1]

The manager defines the limits and requests the group to make a decision. At this point the manager passes to the group (possibly including himself as a member) the right to make decisions. Before doing so, however, he defines the problem to be solved and the boundaries within which the decision must be made.

An example might be the handling of a parking problem at a plant. The boss decides that this is something that should be worked on by the people involved, so he calls them together and points up the existence of the problem. Then he tells them:

> There is the open field just north of the main plant which has been designated for additional employee parking. We can build underground or surface multilevel facilities as long as the cost does not exceed $100,000. Within these limits we are free to work out whatever solution makes sense to us. After we decide on a specific plan, the company will spend the available money in whatever way we indicate.

The manager permits the group to make decisions within prescribed limits. This represents an extreme degree of group freedom only occasionally encountered in formal organizations, as, for instance, in many research groups. Here the team of managers or engineers undertakes the identification and diagnosis of the problem, develops alternative procedures for solving it, and decides on

---

[1] For a fuller explanation of this approach, see Leo Moore, "Too Much Management, Too Little Change," *Harvard Business Review* (January-February, 1956), p. 41.

one or more of these alternative solutions. The only limits directly
imposed on the group by the organization are those specified by the
superior of the team's boss. If the boss participates in the decision-
making process, he attempts to do so with no more authority than any
other member of the group. He commits himself in advance to assist
in implementing whatever decision the group makes.

KEY QUESTIONS

As the continuum in Exhibit I demonstrates, there are a number
of alternative ways in which a manager can relate himself to the
group or individuals he is supervising. At the extreme left of the
range, the emphasis is on the manager—on what *he* is interested in,
how *he* sees things, how *he* feels about them. As we move toward
the subordinate-centered end of the continuum, however, the focus
is increasingly on the subordinates—on what *they* are interested in,
how *they* look at things, how *they* feel about them.

When business leadership is regarded in this way, a number of
questions arise. Let us take four of especial importance.

*Can a boss ever relinquish his responsibility by delegating it to
someone else?* Our view is that the manager must expect to be held
responsible by his superior for the quality of the decisions made,
even though operationally these decisions may have been made on a
group basis. He should, therefore, be ready to accept whatever risk is
involved whenever he delegates decision-making power to his subordinates. Delegation is not a way of "passing the buck." Also, it
should be emphasized that the amount of freedom the boss gives to
his subordinates cannot be greater than the freedom which he himself
has been given by his own superior.

*Should the manager participate with his subordinates once he has
delegated responsibility to them?* The manager should carefully think
over this question and decide on his role prior to involving the
subordinate group. He should ask if his presence will inhibit or
facilitate the problem-solving process. There may be some instances
when he should leave the group to let it solve the problem for itself.
Typically, however, the boss has useful ideas to contribute, and
should function as an additional member of the group. In the latter
instance, it is important that he indicate clearly to the group that
he sees himself in a *member* role rather than in an authority role.

*How important is it for the group to recognize what kind of
leadership behavior the boss is using?* It makes a great deal of

difference. Many relationship problems between boss and subordinate occur because the boss fails to make clear how he plans to use his authority. If, for example, he actually intends to make a certain decision himself, but the subordinate group gets the impression that he has delegated this authority, considerable confusion and resentment are likely to follow. Problems may also occur when the boss uses a "democratic" facade to conceal the fact that he has already made a decision which he hopes the group will accept as its own. The attempt to "make them think it was their idea in the first place" is a risky one. We believe that it is highly important for the manager to be honest and clear in describing what authority he is keeping and what role he is asking his subordinates to assume in solving a particular problem.

Can you tell how "democratic" a manager is by the number of decisions his subordinates make? The sheer *number* of decisions is not an accurate index of the amount of freedom that a subordinate group enjoys. More important is the *significance* of the decisions which the boss entrusts to his subordinates. Obviously a decision on how to arrange desks is of an entirely different order from a decision involving the introduction of new electronic data-processing equipment. Even though the widest possible limits are given in dealing with the first issue, the group will sense no particular degree of responsibility. For a boss to permit the group to decide equipment policy, even within rather narrow limits, would reflect a greater degree of confidence in them on his part.

DECIDING HOW TO LEAD

Now let us turn from the types of leadership that are possible in a company situation to the question of what types are *practical* and *desirable*. What factors or forces should a manager consider in deciding how to manage? Three are of particular importance:

1. Forces in the manager.
2. Forces in the subordinates.
3. Forces in the situation.

We should like briefly to describe these elements and indicate how they might influence a manager's action in a decision-making situation.[2] The strength of each of them will, of course, vary from

---

[2] See also Robert Tannenbaum and Fred Massarik, "Participation by Subordinates in the Managerial Decision-Making Process," *Canadian Journal of Economics and Political Science* (August, 1950), pp. 413-418.

instance to instance, but the manager who is sensitive to them can better assess the problems which face him and determine which mode of leadership behavior is most appropriate for him.

Forces in the manager

The manager's behavior in any given instance will be influenced greatly by the many forces operating within his own personality. He will, of course, perceive his leadership problems in a unique way on the basis of his background, knowledge, and experience. Among the important internal forces affecting him will be the following:

1. *His value system.* How strongly does he feel that individuals should have a share in making the decisions which affect them? Or, how convinced is he that the official who is paid to assume responsibility should personally carry the burden of decision making? The strength of his conviction on questions like these will tend to move the manager to one end or the other of the continuum shown in Exhibit I. His behavior will also be influenced by the relative importance that he attaches to organizational efficiency, personal growth of subordinates, and company profits.[3]
2. *His confidence in his subordinates.* Managers differ greatly in the amount of trust they have in other people generally, and this carries over to the particular employees they supervise at a given time. In viewing his particular group of subordinates, the manager is likely to consider their knowledge and competence with respect to the problem. A central question he might ask himself is: "Who is best qualified to deal with this problem?" Often he may, justifiably or not, have more confidence in his own capabilities than in those of his subordinates.
3. *His own leadership inclinations.* There are some managers who seem to function more comfortably and naturally as highly directive leaders. Resolving problems and issuing orders come easily to them. Other managers seem to operate more comfortably in a team role, where they are continually sharing many of their functions with their subordinates.
4. *His feelings of security in an uncertain situation.* The manager who releases control over the decision-making process thereby reduces the predictability of the outcome. Some managers have a greater need than others for predictability and stability in their environment. This "tolerance for ambiguity" is being viewed increasingly by psychologists as a key variable in a person's manner of dealing with problems.

The manager brings these and other highly personal variables to each situation he faces. If he can see them as forces which, consciously or unconsciously, influence his behavior, he can better understand what makes him prefer to act in a given way. And understanding this, he can often make himself more effective.

---

[3] See Chris Argyris, "Top Management Dilemma: Company Needs vs. Individual Development," *Personnel* (September, 1955), pp. 123-134.

Forces in the subordinate

Before deciding how to lead a certain group, the manager will also want to consider a number of forces affecting his subordinates' behavior. He will want to remember that each employee, like himself, is influenced by many personality variables. In addition, each subordinate has a set of expectations about how the boss should act in relation to him (the phrase "expected behavior" is one we hear more and more often these days at discussions of leadership and teaching). The better the manager understands these factors, the more accurately he can determine what kind of behavior on his part will enable his subordinates to act most effectively.

Generally speaking, the manager can permit his subordinates greater freedom if the following essential conditions exist:

1. If the subordinates have relatively high needs for independence. (As we all know, people differ greatly in the amount of direction that they desire.)

2. If the subordinates have a readiness to assume responsibility for decision making. (Some see additional responsibility as a tribute to their ability; other see it as "passing the buck.")

3. If they have a relatively high tolerance for ambiguity. (Some employees prefer to have clear-cut directives given to them; others prefer a wider area of freedom.)

4. If they are interested in the problem and feel that it is important.

5. If they understand and identify with the goals of the organization.

6. If they have the necessary knowledge and experience to deal with the problem.

7. If they have learned to expect to share in decision making. (Persons who have come to expect strong leadership and are then suddenly confronted with the request to share more fully in decision making are often upset by this new experience. On the other hand, persons who have enjoyed a considerable amount of freedom resent the boss who begins to make all the decisions himself.)

The manager will probably tend to make fuller use of his own authority if the above conditions do *not* exist; at times there may be no realistic alternative to running a "one-man show."

The restrictive effect of many of the forces will, of course, be greatly modified by the general feeling of confidence which subordinates have in the boss. Where they have learned to respect and trust him, he is free to vary his behavior. He will feel certain that he will not be perceived as an authoritarian boss on those occasions when he makes decisions by himself. Similarly, he will not be seen as using staff meetings to avoid his decision-making responsibility. In a climate of mutual confidence and respect, people tend to feel less threatened by deviations from normal practice, which in turn makes possible a higher degree of flexibility in the whole relationship.

Forces in the situation

In addition to the forces which exist in the manager himself and in his subordinates, certain characteristics of the general situation will also affect the manager's behavior. Among the more critical environmental pressures that surround him are those which stem from the organization, the work group, the nature of the problem, and the pressures of time. Let us look briefly at each of these.

Type of organization. Like individuals, organizations have values and traditions which inevitably influence the behavior of the people who work in them. The manager who is a newcomer to a company quickly discovers that certain kinds of behavior are approved while others are not. He also discovers that to deviate radically from what is generally accepted is likely to create problems for him.

These values and traditions are communicated in many ways— through job descriptions, policy pronouncements, and public statements by top executives. Some organizations, for example, hold to the notion that the desirable executive is one who is dynamic, imaginative, decisive, and persuasive. Other organizations put more emphasis upon the importance of the executive's ability to work effectively with people—his human relations skills. The fact that his superiors have a defined concept of what the good executive should be will very likely push the manager toward one end or the other of the behavioral range.

In addition to the above, the amount of employee participation is influenced by such variables as the size of the working units, their geographical distribution, and the degree of inter- and intra-organizational security required to attain company goals. For example, the wide geographical dispersion of an organization may preclude a practical system of participative decision making, even though this would otherwise be desirable. Similarly, the size of the working units or the need for keeping plans confidential may make it necessary for the boss to exercise more control than would otherwise be the case. Factors like these may limit considerably the manager's ability to function flexibly on the continuum.

Group effectiveness. Before turning decision-making responsibility over to a subordinate group, the boss should consider how effectively its members work together as a unit.

One of the relevant factors here is the experience the group has had in working together. It can generally be expected that a group which has functioned for some time will have developed habits of cooperation and thus be able to tackle a problem more effectively than a new group. It can also be expected that a group of people with similar backgrounds and interests will work more quickly and easily than people with dissimilar backgrounds, because the communication problems are likely to be less complex.

The degree of confidence that the members have in their ability to solve problems as a group is also a key consideration. Finally, such group variables as cohesiveness, permissiveness, mutual acceptance, and commonality of purpose will exert subtle but powerful influence on the group's functioning.

The problem itself. The nature of the problem may determine what degree of authority should be delegated by the manager to his subordinates. Obviously he will ask himself whether they have the kind of knowledge which is needed. It is possible to do them a real disservice by assigning a problem that their experience does not equip them to handle.

Since the problems faced in large or growing industries increasingly require knowledge of specialists from many different fields, it might be inferred that the more complex a problem, the more anxious a manager will be to get some assistance in solving it. However, this is not always the case. There will be times when the very complexity of the problem calls for one person to work it out. For example, if the manager has most of the background and factual data relevant to a given issue, it may be easier for him to think it through himself than to take the time to fill in his staff on all the pertinent background information.

The key question to ask, of course, is: "Have I heard the ideas of everyone who has the necessary knowledge to make a significant contribution to the solution of this problem?"

The pressure of time. This is perhaps the most clearly felt pressure on the manager (in spite of the fact that it may sometimes be imagined). The more that he feels the need for an immediate decision, the more difficult it is to involve other people. In organizations which are in a constant state of "crisis" and "crash programing" one is likely to find managers personally using a high degree of authority with relatively little delegation to subordinates. When the time pressure is less intense, however, it becomes much more possible to bring subordinates in on the decision-making process.

These, then, are the principal forces that impinge on the manager in any given instance and that tend to determine his tactical behavior in relation to his subordinates. In each case his behavior ideally will be that which makes possible the most effective attainment of his immediate goal within the limits facing him.

Long-Run Strategy

As the manager works with his organization on the problems that come up day by day, his choice of a leadership pattern is usually limited. He must take account of the forces just described and, within the restrictions they impose on him, do the best that he can. But as he looks ahead months or even years, he can shift his thinking from tactics to large-scale strategy. No longer need he be fettered by all of the forces mentioned, for he can view many of them as variables over which he has some control. He can, for example, gain new insights or skills for himself, supply training for individual subordinates, and provide participative experiences for his employee group.

In trying to bring about a change in these variables, however, he is faced with a challenging question: At which point along the continuum *should* he act?

Attaining objectives

The answer depends largely on what he wants to accomplish. Let us suppose that he is interested in the same objectives that most modern managers seek to attain when they can shift their attention from the pressure of immediate assignments:

1. To raise the level of employee motivation.
2. To increase the readiness of subordinates to accept change.
3. To improve the quality of all managerial decisions.
4. To develop teamwork and morale.
5. To further the individual development of employees.

In recent years the manager has been deluged with a flow of advice on how best to achieve these longer-run objectives. It is little wonder that he is often both bewildered and annoyed. However, there are some guidelines which he can usefully follow in making a decision.

Most research and much of the experience of recent years give a strong factual basis to the theory that a fairly high degree of subordinate-centered behavior is associated with the accomplishment of the five purposes mentioned.[4] This does not mean that a manager should always leave all decisions to his assistants. To provide the individual or the group with greater freedom than they are ready for at any given time may very well tend to generate anxieties and therefore inhibit rather than facilitate the attainment of desired objectives. But this should not keep the manager from making a continuing effort to confront his subordinates with the challenge of freedom.

CONCLUSION

In summary, there are two implications in the basic thesis that we have been developing. The first is that the successful leader is one who is keenly aware of those forces which are most relevant to his behavior at any given time. He accurately understands himself, the individuals and group he is dealing with, and the company and broader social environment in which he operates. And certainly he is able to assess the present readiness for growth of his subordinates.

But this sensitivity or understanding is not enough, which brings us to the second implication. The successful leader is one who is able to behave appropriately in the light of these perceptions. If direction is in order, he is able to direct; if considerable participative freedom is called for, he is able to provide such freedom.

Thus, the successful manager of men can be primarily characterized neither as a strong leader nor as a permissive one. Rather, he is one who maintains a high batting average in accurately assessing the forces that determine what his most appropriate behavior at any given time should be and in actually being able to behave accordingly. Being both insightful and flexible, he is less likely to see the problems of leadership as a dilemma.

---

[4] For example, see Warren H. Schmidt and Paul C. Buchanan, *Techniques That Produce Teamwork* (New London: Arthur C. Croft Publications, 1954); and Morris S. Viteles, *Motivation and Morale in Industry* (New York: W. W. Norton & Company, Inc., 1953).

QUESTIONS

1. What is the dilemma to which Tannenbaum and Schmidt refer?
2. Explain the framework the authors suggest will be useful in "grappling with this dilemma."
3. Briefly explain what is meant by the following:
   a. Forces in the manager.
   b. Forces in the subordinate.
   c. Forces in the situation.
   How do these forces influence the manager's behavior?
4. Explain what the authors mean by "long-run strategy."
5. Summarize the implications of the basic thesis that Tannenbaum and Schmidt developed.

18. THE PROBLEM OF LEADERSHIP: A LOOK AT SOME RECENT FINDINGS OF BEHAVIORAL SCIENCE RESEARCH *

James V. Spotts

INTRODUCTION

The problem of leadership has been one of man's major concerns since the days of antiquity. Leadership was a matter of concern in the days when Alexander set out with a small band of Greeks to conquer the world, when Caesar led his troops across the Rubicon, and when Columbus set out with a mutinous crew in leaky boats to discover a "New World." [1]

Early writers frequently wrote lengthy treatises on problems of leadership. Plato in his *Republic* devoted considerable attention to the characteristics of the "philosopher-king," the ideal and just ruler of men. Machiavelli's *The Prince* presented detailed strategies on how a leader could gain and maintain power over others. Some investigators assert that history itself is a poignant record of the successes and failures of man's leadership efforts. While interest in leadership has been a phenomena of long historical concern, the problem of leadership has become one of crucial importance in our modern era of rapid social change, escalating crises, revolution, and nuclear stalemate. In view of this fact, it seems worthwhile to examine what behavioral scientists have discovered about this aspect of interpersonal behavior.

Although literally hundreds of leadership studies have been conducted during the last two decades, there is, at present, no universally accepted theory of leadership. In fact, many divergent and contradictory theories have been proposed. However, during the last few years, research has reached a point where some consistent findings have begun to emerge. This paper will examine some of the past discoveries that are relevant for understanding leadership phenomena and will provide one assessment of the current status of research in this field.

* From *Kansas Business Review*, Vol. 17, No. 6 (June, 1964). pp. 3-13. Reprinted with permission.
[1] B. Bass, *Leadership, Psychology and Organizational Behavior* (New York: Harper, 1960).

DEFINITIONS OF LEADERSHIP

What do people mean when they talk about leadership? What is a leader? If one were to ask any collection of people what they think about leaders and leadership, he would receive ready answers. Everyone has ideas and opinions about leadership, even children.[2] If a hypothetical investigator were to jot down what people say about leadership, he would probably get a collection of statements something like the following:

> A leader's job is to make decisions and exercise authority.
> A leader's job is to develop responsibility and initiative among his subordinates.
> Most leaders are too bossy, or most leaders are not bossy enough.
> A group is only as strong as its leader.
> The trouble in most groups and organizations is that a few people run everything.
> Once a leader shows weakness he's dead.
> To be a leader you must be aggressive and ambitious and tell people what to do.
> If you want to be a leader you have to be sensitive to the needs of others and tell them what they want to hear anyway.[3]

Thus, it would appear that people have all kinds of ideas about leadership. The general conclusion that one might draw is that there is very little consensus about what leadership *is* or what it *should be*.

The mixed and conflicting assumptions about leadership noted above are, frankly, remarkably similar to ideas held, at one time or another, by investigators who have attempted to study and understand leadership from a scientific point of view. D. Cartwright and A. F. Zander[4] assert that two major problems seemed to have caused behavioral scientists the most trouble. The first is that it has been extremely difficult for investigators to separate and disentangle their assumptions about what leadership *should be* from the straightforward research on the question of *what consequences follow specific leadership practices*. That is, the scientific investigation of problems like leadership is a difficult task; particularly, because it involves value judgments or statements implying that something is "good" or "bad." Scientists are notoriously poor at dealing with questions of value, and it has been difficult for them to separate their own armchair assumptions about what constitutes "good" or "poor" leadership from the variables they are attempting to study. It is only in recent

---

[2] D. Cartwright and A. F. Zander (eds.), *Group Dynamics: Research and Theory* (Evanston, Ill.: Row, Peterson, 1953), p. 535.
[3] *Ibid.*, pp. 535-36.
[4] Cartwright and Zander, *op. cit.*

years that investigators have begun to deal with the value question in empirical terms. Thus, leadership is increasingly being defined in operational terms such as behavior that increases production and employee morale or decreases turnover, absenteeism, and so on.

The second, and perhaps more complex, problem has been that of trying to find acceptable scientific definitions for terms like leader and leadership. For some investigators, leadership is viewed as a *characteristic of the individual*; for others, it is seen as a *property of the group*. Some workers define leadership as anyone who performs leadership *acts*; while others define it in terms of *prestige, status,* or *ability to influence others*. The complexity of the definitional problem is reflected by the fact that in a recent review one investigator compiled a list of 130 different definitions of leadership in a sampling of research literature prior to 1949.[5]

Differing Approaches to the Study of Leadership

Many of the scientist's conceptions about man have their historical roots in philosophical assumptions and ideas that have been a part of the cultural heritage for some time. These philosophical notions are sometimes very valuable in that they sharpen the scientist's conceptions of the phenomena under investigation and help him take into account factors that might otherwise be ignored. However, such ideas can just as easily blind him to other scientific data.

During the eighteenth and nineteenth centuries, philosophers were engaged in heated arguments as to the relative importance of *great men* versus the *situation* these men found themselves in. One group of philosophers believed that the personal characteristics of the great men—men of destiny, such as Napoleon, Caesar, Churchill, and the like—determined the course of history. Some exponents of this view were Thomas Carlyle, Friedrich Nietzsche, Francis Galton, and William James. For example, Carlyle[6] argued vehemently that a true genius would contribute no matter where he was found, and James[7] asserted that the great men were the major forces behind the creative mutations and innovations in society.

Opposed to this group were the environmentalists, a group of thinkers who boldly asserted that it was the *Zeitgeist* or situation rather than the great man that determined the course of history.

---

[5] V. J. Bentz, "Leadership: A Study of Social Interaction" (an unpublished manuscript).

[6] S. Hook, *The Hero in History* (New York: John Day, 1943).

[7] "Great Men, Great Thought and Their Environment," *Atlantic Monthly*, Vol. XLVI (1880), pp. 441-59.

These philosophers declared that the great man was nothing more than an expression of the needs of his time; if one man did not fill this need, another would step forward to do so. This group contended that no man could change society and any changes wrought by a great man were illusory in that they were only another expression of the needs of the period.

There are concrete parallels to these two kinds of thinking and speculation in current leadership research. That is, much of the early work aimed at discovering the *traits* of the leader is a logical outgrowth and development from the philosopher's *great man* theme. Similarly, the modern exponents of the environmentalist position may be reflected in the work of the investigators who have attempted to study the effects of *situational* factors upon leadership behavior.

The trait-oriented approach

One major "vein" of early research focused upon isolating the physical, intellectual, or personality traits that distinguished a leader from his followers. Such studies have found that leaders tend to be somewhat bigger than their followers (but not much) and somewhat brighter than the rest of the group (but not much). Well-accepted leaders also evidence somewhat better adjustment than do followers (but, again, not much).[8]

In one early study, O. Tead [9] reported that the traits of the effective leader were nervous and physical energy, a sense of purpose and direction, enthusiasm, friendliness, integrity, technical mastery, decisiveness, intelligence, teaching skills, and faith! In another study, C. I. Barnard [10] stated that the significant traits that distinguished leaders from their followers were physique, technical skill, perception, knowledge, memory, imagination, determination, persistence, endurance, and courage! Other investigators have asserted that the "successful" leader has an above average education, is active in social organizations, and has high moral and ethical standards.[11] Characteristics such as adjustment, good appearance, need for achievement, assertiveness, and fear of failure have also been reported as necessary leadership traits.[12] While these qualities would be desirable in a

---

[8] Cartwright and Zander, *op. cit.*, p. 536.
[9] *The Art of Leadership* (New York: McGraw-Hill, 1935).
[10] *The Functions of the Executive* (Cambridge, Mass.: Harvard University Press, 1948).
[11] R. M. Wald and R. A. Doty, "The Top Executive: A Firsthand Profile," *Harvard Business Review*, Vol. XXXII (1954), pp. 45-54.
[12] W. E. Henry, "Executive Personality and Job Success," *American Management Association, Personnel Series*, no. 120 (1948).

leader, none of them seem essential. In this context, B. Solomon aptly stated:

> The world has seen numerous great leaders who could hardly lay claim to any kind of formal education. History is replete with non-trained, non-academic Fords, Edisons and Carnegies who could not even claim a grammar school education yet managed to become leaders whose influence was felt around the globe.
>
> As for appearance or robust health, need we mention more than the delicate Ghandi, or George Washington Carver, the frail, shriveled, insignificant little Negro who was one of America's greatest scientists, and so many more like them. As for high ideals, fine character, etc., where would Hitler, Capone or Attila the Hun rate here? [13]

While Solomon characterized some of the exceptions to trait-oriented leadership research, a casual examination of the studies cited above quickly reveals one of the major shortcomings of this kind of approach; namely, that rarely, if ever, do two lists agree on the *essential* characteristics of the effective leader. C. Bird [14] and R. M. Stogdill [15] have surveyed well over one hundred studies in this area. The discouraging finding was that less than five per cent of the traits reported as characteristic of the effective leader were common in four or more of the studies surveyed. Secondly, there is some evidence to suggest that the leaders, in fact, cannot be markedly different from their followers. Thus, while the leader must be intelligent he cannot be—or appear to be—too much more intelligent than the other group members. Extremes in personality are not usually associated with leadership, if for no other reason than they make the person too different from the other members of his group.

Investigators appear to be generally coming to the conclusion that certain minimal abilities may be required of all leaders. However, these same traits will probably be widely distributed among the non-leaders as well. Moreover, there seems to be an increasing recognition of wide variations in the characteristics of individuals who become leaders in similar situations and of even greater divergence in the traits of leaders working in different situations.[16]

The situational approach

General dissatisfaction with the failure to isolate leadership traits led some investigators to focus their research efforts more upon the

[13] B. Solomon, *Leadership of Youth* (New York: Youth Services, 1954), p. 15.

[14] *Social Psychology* (New York: Appleton-Century, 1940).

[15] "Personal Factors Associated with Leadership: A Survey of the Literature," *Journal of Psychology*, Vol. XXV (1948), pp. 35-71.

[16] W. O. Jenkins, "A Review of Leadership Studies with Particular Reference to Military Problems," *Psychological Bulletin*, Vol. XLIV (1947), pp. 54-79.

problem of the situation in which leadership occurs. These workers share the assumption that the traits and skills that characterize a "good" leader will vary from group to group and from situation to situation. Associated with this assumption is the notion of *emergent* leadership, which postulates that temporary or situational leaders will arise in groups when necessary to meet the demands of new situations.

The notion that "new" leaders will emerge when groups are in periods of stress or crisis is well documented. W. Crockett[17] found that, when a designated leader failed to provide the leadership functions he was supposed to perform, other members provided them, so there would be a minimal loss in group effectiveness. Similar results were reported by R. L. Kahn and D. Katz[18] in the work situation. These investigators found that, when foremen failed to provide adequate leadership, informal leaders arose in the work groups and provided the needed functions.

Situation-oriented research has assumed that it is unreasonable to expect one leader to always be able to do everything better than anyone else. In our terms, the question might be posed as follows: Is it reasonable to expect a successful businessman to be equally as "effective" in other types of leadership, such as the president of General Motors, a commander of a B-52, the president of a local P.T.A., or a leader of a Special Forces platoon in the jungles of Viet Nam? Obviously, the situation has much to do with determining what leadership skills will be required. Stogdill cogently stated the problem when he said:

> It is not especially difficult to find persons who are leaders. It is quite another thing to place these people in different situations where they will be able to function as leaders. Thus, any adequate analysis of leadership involves not only a study of the leaders but also of the situation in which leadership acts occur.[19]

There are many studies in the literature that support the notion of situational leadership. For example, F. M. Thrasher[20] in a study of street gangs reported that the particular activity of the group was a major factor in determining who would be the gang leader. In a similar study, W. H. Whyte[21] found that the leaders of these informal

---

[17] "Emergent Leadership in Small, Decision-Making Groups," *Journal of Abnormal & Social Psychology*, Vol. LI (1955), pp. 378-83.

[18] "Leadership Practices in Relation to Productivity and Morale," *Group Dynamics*, eds. D. Cartwright and A. Zander (Evanston, Ill.: Row, Peterson, 1956), pp. 612-27.

[19] Stogdill, *op. cit.*, pp. 64-65.

[20] *The Gang* (Chicago: University of Chicago Press, 1927).

[21] *Street Corner Society* (Chicago: University of Chicago Press, 1943).

gangs actively manipulated their group's activities so as to maintain their leadership. The leader tended to involve his group in activities where he knew he would excel and avoided those situations and activities where his leadership might be threatened.

In a study of the leadership patterns of navy enlisted men on ships during wartime discussed by R. Burke,[22] it was found that three different patterns of leadership emerged depending upon the situation. In combat, the officers were the effective leaders of the enlisted group. However, during the periods of rest and boredom between battles, it was the "jokesters" and entertainers who seemed to occupy major leadership roles. Finally, when the ships were returning to port the men with previous shore "contacts" emerged as leaders. Similarly, M. D. Dunkerly's study [23] of leadership patterns among college women points to the significance of situational factors. Those girls chosen as *intellectual leaders,* such as house president and the like, were found to be superior to their peers in judgment, initiative, and intellectual ability. Those girls selected as *social leaders* were generally superior to others in dress and appearance. Finally, girls selected as *religious leaders* were reported as being less 'neurotic" than the others. Surprisingly enough, or perhaps not so surprisingly, the social leaders were found to be most "neurotic."

Bass [24] reports that cross-cultural studies by anthropologists also support the importance of situational leadership factors. He notes that among the Samoans, where there was a highly developed sensitivity to position and social rank, quite different patterns of leadership were evidenced than were found in the individualistic Eskimo society where no man's importance was considered relative to another. Again, leadership among the Iroquois Indians was attained through acts of generosity, hospitality, and cooperation, but, among the Kwakiutls of the Northwest, leadership was established through one's ability to compete financially with others.

Clearly then, there is a wealth of scientific evidence pointing to the significance of situational factors as determinants of leadership behavior. However, this has been found to be only one facet of the leadership problem.

The functional approach

A third approach to the study of leadership developed from a functional orientation to the problem. This approach developed under

[22] "Approaches to Understanding Leadership" (an unpublished manuscript).
[23] "A Statistical Study of Leadership Among College Women," *Studies in Psychology and Psychiatry* (Washington, D. C.: Catholic University of America), Vol. IV (1940), p. 6.
[24] Bass, *op. cit.*

the influence of Kurt Lewin,[25] founder of field-theory in social science, from subsequent theorizing and research in Group Dynamics and, to some extent, from the Human Relations Movement.

With the Functional Approach, emphasis in research shifted from the study of the leader as a *person* to the study of the *group*. One major aim here has been to discover the kinds of behavior that are necessary for a group to survive and attain its goals. In this context, leadership is defined as all those member acts that aid in the development of the group and accomplishment of the group's task. Thus, leadership may be performed by one or many members of the group. It is viewed as a quality that a person may display in varying degrees rather than as something he possesses entirely or not at all. Consequently, leadership may be "possessed" to some degree by any member of a group, irregardless of his formally designated office or position.

The Functional Approach considers both the individual and the situation in which leadership occurs. This approach assumes that groups (and leaders) are continually faced with two interrelated tasks. The first is that groups must find ways to deal with problems associated with attainment of agreed-upon goals, i.e., resolve *Task Problems*. Secondly, group members must find ways to improve and strengthen the group itself, i.e., resolve internal *Maintenance Problems*, to achieve its goals.

K. D. Benne and P. Sheats,[26] R. F. Bales,[27] and others have attempted to isolate some of the major *Task* and *Maintenance Behaviors* that appear in well-functioning groups. Those member (or leader) functions that seem to be effective in moving groups toward resolution of Task Problems include such acts as asking for clarification of issues at hand, summarizing the contributions of others, proposing new ideas and courses of action, giving and receiving information, coordinating the ideas and suggestions made by others, and so on. Members or leader functions that seem to aid in the resolution of internal problems and maintenance of the group include giving minority views a chance to be heard, mediating and harmonizing conflict within the group, maintaining open channels of communication, ventilating feelings for the group, et cetera.

There are a number of studies to suggest that the behavior of the leader varies considerably depending upon the task at hand. For

[25] *Field Theory in Social Sciences* (New York: Harper, 1951).
[26] "Functional Roles of Group Members," *Journal of Social Issues*, Vol. IV (1948), pp. 41-49.
[27] *Interaction Process Analysis: A Method for the Study of Small Groups* (Cambridge, Mass.: Addison-Wesley Press, 1950).

example, L. Carter and his associates [28] studied the activities of "leaders" on three different tasks; namely, those involving reasoning, mechanical assembly, and group discussion. In the reasoning tasks, the leaders more frequently asked for information or facts. When confronted with the mechanical assembly task, the leader most frequently expressed the need for action and worked actively with his men. Finally, in the group discussion situation, he was most likely to give information and ask for expression of opinions.

The results of the Carter study were based upon data obtained with artificially created laboratory groups. However, similar results have been reported from studies of real-life work groups. R. M. Stogdill,[29] in a study of leadership patterns of officers in 46 naval organizations, found that the relative emphasis placed upon particular leadership functions was highly influenced by the task situation. While all officers did some coordinating, this function was most frequently stressed in the work of the executive officer. The function of exercising administrative control was most prominent in the activities of the district medical officer; technical supervision was most frequently observed with the electrical officer; and consultation was practiced most often by the legal officer.

Two other "classic" studies are worthy of mention in this area. The first, by R. White and R. Lippitt,[30] investigated the effects of three different styles of leadership, which these workers designated as *Democratic*, *Autocratic*, and *Laissez-Faire*, on productivity and member morale.

Democratic leaders generally tended to encourage their members to participate in the decision making, did not give rigid rules as to how things were to be done, and gave suggestions, information, and praise to the groups as a whole rather than to individuals. Autocratic leaders, on the other hand, made all final decisions for the groups, told them how to do things, supervised members closely, and praised and punished individual members. The Laissez-Faire leaders gave no suggestions unless specifically requested to do so. They performed a minimum of leader functions and neither praised nor punished group members.

The results of this investigation show clearly that the behavior of the group members differed markedly under the different patterns

[28] L. Carter, Beatrice Haythorn, and J. Lanzatta, "The Behavior of Leaders and Other Members," *Journal of Abnormal & Social Psychology*, Vol. XLVI (1950), pp. 589-595.

[29] "Studies in Naval Leadership, Part II," *Groups, Leadership and Men*, ed. H. Buetzkow (Pittsburgh, Pa.: Carnegie Press, 1951).

[30] "Leadership Behavior and Member Reaction in Three 'Social Climates,'" *Group Dynamics*, eds. D. Cartwright and A. Zander (New York: Row, Peterson, 1956), pp. 585-611.

of leadership. The following was found in this study:

> Democratic leadership resulted in greater productivity (measured by the amount of work done) than did Laissez-Faire leadership. On the other hand, Autocratic leadership led to greater productivity than did Democratic leadership. However, the quality of work was consistently better in the Democratic than Autocratic groups.
>
> There was more direct and indirect discontent expressed in the Autocratic groups than in Democratic ones. When the Autocratic leaders were absent, their groups collapsed. In Democratic groups, there was only a slight drop in work involvement during "leader-out" periods.
>
> Members of the Democratic groups expressed greater cohesiveness and satisfaction with their group experience than did either the Autocratic or Laissez-Faire group members. In this respect, the Autocratic groups were characterized by two patterns of member behavior: either the greatest amount of hostility, aggressiveness, and scapegoating among members or the greatest apathy.
>
> Democratic groups showed the least absenteeism and dropouts while Autocratic groups evidenced the most absenteeism and terminations.
>
> Group members evidenced more submissive and dependent behavior in the Autocratic groups than in the other two and showed unsurprisingly less "talking back" to leaders.

While the findings reported in this study were based upon data gathered from youth groups, subsequent investigations [31] with a variety of adult work groups yielded highly similar results. Taken together, these studies suggest that the "style" of the leader can have marked effects upon group member performance.

The second "classic" leadership study is by L. Coch and J. French, Jr.[32] In the factory studied, changes in products and methods of doing jobs were a necessary result of existing competitive conditions in the field. In addition, a marked increase in absenteeism and turnover in recent years had resulted in unbalanced production lines and had made frequent shifting of individuals from job to job necessary. Job changes were, therefore, frequent and were nearly always accompanied by sharp drops in employee productivity. One serious problem that had developed out of this situation was an intense resistance by the production workers to the necessary changes in methods and jobs. This resistance was expressed in frequent grievances to the union about the piece rates that accompanied the new methods and in high

---

[31] H. Baumgartel, "Leadership Style as a Variable in Research Administration," *Administrative Science Quarterly*, Vol. 11 (1957), pp. 344-360. E. W. Bovard, Jr., "Group Structure and Perception," *Journal of Abnormal & Social Psychology*, Vol. XLVI (1951), pp. 398-405. A. P. Hare, "Small Discussions with Participatory and Supervisory Leadership," *Journal of Abnormal & Social Psychology*, Vol. LVIII (1953), pp. 273-275. M. G. Preston and R. K. Heintz, "Effects of Participatory Versus Supervisory Leadership on Group Judgment," *Journal of Abnormal & Social Psychology*, Vol. XLIV (1949), pp. 345-355.

[32] "Overcoming Resistances to Change," *Human Relations*, Vol. I (1948), pp. 512-532.

turnover, low efficiency, restriction of output, and marked hostility and aggression towards management.

After an initial survey, the experimenters felt that the reactions described above resulted not from the objective difficulties of changing to a new job but from the difficulty of getting people to accept the need for change and to aid actively in creating change. The investigators, therefore, set up a study based upon the idea that participation in the planning and carrying out of change would be helpful. A total of four different work groups were set up; three, the experimental groups, were allowed to participate in the change in different ways, and the fourth, the control group, was treated the same as the groups had been treated in the past.

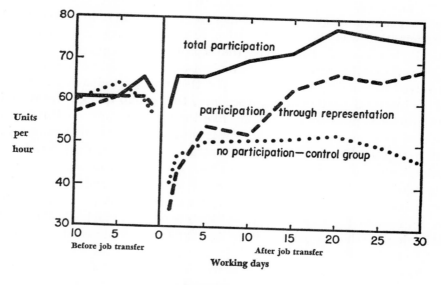

EXHIBIT I

THE EFFECT OF PARTICIPATION ON PRODUCTIVITY

Source: Reproduced by permission from John R. P. French, Jr., C. H. Lawshe, and Floyd C. Mann, "Training for Effective Leadership," *Planning and Training for Effective Leadership* (Ann Arbor, Mich.: The Foundation for Research on Human Behavior, 1956), p. 11.

The control group went through the usual factory routine when jobs were changed. They were told that a change was necessary and that a new piece rate had been set. In this group, there was *no participation* by employees in planning the change though an explanation was given them. The first experimental group involved *participation through representation* in designing the changes to be made;

that is, the group elected representatives who met with management to work out the new methods and piece rates. The third variation, used in the other two experimental groups, involved *total participation* by all of the workers in the designing of the new jobs and establishment of the new rates.

Exhibit I shows rather clearly what happened. The control group showed the usual drop in productivity and did not return to its previous level during the period shown. This group continued to carry grievances to the union about the new rates and showed increased absenteeism, job terminations, deliberate restriction of work output, and hostility towards the foremen and management. The first experimental group, with participation through representation, evidenced an initial drop with fairly rapid recovery. The last two experimental groups (combined in the exhibit), in which total participation was allowed, showed practically no drop and then went to a higher level of productivity than before the change.

Two months after the original study, the control group was involved in a new job transfer using the total participation method. With the total participation procedure, this group quickly recovered its previous efficiency rating and, like the other groups, continued on to new production levels. There was no aggression and turnover in the group for 19 days, a fact that contrasted sharply with its previous behavior after the transfer. From the second experiment, the investigators concluded that the obtained results depended upon the experimental procedures rather than personality factors, such as skill or aggression, since the same individuals evidenced markedly different behavior in the no-participation treatment as contrasted with the total-participation one.

This particular study gives a striking picture of the effects that participatory leadership may have upon productivity. Other data in this study indicated that the morale of the experimental groups was better than that of the control group. Thus, high production apparently was not obtained at the cost of employee morale or satisfaction; in fact, quite the contrary appeared to be true.

It has been argued by some that research developing out of the Functional Approach fosters "group-think," group decision making, and management methods that encourage the supervisor or manager to give his decision-making function to subordinates. For example, W. H. Whyte in his book *The Organization Man* [33] asserts that the current focus upon groups only encourages in leaders a loss of individuality, conformity, and mediocrity. However, it should be noted

[33] (New York: Simon & Schuster, 1956).

that this approach makes no value judgments as to whether a leader should or should not practice a particular leadership pattern. It only asks the question of what consequences are associated with different leadership behavior, and it then leaves the problem of deciding what particular leadership practices will be most effective in a given situation to the practitioner.

Actually, results from studies that have attempted to answer the question of whether leadership should be widely distributed in a group or concentrated in the hands of a few have generally been mixed. For example, A. Bavelas [34] found that concentrated leadership resulted in both more efficient performance and lower morale. Similarly, Kahn and Katz,[35] in a study of a variety of high- and low-producing groups in business and industry, found that the supervisors of high-producing group units tended to take clear control of several leadership functions such as planning, coordinating, et cetera. However, these supervisors were also more inclined to delegate responsibilities to others, encourage subordinates to make decisions, and take initiative in many activities.

The interactionistic approach

Finally, consideration should be given to what may be defined, for lack of a better term, as an *Interactionistic* Approach to the study of leadership. In many respects, this approach is a logical outgrowth and extension of the Functional Approach. However, there is value in distinguishing the two approaches, if for no other reason than to examine the interactionist's methodology. This approach also has a certain uniqueness in that it stresses the quality of the leader-subordinate relationship as an important determinant of productivity, morale, and other goals seen as "good" or desirable by organizations.

One basic assumption of this approach is that leadership cannot be studied in isolation, because it represents an *interaction* between members of a group. One argument leveled at some of the functional studies was that the results were based upon experimentally constituted laboratory groups that were transitory and divorced from the "real-life" conditions in which leadership occurs. Such complaints can hardly be leveled at interactionistic research, since these investigations characteristically have been field studies in all kinds of work groups and organizations.

A favorite methodology in this kind of research is to select "high-productive" and "low-productive" or "effective" and "ineffective"

---

[34] "Morale and Training of Leaders," *Civilian Morale*, ed. G. Watson (Boston, Mass.: Houghton-Mifflin, 1942).
[35] Kahn and Katz, *op. cit.*

work groups doing the same tasks in an organization and then study the leader-follower interactions. In these studies "productive," "effective," and "good" groups are distinguished not on a basis of armchair judgments, such as was observed in some of the earlier leadership research, but on the basis of empirical indices, such as productivity per man, job satisfaction, turnover, absenteeism, costs per man, and so on.

The answer to the question—Are there significant differences in the superior-subordinate relationships of "productive" and "nonproductive" work groups?—seems to be basically "Yes." Evidence from field studies with B-52 bomber crews, factory assembly lines, public utility companies, infantry combat squads, insurance companies, government agencies, petroleum companies, and so on would suggest that the leader-follower interaction may differ quite markedly in "productive" and "nonproductive" groups.[36]

Contrary to what one might suspect, the leaders or supervisors of highly productive units—crews, departments, or divisions—do not appear to devote their greatest time and efforts to technical or job-oriented functions with subordinates. Rather, supervisors or leaders with the best records of performance focus their primary attention upon the human aspects of their subordinate relationships and attempt to build effective work groups with high-performance goals.[37]

High-productive leaders—supervisors and managers—tend to spend more time than low-productive supervisors in motivating their subordinates, providing structure, and keeping them informed as to what is going on, getting their ideas and suggestions on important matters before going ahead, training their subordinates for more responsibilities, trying out new ideas with them, and, in general, showing consideration for the follower and his needs.

At the other extreme, the ineffective or low-production leader frequently demands more from his subordinate than can be done, criticizes them in front of others, treats subordinates without respect for their feelings, rides them for making mistakes, initiates actions without consulting them, and refuses to accept their ideas and suggestions or even explain the actions he has taken.

[36] R. Likert, *New Patterns of Management* (New York: McGraw-Hill, 1961).

[37] Bass, *op. cit.* Likert, *op. cit.* R. Likert and R. L. Kahn, "Planning for Effective Leadership," *Planning and Training for Effective Leadership*, ed. S. Seashore (Ann Arbor, Mich.: Foundation for Research on Human Behavior, 1956), pp. 1-7. F. C. Mann and J. Dent, *Appraisal of Supervisors and Attitudes of Their Employees in an Electric Power Company* (Ann Arbor, Mich.: Institute for Social Research, 1954). D. Katz, N. Maccoby, G. Gurin, and L. G. Floor, *Productivity, Supervision and Morale Among Railroad Workers* (Ann Arbor, Mich.: Institute for Social Research, 1951).

High- and low-production leaders differ not only in their relationships with their subordinates but also in their relationships with their supervisors. D. C. Pelz [38] found that high-production leaders tended to have much greater influence upon their own superiors on matters relating to subordinates' pay, working conditions, promotions, etc. than did low-production leaders. In this study, it was also found that, when leaders who had above average influence with their own bosses followed "good" supervisory practices, the subordinates tended to react favorably. However, when supervisors who were below average in the amount of influence they had with their supervisors practiced these same desirable supervisory procedures, they usually failed to obtain a favorable reaction and not infrequently obtained adverse reactions from their subordinates. Apparently, if the leader is to influence his followers effectively, he must also be able to influence his own supervisor as well.

Interactionistic research findings constitute perhaps the closest thing to what might be regarded as leadership "principles" in the whole literature. Although the maxims are fairly well documented by research and experience, they do not form any kind of compact "cookbook" or guide to effective leadership. None of the findings is universally applicable; in fact, one may sometimes obtain similar results with almost opposite leadership practices. Some representative leadership "principles" that are frequently reported in the research literature are as follows.[39]

> Supervisors of high-productive units spend a greater amount of time developing their work groups into "close," highly cohesive teams than do supervisors or managers of low-productive units.

One assumption here is that a supervisor or leader cannot treat his subordinates with full effectiveness unless he recognizes the work group as a source of morale and motivation. S. Seashore's [40] study of high- and low-"cohesive" work groups in a large manufacturing company indicates clearly the powerful influences a small group can exert upon a member's behavior and adjustment. This investigator found that members of high-cohesive groups exhibited much less anxiety than low-cohesive groups when feeling "jumpy" and nervous, feeling under pressure to achieve higher productivity, and feeling a lack of support from the company were used as measures of anxiety.

[38] "Leadership Within a Hierarchical Organization," *Journal of Social Issues*, Vol. VII (1951), pp. 49-55.

[39] Bass, *op. cit.* Likert, *op. cit.* Likert and Kahn, *op. cit.* Mann and Dent, *op. cit.*

[40] *Group Cohesiveness in the Industrial Work Group* (Ann Arbor, Mich.: Institute for Social Research, 1954), p. 120.

Seashore concluded that membership in a cohesive group provides the worker with effective support in his encounters with work-associated anxiety and provides direct satisfactions that are anxiety reducing.

Similarly, research by E. L. Trist and K. W. Bamforth [41] with English coal miners supports the importance of the group as a determinant of worker effectiveness and morale. As a part of a program of increasing the mechanization and "efficiency" of mining operations, management broke up the miner's small, face-to-face work groups and assigned the workers to more isolated tasks. The reorganization of the small work groups led to serious problems of absenteeism, turnover, and sickness (including psychosomatic disorders). This problem became so acute that it was necessary to alter attempts at increased mechanization and restore the small work groups, even though, from an outsider's point of view, this seemed "inefficient."

While the principle of utilization of group factors such as loyalty and group cohesiveness appears to be one of the most firmly established findings in the literature, highly cohesive groups are *not always* the most productive. In Seashore's study,[42] high productivity among cohesive groups was found *only* if the group members saw the company as a supportive and secure situation. Among crews who saw the company as threatening, high cohesiveness was associated with low productivity.

> General rather than close supervision is more often associated with a high rather than a low level of productivity.

A number of investigators [43] have found that high-production supervisors and managers supervise their employees less closely than low-production supervisors. High-production supervisors make clear to their subordinates what needs to be done then let these subordinates use their own ideas and experience to do the job in the way they find best. Low-production supervisors frequently spend more time with their subordinates than do high-production ones, but the time is broken up into short periods because the supervisors give specific instructions such as "Do this," "Don't do that," et cetera.[44]

An interesting parallel to this proposition is that leaders tend to supervise their subordinates as they themselves are supervised.[45]

---

[41] "Some Social and Psychological Consequences of the Long-wall Method of Coal Getting," *Human Relations*, Vol. IV (1951), pp. 3-38.

[42] Seashore, *op. cit.*

[43] Cartwright and Zander, *op. cit.* Kahn and Katz, *op. cit.* Likert, *op. cit.* Seashore, *op. cit.*

[44] Likert, *op. cit.*

[45] J. M. Pfiffner, "The Effective Supervisor: An Organization Research Study," *Personnel*, Vol. XXXI (1955), pp. 539-40. E. S. Stanton, "Company Policies and Supervisors' Attitudes Toward Supervision," *Journal of Applied Psychology*, Vol. XLIV (1960), pp. 22-26.

Thus, if a department head utilizes general or close supervision, his foremen tend to follow similar practices. It would appear reasonable to assume that low-production subordinates might require more close supervision; however, on the other hand, there is some evidence to suggest that close supervision may actually *cause* poor performance in that it emphasizes precise rules and procedures, at the expense of long-range goals, subordinate morale, and job satisfaction.[46]

While general rather than close supervision practices are often more characteristic of high-producing managers than of low ones, research findings *do not* show that all high-producing managers adhere to this pattern. Some technically competent, job-centered, intensive, and tough managers have achieved impressive levels of productivity. However, the members of these work groups showed unfavorable attitudes towards their work and supervisors, hostility and resentment towards management, a high number of grievances that went to arbitration, frequent slowdowns, work stoppages, waste, and high job turnover.[47]

Likert and Kahn [48] reported a study that attempted to evaluate the effects of (1) tighter controls and direction and (2) greater employee autonomy and participation as alternative ways to achieve high productivity and employee satisfaction in the same organization! In some sections of the company, results were sought through closer supervision, more detailed work procedures, and other forms of tighter control and direction. In other sections, a program of encouraging more autonomy and participation in decision making was followed. Responsibility for decisions was pushed down to lower levels of the organization and greater freedom was given employees. *In both situations, productivity was increased about 15-20 per cent.* Thus, contradictory leadership practices were effective in increasing productivity; however, employee morale changed for the worse in units where tighter controls were imposed and changed for the better in those units where greater autonomy was instituted.

> The greater the amount of unreasonable pressure toward production that men feel from their supervisors, the lower the productivity and the less confidence and trust they have in their supervisors.

Even this finding must be tempered by situational factors; that is, increasing management pressures toward productivity may have different results depending upon the initial level of pressure.[49] At

---

[46] Likert, *op. cit.*
[47] Likert, *op. cit.*
[48] Likert and Kahn, *op. cit.*
[49] Likert and Kahn, *op. cit.*

initially low levels of pressure, an increase in emphasis upon productivity by supervisors not only results in higher productivity but also increases the satisfaction of the men with their supervisor. However, at higher levels of pressure, further increases in emphasis upon productivity by supervisors frequently tend to result in lower productivity and adverse reactions toward the supervisor.

Conclusions

The studies surveyed represent a fair sampling of more than two decades of leadership research, and, on the basis of these findings, some general conclusions can be drawn.

The available evidence seems to indicate that there are probably no personality traits or characteristics that consistently distinguish the leader from his followers. There is some evidence, however, to suggest that the leader probably cannot be markedly different from his subordinates if he is to be followed.

The results of a number of studies indicate that leadership does not occur in a vacuum but at a particular time and place and under a particular set of circumstances. Therefore, the situation determines to some degree the kinds of leadership skills and behavior that may be required. One reassuring finding that has emerged from these studies has been the "discovery" that, when formal or designated leadership fails to provide its required functions, there is a tendency for other members of the group to step in and perform the "needed" functions so that there will be a minimal loss in group effectiveness.

Some workers have investigated the effects of differing kinds of leadership styles and have begun the process of explicating what kinds of leadership acts or behavior helps groups "move forward" and function effectively. Some of these studies suggest that there is a tendency for democratic or participatory leadership behavior to be associated with productivity, increased worker morale, and a number of other factors. Directive leadership has been found to lead to equally high productivity but often results in low morale and commitment to work. However, the relationship between leadership styles and job performance is much too complex to be explained simply by "democratic" or "authoritarian" leadership practices. Different leadership practices seem appropriate for different situations. Thus, under certain conditions, participative leadership may be most effective. Under other conditions, a more directive leadership may be required. Again, the personality characteristics and expectations of subordinates will influence the kinds of leadership practices that are most effective. An increase in the degree of follower participation will often have favorable effects *if* the subordinates have relatively high needs for independence, a readiness to assume responsibility, the necessary knowledge and experience to deal with problems, and an identification with the goals of the organization.[50] However, the use of participatory practices with workers who lack these attributes might have highly adverse and undesirable effects.

There is a growing body of research indicating rather clear differences between the behavior of high- and low-production workers in real-life work situations. These studies suggest that high-production supervisors tend to supervise their subordinates less closely, spend more time consulting with their workers, and give them more opportunities to participate in decisions that affect them than do low-production leaders. The quality of the leader-subordinate relationship—the degree of genuine respect and consideration that the leader shows for the follower's needs—appears to be a crucial factor here. This is perhaps another way of saying that employee-centered leadership tends to be more closely associated with subordinate productivity, morale, and job satisfaction than does production-centered leadership.

On the basis of the research surveyed in this presentation, it would seem clear that leaders accomplish their work through other people and their success as leaders depends upon their ability to enlist and maintain follower commitment and collaboration for the attainment of group or organizational goals. In this respect, some of the research considered here may provide ideas that may be worth considering in the concrete work situation. However, at the present time, there is no straightforward set of supervisory practices that will *always* yield the best results. Research reported in this presentation suggests that a leader's objectives may be reached through multiple and sometimes even contradictory means. At this point, it would appear that the choice of alternative leadership practices for a given individual will depend upon a number of factors, such as the following:

> The leader's personal preference or "style."
> The leader's skill in applying various leadership practices.
> The leader's confidence in his subordinates.
> The leader's value system or the importance that he attaches to organizational efficiency, personal growth of subordinates, company profits, et cetera.
> The leader's assessment of the "situation" of his subordinates.

---

[50] R. Tannenbaum and W. H. Schmidt, "How to Choose a Leadership Pattern," *Harvard Business Review*, Vol. XXXVI (1958), pp. 95-101.

The leader's evaluation of possible undesirable side effects of a particular practice.[51]

Viewed from a historical point of view, the studies considered indicate that behavioral scientists are making progress in understanding the phenomena of leadership. Research has come a long way from the early study of leadership traits, and investigators can now state with some certainty what they know and do not know. Moreover, they are in a position to begin to specify some of the conditions under which given leadership practices may be effective. However, while behavioral scientists may be able to provide managers and supervisors with some tentative "guidelines," leadership research can never specify the "proper" practices for all situations. *In the concrete leadership situtation, the final choice and responsibility for specific action must always fall back upon the judgment and good common sense of frail human beings, and, in all due respects to the "leader," this is as it should be.*

QUESTIONS

1. Explain the two major problems that have caused behavioral scientists the most trouble in their attempts to study and understand leadership from a scientific point of view.
2. Briefly distinguish the various approaches to the study of leadership.
3. Which of these approaches do you believe has the greatest merit? Why?
4. As a result of his study of the available research evidence, what were Spotts' conclusions regarding leadership?
5. Upon what factors does the choice of a leadership style depend? Do you agree? Why? Do Spotts and Golembiewski agree?

GENERAL QUESTIONS ON PART III

1. Distinguish the basic aproaches to the study of leadership. Which approach do you think is best? Why?
2. Compare Jennings' concept of leadership with that of Tannenbaum's.
3. Explain the relationship of leadership to human relations.
4. Discuss the basic problems we face in studying leadership.
5. Prepare a list of five textbook definitions of leadership. Which do you think is the most meaningful? Why?
6. State your own definition of leadership and explain it.
7. How important are personality traits to leadership?
8. Why are all managers, whether they be first-line foremen or company presidents, leaders?
9. What type of leadership accounts for the greatest productivity of groups? Why?
10. Why is it important for the leader to understand himself?

---

[51] Likert and Kahn, *op. cit.* Tannenbaum and Schmidt, *op. cit.*

PART IV. MOTIVATION AND BEHAVIOR

In the introduction to leadership it was stated that the leader's fundamental responsibility in any form of organization is to get work done through people. This statement, it should be noted, makes explicit the fact that the basic objective of all leaders is the effective accomplishment of the duties and the responsibilities necessary for the successful operation of an organization. All activities of people who are in leadership positions must therefore be directed toward this end, for it is this goal that justifies the existence of—in fact, establishes the necessity for—a leader.

Implicit in this statement of leadership is the fact that getting the work of an organization done is immediately and finally dependent upon the behavior of the employees of that organization. The reason for this is obvious. Nothing that must be done in a firm can be done until some person assumes the obligation of and carries out the duties and responsibilities inherent in or delegated to his position. Consequently, whether the employee accomplishes his responsibilities through the use of inanimate and inarticulate tools, such as brooms, lathes, or electronic computers, or solely via cogitative and intellectual powers, all facets of work done in an organization are ultimate manifestations of some manner or form of human behavior. It seems logical to conclude, therefore, that the most immediate objective of leadership is the achievement of that type of employee behavior which will result in the effective accomplishment of the duties and responsibilities required to operate a firm successfully. To understand completely, then, the fundamental nature of human relations and leadership requires some comprehension of the basic aspects of employee behavior, for, in the final analysis, the leader's main task is to influence the behavior of people toward predetermined goals.

WHY PEOPLE BEHAVE AS THEY DO

Although human behavior is a vast and complicated subject composed of and influenced by many variables, it can be simply described as the total response of an individual to various motivating forces.

In other words, all rational human behavior is caused: we behave as we do because we are responding to forces that have the power to prompt—motivate—us to some manner or form of action. In a sense, therefore, behavior *per se* can be considered to be an end result—a response to basic forces. From a more fundamental viewpoint, however, it can be seen that behavior is actually only an intermediate step in a chain of events. Motivating forces lead to some manner or form of behavior, and that behavior must be directed toward some end. That is to say, there must be some reason why we are responding to the motivating force. And that reason could only be to satisfy the force which in the first place motivated us to behave. Consequently, all human beings, whether they do so rationally or irrationally, consciously or subconsciously, behave as they do to satisfy various motivating forces. In diagram form this sequence of human behavior may be summarized as follows:

MOTIVATING FORCES $\longrightarrow$ MOTIVATE $\longrightarrow$ BEHAVIOR $\longrightarrow$ END $\big\langle$ SATISFACTION OF THE MOTIVATING FORCES

Basic motivating forces

The forces that motivate people, that is, the forces that lead to some manner or form of human behavior, are legion in number and vary considerably in degree, not only from individual to individual, but also from time to time within the same person. They range in nature from extremely ethereal and psychological motives, such as truth, love, and beauty, to concrete physical, instinctive, and basic physiological forces, such as hunger, thirst, and avoidance of pain. Because several of the articles that follow explore in detail the nature of some of the specific forces that motivate people, we shall briefly consider here only the major classes or types of forces that can be distinguished. But it should be noted that in this book we shall consider only those motivating stimuli that are inherent in and internal to the human being. These particular forces are commonly called *needs*. We shall purposefully exclude from our analysis consideration of forces such as fire, electricity, and so on. Although such stimuli quite obviously have the power to influence and determine human behavior, they are to a great extent outside the influence of management and hence leadership.

Although there have been many descriptions of the types or classes of needs that motivate human behavior, it is possible to classify most internal human motives under at least three general headings, namely, physiological, sociological, and psychological needs. Whether or not this is a complete classification of all human needs is impossible to say at this time. Our present state of knowledge of the things that motivate human beings is simply not complete enough to give a more definite classification. But the three categories stated here do allow a grouping of the known motives in a manner that makes it convenient to study them and to understand how they influence human behavior.

Physiological needs. Physiological needs are the most primitive and fundamental of all motivating forces. They are identified in both animals and men and are primarily instinctive in nature. They are the most obvious and the most easily observed of all human motives. Included in this class are our needs for food, water, shelter, air, sleep, and so on. In a sense, they are the most powerful of motivating stimuli, for we must satisfy most of them in order to exist. Consequently, they are the needs that we take care of first. They quite obviously exert a tremendous influence on behavior, especially in the world of work, because many of them, like food and shelter, are most easily satisfied with money earned from gainful employment.

Sociological needs. The second basic classification of human needs is that of sociological needs. Motives in this category stem primarily from man's relationship with other people. Unlike physiological needs, which are primitive and instinctive in nature, sociological needs exist on a more refined level and are acquired in the course of everyday existence. They include motives such as the need to belong, the need for love and affection, and the need for acceptance. Although considerably more difficult to observe than physiological motives, sufficient evidence of the operation of these needs is not difficult to find. In particular, one need only to witness the pleasure an individual obtains from acceptance by a group or the potent impact upon a person when members of a group refuse to converse with him.

Psychological needs. The third general group of human motives is classified as psychological needs. Needs in this category are influenced by and are, to a great extent, dependent upon relationships with other people, but they differ from sociological needs because they are concerned only with man's view of himself. Included in this classification are motives such as the need for recognition, achievement, and status, plus many, many others. Unlike physiological and sociological needs, these motivating forces are very difficult to satisfy. But their influence on human behavior is just as important—if not more so in the context of an organization—as the other two basic groups of needs. One has only to examine his own psychological motives to verify this.

Hierarchy of needs

As several of the following articles indicate, one of the most fundamental facets of needs as motivational forces is their hierarchical relationship. Although it is difficult to perceive this character of needs between the sociological and the psychological groups, primarily because of the extent to which these two classifications depend upon relationships with fellow men, it is apparent that physiological needs take precedence over all other needs. In fact, it is only when behavior has satisfied these instinctive motives that satisfaction of other needs becomes important. Consider, for example, the worker faced with continued unemployment. Certainly the loss of earning power is a more important determinant of his behavior than any concern he may have for belonging or recognition. However, when these primitive needs are satisfied—and as long as they are satisfied—sociological and psychological forces take precedence and exert the greatest influence on man's behavior. This point is particularly important in times of full employment, for it is the basic reason why employees are dissatisfied even though their wages, working conditions, and hours are extremely good.

Needs and frustration

Another important aspect of needs as basic motivational forces is the fact that they rarely influence behavior individually. Indeed, there is considerable evidence to prove that most of the time they operate in combination with each other. Consequently, at times the individual may be faced with a situation where his behavior to satisfy one need will frustrate or prevent him from satisfying another need. When such conflicts arise, the person must make a decision as to which need he will satisfy. Depending on the nature of the motives in conflict, he may quickly satisfy one need and forget the other, compromise to some extent, or choose the lesser of two evils. In any case, some degree of frustration will result.

Because frustration occurs whenever needs go unsatisfied, it should be noted that in addition to conflict between motives there are other ways in which an individual can become frustrated. Generally speaking, these obstacles to goal satisfaction are classified under the headings of environmental and personal factors. *Environmental factors* are external to the individual and exist in the situation in which he finds himself. An example of this type of barrier would be a supervisor who so ill-fits his job that he is unable to perceive the true ability of a subordinate and consequently impedes the employee's progress in promotions and wage increases. *Personal factors,* on the other hand, are internal to the individual. They usually result from the individual's overestimation of his capabilities. An example of this type of obstacle would be the employee who wants to become a foreman or a manager, but who simply does not—and never will—possess the abilities for such work. Until such an individual recognizes his limitations and sets different goals for himself, he will remain disappointed and frustrated. This has, of course, drastic implications in the practice of human relations and leadership, for quite frequently the leader will find himself in situations where he must help an employee recognize, understand, and accept the true nature of the employee's capability and potential.

How people react to frustration

Although reaction to frustration varies from individual to individual, there are definite patterns of behavior that can be observed. One common reaction occurs when the individual *compensates* or substitutes one need for another. This means, in essence, that a person simply directs his behavior away from a goal that he finds difficult or impossible to satisfy toward another goal from which he can obtain greater satisfaction. An example of this type of behavior would be the employee who, finding his need for belonging is not satisfied as a member of the organization that employs him, turns his energies toward the satisfaction of his motive by joining and becoming active in a union. It should be noted that this type of reaction can be either advantageous or detrimental to the interest of management, depending upon the nature of the substituted goal. Which behavior pattern the employee selects, however, is frequently a function of how rewarding such a reaction has been in his previous experience. If a particular response has in the past alleviated his frustration, he will more than likely repeat his action when he encounters similar frustrating situations in the future. The main point here, of course, is that if the employee's original motivating force was valid, he should have been able to satisfy it without having to turn his behavior toward a goal that might be contrary to the interest of his employer.

Another common reaction to frustration is *rationalization.* This type of behavior is evidenced by the individual who blames someone else for his failure to satisfy his need or who simply talks himself out of a goal. An example of this response is the worker who, failing to get a promotion, blames his supervisor for having it "in for him" or who maintains he did not want the job anyway. Although rationalization is frequently considered to be a harmless reaction to frustration, it can, unfortunately, lead to more serious responses, such as apathy, indifference, or disinterest, all of which are detrimental to an organization's efficiency.

One of the most serious responses to frustration is that of *aggression*, either in the form of opposition and antagonism or open conflict and physical violence. Whatever form this particular type of response takes, it always involves action against the barriers and obstacles that prevent satisfaction of a motivating force. It is most easily seen in children, who usually vent their frustration directly against the obstacle that deprives them of satisfaction, such as the child who hits his friend with the toy they are arguing about. Adults, on the other hand, most frequently vent their aggression against a barrier in an indirect manner, especially in an employment situation. Thus the foreman who has been reprimanded by his superior may in turn abuse his subordinates. Or the worker whose grievance has gone unnoticed or been improperly handled may resort to petty thievery or sabotage. This tendency of adults to react indirectly to the cause of their frustration is one of the basic reasons why so many people in leadership positions find it difficult or impossible to change the behavior of their subordinates. Altogether too frequently, such leaders "misread" behavioral patterns and make the serious mistake of confusing behavior that is only symptomatic of a more basic cause as a direct reaction to a frustration situation. Any attempt to change symptomatic behavior, therefore, will seldom, if ever, alleviate or change the factor that influenced such behavior in the first place. This is illustrated, perhaps, in the employee who is habitually late for work (indirect reaction to frustration) because the nature of his job is so undemanding of his interest and talents (direct cause of frustration) that he finds very little incentive to get to work on time. Lecturing such a person on the advantages of promptness, therefore, may temporarily change his behavior, but it will in no manner or form remedy or affect the basic underlying cause of his behavior. Unless managers recognize this phenomenon of adult behavior and develop the sensitivity to perceive and separate symptom from cause, they can hardly hope to effectively change the behavior of subordinates, particularly when that behavior is simply a superficial manifestation of a deeply underlying cause. Effective leadership, therefore, quite obviously requires great insight into all the factors that motivate people to behave as they do.

Perhaps the most extreme forms of reaction to frustration are regression and withdrawal. In *regression,* the individual is said to revert from adult levels of behavior to childish levels of behavior. Apparently such a response allows the person to escape the frustrations of adulthood and thereby to gain greater security and satisfaction. In *withdrawal,* the individual retreats from reality to the extent that he is completely out of contact with the situation in which he exists. Both types of behavior are, of course, indicative of serious mental disorders and require professional help. About all the leader can do if he perceives such behavior is attempt to help the individual obtain competent counseling. In no case, of course, should the manager attempt to play the role of a trained psychologist or psychiatrist.

MOTIVATION, ATTITUDES, AND MORALE

There is much evidence today that employers and managers are greatly concerned with employee morale. They tend to believe that if morale is high employees are satisfied and happy about their jobs, working conditions, pay, and other aspects of the employment of situation and are, consequently, producing efficiently and effectively. On the other hand, if they believe morale is low, they assume that employees are dissatisfied with things in general and that quality and quantity of production are accordingly lower. Unfortunately, empirical data to support this assumed correlation between morale and productivity are difficult to obtain, primarily because of difficulties in defining morale and establishing benchmarks to measure it.

Although the term *morale* is used very loosely, there is general agreement that it refers to a combination of employee attitudes toward employment. That is to say, morale is a synthesis of how employees think and feel about their jobs, their working conditions, their superiors, their firm, their fellow workers, their pay, and so on. Defined in this way, the term includes both individual and group aspects of morale, *individual morale* being the structure of an employee's attitudes toward employment, whereas *group morale* is the general tone of employee attitudes in the organization as a whole or in a particular office or department.

Whatever are the difficulties in defining and measuring morale, it is possible to conclude, deductively speaking, that it plays an important role in motivation and behavior, albeit a complex one. The reason for this is obvious. If it is true that employee behavior is directed toward satiation of needs, the result of that behavior must directly influence the attitude of the individual. In other words, if a particular response results in satisfaction of one or more needs, it could be deduced that the individual's attitude with respect to his need, his action, and the result of his action is good. As long as such behavior results in satisfaction, consequent attitudes should remain good. If, on the other hand, behavior does not result in satisfaction, frustration and its consequences will occur and a negative (poor) attitude will result. From a management viewpoint this assumes, of course, that in both cases the employee's need and response are, in the first place, oriented toward the interests of the organization.

The implication of the relationship between morale and behavior is clear: significant attention must be given to morale as an indicator of need satisfaction, both of the individual employee and of the group as a whole. The leader must therefore make every effort possible and use every means at his disposal to determine and be cognizant of employee attitudes. If he will direct his energy toward this task, he should be able to motivate his subordinates more efficiently and, consequently, to improve his effectiveness as a leader.

MOTIVATION AND PERFORMANCE

Although motives are the primary energizers of behavior, they are not the sole determinants of employee performance. In fact, human performance *per se* is largely dependent upon habits and skills that have been acquired through the process of learning and training. To expect effective performance from an employee with high motivation but no skill or potential for the job in question is therefore not only wishful thinking but also downright inefficient management. This quite obviously means that proper motivation of employees presupposes that they have been properly recruited, selected, placed, inducted, and trained.

Assuming, however, that employees possess at least the minimum degree or level of skill required for job performance, there is considerable evidence to prove that increased motivation can improve employee performance of almost any kind. In our everyday experience almost all of us have witnessed this interaction of motivation and skill when we saw the effect of the coach's pep talk or the highly motivated semiskilled person "beat" the performance of the highly skilled but poorly motivated person. In short, if the level of skill is sufficient for the job, the absence or presence of motivation can make a prodigious difference in employee performance.

Total Climate

Although other sections of this book deal more specifically with some of the basic tools (e.g., communications) that leaders can and must use in their efforts to motivate people, it should be noted here that the effective influencing of human behavior cannot be dependent on the use of only several techniques of human relations. The reason for this is clear: it is the total environment in which a person works that influences his behavior. In fact, from a Gestaltic viewpoint it could be said that the total behavior of an individual is greater than the sum of the parts that influence that behavior. Consequently, because the environment in which we live and work contains many factors that influence and cause people to behave as they do, it is imperative for the leader to be sensitive to and develop a total climate that will be conducive to the kind of behavior that is necessary for the accomplishment of the organization's goals. This means, of course, that in addition to being a leader, he must also be a competent manager.

Motivation, Human Relations, and Management

In previous sections of this book emphasis was placed on two important points; namely, (1) that all members of management, whether they be first-line supervisors or chief executives, hold positions of leadership because of the very nature of their jobs, and (2) that human relations, as it is considered in this text, is manifested in the actions and practices of leaders, especially in the environment of the business unit. In this section, heavy emphasis is given to the concept of motivation because, in the final analysis, the leader will get work done efficiently and effectively only if he properly motivates the behavior of his subordinates.

Because the leadership function of motivating people requires a definitive and comprehensive understanding of the causes and effects of human behavior, effort was made to choose a selection of articles that would provide a sound foundation for the practice of human relations. Accordingly, Maslow's article was chosen because it is a classic and fundamental analysis of why people behave as they do. McGregor's article was picked because it is an excellent treatment of employee motivation and behavior in the context of an enterprise. Likert's article was included because it offers concrete proof that proper motivation of employees can increase productivity. The article by Clark was selected because it examines a number of different researches in the field of organizational behavior to see if their similarities can be explained by the use of Maslow's need-hierarchy concept. And, lastly, Herzberg's article was chosen because it presents a new theory of motivation based on research.

19. A THEORY OF HUMAN MOTIVATION *

A. H. Maslow

I. INTRODUCTION

In a previous paper [1] various propositions were presented which would have to be included in any theory of human motivation that could lay claim to being definitive. These conclusions may be briefly summarized as follows:

1. The integrated wholeness of the organism must be one of the foundation stones of motivation theory.

2. The hunger drive (or any other physiological drive) was rejected as a centering point or model for a definitive theory of motivation. Any drive that is somatically based and localizable was shown to be atypical rather than typical in human motivation.

3. Such a theory should stress and center itself upon ultimate or basic goals rather than partial or superficial ones, upon ends rather than means to these ends. Such a stress would imply a more central place for unconscious than for conscious motivations.

4. There are usually available various cultural paths to the same goal. Therefore conscious, specific local-cultural desires are not as fundamental in motivation theory as the more basic, unconscious goals.

5. Any motivated behavior, either preparatory or consummatory, must be understood to be a channel through which many basic needs may be simultaneously expressed or satisfied. Typically an act has *more* than one motivation.

6. Practically all organismic states are to be understood as motivated and as motivating.

7. Human needs arrange themselves in hierarchies of prepotency. That is to say, the appearance of one need usually rests on the prior satisfaction of another, more prepotent need. Man is a perpetually wanting animal. Also no need or drive can be treated as if it were isolated or discrete; every drive is related to the state of satisfaction or dissatisfaction of other drives.

8. *Lists* of drives will get us nowhere for various theoretical and practical reasons. Furthermore any classification of motivations must deal with the problem of levels of specificity or generalization of the motives to be classified.

9. Classifications of motivations must be based upon goals rather than upon instigating drives or motivated behavior.

10. Motivation theory should be human-centered rather than animal-centered.

11. The situation or the field in which the organism reacts must be taken into account but the field alone can rarely serve as an exclusive explanation for behavior. Furthermore the field itself must be

* From the *Psychological Review*, Vol. 50, 1943, pp. 370-396. Reprinted with permission.

[1] A. H. Maslow, "A Preface to Motivation Theory," *Psychosomatic Medicine*, Vol. 5, 1943, pp. 85-92.

interpreted in terms of the organism. Field theory cannot be a substitute for motivation theory.

12. Not only the integration of the organism must be taken into account, but also the possibility of isolated, specific, partial or segmental reactions.

It has since become necessary to add to these another affirmation.

13. Motivation theory is not synonymous with behavior theory. The motivations are only one class of determinants of behavior. While behavior is almost always motivated, it is also almost always biologically, culturally and situationally determined as well.

The present paper is an attempt to formulate a positive theory of motivation which will satisfy these theoretical demands and at the same time conform to the known facts, clinical and observational as well as experimental. It derives most directly, however, from clinical experience. This theory is, I think, in the functionalist tradition of James and Dewey, and is fused with the holism of Wertheimer,[2] Goldstein,[3] and Gestalt Psychology, and with the dynamicism of Freud,[4] and Adler.[5] This fusion or synthesis may arbitrarily be called a "general-dynamic" theory.

It is far easier to perceive and to criticize the aspects in motivation theory than to remedy them. Mostly this is because of the very serious lack of sound data in this area. I conceive this lack of sound facts to be due primarily to the absence of a valid theory of motivation. The present theory then must be considered to be a suggested program or framework for future research and must stand or fall, not so much on facts available or evidence presented, as upon researches yet to be done, researches suggested perhaps, by the questions raised in this paper.

II. THE BASIC NEEDS

The *"physiological"* needs.—The needs that are usually taken as the starting point for motivation theory are the so-called physiological drives. Two recent lines of research make it necessary to revise our customary notions about these needs, first, the development of the concept of homeostasis, and second, the finding that appetites (preferential choices among foods) are a fairly efficient indication of actual needs or lacks in the body.

Homeostasis refers to the body's automatic efforts to maintain a constant, normal state of the blood stream. Cannon[6] has described

[2] M. Wertheimer, unpublished lectures at the New School for Social Research.
[3] K. Goldstein, *The Organism* (New York: American Book Co., 1939).
[4] S. Freud, *New Introductory Lectures on Psychoanalysis* (New York: Norton, 1933).
[5] A. Adler, *Social Interest* (London: Faber & Faber, 1938).
[6] W. B. Cannon, *Wisdom of the Body* (New York: Norton, 1932).

this process for (1) the water content of the blood, (2) salt content, (3) sugar content, (4) protein content, (5) fat content, (6) calcium content, (7) oxygen content, (8) constant hydrogen-ion level (acid-base balance) and (9) constant temperature of the blood. Obviously this list can be extended to include other minerals, the hormones, vitamins, etc.

Young in a recent article [7] has summarized the work on appetite in its relation to body needs. If the body lacks some chemical, the individual will tend to develop a specific appetite or partial hunger for that food element.

Thus it seems impossible as well as useless to make any list of fundamental physiological needs for they can come to almost any number one might wish, depending on the degree of specificity of description. We can not identify all physiological needs as homeostatic. That sexual desire, sleepiness, sheer activity and maternal behavior in animals, are homeostatic, has not yet been demonstrated. Furthermore, this list would not include the various sensory pleasures (tastes, smells, tickling, stroking) which are probably physiological and which may become the goals of motivated behavior.

In a previous paper [8] it has been pointed out that these physiological drives or needs are to be considered unusual rather than typical because they are isolable, and because they are localized somatically. That is to say, they are relatively independent of each other, or other motivations and of the organism as a whole, and secondly, in many cases, it is possible to demonstrate a localized, underlying somatic base for the drive. This is true less generally than has been thought (exceptions are fatigue, sleepiness, maternal responses) but it is still true in the classic instances of hunger, sex, and thirst.

It should be pointed out again that any of the physiological needs and the consummatory behavior involved with them serve as channels for all sorts of other needs as well. That is to say, the person who thinks he is hungry may actually be seeking more for comfort, or dependence, than for vitamins or proteins. Conversely, it is possible to satisfy the hunger need in part by other activities such as drinking water or smoking cigarettes. In other words, relatively isolable as these physiological needs are, they are not completely so.

Undoubtedly these physiological needs are the most prepotent of all needs. What this means specifically is, that in the human being who is missing everything in life in an extreme fashion, it is most

---

[7] P. T. Young, "The Experimental Analysis of Appetite," *Psychological Bulletin*, Vol. 38, 1941, pp. 129-164.
[8] Maslow, *loc. cit.*

likely that the major motivation would be the physiological needs rather than any others. A person who is lacking food, safety, love, and esteem would most probably hunger for food more strongly than for anything else.

If all the needs are unsatisfied, and the organism is then dominated by the physiological needs, all other needs may become simply non-existent or be pushed into the background. It is then fair to characterize the whole organism by saying simply that it is hungry, for consciousness is almost completely preempted by hunger. All capacities are put into the service of hunger-satisfaction, and the organization of these capacities is almost entirely determined by the one purpose of satisfying hunger. The receptors and effectors, the intelligence, memory, habits, all may now be defined simply as hunger-gratifying tools. Capacities that are not useful for this purpose lie dormant, or are pushed into the background. The urge to write poetry, the desire to acquire an automobile, the interest in American history, the desire for a new pair of shoes are, in the extreme case, forgotten or become of secondary importance. For the man who is extremely and dangerously hungry, no other interests exist but food. He dreams food, he remembers food, he thinks about food, he emotes only about food, he perceives only food and he wants only food. The more subtle determinants that ordinarily fuse with the physiological drives in organizing even feeding, drinking or sexual behavior, may now be so completely overwhelmed as to allow us to speak at this time (but *only* at this time) of pure hunger drive and behavior, with the one unqualified aim of relief.

Another peculiar characteristic of the human organism when it is dominated by a certain need is that the whole philosophy of the future tends also to change. For our chronically and extremely hungry man, Utopia can be defined very simply as a place where there is plenty of food. He tends to think that, if only he is guaranteed food for the rest of his life, he will be perfectly happy and will never want anything more. Life itself tends to be defined in terms of eating. Anything else will be defined as unimportant. Freedom, love, community feeling, respect, philosophy, may all be waved aside as fripperies which are useless since they fail to fill the stomach. Such a man may fairly be said to live by bread alone.

It cannot possibly be denied that such things are true but their *generality* can be denied. Emergency conditions are, almost by definition, rare in the normally functioning peaceful society. That this truism can be forgotten is due mainly to two reasons. First, rats have few motivations other than physiological ones, and since so much of the research upon motivation has been made with these animals, it is easy to carry the rat-picture over to the human being. Secondly, it is too often not realized that culture itself is an adaptive tool, one of whose main functions is to make the physiological emergencies come less and less often. In most of the known societies, chronic extreme hunger of the emergency type is rare, rather than common. In any case, this is still true in the United States. The average American citizen is experiencing appetite rather than hunger when he says "I am hungry." He is apt to experience sheer life-and-death hunger only by accident and then only a few times through his entire life.

Obviously a good way to obscure the "higher" motivations, and to get a lopsided view of human capacities and human nature, is to make the organism extremely and chronically hungry or thirsty. Anyone who attempts to make an emergency picture into a typical one, and who will measure all of man's goals and desires by his behavior during extreme physiological deprivation is certainly being blind to many things. It is quite true that man lives by bread alone—when there is no bread. But what happens to man's desires when there *is* plenty of bread and when his belly is chronically filled?

At once other (*and "higher"*) *needs emerge* and these, rather than physiological hungers, dominate the organism. And when these in turn are satisfied, again new (and still "higher") needs emerge and so on. This is what we mean by saying that the basic human needs are organized into a hierarchy of relative prepotency.

One main implication of this phrasing is that gratification becomes as important a concept as deprivation in motivation theory, for it releases the organism from the domination of a relatively more physiological need, permitting thereby the emergence of other more social goals. The physiological needs, along with their partial goals, when chronically gratified cease to exist as active determinants or organizers of behavior. They now exist only in a potential fashion in the sense that they may emerge again to dominate the organism if they are thwarted. But a want that is satisfied is no longer a want. The organism is dominated and its behavior organized only by unsatisfied needs. If hunger is satisfied, it becomes unimportant in the current dynamics of the individual.

This statement is somewhat qualified by a hypothesis to be discussed more fully later, namely that it is precisely those individuals in whom a certain need has always been satisfied who are best equipped to tolerate deprivation of that need in the future, and that furthermore, those who have been deprived in the past will react differently to current satisfactions than the one who has never been deprived.

The safety needs.—If the physiological needs are relatively well gratified, there then emerges a new set of needs, which we may categorize roughly as the safety needs. All that has been said of the physiological needs is equally true, although in lesser degree, of these desires. The organism may equally well be wholly dominated by them. They may serve as the almost exclusive organizers of behavior, recruiting all the capacities of the organism in their service, and we may then fairly describe the whole organism as a safety-seeking mechanism. Again we may say of the receptors, the effectors, of the intellect and the other capacities that they are primarily safety-seeking tools. Again, as in the hungry man, we find that the dominating goal is a strong determinant not only of his current world-outlook and philosophy but also of his philosophy of the future. Practically everything looks less important than safety, (even sometimes the physiological needs which being satisfied, are now underestimated). A man, in this state, if it is extreme enough and chronic enough, may be characterized as living almost for safety alone.

Although in this paper we are interested primarily in the needs of the adult, we can approach an understanding of his safety needs perhaps more efficiently by observation of infants and children, in whom these needs are much more simple and obvious. One reason for the clearer appearance of the threat or danger reaction in infants, is that they do not inhibit this reaction at all, whereas adults in our society have been taught to inhibit it at all costs. Thus even when adults do feel their safety to be threatened we may not be able to see this on the surface. Infants will react in a total fashion and as if they were endangered, if they are disturbed or dropped suddenly, startled by loud noises, flashing light, or other unusual sensory stimulation, by rough handling, by general loss of support in the mother's arms, or by inadequate support.[9]

In infants we can also see a much more direct reaction to bodily illnesses of various kinds. Sometimes these illnesses seem to be immediately and *per se* threatening and seem to make the child feel unsafe. For instance, vomiting, colic or other sharp pains seem to make the child look at the whole world in a different way. At such

---

[9] As the child grows up, sheer knowledge and familiarity as well as better motor development make these "dangers" less and less dangerous and more and more manageable. Throughout life it may be said that one of the main conative functions of education is this neutralizing of apparent dangers through knowledge, *e.g.*, I am not afraid of thunder because I know something about it.

a moment of pain, it may be postulated that, for the child, the appearance of the whole world suddenly changes from sunniness to darkness, so to speak, and becomes a place in which anything at all might happen, in which previously stable things have suddenly become unstable. Thus a child who because of some bad food is taken ill may, for a day or two, develop fear, nightmares, and a need for protection and reassurance never seen in him before his illness.

Another indication of the child's need for safety is his preference for some kind of undisrupted routine or rhythm. He seems to want a predictable, orderly world. For instance, injustice, unfairness, or inconsistency in the parents seems to make a child feel anxious and unsafe. This attitude may be not so much because of the injustice *per se* or any particular pains involved, but rather because this treatment threatens to make the world look unreliable, or unsafe, or unpredictable. Young children seem to thrive better under a system which has at least a skeletal outline of rigidity, in which there is a schedule of a kind, some sort of routine, something that can be counted upon, not only for the present but also far into the future. Perhaps one could express this more accurately by saying that the child needs an organized world rather than an unorganized or unstructured one.

The central role of the parents and the normal family setup are indisputable. Quarreling, physical assault, separation, divorce or death within the family may be particularly terrifying. Also parental outbursts of rage or threats of punishment directed to the child, calling him names, speaking to him harshly, shaking him, handling him roughly, or actual physical punishment sometimes elicit such total panic and terror in the child that we must assume more is involved than the physical pain alone. While it is true that in some children this terror may represent also a fear of loss of parental love, it can also occur in completely rejected children, who seem to cling to the hating parents more for sheer safety and protection than because of hope of love.

Confronting the average child with new, unfamiliar, strange, unmanageable stimuli or situations will too frequently elicit the danger or terror reaction, as for example, getting lost or even being separated from the parents for a short time, being confronted with new faces, new situations or new tasks, the sight of strange, unfamiliar or uncontrollable objects, illness or death. Particularly at such times, the child's frantic clinging to his parents is eloquent testimony to their role as protectors (quite apart from their roles as food-givers and love-givers).

From these and similar observations, we may generalize and say that the average child in our society generally prefers a safe, orderly, predictable, organized world, which he can count on, and in which unexpected, unmanageable or other dangerous things do not happen, and in which, in any case, he has all-powerful parents who protect and shield him from harm.

That these reactions may so easily be observed in children is in a way a proof of the fact that children in our society feel too unsafe (or, in a word, are badly brought up). Children who are reared in an unthreatening, loving family do *not* ordinarily react as we have described above.[10] In such children the danger reactions are apt to come mostly to objects or situations that adults too would consider dangerous.[11]

The healthy, normal, fortunate adult in our culture is largely satisfied in his safety needs. The peaceful, smoothly running, "good" society ordinarily makes its members feel safe enough from wild animals, extremes of temperature, criminals, assault and murder, tyranny, etc. Therefore, in a very real sense, he no longer has any safety needs as active motivators. Just as a sated man no longer feels hungry, a safe man no longer feels endangered. If we wish to see these needs directly and clearly we must turn to neurotic or near-neurotic individuals, and to the economic and social underdogs. In between these extremes, we can perceive the expressions of safety needs only in such phenomena as, for instance, the common preference for a job with tenure and protection, the desire for a savings account, and for insurance of various kinds (medical, dental, unemployment, disability, old age).

Other broader aspects of the attempt to seek safety and stability in the world are seen in the very common preference for familiar rather than unfamiliar things, or for the known rather than the unknown. The tendency to have some religion or world-philosophy that organizes the universe and the men in it into some sort of satisfactory coherent, meaningful whole is also in part motivated by safety-seeking. Here too we may list science and philosophy in general as partially motivated by the safety needs (we shall see later

---

[10] M. Shirley, "Children's Adjustments to a Strange Situation," *Journal of Abnormal (Soc.) Psychology*, Vol. 37, 1942, pp. 201-217.

[11] A "test battery" for safety might be confronting the child with a small exploding firecracker, or with a bewhiskered face, having the mother leave the room, putting him upon a high ladder, a hypodermic injection, having a mouse crawl up to him, etc. Of course I cannot seriously recommend the deliberate use of such "tests" for they might very well harm the child being tested. But these and similar situations come up by the score in the child's ordinary day-to-day living and may be observed. There is no reason why these stimuli should not be used with, for example, young chimpanzees.

that there are also other motivations to scientific, philosophical or religious endeavor).

Otherwise the need for safety is seen as an active and dominant mobilizer of the organism's resources only in emergencies, *e.g.*, war, disease, natural catastrophies, crime waves, societal disorganization, neurosis, brain injury, chronically bad situation.

Some neurotic adults in our society are, in many ways, like the unsafe child in their desire for safety, although in the former it takes on a somewhat special appearance. Their reaction is often to unknown, psychological dangers in a world that is perceived to be hostile, overwhelming and threatening. Such a person behaves as if a great catastrophe were almost always impending, *i.e.*, he is usually responding as if to an emergency. His safety needs often find specific expression in a search for a protector, or a stronger person on whom he may depend, or perhaps, a Fuehrer.

The neurotic individual may be described in a slightly different way with some usefulness as a grown-up person who retains his childish attitudes toward the world. That is to say, a neurotic adult may be said to behave "as if" he were actually afraid of a spanking, or of his mother's disapproval, or of being abandoned by his parents, or having his food taken away from him. It is as if his childish attitudes of fear and threat reaction to a dangerous world had gone underground, and untouched by the growing up and learning processes, were now ready to be called out by any stimulus that would make a child feel endangered and threatened.[12]

The neurosis in which the search for safety takes its clearest form is in the compulsive-obsessive neurosis. Compulsive-obsessives try frantically to order and stabilize the world so that no unmanageable, unexpected or unfamiliar dangers will ever appear.[13] They hedge themselves about with all sorts of ceremonials, rules and formulas so that every possible contingency may be provided for and so that no new contingencies may appear. They are much like the brain injured cases, described by Goldstein,[14] who manage to maintain their equilibrium by avoiding everything unfamiliar and strange and by ordering their restricted world in such a neat, disciplined, orderly fashion that everything in the world can be counted upon. They try to arrange the world so that anything unexpected (dangers) cannot possibly

---

[12] Not all neurotic individuals feel unsafe. Neurosis may have at its core a thwarting of the affection and esteem needs in a person who is generally safe.

[13] A. H. Maslow and B. Mittelmann, *Principles of Abnormal Psychology* (New York: Harper & Bros., 1941).

[14] Goldstein, *loc. cit.*

occur. If, through no fault of their own, something unexpected does occur, they go into a panic reaction as if this unexpected occurrence constituted a grave danger. What we can see only as a none-too-strong preference in the healthy person, *e.g.*, preference for the familiar, becomes a life-and-death necessity in abnormal cases.

The love needs.—If both the physiological and the safety needs are fairly well gratified, then there will emerge the love and affection and belongingness needs, and the whole cycle already described will repeat itself with this new center. Now the person will feel keenly, as never before, the absence of friends, or a sweetheart, or a wife, or children. He will hunger for affectionate relations with people in general, namely, for a place in his group, and he will strive with great intensity to achieve this goal. He will want to attain such a place more than anything else in the world and may even forget that once, when he was hungry, he sneered at love.

In our society the thwarting of these needs is the most commonly found core in cases of maladjustment and more severe psycho-pathology. Love and affection, as well as their possible expression in sexuality, are generally looked upon with ambivalence and are cus-tomarily hedged about with many restrictions and inhibitions. Prac-tically all theorists of psychopathology have stressed thwarting of the love needs as basic in the picture of maladjustment. Many clinical studies have therefore been made of this need and we know more about it perhaps than any of the other needs except the physiolog-ical ones.[15]

One thing that must be stressed at this point is that love is not synonymous with sex. Sex may be studied as a purely physiological need. Ordinarily sexual behavior is multi-determined, that is to say, determined not only by sexual but also by other needs, chief among which are the love and affection needs. Also not to be overlooked is the fact that the love needs involve both giving *and* receiving love.[16]

The esteem needs.—All people in our society (with a few patholog-ical exceptions) have a need or desire for a stable, firmly based, (usually) high evaluation of themselves, for self-respect, or self-esteem, and for the esteem of others. By firmly based self-esteem, we mean that which is soundly based upon real capacity, achievement and respect from others. These needs may be classified into two

[15] Maslow and Mittelmann, *loc. cit.*
[16] For further details see A. H. Maslow, "The Dynamics of Psychological Security-Insecurity," *Character and Personality*, Vol. 10, 1942, pp. 331-344, and J. Plant, *Personality and the Cultural Pattern* (New York: Commonwealth Fund, 1937), Ch. 5.

subsidiary sets. These are, first, the desire for strength, for achievement, for adequacy, for confidence in the face of the world, and for independence and freedom.[17] Secondly, we have what we may call the desire for reputation or prestige (defining it as respect or esteem from other people), recognition, attention, importance or appreciation.[18] These needs have been relatively stressed by Alfred Adler and his followers, and have been relatively neglected by Freud and the psychoanalysts. More and more today however there is appearing widespread appreciation of their central importance.

Satisfaction of the self-esteem need leads to feelings of self-confidence, worth, strength, capability and adequacy of being useful and necessary in the world. But thwarting of these needs produces feelings of inferiority, of weakness and of helplessness. These feelings in turn give rise to either basic discouragement or else compensatory or neurotic trends. An appreciation of the necessity of basic self-confidence and an understanding of how helpless people are without it, can be easily gained from a study of severe traumatic neurosis.[19, 20]

The need for self-actualization.—Even if all these needs are satisfied, we may still often (if not always) expect that a new discontent and restlessness will soon develop, unless the individual is doing what he is fitted for. A musician must make music, an artist must paint, a poet must write, if he is to be ultimately happy. What a man *can* be, he *must* be. This need we may call self-actualization.

This term, first coined by Kurt Goldstein, is being used in this paper in a much more specific and limited fashion. It refers to the desire for self-fulfillment, namely, to the tendency for him to become actualized in what he is potentially. This tendency might be phrased as the desire to become more and more what one is, to become everything that one is capable of becoming.

---

[17] Whether or not this particular desire is universal we do not know. The crucial question, especially important today, is "Will men who are enslaved and dominated, inevitably feel dissatisfied and rebellious?" We may assume on the basis of commonly known clinical data that a man who has known true freedom (not paid for by giving up safety and security but rather built on the basis of adequate safety and security) will not willingly or easily allow his freedom to be taken away from him. But we do not know that this is true for the person born into slavery. The events of the next decade should give us our answer. See discussion of this problem in E. Fromm, *Escape from Freedom* (New York: Farrar and Rinehart, 1941).

[18] Perhaps the desire for prestige and respect from others is subsidiary to the desire for self-esteem or confidence in oneself. Observation of children seems to indicate that this is so, but clinical data give no clear support for such a conclusion.

[19] A. Kardiner, *The Traumatic Neuroses of War* (New York: Hoeber, 1941).

[20] For more extensive discussion of normal self-esteem, as well as for reports of various researches," see A. H. Maslow, "Dominance, Personality and Social Behavior in Women," *Journal (Soc.) of Psychology*, Vol. 10, 1939, pp. 3-39.

The specific form that these needs will take will of course vary greatly from person to person. In one individual it may take the form of the desire to be an ideal mother, in another it may be expressed athletically, and in still another it may be expressed in painting pictures or in inventions. It is not necessarily a creative urge although in people who have any capacities for creation it will take this form.

The clear emergence of these needs rests upon prior satisfaction of the physiological, safety, love and esteem needs. We shall call people who are satisfied in these needs, basically satisfied people, and it is from these that we may expect the fullest (and healthiest) creativeness.[21] Since, in our society, basically satisfied people are the exception, we do not know much about self-actualization, either experimentally or clinically. It remains a challenging problem for research.

The preconditions for the basic need satisfactions.—There are certain conditions which are immediate prerequisites for the basic need satisfactions. Danger to these is reacted to almost as if it were a direct danger to the basic needs themselves. Such conditions as freedom to speak, freedom to do what one wishes so long as no harm is done to others, freedom to express one's self, freedom to investigate and seek for information, freedom to defend one's self, justice, fairness, honesty, orderliness in the group are examples of such preconditions for basic need satisfactions. Thwarting in these freedoms will be reacted to with a threat or emergency response. These conditions are not ends in themselves but they are *almost* so since they are so closely related to the basic needs, which are apparently the only ends in themselves. These conditions are defended because without them the basic satisfactions are quite impossible, or at least, very severely endangered.

If we remember that the cognitive capacities (perceptual, intellectual, learning) are a set of adjustive tools, which have, among other functions, that of satisfaction of our basic needs, then it is clear that any danger to them, any deprivation or blocking of their free use, must also be indirectly threatening to the basic needs them-

---

21 Clearly creative behavior, like painting, is like any other behavior in having multiple determinants. It may be seen in "innately creative" people whether they are satisfied or not, happy or unhappy, hungry or sated. Also it is clear that creative activity may be compensatory, ameliorative or purely economic. It is my impression (as yet unconfirmed) that it is possible to distinguish the artistic and intellectual products of basically satisfied people from those of basically unsatisfied people by inspection alone. In any case, here too we must distinguish, in a dynamic fashion, the overt behavior itself from its various motivations or purposes.

selves. Such a statement is a partial solution of the general problems of curiosity, the search for knowledge, truth and wisdom, and the ever-persistent urge to solve the cosmic mysteries.

We must therefore introduce another hypothesis and speak of degrees of closeness to the basic needs, for we have already pointed out that *any* conscious desires (partial goals) are more or less important as they are more or less close to the basic needs. The same statement may be made for various behavior acts. An act is psychologically important if it contributes directly to satisfaction of basic needs. The less directly it so contributes, or the weaker this contribution is, the less important this act must be conceived to be from the point of view of dynamic psychology. A similar statement may be made for the various defense or coping mechanisms. Some are very directly related to the protection or attainment of the basic needs, others are only weakly and distantly related. Indeed if we wished, we could speak of more basic and less basic defense mechanisms, and then affirm that danger to the more basic defenses is more threatening than danger to less basic defenses (always remembering that this is so only because of their relationship to the basic needs).

The desires to know and to understand.—So far, we have mentioned the cognitive needs only in passing. Acquiring knowledge and systematizing the universe have been considered as, in part, techniques for the achievement of basic safety in the world, or, for the intelligent man, expressions of self-actualization. Also freedom of inquiry and expression have been discussed as preconditions of satisfactions of the basic needs. True though these formulations may be, they do not constitute definitive answers to the question as to the motivation role of curiosity, learning, philosophizing, experimenting, etc. They are, at best, no more than partial answers.

This question is especially difficult because we know so little about the facts. Curiosity, exploration, desire for the facts, desire to know may certainly be observed easily enough. The fact that they often are pursued even at great cost to the individual's safety is an earnest of the partial character of our previous discussion. In addition, the writer must admit that, though he has sufficient clinical evidence to postulate the desire to know as a very strong drive in intelligent people, no data are available for unintelligent people. It may then be largely a function of relatively high intelligence. Rather tentatively, then, and largely in the hope of stimulating discussion and research, we shall postulate a basic desire to know, to be aware of reality, to get the facts, to satisfy curiosity, or as Wertheimer phrases it, to see rather than to be blind.

This postulation, however, is not enough. Even after we know, we are impelled to know more and more minutely and microscopically on the one hand, and on the other, more and more extensively in the direction of a world philosophy, religion, etc. The facts that we acquire, if they are isolated or atomistic, inevitably get theorized about, and either analyzed or organized or both. This process has been phrased by some as the search for "meaning." We shall then postulate a desire to understand, to systematize, to organize, to analyze, to look for relations and meanings.

Once these desires are accepted for discussion, we see that they too form themselves into a small hierarchy in which the desire to know is prepotent over the desire to understand. All the characteristics of a hierarchy of prepotency that we have described above, seem to hold for this one as well.

We must guard ourselves against the too easy tendency to separate these desires from the basic needs we have discussed above, *i.e.*, to make a sharp dichotomy between "cognitive" and "conative" needs. The desire to know and to understand are themselves conative, *i.e.*, have a striving character, and are as much personality needs as the "basic needs" we have already discussed.[22]

III. Further Characteristics of the Basic Needs

The degree of fixity of the hierarchy of basic needs.—We have spoken so far as if this hierarchy were a fixed order but actually it is not nearly as rigid as we may have implied. It is true that most of the people with whom we have worked have seemed to have these basic needs in about the order that has been indicated. However, there have been a number of exceptions.

(1) There are some people in whom, for instance, self-esteem seems to be more important than love. This most common reversal in the hierarchy is usually due to the development of the notion that the person who is most likely to be loved is a strong or powerful person, one who inspires respect or fear, and who is self confident or aggressive. Therefore such people who lack love and seek it, may try hard to put on a front of aggressive, confident behavior. But essentially they seek high self-esteem and its behavior expressions more as a means-to-an-end than for its own sake; they seek self-assertion for the sake of love rather than for self-esteem itself.

(2) There are other, apparently innately creative people in whom the drive to creativeness seems to be more important than any other

---

[22] M. Wertheimer, unpublished lectures at the New School for Social Research.

counter-determinant. Their creativeness might appear not as self-actualization released by basic satisfaction, but in spite of lack of basic satisfaction.

(3) In certain people the level of aspiration may be permanently deadened or lowered. That is to say, the less prepotent goals may simply be lost, and may disappear forever, so that the person who has experienced life at a very low level, *i.e.*, chronic unemployment, may continue to be satisfied for the rest of his life if only he can get enough food.

(4) The so-called "psychopathic personality" is another example of permanent loss of the love needs. These are people who, according to the best data available [23] have been starved for love in the earliest months of their lives and have simply lost forever the desire and the ability to give and to receive affection (as animals lose sucking or pecking reflexes that are not exercised soon enough after birth).

(5) Another cause of reversal of the hierarchy is that when a need has been satisfied for a long time, this need may be under-evaluated. People who have never experienced chronic hunger are apt to underestimate its effects and to look upon food as a rather unimportant thing. If they are dominated by a higher need, this higher need will seem to be the most important of all. It then becomes possible, and indeed does actually happen, that they may, for the sake of this higher need, put themselves into the position of being deprived in a more basic need. We may expect that after a long-time deprivation of the more basic need there will be a tendency to reevaluate both needs so that the more prepotent need will actually become consciously prepotent for the individual who may have given it up very lightly. Thus, a man who has given up his job rather than lose his self-respect, and who then starves for six months or so, may be willing to take his job back even at the price of losing his self-respect.

(6) Another partial explanation of *apparent* reversals is seen in the fact that we have been talking about the hierarchy of prepotency in terms of consciously felt wants or desires rather than of behavior. Looking at behavior itself may give us the wrong impression. What we have claimed is that the person will *want* the more basic of two needs when deprived in both. There is no necessary implication here that he will act upon his desires. Let us say again that there are many determinants of behavior other than the needs and desires.

(7) Perhaps more important than all these exceptions are the ones that involve ideals, high social standards, high values and the

[23] D. M. Levy, "Primary Affect Hunger," *American Journal of Psychiatry*, Vol. 94, 1937, pp. 643-652.

like. With such values people become martyrs; they will give up everything for the sake of a particular ideal, or value. These people may be understood, at least in part, by reference to one basic concept (or hypothesis) which may be called "increased frustration-tolerance through early gratification." People who have been satisfied in their basic needs throughout their lives, particularly in their earlier years, seem to develop exceptional power to withstand present or future thwarting of these needs simply because they have strong, healthy character structure as a result of basic satisfaction. They are the "strong" people who can easily weather disagreement or opposition, who can swim against the stream of public opinion and who can stand up for the truth at great personal cost. It is just the ones who have loved and been well loved, and who have had many deep friendships who can hold out against hatred, rejection or persecution.

I say all this in spite of the fact that there is a certain amount of sheer habituation which is also involved in any full discussion of frustration tolerance. For instance, it is likely that those persons who have been accustomed to relative starvation for a long time are partially enabled thereby to withstand food deprivation. What sort of balance must be made between these two tendencies, of habituation on the one hand, and of past satisfaction breeding present frustration-tolerance on the other hand, remains to be worked out by further research. Meanwhile we may assume that they are both operative, side by side, since they do not contradict each other. In respect to this phenomenon of increased frustration tolerance, it seems probable that the most important gratifications come in the first two years of life. That is to say, people who have been made secure and strong in the earliest years, tend to remain secure and strong thereafter in the face of whatever threatens.

Degrees of relative satisfaction.—So far, our theoretical discussion may have given the impression that these five sets of needs are somehow in a step-wise, all-or-none relationship to each other. We have spoken in such terms as the following: "If one need is satisfied, then another emerges." This statement might give the false impression that a need must be satisfied 100 per cent before the next need emerges. In actual fact, most members of our society who are normal, are partially satisfied in all their basic needs and partially unsatisfied in all their basic needs at the same time. A more realistic description of the hierarchy would be in terms of decreasing percentages of satisfaction as we go up the hierarchy of prepotency. For instance, if I may assign arbitrarily figures for the sake of illustration, it is as if the average citizen is satisfied 85 per cent in his physiological needs, 70 per cent in his safety needs, 50 per cent in his love needs, 40 per cent in his self-esteem needs, and 10 per cent in his self-actualization needs.

As for the concept of emergence of a new need after satisfaction of the prepotent need, this emergence is not a sudden, saltatory phenomenon but rather a gradual emergence by slow degrees from nothingness. For instance, if prepotent need A is satisfied only 10 per cent then need B may not be visible at all. However, as this need A becomes satisfied 25 per cent, need B may emerge 5 per cent, as need A becomes satisfied 75 per cent need B may emerge 90 per cent, and so on.

Unconscious character of needs.—These needs are neither necessarily conscious nor unconscious. On the whole, however, in the average person, they are more often unconscious rather than conscious. It is not necessary at this point to overhaul the tremendous mass of evidence which indicates the crucial importance of unconcious motivation. It would by now be expected, on a priori grounds alone, that unconscious motivations would on the whole be rather more important than the conscious motivations. What we have called the basic needs are very often largely unconscious although they may, with suitable techniques, and with sophisticated people become conscious.

Cultural specificity and generality of needs.—This classification of basic needs makes some attempt to take account of the relative unity behind the superficial differences in specific desires from one culture to another. Certainly in any particular culture an individual's conscious motivational content will usually be extremely different from the conscious motivational content of an individual in another society. However, it is the common experience of anthropologists that people, even in different societies, are much more alike than we would think from our first contact with them, and that as we know them better we seem to find more and more of this commonness. We then recognize the most startling differences to be superficial rather than basic, *e.g.*, differences in style of hairdress, clothes, tastes in food, etc. Our classification of basic needs is in part an attempt to account for this unity behind the apparent diversity from culture to culture. No claim is made that it is ultimate or universal for all cultures. The claim is made only that it is relatively *more* ultimate, more universal, more basic, than the superficial conscious desires from culture to culture, and makes a somewhat closer approach to common-human characteristics. Basic needs are *more* common-human than superficial desires or behaviors.

Multiple motivations of behavior.—These needs must be understood *not* to be *exclusive* or single determiners of certain kinds of behavior. An example may be found in any behavior that seems to be physiologically motivated, such as eating, or sexual play or the like. The clinical psychologists have long since found that any behavior may be a channel through which flow various determinants. Or to say it in another way, most behavior is multi-motivated. Within the sphere of motivational determinants any behavior tends to be determined by several or *all* of the basic needs simultaneously rather than by only one of them. The latter would be more an exception than the former. Eating may be partially for the sake of filling the stomach, and partially for the sake of comfort and amelioration of other needs. One may make love not only for pure sexual release, but also to convince one's self of one's masculinity, or to make a conquest, to feel powerful, or to win more basic affection. As an illustration, I may point out that it would be possible (theoretically if not practically) to analyze a single act of an individual and see in it the expression of his physiological needs, his safety needs, his love needs, his esteem needs and self-actualization. This contrasts sharply with the more naive brand of trait psychology in which one trait or one motive accounts for a certain kind of act, *i.e.*, an aggressive act is traced solely to a trait of aggressiveness.

Multiple determinants of behavior.—Not all behavior is determined by the basic needs. We might even say that not all behavior is motivated. There are many determinants of behavior other than motives.[24] For instance, one other important class of determinants is the so-called "field" determinants. Theoretically, at least, behavior may be determined completely by the field, or even by specific isolated external stimuli, as in association of ideas, or certain conditioned reflexes. If in response to the stimulus word "table," I immediately perceive a memory image of a table, this response certainly has nothing to do with my basic needs.

Secondly, we may call attention again to the concept of "degree of closeness to the basic needs" or "degree of motivation." Some behavior is highly motivated, other behavior is only weakly motivated. Some is not motivated at all (but all behavior is determined).

---

[24] I am aware that many psychologists and psychoanalysts use the term "motivated" and "determined" synonymously, *e.g.*, Freud. But I consider this an obfuscating usage. Sharp distinctions are necessary for clarity of thought, and precision in experimentation.

Another important point [25] is that there is a basic difference between expressive behavior and coping behavior (functional striving, purposive goal seeking). An expressive behavior does not try to do anything; it is simply a reflection of the personality. A stupid man behaves stupidly, not because he wants to, or tries to, or is motivated to, but simply because he *is* what he is. The same is true when I speak in a bass voice rather than tenor or soprano. The random movements of a healthy child, the smile on the face of a happy man even when he is alone, the springiness of the healthy man's walk, and the erectness of his carriage are other examples of expressive, non-functional behavior. Also the *style* in which a man carries out almost all his behavior, motivated as well as unmotivated, is often expressive.

We may then ask, is *all* behavior expressive or reflective of the character structure? The answer is "No." Rote, habitual, automatized, or conventional behavior may or may not be expressive. The same is true for most "stimulus-bound" behaviors.

It is finally necessary to stress that expressiveness of behavior and goal-directedness of behavior are not mutually exclusive categories. Average behavior is usually both.

Goals as centering principle in motivation theory.—It will be observed that the basic principle in our classification has been neither the instigation nor the motivated behavior but rather the functions, effects, purposes, or goals of the behavior. It has been proven sufficiently by various people that this is the most suitable point for centering in any motivation theory.[26]

Animal- and human-centering.—This theory starts with the human being rather than any lower and presumably "simpler" animal. Too many of the findings that have been made in animals have been proven to be true for animals but not for the human being. There is no reason whatsoever why we should start with animals in order to study human motivation. The logic or rather illogic behind this general fallacy of "pseudo-simplicity" has been exposed often enough by philosophers and logicians as well as by scientists in each of the various fields. It is no more necessary to study animals before one can study man than it is to study mathematics before one can study geology or psychology or biology.

---

[25] To be discussed fully in a subsequent publication.

[26] The interested reader is referred to the very excellent discussion of this point in H. A. Murray, *et al.*, *Explorations in Personality* (New York: Oxford University Press, 1938).

We may also reject the old, naive, behaviorism which assumed that it was somehow necessary, or at least more "scientific" to judge human beings by animal standards. One consequence of this belief was that the whole notion of purpose and goal was excluded from motivational psychology simply because one could not ask a white rat about his purposes. Tolman [27] has long since proven in animal studies themselves that this exclusion was not necessary.

Motivation and the theory of psychopathogenesis.—The conscious motivational content of everyday life has, according to the foregoing, been conceived to be relatively important or unimportant accordingly as it is more or less closely related to the basic goals. A desire for an ice cream cone might actually be an indirect expression of a desire for love. If it is, then this desire for the ice cream cone becomes extremely important motivation. If however the ice cream is simply something to cool the mouth with, or a casual appetitive reaction, then the desire is relatively unimportant. Everyday conscious desires are to be regarded as symptoms, as *surface indicators of more basic needs.* If we were to take these superficial desires at their face value we would find ourselves in a state of complete confusion which could never be resolved, since we would be dealing seriously with symptoms rather than with what lay behind the symptoms.

Thwarting of unimportant desires produces no psychopathological results; thwarting of a basically important need does produce such results. Any theory of psychopathogenesis must then be based on a sound theory of motivation. A conflict or a frustration is not necessarily pathogenic. It becomes so only when it threatens or thwarts the basic needs, or partial needs that are closely related to the basic needs.[28]

The role of gratified needs.—It has been pointed out above several times that our needs usually emerge only when more prepotent needs have been gratified. Thus gratification has an important role in motivation theory. Apart from this, however, needs cease to play an active determining or organizing role as soon as they are gratified.

What this means is that, *e.g.*, a basically satisfied person no longer has the needs for esteem, love, safety, etc. The only sense in which he might be said to have them is in the almost metaphysical sense that a sated man has hunger, or a filled bottle has emptiness. If we

[27] E. C. Tolman, *Purposive Behavior in Animals and Men* (New York: Century, 1932).
[28] A. H. Maslow, "Conflict, Frustration, and the Theory of Threat," *Journal of Abnormal (Soc.) Psychology*, Vol. 38, 1943, pp. 81-86.

are interested in what *actually* motivates us, and not in what has, will, or might motivate us, then a satisfied need is not a motivator. It must be considered for all practical purposes simply not to exist, to have disappeared. This point should be emphasized because it has been either overlooked or contradicted in every theory of motivation I know.[29] The perfectly healthy, normal, fortunate man has no sex needs or hunger needs, or needs for safety, or for love, or for prestige, or self-esteem, except in stray moments of quickly passing threat. If we were to say otherwise, we should also have to aver that every man had all the pathological reflexes, *e.g.*, Babinski, etc., because if his nervous system were damaged, these would appear.

It is such considerations as these that suggest the bold postulation that a man who is thwarted in any of his basic needs may fairly be envisaged simply as a sick man. This is a fair parallel to our designation as "sick" of the man who lacks vitamins or minerals. Who is to say that a lack of love is less important than a lack of vitamins? Since we know the pathogenic effects of love starvation, who is to say that we are invoking value-questions in an unscientific or illegitimate way, any more than the physician does who diagnoses and treats pellagra or scurvy? If I were permitted this usage, I should then say simply that a healthy man is primarily motivated by his needs to develop and actualize his fullest potentialities and capacities. If a man has any other basic needs in any active, chronic sense, then he is simply an unhealthy man. He is as surely sick as if he had suddenly developed a strong salt-hunger or calcium hunger.[30]

If this statement seems unusual or paradoxical the reader may be assured that this is only one among many such paradoxes that will appear as we revise our ways of looking at man's deeper motivations. When we ask what man wants of life, we deal with his very essence.

IV. SUMMARY

(1) There are at least five sets of goals, which we may call basic needs. These are briefly physiological, safety, love, esteem, and self-actualization. In addition, we are motivated by the desire to achieve

---

[29] Note that acceptance of this theory necessitates basic revision of the Freudian theory.

[30] If we were to use the word "sick" in this way, we should then also have to face squarely the relations of man to his society. One clear implication of our definition would be that (1) since a man is to be called sick who is basically thwarted, and (2) since such basic thwarting is made possible ultimately only by forces outside the individual, then (3) sickness in the individual must come ultimately from a sickness in the society. The "good" or healthy society would then be defined as one that permitted man's highest purposes to emerge by satisfying all his prepotent basic needs.

or maintain the various conditions upon which these basic satisfactions rest and by certain more intellectual desires.

(2) These basic goals are related to each other, being arranged in a hierarchy of prepotency. This means that the most prepotent goal will monopolize consciousness and will tend of itself to organize the recruitment of the various capacities of the organism. The less prepotent needs are minimized, even forgotten or denied. But when a need is fairly well satisfied, the next prepotent ("higher") need emerges, in turn to dominate the conscious life and to serve as the center of organization of behavior, since gratified needs are not active motivators.

Thus man is a perpetually wanting animal. Ordinarily the satisfaction of these wants is not altogether mutually exclusive, but only tends to be. The average member of our society is most often partially satisfied and partially unsatisfied in all of his wants. The hierarchy principle is usually empirically observed in terms of increasing percentages of non-satisfaction as we go up the hierarchy. Reversals of the average order of the hierarchy are sometimes observed. Also it has been observed that an individual may permanently lose the higher wants in the hierarchy under special conditions. There are not only ordinarily multiple motivations for usual behavior, but in addition many determinants other than motives.

(3) Any thwarting or possibility of thwarting of these basic human goals, or danger to the defenses which protect them, or to the conditions upon which they rest, is considered to be a psychological threat. With a few exceptions, all psychopathology may be partially traced to such threats. A basically thwarted man may actually be defined as a "sick" man, if we wish.

(4) It is such basic threats which bring about the general emergency reactions.

(5) Certain other basic problems have not been dealt with because of limitations of space. Among these are (a) the problem of values in any definitive motivation theory, (b) the relation between appetites, desires, needs and what is "good" for the organism, (c) the etiology of the basic needs and their possible derivation in early childhood, (d) redefinition of motivational concepts, *i.e.*, drive, desire, wish, need, goal, (e) implication of our theory for hedonistic theory, (f) the nature of the uncompleted act, of success and failure, and of aspiration-level (g) the role of association, habit and conditioning, (h) relation to the theory of inter-personal relations, (i) implications for psychotherapy, (j) implication for theory of society, (k) the theory of selfishness, (l) the relation between needs and cultural pat-

terns, (m) the relation between this theory and Allport's theory of functional autonomy. These as well as certain other less important questions must be considered as motivation theory attempts to become definitive.

QUESTIONS

1. Compare the classes of basic needs stated by Maslow with those discussed in the introduction section. Explain any differences you see.
2. Explain what is meant by the "hierarchical" nature of needs. Is this hierarchy "rigid"?
3. What conditions are prerequisites for need satisfaction?
4. Is all human behavior determined by basic needs? Why?
5. Discuss the fundamental characteristics of basic needs.

20. THE HUMAN SIDE OF ENTERPRISE *

Douglas M. McGregor

It has become true to say that industry has the fundamental know-how to utilize physical science and technology for the material benefit of mankind, and that we must now learn how to utilize the social sciences to make our human organizations truly effective.

To a degree, the social sciences today are in a position like that of the physical sciences with respect to atomic energy in the thirties. We know that past conceptions of the nature of man are inadequate and, in many ways, incorrect. We are becoming quite certain that, under proper conditions, unimagined resources of creative human energy could become available within the organizational setting.

We cannot tell industrial management how to apply this new knowledge in simple, economic ways. We know it will require years of exploration, much costly development research, and a substantial amount of creative imagination on the part of management to discover how to apply this growing knowledge to the organization of human effort in industry.

MANAGEMENT'S TASK: THE CONVENTIONAL VIEW

The conventional conception of management's task in harnessing human energy to organizational requirements can be stated broadly in terms of three propositions. In order to avoid the complications introduced by a label, let us call this set of propositions "Theory X":

1. Management is responsible for organizing the elements of productive enterprise—money, materials, equipment, people—in the interest of economic ends.

2. With respect to people, this is a process of directing their efforts, motivating them, controlling their actions, modifying their behavior to fit the needs of the organization.

3. Without this active intervention by management, people would be passive—even resistant—to organizational needs. They must therefore be persuaded, rewarded, punished, controlled—their activities must be directed. This is management's task. We often sum it up by saying that management consists of getting things done through other people.

* From the *Management Review*, Vol. 46, No. 11 (November, 1957), pp. 22-28, 88-92. Copyright, 1957, by the American Management Association. Reprinted by permission of the American Management Association.

Behind this conventional theory there are several additional beliefs —less explicit, but widespread:

4. The average man is by nature indolent—he works as little as possible.

5. He lacks ambition, dislikes responsibility, prefers to be led.

6. He is inherently self-centered, indifferent to organizational needs.

7. He is by nature resistant to change.

8. He is gullible, not very bright, the ready dupe of the charlatan and the demagogue.

The human side of economic enterprise today is fashioned from propositions and beliefs such as these. Conventional organization structures and managerial policies, practices, and programs reflect these assumptions.

In accomplishing its task—with these assumptions as guides— management has conceived of a range of possibilities.

At one extreme, management can be "hard" or "strong." The methods for directing behavior involve coercion and threat (usually disguised), close supervision, tight controls over behavior. At the other extreme, management can be "soft" or "weak." The methods for directing behavior involve being permissive, satisfying people's demands, achieving harmony. Then they will be tractable, accept direction.

This range has been fairly completely explored during the past half century, and management has learned some things from the exploration. There are difficulties in the "hard" approach. Force breeds counter-forces: restriction of output, antagonism, militant unionism, subtle but effective sabotage of management objectives. This "hard" approach is especially difficult during times of full employment.

There are also difficulties in the "soft" approach. It leads frequently to the abdication of management—to harmony, perhaps, but to indifferent performance. People take advantage of the soft approach. They continually expect more, but they give less and less.

Currently, the popular theme is "firm but fair." This is an attempt to gain the advantages of both the hard and the soft approaches. It is reminiscent of Teddy Roosevelt's "speak softly and carry a big stick."

Is the Conventional View Correct?

The findings which are beginning to emerge from the social sciences challenge this whole set of beliefs about man and human nature and about the task of management. The evidence is far from conclusive, certainly, but it is suggestive. It comes from the laboratory, the clinic, the schoolroom, the home, and even to a limited extent from industry itself.

The social scientist does not deny that human behavior in industrial organization today is approximately what management perceives it to be. He has, in fact, observed it and studied it fairly extensively. But he is pretty sure that this behavior is *not* a consequence of man's inherent nature. It is a consequence rather of the nature of industrial organizations, of management philosophy, policy, and practice. The conventional approach to Theory X is based on mistaken notions of what is cause and what is effect.

Perhaps the best way to indicate why the conventional approach of management is inadequate is to consider the subject of motivation.

Physiological Needs

Man is a wanting animal—as soon as one of his needs is satisfied, another appears in its place. This process is unending. It continues from birth to death.

Man's needs are organized in a series of levels—a hierarchy of importance. At the lowest level, but pre-eminent in importance when they are thwarted, are his *physiological needs*. Man lives for bread alone, when there is no bread. Unless the circumstances are unusual, his needs for love, for status, for recognition are inoperative when his stomach has been empty for a while. But when he eats regularly and adequately, hunger ceases to be an important motivation. The same is true of the other physiological needs of man—for rest, exercise, shelter, protection from the elements.

A satisfied need is not a motivator of behavior! This is a fact of profound significance that is regularly ignored in the conventional approach to the management of people. Consider your own need for air: Except as you are deprived of it, it has no appreciable motivating effect upon your behavior.

Safety Needs

When the physiological needs are reasonably satisfied, needs at the next higher level begin to dominate man's behavior—to motivate him. These are called *safety needs*. They are needs for protection against danger, threat, deprivation. Some people mistakenly refer to these as needs for security. However, unless man is in a dependent relationship where he fears arbitrary deprivation, he does not demand security. The need is for the "fairest possible break."

When he is confident of this, he is more than willing to take risks. But when he feels threatened or dependent, his greatest need is for guarantees, for protection, for security.

The fact needs little emphasis that, since every industrial employee is in a dependent relationship, safety needs may assume considerable importance. Arbitrary management actions, behavior which arouses uncertainty with respect to continued employment or which reflects favoritism or discrimination, unpredictable administration of policy —these can be powerful motivators of the safety needs in the employment relationship *at every level,* from worker to vice president.

Social Needs

When man's physiological needs are satisfied and he is no longer fearful about his physical welfare, his *social needs* become important motivators of his behavior—needs for belonging, for association, for acceptance by his fellows, for giving and receiving friendship and love.

Management knows today of the existence of these needs, but it often assumes quite wrongly that they represent a threat to the organization. Many studies have demonstrated that the tightly knit, cohesive work group may, under proper conditions, be far more effective than an equal number of separate individuals in achieving organizational goals.

Yet management, fearing group hostility to its own objectives, often goes to considerable lengths to control and direct human efforts in ways that are inimical to the natural "groupiness" of human beings. When man's social needs—and perhaps his safety needs, too—are thus thwarted, he behaves in ways which tend to defeat organizational objectives. He becomes resistant, antagonistic, uncooperative. But this behavior is a consequence, not a cause.

Ego Needs

Above the social needs—in the sense that they do not become motivators until lower needs are reasonably satisfied—are the needs of greatest significance to management and to man himself. They are the *egoistic needs,* and they are of two kinds:

1. Those needs that relate to one's self-esteem—needs for self-confidence, for independence, for achievement, for competence, for knowledge.

2. Those needs that relate to one's reputation—needs for status, for recognition, for appreciation, for the deserved respect of one's fellows.

Unlike the lower needs, these are rarely satisfied; man seeks indefinitely for more satisfaction of these needs once they have become important to him. But they do not appear in any significant way until physiological, safety, and social needs are all reasonably satisfied.

The typical industrial organization offers few opportunities for the satisfaction of these egoistic needs to people at lower levels in the hierarchy. The conventional methods of organizing work, particularly in mass-production industries, give little heed to these aspects of human motivation. If the practices of scientific management were deliberately calculated to thwart these needs, they could hardly accomplish this purpose better than they do.

SELF-FULFILLMENT NEEDS

Finally—a capstone, as it were, on the hierarchy of man's needs —there are what we may call the *needs for self-fulfillment*. These are the needs for realizing one's own potentialities, for continued self-development, for being creative in the broadest sense of that term.

It is clear that the conditions of modern life give only limited opportunity for these relatively weak needs to obtain expression. The deprivation most people experience with respect to other lower-level needs diverts their energies into the struggle to satisfy *those* needs, and the needs for self-fulfillment remain dormant.

MANAGEMENT AND MOTIVATION

We recognize readily enough that a man suffering from a severe dietary deficiency is sick. The deprivation of physiological needs has behavioral consequences. The same is true—although less well recognized—of deprivation of higher-level needs. The man whose needs for safety, association, independence, or status are thwarted is sick just as surely as the man who has rickets. And his sickness will have behavioral consequences. We will be mistaken if we attribute his resultant passivity, his hostility, his refusal to accept responsibility to his inherent "human nature." These forms of behavior are *symptoms* of illness—of deprivation of his social and egoistic needs.

The man whose lower-level needs are satisfied is not motivated to satisfy those needs any longer. For practical purposes they exist no longer. Management often asks, "Why aren't people more productive? We pay good wages, provide good working conditions, have excellent fringe benefits and steady employment. Yet people do not seem to be willing to put forth more than minimum effort."

The fact that management has provided for these physiological and safety needs has shifted the motivational emphasis to the social and perhaps to the egoistic needs. Unless there are opportunities *at work* to satisfy these higher-level needs, people will be deprived; and their behavior will reflect this deprivation. Under such conditions, if management continues to focus its attention on physiological needs, its efforts are bound to be ineffective.

People *will* make insistent demands for more money under these conditions. It becomes more important than ever to buy the material goods and services which can provide limited satisfaction of the thwarted needs. Although money has only limited value in satisfying many higher-level needs, it can become the focus of interest if it is the *only* means available.

THE CARROT-AND-STICK APPROACH

The carrot-and-stick theory of motivation (like Newtonian physical theory) works reasonably well under certain circumstances. The *means* for satisfying man's physiological and (within limits) his safety needs can be provided or withheld by management. Employment itself is such a means, and so are wages, working conditions, and benefits. By these means the individual can be controlled so long as he is struggling for subsistence.

But the carrot-and-stick theory does not work at all once man has reached an adequate subsistence level and is motivated primarily by higher needs. Management cannot provide a man with self-respect, or with the respect of his fellows, or with the satisfaction of needs for self-fulfillment. It can create such conditions that he is encouraged and enabled to seek such satisfactions for *himself*, or it can thwart him by failing to create those conditions.

But this creation of conditions is not "control." It is not a good device for directing behavior. And so management finds itself in an odd position. The high standard of living created by our modern technological know-how provides quite adequately for the satisfaction of physiological and safety needs. The only significant exception is where management practices have not created confidence in a "fair break"—and thus where safety needs are thwarted. But by making possible the satisfaction of low-level needs, management has deprived itself of the ability to use as motivators the devices on which conventional theory has taught it to rely—rewards, promises, incentives, or threats and other coercive devices.

The philosophy of management by direction and control—*regardless of whether it is hard or soft*—is inadequate to motivate because the human needs on which this approach relies are today unimportant motivators of behavior. Direction and control are essentially useless in motivating people whose important needs are social and egoistic. Both the hard and the soft approach fail today because they are simply irrelevant to the situation.

People, deprived of opportunities to satisfy at work the needs which are now important to them, behave exactly as we might predict—with indolence, passivity, resistance to change, lack of responsibility, willingness to follow the demagogue, unreasonable demands for economic benefits. It would seem that we are caught in a web of our own weaving.

A New Theory of Management

For these and many other reasons, we require a different theory of the task of managing people based on more adequate assumptions about human nature and human motivation. I am going to be so bold as to suggest the broad dimensions of such a theory. Call it "Theory Y," if you will.

1. Management is responsible for organizing the elements of productive enterprise—money, materials, equipment, people—in the interest of economic ends.

2. People are *not* by nature passive or resistant to organizational needs. They have become so as a result of experience in organizations.

3. The motivation, the potential for development, the capacity for assuming responsibility, the readiness to direct behavior toward organizational goals are all present in people. Management does not put them there. It is a responsibility of management to make it possible for people to recognize and develop these human characteristics for themselves.

4. The essential task of management is to arrange organizational conditions and methods of operation so that people can achieve their own goals *best* by directing *their own* efforts toward organizational objectives.

This is a process primarily of creating opportunities, releasing potential, removing obstacles, encouraging growth, providing guidance. It is what Peter Drucker has called "management by objectives" in contrast to "management by control." It does *not* involve the abdication of management, the absence of leadership, the lowering of standards, or the other characteristics usually associated with the "soft" approach under Theory X.

SOME DIFFICULTIES

It is no more possible to create an organization today which will be a full, effective application of this theory than it was to build an atomic power plant in 1945. There are many formidable obstacles to overcome.

The conditions imposed by conventional organization theory and by the approach of scientific management for the past half century have tied men to limited jobs which do not utilize their capabilities, have discouraged the acceptance of responsibility, have encouraged passivity, have eliminated meaning from work. Man's habits, attitudes, expectations—his whole conception of membership in an industrial organization—have been conditioned by his experience under these circumstances.

People today are accustomed to being directed, manipulated, controlled in industrial organizations and to finding satisfaction for their social, egoistic, and self-fulfillment needs away from the job. This is true of much of management as well as of workers. Genuine "industrial citizenship"—to borrow again a term from Drucker—is a remote and unrealistic idea, the meaning of which has not even been considered by most members of industrial organizations.

Another way of saying this is that Theory X places exclusive reliance upon external control of human behavior, while Theory Y relies heavily on self-control and self-direction. It is worth noting that this difference is the difference between treating people as children and treating them as mature adults. After generations of the former, we cannot expect to shift to the latter overnight.

STEPS IN THE RIGHT DIRECTION

Before we are overwhelmed by the obstacles, let us remember that the application of theory is always slow. Progress is usually achieved in small steps. Some innovative ideas which are entirely consistent with Theory Y are today being applied with some success.

Decentralization and delegation

These are ways of freeing people from the too-close control of conventional organization, giving them a degree of freedom to direct their own activities, to assume responsibility, and, importantly, to satisfy their egoistic needs. In this connection, the flat organization of Sears, Roebuck and Company provides an interesting example.

It forces "management by objectives," since it enlarges the number of people reporting to a manager until he cannot direct and control them in the conventional manner.

Job enlargement

This concept, pioneered by I.B.M. and Detroit Edison, is quite consistent with Theory Y. It encourages the acceptance of responsibility at the bottom of the organization; it provides opportunities for satisfying social and egoistic needs. In fact, the reorganization of work at the factory level offers one of the more challenging opportunities for innovation consistent with Theory Y.

Participation and consultative management

Under proper conditions, participation and consultative management provide encouragement to people to direct their creative energies toward organizational objectives, give them some voice in decisions that affect them, provide significant opportunities for the satisfaction of social and egoistic needs. The Scanlon Plan is the outstanding embodiment of these ideas in practice.

Performance appraisal

Even a cursory examination of conventional programs of performance appraisal within the ranks of management will reveal how completely consistent they are with Theory X. In fact, most such programs tend to treat the individual as though he were a product under inspection on the assembly line.

A few companies—among them General Mills, Ansul Chemical, and General Electric—have been experimenting with approaches which involve the individual in setting "targets" or objectives *for himself* and in a *self*-evaluation of performance semiannually or annually. Of course, the superior plays an important leadership role in this process—one, in fact, which demands substantially more competence than the conventional approach. The role is, however, considerably more congenial to many managers than the role of "judge" or "inspector" which is usually forced upon them. Above all, the individual is encouraged to take a greater responsibility for planning and appraising his own contribution to organizational objectives; and the accompanying effects on egoistic and self-fulfillment needs are substantial.

APPLYING THE IDEAS

The not infrequent failure of such ideas as these to work as well as expected is often attributable to the fact that a management has "bought the idea" but applied it within the framework of Theory X and its assumptions.

Delegation is not an effective way of exercising management by control. Participation becomes a farce when it is applied as a sales gimmick or a device for kidding people into thinking they are important. Only the management that has confidence in human capacities and is itself directed toward organizational objectives rather than toward the preservation of personal power can grasp the implications of this emerging theory. Such management will find and apply successfully other innovative ideas as we move slowly toward the full implementation of a theory like Y.

THE HUMAN SIDE OF ENTERPRISE

It is quite possible for us to realize substantial improvements in the effectiveness of industrial organizations during the next decade or two. The social sciences can contribute much to such developments; we are only beginning to grasp the implications of the growing body of knowledge in these fields. But if this conviction is to become a reality instead of a pious hope, we will need to view the process much as we view the process of releasing the energy of the atom for constructive human ends—as a slow, costly, sometimes discouraging approach towards a goal which would seem to many to be quite unrealistic.

The ingenuity and the perseverance of industrial management in the pursuit of economic ends have changed many scientific and technological dreams into commonplace realities. It is now becoming clear that the application of these same talents to the human side of enterprise will not only enhance substantially these materialistic achievements, but will bring us one step closer to "the good society."

QUESTIONS

1. What does McGregor mean by the "conventional view" of the organization of human effort in industry?
2. What are the beliefs behind this "conventional view"? Do you agree with these beliefs? Why?
3. Compare McGregor's classes of needs with those in Maslow's article and the introductory section. What differences exist?
4. What does McGregor mean by the "carrot-and-stick approach" of motivation?
5. What is management's responsibility and task in managing people? What difficulties does it face in applying the "new theory" of management?

21. MOTIVATION AND INCREASED PRODUCTIVITY *

Rensis Likert

Human relations research has great potential value for modern management. Many of its findings can serve as the basis for sound principles of management and good leadership. It is my purpose at this time to talk to you about some of the major conclusions that are emerging from this research.

As a background for stating these conclusions, it will be useful to consider the problem historically by examining two important trends.

The first of these two trends began almost a century ago, and has had by far the greater influence upon both management practices and industrial productivity. I refer to the whole movement in which Frederick W. Taylor and his colleagues provided pioneering leadership. For purposes of brevity, I shall use the term "scientific management" to refer to this whole movement.

Generally speaking, scientific management has brought about a very great improvement in productivity. But associated with these gains have been some serious problems and adverse effects.

Setting production goals through the use of time standards has often been accompanied by an expectation of higher levels of productivity. And, therefore, there has been increased pressure on the workers to produce more. Workers resented and resisted this; and the "speed-up" was and still is a major source of conflict and bitterness. Another aspect of this method of managing which caused resentment was the attitude that workers could contribute nothing of value to the organization of their jobs and to the methods of work to be used. As Henry Ford expressed it, "all that we ask of the men is that they do the work which is set before them."

These and similar adverse effects of scientific management were recognized more and more clearly during the second, third, and fourth decades of this century. The speed-up and "efficiency engineering" were sources of much hostility between workers and their supervisors. And these hostilities manifested themselves in a variety of ways, such as widespread restriction of output (even under incentive pay) and a demand for protection through unions, which eventually led to the Wagner Act.

*From the *Management Record*, Vol. 18, No. 4 (April, 1956), pp. 128-131. Reprinted with permission.

The second trend which I wish to examine started at the end of the First World War when a few business leaders and social scientists began to appreciate some of the problems that were the consequence of scientific management. More general recognition of these problems, however, was brought about dramatically by the famous Western Electric studies. These studies showed conclusively and quantitatively that workers were responding to the methods of scientific management by restricting their production to levels which they felt were appropriate. Moreover, neither group nor individual incentive methods of payment prevented this restriction.

These studies also revealed that the workers had developed an "informal organization" which differed from the "formal." And it was found that this informal organization exercised an important influence on the behavior of the workers, often effectively countermanding the official orders of the formal organization. The Western Electric studies also showed that when the hostilities, resentments, suspicions and fears of the workers were replaced by favorable attitudes, a substantial increase in production occurred, just as it was clear that unfavorable attitudes exerted an appreciable restraining influence upon productivity.

Mathewson, Houser, and others, in a modest number of studies during the Thirties, showed that conditions existing in the Western Electric Company were relatively widespread in American industry. Morale and motivational factors were generally found to influence production. Restriction of output was common, and "informal organizations" were found to exist in most of the companies studied.

During the past decade this second trend, which might be called the human relations trend, has gained greater impetus. The volume of research is still small but it is growing. The findings are consistent with the earlier studies and have important implications for the future trend of management theories and practices.

Some of the results of this more recent research can be shown by briefly presenting a few findings from studies conducted by the Institute for Social Research.

Orientation of Supervision: When foremen are asked what they have found to be the best pattern of supervision to get results, a substantial proportion—usually a majority—will place primary emphasis on getting out production. By this, they mean placing primary emphasis on seeing that workers are using the proper methods, are sticking to their work, and are getting a satisfactory volume of work done.

But other supervisors, whom we have called employee-centered, report that they get the best results when they place primary emphasis on the human problems of their workers. The employee-centered supervisor endeavors to build a team, whose members cooperate and work well together. He tries to have people work together who are congenial. And he not only trains people to do their present jobs well, but tends to train them for the next higher jobs. In other words, he is interested in helping them with their problems, both on and off the job. He is friendly and supportive, rather than punitive and threatening.

Higher levels of management, however, tend to place greater emphasis than do foremen on the production-centered approach as the best way to get results.

But which orientation actually yields the best results? A variety of studies in widely different industries show that supervisors who are getting the best production, the best motivation, and the highest level of worker satisfaction are employee-centered rather than production-centered.

However, there is an important point to be added to this finding. Those employee-centered supervisors who get the best results tend to recognize that high production is also one of their major responsibilities.

Closeness of Supervision: Related to orientation of supervision is closeness of supervision. Close supervision tends to be associated with lower productivity, while more general supervision seems to be related to higher productivity.

Low productivity, no doubt, at times leads to closer supervision, but it is also clear that close supervision causes low productivity. In one of the companies involved in this research program it has been found that when managers of high- and low-production divisions are switched, the high-production manager raises the productivity of the low-production division faster than the former high-production division slips under the low-production manager. Supervisors, as they are shifted from job to job, tend to maintain their habitual attitudes toward the supervisory process and their subordinates.

Both general supervision and close supervision are also related to how workers feel about their supervisors. Workers under foremen who supervise closely, or are production-centered, have a less favorable attitude toward the boss than do workers who are under foremen who supervise more generally or are employee-centered.

As we have seen, the research findings indicate that close supervision results in lower productivity, less favorable attitudes, and less satisfaction on the part of the workers, while more general super-vision achieves higher productivity, more favorable attitudes, and greater employee satisfaction. These results suggest that it should be possible to increase productivity in a particular situation by shifting the pattern of supervision so as to make it more general. To test this, we conducted an experiment involving 500 clerical employees in a large company. The work these employees did was something like a billing operation; there was just so much of it, but it had to be processed as it came along.

Briefly, the experimental procedure was as follows. Four parallel divisions were used, each of which was organized in the same way, used the same technology and did exactly the same kind of work, with employees of comparable aptitude. For the purpose of our experiment, certain changes were initiated. In two of the divisions, decision-making was introduced at lower levels; general supervision of the clerks and their supervisors replaced close supervision; work-ers were given more information about matters that affected them; and their ideas and suggestions were sought before decisions were made. In addition, the managers, assistant managers, supervisors, and assistant supervisors of these two divisions were trained in group methods of leadership. The experimental changes in these two divisions will be called Program I.

We faced many problems in attaining the desired changes. Push-ing downward the level at which decisions were made proved diffi-cult. Managers and supervisors seemed to feel that such action was an admission that they were not essential. Therefore, they made virtually no changes. However, when the general manager asked the managers under him if they would help him with some of his work, they responded favorably. He then asked them if there was work that they could turn over to their subordinates in order to free them to assist in his work. The managers then readily found work which their subordinates could handle. A similar process was used all down the line to get supervisors to turn over work to subordinates, and thereby push decision levels down.

In order to provide an effective experimental control for Program I, in the other two divisions the closeness of supervision was increased and decision-making was pushed upward. This will be called Program II. These changes were accomplished by a further extension of scientific management. One of the first steps was to have the jobs timed by the methods department, and standard times computed. This showed that these divisions were overstaffed by about 30%. The general manager then ordered the managers of these two divisions to cut staff by 25%. This was to be done by transfers and by not replacing persons who left. No one was to be dismissed.

The four divisions participating in the experiment were assigned on the basis of one high- and one low-productivity division to Program I, and one high and one low to Program II.

The experiment at the clerical level lasted for one year. Several months were devoted to planning before the experimental year, and there was also a training period of approximately six months just before the experiment began. Throughout the period of the experiment, productivity was measured continuously and computed weekly. Employee and supervisory attitudes and related variables were measured just before and after the experimental year.

Productivity Reflected in Salary Costs: In Program II, where there was an increase in the closeness of supervision, productivity increased by about 25%. In this group, it will be recalled, the general manager had ordered a 25% cut in staff.

But a significant increase in productivity was also achieved in Program I, where supervision was modified so as to be less close and no reduction in work force was ordered. Although the increase in productivity in Program I was not so great as in Program II, it was nevertheless a little more than 20%. And one of the divisions in Program I increased its productivity by about the same amount as each of the two divisions in Program II. The other division in Program I, which historically had been the poorest of all the divisions, did not do so well.

Productivity and Workers' Responsibility: Although both programs were alike in increasing productivity, they were significantly different in the other changes which occurred. The productivity increases in Program II, where decision levels were moved up, were accompanied by adverse shifts in attitudes, interest, involvement in the work, turnover, and related matters. The opposite was true in Program I. Here it was found that when more general supervision was provided, the employees' feeling of responsibility to see that the work got done increased. In Program II, however, this work responsibility decreased. In Program I, when the supervisor was away, the employees kept on working. When the supervisor was absent in Program II, the work tended to stop.

Effect of Employee Attitudes: The experiment changed the workers' attitudes toward their supervisors. In Program I all the shifts were favorable; in Program II all the shifts were unfavorable.

This very brief description of the experiment, I hope, has made clear the pattern of results. Both experimental changes increased productivity substantially. In Program I this increase in productivity was accompanied by favorable shifts in attitudes, interests, and perceptions. The girls became more interested and involved in their work. They accepted more responsibility for getting the work done. Their attitudes toward the company and their superiors became more favorable. And they accepted direction more willingly. In Program II, however, all these attitudes and related variables shifted in an unfavorable direction. All the hostilities, resentments, and unfavorable reactions which have been observed again and again to accompany extensive use of scientific management manifested themselves.

This experiment with clerical workers is important because it shows that increases in productivity can be obtained with either favorable or unfavorable shifts in attitudes, perceptions, and similar variables. Further application of classical methods of scientific management did substantially increase productivity, but it was accompanied by adverse reactions upon the part of the workers involved. With the other approach used in the experiment, a substantial increase in productivity was also obtained, but here it was accompanied by favorable shifts in attitudes and similar variables. A fundamental conclusion from this experiment and other similar research is that direct pressure from one's superior for greater production tends to be resented, while group pressure from one's colleagues is not.

———

Thus, though scientific management has clearly demonstrated its capacity to get high production, this productivity is obtained at a cost which tends to have serious consequences in the long run.

People will produce at relatively high levels when the techniques of production are efficient, the pressure for production is great, the controls and inspections are relatively tight, and the economic rewards and penalties are sufficiently large. But such production is accompanied by attitudes which tend to result in high scrap loss, lowered safety, higher absences and turnover, increased grievances and work stoppages, and the like. It also is accompanied by communication blocks and restrictions. All these developments tend to adversely affect the operation of any organization.

The critical weaknesses in the scientific management approach, of course, are the resentments, hostilities, and adverse motivational and attitudinal reactions which it tends to evoke. In my judgment, these hostilities and unfavorable attitudes stem from powerful motives which scientific management has ignored in its theoretical basis as well as in the day-to-day operating procedures it has developed. But although scientific management has ignored these powerful motives, it has not been able to avoid the substantial impact of their influence in daily operations.

The fundamental cause, therefore, of the adverse reactions produced by scientific management is the assumption that all persons are simple economic men; that it is only necessary to buy a man's time and he will then willingly and effectively do everything which he is ordered to do. Management textbooks emphasize authority and control as the foundation of administration. They either take for granted the power to control or they hold that the relationship of employer and employee in an enterprise is a contractual obligation entailing the right to command and the duty to obey. The critical weakness of scientific management occurs at precisely the point where the human relations research approach has its greatest strength: motivation.

The power of human relations research findings lies in the understanding and insight which they provide into:

1. The character and magnitude of the powerful forces which control human behavior in working situations;
2. And the manner in which these forces can be used so that they reinforce rather than conflict with one another.

The fundamental problem, therefore, is to develop a management theory, as well as the supervisory and managerial practices needed for operating under this theory, which will make use of the concepts of scientific management while fully utilizing in a positive manner the major forces which influence human behavior in work situations. And, I believe, we are developing just such a theory which effectively combines the resources of scientific management and the findings of human relations research. There is not time here to examine it fully, but one or two aspects can be considered.

———

A basic condition of the theory is that all attempts to influence the behavior of subordinates in an organization should be of such a nature that there is a maximum probability that the subordinates will react favorably. When all of the influence attempts are reacted to favorably by a subordinate, the motivational forces acting upon him will be reinforcing, cumulative and maximized, rather than being minimized by being in conflict.

Two conditions appear to be necessary for a subordinate to react favorably to his superior's attempts to influence his behavior. First the influence attempts should be ones which he has reacted favorably to in the past—that is, they need to be familiar. Second, the influence attempts, as seen by the subordinate, should be supportive rather than threatening. And he will see them this way when they contribute to his sense of importance and personal worth; he will see them as threatening when they decrease his sense of personal worth.

From these conditions it is possible to derive a modified theory of management and the day-to-day operating procedures required to implement it.

Thus, for example, it is possible to state the following principle based on this theory: Any attempt to produce a change in an organization will work best when the people whose behavior needs changing want themselves to change. An attempted change, therefore, will work better when management creates a situation in which people can see the possibility and desirability of change and even initiate the change, rather than merely being ordered to change.

Research findings show that supervisors improve in their handling of human relations much more when provided with objective measurements about their operation and then stimulated to discuss these measurements with their subordinates as a group, than when they are merely given a supervisory training program. A supervisory training program is, after all, just another way of ordering a foreman to change his behavior.

Another operating principle based on this modified theory is also related to the best way to bring about changes and improvements. This principle indicates that an organization will perform more effectively when it functions as a network of integrated and coordinated teams, each of which has a high team spirit, high performance goals related to its part of the total job, favorable attitudes toward its supervision and management, and confidence and trust in them. These teams are knit into an integrated and coordinated organization by supervisors, managers and staff, who hold overlapping memberships in two or more teams or groups.

It is possible to demonstrate theoretically and in actual operation that an organization made up of integrated teams with high team spirit and high performance goals functions better than an organization operating under present managerial systems. The reason for this better performance is that such an organization will have appreciably superior motivation, greater acceptance of influence attempts, more confidence and trust on the part of all its members in one another, better two-way communication, and better decisions at all levels, based on the more accurate and adequate facts provided by the better communication.

The available research findings indicate that high group loyalty has an important influence upon performance at all levels in an organization. The data show that high group loyalty, coupled with high production goals in the work group, result in high productivity, accompanied by high job satisfaction and a feeling of working under little pressure.

QUESTIONS

1. Distinguish the two "trends" that Likert discusses. Show the weaknesses and the strengths of these trends.
2. Briefly explain the experimental procedure used to measure the effect of supervision on productivity.
3. Explain what is meant by "orientation of supervision" and discuss its effect on productivity.
4. What conditions are necessary for supervisors to influence the behavior of subordinates?
5. What are the benefits of human relations research?

22. MOTIVATION IN WORK GROUPS:
A TENTATIVE VIEW *

James V. Clark

This paper represents an attempt to examine a number of different researches in the field of organizational behavior and to see if their similarities can be highlighted and tentatively explained by the use of Maslow's need-hierarchy concept.[1]

A recent research experience of mine (so far published only in case form) [2] suggested for me that this process might be a useful way of generating new hypotheses and methods of measurement. The present paper is presented in the hope that others can be stimulated in the same way.

More specifically, this paper makes no claim that the answers concerning employee motivation and its determinants are all in. Neither does it claim that the questions generated by the examination of several researches from the point of view of the need-hierarchy concept are all presently researchable in a strict operational sense. Rather, the paper puts up what, for me, appears to be a potentially operational scheme for analyzing motivation and its organizational determinants. With such a scheme, it appears possible to study a number of different organizations comparatively, an effort which the field of organizational behavior needs.

I do believe, therefore, that the use of this theory puts us in a somewhat better position than that outlined in a recent research on worker motivation by Herzberg *et al.*:

> This concept [Maslow's need hierarchy] has led many people to feel that the worker can never be satisfied with his job. How are you going to solve the dilemma of trying to motivate workers who have a continuously revolving set of needs? Since each individual may present at any one time a different scramble of his psychological need list, a systematic personnel practice hoping to cater to the most prepotent needs of its entire working force is defeated by the nature of the probabilities. Forgetting for a moment the individual "need hierarchies," it can be argued that there is sufficiently homogeneity within various groups of employees to make for a relative similarity of "need hierarchies" within each group. Even so, the changes in prepotency for the group will occur, and personnel administration will have to

* From *Human Organization*, Vol. 19, No. 4 (Winter, 1960-61), pp. 199-208. Reprinted with permission.
[1] A. H. Maslow, *Motivation and Personality* (Harper and Bros., New York, 1954).
[2] "Century Co. (A)-(I)," Harvard Business School, EA-A 321-29.

keep up with them. For some who hold to this point of view personnel administration is reduced to the essential of labor-management bargaining. For others it means that personnel programs must be geared to be sensitive to the changes that are continually taking place in the needs of the employees. And since this can be done only by the supervisors, the training of supervisors in understanding human motivation, the factors underlying it, and the therapeutic or manipulative skills with which to cope with it, is the most essential ingredient to any industrial relations program.[3]

As this paper will show, I am not opposed to sensitive first-line administrators. However, other variables relating to satisfaction and productivity will be highlighted and in such a way as to suggest that the development of worker motivation is not a random scramble but is perhaps predictable, with only a modicum of sensitivity to employee needs.

The Need-Hierarchy Model

Let us start with McGregor's summary of Maslow's concepts, which is concise and simply put.

As most readers are probably aware, Maslow views an individual's motivations not in terms of a series of drives, but rather in terms of a hierarchy, certain "higher" needs becoming activated to the extent certain "lower" ones become satisfied. McGregor summarized these as follows: [4]

Physiological Needs

Man is a wanting animal—as soon as one of his needs is satisfied, another appears in its place. This process is unending. It continues from birth to death.

Man's needs are organized in a series of levels—a hierarchy of importance. At the lowest level, but pre-eminent in importance when they are thwarted, are his *physiological needs*. Man lives for bread alone, when there is no bread. Unless the circumstances are unusual, his needs for love, for status, for recognition are inoperative when his stomach has been empty for awhile. But when he eats regularly and adequately, hunger ceases to be an important motivation. The same is true of the other physiological needs of man—for rest, exercise, shelter, protection from the elements.

A satisfied need is not a motivator of behavior! This is a fact of profound significance that is regularly ignored in the conventional approach to the management of ["normal"] people. Consider your own need for air; except as you are deprived of it, it has no appreciable motivating effect upon your behavior.

---

[3] Frederick Herzberg, Bernard Mausner, and Barbara Block Snyderman, *The Motivation to Work* (John Wiley & Sons, New York, 1959).

[4] Douglas M. McGregor, 5th Anniversary Convocation, School of Industrial Management, Massachusetts Institute of Technology, Cambridge, Massachusetts.

Safety Needs

When the physiological needs are reasonably satisfied, needs at the next higher level begin to dominate man's behavior, to motivate him. These are called *safety needs*. They are needs for protection against danger, threat, deprivation. Some people mistakenly refer to these as needs for security. However, unless man is in a dependent relationship where he fears arbitrary deprivation, he does not demand security. The need is for the "fairest possible break." When he is confident of this he is more willing to take risks. But when he feels threatened or dependent, his greatest need is for guarantees, for protection, for security.

The fact needs little emphasis that, since every industrial employee is in a dependent relationship, safety needs may assume considerable importance. Arbitrary management actions, behavior which arouses uncertainty with respect to continued employment or which reflects favoritism or discrimination, unpredictable administration of policy— these can be powerful motivators of the safety needs in the employment relationship at *every level*, from worker to vice president.

Social Needs

When man's physiological needs are satisfied and he is no longer fearful about his physical welfare, his *social needs* become important motivators of his behavior—needs for belonging, for association, for acceptance by his fellows, for giving and receiving friendship and love.

Management knows today of the existence of these needs, but it often assumes quite wrongly that they represent a threat to the organization. Many studies have demonstrated that the tightly knit, cohesive work group may, under proper conditions, be far more effective than an equal number of separate individuals in achieving organizational goals.

Yet management, fearing group hostility to its own objectives, often goes to considerable lengths to control and direct human efforts in ways that are inimical to the natural "groupiness" of human beings. When man's social needs—and perhaps his safety needs, too—are thus thwarted, he behaves in ways which tend to defeat organizational objectives. He becomes resistant, antagonistic, uncooperative. But this behavior is a consequence, not a cause.

Ego Needs

Above the social needs—in the sense that they do not become motivators until lower needs are reasonably satisfied—are the needs of greater significance to management and to man himself. They are the *egoistic* needs, and they are of two kinds:

1. Those needs that relate to one's self-esteem—needs for self-confidence, for independence, for achievement, for competence, for knowledge.
2. Those needs that relate to one's reputation—needs for status, for recognition, for appreciation, for the deserved respect of one's fellows.

Unlike the lower needs, these are rarely satisfied; man seeks indefinitely for more satisfaction of these needs once they have become important to him. But they do not appear in any significant way until physiological, safety, and social needs are all reasonably satisfied.

The typical industrial organization offers few opportunities for the satisfaction of these egoistic needs to people at lower levels in the hierarchy. The conventional methods of organizing work, particularly in mass-production industries, give little heed to these aspects of human motivation. If the practices of scientific management were deliberately calculated to thwart these needs, they could hardly accomplish this purpose better than they do.

Self-Fulfillment Needs

Finally—a capstone, as it were, on the hierarchy of man's needs—there are what we may call the needs for *self-fulfillment*. These are the needs for realizing one's own potentialities, for continued self-development, for being creative in the broadest sense of that term.

It is clear that the conditions of modern life give only limited opportunity for these relatively weak needs to obtain expression. The deprivation most people experience with respect to other lower-level needs diverts their energies into the struggle to satisfy those needs, and the needs for self-fulfillment remain dormant.

For purposes of initial explanation and simplicity, McGregor spoke in terms of separate steps or levels. Actually, Maslow suggests that these levels are interdependent and overlapping, each higher-need level emerging before the lower needs have been satisfied completely. In our society, most people tend to be partially satisfied in each need area and partially unsatisfied. However, most individuals tend to have higher satisfaction at the lower-need level than at higher-need levels. Maslow helps to explain this by picturing the average citizen as (for illustrative purposes) 85 per cent satisfied in his physiological needs, 70 per cent satisfied in his safety needs, 50 per cent in his belonging needs, 40 per cent in his egoistic needs, and 10 per cent in his self-fulfillment needs.

SOME SUGGESTED UNIFORMITIES AMONG DIFFERENT RESEARCHES

Exhibit I on p. 379 shows how the need-hierarchy concept might be utilized to relate and explain the findings of a number of different studies. In other words, it takes McGregor's generalization of Maslow's theory, attempts to relate it to some existing studies, and concludes that workers under this or that combination of environmental conditions behave *as if* they were motivated in such-and-such a fashion.

Before we turn to this exhibit, however, a word of caution is in order. This way of relating and thinking about different organizational behavior researches is by no means perfect. First of all, the propositions which follow from the need-hierarchy theory are extremely difficult to test in a research sense. Secondly, the variety of environmental and internal-system factors affecting work-group

CONDITIONS IN THE WORK GROUP'S ENVIRONMENT	(1)	(2)	(3)	(4)	(5)	(6)	(7)
							Company Perceived as Supportive
					Low Perceived Contribution Opportunity	High Perceived Contribution Opportunity	High Perceived Contribution Opportunity
				Production-Centered Leadership	Accommodative Leadership	Accommodative Leadership	Group-Centered Leadership
			Low-Status Congruence	High-Status Congruence	High-Status Congruence	High-Status Congruence	High-Status Congruence
		Low Interaction Opportunity	High Interaction Opportunity	High Interaction Opportunity	High Interaction Opportunity	High Interaction Opportunity	High Interaction Opportunity
	Low Employment Security	High Employment Security	High Employment Security	High Employment Security	High Employment Security	High Employment Security	High Employment Security

NEEDS (NEED ACTIVATION)

SELF-ACTUALIZATION
STATUS-PRESTIGE
SELF-ESTEEM
MEMBERSHIP
SAFETY

(EFFECTS ON PRODUCTIVITY AND TURNOVER - ABSENTEEISM)

	(1)	(2)	(3)	(4)	(5)	(6)	(7)
PRODUCTIVITY	High	Low	Low?	Low	Meets Minimum Requirements	High	High
TURNOVER-ABS.	Low	High	High	?	Average	Low	Low

KEY

☐ = need not activated

▨ (hatched) = need activated but relatively satisfied

▨ (dashed) = need activated but relatively frustrated

EXHIBIT 1

SOME RELATIONS BETWEEN CONDITIONS IN THE WORK GROUP'S ENVIRONMENT MOTIVATION, SATISFACTION, PRODUCTIVITY, AND TURNOVER-ABSENTEEISM

behavior cannot be categorized so as to make all known descriptions of work situations directly comparable from some one point of view. Finally, almost all researches leave out, or find uncontrollable, some variables that are necessary for complete comparability. Nevertheless, some available researches suggest uniformities consistent with the need-hierarchy concept.

Exhibit I shows how a number of different "givens" in a workgroup's environment can prevent or frustrate an individual's opportunity for need satisfaction at different levels of the need hierarchy. The exhibit is based on the assumption that all individuals have a potential for activating all the needs on the need hierarchy. Likewise, the exhibit assumes that an individual does not necessarily suspend or forget his unrealized needs during his hours on the job. Actually, in industrial situations, there are few data to support the first assumption, many data to support the second. Therefore, the exhibit can usefully be regarded as a tentative explanation of how and why most people, or an "average worker," would most typically react under different conditions at work.

The extreme left-hand scale of the middle block of graphs in Exhibit I represents the various levels of the need hierarchy (exclusive of the physiological needs). (In Maslow's description of his need hierarchy, the status-prestige need and the self-esteem need are placed side by side about the membership need. They are placed one on top of the other here for graphic simplicity.)

The remaining columns of the middle block depict the pattern of an individual's need activation and satisfaction under a number of different external conditions. These patterns will be discussed in this paper in relation to certain researches. (It is not possible to show all possible combinations of external conditions: researches have not been conducted under such a wide variety of conditions.)

Across the bottom of the exhibit are two rows which show "productivity" and "turnover and absenteeism" for each column. These are by no means definitely established results but the researches examined in this paper often suggested certain tendencies in regard to these variables which are shown. Consequently, by beginning with human needs, we can move to the relationship between the satisfaction of these needs, external conditions, and productivity and turnover-absenteeism.

Column 1 illustrates a situation in which employment security is extremely low. Such conditions might exist whenever alternative employment is unavailable (as in a depression) or is deemed by the workers to be not as desirable as present employment and where workers feel unprotected from a management which is perceived as arbitrary in its layoff and firing procedures.

Research by Goode and Fowler [5] in an automobile feeder plant illustrates this condition. In their study of a low morale, nonunion plant a small group of high service employees, for whom the job had become an absolute economic necessity, consistently produced according to management expectations. Turnover among other workers, for whom the job was less important, was high. They quit or were fired for not producing enough.

Interestingly enough, related situations were described some time ago, and were alluded to by Mitchell,[6] when he noted that the pace of work was slower in the flush times of 1900–1902 than it had been in the dull times of 1894–1896. He quoted a sample bit of testimony from the period. The superintendent of a company manufacturing electrical machinery said:

> . . . Five years ago men did not restrict their output, union or non-union men, because they wanted to hold their jobs, and a man would do anything and all he was told to do. Now a man knows that all he has to do is walk across the street and get another job at the same rate of pay. . . .

Obviously, a group's productivity does not always increase in depression times: it fell off in the bank-wiring room [7] shortly before the final layoffs. *The suggestion being made here is that under employment conditions which an individual perceives as economically threatening and arbitrary (and such conditions probably exist most often in a depression), his higher needs cannot motivate. He is "stuck" on the safety level and his behavior can only work toward the immediate goal of economic survival. Under conditions of this kind, financial rewards tend to be the primary incentives which motivate workers toward higher productivity.*

Frustrated membership needs

Columns 2 through 4 all show situations in which membership needs are active, but frustrated. They are shown separately, because apparently they occur under different environmental conditions.

[5] W. F. Goode and Irving Fowler, "Incentive Factors in a Low Morale Plant," *American Sociological Review*, XIV, No. 5 (1949).

[6] W. C. Mitchell, *Business Cycles and Their Causes* (University of California Press, Berkeley, Cal., 1941).

[7] F. J. Roethlisberger and W. J. Dickson, *Management and the Worker* (Harvard University Press, Cambridge, Mass., 1952).

Column 2 shows a situation where workers are less concerned with employment security, because they have it, but where the job technology imposes physical or spatial requirements where interaction is impossible or severely restricted. This condition reflects and is labelled "low interaction opportunity." Such conditions and their effects on satisfaction were described in two automobile assembly plant studies.

Walker and Guest [8] rated jobs according to their "mass production characteristics" (noise, repetitiveness, restricted opportunity for movement, etc.). *Workers holding such jobs often reported social isolation to be an important reason for job dissatisfaction.* Moreover, absenteeism and turnover (extremely high throughout the automotive industry) were nearly twice as high for persons whose jobs exhibited "extreme mass production characteristics."

Another study of automobile assembly workers by Jasinski [9] showed that the men resented not being able to follow conventional conversation patterns; looking at the listener, being able to pause for conversation, and to complete the "talk." A correlation was found between an individual's desire to talk on the job and his attitude towards his job: the higher the desire to talk, the less interesting the job.

It is possible that Van Zelst's study [10] of sociometrically restructured construction work groups may be illustrative of what happens when opportunities to interact are increased.

When men were allowed to work alongside others whom they themselves had chosen, turnover, labor cost and materials cost all dropped.

The inference can be drawn that these results occurred because membership level motivation was satisfied and higher needs became activated.

Another Research, "The Case of the Changing Cage," [11] suggests what happens to a work group's productivity and satisfaction when interaction opportunities are suddenly lowered. (In this case, however, interaction opportunity was decreased by a combination of

---

[8] Charles R. Walker and Robert H. Guest, *The Man on the Assembly Line* (Harvard University Press, Cambridge, Mass., 1952).

[9] Frank J. Jasinski, "Technological Delimitation of Reciprocal Relationships: A Study of Interaction Patterns in Industry," *Human Organization*, XV, No. 2 (1956).

[10] R. J. Van Zelst, "Sociometrically Selected Work Teams Increase Productivity," *Personnel Psychology*, V, No. 3 (1953).

[11] Cara B. Richards and Henry F. Dobyns, "Topography and Culture: The Case of the Changing Cage," *Human Organization*, XVI, No. 1 (1957).

physical changes and another variable we will discuss later, leadership behavior.)

Workers in a voucher-check filing unit in an insurance company worked together well, kept up with the work load and expressed feelings of satisfaction. Their work area was inside a wire cage surrounded by filing cabinets and boxes through which the group's supervisors could not see. For efficiency purposes, the cage was moved to a new area in which the filing cabinets were arranged so that supervisors could see into the cage and restrict worker interaction. The workers could no longer engage in social activities which had been important to them (games, chatting, eating, etc.). Their output declined drastically, the amount of time spent in nonwork activities increased substantially, and the workers expressed considerable dissatisfaction with the new setup.

In short, it appears that if there are any major physical or spatial technological factors which restrict opportunities for interaction (under conditions where safety-level needs are not primary) membership needs will be frustrated and, consequently, any higher-need levels will not be activated.

Column 3 illustrates a situation in which safety-level considerations are relatively unimportant because they are satisfied, interaction opportunities are high, but where workers are placed in low-status congruence work groups.

The need-hierarchy explanation of this situation would be as follows: safety needs are not active and membership needs are active but frustrated because social-status differences among persons in the work group are too large for the group to deal with effectively. Therefore no indications of higher-level needs are present. As a consequence, people would not see their work as something to which they could or should contribute. But why should low- or high-status congruence affect membership motivation?

In Zaleznik, Christensen, and Roethlisberger's recent study, a "theory of social certitude" was advanced to explain this on an individual level:

> In the condition of social certitude, the individual may be high, middle, or low in total status. But at whatever level, his status factors are well established. As a social entity, therefore, he can place himself and be placed readily in the structure of a group. People relate to him in terms of common expectations of behavior toward a person well established at his particular level of status. In turn, the individual knows what to expect from others. These expectations may or may not be functional for the group or the individual—there may be a more productive role for an individual than his status, well established as

it is, allows him to play. Nevertheless, in a condition of social certitude the individual becomes "structured" into a group. Whether he is structured into the group at a high rank or low rank will depend on the level of the individual's total status.

The condition of ambiguity, where the individual's status factors are out of line, provides no readily apparent social position for him. As an ambiguous social entity, the group has no clear expectations regarding behavior from or toward such an individual. On the one hand, being high in one or more dimensions of status seems to require the form of behavior associated with a high status person. On the other hand, being simultaneously low in one or more dimensions of status seems to require behavior associated with a low status person. These mixed expectations create ambiguities and consequently anxiety in social relationships.[12]

This theory was advanced to explain why group members are attracted to or repelled by an *individual* whose status factors are out of line: some very high, some very low. Such an individual is ambiguous in relation to the group majority. The term "group-status congruence" refers to a collection of people who share similar status factors, even if the factors themselves may be out of line with one another for a given individual. In this kind of a situation, an individual who exhibits status factors different from the majority tends to be avoided by the majority even if his status factors are in line with one another. He is likely to be described by others as "not our class" or "not our kind of person." [13] The four combinations between an individual and his group (high group-status congruence, high individual-status congruence; low group-status congruence, low individual-status congruence, etc.) have not been studied as such. At the present time, loosely stated, it appears that if, under most conditions, an individual has status factors to some extent different from the majority of people in the small-group social structure to which he belongs, he will tend to be regarded as ambiguous by that majority, and hence will be regarded with anxiety.

Clark's supermarket research [14] was concerned with differences in group-status congruence between stores.

He found that groups with high group-status congruence (which he called "high status factors in common" groups) exhibited low turnover and low absenteeism, both indications of membership-need

---

[12] A. Zaleznik, C. R. Christensen, and F. J. Roethlisberger, *The Motivation, Productivity and Satisfaction of Workers, A Prediction Study* (Harvard University Division of Research, Graduate School of Business Administration, Boston, Mass., 1958).

[13] James V. Clark, *Some Unconscious Assumptions Affecting Labor Efficiency in Eight Supermarkets* (unpublished D.B.A. thesis), Harvard Graduate School of Business Administration, 1958.

[14] *Ibid.*

level satisfaction. Moreover, he further found that stores which had high-status congruent groups in them also tended to have higher labor efficiency ratings. In addition, he found that members of these groups tended to speak of their work as more satisfying.

Adams' bomber crew study [15] was somewhat similar.

He showed that crews with high group-status congruence tended to report feelings of satisfaction with group membership. However, Adams also showed that while crews with high-status congruence showed high technical performance up to a point, beyond that point, as group-status congruence increased, technical performance decreased.

Therefore, while Clark's and Adams' studies showed similar results in the relation between group-status congruence and membership satisfaction, their findings on group-status congruence and performance were less clear.[16] It is difficult to explain with confidence why Adams' highest technical performance groups were low-status congruent. Comparable data on social structure, motivation, satisfaction, and formal leadership might have provided clearer explanations.

Not only the possible difference between these two studies, but the findings of other researches in the general area of status and how people react to it, all indicate that not enough is known yet about this subject to offer inclusive explanations for work-group behavior. For example, Zaleznik's machine shop workers [17] had developed a social structure which offered its members at least a minimal level of satisfaction. In comparison to other studies, his workers could be said to have exhibited low individual and group-status congruence, although the congruence apparently was high enough for the group to form: it contained no Bolsheviks or Andaman Islanders. In short, the existing findings in this area suggest, but not conclusively, that under most industrial conditions, a group will be more cohesive to the extent to which its members exhibit individual and/or group-status congruence. (An important exception will be discussed under Column 7 of Exhibit I.)

---

[15] Stuart Adams, "Status Congruency as a Variable in Small Group Performance," *Social Forces*, XXXII, 16-22.

[16] However, the two studies do not necessarily contradict each other on this point, since Clark studied no stores with status-congruence measures as high as some of the bomber crews studied by Adams. Also, the two studies used different status factors, and different ways to measure group-status congruence. Clark's research is continuing in an attempt to test for lower efficiency under conditions of higher group-status congruence.

[17] A. Zaleznik, *Worker Satisfaction and Development* (Harvard University Division of Research, Graduate School of Business Administration, Boston, Mass., 1956).

The remaining columns, 4 through 7, show those situations where neither technological restrictions on interaction, nor the given sentiments of workers (e.g., notions of member attraction stemming from status factors in common) are such as to prevent the formation of a satisfying social structure. Rather the constrictions on group development portrayed here stem largely from the behavior of the formal leader of the work group.

Leadership behavior

Since leadership is important here, it will be useful, before turning to the columns themselves, to describe roughly the leadership behavior under three different types.[18] The labels "accommodative," "production-centered," and "group-centered" will be briefly described, in that order.

The first, "accommodative," refers to situations where the leader's behavior neither challenges a group, nor seriously violates its norms of how a leader should behave. The group's determination of its own work procedures is left alone. As a result, the formal leader does not seriously threaten the group's survival as a group.

This condition is a common one and was described in the following reports:

In the Whirlwind Corporation [19] a group of workers developed an improved tool capable of increasing their productivity on a certain item fifty per cent. Actually, they increased productivity ten per cent and used the remaining time to improve quality on some other products. A methods engineer was assigned to study the problem but the group withheld information about the tool from him. For some time, the foreman was aware of this but was "satisfied to let the men handle it their own way." He reasoned that at little expense he was able to get out production of high quality on his line.

In Roy's research in a piecework machine shop [20] workers had an elaborate set of restriction-of-output activities. The foreman instructed new men in parts of this system. To one man he said:

> Say, when you punch off day work onto piecework, you ought to have your piecework already started. Run a few, then punch off day work, and you'll have a good start. You've got to chisel a little around here to make money.

---

[18] It is beyond the scope of this article to evaluate these labels or to offer a different classification scheme.

[19] Paul Pigors and Charles H. Myers, *Personnel Administration, A Point of View and a Method* (McGraw-Hill Co., New York, 1956).

[20] Donald Roy, "Efficiency and the Fix: Informal Intergroup Relations in a Piecework Machine Shop," *American Journal of Sociology*, LX, No. 3 (1954).

In the Century Company,[21] workers in one area (B) reported that their foreman left them completely alone and had for several years. Prior to that time, he had supervised the men closely but they had taught him not to, by telling him that they would refuse to work if he didn't let them alone.

Although the three situations above point to different degrees of foreman involvement in the group, the uniformity among them is that the leader has abdicated any influence in the setting of work procedures. The group determines its procedures. A variety of labels other than "accommodative" has been devised to describe such a foreman: "laissez-faire," "abdicratic," etc.

Other researches have pointed to the "production-centered" pattern of leadership behavior (and, moreover, suggested certain relations between such leadership and productivity).

In a study of productivity and leadership in an insurance company,[22] certain leaders were characterized as seeing their job primarily in terms of methods, procedures, and standards of production. Called production-centered leaders, by the researchers, it was noted that such leaders headed seven out of ten low-producing sections.

In the Century Company (I) case,[23] one foreman said this about his idea of a good worker:

> A good man is a man who is reasonable. . . . He does what the company tells him he should do. He does not try to do what he thinks he should do, but he does what he is told.

The people working for this foreman had these kinds of things to say about him:

> Whenever my foreman sees a man sitting down, he comes up to him and gives him something to do. . . . I don't think he'll be happy until he sees everybody running around all the time. [Our] foreman shouldn't yell at a man in front of everybody or nail him down. . . . This makes friction and breaks down the group.

Borrowing the phrase from the above-mentioned insurance company research, the Century Company researchers labelled this foreman "production-centered."

This kind of leader is the direct opposite of the accommodative type, in that he allows the employees little or no influence in the

---

[21] "Century Co. (A)-(1)," op. cit.

[22] Daniel Katz, N. Maccoby, and Nancy Morse, *Productivity, Supervision and Morale in an Office Situation*, Part I (Institute for Social Research, Ann Arbor, Mich., 1950).

[23] "Century Co. (A)-(1)," op. cit.

setting-up of work procedures. Influence is supposed to move downward only according to such a supervisor. Although we are calling such a leader production-centered, others have described him as "authoritarian," "autocratic," and "task-centered."

"Group-centered" leadership was indicated in the same two studies.

In the insurance company,[24] "employee-centered leadership" referred to supervisors who saw their job primarily in terms of the organization, training, and motivation of subordinates. Such supervisors headed six of seven high-producing sections. The researchers said that:

> The supervisors of the high-producing sections . . . regard supervision as the most important part of their work. . . . Their method of supervision appears to be one of setting up certain general conditions for their employees and thus permitting their employees to work out the details of when and how the work will be handled.

In the Century Company case (I),[25] one foreman said this about his idea of a good worker:

> In my estimation, a good furnace worker is a man who has confidence in himself. . . . A foreman should show confidence in his men, and this should be real confidence. I'm always ready to show confidence in a man, even though at first sight I might think he doesn't deserve it. What I do is give some directions to a man and then let him do his work without always being on his back. I want him to be free to do his work. . . . I realize that this requires a lot of talking on the part of the foreman. The men have to learn to trust their foreman. A foreman has to talk to his men to let himself be known by them. . . . Another thing, I like to tease the men, because it's one way for me to talk to them. It shows them I'm not dangerous.

The workers spoke about this foreman as follows:

> Last week when _____ was our foreman we did not have any trouble. There were no complaints, no grievances, no beefs. It was hot and he understood that we were having more difficulty working at this temperature than at other times. After all, a man needs encouragement.
> He knows how to run the men. I wish we could keep him for a long time. . . . We're not the only ones that have noticed he is good. Everywhere he has been in the company, people have been glad to work for him.

The researchers classified this foreman as "group-centered."

---

[24] Daniel Katz, N. Maccoby, and Nancy Morse, *op. cit.*
[25] "Century Co. (A)-(1)," *op. cit.*

This kind of leader has been described as "democratic," "group-centered," "employee-centered," etc. In this paper, the group-centered label will be used. Regardless of the label, however, it can be seen that such a leader allows and encourages a *mutual* influence relationship with his men. Both the leader and his subordinates play a role in the setting-up of work procedures and the mutuality is made legitimate and encouraged by this kind of leader.

Returning to the Exhibit 1 diagram, *Column 4* shows the effects of the production-centered leadership condition in a situation where group formation potential is present. The behavior of a leader allowing low-influence opportunity, as described above, would tend to prevent a group from forming a satisfying relationship with each other and to its environment. Because workers are more consciously forced to attend to their work, their membership needs are frustrated.

The Century Company [26] cases showed two groups of furnace workers, both with equal numbers of high and low individually status-congruent people. Workers in furnace area "A" had a production-centered foreman and exhibited less social development, while workers in furnace area "B" had an accommodative foreman and showed more social development. The researchers made an attempt to assess motivation, also, and there was considerably lower indication of membership need activation in area A than in area B. Moreover, of those judged active at this need level in area A, the majority appeared frustrated.

This study shows an instance in which membership needs were frustrated by a production-centered foreman: by holding workers rigidly to their required activities, he never permitted the social group to form, even though it was potentially capable of so forming. Incidentally, while accurate productivity data were not available for the two particular shift crews studied, area A as a whole (all four shift crews together) was producing much less than area B.

If production-centered leadership is introduced into a group that has already formed, however, there is some evidence to suggest that the group continues to function as a group: they unite around their hostility to management.

The "Case of the Changing Cage" [27] alluded to before illustrates this (although it contains no information about status congruence). The supervisor believed that he could better control output by looking into this cage and thereby reducing nonwork behavior. In the old cage, he could not see in, but in the new cage he could. The result,

---

[26] *Ibid.*

[27] Cara Richards and Henry Dobyns, *op. cit.*

however, was the nonwork activities actually increased (although they were less visible: the group went underground).

Whether or not such a situation is indicative of frustrated memberships needs is difficult to say. Perhaps it can be said, though, that this group was simply elaborating its membership needs: under this condition, the nonwork behavior offered the only *possibility* for need satisfaction.

Columns 1 through 4 have all illustrated how environmental conditions can restrict the development of social structure in work groups. In addition, they also illustrated motivational consequences at lower-need levels only. The remaining columns show situations in which there is indication that higher-need levels can become activated. Since, in a formal organization, people activated at these higher-need levels show a tendency to contribute their judgment and productiveness to the organization's task, the term "contributive motivation" may sometimes be a useful shorthand for all the need levels above the membership level. We shall use it occasionally in the rest of this paper.

Column 5 shows two changes in comparison to Column 4. One, the satisfaction of membership needs, comes from the accommodative leader who, by not threatening the group too much, allows it to form and perpetuate itself. The second change is the frustration of the esteem needs, due to the introduction of a condition which might be labelled "low-perceived contribution opportunity." This refers to a worker's perception of a technological process as being predetermined for the most part. Here, except for the opportunity for an occasional change in setup, technology, etc., a member of a social group at work sees no continuing opportunity to contribute anything, to make a difference, to initiate, along with other members of this group, something useful on his environment. The Column five situation has often been described in organizational behavior research at the worker level because it is undoubtedly the most common. The self-esteem and status-prestige needs are released, because membership needs are relatively satisfied, but, since the workers' jobs prevent any satisfying feelings of group competence or mastery to emerge, and because the accommodative foreman has no concept of getting his group involved in setting up any of its own procedures, the esteem needs are frustrated. Typical comments of workers in such situations are:

A job is a job.

You have to work so it might as well be here as anywhere.

This job isn't bad: it's a nice bunch of guys but any moron could do the work [etc.].

It appears as if the "regulars" in the Zaleznik, Christensen, Roethlisberger prediction study [28] and the famous bank-wiring room workers [29] illustrate this column. Under such conditions, workers' productivity and satisfaction are determined mainly by their position in the social structure, since they are "stuck" on the membership level. Little, if any, opportunity for the satisfaction of contributive motivation exists.

Column 6 differs from Column 5 in that it shows the satisfied self-esteem need under conditions of a high perceived contribution opportunity, but a frustrated status-prestige need (frustrated by the lack of recognition on the part of an accommodative foreman) which the worker would feel was justified by his competence. The accommodative leader allows a group to develop simply by not being around or bothering to impede it. His *not* being around or *not* understanding the forces which motivate productiveness (i.e., self-esteem around job competence) make him less likely to reward the work with verbal or economic recognition of these perceived skills.

This motivational pattern and these environmental conditions were seen in the previously referred to Century Company case.[30] Workers in one furnace area (B) were glad their foreman was not around to interfere with their nonwork activities and their exercising of skill and judgment in their work. However, they resented the fact that he did not *understand* the extent of their technical competence and hence could not reward them adequately when it came time for him to evaluate them.

Before leaving columns 1 through 6, which all illustrate one or another form of what Roethlisberger has called "frozen groups," [31] another condition should be mentioned: "perception of company supportiveness." It has not been studied in enough situations to allow us to place it somewhere in columns 1 through 6; however, two studies nevertheless suggest its importance.

Seashore [32] found that high cohesive groups tended to produce significantly higher than average when they reported a high perception of company supportiveness and to produce significantly lower than average when they reported a low perception of company supportiveness.

[28] A. Zaleznik, C. R. Christensen, and F. J. Roethlisberger, *op. cit.*

[29] Where there is a suggestion (untested) that social structure was determined by individual status congruence. Cf. F. J. Roethlisberger and W. J. Dickson, *op. cit.*

[30] "Century Co. (A)-(I)," *op. cit.*

[31] A. Zaleznik, *op. cit.*

[32] S. F. Seashore, *Group Cohesiveness in the Industrial Work Group* (Survey Research Center, University of Michigan, Ann Arbor, Mich., 1954).

In a piecework machine shop studied by Collins, *et al.*,[33] a work group had an elaborate system of output restriction. The accommodative foreman knew about and actively supported the system. The general superintendent, however, exerted much effort in an attempt to break it up. He told workers they should not accept group pressure to conform and that they were foolish and dishonest if they did. The men saw the over-all company as being hostile toward them and went to considerable lengths to restrict output: they often finished their day's work in three or four hours, they had jigs and fixtures which increased their hourly productivity but which were unknown to management, etc.

Column 7 shows a condition that has only recently been analytically studied on a continuing basis in industry. However, studies concerning group participation in the process of instituting technological change (e.g., the well-known relay assembly test room [34] and Coch and French [35] studies) might illustrate this situation for temporary periods where workers were involved in, and given recognition for, their ability to contribute to important organizational problems. Perhaps, too, the Lamson Company case [36] points to such a condition.

Skilled, experienced oil refinery workers were taken off their old job, given an extensive training course, and placed in a new tower. For several months they worked alongside the engineers who were installing and "de-bugging" the new and complicated equipment. Their suggestions were encouraged and accepted by the engineers and the men's behavior indicated they were highly satisfied with the experience.

Workers in such situations appear to be motivated at the higher need levels and to exist under maximal environmental conditions: they have a high opportunity to interact, a task to which they see a high opportunity to contribute and a leader who sets up a high opportunity for mutual influence between himself and his subordinates. Moreover, we can infer, too, that such workers would exist in an organizational environment which they saw as supportive. In addition, one study in an electronics factory (not yet published) suggests that the remaining environmental condition, high-status congruence, is a prerequisite for the motivation pattern seen in Column 7.

---

[33] Orville Collins, Melville Dalton, and Donald Roy, "Restriction of Output and Social Cleavage in Industry," *Applied Anthropology*, V, No. 3 (1946).

[34] F. J. Roethlisberger and W. J. Dickson, *op. cit.*

[35] L. Coch and J. R. P. French, "Overcoming Resistance to Change," *Human Relations*, I, 512-32.

[36] "Lamson Co.," Harvard Business School, HP 318.

However, in a recently published research by Barnes [37] members of an engineering group exhibited low individual and group-status congruence, yet had high opportunity to interact, high opportunity for mutual influence and a high contribution opportunity. A few individuals, considered as a collection, had high group-status congruence, yet the social structure was not determined by this fact. Moreover, much of the group looked as if they might be exhibiting the need pattern seen in Column 7.

Barnes' research suggests, therefore, that, when all other conditions are met, a group's social behavior is not "frozen" by the status factors its members brought with them. If one is interested in the growth and development of individuals in an organization, Barnes' study points to a helpful situation.

SUMMARY AND CONCLUSION

By carefully examining Exhibit 1 we have attempted to describe factors which both release and constrain different motivations in members of industrial work groups. In addition, we have shown how, according to Maslow's theory, relative satisfaction of certain needs may release other needs which alter the picture. Roughly, the following diagram illustrates this process, and is nothing more than a simplified restatement of Exhibit 1.

Incidentally, the similarity between Exhibit 2 and the small group conceptual scheme of Homans' [38] is obvious. "Contribution opportunity" refers to the extent to which an individual's "required activities" are not so highly programmed that no room is left for the individual's contribution to them. "Interaction opportunity" refers to the extent to which an individual's "required interactions" do not limit him from getting together, on a social as well as task basis, with others. "Influence opportunity," a function of leadership behavior, has an effect on an individual's motivation because of the kinds of "given sentiments" most of us appear to have about leadership: when we are closely controlled or highly programmed, this violates our expectations of a satisfying super-subordinate behavior. "Status congruence" refers to another large body of "given sentiments" most people seem to have: ideas about status and class which are widespread in our culture.

---

[37] Louis B. Barnes, *Organizational Systems and Engineering Groups* (Harvard University Division of Research, Graduate School of Business Administration, Boston, Massachusetts, 1960).

[38] George C. Homans, *The Human Group* (Harcourt, Brace & Co., New York, 1950).

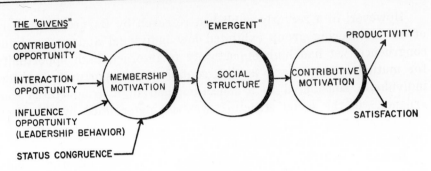

EXHIBIT 2

Any emergent small group behavior feeds back on the givens, however, as Homans and others have observed. And Exhibit 2 is oversimplified insofar as this feedback is not shown. Nevertheless, its importance is obvious, particularly if one must understand and/or deal with a group through time. For example, a foreman of a work group which, for various reasons, was producing too little might change his leadership behavior from accommodative to production-centered, thus, perhaps, frustrating membership and self-esteem needs. Another example of such feedback might exist in a group under a group-centered leader who allowed mutual influence opportunities and whose members were active at the membership and contributive levels. Conceivably, these members would see continuous contribution opportunities in their jobs, thereby releasing further contributive motivation. Another example, and one which a number of my colleagues at the Harvard Business School and myself hope to test specifically in a current project, is the possibility that the structure of a group operating on higher need levels will be less determined by the status congruence of its members than it was at an earlier time, when it was operating more at the membership level.

In conclusion, the obvious fact remains to be emphasized that better techniques for the measurement of need activation in workers must be developed before this broad-stroke explanatory theory can be refined, altered, or rejected in the organizational behavior area. Only one of the studies cited—and that not yet published except in case form [39]—made an explicit attempt to assess motivation in Maslow's terms.

Research takes time, though, and those of us concerned directly with the immediate here-and-now problems of executives cannot always wait for our own and others' patient and time-consuming

---

[39] "Century Co. (A)-(I)," *op. cit.*

testing of intriguing notions of potential utility to practicing administrators. And, it seems to me, an administrator *can* use this general way of thinking to predict, at least on a gross basis, that certain consequences are quite likely to follow from the "givens" in any situation. Such a prediction might be economically valuable to him. He might, for example, behave differently during a technological or organizational change than he would have if he were not aware of the suggested effects of low interaction opportunity and contribution potential on motivation, social structure and productivity, and satisfaction. Conversely, if he were experiencing severe problems of dissatisfaction in his work force, he might seek to understand them in terms of this theory, and thereby highlight some "givens" which might be changed: interaction opportunity, for example. Such a change might cut down grievances, or even avert a strike.

Hopefully, this paper may serve to stimulate some better ways of testing the utility of Maslow's concepts for the study of organizational behavior. Certainly we are in need of integrative and operational concepts that both form the basis for replicable and comparative research and offer some utility to the practicing administrator.

QUESTIONS

1. Briefly describe the basic purpose of Clark's article.
2. Define the following terms and discuss their relationship to leadership and motivation.
   a. Accommodative.
   b. Production-centered.
   c. Group-centered.
3. Explain Exhibit I.
4. Explain the "theory of social certitude."
5. Briefly discuss Clark's general conclusion.

23. THE MOTIVATION-HYGIENE CONCEPT AND PROBLEMS OF MANPOWER *

Frederick Herzberg

I wish to preface my remarks in this article with a disclaimer of competence in the field of manpower. My research and contemplative efforts are more directly related to an equally large and protean problem, that of industrial mental health. From my investigations in the latter area, I have formulated a general theory of mental health, and a specific application to job attitudes that may have bearing on certain aspects of "manpower" questions.

I apologize to the reader who already has familiarity with the Motivation-Hygiene theory of job attitudes for occupying the next few pages with a repetition of data and comments which have appeared a number of times elsewhere. I must lay the groundwork for my thoughts on "manpower" by first presenting my theory of job attitudes, without which I have very little excuse for accepting the invitation to contribute to this issue.

The Motivation-Hygiene theory of job attitudes began with a depth interview study of over 200 engineers and accountants representing Pittsburgh industry.[1] These interviews probed sequences of events in the work lives of the respondents to determine the factors that were involved in their feeling exceptionally happy and, conversely, exceptionally unhappy with their jobs. From a review and an analysis of previous publications in the general area of job attitudes, a two-factor hypothesis was formulated to guide the original investigation. This hypothesis suggested that the factors involved in producing job satisfaction were separate and distinct from the factors that led to job dissatisfaction. Since separate factors needed to be considered depending on whether job satisfaction or job dissatisfaction was involved, it followed that these two feelings were not the obverse of each other. The opposite of job satisfaction would not be job dissatisfaction, but rather *no* job satisfaction; and similarly the opposite of job dissatisfaction is *no* job dissatisfaction—not job satisfaction. The statement of the concept is awkward and may appear at first to be a semantic ruse, but there is more than a play with words when it comes to understanding the behavior of people on jobs. The fact that

* From *Personnel Administration*, Vol. 27, No. 1 (January-February, 1964), pp. 3-7. Reprinted with permission.

[1] F. Herzberg, B. Mausner, and B. Snyderman, *The Motivation to Work* (New York: John Wiley and Sons, 1959).

job satisfaction is made up of two unipolar traits is not a unique occurrence. The difficulty of establishing a zero point in psychology with the procedural necessity of using instead a bench mark (mean of a population) from which to start our measurement has led to the conception that psychological traits are bipolar. Empirical investigations, however, have cast some shadows on the assumptions of bipolarity; one timely example is a study of conformity and non-conformity, where they were shown not to be opposites, but rather two separate unipolar traits.[2]

Methodology

Before proceeding to the major results of the original study, three comments on methodology are in order. The investigation of attitudes is plagued with many problems, least of which is the measurement phase; although, it is measurement to which psychologists have hitched their scientific integrity. First of all, if I am to assess a person's feeling about something, how do I know he has a feeling? Too often we rely on his say so, even though opinion polling is replete with instances in which respondents gladly respond with all shades of feeling when in reality they have never thought of the issue and are devoid of any practical affect. They respond to respond and we become deceived into believing that they are revealing feelings or attitudes. Secondly, assuming the respondent does have genuine feelings regarding the subject under investigation, are his answers indicative of his feelings; or are they rationalizations, displacements from other factors which are for many reasons less easy to express, coin of the realm expressions for his particular job classification, etc.? Those who have had experience with job morale surveys recognize these ghosts and unfortunately some have contributed to the haunting of companies. Thirdly, how do you equate feelings? If two persons state that they are happy with their jobs, how do you know they are equally happy? We can develop scales, but in truth we are only satisfying our penchant for rulers which do not get inside the experience and measure the phenomenological reality, but rather have significance wholly within our devices.

To meet these objections, the methodology of the original study was formulated. It included a study of changes in job attitudes in the hope that if attitudes change there is more likelihood that an attitude exists. Further, it focused on experiences in the lives of the

---

[2] J. P. Guilford, C. R. Christensen, N. Bond, and M. Sutton, "A Factor Analysis Study of Human Interests," *Res. Bull.*, 53-11 (San Antonio: Human Resources Research Center, 1953).

respondents which contained substantive data that could be analyzed apart from the interpretations of the respondents. Finally, rather than attempt to measure degree of feeling, it focused on peak experiences and contrasted negative peaks with positive peaks; without being concerned with the equality of the peaks. Briefly, we asked our respondents to describe periods in their lives when they were exceedingly happy and unhappy with their jobs. Each respondent gave as many "sequences of events" as he could which met certain criteria including a marked change in feeling, a beginning and an end, and contained some substantive description other than feelings and interpretations.

A rational analysis of the "sequences of events" led to the results shown in the accompanying chart. For a more complete description of the methodology as well as the results, see *The Motivation to Work.*[3]

The proposed hypothesis appears verified. The factors on the right that led to satisfaction (achievement, recognition for achievement, intrinsic interest in the work, responsibility, and advancement) are mostly unipolar; that is, they contribute very little to job dissatisfaction. Conversely, the dissatisfiers (company policy and administrative practices, supervision, interpersonal relationships, working conditions, and salary) contribute very little to job satisfaction.

Satisfiers and dissatisfiers

What is the explanation for such results? Do the two sets of factors have two separate themes? It appears so, for the factors on the right all seem to describe man's relationship to what he does, to his job content, achievement on a task, recognition for task achievement, the nature of the task, responsibility for a task, and professional advancement or growth in task capability.

What is the central theme for the dissatisfiers? Restating the factors as the kind of administration and supervision received in doing the job, the nature of interpersonal relationships and working conditions that surround the job, and the amount of salary that accrues to the individual for doing his job, suggest the distinction with the "satisfier" factors. Rather than describing man's relationship to what he does, the "dissatisfier" factors describe his relationship to the context or environment in which he does his job. One cluster of factors relates to what the person does and the other to the situation in which he does it.

---

[3] Herzberg, Mausner, and Snyderman, *op. cit.*

As usual with any new theory, a new jargon is invented, perhaps to add some fictitious uniqueness to the theory, although I prefer to think that these new terms better convey the meaning of the theory. Because the factors on the left serve primarily as preventatives, that is to prevent job dissatisfaction, and because they also deal with the environment, I have named these factors "the hygiene" factors in a poor analogy with the way the term is used in preventive medicine. The factors on the right I call the "motivators" because other results indicate they are necessary for improvement in performance beyond that pseudo improvement which in substance amounts to coming up to a "fair day's work."

In these terms we can recapitulate the major findings of the original study by stating that it is the hygiene factors that affect job dissatisfaction and the motivator factors that affect job satisfaction; with the further understanding that there are two parallel continua of satisfactions. I have only reported on the first study because of the required brevity of this paper. Corroboration can be found in the studies with the following references.[4]

Significance of hygiene factors

Why? We next explore the reasons given by our respondents for the differential effects that the two sets of factors have on job attitudes. In brief, the hygiene factors meet man's need to avoid unpleasantness. "I don't like to be treated this way; I don't want to suffer the deprivation of low salary; bad interpersonal relationships make me uncomfortable." In other words they want their lives to be hygienically clean. The motivator factors on the other hand make people happy with their jobs because they serve man's basic and human need for psychological growth; a need to become more competent. A fuller commentary on these two separate needs of man are contained in the following publications.[5]

---

[4] R. Fantz, "Motivation Factors in Rehabilitation" (unpublished doctoral dissertation, Western Reserve University Library, Cleveland, 1961); J. Gibson, "Sources of Job Satisfaction and Job Dissatisfaction" (unpublished dissertation, Western Reserve University Library, Cleveland, 1961); R. Hamlin and R. Nemo, "Self-Actualization in Choice Scores of Improved Schizophrenics," *J. Clin. Psychol.*, 18, 1962; T. Lodahl, *Patterns of Job Attitudes in Two Assembly Technologies* (Ithaca, New York: Cornell University, Graduate School of Business and Public Administration, 1963); S. Saleh, "Attitude Change and Its Effect on the Pre-Retirement Period" (unpublished doctoral dissertation, Western Reserve University Library, Cleveland, 1962); P. Schwarz, *Attitudes of Middle Management Personnel* (Pittsburgh: American Institute for Research, 1961); and M. Schwartz, E. Jenusaitis, and H. Stark, "Motivation Factors among Supervisors in the Utility Industry," *Personnel Psychology*, 16, 1963.

[5] F. Herzberg, "New Approaches in Management Organization and Job Design," *Industrial Med. and Surgery*, November, 1962; F. Herzberg, "Basic

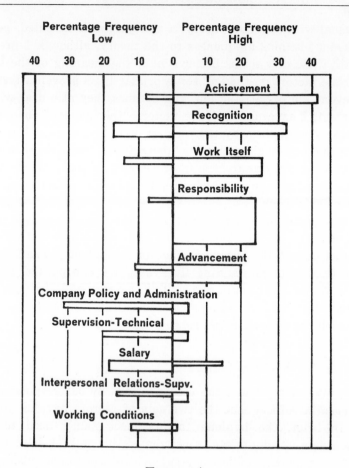

FIGURE 1

COMPARISON OF SATISFIERS AND DISSATISFIERS *

* The wider the box the longer the duration of the attitude. Reproduced from *The Motivation to Work*, Frederick Herzberg, *et al.* John Wiley and Sons, New York, 1959.

This theory opens wide the door for reinterpretations of industrial relations phenomena. To begin with, job attitudes must be viewed twice; what does the employee seek—what makes him happy; and

Needs and Satisfactions of Individuals," *Industrial Relations Monograph*, No. 21 (New York: Industrial Relations Counselors, Inc., 1962); F. Herzberg, "Comment on the Meaning of Work," Proceedings of Symposium of the Worker in the New Industrial Environment, *Industrial Med. and Surgery*, June, 1963; F. Herzberg, "The Meaning of Work to the Individual," in H. Hellerstein (ed.), *Basic Psychology and Physiology of Work* (Ft. Lauderdale: C. C. Thomas Press, In Press); Herzberg, Mausner, and Snyderman, *op. cit.*; F. Herzberg and R. Hamlin, "A Motivation-Hygiene Concept of Mental Health," *Mental Hygiene*, July, 1961; and F. Herzberg and R. Hamlin, "Motivation-Hygiene Concept and Psychotherapy," *Mental Hygiene*, July, 1961.

then a separate question not deducible from the first, what does he wish to avoid—what makes him unhappy? Industrial relations that stress sanitation as their modus operandi can only serve to prevent dissatisfactions and the resultant personnel problems. Of course such attention to hygienic needs is important, for without it any organization, as we well know, will reap the consequences of unhappy personnel. The error of course lies in assuming that prevention will unleash positive health and the returns of increased productivity, lowered absenteeism, turnover, and all the other indices of manpower efficiency. One additional deduction from the theory which is supported by empirical findings should be added. The effect of improved hygiene lasts for only a short time. In fact man's avoidance needs are recurrent and of an infinite variety, and as such we will find that demands for improved salary, working conditions, interpersonal relations and so on will continue to occupy the personnel administrator without any hope of escaping the "what have you done for me lately."

There is nothing wrong with providing the maximum of hygienic benefits to the employee, as much as the society can afford (which appears to be more than the historic cries of anguish which have always accompanied the amelioration of work hygiene would indicate). What is wrong is the summation of human needs in totally hygienic terms. The consequences of this onesided view of man's nature has led to untoward consequences of much greater import than the direct monetary costs of these programs to our organizations. The more pertinent effect has been on the psychological premises of industrial relations and its effect in turn on the self concepts of the employees.

Since hygiene is the apparent key to industrial success, the motivators are given but lip service, and attention to the challenge and meaningfulness of jobs is satisfied via the pious espousal of cultural noises. We are today familiar with the industrial engineering principle of leveling jobs down to the lowest common talent as it applies to the rank and file assembly operation. The same denigration of human talent at the managerial and professional level, the sacrificing of human performance and potentiality to insure that no one will fail or make for unpleasantness, is obscured by referring to the rank and file when acknowledging the lack of meaning in work. At these higher levels, the effects of the assembly line are accomplished by the overuse of rules and regulations, rational organizational principles and the insidious use of interpersonal *skills*. We find that more and more training and education is required to do less and less; more and

more effort on surround and less and less substance on accomplishment. Pride in work, in successful accomplishment, in maximizing
one's talent is becoming socially gauche or more tragically a victim of
progress. We cry for nurturance of human talent and find that we
have no place for most of it; human talent on the job has become as
much of a surplus commodity as our wheat. And where are our
personnel managers? Their problem is hygiene, not the creative function of maximizing human resources.

Significance of motivators

The Protestant Ethic is being replaced by an Avoidance Ethic in
our world of work, and those in charge of personnel utilization have
almost totally directed their efforts to maintenance procedures. This
is seen from the very beginning of employment in the practice of
college recruitment on the campus, where each company sets up its
own enticing tent, and selection is transformed into public relations,
luring of candidates, and in fact the incredible situation of the
candidate interviewing the interviewer.

Job attitude data suggest that after the glow of the initial year
on the job, job satisfaction plummets to its lowest level in the work
life of individuals.[6] From a life time of diverse learning, successive
accomplishment through the various academic stages, and periodic
reinforcement of efforts, the entrant to our modern companies finds,
that rather than work providing an expanding psychological existence, the opposite occurs; and successive amputations of his self-
conceptions, aspirations, learning, and talent are the consequence of
earning a living. Of course as the needs and values of our industrial
enterprises have become the template for all aspects of our lives, the
university is preparing many young people by performing the amputations early, and they enter already primed for work as only a means
of hygienic improvement; or for those still capable of enjoying the
exercise of their human talents, as means of affording off the job
satisfactions. If the number of management development programs
is a valid sign, the educational system has done its job too well.

A reaction to retirement policies is beginning to set in as the
personal consequences of organizational definitions of human obso-
lescence are being told. Prior to retirement, however, are 30 to 40
years of partial retirement and partial commitment to work for the
too many who have not "succeeded" in terms of organizational

---

[6] F. Herzberg *et al.*, *Job Attitudes: Research and Opinion*, Psychological
Service of Pittsburgh, 1957.

advancement. From the first orientation to the farewell party, the history of work careers is a history of human waste. What a paradox we face. There is a shortage of talent in the country at a time when our problems are defined in planetary dimensions and to meet these circumstances we have evolved a system and a philosophy to use and motivate our talent that serves to decrease further this precious resource.

What alternatives are there? A spate of new research and literature is becoming available that is reacting to personnel and managerial psychology that has too long tried to emulate the vast and short term goals of the military. The new literature while encompassing diverse problems, exhortations, solutions and conceptions, seems to have the common theme of emphasizing the motivator needs of man and the necessity for the personnel function of industry to pause in its search for the Holy Grail of instruments, to become creative in finding ways to meet the motivator needs. Man is distinguished from all other animals in that he alone is a determiner. How strange that when it comes to the satisfactions of his special psychological growth needs he finds himself a victim of outside determinisms and helpless in affecting the way he is utilized in work. The short term economic "necessities" cannot justify the larger economic loss and the denial of human satisfaction that the restriction of human talent inevitably costs. I might add that many of the barriers to fuller utilization of manpower that are "justified" by economic reasons, are in reality, devices of fearful and inadequate managers who are not prepared to meet the challenge of managing adults. The philosophy of management which prizes such men is changeable. We need a goal of industry which includes the expansion of manpower utilization in addition to the expansion of productivity and profit. The acceptance of such a goal as basic will lead to the means for its implementation. Personnel cannot remain the one management function that only establishes objectives for which techniques and procedures are available.

Questions

1. Briefly explain the motivation-hygiene theory of job attitudes.
2. Distinguish the relationship between "satisfiers" and "dissatisfiers."
3. Explain the difference between "hygiene factors" and "motivator factors."
4. What is the significance of these factors?
5. What does Herzberg mean by the statement "we need a goal of industry which includes the expansion of manpower utilization in addition to the expansion of productivity and profit"?

GENERAL QUESTIONS ON PART IV

1. Explain how motivation is related to leadership and human relations.
2. Define the following words:
   a. Homeostasis.
   b. Somatically.
   c. Preempted.
   d. Receptors.
   e. Effectors.
3. Distinguish between sociological and psychological motives.
4. Prepare a list of as many basic human needs as you can discover.
5. What is frustration? How do people react to it? Why must the leader be alert to symptomatic behavior?
6. Explain how motivation is related to employee performance and behavior.
7. Explain what is meant by the "total climate." List all the factors that you think are part of this climate.
8. How is morale related to motivation?
9. Is motivation related to productivity? If so, how can this be proved?
10. Why do people behave as they do?

PART V. ORGANIZATION STRUCTURE AND DYNAMICS

The process of management inevitably revolves around some type of formal organization, for by its very nature management is that which deals primarily with the organization of *people* and, to a somewhat lesser degree, physical resources. It follows, therefore, that in industry a large part of the typical manager's job is the *integration* of human and physical resources. To accomplish this integration and to achieve basic business objectives, a company will design a formal organizational structure that sets forth desired job relationships between people and that provides for overall coordination of effort.

Unfortunately, people do not always react or respond properly to formal lines of authority and responsibility. Instead, they tend to form smaller groups of their own, sometimes to overcome restrictions of the formal structure, and at other times to complement and strengthen the formal structure. These groups are most frequently referred to as *informal groups*. We shall see later that they can have a most pronounced effect on the formal structure devised by management and hence on organizational efficiency.

Human beings, since the very beginning of recorded history, have always tended towards "groupism." Psychologists and sociologists teach us that this gregariousness, or the desire for group association, is the ultimate of man's social needs. As such, this phenomenon of group response has probably been a major factor underlying the success of the American business economy. It is important that each and every business organization and the managerial personnel involved give due recognition to this tendency, although a great deal of research is still needed to discover how informal groups can best be blended into the formal structure to achieve optimum productivity and morale. At the same time, it must also be recognized that individuals can become overdependent upon particular groups, thus encouraging manipulation by a select few. Consequently, research effort must also be directed toward discovering "equilibrium points" whereby necessary employee identification can be achieved without making people overdependent on their employer to their own and the company's detriment.

The Formal Structure

Any successful business enterprise goes through certain stages of growth. As a company's size increases, more and more people are put on the payroll, new jobs are created, and additional departments are established. The result of this is that authority and responsibility relationships become increasingly complex, necessitating a more effective type of coordination than can normally be exerted by one person. At this point in time, it becomes necessary for management to determine just exactly what the formal, planned structure of the business should be to best accomplish its objectives. This is typically shown in an organization chart of some type along with job descriptions and man specifications.

Although it becomes mandatory to delegate authority in the large organization, this delegation does create human relations problems, oftentimes very serious ones. For example, some employees resent the control their boss exerts over them, so they join a union and do their best to oppose him and to make him look bad in his job. And if they do not resort to such direct action, more subtle and indirect means may be employed, such as restriction of output, willful damage to machinery, and disobeying of orders. This should indicate that the supervisor-leader, to get work done through others, must understand that he cannot abuse the authority bestowed upon him.

We are all undoubtedly aware that certain people have strong inner drives that motivate them to obtain positions of authority over others. Some researchers even claim this tendency to be a necessary prerequisite for executive success. Not debating this in any way, it nevertheless becomes imperative that management set limits to a man's authority to prevent him from abusing it to the extent that he creates opposition on the part of employees. People will accept only so much control; beyond a certain point they will rebel against it by quitting their jobs or resorting to other means noted above. Obviously many unhealthy situations can result if authority is abused.

Authority limits can be set by a proper organizational structure and by clearly defined job responsibilities. Many human relations problems will be prevented if management observes this fact.

Specialization

Frequently referred to as "division of labor," specialization is a manifestation of the formal organization. Any organized effort of a group of people requires direction and coordination. To accomplish this, employees are grouped according to specific tasks and type of work to be done. This is frequently referred to as horizontal and vertical specialization. *Horizontal specialization* refers to specialization according to different kinds of duties and skills. Typical here are the areas of personnel, purchasing, operating, finance, accounting, and so on. All of these are grouped in terms of a particular type of work. On the other hand, *vertical specialization* refers to a division of authority into levels that are vertically scaled depending upon the degree or amount of authority held by persons in the chain of command. In the ordinary business, authority flows downward from the chairman of the board (assuming a corporate structure), through the president, then to the vice-presidents, and so on down the line until it culminates with the lowest supervisor.

Specialization, therefore, becomes mandatory in a business of any size. Unfortunately, it brings with it many human relations problems. Empire building on the part of various departments, professional jealousy and competition, and group conflicts are but a few. One of the real challenges of the industrial future and this emerging discipline of human relations is somehow to reconcile these problems so that specialization is made compatible with efficient organizational behavior.

Delegation and decentralization

Delegation and decentralization are too often confusedly interpreted to mean the same thing, namely, the extension of authority and responsibility to various individuals and segments of the company. Many firms also use the word "decentralization" to denote a multiplant operation. Be that as it may, the semantical overtones of these terms have created a great deal of misunderstanding in the minds of students.

Delegation is a term best used to describe specific job assignments. To a personnel man, for example, may be delegated the responsibility to recommend people for employment, to train supervisory personnel, to maintain employment records, and to perform many other tasks. How much authority to grant to him for carrying out these responsibilities will depend upon the individual company and its policy along these lines. Clearly, as the number and scope of duties and responsibilities increase in an organization, delegation becomes imperative.

Decentralization, however, is a much broader and more comprehensive term, although its difference is of degree rather than of kind.

It is best used to describe a particular type or philosophy of management. When an executive delegates a job to be done, he normally tells his subordinates not only what to do but how to do it as well, often assigning responsibility but not the full authority to carry out this responsibility. But in a truly decentralized company, when a manager is given a job to do, how he does it, and subsequently the results attained, are left to his own discretion. Above all, he is given appropriate authority to carry out his responsibility. He is held accountable primarily for his results and not the procedural aspects of achieving them. Perhaps the success of well-known companies like General Motors, General Electric, Johnson and Johnson, and Sears, Roebuck and Company can be traced directly to this concept of management.

Line and staff

As organizational theory has developed since the turn of the century, numerous variations in business structures have been introduced, with some having permanent applicability while others have only been passing fancies. One of these variations, the concept of line and staff, originated to allow more specialization within the structure as business units grew in size. It has become an indispensable part of both theory and practice.

The underlying idea behind the line-and-staff principle was simple. Operating men needed help and assistance in those aspects of their jobs that were not directly related to production and for which they had neither the necessary skill nor time. Line-and-staff type of organization, it was argued, would bring needed specialization and professional competence into the industrial picture. The staff man's job and authority relationship to the line would be one of counsel, advice, and assistance. His authority would be absolute only in his own limited sphere of concentration.

Thus the concept of line and staff, previously utilized in the military, the church, and other organizations, was incorporated into the industrial sphere. And with it came a myriad of human relations problems. Line personnel began to guard their authority as a jealous prerogative. The staff man, they felt, was trying to usurp their authority, to extend his influence into matters that did not concern him. Departmental frictions, empire building, overemphasis on professionalism, and countless other human problems have been attributed to line-and-staff organization. But in all fairness, the student should clearly understand that this principle in and of itself is not responsible for these many human problems. Rather, it is the lack of proper application of it to specific organizational needs. The task facing business today is to implement this principle into the formal structure so as properly to insure its adaptability to individual situations and needs.

Policy

One might legitimately ask: "What does policy have to do with the formal structure of a company?" The answer here is fundamental to understanding just how the formal organization operates.

Policy is the lifeblood of any organization. It is an expression of management's intentions for directing and controlling the operations of the company. Policies serve as guides in making decisions and as aids in the accomplishment of objectives. They are set forth to allow many diverse individuals in a firm to make uniform and consistent decisions while acting in virtually complete independence of each other.

It is through formal policy statements that top management gives the necessary directions to people in the company. These statements take many diverse forms, such as policy handbooks, memos, operating letters, and so on. But regardless of form, they all have one thing in common, namely, that they serve as guides for handling recurring situations that arise in day-to-day operations.

Policies also have pronounced effects on people. They cause definite patterns of behavior to occur as individuals respond in different ways to different policies. Occasionally certain persons will disagree with a policy and will either openly or subtly oppose it. It is generally agreed that policies are as effective as supervisors and managers want them to be. Consequently, we can see that serious human relations problems can occur if top management does not give serious attention to how certain policies may affect people.

Informal Organization

The formal structure of a business enterprise illustrated in organization charts and manuals does not really tell us a great deal about the day-to-day relations between employees. Although it is true that this structure does set forth job relations and a limited span of personnel relationships, it is equally true that employees, as time progresses, frequently do not adhere to formal lines of authority and communications and ultimately set up their own network of interpersonal relations. They do this for various reasons, but primarily to satisfy the social aspirations and needs discussed in Part III. Hence, management might designate in detail what it wants the relationships between people and jobs to be, but what management wants and what relationships actually do exist may be two different things.

The company as a social institution

It has taken many years for management to realize that, besides being an economic institution, the business firm is equally as much a *social institution*. People work together, develop friendships on the job, and spend the majority of their lives living and associating with others within the confines of a corporation. This social climate of a business will produce customary and traditional ways of doing work, with behavior to a great extent being influenced by the expectations and hopes of others. Routines and patterns of interaction are developed between and by people and thereby act as sort of a "social cement" for ensuring collaboration and common effort, thus stimulating individual and group security. Friendships will develop, people will begin to share common interests, until finally a man's job and company become an integral part of his life.

This concept of viewing the corporation or any business enterprise as a social institution can be illustrated by the following "culture model" that social scientists use to explain what they feel to be the five basic dimensions of any given group culture:

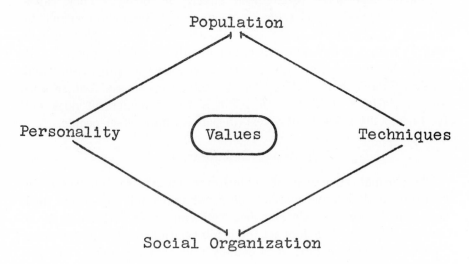

The value dimension in this model is really the core of any culture, regardless of group size, background, or location. These values are shared beliefs—shared by a majority of group members—and although subject to some change over time, they nevertheless remain the pivotal point of any culture. We shall see later that it is principally because of these values that informal groups in industry arise.

Social organization refers to traditional or patterned relations between various types of people. For our purposes, the principal point here is that people at work tend to form or become a member of small groups of their own that are not spelled out by the formal structure. This is usually referred to as *informal organization*, as was noted earlier. Such groups arise because of common beliefs, sentiments, values, attitudes, fears, interests, and so on. In time they develop small cultures of their own, which center around group values as illustrated in the above diagram. Any company, therefore, becomes one large social organization or culture made up of many small, diverse informal groups, each with a culture of its own. Sometimes these groups operate in opposition to the formal organization, but quite often they serve to reinforce and strengthen it.

Personality in a cultural sense refers to how a particular culture trains or shapes an individual to respond in certain ways, especially in terms of the values or beliefs of the culture group. Because our personality largely controls our behavior, our behavior is oriented to group norms or values. In relation to the work situation we can see how our behavior on the job is vitally influenced by associations with fellow workers.

The technology dimension indicates the skill level of a culture. Groups in industry frequently form along functional lines, that is, people doing similar work develop similar patterns of interests, beliefs, and values. It is this technical dimension that is most likely to bring change into the society or group. As skills or tools change, so also may group composition and value systems change. This is one reason why employees often vehemently resist technical or personnel changes that management is desirous of making even though such changes are likely to benefit employees as well as management.

Population, of course, is relatively self-explanatory. In our application of the above culture model to formal and informal organization, population best describes the composition of groups. Although it was stated previously that groups often form along functional lines, it should be recognized that this is not always the case. In many instances they will cross functional lines and other factors will determine their composition, among them being similar attitudes, interests, nationalities, friendships, likes and dislikes, fears, and religious preferences.

Thus the student of business must be cognizant that every company is a vast social network as well as an economic organization. To overlook this fact in the world of today would create serious human relations problems. Perhaps a better understanding of this social structure and its importance could be attained by taking a more detailed look at these informal groups.

The informal group

When we say that a company is a complex social network, we mean that employees interact with each other constantly, not always in a random sense, but rather in habitual, patterned routines. A brief observation of the daily routines of a randomly selected group of individuals would show the same people going to lunch together day in and day out, another group meeting by the coffee machine three times daily to joke and gossip, still another group that always take their breaks together, and so on until just about every employee has one select circle of people with whom he associates.

As to why these groups arise, a multiplicity of answers might be offered. Basically, there does not appear to be any planned reason behind these associations other than that they evidently seem to satisfy social motivations. Most of us have rather strong desires to associate with particular groups, especially if membership will bring with it a psychological feeling of status achievement. We realize, through these informal groups, feelings of prestige and social distinction. We can now exert some influence on the thoughts and actions of others and vice versa. Because the formal structure does not confer this upon us, we achieve it through our informal associations. We will go to great lengths to protect this status, sometimes even to the extent of endangering our position with the company. This is true not only of rank-and-file employees but of those at executive levels as well. Group solidarity becomes all important, and we will do all within our power to protect it. We become very touchy about changes of any kind and either subtly or directly resist them if necessary. Hence, we do all in our power to protect and promote our status and group.

All individuals, however, do not become part of an informal group for status alone. To others, belonging to an informal group is something of an emotionally satisfying experience. They develop certain traditions and customs, which become of paramount importance.

Particular ways of doing things develop to which rigid adherence is paid. Maybe they are of Swedish descent and only want to associate with others who are Swedish; perhaps they will affiliate principally with people of their own religion; or possibly a certain class of employees is held in special esteem by the boss and they also want such a position. Sex, age, type of job, and special interests are other reasons why individual and group relationships occur. Education, office location, and personality are likewise important.

Whatever the reasons are, cliques and informal groupings are common in any firm whenever individuals are grouped together. Habits and customs develop along with group norms and standards of conduct. Value systems are originated to guide, direct, and control the behavior of members; unwritten laws are laid down, quite often in direct contrast to company rules. These values and beliefs will serve to bind people together, strengthen group lines, and, above all, give people a sense of belonging, security, and support.

The relationship of these groups to the effective functioning of the formal organization is of critical importance. Although this will be treated in a following section, attention should be directed to two salient points. First, the attitudes formed and the social satisfactions realized by group associations have a positive correlation with productivity and morale and are as directly related to efficiency as are the money wages a man receives.

Secondly, and also of the utmost importance to managements of today, is the fact that informal leaders arise to give direction and control to most informal groups and cliques. People look up to and respect these leaders *of their own choice*. Generally, informal leaders do not hold appointed leadership positions in the formal structure; yet they exert a profound and distinct influence on the operation of the organization. It therefore becomes necessary for supervisors, managers, and executives to recognize these leaders, to encourage their participation in the management process, and to find ways and means to direct their leadership activities and abilities along positive lines for enhancing departmental and organizational effectiveness.

THE DYNAMICS OF INFORMAL ORGANIZATION

Recognizing that informal groups do exist in business organizations, the question arises as to whether they are of value or hindrance to management. The answer here can be either negative or affirmative, depending upon what approach management decides to take towards the whole social system of the company and upon whether or not management is willing to attempt to utilize social groups to mutual advantage. If management chooses the latter course, informal groups have much to contribute to organizational cohesiveness. If, however, management refuses to recognize their importance, a great deal of internal friction can be generated in the company to the disadvantage of all concerned.

A major function of informal groups is to serve as a means of communications for members. They are a fine example of how a grapevine works and how it influences both upward and downward communications. Good management should therefore see to it that groups are properly and timely informed to prevent the distortion of important information. Too often worker resistance to managerial directives results from the latter's failure to foresee how quickly false rumors can circulate and virtually destroy the true meaning and intent of information.

Another important aspect of informal groups is the relation of these groups to supervisory effectiveness. A supervisor's successful performance on his job can hinge greatly on the degree to which he accepts and utilizes the informal organization existing within his department. A wise supervisor will carefully study and appraise his people to determine which type of group they seem to belong to and will then attempt to motivate employees within this particular context. Worker restriction of output and other resistance to management changes are prevalent in industry and frequently occur because some supervisor failed to perceive how to best integrate company objectives with employee objectives. Management, in selecting supervisors, can do much to overcome this problem by giving serious consideration to matching supervisory type with group type. Many studies on leadership show that better superior-subordinate relationships are attained if similar interests, ideas, and objectives exist between the two.

Research into group activities, supervision, and morale also has directed attention to some interesting evidence that indicates that high employee morale is positively related to the *role expectations of individuals*. Effort along these lines has attempted to relate different types of behavior to the different roles an individual assumes in his job. An individual assumes different types of roles because of the many relationships thrust upon him at work, and his behavior will vary with the role being assumed. Internal conflict can arise within the employee, however, in trying to decide between various roles expected of him and the benefits to be derived from each. Management's job is to recognize how the different demands made upon people will affect their role expectations and, in turn, how these role expectations will influence behavior and adjustment.

Informal group membership, therefore, creates definite roles for people to carry out. In so doing, attitudes and values are created and changed that exert a profound influence on productivity and morale. Although the subject of morale and its determinates is a highly nebulous one, general agreement is usually reached when it is stated that group morale has a strong impact on individual morale, because as people identify themselves with certain groups, group values begin to shape and influence the attitudes and the beliefs of these individuals. In short, we too frequently let the majority will serve as our guide for thinking, and what is good for the group we come to feel is also good for us. So proper recognition and encouragement of group membership, along with policies and procedures designed to foster positive group feelings toward jobs and the company, can go a long way towards raising and maintaining employee morale.

Thus we can readily see that the organization is a living, dynamic organism—a social organism exerting all types of pressures on people, creating conflicts and frustration as well as positive feelings. The task facing managements of today is skillfully to blend together the formal organization with the informal in order to minimize conflict and to encourage healthy adjustment and coordination. This can be achieved by managerial recognition of the importance that informal groups have upon individual attitudes and morale. The supervisor should encourage groups to form; he should recognize their leaders and assign them jobs that reflect their group position; he should see that they are properly informed about policies and procedures. All in all, if proper encouragement is given to informal groups, they will respond in positive rather than negative ways.

ORGANIZATION THEORY AND PRACTICE

In recent years the study of working organizations has increasingly focused on a detailed examination of classical organization theory in light of modern research into behavior at work and organization development and productivity. William G. Scott's article is an excellent overview of classical and modern theory.

Perhaps the most significant development in the study of working organizations has been the heavy emphasis on empirical research for actually testing the validity of traditional organizational principles. When put to the test of reality, many old and comfortable theories of how to best organize people and work "have been weighed in the balance and found wanting." Carzo's and Brown's articles illustrate such criticism. Rensis Likert's article summarizes some of this organizational research, with special regard to significant progress in measuring how effectively organizations perform in light of recent developments in the social and behavioral sciences.

Such research, highlighted not only in this section but in all others as well, has not necessarily invalidated traditional principles of formal organization, but has certainly modified the beliefs and practices of many managers with regard not only to manpower management practices but to integrating the latter with sound formal policies and procedures as well. Questions as to the impact of policies, excessive formal controls, overly rigid formal bureaucratic structures, excessive layers of authority, autocratic leadership practices, etc., have all been and are being studied in the modern working organization. Livingstone's article, for example, examines the many ramifications of formal control systems in the typical firm, illustrating some of the human problems involved with formal controls and their resultant adverse effects on productivity in some situations.

Thus, current research is not necessarily focused on proving traditional, classical principles wrong, but on improving and updating them in a rapidly changing world of work. Emphasis is on finding out what factors really influence organizational effectiveness, growth, vitality, and productivity so that all types and sizes of business firms and related working organizations can continually improve their performance so as to benefit all persons affected by them—managers, employees, customers, stockholders, and the general public as a whole. This research is advancing on all fronts, showing great promise for aiding managers and executives in more effectively utilizing the human and material resources at their disposal in a society which asks not only "how much" but "how good" as well.

24. ORGANIZATION THEORY: AN OVERVIEW AND AN APPRAISAL *

William G. Scott

Man is intent on drawing himself into a web of collectivized patterns. "Modern man has learned to accommodate himself to a world increasingly organized. The trend toward ever more explicit and consciously drawn relationships is profound and sweeping; it is marked by depth no less than by extension." [1] This comment by Seidenberg nicely summarizes the pervasive influence of organization in many forms of human activity.

Some of the reasons for intense organizational activity are found in the fundamental transitions which revolutionized our society, changing it from a rural culture to a culture based on technology, industry, and the city. From these changes, a way of life emerged characterized by the *proximity* and *dependency* of people on each other. Proximity and dependency, as conditions of social life, harbor the threats of human conflict, capricious antisocial behavior, instability of human relationships, and uncertainty about the nature of the social structure with its concomitant roles.

Of course, these threats to social integrity are present to some degree in all societies, ranging from the primitive to the modern. But, these threats become dangerous when the harmonious functioning of a society rests on the maintenance of a highly intricate, delicately balanced form of human collaboration. The civilization we have created depends on the preservation of a precarious balance. Hence, disrupting forces impinging on this shaky form of collaboration must be eliminated or minimized.

Traditionally, organization is viewed as a vehicle for accomplishing goals and objectives. While this approach is useful, it tends to obscure the inner workings and internal purposes of organization itself. Another fruitful way of treating organization is as a mechanism having the ultimate purpose of offsetting those forces which undermine human collaboration. In this sense, organization tends to minimize conflict, and to lessen the significance of individual behavior which deviates from values that the organization has established as worthwhile. Further, organization increases stability in human

* From *Journal of the Academy of Management*, Vol. 4, No. 1 (April, 1961), pp. 7-26. Reprinted by permission of *Journal of the Academy of Management*.
[1] Roderick Seidenberg, *Post Historic Man* (Boston: Beacon Press, 1951), p. 1.

relationships by reducing uncertainty regarding the nature of the system's structure and the human roles which are inherent to it. Corollary to this point, organization enhances the predictability of human action, because it limits the number of behavioral alternatives available to an individual. As Presthus points out:

> Organization is defined as a system of structural interpersonal relations . . . individuals are differentiated in terms of authority, status, and role with the result that personal interaction is prescribed. . . . Anticipated reactions tend to occur, while ambiguity and spontaneity are decreased.[2]

In addition to all of this, organization has built-in safeguards. Besides prescribing acceptable forms of behavior for those who elect to submit to it, organization is also able to counterbalance the influence of human action which transcends its established patterns.[3]

Few segments of society have engaged in organizing more intensively than business.[4] The reason is clear. Business depends on what organization offers. Business needs a system of relationships among function; it needs stability, continuity, and predictability in its internal activities and external contacts. Business also appears to need harmonious relationships among the people and processes which make it up. Put another way, a business organization has to be free, relatively, from destructive tendencies which may be caused by divergent interests.

As a foundation for meeting these needs rests administrative science. A major element of this science is organization theory, which provides the grounds for management activities in a number of significant areas of business endeavor. Organization theory, however, is not a homogeneous science based on generally accepted principles. Various theories of organization have been, and are being evolved. For example, something called "modern organization theory" has recently emerged, raising the wrath of some traditionalists, but also capturing the imagination of a rather elite *avant-garde*.

---

[2] Robert V. Presthus, "Toward a Theory of Organizational Behavior," *Administrative Science Quarterly* (June, 1958), p. 50.
[3] Regulation and predictability of human behavior are matters of degree varying with different organization on something of a continuum. At one extreme are bureaucratic type organizations with tight bonds of regulation. At the other extreme are voluntary associations, and informal organizations with relatively loose bonds of regulation.
This point has an interesting sidelight. A bureaucracy with tight controls and a high degree of predictability of human action appears to be unable to distinguish between destructive and creative deviations from established values. Thus the only thing which is safeguarded is the *status quo*.
[4] The monolithic institutions of the military and government are other cases of organizational preoccupation.

The thesis of this paper is that modern organization theory, when stripped of its irrelevancies, redundancies, and "speech defects," is a logical and vital evolution in management thought. In order for this thesis to be supported, the reader must endure a review and appraisal of more traditional forms of organization theory which may seem elementary to him.

In any event, three theories of organization are having considerable influence on management thought and practice. They are arbitrarily labeled in this paper as the classical, the neo-classical, and the modern. Each of these is fairly distinct; but they are not unrelated. Also, these theories are on-going, being actively supported by several schools of management thought.

THE CLASSICAL DOCTRINE

For lack of a better method of identification, it will be said that the classical doctrine deals almost exclusively with the *anatomy of formal organization*. This doctrine can be traced back to Frederick W. Taylor's interest in functional foremanship and planning staffs. But most students of management thought would agree that in the United States, the first systematic approach to organization, and the first comprehensive attempt to find organizational universals, is dated 1931 when Mooney and Reiley published *Onward Industry*.[5] Subsequently, numerous books, following the classical vein, have appeared. Two of the more recent are Brech's, *Organization*[6] and Allen's, *Management and Organization*.[7]

Classical organization theory is built around four key pillars. They are the division of labor, the scalar and functional processes, structure, and span of control. Given these major elements just about all of classical organization theory can be derived.

(1) *The division of labor* is without doubt the cornerstone among the four elements.[8] From it the other elements flow as corollaries. For example, *scalar* and *functional* growth requires specialization and departmentalization of functions. Organization *structure* is naturally dependent upon the direction which specialization of activities travels in company development. Finally, *span of control* problems

---

[5] James D. Mooney and Alan C. Reiley, *Onward Industry* (New York: Harper and Brothers, 1931). Later published by James D. Mooney under the title *Principles of Organization.*

[6] E. F. L. Brech, *Organization* (London: Longmans, Green and Company, 1957).

[7] Louis A. Allen, *Management and Organization* (New York: McGraw-Hill Book Company, 1958).

[8] Usually the division of labor is treated under a topical heading of departmentation, see for example: Harold Koontz and Cyril O'Donnell, *Principles of Management* (New York: McGraw-Hill Book Company, 1959), Chapter 7.

result from the number of specialized functions under the jurisdiction of a manager.

(2) *The scalar and functional processes deal* with the vertical and horizontal growth of the organization, respectively.[9] The scalar process refers to the growth of the chain of command, the delegation of authority and responsibility, unity of command, and the obligation to report.

The division of the organization into specialized parts and the regrouping of the parts into compatible units are matters pertaining to the functional process. This process focuses on the horizontal evolution of the line and staff in a formal organization.

(3) *Structure* is the logical relationships of functions in an organization, arranged to accomplish the objectives of the company efficiently. Structure implies system and pattern. Classical organization theory usually works with two basic structures, the line and the staff. However, such activities as committee and liaison functions fall quite readily into the purview of structural considerations. Again, structure is the vehicle for introducing logical and consistent relationships among the diverse functions which comprise the organization.[10]

(4) *The span of control* concept relates to the number of subordinates a manager can effectively supervise. Graicunas has been credited with first elaborating the point that there are numerical limitations to the subordinates one man can control.[11] In a recent statement on the subject, Brech points out, "span" refers to ". . . the number of persons, themselves carrying managerial and supervisory responsibilities, for whom the senior manager retains his over-embracing responsibility of direction and planning, co-ordination, motivation, and control."[12] Regardless of interpretation, span of control has significance, in part, for the shape of the organization which evolves through growth. Wide span yields a flat structure; short span results in a tall structure. Further, the span concept directs attention to the complexity of human and functional inter-relationships in an organization.

---

[9] These processes are discussed at length in Ralph Currier Davis, *The Fundamentals of Top Management* (New York: Harper and Brothers, 1951), Chapter 7.

[10] For a discussion of structure see: William H. Newman, *Administrative Action* (Englewood Cliffs, New Jersey: Prentice-Hall, Incorporated, 1951), Chapter 16.

[11] V. A. Graicunas, "Relationships in Organization," *Papers on the Science of Administration* (New York: Columbia University, 1937).

[12] Brech, *op. cit.*, p. 78.

It would not be fair to say that the classical school is unaware of the day-to-day administrative problems of the organization. Paramount among these problems are those stemming from human interactions. But the interplay of individual personality, informal groups, interorganizational conflict, and the decision-making processes in the formal structure appears largely to be neglected by classical organization theory. Additionally, the classical theory overlooks the contributions of the behavioral sciences by failing to incorporate them in its doctrine in any systematic way. In summary, classical organization theory has relevant insights into the nature of organization, but the value of this theory is limited by its narrow concentration on the formal anatomy of organization.

NEOCLASSICAL THEORY OF ORGANIZATION

The neoclassical theory of organization embarked on the task of compensating for some of the deficiencies in classical doctrine. The neoclassical school is commonly identified with the human relations movement. Generally, the neoclassical approach takes the postulates of the classical school, regarding the pillars of organization as givens. But these postulates are regarded as modified by people, acting independently or within the context of the informal organization.

One of the main contributions of the neoclassical school is the introduction of behavioral sciences in an integrated fashion into the theory of organization. Through the use of these sciences, the human relationists demonstrate how the pillars of the classical doctrine are affected by the impact of human actions. Further, the neoclassical approach includes a systematic treatment of the informal organization, showing its influence on the formal structure.

Thus, the neoclassical approach to organization theory gives evidence of accepting classical doctrine, but superimposing on it modifications resulting from individual behavior, and the influence of the informal group. The inspiration of the neoclassical school were the Hawthorne studies.[13] Current examples of the neoclassical approach are found in human relations books like Gardner and Moore, *Human Relations in Industry*,[14] and Davis, *Human Relations in Business*.[15]

---

[13] See: F. J. Roethlisberger and William J. Dickson, *Management and the Worker* (Cambridge: Harvard University Press, 1939).
[14] Burleigh B. Gardner and David G. Moore, *Human Relations in Industry* (Homewood, Illinois: Richard D. Irwin, 1955).
[15] Keith Davis, *Human Relations in Business* (New York: McGraw-Hill Book Company, 1957).

To a more limited extent, work in industrial sociology also reflects a neoclassical point of view.[16]

It would be useful to look briefly at some of the contributions made to organization theory by the neoclassicists. First to be considered are modifications of the pillars of classical doctrine; second is the informal organization.

Examples of the neoclassical approach to the pillars of formal organization theory

(1) The *division of labor* has been a long standing subject of comment in the field of human relations. Very early in the history of industrial psychology study was made of industrial fatigue and monotony caused by the specialization of the work.[17] Later, attention shifted to the isolation of the worker, and his feeling of anonymity resulting from insignificant jobs which contributed negligibly to the final product.[18]

Also, specialization influences the work of management. As an organization expands, the need concomitantly arises for managerial motivation and coordination of the activities of others. Both motivation and coordination in turn relate to executive leadership. Thus, in part, stemming from the growth of industrial specialization, the neoclassical school has developed a large body of theory relating to motivation, coordination, and leadership. Much of this theory is derived from the social sciences.

(2) Two aspects of the *scalar and functional* processes which have been treated with some degree of intensity by the neoclassical school are the delegation of authority and responsibility, and gaps in or overlapping of functional jurisdictions. The classical theory assumes something of perfection in the delegation and functionalization processes. The neoclassical school points out that human problems are caused by imperfections in the way these processes are handled.

For example, too much or insufficient delegation may render an executive incapable of action. The failure to delegate authority and responsibility equally may result in frustration for the delegatee. Overlapping of authorities often causes clashes in personality. Gaps

---

[16] For example see: Delbert C. Miller and William H. Form, *Industrial Sociology* (New York: Harper and Brothers, 1951).
[17] See: Hugo Munsterberg, *Psychology and Industrial Efficiency* (Boston: Houghton Mifflin Company, 1913).
[18] Probably the classic work is: Elton Mayo, *The Human Problems of an Industrial Civilization* (Cambridge: Harvard University, 1946, first printed 1933).

in authority cause failures in getting jobs done, with one party blaming the other for shortcomings in performance.[19]

The neoclassical school says that the scalar and functional processes are theoretically valid, but tend to deteriorate in practice. The ways in which they break down are described, and some of the human causes are pointed out. In addition the neoclassicists make recommendations, suggesting various "human tools" which will facilitate the operation of these processes.

(3) *Structure* provides endless avenues of analysis for the neoclassical theory of organization. The theme is that human behavior disrupts the best laid organizational plans, and thwarts the cleanness of the logical relationships founded in the structure. The neoclassical critique of structure centers on frictions which appear internally among people performing different functions.

Line and staff relations is a problem area, much discussed, in this respect. Many companies seem to have difficulty keeping the line and staff working together harmoniously. Both Dalton [20] and Juran [21] have engaged in research to discover the causes of friction, and to suggest remedies.

Of course, line-staff relations represent only one of the many problems of structural frictions described by the neoclassicists. As often as not, the neoclassicists will offer prescriptions for the elimination of conflict in structure. Among the more important harmony-rendering formulae are participation, junior boards, bottom-up management, joint committees, recognition of human dignity, and "better" communication.

(4) An executive's *span of control* is a function of human determinants, and the reduction of span to a precise, universally applicable ratio is silly, according to the neoclassicists. Some of the determinants of span are individual differences in managerial abilities, the type of people and functions supervised, and the extent of communication effectiveness.

Coupled with the span of control question are the human implications of the type of structure which emerges. That is, is a tall structure with a short span or a flat structure with a wide span more conducive to good human relations than high morale? The answer is situational. Short span results in tight supervision; wide

---

[19] For further discussion of the human relations implications of the scalar and functional processes see: Keith Davis, *op. cit.*, pp. 60-66.

[20] Melville Dalton, "Conflicts Between Staff and Line Managerial Officers," *American Sociological Review* (June, 1950), pp. 342-351.

[21] J. M. Juran, "Improving the Relationship Between Staff and Line," *Personnel* (May, 1956), pp. 515-524.

span requires a good deal of delegation with looser controls. Because of individual and organizational differences, sometimes one is better than the other. There is a tendency to favor the looser form of organization, however, for the reason that tall structures breed autocratic leadership, which is often pointed out as a cause of low morale.[22]

The neoclassical view of the informal organization

Nothing more than the barest mention of the informal organization is given even in the most recent classical treatises on organization theory.[23] Systematic discussion of this form of organization has been left to the neoclassicists. The informal organization refers to people in group associations at work, but these associations are not specified in the "blueprint" of the formal organization. The informal organization means natural groupings of people in the work situation.

In a general way, the informal organization appears in response to the social need—the need of people to associate with others. However, for analytical purposes, this explanation is not particularly satisfying. Research has produced the following, more specific determinants underlying the appearance of informal organizations:

1. The *location* determinant simply states that in order to form into groups of any lasting nature, people have to have frequent face-to-face contact. Thus the geography of physical location in a plant or office is an important factor in predicting who will be in what group.[24]
2. *Occupation* is key factor determining the rise and composition of informal groups. There is a tendency for people performing similar jobs to group together.[25]
3. *Interests* are another determinant for informal group formation. Even though people might be in the same location, performing similar jobs, differences of interest among them explain why several small, instead of one large, informal organizations emerge.
4. *Special issues* often result in the formation of informal groups, but this determinant is set apart from the three previously mentioned. In this case, people who do not necessarily have similar interests, occupations, or locations may join together for a common cause. Once the issue is resolved, then the tendency is to revert to the more "natural" group forms.[26] Thus, special issues give rise to a

---

[22] Gardner and Moore, *op. cit.*, pp. 237-243.
[23] For example: Brech, *op. cit.*, pp. 27-29; and Allen, *op. cit.*, pp. 61-62.
[24] See: Leon Festinger, Stanley Schachter, and Kurt Back, *Social Pressures in Informal Groups* (New York: Harper and Brothers, 1950), pp. 153-163.
[25] For example see: W. Fred Cottrell, *The Railroader* (Palo Alto: The Stanford University Press, 1940), Chapter 3.
[26] Except in cases where the existence of an organization is necessary for the continued maintenance of employee interest. Under these conditions the previously informal association may emerge as a formal group, such as a union.

rather impermanent informal association; groups based on the other three determinants tend to be more lasting.

When informal organizations come into being they assume certain characteristics. Since understanding these characteristics is important for management practice, they are noted below:

1. Informal organizations act as agencies of *social control*. They generate a culture based on certain norms of conduct which, in turn, demands conformity from group members. These standards may be at odds with the values set by the formal organization. So an individual may very well find himself in a situation of conflicting demands.
2. The form of human interrelationships in the informal organization requires *techniques of analysis* different from those used to plot the relationships of people in a formal organization. The method used for determining the structure of the informal group is called sociometric analysis. Sociometry reveals the complex structure of interpersonal relations which is based on premises fundamentally unlike the logic of the formal organizations.
3. Informal organizations have *status and communication* systems peculiar to themselves, not necessarily derived from the formal systems. For example, the grapevine is the subject of much neoclassical study.
4. Survival of the informal organization requires stable continuing relationships among the people in them. Thus, it has been observed that the informal organization *resists change*.[27] Considerable attention is given by the neoclassicists to overcoming informal resistance to change.
5. The last aspect of analysis which appears to be central to the neoclassical view of the informal organization is the study of the *informal leader*. Discussion revolves around who the informal leader is, how he assumes this role, what characteristics are peculiar to him, and how he can help the manager accomplish his objectives in the formal organization.[28]

This brief sketch of some of the major facets of informal organization theory has neglected, so far, one important topic treated by the neoclassical school. It is the way in which the formal and informal organizations interact.

A conventional way of looking at the interaction of the two is the "live and let live" point of view. Management should recognize that the informal organization exists, nothing can destroy it, and so the executive might just as well work with it. Working with the informal organization involves not threatening its existence unnecessarily, listening to opinions expressed for the group by the leader,

---

[27] Probably the classic study of resistance to change is: Lester Coch and John R. P. French, Jr., "Overcoming Resistance to Change," in Schuyler Dean Hoslett (editor) *Human Factors in Management* (New York: Harper and Brothers, 1951) pp. 242-268.

[28] For example see: Robert Saltonstall, *Human Relations in Administration* (New York: McGraw-Hill Book Company, 1959), pp. 330-331; and Keith Davis, *op. cit.*, pp. 99-101.

allowing group participation in decision-making situations, and controlling the grapevine by prompt release of accurate information.[29]

While this approach is management centered, it is not unreasonable to expect that informal group standards and norms could make themselves felt on formal organizational policy. An honestly conceived effort by managers to establish a working relationship with the informal organization could result in an association where both formal and informal views would be reciprocally modified. The danger which at all costs should be avoided is that "working with the informal organization" does not degenerate into a shallow disguise for human manipulation.

Some neoclassical writing in organization theory, especially that coming from the management-oriented segment of this school, gives the impression that the formal and informal organizations are distinct, and at times, quite irreconcilable factors in a company. The interaction which takes place between the two is something akin to the interaction between the company and a labor union, or a government agency, or another company.

The concept of the social system is another approach to the interactional climate. While this concept can be properly classified as neoclassical, it borders on the modern theories of organization. The phrase "social system" means that an organization is a complex of mutually interdependent, but variable, factors.

These factors include individuals and their attitudes and motives, jobs, the physical work setting, the formal organization, and the informal organizations. These factors, and many others, are woven into an overall pattern of interdependency. From this point of view, the formal and informal organizations lose their distinctiveness, but find real meaning, in terms of human behavior, in the operation of the system as a whole. Thus, the study of organization turns away from descriptions of its component parts, and is refocused on the system of interrelationships among the parts.

One of the major contributions of the Hawthorne studies was the integration of Pareto's idea of the social system into a meaningful method of analysis for the study of behavior in human organizatins.[30] This concept is still vitally important. But unfortunately some work in the field of human relations undertaken by the neo-

---

[29] For an example of this approach see: John T. Doutt, "Management Must Manage the Informal Group, Too," *Advanced Management* (May, 1959), pp. 26-28.

[30] See: Roethlisberger and Dickson, *op. cit.*, Chapter 24.

classicists has overlooked, or perhaps discounted, the significance of this consideration.[31]

The fundamental insight regarding the social system, developed and applied to the industrial scene by the Hawthorne researchers, did not find much extension in subsequent work in the neoclassical vein. Inded, the neoclassical school after the Hawthorne studies generally seemed content to engage in descriptive generalizations, or particularized empirical research studies which did not have much meaning outside their own context.

The neoclassical school of organization theory has been called bankrupt. Criticisms range from, "human relations is a tool for cynical puppeteering of people," to "human relations is nothing more than a trifling body of empirical and descriptive information." There is a good deal of truth in both criticisms, but another appraisal of the neoclassical school of organization theory is offered here. The neoclassical approach has provided valuable contributions to lore of organization. But, like the classical theory, the neoclassical doctrine suffers from incompleteness, a shortsighted perspective, and lack of integration among the many facets of human behavior studied by it. Modern organization theory has made a move to cover the shortcomings of the current body of theoretical knowledge.

Modern Organization Theory

The distinctive qualities of modern organization theory are its conceptual-analytical base, its reliance on empirical research data and, above all, its integrating nature. These qualities are framed in a philosophy which accepts the premise that the only meaningful way to study organization is to study it as a system. As Henderson put it, the study of a system must rely on a method of analysis, ". . . involving the simultaneous variations of mutually dependent variables." [32] Human systems, of course, contain a huge number of dependent variables which defy the most complex simultaneous equations to solve.

Nevertheless, system analysis has its own peculiar point of view which aims to study organization in the way Henderson suggests. It treats organization as a system of mutually dependent variables.

---

[31] A check of management human relations texts, the organization and human relations chapters of principles of management texts, and texts on conventional organization theory for management courses reveals little or no treatment of the concept of the social system.

[32] Lawrence J. Henderson, *Pareto's General Sociology* (Cambridge: Harvard University Press, 1935), p. 13.

As a result, modern organization theory, which accepts system analysis, shifts the conceptual level of organization study above the classical and neoclassical theories. Modern organization theory asks a range of interrelated questions which are not seriously considered by the two other theories.

Key among these questions are: (1) What are the strategic parts of the system? (2) What is the nature of their mutual dependency? (3) What are the main processes in the system which link the parts together, and facilitate their adjustments to each other? (4) What are the goals sought by systems? [33]

Modern organization theory is in no way a unified body of thought. Each writer and researcher has his special emphasis when he considers the system . Perhaps the most evident unifying thread in the study of systems is the effort to look at the organization in its totality. Representative books in this field are March and Simon, *Organizations*,[34] and Haire's anthology, *Modern Organization Theory*.[35]

Instead of attempting a review of different writers' contributions to modern organization theory, it will be more useful to discuss the various ingredients involved in system analysis. They are the parts, the interactions, the processes, and the goals of systems.

The parts of the system and their interdependency

The first basic part of the system is the *individual*, and the personality structure he brings to the organization. Elementary to an individual's personality are motives and attitudes which condition the range of expectancies he hopes to satisfy by participating in the system.

The second part of the system is the formal arrangement of functions, usually called the *formal organization*. The formal organization is the interrelated pattern of jobs which make up the structure of a system. Certain writers, like Argyris, see a fundamental conflict resulting from the demands made by the system, and the structure of the mature, normal personality. In any event, the individual has expectancies regarding the job he is to perform; and, conversely, the job makes demands on, or has expectancies relating to, the performance of the individual. Considerable attention has

---

[33] There is another question which cannot be treated in the scope of this paper. It asks, what research tools should be used for the study of the system?

[34] James G. March and Herbert A. Simon, *Organizations* (New York: John Wiley and Sons, 1958).

[35] Mason Haire (editor), *Modern Organization Theory* (New York: John Wiley and Sons, 1959).

been given by writers in modern organization theory to incongruencies resulting from the interaction of organizational and individual demands.[36]

The third part in the organization system is the *informal organization*. Enough has been said already about the nature of this organization. But it must be noted that an interactional pattern exists between the individual and the informal group. This interactional arrangement can be conveniently discussed as the mutual modification of expectancies. The informal organization has demands which it makes on members in terms of anticipated forms of behavior, and the individual has expectancies of satisfaction he hopes to derive from association with people on the job. Both these sets of expectancies interact, resulting in the individual modifying his behavior to accord with the demands of the group, and the group, perhaps, modifying what it expects from an individual because of the impact of his personality on group norms.[37]

Much of what has been said about the various expectancy systems in an organization can also be treated using status and role concepts. Part of modern organization theory rests on research findings in social-psychology relative to reciprocal patterns of behavior stemming from role demands generated by both the formal and informal organizations, and role perceptions peculiar to the individual. Bakke's *fusion process* is largely concerned with the modification of role expectancies. The fusion process is a force, according to Bakke, which acts to weld divergent elements together for the preservation of organizational integrity.[38]

The fifth part of system analysis is the *physical setting* in which the job is performed. Although this element of the system may be implicit in what has been said already about the formal organization and its functions, it is well to separate it. In the physical surroundings of work, interactions are present in complex man-machine systems. The human "engineer" cannot approach the problems posed by such interrelationships in a purely technical, engineering fashion. As Haire says, these problems lie in the domain of the social theorist.[39] Attention must be centered on responses demanded from a

---

[36] See Chris Argyris, *Personality and Organization* (New York: Harper and Brothers, 1957), esp. Chapters 2, 3, 7.

[37] For a larger treatment of this subject see: George C. Homans, *The Human Group* (New York: Harcourt, Brace and Company, 1950), Chapter 5.

[38] E. Wight Bakke, "Concept of the Social Organization," in Mason Haire (editor), *Modern Organization Theory* (New York: John Wiley and Sons, 1959) pp. 60-61.

[39] Mason Haire, "Psychology and the Study of Business: Joint Behavioral Sciences," in *Social Science Research on Business: Product and Potential* (New York: Columbia University Press, 1959), pp. 53-59.

logically ordered production function, often with the view of minimizing the error in the system. From this standpoint, work cannot be effectively organized unless the psychological, social, and physiological characteristics of people participating in the work environment are considered. Machines and processes should be designed to fit certain generally observed psychological and physiological properties of men, rather than hiring men to fit machines.

In summary, the parts of the system which appear to be of strategic importance are the individual, the formal structure, the informal organization, status and role patterns, and the physical environment of work. Again, these parts are woven into a configuration called the organizational system. The processes which link the parts are taken up next.

The linking processes

One can say, with a good deal of glibness, that all the parts mentioned above are interrelated. Although this observation is quite correct, it does not mean too much in terms of system theory unless some attempt is made to analyze the processes by which the interaction is achieved. Role theory is devoted to certain types of interactional processes. In addition, modern organization theorists point to three other linking activities which appear to be universal to human systems of organized behavior. These processes are communication, balance, and decision making.

(1) Communication is mentioned often in neoclassical theory, but the emphasis is on description of forms of communication activity, i.e., formal-informal, vertical-horizontal, line-staff. Communication, as a mechanism which links the segments of the system together, is overlooked by way of much considered analysis.

One aspect of modern organization theory is study of the communication network in the system. Communication is viewed as the method by which action is evoked from the parts of the system. Communication acts not only as stimuli resulting in action, but also as a control and coordination mechanism linking the decision centers in the system into a synchronized pattern. Deutsch points out that organizations are composed of parts which communicate with each other, receive messages from the outside world, and store information. Taken together, these communication functions of the parts comprise a configuration representing the total system.[40] More is

---

[40] Karl W. Deutsch, "On Communication Models in the Social Sciences," *Public Opinion Quarterly*, 16 (1952), pp. 356-380.

to be said about communication later in the discussion of the cybernetic model.

(2) The concept of *balance* as a linking process involves a series of some rather complex ideas. Balance refers to an equilibrating mechanism whereby the various parts of the system are maintained in a harmoniously structured relationship to each other.

The necessity for the balance concept logically flows from the nature of systems themselves. It is impossible to conceive of an ordered relationship among the parts of a system without also introducing the idea of a stabilizing or an adapting mechanism.

Balance appears in two varieties—quasi-automatic and innovative. Both forms of balance act to insure system integrity in face of changing conditions, either internal or external to the system. The first form of balance, quasi-automatic, refers to what some think are "homeostatic" properties of systems. That is, systems seem to exhibit built-in propensities to maintain steady states.

If human organizations are open, self-maintaining systems, then control and regulatory processes are necessary. The issue hinges on the degree to which stabilizing processes in systems, when adapting to change, are automatic. March and Simon have an interesting answer to this problem, which in part is based on the type of change and the adjustment necessary to adapt to the change. Systems have programs of action which are put into effect when a change is perceived. If the change is relatively minor, and if the change comes within the purview of established programs of action, then it might be fairly confidently predicted that the adaptation made by the system will be quasi-automatic.[41]

The role of innovative, creative balancing efforts now needs to be examined. The need for innovation arises when adaptation to a change is outside the scope of existing programs designed for the purpose of keeping the system in balance. New programs have to be evolved in order for the system to maintain internal harmony.

New programs are created by trial and error search for feasible action alternatives to cope with a given change. But innovation is subject to the limitations and possibilities inherent in the quantity and variety of information present in a system at a particular time. New combinations of alternatives for innovative purposes depend on:

1. The possible range of output of the system, or the capacity of the system to supply information.
2. The range of available information in the memory of the system.

---

[41] March and Simon, *op. cit.*, pp. 139-140.

3. The operating rules (program) governing the analysis and flow of information within the system.
4. The ability of the system to "forget" previously learned solutions to change problems.[42] A system with too good a memory might narrow its behavioral choices to such an extent as to stifle innovation. In simpler language, old learned programs might be used to adapt the change, when newly innovated programs are necessary.[43]

Much of what has been said about communication and balance brings to mind a cybernetic model in which both these processes have vital roles. Cybernetics has to do with feedback and control of all kinds of systems. Its purpose is to maintain system stability in the face of change. Cybernetics cannot be studied without considering communication networks, information flow, and some kind of balancing process aimed at preserving the integrity of the system.

Cybernetics directs attention to key questions regarding the system. These questions are: How are communication centers connected, and how are they maintained? Corollary to this question: what is the structure of the feedback system? Next, what information is stored in the organization, and at what points? And as a corollary: how accessible is this information to decision-making centers? Third, how conscious is the organization of the operation of its own parts? That is, to what extent do the policy centers receive control information with sufficient frequency and relevancy to create a real awareness of the operation of the segments of the system? Finally, what are the learning (innovating) capabilities of the system? [44]

Answers to the questions posed by cybernetics are crucial to understanding both the balancing and communication processes in systems.[45] Although cybernetics has been applied largely to technical-engineering problems of automation, the model of feedback, control, and regulation in all systems has a good deal of generality. Cybernetics is a fruitful area which can be used to synthesize the processes of communication and balance.

(3) A wide spectrum of topics dealing with types of decisions in human systems makes up the core of analysis of another important process in organizations. Decision analysis is one of the major contributions of March and Simon in their book *Organizations*. The

---

[42] Mervyn L. Cadwallader, "The Cybernetic Analysis of Change in Complex Social Organization," *The American Journal of Sociology* (September, 1959), p. 156.

[43] It is conceivable for innovative behavior to be programmed into the system.

[44] These are questions adapted from Deutsch, *op. cit.*, 368-370.

[45] Answers to these questions would require a comprehensive volume. One of the best approaches currently available is Stafford Beer, *Cybernetics and Management* (New York: John Wiley and Sons, 1959).

two major classes of decisions they discuss are decisions to produce and decisions to participate in the system.[46]

Decisions to produce are largely a result of an interaction between individual attitudes and the demands of organization. Motivation analysis becomes central to studying the nature and results of the interaction. Individual decisions to participate in the organization reflect on such issues as the relationship between organizational rewards versus the demands made by the organization. Participation decisions also focus attention on the reasons why individuals remain in or leave organizations.

March and Simon treat decisions as internal variables in an organization which depend on jobs, individual expectations and motivations, and organizational structure. Marschak[47] looks on the decision process as an independent variable upon which the survival of the organization is based. In this case, the organization is viewed as having, inherent in its structure, the ability to maximize survival requisites through its established decision processes.

The goals of organization

Organization has three goals which may be either intermeshed or independent ends in themselves. They are growth, stability, and interaction. The last goal refers to organizations which exist primarily to provide a medium for association of its members with others. Interestingly enough these goals seem to apply to different forms of organization at varying levels of complexity, ranging from simple clockwork mechanisms to social systems.

These similarities in organizational purposes have been observed by a number of people, and a field of thought and research called system theory has developed, dedicated to the task of discovering organizational universals. The dream of general system theory is to create a science of organizational universals, or if you will, a universal science using common organizational elements found in all systems as a starting point.

Modern organization theory is on the periphery of general system theory. Both general system theory and modern organization theory studies:

1. The parts (individuals) in aggregates, and the movement of individuals into and out of the system.

[46] March and Simon, *op. cit.*, Chapters 3 and 4.
[47] Jacob Marschak, "Efficient and Viable Organizational Forms" in Mason Haire (editor), *Modern Organization Theory* (New York: John Wiley and Sons, 1959), pp. 307-320.

2. The interaction of individuals with the environment found in the system.
3. The interactions among individuals in the system.
4. General growth and stability problems of systems.[48]

Modern organization theory and general system theory are similar in that they look at organization as an integrated whole. They differ, however, in terms of their generality. General system theory is concerned with every level of system, whereas modern organizational theory focuses primarily on human organization.

The question might be asked, what can the science of administration gain by the study of system levels other than human? Before attempting an answer, note should be made of what these other levels are. Boulding presents a convenient method of classification:

1. The static structure—a level of framework, the anatomy of a system; for example, the structure of the universe.
2. The simple dynamic system—the level of clockworks, predetermined necessary motions.
3. The cybernetic system—the level of the thermostat, the system moves to maintain a given equilibrium through a process of self-regulation.
4. The open system—level of self-maintaining systems, moves toward and includes living organisms.
5. The genetic-societal system—level of cell society, characterized by a division of labor among cells.
6. Animal systems—level of mobility, evidence of goal-directed behavior.
7. Human systems—level of symbol interpretation and idea communication.
8. Social system—level of human organization.
9. Transcendental systems—level of ultimates and absolutes which exhibit systematic structure but are unknowable in essence.[49]

This approach to the study of systems by finding universals common at all levels of organization offers intriguing possibilities for administrative organization theory. A good deal of light could be thrown on social systems if structurally analogous elements could be found in the simpler types of systems. For example, cybernetic systems have characteristics which seem to be similar to feedback, regulation, and control phenomena in human organizations. Thus, certain facets of cybernetic models could be generalized to human organization. Considerable danger, however, lies in poorly founded analogies. Superficial similarities between simpler system forms and social systems are apparent everywhere. Instinctually based ant societies, for example, do not yield particularly instructive lessons for understanding rationally conceived human organizations. Thus,

---

[48] Kenneth E. Boulding, "General System Theory—The Skeleton of a Science," *Management Science* (April, 1956), pp. 200-202.
[49] *Ibid.*, pp. 202-205.

care should be taken that analogies used to bridge system levels are not mere devices for literary enrichment. For analogies to have usefulness and validity, they must exhibit inherent structural similarities or implicitly identical operational principles.[50]

Modern organization theory leads, as it has been shown, almost inevitably into a discussion of general system theory. A science of organization universals has some strong advocates, particularly among biologists.[51] Organization theorists in administrative science cannot afford to overlook the contributions of general system theory. Indeed, modern organization concepts could offer a great deal to those working with general system theory. But the ideas dealt with in the general theory are exceedingly elusive.

Speaking of the concept of equilibrium as a unifying element in all systems, Easton says, "It (equilibrium) leaves the impression that we have a useful general theory when in fact, lacking measurability, it is a mere pretense for knowledge." [52] The inability to quantify and measure universal organization elements undermines the success of pragmatic tests to which general system theory might be put.

Organization theory: quo vadis?

Most sciences have a vision of the universe to which they are applied, and administrative science is not an exception. This universe is composed of parts. One purpose of science is to synthesize the parts into an organized conception of its field of study. As a science matures, its theorems about the configuration of its universe change. The direction of change in three sciences, physics, economics, and sociology, are noted briefly for comparison with the development of an administrative view of human organization.

The first comprehensive and empirically verifiable outlook of the physical universe was presented by Newton in his *Principia*. Classical physics, founded on Newton's work, constitutes a grand scheme

---

[50] Seidenberg, *op. cit.*, p. 136. The fruitful use of the type of analogies spoken of by Seidenberg is evident in the application of thermodynamic principles, particularly the entropy concept, to communication theory. See: Claude E. Shannon and Warren Weaver, *The Mathematical Theory of Communication* (Urbana: The University of Illinois Press, 1949). Further, the existence of a complete analogy between the operational behavior of thermodynamic systems, electrical communication systems, and biological systems has been noted by: Y. S. Touloukian, *The Concept of Entropy in Communication, Living Organisms, and Thermodynamics*, Research Bulletin 130, Purdue Engineering Experiment Station.

[51] For example see: Ludwig von Bertalanffy, *Problem of Life* (London: Watts and Company, 1952).

[52] David Easton, "Limits of the Equilibrium Model in Social Research," in *Profits and Problems of Homeostatic Models in the Behavioral Sciences*, Publication 1, Chicago Behavioral Sciences (1953), p. 39.

in which a wide range of physical phenomena could be organized and predicted. Newtonian physics may rightfully be regarded as "macro" in nature, because its system of organization was concerned largely with gross events of which the movement of celestial bodies, waves, energy forms, and strain are examples. For years classical physics was supreme, being applied continuously to smaller and smaller classes of phenomena in the physical universe. Physicists at one time adopted the view that everything in their realm could be discovered by simply subdividing problems. Physics thus moved into the "micro" order.

But in the nineteenth century a revolution took place motivated largely because events were being noted which could not be explained adequately by the conceptual framework supplied by the classical school. The consequences of this revolution are brilliantly described by Eddington:

> From the point of view of philosophy of science the conception associated with entropy must I think be ranked as the great contribution of the nineteenth century to scientific thought. It marked a reaction from the view that everything to which science need pay attention is discovered by microscopic dissection of objects. It provided an alternative standpoint in which the centre of interest is shifted from the entities reached by the customary analysis (atoms, electric potentials, etc.) to qualities possessed by the system as a whole, which cannot be split up and located—a little bit here, and a little bit there. . . .
> We often think that when we have completed our study of *one* we know all about *two*, because "two" is "one and one." We forget that we have still to make a study of "and." Secondary physics is the study of "and"—that is to say, of organization.[53]

Although modern physics often deals in minute quantities and oscillations, the conception of the physicist is on the "macro" scale. He is concerned with the "and," or the organization of the world in which the events occur. These developments did not invalidate classical physics as to its usefulness for explaining a certain range of phenomena. But classical physics is no longer the undisputed law of the universe. It is a special case.

Early economic theory, and Adam Smith's *Wealth of Nations* comes to mind, examined economic problems in the macro order. The *Wealth of Nations* is mainly concerned with matters of national income and welfare. Later, the economics of the firm, microeconomics, dominated the theoretical scene in this science. And, finally, with Keynes' *The General Theory of Employment Interest*

---

[53] Sir Arthur Eddington, *The Nature of the Physical World* (Ann Arbor: The University of Michigan Press, 1958), pp. 103-104.

and Money, a systematic approach to the economic universe was re-introduced on the macro level.

The first era of the developing science of sociology was occupied by the great social "system builders." Comte, the so-called father of sociology, had a macro view of society in that his chief works are devoted to social reorganization. Comte was concerned with the inter-relationships among social, political, religious, and educational insti-tutions. As sociology progressed, the science of society compressed. Emphasis shifted from the macro approach of the pioneers to de-tailed, empirical study of small social units. The compression of sociological analysis was accompanied by study of social pathology or disorganization.

In general, physics, economics, and sociology appear to have two things in common. First, they offered a macro point of view as their initial systematic comprehension of their area of study. Second, as the science developed, attention fragmented into analysis of the parts of the organization, rather than attending to the system as a whole. This is the micro phase.

In physics and economics, discontent was evidenced by some scientists at the continual atomization of the universe. The reaction to the micro approach was a new theory or theories dealing with the total system, on the macro level again. This third phase of scientific development seems to be more evident in physics and economics than in sociology.

The reason for the "macro-micro-macro" order of scientific pro-gress lies, perhaps, in the hypothesis that usually the things which strike man first are of great magnitude. The scientist attempts to discover order in the vastness. But after macro laws or models of systems are postulated, variations appear which demand analysis, not so much in terms of the entire system, but more in terms of the specific parts which make it up. Then, intense study of microcosm may result in new general laws, replacing the old models of organiza-tion. Or, the old and the new models may stand together, each explaining a different class of phenomenon. Or, the old and the new concepts of organization may be welded to produce a single creative synthesis.

Now, what does all this have to do with the problem of organiza-tion in administrative science? Organization concepts seem to have gone through the same order of development in this field as in the three just mentioned. It is evident that the classical theory of organization, particularly as in the work of Mooney and Reiley, is concerned with principles common to all organizations. It is a macro-organization view. The classical approach to organization, however, dealt with the gross anatomical parts and processes of the formal organization. Like classical physics, the classical theory of organization is a special case. Neither are especially well equipped to account for variation from their established framework.

Many variations in the classical administrative model result from human behavior. The only way these variations could be understood was by a microscopic examination of particularized, situational aspects of human behavior. The mission of the neoclassical school thus is "micro-analysis."

It was observed earlier, that somewhere along the line the concept of the social system, which is the key to understanding the Hawthorne studies, faded into the background. Maybe the idea is so obvious that it was lost to the view of researchers and writers in human relations. In any event, the press of research in the microcosmic universes of the informal organization, morale and productivity, leadership, participation, and the like forced the notion of the social system into limbo. Now, with the advent of modern organization theory, the social system has been resurrected.

Modern organization theory appears to be concerned with Eddington's "and." This school claims that its operational hypothesis is based on a macro point of view; that is, the study of organization as a whole. This nobility of purpose should not obscure, however, certain difficulties faced by this field as it is presently constituted. Modern organization theory raises two questions which should be explored further. First, would it not be more accurate to speak of modern organization theor*ies*? Second, just how much of modern organization theory is modern?

The first question can be answered with a quick affirmative. Aside from the notion of the system, there are few, if any, other ideas of a unifying nature. Except for several important exceptions,[54] modern organization theorists tend to pursue their pet points of view,[55] suggesting they are part of system theory, but not troubling to show by what mystical means they arrive at this conclusion.

The irony of it all is that a field dealing with systems has, indeed, little system. Modern organization theory needs a framework, and it needs an integration of issues into a common conception of organization. Admittedly, this is a large order. But it is curious not to

---

[54] For example: E. Wight Bakke, *op. cit.*, pp. 18-75.
[55] There is a large selection including decision theory, individual-organization interaction, motivation, vitality, stability, growth, and graph theory, to mention a few.

find serious analytical treatment of subjects like cybernetics or general system theory in Haire's *Modern Organizational Theory* which claims to be a representative example of work in this field. Beer has ample evidence in his book *Cybernetics and Management* that cybernetics, if imaginatively approached, provides a valuable conceptual base for the study of systems.

The second question suggests an ambiguous answer. Modern organization theory is in part a product of the past; system analysis is not a new idea. Further, modern organization theory relies for supporting data on microcosmic research studies, generally drawn from the journals of the last ten years. The newness of modern organization theory, perhaps, is its effort to synthesize recent research contributions of many fields into a system theory characterized by a reoriented conception of organization.

One might ask, but what is the modern theorist reorienting? A clue is found in the almost snobbish disdain assumed by some authors of the neo-classical human relations school, and particularly, the classical school. Re-evaluation of the classical school of organization is overdue. However, this does not mean that its contributions to organization theory are irrelevant and should be overlooked in the rush to get on the "behavioral science bandwagon."

Haire announces that the papers appearing in *Modern Organization Theory* constitute, "the ragged leading edge of a wave of theoretical development." [56] Ragged, yes; but leading no! The papers appearing in this book do not represent a theoretical breakthrough in the concept of organization. Haire's collection is an interesting potpourri with several contributions of considerable significance. But readers should beware that they will not find vastly new insights into organizational behavior in this book, if they have kept up with the literature of the social sciences, and have dabbled to some extent in the esoteria of biological theories of growth, information theory, and mathematical model building. For those who have not maintained the pace, *Modern Organization Theory* serves the admirable purpose of bringing them up-to-date on a rather diversified number of subjects.

Some work in modern organization theory is pioneering, making its appraisal difficult and future uncertain. While the direction of this endeavor is unclear, one thing is patently true. Human behavior in organizations, and indeed, organization itself, cannot be adequately understood within the ground rules of classical and neo-classical doc-

---

[56] Mason Haire, "General Issues," in Mason Haire (editor), *Modern Organization Theory* (New York: John Wiley and Sons, 1959), p. 2.

trines. Appreciation of human organization requires a *creative* synthesis of massive amounts of empirical data, a high order of deductive reasoning, imaginative research studies, and a taste for individual and social values. Accomplishment of all these objectives, and the inclusion of them into a framework of the concept of the system, appears to be the goal of modern organization theory. The vitality of administrative science rests on the advances modern theorists make along this line.

Modern organization theory, 1960 style, is an amorphous aggregation of synthesizers and restaters, with a few extending leadership on the frontier. For the sake of these few, it is well to admonish that pouring old wine into new bottles may make the spirits cloudy. Unfortunately, modern organization theory has almost succeeded in achieving the status of a fad. Popularization and exploitation contributed to the disrepute into which human relations has fallen. It would be a great waste if modern organization theory yields to the same fate, particularly since both modern organization theory and human relations draw from the same promising source of inspiration—system analysis.

Modern organization theory needs tools of analysis and a conceptual framework uniquely its own, but it must also allow for the incorporation of relevant contributions of many fields. It may be that the framework will come from general system theory. New areas of research such as decision theory, information theory, and cybernetics also offer reasonable expectations of analytical and conceptual tools. Modern organization theory represents a frontier of research which has great significance for management. The potential is great, because it offers the opportunity for uniting what is valuable in classical theory with the social and natural sciences into a systematic and integrated conception of human organization.

QUESTIONS

1. Explain in detail the three theories of organization presented in Scott's article.
2. Why does he consider decision making as part of an organizational linking process?
3. What is meant by general systems theory? How is it related to the usual organization of a business firm?
4. What is your opinion of modern organization theory? Do you feel it is applicable in a firm like General Motors? Your local Ford dealership? The university you are attending?
5. Explain the following: (a) social control in the working organization; (b) scalar and functional processes; (c) formal structure; (d) organizational systems.

25. ORGANIZATIONAL REALITIES *

Rocco Carzo, Jr.

Organizing is easy—at least, that is what one is led to believe from traditional writings on the subject. Traditional theory prescribes that organization be built around the work to be done. For maximum efficiency, this theory specifies that the work be divided into simple, routine, and repetitive tasks. These tasks or jobs should then be grouped according to similar work characteristics and arranged in an organization structure in which an executive has a limited number of subordinates reporting directly to him. Also, every member of the organization should be accountable to only one boss. Personnel assignments are to be made on the basis of the requirements of the job and each individual's ability to do the work.

These are not doctrinaire beliefs reserved for academic minds. In many quarters, they have gained enough stature to be called "principles" of management and/or organization, and they are also widely accepted in practice. Administrators and academicians will recognize the traditional organization pyramids that are based on these seemingly reasonable propositions. As an example, one administrator recommends the following for a "sound, flexible, and dynamic" organizational structure: [1]

1. Determine the objectives and the policies, programs, plans, and schedules that will best achieve these objectives for the company as a whole and, in turn, for each component of the business.
2. Determine the work to be done to achieve those objectives under such guiding policies.
3. Divide and classify or group related work into a simple, logical, understandable, and comprehensive organizational structure.
4. Assign essential work clearly and definitely to the various components and positions.
5. Determine the requirements and qualifications of personnel to occupy such positions.
6. Staff the organization with persons who meet these qualifications.
7. Establish methods and procedures that will help to achieve the objectives of the organization.

Now, however, there is enough research evidence to raise some significant doubts about the validity of prevailing organizational

* From *Business Horizons*, Vol. 4, No. 1 (Spring, 1961), pp. 95-104. Reprinted with permission.
[1] Ralph J. Cordiner, *New Frontiers for Professional Managers* (New York: McGraw-Hill Book Company, Inc., 1956), pp. 52-53.

theories. Traditional theory is based on logical division of work. More recent social research is concerned with organizational arrangements that will facilitate the joining of human efforts. Realistic organizational theory must be based on the real behavior of real people in real organizations, that is, the ways in which people join their efforts in any kind of cooperative system. The real test of organizational theory is not abstract logic based on work but on arrangements that facilitate effective cooperative relationships. These relationships are the key to productivity. It is the purpose of this article to explain and illustrate the lack of concern for these realities in the traditional approach. In addition, some suggestions will be made for realistic organization.

TRADITION VS. RESEARCH

Specialization

The advantages of specialization are primarily economic. Both economists and formal organization theorists emphasize that greater efficiency and productivity are achieved through division of work. Adam Smith, in his *Wealth of Nations*, illustrated his thinking with his description of a pin factory. By dividing the work into specialized tasks, the factory could produce thousands of pins per man per day. But if the complete manufacturing process were left to individual workmen, each might produce only a few dozen per day. F. W. Taylor went a step further by proposing that management jobs be specialized so that "each man from the assistant superintendent down shall have as few functions as possible to perform. If practicable, the work of each man in the management should be confined to the performance of a single leading function." [2]

The approach that divides the work into simple, routine, and repetitive tasks utilizes *minimum* skills and abilities. James Worthy has attacked this approach as follows:

> The gravest weakness [of specialization] was the failure to recognize and utilize properly management's most valuable resource: the complex and multiple capacities of people. On the contrary, the scientific managers deliberately sought to utilize as narrow a band of personality and as narrow a range of ability as ingenuity could devise. The process has been fantastically wasteful for industry and society.[3]

[2] Frederick W. Taylor, *Scientific Management* (New York: Harper & Brothers, 1941), p. 99.
[3] James C. Worthy, *Big Business and Free Man* (New York: Harper & Brothers, 1959), pp. 69-70.

Recently, the effect of specialization on employee attitudes have received more study. For example, Chris Argyris feels that congruency is lacking between the needs of healthy individuals and the demands of the formal organization. In his research of a seemingly healthy manufacturing operation that had very low indexes of employee turnover, absenteeism, and grievances, Argyris found the employees to be apathetic and indifferent toward management and the organization. He has said that the formal organization, with its emphasis on task specialization, utilizes a narrow range of skills and minimum abilities, and tends to create needs that are not characteristic of healthy, mature individuals.

The administrator and the social scientist might argue that these criticisms involve value judgments and are not really their concern. They may ask: Does it matter if human resources are not fully utilized; and does it matter that employees are apathetic and indifferent, as long as organization objectives are accomplished efficiently or as long as profits are maximized in the case of a business enterprise? The administrator may argue further that he is forced to adopt specialization because it promises the greater efficiency and productivity. The social scientist may point out that, as a scientist, he cannot consider values; his concern must be limited to means and not ends.

Both administrators and social scientists would accept the position, however, that greater utilization of the physical and mental capabilities of the human resource may increase the scope of organizational accomplishment. They would also accept the argument that apathy and indifference may have long-run implications for the efficient attainment of goals. For example, Argyris predicts that the dissatisfaction of employees manifested by apathy and indifference will result in demands for increased wages; these increases will be viewed "not as rewards for production but as management's moral obligation for placing the employees in the kind of working world where frustration, failure, and conflict are continuously being experienced." According to this thesis, wage costs will tend to rise regardless of productivity changes. The employee in this situation views the increase as compensation for continued frustration.

Perhaps these realities imply even broader organizational objectives than those of maximum efficiency, productivity, and profits. The narrower view of organizations in terms of material achievements, such as profits as the prime goal (and some say the only goal) of business institutions, has permeated the classical as well as the popular and current versions of organized activity. The materialistic goals attributed to organizations are abstractions and serve only to facilitate simplified descriptions of organization and group behavior. These descriptions are usually devoid of human and moral values. Such values are important not only as ends in themselves but also for understanding human behavior. Over-simplification with regard to the multiple objectives of organizations and the complex motivations of individuals will not lead to realistic organizational structure. Worthy has decried the prevailing theories of business organization and has called for a new theory that more adequately reflects and explains reality:

> Such a theory will recognize that business is a social organ with functions far beyond the mere promotion of material prosperity, and with motivations far broader than simple self-interest. It will give consideration to the pervasive influence of religious forces in American life, the profound consequences of the rise of the large, publicly owned corporation, and certain unique features of American historical development. It will, in other words, shake off outmoded economic doctrine and take a fresh look at the truth about today's business.[4]

This broader view of organizational goals implies that the administrator has responsibilities far beyond those dictated by material achievements. The fragmentation and routinization of work to the point where it loses significance has dire implications, not only for organizations that live by this action, but also for society in general. The organization may suffer because the rewards for submissive compliance produce apathy, indifference, noninvolvement, and alienation on the part of group members. They become highly dependent and incapable of solving problems and making decisions. The organization may become rigid and its members unwilling to accept and adapt to changes necessary for growth and changing socio-economic conditions. Furthermore, a democracy built on a foundation of free choice will suffer because the dependency rewarded and fostered in organizations may carry over into everyday life.

Grouping

After the work has been divided into specialized tasks, the advocates of formal organization prescribe the grouping of these tasks according to similar work characteristics. This is called the principle of "functional homogenity." According to one definition, the principle ". . . says that organizational effectiveness is increased and the cost of executive and operative labor is reduced when duties are

---

[4] *Big Business and Free Man*, pp. 31-32.

grouped in accordance with functional similarities. The members of a group are able to *coordinate* and *cooperate* with one another directly when they are dealing with similar problems." [5]

The grouping of persons according to similarities in their work may be contrary to the natural development of human organization. Early researchers found that people tend naturally to organize on a basis other than the technical requirements of work. They organize in terms of sentiments, social customs, codes of behavior, status, friendships, and cliques. The significance of these findings lies in the researchers' conclusions that cooperation depends upon the natural relationships of informal organization and not necessarily on groupings based on work arrangements and/or economic incentives.

The simplicity and rationale of formal structuring is open to further criticism when one examines another prescription for organizing. The principle of "span of control" stipulates that the number of subordinates supervised directly by any one executive be limited. Some eminent students of administration have gone so far as to specify how many subordinates a superior can effectively manage. Urwick, for example, has said, "No superior can supervise directly the work of more than five or, at the most, six subordinates *whose work interlocks*." [6] Two of the most outstanding criticisms (many have been made) of the span of control are those of Herbert A. Simon and Waino W. Suojanen. Simon points out that there is a basic contradiction between this principle and the principle that there should be as few levels as possible in an organization. By restricting or limiting the span of control, an organization—especially one that is growing—must increase the number of scalar levels and the administrative distance between individuals. This development inevitably produces excessive red tape and waste of time and effort. Obviously, adherence to the principle of span of control conflicts with the principle that requires a minimum number of organizational levels. Suojanen states:

> If both principles are actually applicable to the large organization, then it must follow that many large government agencies and business corporations are less efficient than their smaller counterparts. However, large corporations not only continue to grow in size but also comparisons of various sizes of corporations are not convincing as to the superiority of smaller, as opposed to larger corporations. [7]

---

[5] Ralph C. Davis, *Industrial Organization and Management* (New York: Harper & Brothers, 1957), p. 70. The emphasis is mine.

[6] Lydall F. Urwick, "The Manager's Span of Control," *Harvard Business Review*, XXXIV (May-June, 1956), p. 41.

[7] Waino W. Suojanen, "The Span of Control—Fact or Fable," *Advanced Management*, XX (November, 1955), p. 5.

While Urwick's argument for the span-of-control concept is based on those situations where the work of subordinates interlocks, Suojanen offers this very reason as an explanation for the success of large organizations. Common purpose, willingness to cooperate, and coordinated action are characteristics of the executive unit. According to Suojanen, the ease of communication, the informality of relationships, and the personal satisfactions gained in association actually reduce rather than increase the number of relationships and the demands made on the superior.

If this is not enough to raise doubts about the span-of-control doctrine, one can consider the research done at the Institute for Social Research, University of Michigan. One of the researchers there has concluded that an organization will function best and will achieve the highest motviation when the people in the organization hold overlapping group memberships.[8] The very characteristic (interlocking relationships) that seems to make the span of control operative is in reality a necessity for cooperative and coordinated effort.

Effects of interaction. Evidence indicates that an organization initially framed according to work groupings will eventually function in a manner that parallels the natural social tendencies and personality characteristics of the persons in it.

In laboratory research undertaken by the author (the results have not yet been published), an attempt is being made to predict organizational success on the basis of the composition and interaction of group members. We have seen organizations, initially departmentalized according to similarities in work, actually operate under different systems. The new systems were based on the personalities and interaction of group members. In another study, where departments were established on the basis of work similarities and authority was delegated on the basis of work performance, researchers found that a system of relations had developed that was quite distinct from the formal organization. Furthermore, they suggest that difficulties of industrial cooperation could be avoided if organization would adapt the formal organization to the real relationships that develop over a period of time.[9]

---

[8] Rensis Likert, "A Motivational Approach to a Modified Theory of Organization and Management," in Mason Haire (ed.), *Modern Organization Theory* (New York: John Wiley & Sons, Inc., 1959), pp. 184-217.

[9] Conrad M. Arensberg and Douglas McGregor, "Determination of Morale in an Industrial Company," *Applied Anthropology*, I (January-March, 1942), p. 12-34. In a more recent study, Melville Dalton, *Men Who Manage* (New York: John Wiley & Sons, Inc., 1959), Chapter 3, the author found that "real" or "actual" organization and authority differed from prescribed or formal organization and authority.

Separation of line and staff

Another area where reality differs from theoretical prescriptions is the traditional separation of line (command) and staff (advisory) authority. According to traditional theory, staff departments are recommended for assisting line executives in work that requires technical knowledge and detailed attention. While the staff is supposed to remain advisory, it usually develops into a line capacity with both the higher and lower elements of the organizational hierarchy. Staff specialists become "experts" in their specialty and top management officials rely on them for "authoritative" advice. As lower management officials realize that staff recommendations are backed by top management, a line of command is established that covers a particular aspect of the work—in addition to general supervision of the line.

The development of this arrangement serves to obviate the neat separation of line and staff. Also, there is reason to question whether the unity-of-command doctrine (one boss) really operates in practice. The acceptance of staff recommendations and suggestions by lower management officials as authoritative and representative of the views of higher management creates a much more complicated organization than that portrayed by the simple line-and-staff (unity-of-command) type of structure.

The line-and-staff type of structure seems to suffer from some false assumptions: (1) staff specialists are able and willing to operate without formal authority, and (2) their advice, suggestions, and recommendations will readily be accepted and applied by lower line officials. Under the true line-and-staff arrangement as it works out in practice, the staff officer finds he has little power. His advice may go unheeded and unheralded because he has no authority to implement his decisions in the organization. The lower line officers may resent and reject staff advice because it threatens the sacred position of the line. Melville Dalton, after a study of three industrial plants, concluded that line officers fear staff innovations for a number of reasons.

> In view of their longer experience, presumably intimate knowledge of the work, and their greater remuneration, they fear being "shown up" before their line superiors for not having thought of the processual refinements themselves. They fear that changes in methods may bring personnel changes . . . and quite possibly reduce their area of authority. Finally, changes in techniques may expose forbidden practices and departmental inefficiency.[10]

---

[10] Melville Dalton, "Conflicts Between Staff and Line Management Officers," *American Sociological Review*, XV (June, 1950), p. 349. Also see *Men Who Manage*, Chapter 4.

These frustrations lead to a power struggle. The staff officer seeks more authority by reporting his frustrations and criticisms of line operations to higher line officials. Evidence indicates that staff officers, by virtue of their specialized knowledge, their continual contact with top management, and better education, are able to gain from top management the necessary functional authority over line operations. Some would bemoan this development because it violates the principle of unity of command and causes the lower line officials no end of confusion. However, as explained earlier, the overlapping and the various relationships are the basic ingredients for cooperation and coordination. Thus they should be encouraged, not circumscribed by the contrivances of those who draw organization charts.

Motivation

The doctrine of self-interest has long prevailed in traditional theory as well as in practice. The self-interest doctrine is illustrated in one of Adam Smith's basic assumptions: Every individual is continually exerting himself to discover the most advantageous employment for whatever captial he can command. It does not take much study to realize that this same doctrine still prevails. As an example, note the view of the president of one of the world's largest corporations: "Of all the motivations to which the human mechanism responds, none has proved so powerful as that of financial gain . . . self enrichment is a dream which must rank with the most compelling forces in shaping the destinies of the human race." [11]

While the concept of self-interest based on financial reward is important in explaining human behavior, it presents an incomplete and inadequate picture of human needs. It says nothing of the desire to feel important, to be respected, and to have prestige. Of even greater significance for the study of organizations is the basic human desire to associate, to belong, or to be accepted as a member of a group. This need far exceeds monetary enrichment as a factor in motivating human behavior. Elton Mayo has said, "The desire to stand well with one's fellows, the so-called human instinct of association, easily outweighs the merely individual interest and the logical reasoning upon which so many spurious principles of management are based." [12] He concluded that "If one observes either industrial

---

[11] Crawford H. Greenewalt, *The Uncommon Man* (New York: McGraw-Hill Book Company, Inc., 1959), pp. 37-38.
[12] Elton Mayo, *The Social Problems of an Industrial Civilization* (Boston: Division of Research, Graduate School of Business Administration, Harvard University, 1945). This and the following quotation are from p. 43.

workers or university students with sufficient care and continuity, one finds that the proportionate number actuated by motives of *self-interest logically elaborated* is exceedingly small. They have relapsed upon self-interest when social association has failed them."

The self-interest thesis falls down in another important respect. It was stated earlier that people organize naturally on a basis other than the technical requirements of work. This organization has been called the social structure or the informal organization. By satisfying men's basic needs for association, friendship, and belonging, it provides the setting that makes them willing to cooperate. Furthermore, individual behavior is influenced by the customs, traditions, and pressures of the group. Thus, individual interests and desires become subordinated to those of the social organization.

In this respect, one is reminded of the Coch and French experiments, which dealt with the problem of employee resistance to change at the Harwood Manufacturing Corporation.[13] The company had tried to solve this problem with monetary allowances for transfers. It would seem from the self-interest doctrine that economic incentives such as a transfer bonus should create acceptance toward job changes and attitudes favorable to relearning after transfer. On the contrary, the researchers found the general attitudes toward job changes markedly negative. Analysis of the relearning curves of several hundred experienced operators, rating standard or better prior to change, showed that 38 percent of the operators recovered to the standard unit rating; the other 62 percent either became chronically substandard operators or quit during the relearning period.

Four different groups were studied. One group was merely told of planned changes; a second group was allowed to participate through representation in designing changes; and the two remaining groups participated fully. The researchers found that the total participation groups not only returned to the previous production rate faster than the other groups, but showed sustained progress toward a higher rate. Coch and French concluded that resistance to change in methods of work can be overcome by stimulating group participation in planning the changes.

This study dramatizes the significance of factors other than financial gain in motivating human behavior. First of all, the researchers observed that work standards, informally set by the groups, were important in determining output levels before and after the change.

---

[13] Lester Coch and John R. P. French, Jr., "Overcoming Resistance to Change," *Human Relations*, I (August, 1948), p. 512-32.

The nonparticipation group seemed to be governed by a standard set before the change, while the two total-participation groups were governed by a standard set when competition developed between them. However, it is important to note the authors' observation that a major determinant of the strength of these standards was probably the cohesiveness of the group. The power of the group over the members to increase or decrease productivity seemed to depend upon the amount of participation.

Secondly, changes in the social system that would be produced by technical or work changes may cause resistance to change. For example, the researchers indicated that employees would resist change because of the possibility of failure on the new job and a loss of status in the eyes of fellow employees. Furthermore, employees may resist because they are reluctant to leave friends or break social ties and are uncertain about being accepted in a new and different social system.

Thirdly, and most important for overcoming resistance and motivating human behavior, is the very nature of participation. Participation requires interaction, association, and involvement; as noted earlier, these are essential for cooperative effort.

Comparison and evaluation. The self-interest doctrine has prompted another organizational practice that is believed to stimulate greater productivity. This is the arrangement of individuals in a manner that permits their performance to be compared and evaluated. Rating and reward are based on how one individual compares to another doing similar work. Control is supposed to be easier because the organization has built-in standards for comparison and evaluation. Furthermore, it is believed that individuals will compete when they learn that they are being compared, and greater productivity will result.

Does competition increase production? Perhaps a more important first question is: Does competition stimulate cooperation? Competition is characterized by rivalry; one organization member strives against another for an objective of which he will be the principal beneficiary. Cooperation, on the other hand, is characterized by collaborative behavior; group members strive together for the attainment of a goal that is to be shared equally by each participating individual or unit. Cooperation, therefore, suppresses individual drives and goals so that common group objectives may be attained. An organization that promotes competition among its members will not have cooperation; it will have conflict. Group members have little reason to act jointly or collaborate with those against whom they are being measured or compared, or with whom they are competing.

Moreover, evidence indicates that a group will be more productive when its members are cooperative rather than competitive. Morton Deutsch, in an experiment designed to study the behavior of different groups (some cooperative, others competitive), found greater productivity among the cooperative groups.[14] Also, he found that the productivity was of a higher quality; these groups produced more fruitful ideas and showed more insight and understanding of problems. Measurement and reward of individual performance in the cooperative groups were made on the basis of group achievement. In this situation, each member received the same reward. Each member in the competitive groups was rated and rewarded on the basis of comparison with the efforts of the members in his group. In this situation, the reward each member received was different and was determined by his relative contribution to the solution of the problem with which the group was confronted. In contrast, the emphasis on group behavior in the cooperative groups produced the motivation, cooperation, and coordination that is necessary for the successful achievement of organization objectives.

Decentralization. Decentralization and "management by objectives" have often been offered by administrators and theorists as the best organizational arrangement for overcoming the suppressive aspects of a large organization while providing for the greatest motivation. Decentralization, as defined by its advocates, gives maximum authority and responsibility to the manager of each decentralized unit. Control by top management is exercised primarily by measuring end results and comparing performance with predetermined standards and the performance of other units. Once these measurements have been defined and applied, they are supposed to provide motivation. They are also used by top management as a basis for giving rewards such as promotions and bonuses. This practice may not only emphasize the wrong things in cooperative behavior, as explained earlier, but there is the possibility that measurements based on end results, such as earnings, production, costs, and sales, will encourage managers of decentralized units to adopt a pressure-oriented management. In other words, they may exercise

---

[14] Morton Deutsch, "A Theory of Co-operation and Competition," *Human Relations*, II (April, 1949), pp. 129-52, and "An Experimental Study of the Effects of Cooperation and Competition Upon Group Process," *Human Relations*, II (July, 1949), pp. 199-231.

pressure on the organization to meet the end results expected, while ignoring the quality of the human organization.

From a number of research studies, Rensis Likert has found that pressure-oriented supervision can achieve impressive short-run results. He reports that:

> . . . Putting pressure on a well-established organization to produce can yield substantial and immediate increases in productivity. *This increase is obtained, however, at a cost to the human assets of the organization.* In the company we studied, for example, the cost was clear: hostilities increased, there was greater reliance upon authority, loyalties declined, and motivations to produce decreased while motivations to restrict production increased. In other words, the quality of the human organization deteriorated as a functioning social system.[15]

On the other hand, he has found that managers who are employee-centered and who support their subordinates will foster team spirit, greater productivity, and better employee satisfaction than pressure-oriented or production-centered managers.

Decentralization can, of course, provide the means for maximum utilization and development of the human resource as well as the basis for cooperative behavior. In contrast to organizations where there are many levels of supervision and elaborate systems of control, Worthy found that the flat type of structure with maximum decentralization develops self-reliance and initiative, and more fully utilizes individual capacities. At Sears, Roebuck and Co., for example, the typical store manager has forty-odd department managers reporting directly to him (thus violating the traditional limitations of the span-of-control doctrine), and has no alternative but to delegate decision-making authority to subordinates. When managers of departments were asked to manage, they learned to manage. Having to rely heavily on department managers, store managers at Sears took greater care in the selection, placement, and development of subordinates. Furthermore, Worthy says:

> This pattern of administration not only gets today's job done better, but permits the individual to grow and develop in a way that is impossible in more centralized systems. Furthermore, it contributes strongly to morale because employes work in an atmosphere of relative freedom from oppressive supervision and have a sense of individual importance and personal responsibility which other types of arrangements often deny them.[16]

---

[15] Rensis Likert, "Measuring Organizational Performance," *Harvard Business Review*, XXXVI (March-April, 1958), p. 48.

[16] James C. Worthy, "Organizational Structure and Employe Morale," *American Sociological Review*, XV (April, 1950), p. 178. Worthy also observes that not all individuals can function effectively in this type of arrangement and that the system will tend to weed them out.

It is important to note also that Worthy attributes much of the success of the Sears organization to its ability to meet the personal and social demands of its employees and not to any "logical technology, division of labor, or hierarchy of control." The study showed that both low output and low morale prevailed where jobs were broken down minutely. The most sustained efforts were exerted by employees who performed the more complete sets of tasks; these likewise exhibited the highest levels of morale and *esprit de corps*. Further, the research revealed that size of the organization unit was unquestionably a most important factor in determining the quality of employee relationships: the smaller the unit the higher the morale, and vice versa. It was clear that closer contact between executives and the rank and file in smaller organizations tends to result in friendlier, easier relationships.

In Perspective

The research results that have been described are not conclusive, of course, but they do suggest that many of the so-called principles of management and organization are preconceived and have little value as descriptions of behavior or as prescriptions for success. Though specialization has its advantages, it may create employee attitudes and demands that are injurious to the organization. Similarly, efforts to departmentalize according to the requirements of work—while necessary for some degree of order, planning and control—may create arrangements that are contrary to the requirements for cooperative behavior. Also, while the importance of economic and material incentives cannot be denied, reliance on them as the prime or only means of motivation may produce behavior that is contrary to organization needs such as loyalty, honesty, and initiative.

The administrator's task is a difficult one. According to what has been suggested here, the administrator must provide a structure that is loose enough to gain the motivational benefits from the natural social inclinations of organization members, yet he must impose the technical or formal organization and controls so necessary for efficient goal achievement.

As an example of organizing on the basis of natural tendencies, consider the way people associate in small informal groups. They are not only influenced by customs, traditions, and structure, but also receive many satisfactions from and are motivated by membership in these simple social systems.

It seems appropriate, therefore, that the formal organization be structured to take advantage of the benefits provided by smallness. Small, loosely structured organizational units, coupled with maximum employee involvement in organization affairs, can provide the cooperation necessary for successful performance. Seemingly, as the number of organizational units increases, the task of coordination and control will become more difficult. However, the converse may be true, depending on the number of levels, the directness of communication, the amount of interaction and involvement that takes place in an organization. The flat or horizontal type of arrangement (wide spans of supervision and few levels), where the lines of communication are simple and direct, can more readily be coordinated than the organization with many levels where communication is relatively slow and subject to many interpretations. The coordination problem becomes simpler when components of the organization operate autonomously. Left to operate on their own, decentralized units need only to be coordinated on end results.

It is important to re-emphasize that overspecialization and overfunctionalization in decentralized units can create not only the same problems as those experienced in the larger, more centralized organization but also more complex ones. The more a functional unit is defined as a separate entity, the greater the possibility that it will neglect its integrative purpose and be at odds with the over-all objectives of the decentralized unit as well as the whole organization. Furthermore, overfunctionalization may tend to make relationships at both the management and employee levels too formal. Cooperation may then be limited to that required by organization policy or the management hierarchy. Thus, the task of coordination becomes even more burdensome, increasing the necessity for elaborate systems and formal controls. This type of system, characterized by pressure-oriented management with undue regard for end results, can also be detrimental to the human organization. A loosely structured organization, where the emphasis is on teamwork and where there is a high degree of compatibility between goals of group members and the overall objectives of the organization, produces a human organization that is much more cooperative and productive.

Those who argue against organizing on the basis of human characteristics and tendencies emphasize the difficulties inherent in trying to diagnose human problems and in predicting human behavior. Diagnosis, of course, requires a much more learned and analytical administrator. He must be aware of and understand the research on organization behavior. He must be able to conduct and supervise research in his own organization concerning problems peculiar to his situation. With understanding and analysis, he should be better equipped to predict the outcome of anticipated courses of action and choose those that promise continued organizational success. Granted, this requires administration of a high order. It is, however, a necessity if organization in accord with reality is desired.

Questions

1. What is an organizational pyramid? How is this related to managerial authority?
2. What are the primary arguments for and against specialization in the formal working organization?
3. What does Carzo feel can be done to increase organizational accomplishment and individual contribution within the work organization?
4. What is the self-interest doctrine? How is it promoted in the firm?
5. Do you agree with Carzo's views about traditional versus contemporary organizational issues? In what ways do you agree and/or differ? Explain.

26. MEASURING ORGANIZATIONAL PERFORMANCE *

Rensis Likert

❡ *Does top management's emphasis on immediate earnings, production, cost reduction, and similar measures of end results encourage division managers to dissipate the organization's human assets?*

❡ *What measurable changes occur in the productivity, loyalty, attitudes, and satisfactions of an organization where decision levels are pushed down and group methods of leadership are employed? What measurable changes occur in an organization where decision levels are pushed upward and close control is exercised at the top? How do the results of each type of management compare in the short and long run?*

❡ *What qualities of an organization can and should be measured for the purposes of appraising the leadership of division managers and others to whom authority is delegated?*

Decentralization and delegation are powerful concepts based on sound theory. But there is evidence that, as now utilized, they have a serious vulnerability which can be costly. This vulnerability arises from the measurements being used to evaluate and reward the performance of those given authority over decentralized operations.

This situation is becoming worse. While companies have during the past decade made greater use of work measurements and measurements of end results in evaluating managers, and also greater use of incentive pay in rewarding them, only a few managements have regularly used measurements that deal directly with the human assets of the organization—for example, measurements of loyalty, motivation, confidence, and trust. As a consequence, many companies today are encouraging managers of departments and divisions to dissipate valuable human assets of the organization. In fact, they are rewarding these managers well for doing so!

NEW MEASURES NEEDED

The advocates of decentralization recognize that measurements play a particularly important function. Ralph J. Cordiner, one of the

* From *Harvard Business Review*, Vol. 36, No. 2 (1958), pp. 41-50. Reprinted with permission.

most articulate spokesmen, has stated his views on the question as follows:

> Like many other companies, General Electric has long felt a need for more exact measurements and standards of performance, not only to evaluate past results, but to provide a more accurate means for planning future activities and calculating business risks. The traditional measures of profits such as return on investment, turnover, and percentage of net earnings to sales provide useful information. But they are hopelessly inadequate as measures to guide the manager's effectiveness in planning for the future of the business—the area where his decisions have the most important effects.
>
> When General Electric undertook the thorough decentralization . . . , the need for more realistic and balanced measurements became visibly more acute. For with the decentralization of operating responsibility and authority to more than a hundred local managerial teams, there was a need for common means of measuring these diverse business operations as to their short-range and long-range effectiveness. . . .
>
> It was felt that, if a system of simple, common measurements could be devised, they would have these important values. . . .
>
> 1. Common measurements would provide all the managers of each component, and the individual contributors in the component, with means to measure and plan their own performance, so that their individual decisions could be made on the basis of knowledge and informed judgment.
>
> 2. Common measurements would provide each manager with a way of detecting deviations from established standards in time to do something about it—the feedback idea, in which current operations themselves provide a means of continuous adjustment of the operation.
>
> 3. Common measurements would provide a means of appraisal, selection, and compensation of men on the basis of objective performance rather than personality judgments, which is better for both the individual and the Company.
>
> 4. Common measurements would provide an important motivation for better performance, since they make clear on what basis the individual is to be measured and give him a way of measuring his own effectiveness.
>
> 5. Common measurements would simplify communications by providing common concepts and common language with which to think and talk about the business, especially in its quantitative aspects.
>
> You will notice that all these points are directed at helping each decentralized manager and individual contributor measure and guide his own work, through self-discipline; they are not designed as a way for others to "second-guess" the manager of a component or the workers in his component. When measurements are designed primarily for the "boss" rather than for the man himself, they tend to lose their objectivity and frequently become instruments of deception.
>
> An adequate system of common measurements, moreover, would have the additional advantage of providing the company's executives

with a way of evaluating performance in some hundred different businesses without becoming involved in the operational details of each of them.[1]

Traditional theory

These specifications point to serious inadequacies in the measurements now being obtained. Virtually all companies regularly secure measurements which deal with such end results as production, sales, profits, and percentage of net earnings to sales. The accounting procedures of most companies also reflect fairly well the level of inventories, the investment in plant and equipment, and the condition of plant and equipment.

But much less attention is given to what might be called "intervening factors," which significantly influence the end results just mentioned. These factors include such qualities of the human organization that staffs the plant as its loyalty, skills, motivations, and capacity for effective interaction, communication, and decision making. At present there is not one company, to my knowledge, that regularly obtains measurements which adequately and accurately reflect the quality and capacity of its human organization. (But in two companies experimental programs are underway to develop measurements of this kind.)

There are two principal reasons for this situation: (1) The traditional theory of management, which dominates current concepts as to what should be measured, largely ignores motivational and other human behavior variables. (2) Until recently the social sciences were not developed enough to provide methods for measuring the quality of the human organization.

The traditional theory of management is based on scientific management, cost accounting and related developments, and general administrative concepts taken from military organizational theory. As a consequence, it calls for measurements that are concerned with such end result variables as profits and costs, or with such process variables as productivity.

Substantial research findings show, however, that the managers in business and government who are getting the best results are systematically deviating from this traditional theory in the operating procedures which they use.[2] The general pattern of these deviations

---

[1] Ralph J. Cordiner, *New Frontiers for Professional Managers* (New York: McGraw-Hill Book Company, Inc., 1956), pp. 95-98; this volume comprises the McKinsey Lectures, which Mr. Cordiner delivered in 1956 at the Graduate School of Business, Columbia University.

[2] See, for example, R. Likert, "Motivational Dimensions of Administration," *America's Manpower Crisis* (Chicago Public Administration Service, 1952), p. 89,

is to give much more attention to motivation than the traditional theory calls for. High-producing managers are not neglecting such tools and resources provided by scientific management as cost accounting; quite to the contrary, they use them fully. But they use these quantitative tools in special ways—ways that achieve significantly higher motivation than is obtained by those managers who adhere strictly to the methods specified by the traditional theory of management.

Modified theory

The exact principles and practices of high-producing managers have been integrated into a modified theory of management, which has been discussed elsewhere.[3] What I am interested in discussing here are the implications of this modified theory for control. Management needs to make extensive changes in the measurements now being obtained. It should take into account such factors as the levels of confidence and trust, motivation, and loyalty, and the capacity of the organization to communicate fully, to interact effectively, and to achieve sound decisions.

It is important for all companies to obtain these new kinds of measurements to guide their operations, but it is especially important for companies making extensive use of decentralization to do so. The logic of decentralization and the underlying theory on which it is based point to the need for this. In the absence of the new measurements, as we shall see presently, many managers are enabled and may even be encouraged to behave in ways which violate the logic of decentralization and which run contrary to the best interests of their companies.

It is easy to see why. Managers, like all human beings, guide their behavior by the information available to them. The measurements which a company provides them as a basis for decision making are particularly important. They are used by top management not only to judge the performance of departmental and division heads but also, through promotions, bonus compensation, and similar devices, to reward them. If the measurements which companies use for these purposes ignore the quality of the human organization and deal primarily with earnings, production, costs, and similar end results,

and "Developing Patterns of Management," *General Management Series, No. 178* (New York: American Management Association, 1955), pp. 32-51; and D. Katz and R. Kahn, "Human Organization and Worker Motivation," in L. Reed Tripp (ed.), *Industrial Productivity* (Madison: Industrial Relations Research Association, 1952), p. 146.

[3] R. Likert, "Developing Patterns of Management: II," *General Management Series, No. 182* (New York: American Management Association, 1956), pp. 3-29.

managers will be encouraged to make a favorable showing on those factors alone.

Management & productivity

Let us examine the evidence for these statements. A central concept of the modified theory is (1) that the pattern of interaction between the manager and those with whom he deals should always be such that the individuals involved will feel that the manager is dealing with them in a supportive rather than a threatening manner. A related concept is (2) that management will make full use of the potential capacities of its human resources only when each person in an organization is a member of a well-knit and effectively functioning work group with high interaction skills and performance goals.

A test of these concepts, and thereby of the modified theory, was made recently using attitudinal and motivational data collected in 1955 in a study done by the Institute for Social Research, University of Michigan:

> Data are from a company that operates nationally. The company comprises 32 geographically separated units, varying in size from about 15 to over 50 employees, which perform essentially the same operations, and for which extensive productivity and cost figures are available continuously.
>
> A single score was computed for the manager in charge of each of the 32 units. These scores, based on seven questions in the managers' questionnaire, measure the manager's attitude on the two concepts which represent the modified theory. These two concepts were found to be highly related, and consequently have been handled in the analysis as a single combined score—labeled, for convenient reference, *attitude toward men*. The results obtained are shown in Exhibit I.

This study demonstrates clearly that those managers who, as revealed in their questionnaires, have a favorable *attitude toward men* score achieve significantly higher performance than those managers who have an unfavorable score. Managers who have a supportive attitude toward their men and endeavor to build them into well-knit teams obtain appreciably higher productivity than managers who have a threatening attitude and rely more on man-to-man patterns of supervision. (The correlation coefficient is 0.64.)

Information obtained from the nonsupervisory employees under these managers confirms the supervisory pattern reported by the managers. The material from the employees also confirms the character of the important intervening human variables contributing to

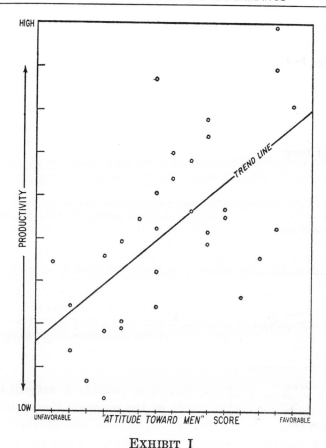

EXHIBIT I

RELATIONSHIP OF *ATTITUDE TOWARD MEN* SCORE OF MANAGER TO UNIT'S PRODUCTIVITY

the better productivity of the high-performance units. The men in those units in which the manager has an above-average *attitude toward men* score differ in their descriptions of their supervision and experience from the men in units whose managers are below average in their *attitude toward men* score. More specifically, the men in units whose managers had a favorable *attitude toward men* score are more likely than the men in the other units to indicate that:

1. The supervision of their unit is of a supportive character. This involves such supervisory behavior as being more interested in the men, friendlier, more willing to go to bat for them, and being less threatening, less punitive, less critical, and less strict (but still having high performance expectations).
2. There is more team spirit, group loyalty, and teamwork among the men and between the men and management.

3. The men have more confidence and trust in management and have higher motivation. Moreover, there is better communication between the men and management.
4. The men work under less sense of pressure, feel much freer to set their own work pace, and yet produce more.

The findings from this study are consistent with the results obtained in a number of other studies in widely different industries.[4] These other studies have also yielded evidence showing important differences in the way the managers of high- and low-producing units conceive of their job and deal with their subordinates:

1. The units achieving the best performance are much more likely than the poor performance units to have managers who deal with their subordinates in a supportive manner and build high group loyalty and teamwork.
2. The poor performance units are much more likely than the best units to have managers who press for production and treat their subordinates as "cogs in a machine."
3. The supportive managers tend to supervise by establishing goals and objectives for their subordinates; in contrast, the pressure-oriented managers tend to focus on the processes they want their employees to carry out in order to achieve the objectives of the manager.

Dangers of pressure

These research findings, therefore, provide a pattern of results which confirms central concepts of the modified theory of management. These results demonstrate that, on the average, *pressure-oriented, threatening, punitive management yields lower productivity, higher costs, increased absence, and less employee satisfaction than supportive employee-centered management which uses group methods of supervision coupled with high-performance expectations.*

Since the supportive pattern of supervision tends to yield the best results, clearly this is the pattern which boards of directors and top company officials should foster in all situations including those that involve decentralization and delegation. Company officers believe, no doubt, that they are achieving this pattern of management in their operations. But, unfortunately, the performance measurements now being used by most top managements put pressures on lower levels of management to behave otherwise.

---

[4] R. Kahn, "The Prediction of Productivity," *Journal of Social Issues*, Vol. 12, No. 2 (1956), p. 41; D. Katz, N. Maccoby, G. Gurin, and L. G. Floor, "Productivity, Supervision and Morale among Railroad Workers," *SRC Monograph Series No. 5* (Ann Arbor: Institute for Social Research, 1951); D. Katz, N. Maccoby, and N. Morse, "Productivity, Supervision and Morale in an Office Situation, *SRC Monograph Series No. 2* (Ann Arbor: Institute for Social Research, 1950); and R. Likert, "Motivation: The Core of Management," *Personnel Series A155* (New York: American Management Association, 1953), pp. 3-21.

What often confuses the situation is that pressure-oriented, threatening supervision can achieve impressive *short-run* results, particularly when coupled with high technical competence. There is clear-cut evidence that for a period of at least one year supervision which increases the direct pressure for productivity can achieve significant increases in production. However, such increases are obtained only at a substantial and serious cost to the organization.

TESTING PERFORMANCE

To what extent can a manager make an impressive earnings record over a short-run period of one to three years by exploiting the company's investment in the human organization in his plant or department? To what extent will the quality of his organization suffer if he does so?

Contrasting programs

On this further question, we also have some concrete evidence from an important study conducted by the Institute for Social Research in a large multidivision corporation:

The study covered 500 clerical employees in four parallel divisions. Each division was organized in the same way, used the same technology, did exactly the same kind of work, and had employees of comparable aptitudes.

Productivity in all four of the divisions depended on the number of clerks involved. The work was something like a billing operation; there was just so much of it, but it had to be processed as it came along. Consequently, the only way in which productivity could be increased under the existing organization was to change the size of the work group.

The four divisions were assigned to two experimental programs on a random basis. Each program was assigned at random a division that had been historically high in productivity and a division that had been below average in productivity. No attempt was made to place a division in that program which would best fit its habitual methods of supervision used by the manager, assistant managers, supervisors, and assistant supervisors.

The experiment at the clerical level lasted for one year. Beforehand, several months were devoted to planning, and there was also a training period of approximately six months. Productivity was measured continuously and computed weekly throughout the year.

Employee and supervisory attitudes and related variables were measured just before and after the period.

Turning now to the heart of the study, in two divisions an attempt was made to change the supervision so that the decision levels were pushed *down*. More *general* supervision of the clerks and their supervisors was introduced. In addition, the managers, assistant managers, supervisors, and assistant supervisors of these two divisions were trained in group methods of leadership, which they endeavored to use as much as their skill would permit during the experimental year. (To this end we made liberal use of methods developed by the National Training Laboratory in Group Development.) For easy reference, the experimental changes in these two divisions will be labeled the "participative program."

In the other two divisions, by contrast, the program called for modifying the supervision so as to increase the closeness of supervision and move the decision levels *upward*. This will be labeled the "hierarchically controlled program." These changes were accomplished by a further extension of the scientific management approach. For example, one of the major changes made was to have the jobs timed by the methods department and to have standard times computed. This showed that these divisions were overstaffed by about 30%. The general manager then ordered the managers of these two divisions to cut staff by 25%. This was to be done by transfers without replacing the persons who left; no one was to be dismissed.

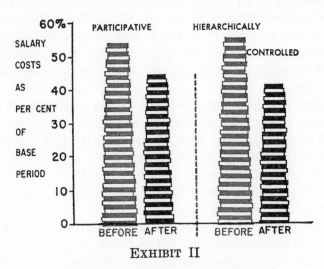

EXHIBIT II

CHANGES IN PRODUCTIVITY

As a check on how effectively these policies were carried out, measurements were obtained for each division as to where decisions were made. One set of these measurements was obtained before the experimental year started, and the second set was obtained after the completion of the year. The attempts to change the level at which decisions were made were successful enough to develop measurable differences. In the hierarchically controlled program a significant shift upward occurred; by contrast, a significant shift downward occurred in the levels at which decisions were made in the participative program. Also, in the participative program there was an increase in the use of participation and in the extent to which employees were involved in decisions affecting them.

Changes in productivity

Exhibit II shows the changes in salary costs per unit of work, which reflect the changes in productivity that occurred in the divisions. As will be observed, the hierarchically controlled program increased productivity by about 25%. This was a result of the direct orders from the general manager to reduce staff by that amount. Direct pressure produced a substantial increase in production.

A significant increase in productivity of 20% was also achieved in the participative program, but this was not so great an increase as in the hierarchically controlled program. To bring about this improvement, the clerks themselves participated in the decision to reduce the size of the work group. (They were aware, of course, that productivity increases were sought by management in making these experiments.) Obviously, deciding to reduce the size of a work group by eliminating some of its members is probably one of the most difficult decisions for a work group to make. Yet the clerks made it. In fact, one division in the participative program increased its productivity by about the same amount as each of the two divisions in the hierarchically controlled program. The other participative division, which historically had been the poorest of all of the divisions, did not do so well and increased productivity by only about 15%.

Changes in attitudes

Although both programs had similar effects on productivity, they had significantly different results in other respects. The productivity increases in the hierarchically controlled program were accomplished by shifts in an *adverse* direction in such factors as loyalty, attitudes, interest, and involvement in the work. But just the opposite was true in the participative program.

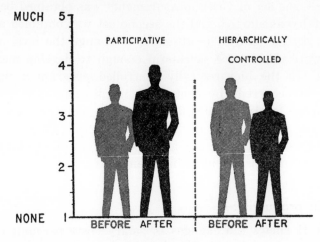

EXHIBIT III

EMPLOYEES' FEELING OF RESPONSIBILITY TO SEE
THAT WORK GETS DONE

For example, Exhibit III shows that when more general supervision and increased participation were provided, the employees' feeling of responsibility to see that the work got done increased. Again, when the supervisor was away, they kept on working. In the hierarchically controlled program, however, the feeling of responsibility decreased, and when the supervisor was absent, the work tended to stop.

Another measurement of the extent to which an employee feels involved in his work is his attitude toward workers who are high producers. The changes in attitudes toward the high producer by the employees in the two programs are shown in Exhibit IV. Here again there was a statistically significant shift in opposite directions. In the participative program the attitudes became more favorable, and there was less pressure to restrict production. In the hierarchically controlled program the opposite effect occurred.

In industrial organizations that are effective in achieving their objectives, extensive research in a variety of organizations shows that superiors and subordinates are linked by loyalty, a mutual feeling of understanding and closeness, and a feeling that influence and communication (both upward and downward) function well.[5] How

───────────
⁵ R. Kahn, F. Mann, and S. Seashore (eds.), "Human Relations Research in

are these attitudes and feelings achieved? Our study of the four divisions throws some light on the answer.

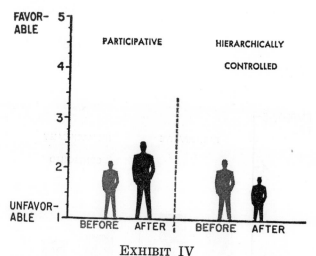

EXHIBIT IV

EMPLOYEE ATTITUDES TOWARD HIGH PRODUCER

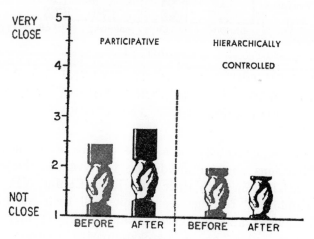

EXHIBIT V

HOW CLOSE MANAGER AND ASSISTANT MANAGER
WERE FELT TO BE TO EMPLOYEES

As Exhibit V shows, the employees in the participative program at the end of the year felt that their manager and assistant manager were "closer to them" than at the beginning of the year. The opposite was true in the hierarchically controlled program. Moreover, as Exhibit VI shows, employees in the participative program felt that their superiors were more likely to "pull" for them, or for the company *and* them, and not be solely interested in the company; while in the hierarchically controlled program, the opposite trend occurred.

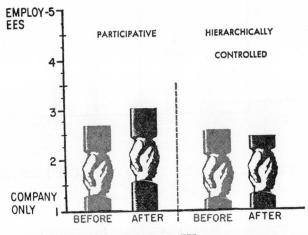

EXHIBIT VI

EMPLOYEE OPINIONS AS TO EXTENT TO WHICH SUPERIORS "PULLED" FOR COMPANY ONLY OR FOR EMPLOYEES AND COMPANY

As might be expected from these trends, a marked shift in opposite directions showed up during the year in the employees' feeling of satisfaction with their superiors. Exhibit VII shows the shifts in employees' feelings as to how well their superiors communicated upward and influenced management on matters which concerned them. Once again the participative program showed up better than the hierarchically controlled program. One significant aspect of the changes in attitude in the hierarchically controlled program was that the employees felt that their superiors were relying more at the end of the year on rank and authority to get the work done than was the case at the beginning of the year. "Pulling rank" tends to become self-defeating in the long run because of the hostilities and counterpressures it evokes.

The deterioration under the hierarchially controlled program showed up in several other ways. For instance, turnover increased.

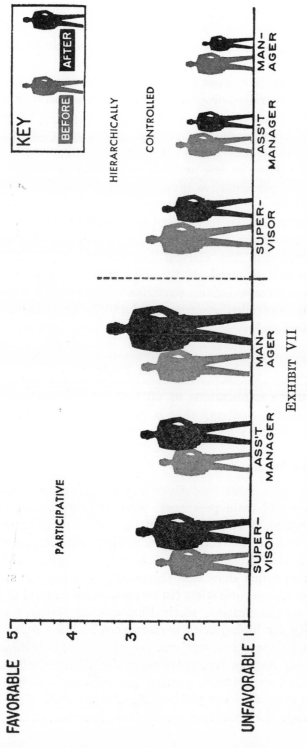

EXHIBIT VII

EMPLOYEES' SATISFACTION WITH SUPERIORS AS REPRESENTATIVES

Employees began to quit because of what they felt to be excessive pressure for production. As a consequence, the company felt it desirable to lessen the pressure. This happened toward the end of the experimental year.

Unfortunately, it was not possible to conduct the participative and hierarchically controlled programs for more than one year because of changes in the over-all operations of the company. However, the significant trends in opposite directions which occurred in these two programs are the trends which would be expected in the light of the studies cited earlier in the article. The attitudes which improved the most in the participative program and deteriorated the most in the hierarchically controlled program are those which these studies have consistently shown to be most closely related *in the long run* to employee motivation and productivity. This gives us every reason to believe that had the clerical experiment been continued for another year or two, productivity and quality of work would have continued to increase in the participative program, while in the hierarchically controlled program productivity and quality of work would have declined.

IMPLICATIONS FOR POLICY

What are the implications of all this for management policy—particularly in the company that is decentralizing its operations or otherwise delegating a good deal of authority to various managers?

Treatment of human assets

To begin with, most executives will readily agree that it costs money to hire and train personnel. And, after personnel have been hired and trained, it takes additional time and money to build them into a loyal, well-knit, effectively functioning organization with well-established goals. Most businessmen will also agree with the research findings which show that the more supportive the supervision and the better the organization (in terms of loyalty, level of performance goals, communication, motivation, and so forth), the greater is its capacity for high-quality performance at low cost.

If we make these assumptions, we can come, I believe, to only one conclusion. As was demonstrated in the hierarchically controlled program of the experiment, putting pressure on a well-established organization to produce can yield substantial and immediate increases in productivity. *This increase is obtained, however, at a cost to the human assets of the organization.* In the company we studied, for example, the cost was clear: hostilities increased, there was greater reliance upon authority, loyalties declined, and motivations to produce decreased while motivations to restrict production increased. In other words, the quality of the human organization deteriorated as a functioning social system.

If the company had had an accounting procedure which showed the investment in the human organization, it would have shown that in the two divisions in the hierarchically controlled program the value of the human organization was less at the end of the experimental year than at the beginning. In other words, some of the increased productivity was achieved actually by liquidating part of the investment which the company had in the human organization in these divisions. The increase in productivity should have been charged with this cost.

On the other hand, had the company's accounting records reflected the value of the company's investment in the human organization in the two divisions in the participative program, they would have shown an opposite picture. During the year, the value of this investment increased. The management of the two divisions had been of such a character as to increase the productive capacity of the organization as a functioning social system: loyalties had increased, hostilities had decreased, communication was improved, decisions were better since they were based on more accurate and adequate information, and production goals and motivations to produce were increasing.

While a company's investment in its human organization is less tangible than the investment in plant and equipment, and therefore has not yet been given the kind of evaluation an accountant would give it, *it can be measured approximately with the methods now available.* These methods can enable management to size up present trends, analyze their relationships, and guide company operations accordingly.

Quantitative controls

Companies are very careful not to let managers of decentralized plants show spurious profits and earnings by juggling inventory or by failing to maintain plant and equipment. Their accounting procedures measure and report regularly on inventory and condition of plant and equipment. "Earnings" achieved by liquidating the assets represented in the human organization are just as spurious as though achieved by liquidating the investment in plant. Yet they are encouraged by compensation formulas that urge managers to press unduly for immediate production, cost reduction, and similar goals; by the present-day emphasis on measuring only the end results of the activities of the lower echelons or of decentralized operations; and by job evaluations focused on the immediate contribution to earnings and profits.

In the long run, of course, such measurements are valid. The executive who "milks the human franchise" today will not be in a position to show good profit-and-loss figures tomorrow. The catch is that, by the time the symptoms of trouble are clear, the human organization has deteriorated to a point where steps to correct it are difficult and costly. As a practical matter, moreover, there is often so much rotation in executive responsibilities, and so much change in the conditions of business, that short-run tests which will provide adequate measures of current performance, including trends in the human organization, are worth much more than long-run evaluations.

There is only one solution to this problem, and it does not yet lie in more precise accounting data. The solution is to obtain adequate periodic measurements of the character and the quality of the human organization. Judgment alone is notoriously inaccurate and tends to be most inaccurate in those situations which are unsatisfactory or deteriorating. Measurements and compensation formulas are needed which will penalize managers financially and otherwise when they permit the quality of the human organization under them to deteriorate, and reward them when they improve the quality of this organization.

Identically the same point can be made with regard to consumer attitudes, good will, and confidence in the company, in its products, and in its service. A manager of a decentralized operation can substantially increase current earnings by reducing the product quality with low-cost, shoddy output. However, the immediate earnings shown on the company books would be spurious and would actually represent a substantial liquidation of the investment made in developing consumer confidence and acceptance. Therefore, periodic measurements of consumer perceptions, attitudes, and acceptance should be made not only for the usual purposes, such as to provide direction in product development and to guide advertising and marketing, but also to protect the company's investment in consumer good will.

Adequate appraisals

It is not sufficient merely to measure morale and the attitudes of employees toward the organization, their supervision, and their work. Favorable attitudes and excellent morale do not necessarily assure high motivation, high performance, and an effective human organization. A good deal of research indicates that this relationship is much too simple. Favorable attitudes may be found, for example, in situations where there is complacency and general contentment but where production goals are low and there is little motivation to achieve high performance.

Similarly, measurements of behavior which reflect the past condition of the human organization, while useful, are also inadequate for current appraisals. Such measurements as absence, turnover, and scrap loss tend not only to be insensitive measurements but also to reflect changes in the human organization *after* they have become substantial. More sensitive and more current measurements than those are needed.

Progress in the social sciences in recent years enables any company which so desires to obtain measurements needed for adequate appraisals of the quality and performance capacity of its human organization. Instruments to measure many of the important variables are now available; for those variables for which measuring instruments are not now available, the basic methodology now exists to develop the necessary tools. The organization for which these measurements are obtained can be an entire corporation or any of its divisions.

The following illustrate the kinds of variables which are now being measured in some companies or for which satisfactory measuring instruments can be developed:

1. Extent of loyalty to and identification with the institution and its objectives.
2. Extent to which members of the organization at all hierarchical levels feel that the organization's goals are consistent with their own needs and goals, and that the achievement of the company's goals will help them achieve their own.
3. Extent to which the goals of units and of individuals are of a character to enable the organization to achieve its objectives.
4. Level of motivation among members of the organization with regard to such variables as:

   a. Performance, including both quality and quantity of work done;
   b. Concern for elimination of waste and reduction of costs;
   c. Concern for improving product;
   d. Concern for improving processes.

5. Degree of confidence and trust among members of the organization in each other and in the different hierarchical levels.
6. Amount and quality of teamwork in each unit of the organization and between units.
7. Extent to which people feel delegation is being effectively achieved.
8. Extent to which members feel that their ideas, information, knowledge of processes, and experience are being used in the decision-making processes of the organization.
9. Level of competence and skill of different groups in the organization to interact effectively in solving problems and other tasks.
10. Efficiency and adequacy of the communication process upward, downward, sidewise.
11. Level of the leadership skills and abilities of supervisors and managers, including their basic philosophy of management and orientation toward the processes of leadership.
12. Aptitude scores of the members of the organization. If aptitude scores are obtained as people join the organization, then trends in these scores will show whether the current management is improving the basic quality of the personnel through its hiring practices or is letting quality deteriorate through unfavorable turnover.

Job for experts

The measurement of these variables is a complex process and requires a high level of scientific competence. It cannot be done by an untrained person, no matter how intelligent he is. Nor can it be done simply by asking people questions that have not been pretested or by handing them a ready-made questionnaire. Few companies trust cost figures obtained by inexperienced personnel. It is equally dangerous to trust the untrained to obtain measurements of the state of a human organization.

CONCLUSION

Industry needs more adequate measures of organizational performance than it is now getting. Progress in the social sciences now makes these measurements possible. As a consequence, new resources are available to assist company presidents in their responsibility for the successful management of their companies.

The president's responsibility requires that he build an organization whose structure, goals, levels of loyalty, motivation, interaction skills, and competence are such that the organization achieves its objectives effectively. As tools to assist him and the other members of management, a president needs a constant flow of measurements reporting on the state of the organization and the performance being achieved. The measurements proposed here would provide a president with data which he needs to fill the current serious gap in the information coming to him and to his organization.

QUESTIONS

1. What are the principal variables for measuring organization performance as set forth by Likert?
2. Is he for or against formal organizational controls? What are some of the human problems they present?
3. What factors are presented in this article as being related to high employee productivity? Do you agree with his analysis of these factors?
4. How would you compare Likert's major arguments with the material presented on motivation in Part IV?
5. If you were a practicing manager, what would be the three most important ideas you have picked up from reading and studying this article?

27. MANAGEMENT CONTROLS AND ORGANIZATIONAL PERFORMANCE *

John Leslie Livingstone

Inevitably there are conflicts between the motives of individuals and the demands of the organization. Organization implies some subordination of individual objectives to those of the group. Processes tending to constrain idiosyncratic behavior and to promote conformity with organizational norms are "controls." This usage is very broad, as it includes *incentives* under the classification of controls. However, incentives are often linked with controls—for instance, rewards for exceeding budgeted sales quotas. Therefore, we have explicitly recognized this interdependence by regarding controls broadly as reward-punishment processes aimed at ensuring that members of the organization do work toward its goals.

Individuals in their work are likely to seek ways of fulfilling their personal needs, very possibly at the expense of formal objectives. This tendency is countered, among other things, by budgets, standards, quotas, internal audit, etc. Generically these instruments are usually referred to as "management controls." In this paper I shall examine the impact of management controls on organizational performance.

How do management controls control?

Management controls, in the form of standards or budgets, are simply quantified statements of management's goals. As Stedry observes, "The setting of the standard is not sufficient of itself to assure or even invite compliance. The problem of directing activity toward a goal is one of 'motivation' . . . a goal, even if externally imposed, must receive . . . internal recognition . . . to be at all effective." [1] This statement has important implications.

The setting of standards requires measurements to be made. In the environment of the organization, however, measurement takes on special characteristics. Using Drucker's example: [2] when we measure

* From *Personnel Administration*, Vol. 28, No. 1 (January-February, 1965), pp. 37-43. Reprinted with permission.
[1] A. C. Stedry, *Budget Control and Cost Behavior* (Englewood Cliffs, N. J.: Prentice-Hall, 1960), p. 12.
[2] P. F. Drucker, "Controls, Control and Management" (Papers from Seminar on Basic Research in Management Controls, Graduate School of Business, Stanford University, February 20, 21, and 22, 1963), p. 3.

the rate of fall of a stone, we are outside the event itself. By measuring we do not change the event, and it does not change us. Therefore measuring is *neutral*. Furthermore, measurements are not likely to vary significantly with different observers—because accurate physical measuring instruments may be used and because there is little probability that different observers would have different perceptions of the event. Therefore measuring is *objective*.

Unlike physical measurement, the measurement of organizational performance is not independent of the events, the persons being evaluated and the observers. It is not neutral. It is subjective and necessarily biased. Management controls are ". . . goal-setting and value-setting . . . They endow events not only with meaning, but with value." [3]

Therefore, in asking how management controls control, we have to consider not only organizational goals and individual goals, but also the interactions between these sets of goals and the values perceived in the management control system itself. Haire gives an example of this interaction:

> Bank managers often complain that their tellers lack zeal in building customers good will. When a customer approaches, the teller has an air of regretfully interrupting his important work to serve the customer. The customer may even be kept waiting while the teller continues to add his column of figures, concerned that the customer will throw his figures out of balance by making a transaction.[4]

Why should this sort of thing happen? Perhaps management has trained the tellers to act just this way. The teller may have been rewarded in the past only for conscientious balancing of his books, and been punished only for failing to balance. Probably he has never had reward or punishment for his handling of customers.

Because control is such an important feature of banking, bank management may have slid involuntarily into a policy they would not deliberately adopt: balancing the books is all that matters. They never decided to train tellers this way. But the silent emphasis on control has had the effect of a training policy.

The management control process has frequently been identified with servomechanisms,[5] feedback circuits,[6] feedback,[7] and feedback

---

[3] *Ibid.*, p. 4.

[4] M. Haire, *Psychology in Management* (New York: McGraw-Hill, 1956), pp. 16-17.

[5] C. J. Haberstroh, "Goals, Programs and the Training Function" (Papers from Seminar on Basic Research in Management Controls, Graduate School of Business, Stanford University, February 20, 21 and 22, 1963).

[6] L. Petrullo and B. M. Bass (editors), *Leadership and Inter-Personal Behavior* (New York: Holt, Rinehart & Winston, 1961), p. 14.

[7] W. T. Jerome, *Executive Control—The Catalyst* (New York: John Wiley & Son, 1961), p. 26.

response.[8] This analogy is useful in stressing the importance and worth of feedback. But it is easy, with only a little stretch of the imagination, to assume that the management control system is an *efficient* servomechanism for keeping key variables "in control."

Servomechanisms, however, are sophisticated engineering systems with programmed response patterns. Due to the complex human dynamics of organizational behavior and to the ". . . deficiencies in the available methods of (financial) measurement" [9] this is not true of management control systems—as the example quoted from Haire illustrated.

Management controls and employees

Argyris contends that management controls tend to take away from workers their planning of the work and participation in important decisions affecting them. This loss of control tends to cause employees to feel psychological failure. People experiencing failure may reduce their work aspirations much below their capability, leading to increased failure.[10]

> The data suggest that the supervisors dislike budgets of all types because (1) they tend to report only results, not reasons; (2) they emphasize the past and not the present; (3) they are rigid; (4) they apply pressure for an ever-changing goal; (5) they tend to create failure for the supervisor. . . .
> As a result of the pressure, tension, and general mistrust of management controls, employees tend to unite *against* management. Psychological research shows that people can stand only a certain amount of pressure and tension. . . . In short, new cohesive groups developed to *combat* management pressure.[11]
> . . . management diagnoses the employees to be at fault for high turnover; high absence rates; low productivity, apathy, disinterest. . . . They conclude that stronger dynamic leadership, management controls, and 'human relations' are the answers. Our analysis suggests that instead of ameliorating the basic causes, these three practices tend to reinforce the problems caused by the organization, thus increasing the very behavior these practices were supposed to decrease.[12]

Argyris has been criticized for assuming that man must be in conflict with the organization.[13] Yet most of his critics do not deny

---

[8] G. Shillinglaw, "Division Performance Review: An Extension of Budgetary Control" (Papers from Seminar on Basic Research in Management Controls, Graduate School of Business, Stanford University, February 20, 21 and 22, 1963), p. 4.

[9] *Ibid.*, p 6.

[10] C. Argyris, *Personality and Organization* (New York: Harper and Brothers, 1957), pp. 132-34.

[11] *Ibid.*, p. 137.

[12] *Ibid.*, p. 162.

[13] J. M. Pfiffner and F. P. Sherwood, *Administrative Organization* (Englewood Cliffs, N. J.; Prentice-Hall, 1960), pp. 434-35.

the widespread existence of this conflict—rather they ascribe much of it to social attitudes and beliefs. It would, therefore, be dangerous to conclude that management's use of controls is necessarily as deleterious to employee needs as Argyris concludes. It would, however, be no less dangerous to dismiss his conclusions lightly, for many agree with him—Robert K. Merton and C. Wright Mills, to name but two.[14]

Management controls and managers

The evaluation and compensation of managers is frequently based on production oriented accounting measurements. Successful performance, so measured, usually leads to transfers and promotion. Therefore many managers recognize that

> . . . they can get increased performance and earnings by direct, threatening pressure on their subordinates and their organization . . . such pressure is apt to lead to undesirable turnover . . . and to other forms of organizational deterioration . . . If (a manager's) experience shows that the odds are against his staying in his present job for more than two or three years, he is apt to appreciate that he will probably not be adversely affected by any of the resentments, hostilities, and turnover he creates through hierarchical pressure. . . . Ironically, these managers often achieve a reputation with their top management of being outstandingly able . . . and . . . are not only permitted to dissipate company assets but are rewarded for doing so.[15]

Likert suggests that the remedy is to make periodic approximations of employee attitudes and other human variables. Argyris, however, is very skeptical of the validity of such criteria for organizational well being. What may really be happening, despite the sanguine indices of attitudes, is that employees have simply grown apathetic, devitalized and alienated. Their aspirations fall so low that they accept mediocre performance and resist change.[16]

Individual adjustment to management controls

Research has sought to discover individual predispositions to varying patterns of control. Findings suggest that individual reactions to control patterns tend to differ according to personality. Tannenbaum reviews several studies.[17] Two of these dealt with

---

[14] *Ibid.*, p. 433.
[15] R. Likert, *New Patterns of Management* (New York: McGraw-Hill, 1961), pp. 75-76.
[16] Pfiffner and Sherwood, *op. cit.*, pp. 420-21.
[17] A. S. Tannenbaum, "Control in Organizations: Individual Adjustment and Organizational Performance" (Papers from Seminar on Basic Research in Man-

individual employees' reactions towards a shift to less authoritarian, more participative work organization. Most employees reacted favorably. A few, however, did not—largely those whose personalities were not suited to the new type of authority relations introduced. They preferred to be submissive, dependent and directed. Workers who judged their supervisors to employ participative methods were generally higher in productivity than the remaining workers *providing* subordinates had low scores on measures of authoritarianism.

Despite the existence of different individual preferences for types of authority relations, employees generally felt they had too little control, rather than too much, in their work. They felt they did not, as a group, have as much control as they should, although they did not believe that workers should exercise more control than management. In reply to the same questions, supervisory groups unanimously agreed that workers should not exercise more control than they presently did.

Tannenbaum notes that, whatever the reasons, power is desired. Power can urge the individual toward a greater and greater share of the work load of the organization. Added dimensions of his personality came into play, increasing his effort. He gives more of himself to his work, and is probably more identified, more loyal and more active on behalf of the organization.[18]

However, greater work satisfaction may also be accompanied by greater personal frustration. The responsibility for making big decisions creates strong personal identification with the success or otherwise of the results. This intense personal involvement may be gratifying, perhaps elating, but can also be extremely anxiety-producing. Tannenbaum quotes studies where clerks given increased responsibility, felt greater work satisfaction but less sense of accomplishment; and workers in a newly automated plant, with heightened responsibility and control due to automation, felt generally improved morale but found that their new work made them feel "jumpy" and tense (despite slightly reduced accident danger in the new plant). Some evidence suggests that individuals in positions of control and responsibility also tend to have an above-average incidence of psychosomatic illnesses.[19]

---

agement Controls, Graduate School of Business, Stanford University, February 20, 21 and 22, 1963), pp. 6n.
   [18] *Ibid.*, p. 9.
   [19] *Ibid.*, p. 12.

Control as a zero-sum game

If the total amount of control exercised in an organization were fixed in quantity, increments in the influence of certain individuals and groups would lead to decrements in the power of others. There is, however, strong reason for believing that the "influence pie" need not have constant dimensions. A *laissez faire* leader, exercising little control, may be indifferent to his subordinates' wishes. There is not much influence either way, and the total amount of control is relatively small.

> . . . as seen by them and as seen by the men, the managers in the high-producing departments have much more influence than do the managers in the low-producing departments. The 'influence pie' is seen as being bigger in the high-performing departments than in the low. . . . Evidently, the manager's leadership methods and skills, including the extent to which he builds his men into a well-knit loyal group with efficient communication, as well as the capacity to *exert influence upward*, affect the amount of authority the manager really has. . . . this better management system, while giving the men more influence, also gives the high-producing managers more influence. The high-producing managers have actually increased the size of the "influence pie' by means of the leadership processes which they use.[20] (Italics added).

In Likert's terms, a more substantial "interaction-influence" system increases the total amount of control, with benefit to all members of the organization. These findings are not isolated. They are corroborated by similar studies in several different types of organization.[21] However, Likert is careful to point out that the research findings do *not* suggest that *every* organization in which there are high degrees of confidence and trust and favorable attitudes will be highly efficient. High performance goals as well as favorable attitudes are needed if an organization is to achieve high productivity.[22] Also, of course, supervisors' attitudes are critical. Unless supervisors are genuinely interested in subordinates' ideas and prepared to act on them, any pretended use of participative devices is likely to be futile.

Management controls and managers' aspirations

Stedry has investigated interactions between self-performance aspirations, budget administration and actual achievement. His experiments showed that where subjects know that goal attainment will be

---

[20] Likert, *op. cit.*, p. 58.
[21] Tannenbaum, *op. cit.*, p. 17.
[22] Likert, *op. cit.*, p. 59.

rewarded and nonattainment penalized, performance is significantly affected by the way in which task aspiration levels are determined and the demand of the budget ("high," "medium," "low" or "implicit," i.e., no budget imposed).

An "implicit" budget produced the best performance, followed respectively by "medium," "high" and "low" budgets. However, there was strong interaction between budgets and aspiration levels. The "high" budget group, who received their budgets prior to setting their aspiration levels, outperformed *any* other group. The "high" budget group, who set aspirations before receiving the budget, were outperformed by *all groups*.[23] Stedry admits [24] that only a short span of time was covered by the experiment, and he suggests that further research over an extended period is desirable.

Therefore, his findings are somewhat tentative in their relation to business organizations, especially as it is unlikely that situations will frequently be encountered where the setting of aspiration levels can be delayed until budgets have been received. In a continuing organization one would expect aspiration levels to be perpetually projected out over time, with budgets being introduced at regular intervals. This assumption limits speculation to groups forming aspirations before receiving budgets. In this category, "high" budgets result in lowest performance, "medium" and "implicit" budgets together come extremely close in achieving the best performance and "low" budgets produced performance approximately midway between best and worst. Stedry points out that the group which determines its aspiration level first, in the experimental situation, is closest to the solution proposed by MacGregor,[25] who suggests that the department head should plan the budget and then take it to his supervisor who will give him his budget based on his estimate.[26] This is in close accord with the suggestions of Argyris.[27]

Management controls and conflict

If any theme has consistently underlain our discussion, it is that of inevitability of *conflict*—conflict between the accuracy and the imprecision of control instruments; between short-run manager

---

[23] Stedry, *op. cit.*, pp. 80-90.
[24] *Ibid.*, p. 154.
[25] D. McGregor, "An Uneasy Look at Performance Appraisal," *Harvard Business Review*, May-June, 1957.
[26] Stedry, *op. cit.*, p. 9.
[27] C. Argyris, *The Impact of Budgets on People* (New York: Controllership Foundation, Inc., 1952), p. 28.

rewards and long-run organizational health; between individual needs and management pressure; between workers' and supervisors' perceptions of the amount of control respectively they should have; between work satisfaction from participation and the frustrations that accompany responsibility; between managers' performance aspirations and the unilateral issue of "high" budgets by their superiors.

Are management controls inexorably linked with conflict? Argyris would have it so. He believes that conflict may be lessened by the ". . . use of job and role enlargement, employee-centered and reality-centered leadership." But:

> Much more research needs to be done . . . the behavioral scientists have little to say on this subject and even less on how one may try to create a formal organization . . . which does not rely for part of its health on a basically antagonistic sub-system.[28]

Likert, too, stresses the ubiquity of conflict. He refers to the increased use of performance measurements and budgets, with the decisions on budgets often highly centralized, and believes that these developments are accompanied by feelings of increased hierarchical pressure and growing resentment against it.[29]

Against this background of greater imposition of controls, suggestions for more employee-centered, participative management may well be perceived by some managers as appeals for anarchy. Is management to abandon its prerogatives? Are decisions to be turned over to the workers?

This does injustice to participative management.

> Democratic leadership is not an absence of leadership . . . We know from experiments and field research that *laissez-faire* leadership creates more tension and anxiety than does *either* democratic or autocratic. Subordinates are frustrated from lack of leadership which in turn frustrates their need for clarity, sense of direction and accomplishment . . .
>
> Nor are we suggesting that democratic leadership is the answer. . . . 'democratic' leadership fulfills primarily the individual's needs. But this is not all of the organization. What is also needed is leadership that tries to fulfill the demands of the organization.[30]

If there are no pat answers to the perplexing problems of control and conflict, let us see what constructive part-answers may exist.

---

[28] Argyris, *Personality and Organization*, p. 232.
[29] Likert, *op cit.*, p. 84.
[30] Argyris, *Personality and Organization*, pp. 192-93.

The merits of measurement

Likert comments that research findings show that the relationships observed between productivity on the one hand and management principles and practices on the other hand, grow sharper as more accurate measurements of productivity are made. Productivity ratings appear to be least accurate when based only on the judgments of the superior, because the superior tends to base his judgment largely on his perception of how the supervisor manages his unit, rather than on actual output. "Superiors tend to rate favorably those supervisors whose pattern of supervision corresponds to the pattern which the superior feels should be used to obtain the best production. Thus, if a superior feels that job-centered supervision yields the best results, he will rate highest those supervisors who use this kind of supervision." [31]

Therefore, measurement plays a powerful part in reducing this perceptual miasma. Accuracy in measurement potentially leads to better decisions, based on better information, and greater motivation to implement these decisions. Likert quotes Mary Parker Follett, "My solution is to depersonalize the giving of orders, to unite all concerned in a study of the situation, to discover the *law of the situation* and obey that . . . One *person* should not give orders to another *person*, both should agree to take their orders from the situation . . . Of course we should exercise authority, but always the authority of the situation." [32] However blunt and imprecise the available measuring instruments may be, they are less personally biased than purely subjective opinions.

Under formal organization theory, all planning and central information is sent from the top of the organization downwards. Performance measurements travel upwards for evaluation. This is known as "feed-back." [33] Under the law of the situation, this flow is inadequate. Each work group should receive the measurements needed for it to see how well it is performing and to make intelligent decisions.

But however free and efficient the dissemination of information, this alone cannot result in depersonalizing its use. Controls may still be perceived as threatening if there are punitive managerial pressures for desired results. There are incentives, then, for the distortion of

---

[31] Likert., *op. cit.*, p. 13.
[32] H. C. Metcalf and L. Urwick, *Dynamic Administration, The Collected Papers of Mary Parker Follett* (New York: Harper, 1940), pp. 58-59.
[33] See Shillinglaw, *op. cit.*

data that are notorious—withholding of output, spending of over-generous budget allowances for fear of future cuts, fudging favorable performance results to prevent tighter budgets in subsequent periods, and so on.

Certainty and uncertainty

Budgets and standards tend to be deterministic. They express unequivocal performance criteria with aura of exactitude and rectitude. There is no attempt to measure the standard error of the measurements themselves. This is in sharp contrast with the risk and uncertainty characteristic of the business environment. On the other hand, it fits strikingly well with certain authoritarian personality traits:

> Tends to think in rigid dichotomies. He thinks in 'black or white' terms.
> Tends to be more concrete in his thinking. Ambiguity threatens him. He sticks close to the everyday details of life.[34]

Accounting estimates are commonly referred to as "measurements." It is true that these "measurements" are often the best available information. But strictly they are not measurements at all, because they do not measure their own error. For instance, it is one thing to say that there is 90% confidence that output will be between 95 and 105 units a day. It is quite another to say that there is 30% confidence that output will be between 50 and 150 units a day. In both cases the accounting "measurement" is likely to be the mean of 100 units a day—but nothing is said about the reliability of the "measurement" itself, despite the significant difference in precision between the two cases.

It is also true, of course, that expected values and dispersion cannot be measured under uncertainty. Also, few managers would expect performance to be exactly equal to the budget or standard in practice. But the spurious air of precision in performance "measurement," and its appeal for the authoritarian mind, may readily cause management controls to be perceived by subordinates as directive, pressure-oriented and subjectively arbitrary. This is remote from the "law of the situation."

Supportive atmosphere

If managers, in using measurements, are sensitive to the randomness of performance measurement data and, therefore, expect

---

[34] Argyris, *Personality and Organization*, p. 217.

deviations to occur through chance as well as performance variations, perhaps their reactions to information may be less likely to lead to unilateral exercise of authority. Individuals could feel that information is used to help them, not harm them. Errors, instead of being simply *tolerated*, would be *expected*. The emphasis would be placed not so much on avoiding errors, but on quick recognition and correction. Managers willing to develop this leadership pattern should be able to do so. Whether basically authoritarian managers could— or should—be influenced in this direction is doubtful.

Measurements should be regarded as primarily for self guidance, for enabling workers to keep the processes for which they are responsible "in control"—in the statistical sense. The users of measurements should have a say in deciding what measurements should be used so that decisions can be made and implemented ". . . with cooperative motivation . . . the men are able through group processes to exercise influence on the decisions. Both managers and man, as a consequence, have more influence on what goes on, and there is greater coordinated effort and better performance." [35]

In short, the supportive and cooperative use of measurements and controls is simply an inseparable part of Likert's general "linking-pin," "interaction influence" system of organization.[36]

There are research findings sufficient to hypothesize on the nature of highly effective groups and to advance the suggestions we have made above. But, in going from theory to practice, the way is riddled with pitfalls. Some, such as different individual reactions to authority relations and the error of confusing democratic with *laissez-faire* leadership, we have mentioned. There are many others.

Also, it is not suggested that there is any "frictionless" or near-perfect organizational state. Conflicts will probably always be a *sine qua non* of organizations. Discontent is essential to progress. "Is growth and self-fulfillment possible . . . without pain and grief. . . ? If grief and pain are sometimes necessary for growth of the person, then we must learn not to protect people from them automatically as if they were always bad." [37]

The question, then, is not how to suppress conflict but rather how to use it constructively.

Effective organizations have extraordinary capacity to handle conflict. Their success is due to three very important characteristics:

[35] Likert, *op. cit.*, p. 180.
[36] *Ibid.*, Chapters 8, 11, and 12.
[37] A. H. Maslow, *Toward a Psychology of Being* (Princeton, N. J.: Van Nostrand, 1962), p. 8.

1. . . . They have an organizational structure which facilitates constructive interaction between individuals and work groups.
2. The personnel of the organization is skilled in the processes of effective interaction and mutual influence. . . .
3. There is a high confidence and trust among the members of the organization in each other, high loyalty to the work group and to the organization, and high motivation to achieve the organization's objectives. . . .[38]

These characteristics are not easily developed in an organization, although sometimes they may be present without full realization of the significance and unified philosophy they connote. Depersonalized performance measurements create forces to move toward development of these characteristics. Therefore, we conclude that the instruments of "management controls" are invaluable. But the emotional connotation and authoritarian flavor of "management controls" make the term—and the concepts it denotes—incongruent with democratic leadership.

QUESTIONS

1. What usefulness do formal controls provide for managers and management?
2. What are some of the problems of formal controls as presented by Argyris, etc.?
3. What is an "influence system"? What is its impact on a firm's control system?
4. What is the impact of formal controls on conflict and creativity in the firm?
5. What traditional management controls do you feel are necessary and indispensable to an organization? Which ones could possibly be eliminated? Why?

---

[38] Likert, *op. cit.*, p. 117.

28. A CRITIQUE OF SOME CURRENT IDEAS ABOUT ORGANIZATION *

Wilfred Brown

Much of the current teaching in the field of management is based on ideas which seem to be inconsistent with experience and perceptions which are available to practising managers. The first part of this paper attempts, briefly, to formulate these ideas; the rest of it is an examination and criticism.

I believe that everyone who is seriously concerned with organization accepts that, for personal fulfilment, a person has to be able to indulge in creative activity at work by being placed in a position where he is best able to make that optimum contribution to the work of an enterprise which his particular capacity makes possible. I want to criticize a whole spectrum of ideas which are advocated as a means of accomplishing the foregoing aim. It seems to include the following notions:

1. That we must have a degree of formal organization to co-ordinate the activity of the business. Nevertheless, if the resultant delineation of task and activity are regarded as limits to activity, then we clog up the whole organization. Unforeseen circumstances occur and if there are not many Admiral Nelsons about, vital decisions remain undone and the business will suffer. Therefore, organization must be regarded as something that sets up "soft" bounds to activity; guide lines to be crossed as necessary rather than rigid fences.
2. We must state "who is responsible for what" so that in the last analysis we can hold an individual responsible if things go wrong, but we must also recognize that there are such things as personal networks, group pressures and orders and that the interplay of these things with formal organization will, in fact, decide who does what.
3. That there is an informal organization inherent in every company upon which we are dependent if its work is to be accomplished. This informal organization stems from group culture and individual psychology and is not capable of being explicitly stated because it is always changing. If those involved have a sufficient general idea of the purpose of and a sufficient sense of participation and identification with the business, then all will be well; but if this is lacking, then the informal organization will fail to assist the company or will even drag it down.
4. That because each individual is different, any attempt to set up a series of roles, each with a given pattern of work embodied in it, is not viable because a match between role and individual characteristics is fortuitous. There is a gap which must be bridged if there is to be an integration between the organization and the individual.

* Reprinted from the *California Management Review*, Volume VI, No. 1, Fall, 1963. Copyright 1963 by The Regents of the University of California.

The attempt to fill this gap leads to concern with sensitivity training of managers so that they may become perceptive about social pressures which are affecting the behaviour of those around them; to the emergence of theories which seek to predict the effect of varying circumstances on the degree of identification of the individual with his work; and to the idea that individuals must have freedom to create roles for themselves which fit their personal psychological characteristics.

5. That many of those who now manage industry are socially blind to the boring lack of creativity in the way in which they organize work and that, therefore, one of the main purposes of management education is to breed insight into the dangers inherent in formal organization and the need to refrain from acts which tamper with the helpful underlying, unformulated organization which really gets the work done.

This thinking seems to be based on the inference that a series of compromises between the design of organization and the needs of the individual are required; that the object of organization is to serve the needs of the business and that these are inimicable to the needs of the individual. It deprives organization itself of the positive goal of so arranging matters as to make work itself the object of creative endeavour by people. I find myself unable to agree with the whole frame of reference.

Essential conditions

What are the essential conditions for creative activity? It is in this area that some of the main arguments lie. Consider the case of an emerging society. In one sense it can be regarded as a group of people in search of formal organization. A group trying to discover what type of social institutions it requires in order that some freedom for the individual from interference by others may be ensured and that the work which is necessary to sustain life is completely done. Sophisticated societies are able to describe the social institutions which they have built, with reasonable accuracy. Primitive societies, on the other hand, live in a greater or lesser degree of fantasy; their notions about the organization of their own society are characterized by mysticism and superstition. Their perception of the workings of these institutions is often at variance with the description that an independent observer would give.

Change is feared because its effects cannot be explicitly stated and understood until both the current and the future position have been identified and described with reasonable accuracy. Change, in a primitive situation, is based on intuition and is not under explicit intellectual control and its acceptance tends to be dependent on the character of the leader who proposes it rather than on its content. It becomes a matter of faith in leadership rather than objective assessment.

Power and freedom

In the primitive society, the individual often lies in constant fear of the personal power of the few whose dictates take the place of the laws; in the sophisticated society a higher degree of personal freedom is attained by setting bounds to the discretion of everybody through the building of social institutions, laws, etc.

Modern businesses are sophisticated about technical matters. They can describe, with a highly developed series of concepts and language, the processes which they use; but sociologically, they are still somewhat primitive. They do not see organization as a complex series of social mechanisms which require analysis and description. For example, the system of work roles, which is the central institution of a business, has not yet achieved a precise label. It is variously referred to as "the hierarchy," "the organization," "the organization chart," or simply as "the company." (In the interests of clarity I shall refer to this system of work roles which embraces all employees of a company from president to the rank and file members as "The Executive System.")

Managers and teachers of the subject often lack an explicit appreciation that this executive system is brought into being to perform the work of the company, that its structure must be a function of such work, that it must be capable of constant adaptation to match the changes in the work, and that the total work must be divided between all the roles in the Executive System. To what extent is this to be done with deliberation and in a stateable manner, and to what extent is it to be left to be decided by the pressure generated by group and individual interaction? The salient result of the latter process is that the people involved in the situation lack full and consistent knowledge of who does what. The assumption made by some is that this is a situation of liberty for the individual, but is it not more accurate to say that such a situation is one where the right to do certain types of work is decided by the competitive ambitions and power positions of the individuals concerned? Jones may well feel a need to carry a certain area of responsibility but, supposing that Smith equally feels that his needs can be met only by carrying that same responsibility, what then? If they are left to fight it out, that can scarcely be called a situation of freedom for either of them.

Group decision

Perhaps it may be argued that a decision on this matter would be arrived at by the culture of the group, that certain norms of behaviour are always established by groups, certain conventions come into play and that these would be the factors which would decide who did which job. Supposing, however, that this process produces decisions that are not consistent with the success of the business? Is there not then a strong danger that the group, being unaware of the total nature of the business, would be likely to arrive at decisions which would be inconsistent with its efficiency or survival?

This dilemma of thinking need not arise if we take more account of our perceptions of the nature of work. If we have a chain of command stretching down from the president of the company to its plant manager and, from him, to the superintendent and to the foreman, it is commonplace to hear people saying, of each of these roles, that they are "responsible for production." If we ask what particular part of the "responsibility for production" each role in the chain does, we are unlikely to get anything in the way of a concrete answer because business has not got an objective mode describing work.

One of the things that has emerged from our research project is such a mode of description. We have observed that the occupant of any role has to carry out certain prescribed tasks and must use his judgment within the boundaries set by policies to make specific types of decisions. Whatever the level or nature of work carried out by people, it involves the use of personal judgment.

Elliott Jaques has described this approach to the description of work, in a recent book.[1] His definition of employment work is as follows:

> *Employment Work* is the application of knowledge and the exercise of discretion within the limits prescribed by the immediate manager and by higher policies in order to carry out the activities allocated by the immediate manager, the whole carried out within an employment contract for a wage or salary.

In short, our current perception of organization can be described in the following terms:

1. A structure of roles derived from the nature of the work to be done.
2. A series of defined inter-relationships between all these roles.
3. A splitting up of the total work of the business between all the roles in this structure in terms of their prescribed and discretionary content.

[1] Elliott Jaques, *Equitable Payment* (New York and London: John Wiley & Sons, 1961).

4. Dynamic adaptation of the rule structure and the work content of the role in accordance with the change in the total work to be done.
5. Periodic survey by managers of changes in individual performance and changes in the work which they allocate to the roles subordinate to them.
6. Mobility of individuals from role to role so that when the level of their capacity and the level of work is not in balance, then a better fit can be achieved by a change to another role within limits of the work available.
7. Continuous endeavour by managers to maintain a balance between that portion of their work which they allocate to an individual subordinate and the capacity for work of that individual.

Just as people in our society need and bring into existence institutions and laws, so the needs of the individual in industry require the institutions I have listed above. In the absence of a clearly structured system of roles and definition of the work allocated to each of them, there is too little creative freedom for the individual because he works within a halo of uncertainty.

One of the most important modes by which a society advances toward a higher level of civilization lies in its capacity to set up institutions endowed with the authority to make, implement, and supervise the working of the law. This is one of the major means by which it has assured the freedom of the individual. It is not absence of law which allows creative use of discretion, but an explicit area of freedom bounded by the law which reduces anarchy and allows the individual to make his contribution to a society. A little reflection will surely enable each of us to see that we want a system of law, despite the fact that at times we find it irksome, first, because we desire to be protected from the effect of the unlimited decisions of our fellows and, secondly, because without limitations on our own freedom of decision, we must carry unlimited responsibility.

Thus, while agreeing that the individual needs freedom at work to use his creative imagination, I contest the idea that this is to be achieved by failing to formalize organization. I take a very different view based on different perceptions about the work situation. Creative freedom for the individual can be assured by building discretion into the role which he occupies. Soundly organized companies do that, though they do not always recognize what they have done. Whether they are recognized or not, these boundaries exist and can be discovered. If a company desires to establish role discretion within its organization that is consistent with work and with individual capacity, it must necessarily make these boundaries explicit.

People in industry contrast mental and manual work; skilled or unskilled work and responsible and routine jobs. These dichotomies indicate the existence of an active assumption that, in many of the roles at lower levels in the executive system, no responsibility exists for making decisions. An examination of even the simplest of jobs demonstrates that this assumption is not valid. I have never come across work done by a person which did not involve him in the use of discretion. (If such work could be discovered, then it would be extremely simply mechanized.) Those who doubt this statement might test it by meeting a person doing what they feel is a very low-level job and getting a description in detail. The setting up of a role from which all discretion is excluded postulates the ability to foresee in detail the nature of all the almost infinite variety of future situations that might arise and of being able to prescribe exactly what the occupant of the role should do in each.

Opportunity for judgment

The assumption that most low-level jobs give the individual too little opportunity for the use of judgment (and this assumption underlies a great deal of theorizing about management), is not consistent with our experience. The idea obstinately persists for several reasons:

1. In the absence of an objective mode of describing work it cannot be put to the test.

2. Failure to perceive that the level of capacity of people to do work, the level of work itself, and the level of pay are independent variables and that a sine qua non of optimal personal satisfaction is to get these three variables into reasonable equilibrium.

3. In the absence of this latter perception, we project ourselves into some role which contains low-level work, realize that it would be totally unsatisfactory to us, and make the emotional assumption that it must have the same effect on the person in the job.

One can, of course, have a dysfunctional form of organization where the amount of discretion allotted is lower than the potential of the individual who occupies the role or where too much of the discretion and responsibility is carried in the higher levels of the executive system and too little at the lower levels or where two individuals, in two different roles, are given a degree of responsibility for making decisions which are in conflict with each other. These, however, are examples of dysfunctional organization and indicate the use of bad discretion by the person who decided upon that form of organization.

Source of confusion

The constant reiteration by people in business that they ought to have more responsibility for making decisions than they, in fact, *feel* that they have, is another source of confusion. This leads some to the assumption that most people at work are given less responsibility than their level of capacity warrants. So long as there is no mode of objective definition of work, then there is no way of explicitly varying the amount of responsibility which an individual carries, in order to test its validity. Our experience, since we have been able to describe responsibility objectively, is that the majority of people abdicate from some part of their responsibility for making decisions. One of the methods of indulging in such abdication is for the person to seek a meeting with his manager and say: "I have a problem which I wish to discuss with you." His manager may say: "Make your own decision; I trust your judgment; it is part of your responsibility to come to such decisions." But the individual will say: "I prefer to discuss it with you."

At one stage our foremen, whilst carrying the responsibility for the work of machine operators subordinate to them, were denied the authority to reject candidates for vacant roles subordinate to them, or to decide which of their subordinates was the most able and should be paid the most, or to decide that a subordinate was not suitable for retention in his role. In short, our foremen were not given managerial authority. We became convinced that it was illogical to hold them responsible for the work of their subordinates without giving them such authority. This was, indeed, just what they had been seeking for years. When we took the step of giving this managerial authority, a high proportion abdicated from taking the new range of decisions which had become their own responsibility. We still find it difficult to fill these foremen roles with men who will accept the full responsibility for such decisions.

In the conditions of the postwar era, there has been a consistent hunt by most companies for managers capable of continuously making sound decisions about their own work without aid from their managers. This does not tie up with the picture of thousands of people who could carry more responsibility being denied it. The major problem, in Western society, is not one of widespread under-employed individual capacity, but of difficulty in discovering sufficient people with the necessary capacity to do the work available. I have little doubt that a hundred years ago there were vast numbers of people who were denied work of a sufficiently high level but the general rise in the size of companies, the sophistication of our techniques, and the complexity of our products has changed the situation. This is not being faced. Indeed, there are still many who proclaim that automation and mechanization produce routine jobs. In fact, as we know, these techniques take over from people not the complex jobs, but the simplest.

"Formalizing" organization

Some managers take up a very positive stance against "formalizing" organization. In a conversation such a manager informed me that there were no limits on the discretion of the managers who ran the many branches of his company. I suggested that what he meant was that they had not made the limits explicit, but this he denied. I demonstrated the validity of the point I had made by asking him a series of questions, which provided me with the following information:

1. The branch managers had discretion to spend up to £ 500. at a time on the repair of buildings and equipment, but none on new equipment.
2. Decisions about the purchases of merchandise were subject to separate financial limits for different types of stock and a total financial limit.
3. No staff beyond the current numbers employed could be engaged without head office sanction.
4. Staff had to be paid within a precise range of salary brackets established by head office.

Further questioning brought to light a most extensive array of policy covering all aspects of the work done. Managers carrying out their tasks, in fact, work within a range of policies, they set policies for their subordinates, they insist on the use of discretion by their subordinates, and yet they will deny not only the existence but the need for such a framework for getting work done.

We are, indeed, face to face with a peculiar phenomenon. An attempt to state in objective terms, perceptions which are available to all of us raises very deep anxiety. We share a desire that people doing the simpler jobs should be asked to carry responsibility consistent with their ability and yet many of us shy away from any attempt to state that responsibility in explicit terms. This is, indeed, ambivalence. It is almost the equivalent of saying: "Yes, they have responsibility. I want them to have it but not to know how much— keep the organization informal therefore."

Routine work

Perhaps deeply buried somewhere in the minds of many business managers lies a thought such as: "down at the lower levels of this business, people do routine work involving no judgment; in the middle levels and at the top we are happily freed from this depressing situation. We, at the higher levels, make such decisions as we see fit; there are no bounds to our use of discretion except our own common-sense and experience; do not, therefore, formalize organization."

Thus, the institution of a higher degree of formal organization is merely a sophisticated recognition of what already exists. The act of recognition, however, carries advantages with it. If one knows, in objective terms, the work content of roles, then it becomes possible to teach people what work they have to do. Once something is stateable, then it comes under intellectual control; it can be talked about or thought about in explicit terms. This leads to adaptability and makes the result of change more predictable. As long as it remains non-explicit, it cannot be thought about or discussed in objective terms and adaptation, which must rest on intuition, is rendered more difficult and more dangerous. Informal, non-explicit organization is felt to be necessary because it enhances adaptability; explicit or formal organization is rejected because it is felt to make for rigidity. Both of these statements are the converse of my business experience.

Explore roles

What I have said above might imply that the prescribed and discretionary content of every role should be explored and committed to paper; that every routine should be set out in all its detail in writing; that a record should be kept of every minute change of policy that took place in a company. We need a situation where every manager has an explicit knowledge, without necessarily recording it, of the tasks and of the prescribed and discretionary authority for their discharge which he has set up for each of his subordinates. These subordinates will then know enough to get on with the job without wondering most of the time what is really required of them and how far they can go in the use of resources and the commitment of their manager. The essence of work is the making of decisions, and the burden of work is the carrying of anxiety about the efficacy of such decisions until the results pass under the scrutiny of higher authority. It is the intuition and the imagination which have to be summoned to their making, which are the creative part of work. It seems essential, in the interests of psychological health and efficiency, that people should not have to carry the added burden, each time they have to make a decision, of wondering whether or not that decision lies within their sphere of responsibility. They ask themselves: "Is this one of those situations when one takes chances and throws one's weight about or shall I work to rule? If I do the latter, I may be assessed as lacking initiative; if I have a go, I may be classed as one who jumps the gun too often." On too many occasions one hears either: "You had no right to make such a decision," or "Why did you not make a decision on the spot instead of wasting all this time?" Neither criticism can be valid unless the discretion in the role has been made explicit. There is need to avoid situations where the use of personal networks, manipulation of other people, lobbying of support, etc., is required by an individual in order to discharge the duties of his role. The absence of clear-cut statements about authority, responsibility, and task create such situations. The assumption seems to be that these informal mechanisms based on personal prestige and power rather than on role authority and responsibility, must not be disturbed by the invasion of formal organization.

The degree of formal organization required is that which will ensure that all necessary decisions are made, which will keep at a low level interpersonal jealousy and confusion about authority, which will avoid leaving people in a continual state of uncertainty as to how far they can go in making decisions, and which will prevent individuals assuming personal positions of power and influence which have no connection with the proper authority required by them to do the work allotted to them.

Formulating policy

There is a need for and, indeed, an insistence on the part of people that they should take part in the formulation of policies governing their work and their working conditions. Many writers in the management field clearly believe that as long as the organization remains informal then this opportunity for people to influence policy exists but, if formalized, then they are deprived of this opportunity. This thinking is inconsistent with everyday perceptions of people at work. People can be seen to exercise a vital influence on the formulation of the policy which controls their working conditions. Important changes in wages, conditions of employment, the authority of managers and the privileges attached to different roles do, in fact, take place with regularity in companies but they are not accounted for by group decision theory. The culture of the groups of people concerned influences the goals they seek to achieve but it does not explain their mode of participation in the construction of the policies which determine the extent to which these goals are achieved.

There is a failure to perceive the existence of other social systems side by side with the executive system. These are the representative system, the system of stockholders, and the customer system. These four systems are in constant interaction. It is interaction between these power groups which produces the basic policies which govern the running of the company and the work of its executive system. This interaction of role systems we call the legislative system.

It is demonstrable that the chief executive cannot implement any change in the executive system which is not at least tolerated by each of these three other systems. The board of directors (the representatives of the stockholders) can legally prevent him from pursuing any course of action to which it objects. Customers withdraw their business if the chief executive insists on innovation with regard to price, quality, performance, etc., which is not acceptable to them. Representatives of the employees of the business initiate strikes or use the threat of strike to inhibit the implementation of policies which are inimicable to the interests of those who elect them.

Toleration for change

A chief executive has sophisticated means of discovering the degree of toleration for change, in the case of the stockholder system, in the form of the board of directors, annual and special meetings of stockholders, etc. His means of discovering the acceptability of innovation to customers are his sales organization, market research techniques, etc. But in the case of the employee group, his mechanisms for discovering the degree of toleration or the consensus of opinion are often primitive. Social institutions within which interaction between these four systems about policy can take do not exist in explicit form. Indeed, many chief executives not only fail to recognize the existence of such institutions, but would deny the appropriateness of employees taking part in the formulation of the policy which affects them. These are false perceptions because those who deny the need most vigorously in fact have to argue policy with representatives of their employees, particularly to end the strike which was caused by those innovations in policy which they would not tolerate.

There is not space in this article to describe in detail the form which an explicit legislative system within a company can take. Nor will space permit argument to support the notion that whether or not such an institution is set up explicitly, the chief executive's policy is a result of interaction of his views with those of these power groups (the stockholder, customer, and representative systems) which exist side by side with the executive system. My book, *Exploration in Management,*[2] discusses these matters in greater detail. Briefly, however, it seems clear from prolonged study of the ways in which companies operate that:

1. Executive systems form part of and exist within an embracing legislative framework which is unique to each company.
2. Such legislative systems, whether explicitly recognized or not, formulate the major policies which the executive system operates.
3. When explicit legislative institutions are formed, it becomes possible for employees to recognize the part they are playing in the formulation of those policies which are of concern to them. This makes possible the realization that the implementation of such policies depends on the sanctioning by them of the necessary degree of authority in the executive system.
4. This in turn leads to the appreciation that the use of threats, power, etc., by representatives not only weakens the executive system but threatens the legislative system through which they exercise their own capacity to take part in the formulation of policy.
5. The recognition of the existence of these social systems not only aids participation of employees in the formulation of policy but, at the same time, adds greatly to the responsibility and authority of managers.

Thus, in our company, where these systems are recognized, managers cannot change policy without the agreement of representatives, but representatives are agreed that the reverse is also true and that any attempt on their part to use the threat of force to bring about revision of policy is a breach of our constitution. Furthermore, managers have clear authority from the representative system itself to discipline those who attempt to breach agreed policies. Part of the preamble to our Company Policy Document reads as follows:

> This policy assumes that shareholders and employees individually and collectively want to go to the very limit in trying to work out policies which are in the best interests of the Company and its employees as a whole, and that they are willing to tolerate some shortcomings in policy in order to achieve this end. These assumptions are embodied in the principle that Councils[3] shall pursue their deliberations until they reach unanimous agreement.

---

[2] Wilfred Brown, *Exploration in Management* (London: Heinemann Educational Books; New York: Wiley; and Sweden: Stromberg). In preparation for publication in German, Girardet; French, Editions de la Baconniere; Dutch, Royal van Gorcum, Ltd.; Japanese, Diamond Publishing Co.

[3] A council is the body within which interaction between a manager of an

It is realized that when, after a serious attempt to reach unanimous agreement has been made, differences of viewpoint prove irreconcilable, action may be forced by the section which has the most power. The use of power in this way shall be regarded not as a normal alternative to the methods of legislation laid down in this document, but as the inevitable consequence of a breakdown in these methods.

> The desired interaction between the Executive and Representative Systems does not impair the scope either of managers or of representatives. Indeed, great responsibility and authority will have to be accepted by managers for the leadership of their subordinates; and elected representatives will have to occupy fully their elected roles in the sense of knowing policy, of being able to speak responsibly on behalf of their constituents, and of being able to integrate their views with those of representatives of other groups.

Some of the current theories about organization simply make no reference to representative systems and seek to explain the impact of people on the policies which govern the operation of the company in terms of theories about the psychological interaction of groups and the degree of identification of the individual with the company. Formal organization is thus seen as something that may disrupt these informal mechanisms of association. Such failure to observe the existence of vital social institutions distorts the whole frame of reference within which organization as a subject is considered.

"Behaviouristic" mode

Between 1939 and 1947, as a chief executive, I followed the "behaviouristic" mode of thought about organization. By the end of that period I had managed to get the executive, representative and embryo legislative systems hopelessly confused. The result was a dangerous weakening of the authority of managers and no consequential feelings of freedom or satisfaction on the part of other members of the Company. Elliott Jaques has described, in *The Changing Culture of a Factory*,[4] the situation which resulted and the thinking which enabled it to be untangled. In short, failure to recognize the existence of role systems other than executive systems leads to the attempt to use the latter not only for the co-ordination and execution of work but also for other purposes for which its

---

area of the company and representatives and all people in his command takes place.

[4] Elliott Jaques, *The Changing Culture of a Factory* (New York: Tavistock Publications Ltd., 1951, and Dryden Press, 1952).

structure is not appropriate. The resulting confusion of executive, representative, and legislative institutions weakens all of them and deprives employees of opportunities to participate in policy-making and managers of the necessary degree of responsibility and authority to implement those policies. We must take more account of the phenomena.

The increasing degree to which social conscience is affecting the thinking of managers leads inevitably, I think, to feelings of concern about the possibility that many of their decisions could be highly unjust in their effects on the individual. Is it possible that here again we face one of the sources of felt need to keep organization informal? Perhaps the feeling is that if organization is not formalized, these occasional acts of injustice will find their way to the surface for correction whereas, if everything is cut and dried, the cry for justice would be stifled by the "establishment."

Societies need law and, inevitably, once laws are established, they require not only executive systems to implement them but a judiciary to which the individual can appeal if he feels that the way in which the law is implemented is unfair to him. One of the missing institutions in industry is a formal appeal mechanism through which the individual can cause a decision of his manager which bears hard on him to be reviewed at higher levels. I realize that many forms of arbitration procedure for the settlement of industrial disputes do exist, but most of them are cumbersome, slow, difficult to actuate on the basis of the feelings of a single individual and are often confusedly intertwined with policy-making systems. Again, I must refer my readers to *Exploration in Management* for a discussion of an appeal mechanism which has been in operation for 22 years in our company. It is but a sample of the form which such mechanisms can take.

Appeal mechanism

Returning to the main theme, however, I must ask the question— would the setting up of a formalized appeal mechanism help to lower the feelings of resistance of the behaviourist school of thinking to an explicit and more formal organization? The absence of such judicial institutions in industry is the cause of much social friction. It is surprising, therefore, that so few organization theorists have much to say on the subject. I am left with the inference that they hope, that in some undefined way, informal organization will render appeals mechanisms unnecessary.

Is the current insistence of so many people on keeping organization informal based on the desire to ensure that as a man's ability grows he can expand, raise the level of his work at will? This is what I read into much that is written.

Such an approach to the problem of equating the level of capacity of the individual to the level of work in his role is, in my experience, not viable. Business organization requires the allocation of specific work to specific roles. There is not a bank of work waiting to be drawn upon by men who feel they can carry a greater load of responsibility for, unless all the necessary work is allocated into specific roles, there is no guarantee that it will be done. We perceive the need for the following situations:

1. Where managers allocate explicitly described parts of their tasks to their subordinates.
2. Where managers (as far as their own work permits) vary the level of work allocated to subordinates consistently with their intuitive assessments of those subordinates' capacities; always holding subordinates responsible for dynamic development of their area of responsibility and for the making of recommendations on those matters where discretion is not allocated.
3. Where new or vacant posts are advertised within the organization as well as outside so that a current employee may avail himself of such opportunities for promotion.
4. Where, at regular intervals, review takes place by the manager and the manager once removed, of the work allocated to specific roles and the performance of people in them so that planned progression may take place.
5. And above all, a situation of full employment in society where people have the possibility of leaving one company and joining another if work consistent with their ability is not available to them.

I suggest that the free play of group culture, sociometric forces, individual and group motivation, etc., within a framework of permissive management and informal organization, will lead neither to effective work output nor to a situation where the individual achieves that level of work which is consistent with his personal capacity. If those responsible for a company want people to be given the opportunity of performing that work which they are best suited for psychologically, then they must plan for it to happen. Where is the evidence to suggest that if a management abdicates from their responsibility for trying to bring about that result that it will just happen?

Room for research

There is room for research here. Jacques, working with our Company, has organized the plotting of career curves of thousands of people working in business from chief executives to rank and file employees. A career curve is based on plotting the corrected earnings of an individual against his age over his period of employment. Earnings are corrected in the United Kingdom by the use of the National Wage Index and, in other countries, by reference to some similar index of general standards of living. These graphs are found consistently to conform to a general pattern of growth curves which are the same for the six or seven countries which have provided data. These curves are predictive indices for the careers of individuals. With the use of such data, planned progression for the individual is aided. Initial results over the last few years indicate that if work level and pay progression along these curves is available, then the psychological satisfaction of the individual is more consistently assured than by any other method of which I am aware. This work has been described fully by Jaques in his book, *Equitable Payment*. Here is an example of the sort of approach that is required, and I contrast it with what seems to me to be the barrenness of that postulated by theories of informal organization.

Psychological contributions

Business work, so long as it is serving objective social needs, requires an imaginative psychological contribution from everybody whatever the level at which they are working. The need for wise decision exists in every role. The provision of work which appeals to the creative instincts of the individual is, therefore, a matter of matching human capacity and work. Can anybody doubt that this requires explicit intellectualization, planning, and execution?

There are those who believe that the advance of modern industry continually creates an ever-growing array of jobs fit to be performed only by morons. Others believe that the industrial machine operator is gradually becoming a mere button-pusher. Such views are clearly inconsistent with what is happening in Western society where each year sees the spending of ever-increasing resources on the training of increasing numbers in the acquirement of knowledge and skills at all levels. Despite this vast social effort to train people, a shortage of people with the necessary capacity to perform increasingly complex work continues to exist. Economic success today goes to the society which can provide the largest number of people competent to carry increasing levels of authority and responsibility. But it depends also on the ability of organization to see that the work allotted to the individual matches his ability. That is one of the major functions of well constructed organization. We must face the need for an explicit intellectual effort and an explicit series of plans and policies if we are to avoid the ultimate form of waste—that of human capacity.

QUESTIONS

1. Briefly summarize Brown's major criticisms of formal organization theory.
2. Why does he feel creativity is hindered in the typical organization? Why is it important?
3. What is meant by organizational roles? How are individual roles related to the logic of organization structure?
4. Do organizations need appeal mechanisms and systems? Why or why not? If so, how can these be designed and implemented?
5. Do business firms need legislative, executive, and judicial systems? Why or why not?

GENERAL QUESTIONS ON PART V

1. How does the formal organization structure influence the formation of informal groups?
2. How does the informal organization, in turn, affect the formal structure of a company?
3. How would Likert respond to the above question?
4. What is organization theory? What help can such theoretical propositions be to the working manager?
5. What are the most important variables presented in this chapter which influence employee productivity and morale?
6. Contrast Brown's article to that of Carzo. How are they similar? Different?
7. Should business firms—or any working organization—formalize some form of a judicial system? If so, how can this be done? What arguments can be presented against such a system?
8. What are the three major arguments against formal management controls? What points in their favor can be presented? Is there a balance between the two?
9. What are the purposes of a formal organization structure? In what ways is it self-defeating?
10. Do managers view organizational procedures and regulations differently than rank-and-file employees? If so, in what ways? Is this good or bad?

PART VI.   COMMUNICATION

Communication, the process of transmitting and receiving information, is so fundamental to the practice of management that without it an organization could not exist. The reason for this is very apparent. If we could not communicate with employees, we could not inform them of the work we want done, how we want it done, when we want it done, who we want to do it, and so on. We could not in any way possible practice human relations, motivate people, or exercise the functions of leadership. In short, we could get nothing—absolutely nothing—done.

From a very basic viewpoint the absence of communication would also result in the denial of existence to the human being, for every aspect of human behavior is related in some manner or form to the process of sending and receiving information. Our physiological needs, for example, have the ability to motivate our behavior because they possess the power to send to us, primarily via neurological pathways, the information we need to satisfy our primitive motives. Thus we know we are hungry when we experience pangs of hunger in the stomach. Or we know we are thirsty or need warmth and shelter when we "feel" the dryness in our mouth or the coldness of our skin. On a considerably more complex and emotional level, the same concept is true of our reaction to sociological and psychological needs. We know we "belong," for example, when something has communicated to us that we have been accepted as a member of a group or organization. Or our desire for recognition is satisfied when our responses lead someone or something to convey to us in some manner or form that we have performed our work well. Whatever our needs be, therefore, our reaction to their motivational force is completely dependent upon the transmission and reception of some type or kind of information. In the employment situation, consequently, employee performance is directly correlated with the efficiency of the communication process.

Evidence to prove the importance of communication to the existence of an organization or a human being is not difficult to find. In almost any firm there can be found examples of inefficiency, waste and spoilage, misunderstandings, and so forth, all of which can be traced to some form of communication. One then need only to extrapolate these particular incidents to "see" their effect on the organization as a whole. And as far as the impact of communication on the human being is concerned, almost every hospital in the world contains an abundance of evidence. Perhaps the reader has seen or heard of the effect of a damaged or destroyed neurological system, or the result of the loss of hearing, sight, and speech. In fact, recent research has proved that man, when denied (to the extent that he can be denied in a controlled laboratory experiment) use of his communicative faculties (sight, touch, hearing, and so on) at the same time, can tolerate this condition for only a short length of time. Beyond a certain point, continued deprivation of his senses will result in psychological damage or even death.

Because the process of communication is so important to human relations and motivation, it is unfortunate that many managers, that is, people in leadership positions, are extremely poor communicators. In fact, of all the abilities required for successful management and leadership, the ability to communicate is undoubtedly the one ability that most managers are commonly deficient in. It is not surprising to find, therefore, so many subordinates in business today who do not clearly understand what they are doing, why they are doing it, how they should do it, and so on. Nor is it surprising to find, as a consequence, so many people who are dissatisfied with their work environment in general because they have not found the means to satisfy their basic motivational forces, especially their sociological and psychological needs. This situation is all the more unfortunate because many managers quite frequently think they are properly communicating to their subordinates when in reality they are not. Communication, as we shall see in the following paragraphs and articles, consists of far more than merely telling people things. Until managers learn this—in fact, until they learn, understand, and become skilled in the basic process of transmitting and receiving information—they cannot possibly lead and motivate people in the manner required to get work done efficiently.

WHY WE COMMUNICATE

The basic reason for any kind or type of communication, whether it be in the form of a nerve sending impulses to the brain or a foreman instructing a subordinate on how to do a job, is to get some manner or form of action (behavior). In the context of a business enterprise, the action desired is usually related, either directly or indirectly, to the efficient performance of duties and responsibilities. This does not mean, incidentally, that the action wanted must necessarily be only in the form of concrete physical behavior, such as a worker operating a machine after receiving instruction on how to do so. On the contrary, action resulting from communication frequently can be and is in the form of an attitudinal response, the accepting of an idea, or a willingness not to behave in a particular way. This latter point, it should be noted, is especially true in counseling, particularly when it is disciplinary in nature.

Because some form of behavioral response will ultimately result from communication, it should not be inferred that overt or covert action will take place immediately or that it will always be observable to the eyes of men. Quite frequently behavior resulting from the receiving of information may not take place for many years. This is particularly true of formal education, of course. What the student learns in college may not actually influence his behavior until years later. The same is also true of present-day management development programs and other forms of executive development. Anything the young executive may learn about the subjects communicated to him during the course of such programs may not become manifested in his actions until considerably later in his career. And even then we may notice no apparent change in his behavior, especially if only an attitudinal response has occurred.

Although some manner or form of response is the basic objective of communication, especially in the context of a business organization, it must also be recognized that the type or kind of response desired by management of its subordinates, whether they be vice-presidents or operative employees, may not always materialize. Undoubtedly, one of the fundamental reasons why people sometimes fail to respond properly is because of various barriers to effective communication, a subject that will be considered in detail later in this part. Whatever the reasons why people fail to respond properly to communication, however, it should always be remembered that some manner or form of behavior (response) is going to result whenever we communicate. It is imperative, therefore, that every effort be made to prevent the various barriers to effective communication from operating. Unless this is done, it is very possible that employee response to communication may be unacceptable to management.

How We Communicate

How we transmit information

Perhaps the two most frequently used methods of communicating to people are the spoken and the written word. Oral communication, of course, takes place primarily in a face-to-face situation. It is, generally speaking, the most preferred method of transmitting information, principally because it is more personal in nature and because it more conveniently allows the transmitter to determine if the receiver understands and accepts what has been communicated to him. In addition, it possesses the advantages of being the fastest form of communication and of allowing both parties to participate in the situation and to share their opinions and feelings, advantages which are most important to motivation and the practice of human relations.

Written communication, although considerably less personal and participative in nature than oral transmission, is an essential part of any organization. Whenever information concerns many people, is very complex and extremely important, or has long-term significance, written media must almost always be used. However, because writing lacks the advantages of oral communication, skill is required to design properly the various forms used to convey the written word. But even when forms such as letters, manuals, handbooks, posters, and other media have been properly constructed, it is frequently necessary to explain orally and to clarify written information.

Other ways of communicating information to people include signs and symbols, pictures, facial expressions, gestures, what people do (the actions of others), silence, and so on. Although almost all of us utilize these means of communication every day of our lives, few of us recognize how powerful and significant these media are. And yet evidence of their impact and motivational force is not difficult to find. One need only to recall his reaction to a friend's facial expression or gesture, or how he was influenced by someone's action, or the purposeful silence of an acquaintance to understand the inherent nature of these forms of information transmission. Inanimate and inarticulate as they are, they most certainly speak "louder than words." As such, they play, along with oral and written communication, an extremely important part in the process of transmitting information.

How we receive information

Because we tend to use oral and written communication more than other forms of transmitting information in the business enterprise, we must of necessity receive information more by listening and seeing than by any other means of reception. This does not mean that other ways of receiving information are less important or useful to the communication process. On the contrary, if the transmitting media discussed in the preceding paragraph are important to communication, then the receptors required to receive the information transmitted by them are equally important. Accordingly, our senses of touch, smell, and taste also play important roles in the process of receiving information. But it should be emphasized that hearing and seeing, especially the hearing of spoken words and the seeing of written words, actions, gestures, and facial expressions, are by far our most relied upon means of receiving communication.

The Dimensions of Communication

Downward communication

In every business organization the most frequently used and relied upon dimension of communication is the downward direction. This refers, of course, to the process of transmitting information from the top of the organization (management) down through various levels to the bottom of the organization (workers). It is an essential dimension of transmission because without it a firm would cease to function. Accordingly, it is the direction used by management to communicate to employees information on company objectives, policy, procedure, and so on.

Upward communication

A second but equally important dimension of information transmission is that of upward communication. This direction of communication is predicated on the fact that employees not only possess the ability to receive communication, but also possess and must be allowed to use the capacity to transmit information. It is the only dimension of communication via which employees can convey to their superiors their actions, attitudes, and opinions about a multitude of subjects of vital concern to the efficient operation of a business enterprise. As such, it is the only means by which management can determine if the information it has transmitted has been received, understood, and accepted and if proper action has been taken or is being taken to accomplish the objectives of the company. Most important of all is the fact that this direction of information flow is the only way management can discover if the needs of subordinates are being satisfied. In other words, whether it be evidenced through records, reports, grievances, attitude surveys, interviews, suggestion systems, and so on, it is the only dimension that can communicate to superiors whether or not employees are being properly motivated. It is therefore unfortunate that it has only been in the past decade or so that management has recognized the inherent importance of facilitating the flow of information from the bottom to the top of the organization. But even today there are many managers who believe that the process of transmitting and receiving information means that they, the managers, transmit and that their subordinates, the employees, receive. What makes this situation all the more worse is, as we said before, the fact that many of the managers who think this way are, in the first place, extremely poor transmitters. Until such people recognize that, no matter what direction it takes, communication is inherently two-way in nature, they cannot possibly hope to practice human relations effectively.

Evidence that proves the importance of upward communication can be found in any efficiently managed firm. Successful suggestion systems, for example, have long been demonstrating their effectiveness as an upward communication medium by saving numerous organizations millions of dollars as a result of employees contributing their ideas. Encouraging workers to bring their grievances out into the open has resulted in the prevention of many major problems. And so on. But it should be emphasized that these examples materialize only when management, first, recognizes the importance of employees' communicating information to them and, second, facilitates the flow of such information. Unless recognition and facilitation exist, along with proper action by management with respect to the nature of the information transmitted, the inherent desire of people to communicate will be thwarted, and frustration, with all its dire implications to a firm, will result. In this respect it should be noted that some people believe that a basic reason for the formation of unions and the willingness of employees to join them is the lack of an effective upward communication system in the organization concerned. The theory here is that the union becomes the medium by which employees can convey their attitudes, opinions, wants, and needs to management.

Horizontal communication

A third dimension of communication necessary for the efficient operation of any business is called horizontal communication. This term refers to the flow—transmitting and receiving—of information between departments or people on the same level in an organization. It is a direction of communication that is absolutely essential to the success of any firm, for without it the activities of various functions, such as production, sales, personnel, purchasing, and finance, could not possibly be coordinated. An example that effectively illustrates this point occurred in a large manufacturing organization several years ago. The vice-president of sales of the company concerned, being disappointed over the sales volume of his organization, encouraged his sales personnel to do everything they could to improve conditions. He so thoroughly motivated his subordinates that within days orders began to flow in. Unfortunately, because this vice-president had not informed—horizontally communicated to—the manufacturing department of the nature of his plans, production quickly became bogged down by a load it was not geared to carry. The net result was that buyers, who had geared their own production to receipt of their orders within a certain period of time, canceled their orders and switched their business to other firms. This fiasco, it was estimated, cost this company approximately three hundred thousand dollars in business—sales lost to competitors. And all because of an absence of horizontal communication.

FORMAL AND INFORMAL COMMUNICATION

Formal communication

The directions of information transmission that were discussed above, particularly downward and upward communication, represent what is frequently termed formal communication within an organization. The reason for this is that they are directions of communication that result from the delegation of authority and responsibility in the creation of a formal organization structure. In other words, when an individual has been given the authority and the responsibility to get work done, there is immediately created an upward line of communication that he should use to transmit information to and receive information from his superiors, and a downward line of communication that he should use to transmit information to and receive information from his subordinates. In many cases, especially in well-run organizations, these transmitting and receiving "lines" are clearly indicated on organization charts and in job descriptions. This is particularly true of horizontal communication, primarily because this dimension of information flow does not follow normal lines of authority and responsibility; consequently, because of its importance to overall organizational efficiency, many managers formally determine its path.

Although there are inherent disadvantages in all forms of formal communication, primarily because of the authoritarian and superior-subordinate relationships established by them, there are several advantages of this type of communication that deserve mention. For example, horizontal communication, as was mentioned earlier, allows management to coordinate the various functions necessary to the organization. Formal downward communication allows management directly and immediately to send to or give employees information important to the operation of a company. And formal upward communication possesses the advantage of allowing management to establish lines that subordinates can use to convey information, such as suggestions and grievances, to superiors who have been delegated the authority and the responsibility to act upon it. This latter point illustrates, incidentally, a common misunderstanding of what is frequently called an open-door policy. If the chief executive of an organization, especially a large organization, literally left his door open to every conceivable type and kind of upward communication, he would have little time to devote to the top management aspects of running the business. What the term "open-door" really means is that communication from employees, if exceptional enough in nature to prohibit lower level managers and supervisors from acting on it, will be received personally by the chief executive. To allow otherwise would mean inefficient utilization of the executive's time and under-utilization of the time of lower-level managers. This does not mean to imply, however, that there should be no exceptions to this rule. On the contrary, in every organization there will occur times when employees, because of the personal nature of their information, should be allowed to see the "big boss." Unfortunately, it is always difficult to determine whether or not the nature of the information is personal enough to warrant consideration by the top man, especially when the employee, because of personality or other reasons, refuses to reveal what he wants to communicate. In addition, psychological and sociological barriers quite frequently make people reluctant just to "walk in."

Informal communication

As the section on organization pointed out, there also exists in every company a system of informal communication. This type of communication is a result of the natural desire of people to communicate with each other and arises from the social interaction of individuals. It is multidimensional in nature and is as flexible, dynamic, and varied as are the people who communicate along its paths. As a system of communication it is limited in direction and degree only to the extent that limits are self-imposed by members of an organization. As such, it contrasts sharply with the formal communication system because it frequently ignores or trespasses upon formally delegated lines of authority and responsibility. It is usually, but sometimes mistakenly, called the grapevine.

Although some people consider informal communication undesirable, undoubtedly because they do not understand it and utilize it properly, this system of transmitting and receiving information has several important characteristics that should be mentioned here. Perhaps one of its most important functions, if it is properly utilized, is to help disseminate and clarify management's formal communication. In this way it helps to improve overall communication or, more frequently, to overcome management's failure to transmit information properly in the first place. Another important quality is that it allows employees to express their emotions orally to other people without fear of repercussion. This safety-valve feature plays an important role in human relations, because the cathartic value of "blowing-off steam" frequently alleviates employee problems or prevents them from growing larger.

One of the most important disadvantages of informal communication is that it frequently spreads rumor, untruth, and distorted information with an alarming rate of speed. Perhaps the basic reason for this is lack of proper formal communication. Consequently when employees do not understand or are "left-in-the-dark" about something, they immediately interpret actions and procedures as they want to see them. The net result is rumor and untruth. It should be noted, however, that many times the transmitter is unaware that he is transmitting such items of information. As a receiver he frequently assumes that the information he sees or hears is reliable and truthful and that he is passing it on exactly as he received it. Unfortunately there are also people who purposefully concoct misinformation. Perhaps the best way to deal with such individuals—in fact, the best way to deal with all rumors and untruths—is to establish a rumor board or some similar medium of communication. The basic purpose of such a device is to answer the rumor or untruth immediately and thereby to stop it before it becomes serious. This means that management must constantly listen to the grapevine and act immediately when necessary.

Another undesirable characteristic of informal communication, so some managers think and fear, is that unlike formal communication it is very difficult to control. In other words, it is believed that management has little to say about what will be commnuicated, when it will be transmitted, who will receive it, and so forth. Although this quality exists to some degree, its manifestation actually depends upon the ability of the managers involved. If people ignore the grapevine and make no attempt to listen to it and combat the misinformation being transmitted, then, of course, it cannot be controlled. If, on the other hand, managers study the grapevine by listening to it and by determining who its leaders are and what information it transmits, they can take intelligent actions that will ultimately lead to an integration of informal communication with the formal communication system.

Barriers to Effective Communication

In a previous part of this section it was pointed out that some manner or form of action is the basic objective of all communication. It was also stated that the type or kind of response desired by management may not always result, primarily because of various barriers that thwart proper behavior. The purpose of this section is to consider briefly the nature of some of the more important obstacles to efficient communication.

Semantics

The meaning of words is undoubtedly one of the more important barriers to effective communication. Altogether too frequently we feel that because we undertand the meaning of the terms we use, our subordinates will likewise understand them. Unfortunately, what we fail to recognize is that words mean different things to different people. The level of our education, the part of the country we come from, the ethnic group to which we belong—these and many other factors determine what words mean to us. Managers must consequently take this fact into consideration when they communicate. In other words, they must in the first place carefully choose the words—frequently simple, single-syllable words—that they wish to transmit to people. When the nature of the communication is such that it is impossible to use universally understandable terms, then every effort must be made to interpret the meaning of the message to the various individuals or groups concerned. If this is not done, people will automatically interpret the communication in accordance with their understanding of the words used. The net result is usually misinterpretation and undesired action.

Too many words

In addition to using complex and difficult-to-understand words and terms, many managers also clutter up their communications with too many words. Consider, for example, the following illustration. In a well-known organization, the office manager recently sent this memo to employees:

> Employees of the XYZ Company who are desirous of receiving additional copies of the form which accompanies this memo should inform the receptionist of this office of the nature of their request in order to obtain without delay the extra copies they should like to have.

Although the nature of this communication may not be too difficult to understand, think how much simpler it would have been had the office manager simply written:

> If you want additional copies of this form, ask the receptionist.

When we fail to condense our communication, we leave the door wide open to time-consuming misunderstanding and improper response. This is especially true of communication requiring immediate action of employees.

Physical distance

Another important barrier to effective communication, particularly in the larger organization, is physical distance between people. When we are far away from the persons to whom we wish to communicate, it becomes very difficult for us to determine if they receive, understand, accept, and properly react to what we have transmitted. We must also rely more and more on written media, which means that we encounter additional problems of construction and interpretation. To overcome the disadvantage of distance, we must utilize, where possible, physical devices such as telephones and intercommunication systems, and we must make sure that the people on the various levels through which our information is sent understand, accept, and pass on our message up or down the line. In particular we must make sure that the people on these levels communicate intact the nature of our information. That is to say, we must make sure that our information is not misinterpreted, distorted, or stopped by the people who are responsible for passing it on to and interpreting it for other people. As difficult as this is to do, we must do it if we want proper employee behavior.

People

In addition to being the basic cause of many of the barriers to effective communication, it should be noted that people *per se* are an important obstacle to information transmission. This type of barrier occurs when information that must be transmitted through other people is stopped before it reaches its final objective. Included among reasons why people hinder the flow of communication are factors such as misunderstanding of the original message (poor communication in the first place) and fear of passing on information because it might indicate inefficiency or inability to handle certain situations. This latter point is extremely relevant to upward communication. Altogether too frequently foremen and supervisors hestitate or fail completely to pass important information, such as employee attitudes, opinions, grievances, and suggestions, on to their superiors because they believe such information will impair their status or prestige or reflect on their supervisory ability. When such stoppages occur, problems that could have been prevented usually develop into situations that ultimately require drastic remedial action. It is important, therefore, for people to recognize that the stopping of information, rather than the content of the message stopped, is an indication of poor leadership ability.

Another very common way people serve as barriers to effective communication, that is, communication designed to elicit proper response from employees, concerns the way some people behave on the job. A frequently occurring illustration of this is the supervisor who consistently breaks many rules and regulations that have been established for safety or other reasons. When employees see such a person smoking in a no-smoking area or being frequently late to or absent from work, it is extremely difficult to obtain proper response from them no matter how well we communicate the rules themselves and the reasons for them. When such actions occur on the supervisory level, they are, of course, indicative of extremely poor leadership ability. But they serve as very effective barriers to communication.

Interest

As several of the following articles point out, one of the most fundamental obstacles to communication is that we do not pay as much attention as we should to the interests of the people to whom we communicate. This concept is based on the fact that we listen (or look) more attentively to communications that are geared to our interests and our basic needs. When we listen in this manner, we facilitate understanding and acceptance of the information transmitted and usually respond with the proper type of behavior. Until management recognizes this important aspect of communication and keys its information transmission to it, it will seldom achieve the benefits desired from training, cost reduction programs, quality improvement programs, suggestion systems, and so forth. It is fortunate, therefore, that the simple explanation of the "why" of a particular communication is frequently sufficient to relate the response desired to employee interests.

COMMUNICATION: THE BASIC PROCESS

Although the achievement of some manner or form of human behavior is the basic objective of all communication, especially in the context of a business enterprise, it should be apparent by now that the accomplishment of this goal requires more than telling, writing, or indicating something to people. In fact, it should be obvious that the basic process of communication, if it is to achieve proper employee response, must of necessity give attention to three important and sequentially related concepts. In the first place, it must begin with the proper transmission of information. In the second place, the receiver must understand this information. And in the third place, the receiver must accept the information transmitted to him. Unless these three conditions exist in the order stated, the fourth part of the process of communication, namely, action, will be seriously thwarted or left completely to chance. Let us briefly consider the nature of these facets of communication.

Transmitting information

The transmitting of information to people, particularly if it is done with written media, requires considerable planning on the part of the transmitter. Detailed attention must be given to the nature of the communication *per se*, the best medium to use, the people who should receive it, the interests and the needs of the people who will receive it, and the various barriers that could impede its effectiveness. In other words, every effort should be made to insure that what people are to receive is receivable. If this is not done—and it frequently isn't—it is senseless to expect understanding, acceptance, and proper action.

Understanding information

It is obvious that the understanding of communication is dependent to an infinite degree on how well the communication was planned and transmitted in the first place. Not so obvious, however, is the fact that we frequently assume that the receiver understands what has been communicated to him. Because sound communication does not rest upon a structure of assumptions, primarily because even the best communication is sometimes misunderstood, it is therefore necessary that the transmitter determine whether or not the receiver comprehends his message. In essence, this requires the transmitter now to become the receiver and the receiver to become the transmitter. In other words, after communicating information to an employee, we must do everything possible to encourage that person to indicate to us the degree of his understanding. We must facilitate the transmission of this information and, most important of all, listen attentively to it. This is why most people prefer oral communication. In a face-to-face situation it is considerably easier to determine whether or not the receiver understands us. It is also easier, of course, for the receiver to transmit to us. No matter what dimension or medium of communication is used, however, it is imperative that we recognize that understanding can be determined only if we utilize the inherent two-way nature of the process of communication. That is to say, we must be both transmitters and receivers. Unless we accept this dual role, it is impossible to communicate effectively with and hence to motivate people.

Accepting information

Many people fail to recognize that in addition to proper transmission and understanding of communication, action is also dependent to a great degree upon acceptance of the information received. Perhaps the basic reason for this is the assumption that people accept what they understand. Unfortunately for the manager, however, this assumption is not always true, especially when consideration is given to the nature and the degree of the understanding involved. Consider, for example, the case of the older worker who was given detailed and explicit instructions on how to operate a new machine. According to tests and demonstrations there was no doubt that this individual understood how to run the machine and had the ability to do so. Yet the quality and the quantity of his production were disappointingly low. Why? Although he understood how to operate the new machine, he did not understand why the machine was necessary, how it would affect his status, or what influence the potential increase in productivity would have on his pay. As a consequence, he covertly refused to accept the machine and accordingly produced at a lower level than his ability warranted. In this case and thousands similar to it the only answer is to explore thoroughly via two-way communication the nature and the degree of the employee's understanding. Where voids in his information exist, he must have communicated to him the information he needs to satisfy his interests. Difficult as this is to do, it must be done if action based on acceptance, rather than behavior based on rejection, is to result.

The articles that follow were purposefully selected to help the reader gain greater understanding of the nature and the facets of the basic process of communication. Gibb's article was chosen because it is an incisive analysis of managerial communication. Higham's article was included because, as its title suggests, it gives consideration to some important basic psychological factors that are deeply involved in communication. The article by Nichols was selected because it is an excellent analysis of one of the most critical aspects of communications, namely, listening. The article by Stieglitz was picked because it explores the myriad barriers to effective communication. And, lastly, the article by Bavelas and Barrett was selected because the well-informed reader should be acquainted with experimental approaches to organizational communication.

29. COMMUNICATION AND PRODUCTIVITY *

Jack R. Gibb

Communication is a process of people relating to other people. As people relate to each other in doing work and in solving problems they communicate ideas, feelings and attitudes. If this communication is effective the work gets done better and the problems are solved more efficiently. Thus, in one sense, at this level of abstraction, there is an obvious relationship between communication and productivity.

Work and problem solving can each be viewed as the taking of appropriate roles at appropriate times as the task or problem evolves. Role taking *is* communication. This apparent and real relationship has caused management to take an increasing interest in all phases of communication. Books are written, training courses are devised, and communications specialists are created and demanded. The rapid growth of literature and programs has far outdistanced the relevant research and the clear knowledge that management can use in making decisions about communications programs. The literature is confusing, contradictory and voluminous.

Although in the most global sense it is fairly obvious that communication is related to productivity, it is very difficult to find satisfying evidence of clear relationships between specific communicative programs or acts, on the one hand, and measures of productivity, profit or corporate vitality on the other. Most studies of communication are short term in nature and relate aspects of communication to various personal and group variables that are perhaps assumed to be related to productivity in the long run, but whose relationships are tenuous at best.

It is the purpose of this paper to look at the over-all problem from the standpoint of managerial decision making. What does top management or the individual manager do? The paper is organized around nine fundamental communication issues that confront management in today's corporate world. These issues grow out of research, theory and management experience. While it is true that in both practice and theory there are many and varied legitimate positions on each issue, it is possible to distinguish two clusters of related managerial behaviors that are fairly consistently antithetical on each of the fundamental issues. In Table 1 are summarized the

* From *Personnel Administration*, Vol. 27, No. 1 (January-February, 1964), pp. 8-13, 45. Reprinted with permission.

extreme positions of the conflicting views—the views of the "persuasion manager" and of the "problem-solving manager"—on each of the nine issues. Each issue is stated in more detail at the beginning of each of the nine sections of the paper. The issues are practical, overlapping and in general are worded in the language of management rather than in the language of the specialist.

In general, the *persuasion approach* to communication tends to assume that it is the responsibility of management to regulate the flow of fact and feeling through the organization, to use such regulation as a convenient managerial tool, to build staff roles to work on communication problems, to spend a great deal of time and energy building "communications" programs, and to show a high concern about the information flow in the organization, particularly about verbal and written messages downward.

An alternative approach, designated for convenience as the *problem-solving approach*, is to assume that effective communication is an intrinsic component of effective work and efficient problem solving, that if communications problems exist they are symptoms of aberrant organization or poor line management, that communication is improved by more adequate line management action and problem solving rather than by staff action, and that by creating a managerial climate in which trust and openness is a norm appropriate facts, attitudes and feelings tend to be spontaneously fed into the process of getting the job done.

In each of the following sections a focus or viewpoint consistent with each of the two above approaches is discussed.

TABLE 1

TWO ALTERNATIVE VIEWS OF THE COMMUNICATION PROCESSES

A Persuasion Approach—	A Problem-Solving Approach—
The focus is on:	*The focus is on:*
1. Remedial programs	1. Diagnosis and etiology
2. Staff responsibility	2. Line responsibility
3. Morale and hygiene	3. Work product and job requirements
4. Persuasion	4. Problem solving
5. Control of communication flow	5. Trust and openness
6. Verbal communication	6. Management actions
7. One-way messages	7. Interaction and climate
8. Knowledge and logic	8. Attitudes and feelings
9. Output and telling	9. Input and listening

Symptom or cause

Is communication seen primarily as a symptom of more basic organizational processes or as itself a fundamental factor to be manipulated by management in the quest for greater productivity and organizational vitality? Is communication best viewed as a symptom or as a cause?

A manager with what might be termed a persuasion approach to management sees communication primarily as a management tool to be used in getting people to get the job done. When he sees some defect in the work pattern that must be remedied he tends to attempt to manipulate the flow of communications as a remedial action. Communicative distortion is seen as a basic cause of poor work or problem solving and is worked on directly by altering managerial communications.

A manager with what might be termed a problem-solving approach to management tends to see communication primarily as a symptom or indicator of more basic organizational or managerial inadequacy. Information about communicative distortion is used as diagnostic data which will guide the manager in taking new managerial actions, reorganizing work patterns, or achieving new attitudes toward the organization or the people in it.

The evidence is fairly clear that when people are in an effective problem-solving or work relationship with each other they tend to communicate relevant feelings, ideas and perceptions with each other. When there is a goal ambiguity, poor supervision or role inadequacy, then communicative distortion occurs as a symptom of these more basic problems.

An analog occurs in the concurrently flowering field of human relations. Human relations can be viewed as a symptom or as a cause. The growing awareness of human relations and communications problems is symptomatic of growing feelings of inadequacy on the part of management, and of a growing awareness of basic inadequacies in both management and organization theory and practice. When people have trouble getting along with each other and understanding each other, it is probably an indication that somehow they have been unable to create satisfactory jobs or a satisfying and effective work organization. The way to improve human relations and communications is to evolve new job prescriptions and more adequate work organizations—to change managerial actions. It may be a temporary solution to build human relations training programs and communications workshops—but this is at best a *temporary* or intermediate solution, a step that is getting at symptoms rather than more basic causes, and that is working on the shadow of the problem rather than on the problem itself.

Staff or line

Who is primarily responsible for effective communication—staff or line? The persuasion manager tends to emphasize the staff role in improvement of communications. The problem-solving manager tends to build responsibility for communications and human relations directly into the line functions.

A differentiating characteristic between the persuasion manager and the problem-solving manager is his emphasis upon one or two paths. The persuasion manager tends to build a communications staff with many responsibilities for studying communications, instituting programs, managing information and data flow within the organization, training people to communicate, and using various media to *persuade* people to change behavior or to communicate more adequately.

The problem-solving manager makes the assumption that communication is a direct line responsibility, that communication *must* occur in the process of doing work, solving problems, controlling distribution, or getting the job done. He works directly on the line causes of communicative errors. He works with others towards recomposing work groups, changing organizational patterns, reorganizing work space, or creating more adequate man-job relationships. He tends to change his behavior rather than his speech. He tends to control actions rather than to control talk.

It seems well at this point to call attention to the fact that we are describing two extreme typologies of management. In one sense the two types of managers being considered are hypothetical or "ideal" cases. The pure cases do not exist in the natural state. However, anyone with wide experience on the industrial scene can recognize the *genre*. The intent is to sharpen assumptions and to focus attention upon the implications of communications research for management practices. In practice individual managers tend to show mixtures of the above patterns.

Hygiene or production

If there is a "communications program" is it primarily centered upon the requirements of the job and the product or is it primarily remedial in nature? Is it directed toward morale, hygiene and human relations or is it directed toward work and productivity?

The persuasion manager tends to direct the communication program toward improvement of morale and hygiene around the plant. He fights fires, drops verbal bombs where they are presumed to do the most good, centers upon remedial aspects of the situation, and directs plant and company campaigns toward curing ills such as absenteeism and waste.

The problem-solving manager tends to have no special communications program as such. When he does create such a program he tends to deal with analyses of job requirements, production schedules, goals of the enterprise, information storage and retrieval, efficiency of work flow, and other aspects of communication flow that are directly relevant to job performance and problem solving.

Hygiene-centered communication programs tend to send out information that is irrelevant, distorted to fit management goals, camouflaged to cover management errors, sent in too great a quantity, irrelevant to the concerns of the moment that *grow out of* task and problem demands or out of spontaneous group maintenance demands. Such programs are often met with suspicion and apathy, and may be seen as propaganda or as attempts to meet management needs rather than work needs or worker needs.

There is some evidence that communication is best when it is in response to natural interaction on the job between people who are learning appropriate trust, when it is in small groups or face-to-face situations, when it is asked for, and when it is between members who do not have too great psychological or hierarchial distance. The most effective communication thus tends to arise spontaneously out of situational demands.

Effective communication tends to be best in work units, where line managers and co-workers are learning a degree of trust appropriate to their relationship, and are learning to send and receive attitudes, feelings and information that are necessary for appropriate job performance. The interrelated assumptions here are that people like to do meaningful work, feel good when they have satisfactory job relationships, have good morale when they do challenging work that is related to their own choices, goals, and abilities, and that effective communication is a residual property of effective work and problem solving.

Persuasion or problem-solving

Is the communication problem focussed upon persuasion of people or upon individual and team problem solving?

The persuasion manager tends to see communication as primarily an influence process through which people can be changed, controlled, guided, or influenced. Communication becomes education, propaganda, leadership, or guidance. Managers try to sell ideas, or to motivate others to work harder, feel better, have higher morale, and be more loyal.

The problem-solving manager sees communication primarily as a necessary adjunct of the process of doing work or solving problems. In order to solve the problem or get the job done certain information must be obtained, certain feelings must be expressed, and a certain amount of interpersonal perceptions must be exchanged in order for a team to be a healthy work or problem-solving unit. Job demands or team maintenance demands determine the amount and kind of communication that is necessary. Communication *is* problem solving.

The difference in the two approaches is one of *focus*. Communication is *both* influence and problem solving. The emphasis and the approach are the significant things. Persuasive communication tends to produce resistance, distrust, circumvention, or counter-persuasion. It is seen by the worker or subordinate as "news management," as propaganda, or as an effort to get him to do what he may not want to do. Research has shown persuasion-centered communications programs to be discouragingly ineffective in accomplishing management goals.

Problem-solving communication is subordinate to the demands of the job or the problem. The nature of the job or the problem calls forth certain bits of information, feelings or perceptions that are relevant to job accomplishment or problem solution. In general, the research shows that when conditions are created which produce relevant *emergent* communications out of the work situation, that communications problems are reduced. Thus, face-to-face communications in small groups tend to be superior to other forms of communication because there is a greater likelihood that communications will emerge from interactive job and problem demands.

Regulation or trust

Does one trust the manager and the worker or does one regulate the communication flow?

An increasingly clear body of evidence indicates that communication is related to the trust level in the relationship or in the organization. People who trust each other tend to be more open with each other. With high trust people are free to give information and feelings and to respond spontaneously to questions, are less apt to devise control strategies to manipulate others, are less apt to be closed and devious, are less apt to manufacture rumors or distortions, perhaps have less need to engage in extra communication, and thus they lay the groundwork for higher productivity. With low trust, people use more strategy, filter information, build interpersonal facades, camouflage attitudes, deliberately or unconsciously hold back relevant feelings and information in the process of interpersonal infighting, distort feedback upward in the direction of personal motivations, engage in extra communication, and thus indirectly sabotage productivity.

Managers tend to regulate the communication flow when distrust is high and tend to be more spontaneous and open with feelings and information when distrust is low. The persuasion manager tends to regulate communication flow—both in his personal actions and in his managerial policies. The problem-solving manager tends to create trust by allowing communications to follow the demands of the work situation. The openness-trusting stance is antithetical to the persuasion stance. Experimentation indicates that work and problem-solving efficiency is dependent upon the spontaneous flow of information and feelings through the system. Trust and openness are related to productivity.

Talk or action

Does a manager talk or act? Given a choice of where to focus effort, does management spend energies getting the problems solved and the jobs done or deciding what kinds of communications to send to the subordinate and the worker?

With articulate people words can become a fetish. What shall we say to the worker? What can I tell my subordinate? How shall I word the message? Part of this word-focus habit arises from a naive confidence that people will take the words at face value, part of it perhaps from an unconscious protest to one's intuitive understanding that talk will make little difference and that people won't listen at all. Interviews with managers indicate bimodal reactions of naive trust or equally naive cynicism about the effectiveness of words in communication.

Experimental and field studies can be interpreted to show that actions are more significant than words in communication. Gestures, bodily attitudes, emphatic postures, and management actions communicate a great deal more than words do. A manager who says verbally that he trusts a subordinate and then proceeds to require detailed and frequent reports, or to make frequent checks on the subordinate's work, usually is *perceived* as distrusting the subordinate. Actions take priority over words in the communication channels.

The persuasion manager tends to ascribe an inordinately high value to words, symbols, pictures, and formal communications. Most people would perhaps agree that both words and actions communicate. The difference in management technologies lies in the relative emphasis in day to day management decision. The problem-solving manager tends to rely upon actions to communicate rather than upon words. He tends to use words more for information than for influence.

Traffic or climate

Is the "communication problem" basically a climate problem or a traffic problem? Do we focus attention upon refining the message we send or upon creating a climate in which "messages" are decreasingly necessary? Is communication primarily directional or is it an interaction among people doing a job? Is the management problem one of creating a climate for interaction or one of regulating the message traffic?

The persuasion manager tends to be a traffic man, usually centering attention upon the one-way channels down the hierarchy or command channel. Great attention is paid to the mass media, refinement of the message, timing of the presentation, organizing the campaign, hitting at the psychological moment, and devising an appropriate propaganda strategy. Public relations, advertising and visual aids are in great demand. The problem is control of the traffic patterns of communication. Communication is often one-way.

The problem-solving alternative to such action is to focus upon the interactive climate of work, to rely upon face-to-face interaction in line units who are working or solving problems together, to give all relevant information to line managers with maximum openness, to arrange the geography of work in such a way as to optimize relevant interaction, and to encourage questions, criticisms and all forms of informal interaction. Group discussions, small, flexible and overlapping work teams, and open channels are seen as communication tools. The problem is seen as one of creating a climate for work and problem solving. Communication is seen as flowing in a field of interaction, rather than as occurring on a one-way street—or even on a two-way street. Communication is a relationship.

Knowledge or attitude

Which is more central in determining effective communication—information and logic or attitudes and feelings? If communication is seen as poor, does the manager direct his energies toward refining the flow of information or toward changing the attitudes of persons engaged in communicating? Which is a more critical "leverage point" in adequate communication—knowledge and logic or attitudes and feelings?

The persuasion technologist tends to place an emphasis upon information and upon getting the "facts" to the right people. He tends to assume that information will change attitudes and behavior, and that information can be transmitted with acceptably high reliability through formal channels.

The evidence seems to point to the relative importance of attitudinal and motivational factors over informational factors in management and in behavior change. Campaigns to increase information usually accomplish considerably less than management would hope. Information does not necessarily change attitudes, value systems, or even perceptions. People tend to perceive information or reinterpret data in the direction of their motivations and wishes. People hear what they want to hear. They forget what they want to forget. There are various motivational reasons why people select from available information, ignore posters and pamphlets, over-perceive or underperceive the "facts," and in general add their own distortions to the information that they receive.

The communication of intangibles like warmth, acceptance, respect, and trust are complex processes which are poorly correlated with the words people use and the information that is conveyed. The problem-solving manager tends to place emphasis upon feelings and perceptions of people, and to focus upon the work climate which will determine the way information is received and which may make special communication decreasingly necessary.

Output or input

If something goes wrong, does the manager start telling or listening? If a manager wishes to take a diagnostic stance toward the communication problem in his company, does he accomplish more by refining the outputs or the inputs? Supposing we knew no other information about the alternatives than the titles of the courses, which management development course would we keep going: "Management Public Speaking" or "Management Listening?"

The persuasion manager tends to think in terms of output. He tends to talk of getting the message across, telling subordinates about the goals of the company, motivating people to work, seeing that people understand what management is trying to do, and putting out the message efficiently and quickly with a minimum of effort.

The problem-solving manager tends to think more in terms of input. He may ask himself such questions as the following. What information is needed? How do others look at the problem? What other solutions are there to problems that face us? How can we get more data? How can we interpret what information is available? What cues are we failing to process?

In examining the above clusters of management behavior we find that tradition and precedent are on the side of the persuasion manager. Most of the scientific evidence where it is available is on the side of the problem-solving approach. The skills and habits of persuasion are readily available. The skills, habits, and attitudes appropriate to the problem-solving approach are less easily acquired. The paths to creative problem solving are unclear. The managerial rewards are presumably great.

QUESTIONS

1. Briefly distinguish between the persuasion approach and the problem-solving approach.
2. Explain the assumptions of each of the above approaches.
3. What does Gibb suggest as the way to improve human relations and communications? Do you agree? Why?
4. Explain the relationship of the following to the two approaches Gibb discusses:
   a. Staff or line.
   b. Hygiene or production.
   c. Regulation or trust.
   d. Traffic or climate.
5. What is Gibb's general conclusion? Do you agree? Why?

30. BASIC PSYCHOLOGICAL FACTORS
IN COMMUNICATION *

T. M. Higham

A celebrated authority on Canon law and mediaeval Universities, Dr. Hastings Rashdall, was one of those who could ride, but not understand a bicycle. One day, for example, having had a puncture in his front tyre, he was found vigorously pumping up the back one; when a passer-by pointed this out to him, he remarked, "What? Do they not communicate?" I sometimes wonder whether, in our present-day eagerness to "put people in the picture," we do not behave rather like Dr. Rashdall, strenuously pumping in information at one end of a firm, in the hopeful expectation that it will somehow find its way to the other. Perhaps we too ride, but cannot understand.

In the last few years, a great deal has been written on this topic of "communications," mainly to the effect that communication must be "two-way," a comment of unstartling originality, as anyone familiar with the derivation of the word must realise. Today you can hardly open one of the many journals, English or American, in the personnel field, without finding some article on the subject, or some review of the latest authoritative work on it; there is even a "Communications Training Centre" in existence, and one firm, at any rate, now has its "Communications Manager"; Technical Colleges, Evening Institutes and other organisations run courses in clear expression, and the art of speaking or writing; you can be trained in running a meeting or leading a conference. Training Officers and others make increased use of visual and other aids, as a help in putting their teaching across; industries make use of suggestion schemes, joint consultative committees, broadcast address systems and similar devices to try to ensure that information reaches to all levels in the business and is fed back again to the top. But, as P. H. Cook [1] (1951) has said:

> "There is as yet no firmly-established theory of communication which can provide guiding principles guaranteeing that effective communications will be achieved. As a result, much communication practice is dependent on unconfirmed hypotheses, personal hunches and techniques and tricks of doubtful merit."

* From *Occupational Psychology*, Vol. 31, No. 1 (January, 1957), pp. 1-10. Reprinted with permission.
[1] P. H. Cook, *The Productivity Team Technique* (London: Tavistock Institute of Human Relations, 1951).

The nearest approach to a theory of communications has probably come from students of cybernetics and information theory. The new science of "Communication Engineering," as Professor Meredith [2] (1955) pointed out recently, is so highly developed that "we are strongly tempted to use it as a ready-made frame of reference, and to fit all our ideas about communication into this frame." That I believe to be a mistake—not so much because it is difficult to see what relevance a man-made machine has in considering the problems of a God-made man, but rather because, in everyday life, at home, in industry, in social life generally, the problems of communication (that is, of the transmission of ideas and attitudes) between people and groups are not those which can be solved, or even greatly understood, by means of a knowledge of information theory. Until such time as a machine is developed which can not only interpret information, but also convey its like or dislike of its informant, I believe we should do well to stick to our knowledge of human and animal psychology in trying to understand the problems and workings of communication between individuals and groups.

In most of the studies of communication between individuals and groups which I have come across, scant recognition is given to what is, perhaps, the one fact which we do know from experience about it— that if a person dislikes or mistrusts us, he is not likely to be receptive to what we have to say, and his version of our words is likely to be distorted by his personal opinions of us, or his preconceived notions about our motives. For that reason a study of communication could well begin with an examination of the problems of the reception of information—that process by which we perceive what is said against a background of who says it. It is there that the work of animal psychologists, and the many experimental studies of perception, can help us.

The experiments of Schelderup-Ebbe [3] (1935) with hens, Maslow [4] (1936) with apes, and Lorenz [5] with dogs have shown clearly that a sizing-up process goes on when two animals meet, which subsequently merges into a dominance-submission relationship. Of these, the most vivid is probably Lorenz's description of the encounter of two adult male dogs.

---

[2] G. P. Meredith, "The Flow of Information," *Occupational Psychology*, Vol. 29, 1955, pp. 99-103.

[3] T. Schelderup-Ebbe, "The Social Behaviour of Birds," in C. Murchison, *A Handbook of Social Psychology* (Worcester: Clark University Press, 1935).

[4] A. H. Maslow, "The Dominance Drive as a Determiner of the Social and Sexual Behaviour of Infra Human Primates I-IV," *Journal of Genetic Psychology*, Vols. 48 and 49, 1936.

[5] K. Lorenz, *Man Meets Dog* (London: Methuen, 1954).

"Two adult male dogs meet in the street. Stiff-legged, with tails erect and hair on end, they pace toward each other. The nearer they approach, the stiffer, higher and more ruffled they appear, their advance becomes slower and slower. . . . They do not make their encounter head to head, front against front, but make as though to pass each other, only stopping when they stand at last flank to flank, head to tail, in close juxtaposition. Then a strict ceremonial demands that each should sniff the hind regions of the other. Should one of the dogs be overcome with fear at this juncture, down goes his tail between his legs and he jumps with a quick, flexible twist, wheeling at an angle of 180 degrees, thus modestly retracting his former offer to be smelt. Should the two dogs remain in an attitude of self-display, carrying their tails as rigid as standards, then the sniffing process may be of a long protracted nature. All may be solved amicably and there is still the chance that first one tail and then another may begin to wag with small but rapidly increasing beats and then this nerve-racking situation may develop into nothing worse than a cheerful canine romp."

Apart from the fact that such encounters take place primarily on a symbolic level, is the encounter between two humans so very different? When two individuals meet for the first time, there is usually a rather more refined process of 'sniffing over'—an interchange of neutral information (the weather, for example, or a search for mutual acquaintances) which serves the same purpose. An attempt to set up a dominance-submission relationship also emerges on some occasions, as Maslow [6] (1937) has shown. Pear [7] (1955) has explored with skill the part played by voice and social differences in the same situation. The fact that this process may be going on below the level of consciousness is a further factor: there are still, for example, some managers who sit with their backs to the light, in a chair just a little higher than that of their visitors, and continue to write after someone enters their office; but luckily their numbers are dwindling. But these, unlike the Admiral's gold braid and the peacock's tail, are more often than not unconscious ways of conveying an impression of importance. None the less, their effect on recipients is much the same.

What has not yet been satisfactorily demonstrated is the opposite of that—the approach or manner which makes for confidence and an easy reception. If there are mannerisms which tend to put the recipients of information in a subordinate position, by conveying an attitude of superiority, are there other ways in which an atmosphere of trust and confidence can be built up without loss of status by either party?

---

[6] A. H. Maslow, "Dominance-Feeling, Behavior and Status," *Psychological Review*, Vol. 44, 1937, pp. 404-429.
[7] T. H. Pear, *English Social Differences* (London: Allen and Unwin, 1955).

If we recall the two dogs sniffing each other over, I believe we can say that such a situation is possible—and in fact many well-trained interviewers and counsellors are creating such a situation every day. Every interviewer is taught to "put the candidate at his ease"—in other words to make him receptive, whether it be to questions about himself or to advice and guidance. The exact ways in which this is done vary, but the essential part has been well put by Oldfield [8] (1941):

> "The adoption of an appropriate *general attitude* at the outset of the interview is a matter of greater importance than the maintenance of an effort to *behave* appropriately throughout its course. As an eminent psychologist remarked apropos this question, 'each interview is a world to itself. One hour I am a schoolmaster, the next a parson'."

It seems clear that to ensure good reception, you must create the right atmosphere. This is, perhaps, the one pre-requisite for effective communication. Where it does not exist, communication will be difficult, and all that is said is likely to be distorted. A further complication is that two people, or two groups, rarely if ever meet with what is called an "open mind." Each comes together, instead, with preconceived ideas about the other, and about the other's preconceived ideas about them.

During the preliminary "sniffing over," any small clues that can be fitted into the pre-existing picture will be readily grasped. The ingenious experiments of Asch [9] (1946) demonstrate this point neatly. It will be remembered that he read two lists of personality traits to two different groups of people. The first group's list was "Kind, Wise, Honest, Calm, Strong." The second group's list was "Cruel, Shrewd, Unscrupulous, Calm, Strong." The last two epithets in both lists were the same. After hearing the lists, separately, the two groups were told, "Suppose you had to describe this person in the same manner, but without using the terms you heard, what other terms would you use?" The first group, who heard the list "Kind, Wise, Honest, Calm, Strong," gave the following synonyms for "calm"—soothing, peaceful, gentle, tolerant, mild-mannered. But the second group, who heard "Cruel, Shrewd, Unscrupulous, Calm, Strong," produced synonyms for "calm" like cold, frigid, calculating. Similar results were got from the two groups with synonyms for "strong"—the first group listing such terms as fearless, helpful, just, forceful; the second group giving ruthless, overbearing, hard, inflexible, dominant. Both groups on

---

[8] R. C. Oldfield, *The Psychology of the Interview* (London: Methuen, 1941).
[9] S. E. Asch, "Forming Impressions of Personality," *Journal of Abnormal and Social Psychology*, Vol. 41, 1946, pp. 258-290.

hearing the first few epithets, got a fixed idea about the sort of person described; the later terms were merely fitted into the existing pattern.

This is not merely an academic point, illustrated by carefully controlled laboratory experiments; it is a very real factor in communication, simply because "the past in the worker's mind," as Zweig [10] (1952) calls it, is so strong and potent a factor in his reactions. The truth of that is seen in the study made recently by the Acton Society Trust [11] (1952) of communications in the coal mining industry. In an attempt to raise the output of coal, many attempts were made to tell the miners why a higher output was necessary; pamphlets, magazines, even a personal letter from the then Prime Minister, Mr. Attlee, were employed. But, as the report makes clear:

> "The mere provision of information . . . does not reduce proneness to prejudice . . . it does not succeed in modifying the underlying attitude of mistrust upon which credulity seems to be based."

In a later report, *Management under Nationalisation*, the Trust [12] (1953) quoted the comment of an Area Manager in the Coal Industry, pointing out that he:

> "can never forget that the (Coal) Board's biggest headache is the attitude of the miners and their misconceptions about the work the Board and its staff perform, and, perhaps most important, about the need for economic efficiency."

Then follows the comment of the Area General Manager:

> "We have issued booklets, but nobody bothered to read them. We had a few questions when we started joint consultative committees, but even these have now petered out. We have tried to put explanations into the minutes and put them up on the notice-board, but nobody bothered to read them. It is no use trying to put it over at the lodge meetings of the union, for only a few miners attend them. This is really our major difficulty, how to put this information across and how to rid the minds of the men of misconceptions."

The pathetic notion that you can improve communications by giving more and better information should surely be allowed to die a natural death; you will not get any reception if you are not trusted; but if relations are good, then there is a good chance that what you say will be received, and that you will get co-operation in return.

---

[10] F. Zweig, *The British Worker* (London: Penguin Books, 1952).
[11] Acton Society Trust, *The Worker's Point of View* (London: Acton Society Trust, 1952).
[12] Acton Society Trust, *Management under Nationalisation* (London: Acton Society Trust, 1953).

But even where trust and mutual confidence do exist, that tendency to come to an interview, meeting or conference with preconceived notions is still found, and we cannot afford to forget that the same situation is almost always seen in different ways by different people, depending on their personal capacities, inclinations and background. Zangwill's [13] (1937) experiment on "Aufgabe" showed the importance of that. Two groups of subjects were shown, separately, a vague, ill-determined ink-blot. They were not told what it represented, but one group was told that it might be like an animal; and the second group was told that it might resemble a landscape. Both groups drew and described what they had seen. The first group all drew cats, rabbits, or similar animals, while the second group drew mountains and hills. The same stimulus confronted both groups, but their preconceived ideas about it determined their reactions to it.

I believe, therefore, that in trying to understand human communication, we would be well advised to study the basic mental processes that underlie so much of everyday human behaviour—the study of perception in particular, and the many experiments on "Aufgabe" and attitude formation.

But further problems arise. Suppose that a person to whom we wish to communicate something has sniffed us over, asking unconsciously, "Is he friendly, can I trust him?", and decided that he is disposed to listen to us, we still need to know whether what we say will be understood, and if so, whether, at a later date, it will be recalled or repeated accurately. So I would suggest that comprehension and recall are legitimate subjects for research and study when considering human communications.

Both of these, as it happens, have been studied fully in recent years. I should like, therefore, only to point out a few of the researches or experiments which seem to me to throw light on how we succeed or fail in comprehending information and recalling it accurately.

Bartlett [14] (1951) has suggested that one of the chief functions of the mind, when it is active, is "filling up gaps"; that is, it is constantly trying to link new material into the pattern of older material, in order to make it meaningful. Our minds seem to prefer the simple and regular to the complex and irregular, and to organise what is received into tidy, meaningful bundles. That is why it is so difficult

[13] O. L. Zangwill, "A Study of the Significance of Attitude in Recognition," *British Journal of Psychology*, Vol. 28, 1937, pp. 12-17.
[14] F. C. Bartlett, *The Mind at Work and Play* (London: Allen and Unwin, 1951).

to get a new idea across; for a new idea has to be fitted into the existing structure in the mind, and it is often quite a struggle to do so. A simple demonstration of that difficulty was given by Wertheimer; to give you an example of it, suppose you look at these four words:

MAN   TABLE   KNIFE   CLOTH

You can, without much difficulty, form some kind of mental picture out of them. If I add the word TROLLEY, you can probably fit that in quite easily to your already established picture. But if I now add the words:

SURGEON   BLOOD   ANAESTHETIC

you will probably have a few puzzled moments before you are able to reorganise the picture in your mind. The meaning of the isolated words changes as the pattern alters, so that the table, once laid for a meal, with a knife handy for cutting a cake, becomes an operating table, with the knife poised over the man who a few moments earlier was sitting down to his tea.

Our mental habits persist and may help or hinder us; they will only do the former if we can link what we have to say on to what our listeners already know; for in that way, the new can be assimilated to the old.

But there is more to comprehension than mental habits; the interest of the subject matter and our own intelligence are also involved. Some idea of the extent of these factors can be seen in two very detailed and careful experiments carried out by the BBC Audience Research Department [15] (1950, 1951, 1952).

The first of these researches was an attempt to assess the intelligibility of a series of Forces Educational Broadcasts; the second was concerned with the comprehensibility of the five minute programme "Topic for Tonight" which follows the 10 o'clock news. What was particularly striking about both these researches was that they demonstrated that understanding was largely based on intellectual capacity—not perhaps a very new finding, but an interesting one because it showed the extent to which comprehension relies on intelligence. To quote from the report:

---

[15] P. E. Vernon, *An Investigation into the Intelligibility of Broadcast Talks*, Audience Research Department Report (London: British Broadcasting Corporation, 1950); R. Silvey, "The Intelligibilty of Broadcast Talks," *Public Opinion Quarterly* (Summer, 1951); W. A. Belson, *An Inquiry into the Comprehensibility of "Topic for Tonight,"* Audience Research Department Report (London: British Broadcasting Corporation, 1952).

"It would seem that the talk which is couched at a level of difficulty appropriate to the top third of the population can rarely convey much to people of even average intelligence and little or nothing to the backward quarter (of the population)."

But something else came out of the first research too; that was the finding that, apart from intellectual capacity, comprehension was "profoundly influenced by the extent to which (people) are interested in the subject, or have their interest in it aroused. The greater the listeners' interest, the greater their understanding is likely to be, and vice versa." This factor of interestingness was more important for intelligibility than any factor of style, language, and delivery. Certainly, such factors as limiting the number of main points, providing clear summaries, a lucid and lively style, concrete treatment, and the illustration of abstract points all *make for* intelligibility—the research proved that—but they do not *guarantee* intelligibility; they only come into play if the talk is interesting in the first place.

Although these studies are of great value in showing just how complicated a matter it is to get information across that will be remembered with any accuracy, a broadcast talk is not the same as face-to-face contact; there are, unfortunately, to my knowledge, no scientific studies of the intelligibility of personal talks to an audience as compared with broadcast talks. The nearest approach to such an investigation is the series of experiments conducted by Lewin [16] (1947) on the respective values of lectures and group discussions in changing food habits. It will be remembered that the latter proved far more effective because the audience participated in a decision. They were, in fact, "ego-involved." I should like to suggest that it is that factor of ego-involvement which lies behind the importance of interest in the subject matter of a talk, which was so well shown in the BBC researches.

Some years ago, I carried out some experiments on the transmission of rumour (Higham,[17] 1951). The method I used was to get someone to recount a short tale to a second person, who repeated it to a third, and so on; each version of the story was recorded on a recording machine, so that a permanent record was available; by those means the successive reproductions could be analysed to see what changes had taken place in the narrative. I used different types of story and different groups of subjects; one day, quite by accident

[16] K. Lewin, "Frontiers in Group Dynamics (II)," *Human Relations*, Vol. 1, 1947, pp. 143-153.

[17] T. M. Higham, "The Experimental Study of the Transmission of Rumour," *British Journal of Psychology (General Section)*, Vol. 42, 1951, pp. 42-55.

(as I must admit), I made up a short tale about a professor discussing the prospects of his students in their forthcoming examinations; I tried this out on just such a group of his students as might be involved in this sort of discussion. To my surprise, I found that reproduction of the story showed few changes and comparatively small loss of detail, whereas all the other stories produced many changes and a great loss of content with successive reproductions. Applying an appropriate statistical technique, I found that such a result was unlikely to have happened by chance. The explanation was that the students were personally involved in the story; it was about something that affected their interests; and for all they knew it might have been true, or a prophetic warning! Because of this personal interest they remembered it better.

Joint Consultation, particularly through Works' Councils, shows this sort of thing well: matters which management thinks of burning interest are passed by almost without comment; but if an announcement is made that the price of tea in the canteen is going up, discussion is animated and prolonged. People will show most interest in things which concern them personally, or which are linked to their basic needs; that is perhaps why discussion methods seem to be more successful in bringing about change than are formal lectures, for if you take part in a discussion you become involved in it, and it means more to you.

None the less, I think we would be unwise to neglect the importance of the personal factor even in the comprehension of information. For, as many will testify, a good speaker can arouse interest in his audience, even if he breaks every known rule of lecturing. Professor Meredith [18] (1950) has given an excellent example of this in a talk he gave some time ago:

> "I am not a theologian, but I was once privileged to attend, at a weekend conference, a lecture by a professor of theology. It was twenty-five years ago and it is still vivid to me today. The subject was Amos, of whom I previously knew precisely nothing. By the end of the lecture I had not only a dynamic impression of the character and message of the prophet but also a clear and colourful picture of the contemporary economic, political, and social structure of the people of Israel. The professor used no notes. He padded round the room, with his hands behind his back, and wearing felt slippers. From time to time he raised one foot to scratch the calf of the other leg. Now and then he looked at one or other of us directly in the eyes, with a kind of challenging glare. At other times he gazed through the window into the extreme

[18] G. P. Meredith, "The Art of Lecturing," *British Medical Journal*, 26 August, 1950.

distance, as if looking at Palestine, and describing what he saw, taking our gaze with him. I recall that he pronounced Jahweh with the sort of sound one makes in clearing one's throat."

Later Professor Meredith gives his views on why the professor of theology, and other lecturers he had heard, succeeded in communicating to their listeners. He says:

"You can wander about, you can indulge in irritating mannerisms, you can hum and haw, you can remain glued to a desk, you can twiddle your fingers, you can commit all the crimes on the statute book (the latter would make entertaining reading if someone would write it: 'The Deadly Sins of the Lecture Theatre'), and you can get away with all of them if only you have the one supreme virtue. What is that virtue? The name I would give it is *vitality*. This was the common factor in all my remembered lectures."

I suggested earlier that the recall of information was a part of the process of communication which could well be studied. Indeed it has been thoroughly explored, notably and perhaps primarily by Sir Frederic Bartlett [19] (1932) whose book *Remembering* is still the classic on that subject. Later work by Allport and Postman [20] (1948) and others on rumour has supported these earlier findings. The factors of interest and personal involvement, which I mentioned earlier, are important in recall, because we tend to remember better and more accurately those things in which we have been personally interested; but with matters less personal, or less interesting, our minds tend to transform what we have heard, until our final recollection may be quite different from what actually took place. This is an important factor in two way information, because if, for example, a Works' Council holds a meeting, it is attended by delegates from different sections of the organisation, who have to report back to their constituents; and it is in this reporting back that mistakes and falsifications—albeit involuntary ones—are apt to occur.

Another BBC experiment has shown the importance of some other factors in recall as well. This experiment [21] (1954) was about the immediate memory of a feature programme, one of the "This is the Law" series, in which the script was enlivened by dramatisation, and by being cast in the form of a continuous story. In addition the subjects were all personally invited to the BBC to take part in the

[19] F. C. Bartlett, *Remembering* (London: Cambridge University Press, 1932).

[20] G. W. Allport and L. Postman, *The Psychology of Rumour* (New York: Holt, 1948).

[21] A. H. W. Nias and H. Kay, "Immediate Memory of a Broadcast Feature Programme, *British Journal of Educational Psychology*, Vol. 24, 1954, pp. 154-160.

experiment. Under such conditions about 80 per cent of the story was recalled accurately, with the same variations according to intelligence, occupation, etc. as had been found previously. What is interesting, though, is that the material—a connected story, dealing with everyday people and incidents in everyday language—"lent itself to quick and easy assimilation." But illustrations and dramatisations cannot just be left to make their point; as Vernon [22] has pointed out (1946) they must be related to the subject matter as a whole, otherwise the point is apt to be forgotten.

Here, as in the other aspects of communication which I have touched on, much work remains to be done. So much of what passes for "communication theory" (in the non-engineering sense) is based on hunches and prejudices that further careful experiments are needed. It is the importance of the personal factor in communication that particularly needs to be examined. Simply because we almost all have to live and work among other human beings, we all tend at times to be like the character in Shaw's "Fanny's First Play," who was asked to comment on a production. "You don't expect me to know what to say about a play," she said, "when I don't know who the author is, do you?"

If subjective evidence is acceptable, we have the testimony of teachers, sages and others over the centuries, that people tend to weigh up who we are before listening to what we have to say.

St. Thomas Aquinas warned his pupils "Non respicias a quo sed quod sane dicetur memoriae recommenda." Dr. Johnson said of someone, "What have you to say about Aristotle tells me very little about Aristotle, but a great deal about you." Emerson puts it more forcefully, "What you are sounds so loudly in my ears that I cannot hear what you say." In many speeches, talks, and other forms of communication, it is often the character of the man that shows through the words he uses, as for example in Sir Winston Churchill's war-time speeches. What is said, and how it is said, often matter less than who says it. As Lord Rosebery said of William Pitt the Elder:

> "It is not merely the thing that is said, but the man who says it that counts, the character which breathes through the sentences."

There needs to be some degree of warmth in a personal relationship for real communication to exist. When people in conference or consultation have built up stable and firm relationships, then com-

---

[22] P. E. Vernon, "An Experiment on the Value of the Filmstrip in the Instruction of Adults," *British Journal of Educational Psychology*, Vol. 16, 1946, pp. 149-162.

munication is not only easier, but, usually, better. As Sir Geoffrey Vickers [23] (1954) has put it:

> "Consider how much easier it is to communicate on a standing committee, the members of which are used to deliberating together, than on an ad hoc committee which has never met before. Consider also, how, if the atmosphere of a conference begins to deteriorate, all the experienced members will set to work to put it right again, that is, to recreate the mutual attitudes without which it is a waste of time to confer."

So I should like to suggest to you that successful communication will come about by careful placement of key-men—men, that is, who command trust and respect, who are sympathetic and intelligent; they are your eyes and ears, the people through whom information will flow to you and from you. As to most operatives, the foreman, not the Board of Directors, *is* the firm, it means careful selection and training of your supervisors. On a higher level, it means equally careful selection and training of junior staff. But a fundamental attitude of "consistent and fair treatment of employees, pursued in good times and bad, and humour and common sense in day to day relationships," as John Marsh of the Industrial Welfare Society put it recently, is not something you can just lay on; it is not a technique; it springs from qualities of character and personality, which is why selection is so important. As March [24] (1954) says:

> "The fully fashioned personnel or welfare service cannot be effective unless the foreman—who is 'the firm' to most employees—is efficient, just and consistently humane in his leadership. One knows of instances where the results of years of patient endeavour in building up morale have been dissolved within a few hours of a manager losing his temper. All this goes to show that there are no final answers to human relations questions."

And if at times we tend to forget that last sentence, and to think that we really have at last found the means to cure the human ills of industry once and for all—and judging by the rise and fall in the popularity of such means to that end as welfare schemes, joint consultations, communications and co-partnerships, at times we all do think that—then we would do well to remember the warning of Sir Thomas More:

> "It is not possible for all things to be well unless all men are good, which I think will not be for these many years."

[23] C. G. Vickers, "Human Communication," *British Management Review*, Vol. 12, 1954, pp. 71-79.

[24] J. Marsh, "Human Relationships in Industry," *Financial Times*, 30 September, 1954.

Questions

1. What are some of the basic reasons why people are not receptive to what we have to say?
2. How can the receptivity of people be improved?
3. What are some of the basic subjects that should be studied when considering human communications?
4. What does Higham recommend for successful communication?
5. Illustrate Higham's psychological factors with examples from your own experience.

31. LISTENING IS GOOD BUSINESS *

Ralph G. Nichols

In the year 1940, Dr. Harry Goldstein completed an important educational research project at Columbia University. It was underwritten by one of our educational foundations, was very carefully drawn. Two very important observations emerged from it. *One:* he discovered that it is perfectly possible to listen to speech at a rate more than three times that which we normally hear it without any significant loss of comprehension. *Two:* he suggested that America may have overlooked a very important element in her educational system, that of refining our ability to listen.

Quite a few people read this study, and wondered about it; but not very many did anything about it. Shortly after that, however, a chap named Richard Hubbell, an important figure in the television industry, produced a new book. In it he declared without equivocation that 98 per cent of all that a man learns in his lifetime he learns through his eyes or through his ears.

Hubbell's book threw a spotlight upon a long-neglected organ we own—our ears; and it threw into focus one of the most important educational researches of our time. Dr. Paul Rankin of Ohio State University was determined to find out what proportion of our waking day we spend in verbal communication. He kept a careful log on 65 white-collar workers at 15-minute intervals for two months on end. Here is what he found:

> Seven out of every ten minutes that you and I are conscious, alive and awake we are communicating verbally in one of its forms; and that communication time is devoted 9 per cent to writing, 16 per cent to reading, 30 per cent to speaking, and 45 per cent to listening.

Our Upside-Down Schools

With respect to training in these communication skills, America has built her school system upside-down. Primary and secondary schools devote some 12 years to teaching a youngster how to write a sentence, in the hope that sometime he will be able to write a full paragraph, and then a complete report. Countless tax dollars and teacher hours of energy are spent in improving the least-used channel of communication.

* From *Personnel Management: New Perspectives*, Bulletin No. 29, Bureau of Industrial Relations, University of Michigan, 1961. Reprinted with permission.

For some inexplicable reason we chop off all reading improvement training at the end of the eighth grade. From that time on the reading we do is of an extensive, voluntary and general character. Then we moan because America averages out as a nation of eighth grade readers. In view of the eight years of training we receive at best, we shouldn't be shocked at that fact. However, a lot of tax dollars are devoted to improving this second least-used channel of communication.

Then we come to something important quantitatively—speech itself. Thirty per cent of our communication time is spent in it; yet speech training in America is largely an extra-curricular activity. In a typical school you will find an all-school play once or twice a year. There may be a debating team with a couple of lawyers' sons on it. There will be an orator, an extemporary speaker, and that is about the size of it. You will find it very difficult to discover a high school where even one semester of speech training is required of the students.

Then we come to listening. Forty-five per cent of our communication time is spent in it. In 1948, when I first became concerned about this field, hardly anyone had considered refining his listening ability.

I asked my University for a sabbatical leave that year, and spent 12 months doing research, trying to identify the characteristics of a good and bad listener. First, I learned that nobody knew much about effective listening. Only one small girls' college in Missouri, Stephens College, was teaching listening. Only three experimental and scientific research reports in the field of listening comprehension had been published in 1948. By comparison, over 3,000 scientific studies had been published in the field of reading comprehension.

TEN YEARS MAKE A DIFFERENCE

By 1958 a very dramatic change had occurred. Most of our leading universities were teaching listening under that label. Today these schools are not only teaching listening—they are conducting graduate-level research in the field. Today scores of businesses and industries have instituted listening training programs for selected management personnel. Several departments of the Federal Government have followed suit.

A number of units of our military service have started listening training programs. Effective listening has practical application to current business practices. For example, there is a growing conviction that most salesmen talk too much and listen too little. There is a good deal of evidence accumulating to support this conviction.

Two Central Questions

In view of this tremendous surge of interest in listening in just ten years' time, I should like to raise two questions and very closely pursue answers to them.

Question No. 1: Is efficient listening a problem in business and industrial management?

For our first bit of insight on this, I should like to revert to the classroom for just a moment, for the first person to produce important evidence on it was H. E. Jones, a professor at Columbia University. He was in charge of all the beginning psychology classes there, and he frequently lectured to a population of some 476 freshmen.

It seemed to him, when he gave comprehensive tests on his lecture content, that the students weren't getting very much of what he was trying to say. He hit upon a novel idea for an experiment and, with the cooperation of 50 of his colleagues on the Columbia faculty, he proceeded with the study. Each professor agreed to prepare and deliver a ten-minute lecture on his own subject to Jones' students. Each one submitted his lecture excerpt to Jones ahead of time, and Jones painstakingly built an objective test over the contents. Half of the questions in each quiz demanded a recalling of facts, and the other half required the understanding of a principle or two imbedded in the lecture excerpt.

Efficiency Level—25 Per Cent

Professor No. 1 came in, gave his ten-minute lecture, disappeared, and the group was questioned on its content. No. 2 followed. At the end of the 50th presentation and the 50th quiz, Jones scored the papers and found that freshmen were able to respond correctly to only about 50 per cent of the items in the test. Then came the shock. Two months later he assembled the 476 freshmen and gave them the whole battery of tests a second time. This time they were able to respond correctly to only 25 per cent of the items in the quizzes. Jones was forced to conclude, reluctantly, that without training, Columbia University freshmen operate at a 25 per cent level of efficiency when they listen.

I couldn't believe it could be that bad. I decided to repeat the experiment at the University of Minnesota, and did so. I didn't let two months go by, for I was pretty certain that the curve of forgetting takes the downward swoop long before two months pass.

I let two weeks pass, and got exactly the same statistics: 50 per cent response in the immediate test situation; 25 per cent after two weeks had passed. Several other universities have conducted the same experiment, and all have come up with similar statistics.

I think it is accurate and conservative to say that we operate at precisely a 25 per cent level of efficiency when listening to a ten-minute talk. How do you like that? I know you are interested in efficiency. Some of us like to talk in terms of 90, 93, 95 or even 98 per cent efficiency in the things we do—yet in the thing we do most frequently in all our lives (save possibly for breathing), we probably operate at about a 25 per cent level of efficiency.

Is this important in business and industrial management? Let us consider some evidence that will be nearer to your heart.

EVIDENCE FROM INDUSTRY

A few years ago a young man went to a speech professor at a large state university and said that he would like to acquire a Ph.D. degree in the field of speech. My professional friend said, "Well, your credentials look good enough; but instead of doing a Ph.D. in the speech field, I would like you to do it in the field of listening. I have a project in mind. Take a notebook; go to this firm in New Orleans; and interview all the management people you can get in to see during one week. Ask them these questions." Then he gave the student a list of questions he was to ask of each manager.

The young man disappeared, and came back a week later. He had a little notebook full of testimony that he had acquired from these management people. The gist of it was that they worked for a tremendous organization, that they had a great future, that they felt they had one of the finest communication systems ever devised in any business or industry.

They said, "Our workers know what they are trying to do. They understand our program. We have the most loyal group of employees to be found anywhere. The morale in our outfit is tremendous. The future looks good."

"Okay," said my friend the speech professor. "Put on a pair of coveralls. Go down to that same firm and see Joe Walker, head of the company's trucking department. You are to work for him for one year. Every day, carry a notebook in your inside pocket, and whenever you hear the employees say anything about their management—write it down in your notebook."

Twelve months later the student came back with a great stack of notebooks. My friend spent several weeks pouring over the testimony in them, and when he got through announced that it was the most vicious, malicious, denunciatory attack of one group upon another he ever had seen.

Trying to find out what the employees really knew of their firm's policies, procedures, and philosophy, he concluded that the workers understood *less* than 25 per cent of what their managers thought they understood.

I doubted this generalization and discussed my skepticism with Erle Savage, a senior partner of the Pidgeon Savage Lewis Cor-

Dilution of information occurs as a result of improper Communications flow . .

100%	63%	56%	40%	30%	20%
BOARD	VICE PRESIDENT	GENERAL SUPERVISOR	PLANT MANAGER	GENERAL FOREMAN	WORKER

Reproduced By Special Permission of Pidgeon Savage Lewis, Inc.

poration of Minneapolis, an advertising and communications firm. He looked at me when I told him about the study, and said, "Professor, don't be so skeptical. As a matter of fact, the picture is even worse than your friend reports it to you. My company has just made a very careful study of the communicative efficiency of 100 representative business and industrial managements. This chart shows the composite picture of what we discovered."

As you can see, there is a tremendous loss of information—37 per cent—between the Board of Directors and the Vice-Presidential level.

General supervisors got 56 per cent of the information; plant managers 40 per cent; and general foremen received only 30 per cent of what had been transmitted downward to them. An average of only 20 per cent of the communication sent downward through the five levels of management finally gets to the worker level in the 100 representative American companies.

Studies have dug deeper. What kind of person is the employee who understands only 20 per cent of what his management thinks (and hopes) he understands? The 20 per cent-informed individual is usually a negative-minded fellow. He believes that there are big fat managers up there at the top, exploiting him, hogging most of the profits and not giving a proper share to him. His first inclination may be to steal something in order to get even—and the easiest thing to steal in our economy is time. One can check in late and pretend he got there early. Or he can leave early and report he left late. It is always easy to slow down at the desk or on the assembly line or wherever one is working. All this is costly business. If this doesn't satisfy him, a person can start stealing tools or equipment. People have been found carrying out a hammer or saw beneath overcoats as they walk out at night. One person was even caught with a nickel roll of toilet tissue under his jacket—trying to get even.

Upward Communication

Communicative efficiency down through the levels of management is terribly poor, and we are only beginning to appreciate the enormity of the problem. But I am much more concerned about another kind of communication. I am much more excited about the efficiency or inefficiency of upward communication than of that which passes downward through the channels. Why? Because I hold the deep conviction that the efficiency of downward communication is going to be improved significantly only when top management better understands the attitudes, the opinions, the ideas and the suggestions of the people at the bottom of the whole structure.

What kind of efficiency do we have when the levels of management report upward? We have begun to collect a lot of evidence on that. A recent study made of 24 industrial plants reveals a very peculiar thing. In the early stages of their study the researchers recognized that ten distinct factors are probably the most important in the morale of any employee group. They asked managers to rate these ten morale factors in the order of their importance as they thought they were influencing the employee group.

The managers put these three factors in the bottom three ranks. Eight: full appreciation of work done. Nine: feeling "in" on things. Ten: sympathetic help on personal problems.

Then the researchers went to the employee group and asked them to rate the ten morale factors in the rank-order of their actual influence. They rated these factors as follows: First: full appreciation of work done. Two: feeling "in" on things. Three: sympathetic help on personal problems.

It is almost incredible that management could guess exactly wrong, putting the three most important factors in the three least important spots; but this kind of evidence emerges again and again when objective studies are made of how well management really understands the attitudes and opinions of the employee group.

Attempts to Improve

Knowing this, a number of forward-looking firms and businesses in America are making very serious attempts to do something about it. A lot of different techniques have been tried. The old one, of course, was to have the boss know everybody. Many a president took great pride in the fact that he knew everybody on his payroll. Many of them liked to spend half a day walking through the shop or plant, shaking hands with all the workers.

This didn't work badly as long as the number was small enough to make it possible. But soon our companies got too big; so then we tried different systems.

We have had labor-management meetings in which labor was supposed to "speak out." We have had elected representatives of labor meet with selected management people. Neither of these things worked very well. We have tried hiring a chaplain as a special counselor, with the open invitation to everyone in the whole organization to go and talk to the chaplain at any time. This method might have succeeded had not some malcontented employee started a rumor that the chaplain was a stool pigeon "planted" by the board of directors. Of course, the potential value of this technique was soon lost.

Labor reporters for the house publications have been tried. We have tried suggestion and complaint boxes, father confessors, opinion and attitude surveys; and even though each device probably has some merit to it, in every case it has a built-in weakness.

The Central Remedy

Their failing is that they *are* merely devices or techniques, and as such it seems to me they do not get at the head of the problem, which is sympathetic listening by one man to another. My feelings were pretty well restated in a study made by Loyola University researchers. They spent 18 months making this study. They were trying to find out what the attributes of a good manager really are. They finally came up with this generalization:

> Of all the sources of information a manager has by which he can come to know and accurately size up the personalities of the people in his department, listening to the individual employee is the most important.

The most stereotyped report they got from worker after worker who like their superiors was this one: "I like my boss. He listens to me. I can talk to him."

Frank E. Fischer, managing director of the American Management Association's School of Management, summarizes the situation in one sentence. He says, "Efficient listening is of such critical importance to industry, that as research and methodology improve, I feel that training departments will have to offer courses in this field."

Granted that such a course is needed, how do you keep a listening training program alive in an industry? There is only one possible justification for keeping it alive, and that is if it is paying you money. If it is not paying off, get rid of it.

A few years ago a large firm located near Chicago was having a lot of trouble. They had been losing money in one particular plant for several months, and they tried a number of devices to get the plant operating productively again. Finally, hunting around for some new idea, they hired an outside psychologist to come in to teach all of their foremen how to listen. The psychologist got all the foremen into a room and essentially taught them how to grunt. He said, "When your men come in and complain to you about not having enough baths or not enough rest rooms or all of the other grievances they have, I want you to look sympathetic and say 'hmmm' and nod affirmatively to them. Don't argue or talk back. Ask questions if you want to, such as, 'Well, what did your wife say?' or 'Do all the boys think this way?' Throw out little questions like these, but you are never to debate with one of these fellows. And you must all practice until you can say 'hmmm,' looking sympathetic while you're saying it." He coached these fellows for a couple of weeks and sent them back to their jobs.

As usual, streams of complainers made their way to the foremen's offices. To their surprise, instead of getting rude treatment, they found a man saying, "Hmmm, is that so? Well, what did you do then, Joe?" Several of them acted as though they were bulls in a china shop, muttered a half-baked apology of some kind, and backed out. The result was that after three months had gone by some 90 per cent of the grievances had disappeared, and the plant was making money again. The management of the plant was so sold on listening training that they decided if it was good for foremen, it would be just as well to have the plant managers learn how to listen too. They soon spread it through all of their levels of management.

I have pursued my first question long enough, is inefficient listening a problem in business and industrial management? I trust that perhaps you will concede it is.

Question No. 2: What can be done about it?

A few years ago I screened out the 100 worst listeners and the 100 best listeners I could identify in my University's freshman population. Standardized listening tests and lecture-comprehension tests were used, and we had two widely contrasting groups. These poor suffering 200 freshmen were then subjected to about 20 different kinds of objective tests and measures. I got scores on their reading, writing, speaking, mathematical and scientific aptitudes; six different types of personality inventories and each one filled out a lengthy questionnaire. In addition, I had a personal interview with each of the 200.

TEN BAD HABITS

When I got all done it seemed to me that ten things clearly differentiated a good listener from a bad one. I published an article about "The Ten Worst Listening Habits of the American People." Other universities read the article and repeated the study. Essentially, they came to the same conclusions. Thus, for whatever it is worth, I should like to enumerate and comment briefly on what seems to be the ten worst listening habits that afflict us. Why? Because listening training is largely the business of eliminating these bad listening habits, and replacing them with their counterpart skills.

I. Calling the subject uninteresting

Bad listening habit number one is to declare the subject uninteresting. The chairman announces a topic, or perhaps the bad listener reads it on the program and says to himself, "Gee, how dull can they get, anyhow? You'd think for the money they shell out they could get a decent speaker on a decent subject. This is such a dull topic that I think I'll worry about that secretary of mine. Am I going to keep her on another year, or am I going to sack her right now?" A lot of us store up these mental tangents to use in moments of boredom, and this is what the bad listener *always* does.

The good listener starts at the same point, but goes to a different conclusion. He says, "Gee, that sounds like a dull subject. I don't know what it has to do with me in my business. However, I'm trapped here, I can't get up and walk out. It would be terribly embarrassing and very conspicuous. Inasmuch as I am trapped, I guess I'll tune in on this guy to see if he has anything to say that I can use."

And the key to good listening in the first instance is that three-letter word—"use." The good listener is a sifter, a screener, a winnower, always hunting for something worthwhile or practical that he can store away in the back of his mind and put to work for him in the days or months ahead.

This is a selfish activity, but a very profitable one. We openly acknowledge the selfish character of it, and urge our trainees to become better listeners by hunting for the useful and practical. G. K. Chesterton put it beautifully many years ago in these words: "In all this world there is no such thing as an uninteresting subject. There are only uninterested people."

2. Criticizing the delivery

Bad listening habit number two is criticizing the speaker's delivery. A bad listener does it almost every time. The speaker starts to talk, and the man thinks, "Gee, is that the best they can get? This man can't even talk. All he does is try to read from his notes. Hasn't anyone ever told him to look his listeners in the eye when he talks to them? I have never heard a voice as unpleasant as this fellow's. All he does is fidget, snort and cough. Nobody could get anything from such a character. I'll tune him out and worry about that sales pitch I have to make next week." And off he goes on a mental tangent.

The good listener moves in a different direction. He says, "I don't know when I have heard such an inept speaker. You'd think they would get a better man than that for what they pay him. But wait a minute! This guy knows something I don't know, or he wouldn't be up there. Inasmuch as I have paid tuition or a registration fee, I'll dig his message out of him if it kills me. I'll concentrate on his content and forget about the lack of smoothness in this character's delivery."

After an hour or two of concentrating on content, he doesn't even remember the eccentricities and the oddities of the speaker. He begins to get interested in the subject. Actually, the speaker does very little of the learning. If learning takes place, it is because of action inside the brain of the listener—the man out front.

Suppose that right now a janitor interrupted you, yelling in broken, profane English, "Get the hell out of here! The building is on fire!" You wouldn't lean backward and say, "Please, sir, will you not couch that admonition in better rhetoric?" You would rush pell-mell out of the room, as you know. That is my point. The message is ten times as important as the clothing in which it comes. Form has little to do with the significance of the communication taking place.

3. Getting overstimulated

I feel like an authority on this one, for I have been overstimulated as long as I can remember. I get so excited about people and things that I just can't control myself. How does it work? A speaker starts to develop his topic. I am out in the audience, and before he talks three or four minutes he walks rough-shod on one of my pet biases or convictions. Immediately, I want to throw up my hand and challenge him on the spot. If it is too formal a spot, I will sit there and gnash my teeth and figure out the meanest, dirtiest, most embarrassing question I can hurl at him. I have often sat for 30 minutes composing the most embarrassing question that could possibly be phrased for the speaker to answer. If that doesn't fit, I will sit and build a great rebuttal speech. Maybe I know of a little evidence that contradicts something he has presented, and I will plan my rebuttal effort.

All too often I have hurled my nasty question or great rebuttal at the speaker, only to find him looking at me in complete wonderment and saying, "Nichols, didn't you hear when I went on to say that so-and-so was also true?" I hadn't. My listening efficiency had dropped to a zero per cent level because I had been overstimulated and excited about my contribution to come.

It happens all the time. And it is important! We now think it is so important that we put at the top of each blackboard in every classroom where we teach listening—and, by the way, we teach 25 per cent of the incoming freshmen on my campus to be better listeners because we don't think many will get through college if we don't—this slogan: "Withhold Evaluation until Comprehension is Complete." It sounds kind of abstract and meaningless, but it isn't. In smaller words we might say, "Hear the man out before you judge him." Unless you fully comprehend his point, you are going to make a snap judgment of it, and at least half the time you are going to guess wrong.

4. Listening only for facts

Bad listening habit number four is listening only for facts. I know that you have great respect for facts. I have, too; but a curious thing exists about those facts. I personally asked the 100 worst listeners I could locate what they concentrated on in a listening situation. Ninety-seven of the 100 testified proudly that they "listened for the facts." The truth was that they got a few facts, garbled a shocking number, and completely lost the bulk of them.

I asked the 100 best listeners what they concentrated on in a listening situation, and a bit timidly and apologetically they testified in equal proportion, "When we listen we try to get the gist of it—the main idea."

The truth was that these idea listeners *had* recognized generalizations or principles, and had used them as connecting threads to give sense and system to the whole talk. Two days later they somehow appended more facts to these connecting threads than the bad listeners were able to catalogue and report.

We had to conclude that if one wants to be a good listener he should try to get the gist of the discourse—the main thread, the idea, the principle, the concept, the generalization. We should quit worrying about the facts. Facts can be retained only when they make sense, and they may make sense only when they support a generalization of some kind.

5. Outlining everything

Bad listening habit number five is trying to make an outline of everything. This is a curious business. We found that the 100 worst listeners thought that notetaking and outlining were synonymous. They knew only one way to take notes—to make an outline of the speech. There is nothing wrong with outlining if the speaker is following an outline pattern of organization. He should be, I would concede. However, between today and the day you and I die, probably not one-third of the speakers we hear are going to have organized their discourses carefully on an outline pattern or scheme—and one of the most frustrating things in this world is to try to outline the un-outlinable.

The student who does it always comes out with a sheet of notebook paper that is a perfect and beautiful thing in terms of symmetry— all the margins and indentations perfectly ordered, the symbols all nicely subordinated; and there is meaningless jargon after each symbol. Two months later, when he tries to review his notes, they have no meaning whatsoever.

We asked the 100 best listeners what they did for notetaking and they said, "It all depends on the speaker. We listen for a while and do nothing. When we figure out if he is organized or not, we sometimes write little abstracts. We listen three or four minutes and write a one-sentence summary of what has been said. Sometimes we annotate the workbook or textbook as we listen. Sometimes we use the 'fact versus principle' technique."

I am fascinated about this last technique for I feel it is highly effective. They have two sheets of notebook paper side by side when they go in to hear a lecture. At the top of one sheet they write the word "facts," and at the top of the opposite sheet they write the word "principles." Then they sort of lean back thinking. "Produce, Mister, produce!" They merely list in vertical columns the facts or principles produced. The system calls for a minimum of writing. If the man is a phony and has no ideas, they have two blank sheets of paper. If he happens to be a producer (and some of them are), you will find him grinding out from 20 to 40 facts every time he gives a talk, with two or three very important principles on the other side. These are the best possible notes to have when we come to a period for review.

Our conclusion had to be that the good listener is a flexible character who has many systems of taking notes, and that he carefully picks out the best one for the type of speaker he hears.

6. Faking attention

Bad listening habit number six is faking attention to the speaker. As a schoolteacher, for many years I felt I was going over big if I looked over the classroom and saw the bulk of my students with their chins in their hands looking up at me in this fashion. I was always pleased to see the girls in the first rows in this posture. I thought they were tuning me in.

We now know that the surest index to inattention in all this world is this posture on the part of the listener. Having paid the speaker the overt courtesy of appearing to tune him in, the listener feels conscience-free to take off on one of a thousand mental tangents, and that is precisely where he has gone. If you ever face an audience and, looking out across the room, see the bulk of your listeners in this pose, stop short in your talk and tell them to stand up and do calisthenics with you to get their blood circulating again.

Efficient listening is characterized by a quicker action of the heart, a faster circulation of blood, a small rise in body temperature. It is energy-burning and energy-consuming. It is dynamic and constructive.

7. Tolerating or creating distractions

Bad listening habit number seven is . . . so obviously clear that I will not elaborate on it.

8. Evading the difficult

Bad listening habit number eight is much more important. This is avoiding difficult and technical presentations.

We asked our 100 worst listeners what they did in terms of listening to radio and television. We found that these 100 worst listeners were authorities on Bob Hope, Red Skelton and the Lone Ranger. Apparently they had spent their lives listening to these programs. Not one of those bad listeners had ever sat clear through the "Chicago Round Table," "Town Meeting of the Air," "Meet the Press," "Invitation to Learning," "See It Now," or "You Are There."

We asked the 100 best listeners, and they knew all about Bob Hope and Red Skelton, to be sure; but, voluntarily or otherwise, they had many times sat through some of these more difficult, technical and educational programs on radio and television.

Pursuing this aspect of good listening, we finally concluded that the one word in the dictionary that best describes the bad listener is the word "inexperienced." It is true he spends 45 per cent of his communication day listening to something, but that something is always easy, recreational or narrative in character. He avoids, as though it were poison, anything tough, technical or expository in character.

Take a youngster who has never heard anything more difficult than Bob Hope and put him in an auditorium with 300 other freshmen; trot out the best professor of biochemistry on the faculty and let him start a lecture. The boy says, "Gee, what am I doin' here? What's he talkin' about?" He cancels that course and maybe heads into an economics class. It is just as rough over there. Inside of three months he washes out of school and is gone. He is inundated. For every two freshmen who come to our university and college campuses in America today, one washes out before the end of his sophomore year—and often before the end of his freshman year.

At the other end of the curriculum, in most instances, for every one graduate to whom we can award a four-year degree there are two employers waiting to bid for his services. Fifty per cent mortality on the intake! And we meet half of the demand on the outgo! I claim this is critical.

I am not sure how long we can stay in the world competition we are engaged in with this horrible loss of trained manpower. I get excited about it, perhaps overexcited. I actually feel that if we could get a little training grade by grade, ten minutes a week, in tough technical material, we would have a tremendous decrease of that 50 per cent mortality at the college level. America needs more educated men and women to improve her economy and her culture.

9. Submitting to emotional words

Bad listening habit number nine is letting emotion-laden words throw us out of tune with the speaker.

This is a curious business; but it is a fact that a single word may have such an emotional load in it that it throws some listener or group of listeners right out of perspective.

When I was in college I was on the debate team, and my colleague was a Negro boy whose first name was Lionel. He was intelligent and an excellent speaker; and we did all right until we met a certain college away from home. Inadvertently in that debate one of the opposition said, "The niggers will be coming over." I happened to be looking at Lionel's black throat, saw the blood rush upward into his black face, and realized he was the next speaker in the debate, and he went out and made a tremendous ten-minute speech on the race problem in America. It was a great talk—but we were supposed to be debating the Philippine Island question. We lost that debate.

Word got around, and every debate tournament we entered we lost because the opposition soon learned that all they had to do to lick us was to drop the word "nigger" into the conversation and we would go berserk. To this day if anybody says that word in my hearing, I begin to erupt emotionally and am unable to think for three or four minutes.

I don't know what words throw you out of tune with a speaker, but I will warrant that a few of these may affect you. We have pinned down a number of them. We know that the word "mother-in-law" sometimes does it. The word "evolution" does it sometimes. "Automation" and "big business" are troublemakers. "Income tax," "landlord," "landlady," "Harry Truman," and "Sherman Adams" are all fighting words that have tended to disrupt listening efficiency for some people at some time or other. Last year I learned that department store personnel do not want to be called "clerks." Unfortunately I had used the word "clerks" in a talk, and I had five women reproach me afterwards. They wished to be called "retail sales personnel."

One of the most important studies that could be made would be for some researcher to identify the 100 greatest word barriers to learning. I wish I knew what they were. If we knew what 100 words cause most of our difficulty as barriers to communication, we could consider them grade by grade; we could lay them out in the open, discuss them, rationalize them and get them behind us. How silly it is to let a simple word—merely a symbol of something—get us so excited as to disrupt our listening efficiency; yet this goes on all the time.

10. Wasting through power

I have left bad listening habit No. 10 until the last because I think it is by far the most important of all. It is wasting the differential between thought speed and speech speed.

On the average in America we talk 125 words per minute; but if you put a man up in front of an audience and get that degree of formality in the situation that always ensues when he starts speaking informatively or instructionally to a group seated before him, he slows down. In America we average 100 words per minute when we speak informatively to an audience. How fast do people out front listen? Or, to put it more accurately, how fast do listeners think in words per minute when they listen? We know from three different studies that you will never face an audience of any size at all that does not think at an easy cruising speed of 400 to 500 words per minute. The difference between speech speed and thought speed operates as a tremendous pitfall. It is a snare and a delusion. It is a breeder of false security, and a breeder of mental tangents.

MENTAL TANGENTS AT WORK

I believe I can give you fairly good insight as to what a male engineer thinks about when he is listening to a professor of engineering. Travel with me mentally, and imagine you are a group of senior engineering students about ready to graduate.

I am an old professor of engineering, and I walk in and glower at you at the beginning of your class in your senior year, and I say, "Well, you think you're going to make it, eh? Some of you are going to get your sheepskins—but I'll tell you now that there are a few of you who aren't going to make it. We're going to flunk a couple of you. If you *do* make it, there is something you must remember as long as you live. The successful engineer is the man who appreciates the value and worth of a slide rule! He is the man who never goes anywhere without one in his pocket or at his belt.

"Because a slide rule is the most important requirement for a successful career in engineering, I am going to spend this last class hour with you reviewing the mathematic computations possible when using it."

What do the students think about? One is thinking: "This old goat going over that again? I got that in physics when I was a junior in high school. They told me all about it again in my senior year, and again as a freshman and sophomore in college. How can a man stall that way and take taxpayers' money for a salary? Guess I'll worry about that soft tire on my Ford. I noticed the right rear was a little soft this morning. If that darned thing is flat when I get out of here, am I going to change it or let 'er sit until tomorrow, and get some help on it?"

He worries 50 seconds about the tire and then he checks in on the professor. The professor is now adding two digit figures on the slide rule. It is old stuff. Out goes the student worrying now about an approaching chemistry quiz. He spends 50 seconds on the chemistry quiz and ten seconds on the professor. In again, and out again. It wouldn't be so bad, if he always checked in for the ten!

Sooner or later this male engineering student gets to that inevitable tangent that occurs to every male at the college level. He begins to wonder which woman to call for a date Saturday night. "I wonder if I should call Susie. She's plump and jolly and I've had her out a lot of times and she's a lot of fun. She always make candy that's so darned good!" He figures he could easily get a date with Susie—and then a thought strikes him. "I wonder if I could rate a date with Martha who came in from out of town. I don't know her last name, but gee, what a woman! That gal is tall, sinuous and glamorous. When she walks it's like watching a snake crawl. If I could rate a date with that creature, brother!" And this lad is off on a mental tangent from which there is no return!

The next thing he hears is the bell at the end of the hour.

As the bell rings he hears the old professor say, "Remember, when you take the cube root do it step by step, as a. . . ."

"Cube root? I never heard of it!" In absolute panic he grabs a friend going out the back door and he says, "How do you do cube root?" And the friend doesn't know either, for he has been out on a mental tangent too.

This is why we listen at an average efficiency level of 25 per cent. It is because of the constant allurement of mental tangents. It seems to be almost impossible to keep our minds free from them.

What is the answer? It is obvious. If you can think four times faster than any man can talk to you, this should be a source of power; it should not be a weakness. As it operates without training it is a liability, but with training it can be converted into a tremendous asset.

Mental Manipulations

These activities, these mental manipulations, are three in number. Wherever you find listening training succeeding today, you will find them in the training program.

1. Anticipate speaker's next point

Number one is to anticipate what the speaker is going to say next. One of the best things we can possibly do is to dash ahead of him mentally and try to guess what his next main point is likely to be. If we guess it is going to be point A and it turns out to be point A, learning is reinforced, nearly doubled; for that point comes twice into our brain centers instead of once.

If we guess wrong, what then? If we guess it is going to be point A and it turns out to be point Z, we can't help ourselves. We begin to compare Z with A, and wonder why he didn't make A his next point.

When we compare the thought we felt he was going to make with the one he actually produced, we begin to apply the oldest law of learning in the books—which is that we learn best by comparison and contrast. To anticipate—to "guess ahead," is the one wager in life we cannot lose. Whether we guess right or wrong, we win.

2. Identify elements

Mental exercise number two is to identify the supporting elements the speaker uses in building his points. By and large, we use only three ways to build points. We explain the point, we get emotional and harangue the point, or we illustrate the point with a factual generalization following the illustration.

The sophisticated listener knows this. He spends a little of the differential between thought speed and speaking speed to identify what is being used as point-support material. This becomes very profitable in terms of listening efficiency.

3. Make mental summaries

Finally and most important, the good listener throws in periodic mental summaries as he listens. At the end of about three or four minutes, if the speaker draws a long breath or walks around the lectern, or takes a swallow of water, or if there is any pause at all, the sharp listener dashes clear back to the beginning of the discourse and makes a quick mental summary of what has been said up to the point of the break. We call these "dashes" mental recapitulations. There ought to be half a dozen or more in every lengthy talk we hear. They are the greatest dividend-payer in listening efficiency that we can possibly master and practice.

These periodic listening summaries are tremendous reinforcements of learning; and the beautiful thing about it is that we use to our own profit the ever-present differential between thought speed and speech speed.

A Look Ahead

I would predict that within another five years or so no employer of white-collar personnel in America is going to sign up a young college or high school graduate without first inquiring about his listening index. If the young man asking you for a job says, "Well, my index is 17," I would advise you not to sign him up. We can no longer afford the luxury of a bad listener on our payrolls. One bad listener can cause more damage in the complex economy in which we operate than all your good listeners can compensate for. But if he says, "My listening index is 91," sign him up; for he is going to be a producer for you.

QUESTIONS

1. Is listening a problem in management? Why?
2. What is the relationship of listening to upward and downward communication?
3. List the ten bad habits of listening. Add to this list from your own experience.
4. What activities does Nichols recommend to improve one's listening ability?
5. How is listening related to leadership and motivation?

32. BARRIERS TO COMMUNICATION *

Harold Stieglitz

It is pretty much taken for granted that communication is essential to sound personnel administration. But as the understanding of communication increases, the degree of satisfaction with communication decreases. More and more, management becomes aware of barriers to communication. And more and more, it seeks ways to overcome them.

What are the barriers? Well, words themselves may be barriers to communication. Words, of course, are merely symbols or substitutes for things or ideas. Too soon, however, especially in the realm of ideas, the word itself becomes separated from what it represents. Too often, homage is paid the word, with little thought given to the concept it stands for.

An example might be the opening statement of this article: "It is pretty much taken for granted that communication is essential to sound personnel administration." Many times, this amounts to an anesthetizing cliché—and very little else—to which most managers will nod their heads.

But, what does it really mean? The key terms are "personnel administration" and "communication." Personnel administration, it is generally agreed, is a process designed to enable each individual to make his maximum contribution to the enterprise as well as gain maximum satisfaction from his work experience. Communication is the interchange of information and ideas among all individuals in the enterprise. It provides an opportunity for each person to know what is going on, to contribute his ideas, to have a say in all matters that affect him. Thus it is one of the means of assuring that the individual gains satisfaction from his work. For the desire to communicate, to have a say in matters affecting him, is one of the basic desires of every employee.

Communication, in this sense, obviously connotes far more than just letters, bulletin board notices, magazines, suggestion systems, grievance procedures or other means of communication. It is a continuing process that can't be compartmentalized or reduced to one or more communication programs. For the goal of communication is complete understanding. And this requires a never ending process of listening and telling—of consultation between the employee and his

* From *Management Record*, Vol. 20, No. 1 (January, 1958), pp. 2-5. Reprinted with permission.

supervisor. For this goal to be achieved, communication must be constant, indeed habitual and automatic.

Actually, it is in terms of this concept of communication that many companies are dissatisfied with what they now call their "communication program." It is in terms of this concept that the question, "Is anybody listening?" is raised. For the company may publish beautiful employee magazines, write glowing letters to employees, have neon bulletin boards—and yet find communication just isn't taking place.

Why? What are the barriers to communication within a company? It is a large problem toward which much research has been and still is directed. Chances are that the problems of space travel will be solved long before this problem of human relations. But on the assumption that people who engage in communication may have some insights, THE CONFERENCE BOARD over a period of time has asked this question of more than 750 employees (representing over 500 companies) whose general level of responsibility places them in the management category.

The barriers cited by these management representatives can be categorized into three major groups:

1. Barriers arising from the fact that individuals are involved in communication—and individuals differ. These might be called pre-existing barriers to communication, which a company inherits because they are common to society.
2. Barriers arising from the company's "climate," or atmosphere, which tend to stultify communication.
3. Barriers that are largely mechanical in the sense that they stem from lack of proper facilities or means of communication.

INDIVIDUAL DIFFERENCES

"People differ," "personalities differ," "they come from different backgrounds," "have preconceived opinions or prejudices," "listen with a selective ear"—these are items often cited as barriers to communication. These shorthand terms are another way of saying that words and actions have different meanings to different people. The fact that the different people come from different backgrounds—geographic, economic, social, educational and occupational—may mean that each puts a different interpretation on what he sees or hears. They may even use a different vocabulary. This is apparent in magazine articles today that attempt to explain the lexicon of the teenager to the bewildered parents. It is apparent in the existence of such labels as "Madison Avenue jargon," the "language of Wall Street," "shop talk," "political double talk," etc.

Also encompassed in this barrier is the fact that individual interests vary: "What is important to one man may not be important to another." So, because of individual interests, or group interests, individuals place different interpretations on words. Epitomizing this is an anecdote being heard more frequently these days: a man explains that "a recession is when my neighbor is laid off; a depression is when I am laid off."

CORPORATE CLIMATE

The barriers arising from the fact that people are different are inherited by a company. To a certain extent, they contribute and magnify another set of barriers to communication that exists within the company. For example, those discussing the problem frequently cite the "caste system" within the company as a barrier; various hierarchies either find it difficult or don't want to communicate with each other. Each has its own set of problems and, presumably, the status-factor impinges upon their ability to exchange thoughts. This is evident when the man from the ranks moves up and becomes foreman; when the junior executive finally makes the executive dining room.

Communication may become stratified within the organization level. Undoubtedly, this type of barrier has its roots partly in the individual differences already cited.

But there is a whole set of barriers, which the management representatives cite, that are somewhat indigenous to the company itself.

The top man

One of the major barriers that management people often point to is the "boss," the top man in the company. How is he a barrier? He may be unwilling to communicate. He may feel that he supplies the ideas and they are not subject to question. He may afford no means of communication to those he supervises. Or, more correctly, he only practices one-way communication, which is not really communication but order giving.

Or, he may not understand the need for communication. To him communication may denote idle chit-chat; meetings that are a waste of time; listening to the thoughts of people he believes are not qualified by position or function to have thoughts. Regardless of the reason, his very lack of communication in itself becomes a message that is pervasive throughout the company.

Lack of policy

However, even if the top man is willing and does practice good communication, his example alone does not suffice to bring about constant listening and telling at all levels in the organization. Top management's belief in the desirability of communication must be spread throughout the organization in the form of a written statement of policy. Lack of such a policy statement is cited by many of the management men who were interviewed as another barrier to communication. For without this company commitment, communication may be sporadic, may be turned on or off depending upon the situation. Communication, or lack of it, may be by whim of the individual supervisor rather than an experience that is company-wide. Lack of company policy may be interpreted by some supervisors as a lack of desire on the part of the company to foster communication. In short, lack of a positive statement is interpreted as a negative attitude.

Fears

There are several fears that stunt communication, according to those close to the problem. Fear of misinterpretation, for example, is a barrier often cited. "If we tell them we had a good year, they'll think we are in a better position to grant a raise." "If I ask the boss about chances for promotion, he'll think I am dissatisfied here." There are many examples that show communication is blocked because the teller fears that the listener may misinterpret his message.

Fear of distortion, whether by the individual, by the grapevine, or by the union, is also cited as a barrier. The speaker may say, "Your work can be improved." The individual listener may hear, "Your work is no good." A remark in the upper levels of the company concerning a batch of rush orders may emerge in the lower levels as a cancellation of vacations. Management may request suggestions on possible improvements, even express a willingness to pay for worthwhile suggestions. But a union may state management's proposal a little differently: "They'll take your suggestions, give you token payment, and end up displacing your buddy and maybe even you."

So rather than risk possible distortion, some don't communicate.

Fear of exposing a lack of knowledge or having too little to offer also is a barrier. So is fear of exposing oneself to criticism. For in these situations, there is a holdback. The employee, at any level, may deliberately withdraw, lest his suggestion be scoffed at or provoke a derisive look. Or if he is involved in finding a solution to an operating problem, he may hold back in discussing it. He may camouflage his answers so that they won't reflect badly on him.

To a certain extent, these fears may be part of another fear very often mentioned as a barrier: fear of reprisal. For much of the hold-back is caused by the employee's fear that a frank criticism, a voiced grievance, a nonconforming opinion may mark him for odious duties, may cost him a raise or promotion, or may even result in the loss of his job. Actually, what constitutes reprisal in the eyes of the employee may vary with his status and level in the organization. But rather than risk reprisal in any form, the vice-president or rank-and-file employee may limit his communication to areas or remarks that he believes are guaranteed not to offend the person who has some control over his welfare in the company.

In discussing these barriers, the management representatives stressed *fear* of distortion, of misinterpretation, of reprisal. However, they go on to emphasize that actual distortion, actual misinterpretation and actual reprisal, not just the fear of them, are even greater barriers to good communication.

Poor supervision

The poor supervisor, whether he is at a high or a low level, is another barrier to communication that many of the management men point to. The supervisor may act as a self-appointed censor and block information going down or up. He may not invite consultation with employees because he is insecure or jealous of his status. He may fail to listen or listen only with a closed mind. In a sense, the supervisor can have a dampening effect on communication in the same way as the top man in the organization. For to the group he supervises, he *is* top man. His unwillingness to communicate, his failure to understand the need for communication, while more limited in scope, still makes for dead spots in communication.

Insincerity and lack of confidence

Whether insincerity and lack of confidence result from the already mentioned barriers or are the root causes of these barriers is difficult to determine. But most of the management men interviewed agree that these two are major barriers of communication. Actually they may be two sides of the same barrier. Insincerity breeds lack of confidence and vice versa.

By insincerity, those suggesting this as a barrier imply the type of communication that is superficial. The supervisor may ask for an employee's opinion when he really doesn't want or doesn't care about the opinion. Employees' views on the solution of a problem may be solicited after the answer is already decided upon. In these and other cases the lack of sincerity becomes quite apparent to the employees. The resulting conviction that management is "putting on an act" effectively forestalls further communication.

Those suggesting "lack of confidence" as a barrier imply that what is being communicated or who is communicating is distrusted. For a variety of reasons, one person just doesn't believe the other. The listener suspects that the motive behind the communication is not in his best interest. The teller might say "I am considering recommending you for promotion for another job." The listener may believe that he is being eased out, that he is being switched to a dead-end job. The company may say "We can't afford a pay increase." The employees reject this because they feel the company is more interested in higher profits.

Essentially then, the barriers of insincerity and lack of confidence go back to the fact that people have different interests. To the extent that either party thinks the other is not genuinely concerned with his interest, communication suffers.

MECHANICAL BARRIERS

By comparison with the barriers to communication posed by individual differences and the corporate climate, the mechanical barriers are mere hurdles. For here, the management people discussing the problem were not talking about attitudes or fears but were speaking about specific technical impediments in the way of communication within the company.

Organization structure

The cooperators assessing this area of the problem label poor organization as a major obstacle to communication. For good organization requires the proper delineation and grouping of functions. It establishes proper relationships among functions. And it concerns the assignment of responsibility and authority for the functions. In short, organization is the basic determination of "who said what": who does what job, who makes what decision, who tells what to whom.

Organization necessarily sets out the chain of command and reporting relationships within the company. This in turn marks the main channels of regular, systematic communication. If the channels aren't clear, if there are dead ends, blocked passages or bottlenecks, communication is chaotic or nonexistent.

Those who point this out are, in effect, saying that violation of the principles of sound organization necessarily hinders communication. As examples, consider unity of command, span of control, and levels of authority.

Unity of command means no one in the organization should report to more than one supervisor; no one should have more than one boss. If this principle is violated and if Joe has two bosses, he is getting information and orders from two sources. These may conflict or be inconsistent. Not only that, but Joe may be shunted from one to the other when he has something on his mind.

The span of control principle merely states that there is a limit to the number of positions that can be coordinated by a single executive. If Mr. Smith has too many foremen, section heads, or department heads reporting to him, some of them may give up before they can get his ear. In this case communication is bottlenecked. Possibly, those reporting to Mr. Smith may seek out others for advice, recommendations, or counsel. In such an event, the chain of command is diluted. Mr. Smith isn't getting all the information he needs to do his job, and the foremen may be getting misinformation because it is not coming directly from their supervisor.

Third, the principle dealing with levels of authority indicates that the number of such levels should be kept to a minimum. Delays in communication and "informal" lines of communication occur when the chain of command is cluttered with too many "bosses." It is harder for information to move down the line; and it is even more difficult for upward communication to occur.

When too many levels of authority are linked with too broad spans of control, the frequent warning is that communication up, down, and across will be too little and too late—if at all.

Functional responsibility

Related to the barrier presented by poor organization is another obstacle quite frequently mentioned: no one is responsible for seeing to it that communication takes place. This is stated in various ways. Some say, "we don't have experts to handle communication." Others say, "nobody sets up the media of communication to be used." Still others say, "there is no central control deciding what should be communicated, when, and how." Summarizing the thinking on this barrier, the point being made is that willingness to communicate is not enough; somebody must be in charge of the function. His job is not to relieve everyone else from communicating, but rather to aid them in their communication.

Other barriers

Some of the other impediments to communication cited by management people are geographic dispersion (how can you have good communication when you are spread all over the country?), lack of time (the pressure of events, of things to do, leaves no time for communication), and lack of training (the supervisors just don't know how to communicate, they don't know how to run a meeting, they don't know how to draw out an employee).

OVERCOMING THE PROBLEM

This list of barriers is by no means exhaustive. It merely represents some of the more apparent difficulties in achieving constant, automatic and habitual listening and telling within the company. But the management personnel involved in this exercise find that identifying and analyzing the barriers is the first step toward their removal. Actually, what becomes apparent is that the structure of the barriers is interlocking; remove one barrier and several others fall with it. For example, eliminate lack of confidence and many of the fears that forestall communication disappear too.

Within a company, what are the key barriers? Those who were asked to analyze this answered: negative attitude toward communication on the part of the top man, lack of policy, and poor organization.

The top man, they insist, must be convinced of the need for communication. He must be convinced that good communication is good human relations; that good communication is good business. Not only must he be convinced (sold is the word some of them used) but he must practice it. His practices, they emphasize, are contagious.

The necessity for a clear written statement of policy is emphasized as the best means of letting everyone in the organization know just how the company feels about communication. It sets the tone for the type of communication that everyone throughout the organization is to have. It sets the basis for the procedures and practices that will be used to implement the policy. And its formulation forces a consideration of such difficult questions as:

1. What and how much should employees be told: How about good news, bad news, sensitive information?
2. On what matters should employees have a chance to be heard—grievances, gripes, methods, products, profits?
3. How can the company insure day-to-day acceptance and conformity with the communication policy? How can it protect the employees from reprisal?

Good organization, the management representatives insist, will do away with many mechanical barriers to communication. Points emphasized here are: the job specification of each supervisor should include the responsibility for communication; the organization structure should clearly designate the channels of communication; the staff responsibility for coordinating and controlling communication processes should be clearly fixed.

Once these chief barriers are removed, will good communication automatically follow? The answer THE CONFERENCE BOARD repeatedly gets is "no." But it seems to be an optimistic "no." When amplified, it becomes, "no—but by correcting these things the company takes a giant step toward creating a climate for good communication. It is only through constant practice, under the aegis of the right man at the top, good policy, and sound organization that any company can eventually achieve communication that is constant, habitual and automatic."

QUESTIONS

1. Explain what is meant by "barriers to communication."
2. Why must the leader be aware of barriers to communication?
3. How do individual differences affect communication?
4. Briefly discuss the barriers that arise from corporate climate.
5. What other barriers does Stieglitz present? What does he recommend to overcome barriers to communication?

33. AN EXPERIMENTAL APPROACH TO
ORGANIZATIONAL COMMUNICATION *

Alex Bavelas and Dermot Barrett

Communication as a critical aspect of organization has been attracting more and more attention. If one may judge from articles and speeches, much of the current thinking on communication centers around categories of problems which arise in day-to-day operations—"getting management's point of view to the workers," "stimulating communication up the line as well as down," "obtaining better communication with the union," "establishing more effective communication within management, and especially with the foremen." Knowing how such questions usually arise, it is not surprising that their discussion invariably resolves itself into considerations of *content* and *technique*: on the one hand, analyses of what management ought to be saying to the worker, the union, the foreman; on the other hand, descriptions of devices which can best say it—bulletin boards, letters, films, public address systems, meetings, etc. In its extreme form this approach becomes one of searching for a specific remedy for a specific ill. Helpful and practical as this may be, it is doubtful that such activity can lead to the discovery and understanding of the basic principles of effective organizational communication. Breakdowns and other difficulties at some point of a communication system are often only superficially related to the local conditions which appear to have produced them. They may, rather, be cumulative effects of properties of the entire communication system taken as a whole. But what are these properties, if, indeed, they exist?

Formal and informal systems

An organizational system of communication is usually created by the setting up of formal systems of responsibility and by explicit delegations of duties. These categories include statements, often implicitly, of the nature, content, and direction of the communication which is considered necessary for the performance of the group. Students of organization, however, have pointed out repeatedly that groups tend to depart from such formal statements and to create other channels of communication and dependence. In other words,

* From *Personnel*, Vol. 27, No. 5 (March, 1951), pp. 366-371. Copyright, 1951, by the American Management Association. Reprinted with permission of the American Management Association.

informal organizational systems emerge. One may take the view that these changes are adaptations by the individuals involved in the direction of easier and more effective ways of working, or, perhaps, not working. It is no secret that informal groups are not always viewed by managers as favorable to the goals of the larger body. Also, it is by no means obvious that those informal groupings which evolve out of social and personality factors are likely to be more efficient (with respect to organizational tasks) than those set up formally by the managers. Altogether, if one considers how intimate the relations are between communication channels and control, it is not surprising that the managers of organizations would prefer explicit and orderly communication lines.

Is there "one best way"?

Unfortunately, there seems to be no organized body of knowledge out of which one can derive, for a given organization, an optimal communication system. Administrative thinking on this point commonly rests upon the assumption that the optimum system *can* be derived from a statement of the task to be performed. It is not difficult to show, however, that from a given set of specifications one may derive not a single communication pattern but a whole set of them, all logically adequate for the successful performance of the task in question. Which pattern from this set should be chosen? The choice, in practice, is usually made either in terms of a group of assumptions (often quite untenable) about human nature, or in terms of a personal bias on the part of the chooser. The seriousness of this situation is illustrated by the following example.

Let us assume that we have a group of five individuals who, in order to solve a problem, must share as quickly as possible the information each person possesses. Let us also assume that there are reasons which prevent them from meeting around a table, and that they must share this information by writing notes. To avoid the confusion and waste of time of each person writing a message to each of the others, a supervisor decides to set up channels in which the notes must go. He strikes upon the pattern shown in Fig. 1.

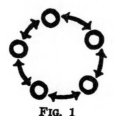

FIG. 1

In this arrangement each individual can send to and receive messages from two others, one on his "left" and one on his "right." Experiments actually performed with this kind of situation show that the number of mistakes made by individuals working in such a "circle" pattern can be reduced by fully 60 per cent by the simple measure of *removing one link,* thus making the pattern a "chain" as shown in Fig. 2. The relevance of such a result to organization communication is obvious, simple though the example is. The sad truth, however, is that this phenomenon is not clearly derivable either from traditional "individual psychology" or from commonly held theories of group communication.

Fig. 2

An integral process of organization

Perhaps some headway can be made by approaching the general problem from a somewhat different direction. In the affairs of organizations, as well as in the affairs of men, chance always plays a part. However good a plan may be, however carefully prepared its execution, there is a point beyond which the probability of its success cannot be increased. With the firmest of intentions, agreements and promises may be impossible to carry out because of unforeseen events. Nevertheless, an organization whose functioning is too often interrupted by unforeseen events is looked upon with suspicion. Bad luck is an unhappy plea, and it may well be that the "unlucky" organization is more to be avoided than the simply incompetent one. On the other hand, few things about an organization are more admired and respected than the ability to "deliver" despite widely varying conditions and in the face of unusual difficulties.

In a very broad sense, it may be argued that the principal effort of organizational activities is the making of favorable conditions for the achievement of certain goals. In other words, an effort is made to increase, as much as the economics of the situation will permit, the probabilities of succeeding. This is the essence of the manager's job. The development of training and selection programs, the improvement of methods and the specification of techniques, the organization of research and development activities, the designation of responsibility and the delegation of duties—all these processes have one organizationally legitimate purpose: to increase the chances of organizational success. Upon this point rest almost all of the notions by which we are accustomed to evaluate organizations—in part or as a whole.

An organization is, in short, a social invention—a kind of "machine" for increasing certain sets of probabilities. (Which sets of probabilities are given to it to increase, which it chooses, how freely and by what means will not be discussed here. These problems, although they lie well within the scope of this subject, are outside the range of this paper. We will confine ourselves to a consideration of the process by which an accepted set of probabilities is optimized.) Probabilities of success are increased, however, only by taking relevant and appropriate actions. For the manager, these actions reduce in most instances to the gathering and evaluating of information in the form of reports, schedules, estimates, etc. It is entirely possible to view an organization as an elaborate system for gathering, evaluating, recombining, and disseminating information. It is not surprising, in these terms, that the effectiveness of an organization with respect to the achievement of its goals should be so closely related to its effectiveness in handling information. In an enterprise whose success hinges upon the coordination of the efforts of all its members, the managers depend completely upon the quality, the amount, and the rate at which relevant information reaches them. The rest of the organization, in turn, depends upon the efficiency with which the managers can deal with this information and reach conclusions, decisions, etc. This line of reasoning leads us to the belief that communication is not a secondary or derived aspect of organization—a "helper" of the other and presumably more basic functions. Rather it is the essence of organized activity and is the basic process out of which all other functions derive. The goals an organization selects, the methods it applies, the effectiveness with which it improves its own procedures—all of these hinge upon the quality and availability of the information in the system.

Patterns of communication

About two years ago a series of studies was begun whose purpose was to isolate and study certain general properties of information handling systems. The first phase of this research program [1] is

---

[1] These studies are supported jointly by the Rand Corporation and the Research Laboratory of Electronics at M.I.T.

directed at a basic property of all communication systems, that of connection or "who can talk to whom."

FIG. 3

This property of connection can be conveniently expressed by diagrams. The meaning of the picture in Fig. 3 is obvious. Individuals A and B can send messages to C but they can receive messages from no one; C and D can exchange messages; E can receive messages from D, but he can send messages to no one. The pattern shown in Fig. 3, however, is only one of the many that are possible. A group of others is shown in Fig. 4. An examination of these patterns will show that they fall into two classes, separated by a very important difference. Any pair of individuals in each of the patterns, d, e, and f can exchange messages either directly or indirectly over some route. No pair of individuals in each of the patterns a, b, and c can exchange messages. Patterns like a, b, and c obviously make any coordination of thought or action virtually impossible; we will be concerned from this point on only with patterns like d, e, and f.

Since the individuals in any connected pattern like d, e, and f can share ideas completely, should we expect that the effectiveness of individuals in performing group tasks or solving group problems would be the same in patterns d, e, and f except for differences in ability, knowledge, and personality? Should we expect differences in quality and speed of performance? Is it likely that the individuals

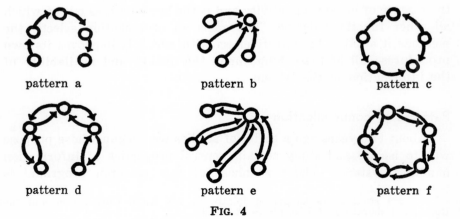

FIG. 4

working in one pattern would show significantly better morale than the individuals working in a different pattern? Sidney Smith and Harold J. Leavitt conducted a series of experiments [2] which yielded very definite answers to these questions. An experimental design was used which made it possible to equate the difficulty of the tasks which the groups performed, and which permitted the cancelling of individual differences by randomizing the assignment of subjects to patterns. Also, the experiment was repeated with different groups enough times to establish the consistency of the results. A brief summary of the findings is given in Fig. 5. The use of qualitative terms in Fig. 5 in place of the quantitative measurements which were actually made blurs the comparison somewhat, but it gives a fair picture of the way these patterns performed. Since the original experiments were done by Smith and Leavitt, this experiment has been repeated with no change in the findings.

Speed	slow	fast	fast
Accuracy	poor	good	good
Organization	no stable form of organization	slowly emerging but stable organization	almost immediate and stable organization
Emergence of Leader	none	marked	very pronounced
Morale	very good	poor	very poor

FIG. 5

The question very properly arises here as to whether these findings can be "explained" in the sense of being related to the connection properties of the patterns themselves. The answer to this question is a qualified yes. Without developing the mathematical analysis, which can be found in Leavitt's paper, the following statements can be made:

For any connected pattern, an *index of dispersion* can be calculated. Relative to this index, there can be calculated *for each position in each pattern* an *index of centrality*, and an *index of peripher-*

[2] Harold J. Leavitt reports these experiments in detail in the January, 1951, issue of the *Journal of Abnormal and Social Psychology.*

ality. The data suggest strongly that the rapidity with which organization emerges and the stability it displays are related to the gradient of the indices of centrality in the pattern. In Fig. 6 these indices are given for each position. It should be added at this point that in the patterns in which leadership emerged, the leader was invariably that person who occupied the position of highest centrality.

The index of peripherality appears to be related strongly to morale. In Fig. 7 the indices of peripherality are given by position. Those individuals who occupied positions of low or zero peripherality showed in their actions as well as in self-ratings (made at the end of the experiments) that they were satisfied, in high spirits, and generally pleased with the work they had done. Those individuals who occupied positions of high peripherality invariably displayed either apathetic or destructive and uncooperative behavior during the group effort, and rated themselves as dissatisfied and critical of the group's operation.

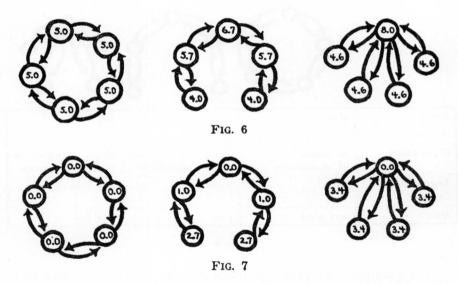

Fig. 6

Fig. 7

A word of caution should be given concerning the slow, inaccurate, but happy "circle" pattern. Subsequent experiments by Sidney Smith indicate that this pattern possesses unusual abilities for adaptation to sudden and confusing changes of task—a quality lacking in the other two patterns.

A promising field for research

Clearly, these experiments are only the beginning of a long story. The findings, although they promise much, settle nothing; but they do suggest that an experimental approach to certain aspects of organizational communication is possible and that, in all probability, it would be practically rewarding. As the characteristics of communication nets and their effects upon human performance *as they occur in the laboratory* become better understood, the need will grow for systematic studies of actual operating organizations. The job of mapping an existing net of communications even in a relatively small company is a complicated and difficult one, but it is not impossible. Some work is beginning on the development of field methods of observation. The importance of bridging the gap between the simple, directly controlled experiment and the very complex, indirectly controlled social situation cannot be overestimated.

QUESTIONS

1. What, apparently, does current thinking on communication center around? What are the limitations of this approach?
2. Describe the influence of informal systems on organizational communication.
3. Can an optimal communication system be derived for an organization? Why?
4. Explain what is meant by the statement "A basic property of all communication systems is that of connection."
5. Briefly outline the conclusions of this article.

GENERAL QUESTIONS ON PART VI

1. Discuss the relationship of communication to leadership and motivation.
2. Explain what is meant by "two-way" communication.
3. What is the basic reason for communication?
4. What are the fundamental dimensions of communication? Which of these dimensions is most important to organizational efficiency? Why?
5. Distinguish between formal and informal communication. Of what significance is the latter to the leader?
6. Why do misunderstandings arise between people?
7. Prepare a list of barriers to communication.
8. How important is listening to communication? Why?
9. Explain the basic process of communication.
10. Prepare a list of the communication media that can be used in a typical organization.

PART VII. PARTICIPATION AND GROUP DYNAMICS

Whatever his duties or responsibilities may be, the typical American workman of today is surrounded by a complex technological maze. This means he must reconcile systems and procedures, understand and execute company policies, develop essential technical skills to perform his job properly, and so forth. Quite clearly he faces an extremely difficult task.

One factor that has contributed greatly to this complex task is the corporate form of organization. Layer upon layer of "managers" has been added to what was originally a simple business structure. Lines of communications have become complicated and easily snarled; confusion has arisen as to responsibility and authority; and, most important of all, the social and physical distances between managers and workers have become greater and greater.

The result has been that for some people a job is only a job— work that must be performed in order to earn a living. Resigning themselves to the complexity of the maze, workers lose interest, not only in their work, but in the company as well. Some become chronic "job shoppers," whereas others develop apathy towards their work and perform at a level that is just good enough to keep them employed. Still others become agitators, endeavoring to stir up malcontentment in their departments by constant complaining or by disseminating false information. Thus, the corporation and its evolving technology, although largely responsible for unprecedented prosperity, have also fostered much discontent and unrest.

Now we are not making the claim that this is generally true of all industry. Obviously it is not; certainly many of us are well satisfied with our jobs, do our best at them, and do not as a rule fall into the categories just described. So the question arises: "Why this difference between workers? Why are some of us inspired by our job and its responsibilities while others find themselves wallowing in the doldrums?"

Needless to say, a myriad of answers may be offered. Volume upon volume has been written along these lines, and a great portion of this book is devoted to just this subject. Our concern in this part, however, is with something so basic to any and all organizations that, indeed, it is possibly the most vital link between the worker, his job, and the company.

We are referring, of course, to *employee participation*—psychologically as well as physically—in the many phases of the management process. It has been shown in countless numbers of studies that participation on the part of employees exerts profound effects on quality of work, acceptance of changes, and on overall morale, loyalty, and productivity. Furthermore, employees who are psychologically and mentally involved in their jobs display a much greater degree of identification with the company and its goals, thereby creating a climate conducive to individual growth and development. In turn, it is this very growth and development that so vitally affects the expanding company and the business economy as well.

A Theoretical Framework for Participation

One of the truly perplexing problems we face as we go through life is that we cannot always prove, with facts and figures, all of our opinions and ideas. Many things in life we have to accept at face value or on the basis of sheer faith alone. For example, what about the advantages to be derived from going to college? Can one actually prove conclusively that he will have a better life if he obtains an academic degree and becomes a lawyer, businessman, or politician? The answer is fairly simple—no, he cannot. But he can obviously *assume* that a college education will help him to achieve goals that will make him a more satisfied, happy person since research indicates that this does happen for many college graduates.

The same thing can be said of quite a few of the practices and procedures that one uses as a manager or executive in the business world. Everything cannot simply be measured in terms of dollars and cents, in inches and feet, or in terms of absolute cost. In short, the benefits to be derived from many practices and/or policies have to be assumed and taken for granted. Certain indirect measurements are frequently utilized, but exclusive reliance upon them is not feasible. Employee fringe benefits are a good example. Although management assumes that benefits contribute to productivity and morale, the extent of their contribution cannot be directly and exactly ascertained.

The theory behind securing employee participation in group endeavor is of the same nature. It remains an impossibility to measure or calculate exactly the benefits attained by running an organization on a participative-democratic basis rather than on a highly autocratic basis. Because the best measurement we have to date is accomplishment, it is along these lines that leading enterprises of today's economy, utilizing participative management, rank first and foremost in terms of profits, assets, research and development, and so on. These companies have devised ways and means for achieving ego-involvement on the part of workers within the organization. And it is upon this ego-involvement that the success of participative management depends, for people will only take an active interest in the forces that shape their industrial destinies if they are given free opportunity and encouragement to do so.

Industrial organizations, because of their form of organization, are highly autocratic. As was discussed earlier, leaders or managers are appointed to their leadership positions and are vested with authority to compel obedience from their subordinates. Consequently, many employees have little or nothing to say about the whole procedure, except perhaps the freedom to quit their jobs, although circumstances frequently preclude this. In other words, they have little choice but to accept their appointed "boss," even though the goals that each party seeks to attain are probably directly opposing. Because successful leadership is heavily contingent upon leaders and followers viewing each other as "mutual means" for achieving similar goals, a serious dichotomy arises.

Those of us fortunate enough to have been born and raised in the democratic atmosphere of the United States have gone through a long process of inculcation in democratic processes. Consequently, we expect to have something to say about actions and plans that affect our way of life in industry and society. If others attempt to deprive us of this right, we will do all in our power to do something about it.* The growth of unionism, for example, shows how this has affected industry.

We are not trying to say that the autocratic type of industrial organization is essentially bad or purposefully opposed to democracy. Obviously, certain authority relationships are necessary to provide direction and coordination in any working organization. Our principal claim, however, is that by introducing and blending into this autocratic structure as many participative devices as are feasible, advantages will accrue that tend to minimize some of the more psychologically adverse effects of autocracy. Just how much participation is feasible

---

* The authors are fully aware of the limits of reality; certainly our democratic processes are imperfect and often leave much to be desired. Nevertheless, this does not disqualify the basic assumptions upon which such processes rest, nor does it imply that, because some imperfections exist, the entire system is imperfect.

will depend upon individual managements and their philosophies. Davis, in a following article, demonstrates that proper focus on participation enhances democratic action. The last twenty years have shown that industry is fully aware of these potentialities. The critical question now becomes one of how far management is willing to go with participative management.

Although our thoughts have so far been directed towards management's approach to participation, the individual employee deserves equal attention. Tannenbaum and Massarik's article states that "the subordinate must be capable of becoming psychologically involved in the participational activities." In other words, not only must he be conditioned to participating in decisions that affect him in his work, but he has to possess the necessary intelligence and desire to do so. Thus, several conditions have to be met by both the management and the worker before participative management can successfully be applied in any enterprise.

In summary, it is important to bear in mind the psychological basis upon which employee participation rests. The psychologist has proven most conclusively that people are more creative, exhibit greater degrees of initiative, and become more responsible when given the opportunity to express themselves and share in the decisions affecting them. Not only is this true of our democratic society as a whole, but of industry as well. Therefore, industry must provide means for allowing employees to participate actively—psychologically as well as physically—in their work. The problem of "how" is the subject of following sections.

PARTICIPATIVE LEADERSHIP

Parts I and III have already sketched the different approaches one can take towards leadership. Admittedly, it is a vast and complex subject. If we were to query a random sample of successful executives about the worthwhileness of using the participative approach in directing the work of subordinates, unquestionably a variety of answers would be received. Depending upon their background and function, some would undoubtedly be highly in favor of such techniques, while others would be quite skeptical.

We can see also that managerial attitudes will differ for varying reasons. The old-line manager who insists he "came up the hard way" will consider participation as nonsense, insisting that workers are paid to do, not think. He gives the orders and makes the decisions. Or an executive's personality may be such that he cannot relinquish any of his authority. Furthermore, he may fear that increased participation will result in his authority being taken away from him or that it will give the union more and more power.

These and many other negative attitudes regarding participation still persist in the industrial scene. However, they are slowly but surely changing with the passage of time. As the old-timers begin to relinquish the reins to younger men, the latter tend to bring newer concepts of management into their jobs, among them being the idea of securing subordinate participation. Recognition is given to the fact that authority really flows from the bottom up and not exclusively from the top down. Today employees are better educated and therefore expect more from their boss and from the company as a whole. Jobs are not scarce, and manpower is at a premium. All in all, people know more and want more. The democratic system has instilled in the majority of us the desire to get ahead and to improve our way of life. Once we have had the taste of opportunity, we are not likely to give it up.

So the modern executive has to admit to his own limitations. He cannot do all that has to be done by himself. He must, of necessity, depend upon others. No longer is he the indispensable man, what with the emergence of the management profession. This does not imply, however, that he can pass on his responsibilities to those below him. Indeed, participative management does not lighten the executive load, for he still must make final decisions and be accountable for performance and getting the work done. It simply means he must now be willing to share his authority and responsibility with his subordinates.

To practice participative leadership, the executive or supervisor has to admit that his people have talents and abilities other than what they can do with their hands. He must recognize that his subordinates have the ability to think, to come up with new ideas, and to initiate new procedures and ways of doing things. In fact, countless numbers of innovations have stemmed directly from employees on the assembly line. As more executives and their companies open their minds to this talent and allow it to express itself, productivity will increase in rapid strides as Likert demonstrates in his article.

But it must be emphasized that participation is not a one-way street. Participation requires joint response on the part of *both* superior and subordinate. Both have to share a zone of interest, recognizing that theirs is a joint endeavor. In today's technical world, the manager and the worker cannot walk separate paths. The success of one depends upon the success of the other. The assembly line, for example, cannot roll unless the salesman gets the order, the engineer designs the product, the supervisor lays out the needed processing, and the worker performs his diverse functions.

The modern executive job is thus increasingly becoming one of a participative nature. Executives and supervisors are today turning to their subordinates for more help in the decision-making process. How far to extend this participation throughout the organization now becomes a perplexing question. There is no simple solution here. It depends upon the individual situation and how ready the organization and its people are for participation. Certain limits have to be established, but the question of where and how to draw the line is a problem for top management to resolve.

TYPES OF PARTICIPATION

Multiple management

"Multiple management" is a term coined to describe a certain type of participation. It best describes how some companies establish permanent committees to assist and advise operating executives.

These companies, for example, establish committees at different levels made up of representatives from many different departments. Such committees exist to give advice to key executives in particular functions. Perhaps the vice-president in charge of sales will have a sales committee made up of people from personnel, finance, production, the legal department, and so on, which will meet at intervals to discuss with the vice-president various policies or actions that he has taken or possibly will take. Ordinarily these committees have no decision-making power. Instead, their job is to recommend, discuss, and review. One of their principal advantages is that they serve as a fine training technique for people in different functions. By participating in these committee meetings, people from different jobs learn more about the sales function, its responsibilities and problems.

Consultative management

The multiple management type of participation is found in a relatively few number of firms. Other companies, however, have found that committees do serve as an excellent device for obtaining participation, although these companies do not ordinarily set up such an elaborate system of committees as do firms utilizing the multiple management concept. Rather than set up formal, standing committees, their preference, especially at the middle and lower levels of the organization, seems to be for *ad hoc* committees. To distinguish between the two different approaches to using committees, we can label the latter approach "consultative management."

Regardless of what committee system is used, of fundamental importance is the fact that committees do serve as excellent providers for participative effort. Through them, people are asked to share in solving problems, to discuss and analyze various situations, and to add their ideas to the ideas of their peers and superiors. Along these same lines, many companies urge supervisors to hold periodic staff conferences and meetings for attaining the same results. Here people are informed of past and coming events that may affect them in their work. Again their comments and ideas are solicited and their opinions are asked for. This, too, is a part of consultative management.

Suggestion systems

Company-wide suggestion systems are another technique for obtaining participation, especially at the rank-and-file level. Some persons undoubtedly feel that suggestion systems are of little importance, and in some companies this might be entirely correct. The success of such systems depends heavily upon how well they are implemented and administered, and upon a firm belief by management in their importance. If management displays a sincere interest in the system, it can be a very effective participation device. If, however, it is installed just because it looks good to have one and because other companies have them, employees are quick to sense these attitudes, and the results will probably be solely on the negative side.

These are but a few techniques a business can use to encourage active participation on the part of all employees. Many other techniques, too numerous for special mention here, are also available to the progressive concern. Of the utmost importance, however, is not what specific techniques to use, because they will depend upon the situation, but rather that the manager-leader realize that the desire to participate is a basic drive in all employees, and thus certain conditions must prevail before this need can be accommodated. We shall now look at these in some detail.

ORGANIZATION STRUCTURE AND PARTICIPATION

Before any kind of participative leadership or consultative management can be applied in an organization, there must be a firmly rooted belief on the part of the "executive class" that participation by employees is not only desirable but essential as well. In turn, executive attitudes regarding participation will depend upon whether their company is highly centralized or whether it is decentralized in terms of authority.

The highly centralized company tends to restrict managerial authority to the uppermost levels of management. All important decisions, and many unimportant ones as well, are reserved for top officials and are, for all practical purposes, divorced from the operating manager who should be making them. His job is to implement whatever the decisions might be. When this is the situation, how can operating managers be expected to invite participation on the part of their own subordinates when their own superiors do not offer them this opportunity? Indeed, active, ego-involved participation will be virtually nonexistent in this type of organization.

The decentralized structure presents a different picture, however. When managers are given full authority to make decisions commensurate with their responsibility, they are more likely to extend this policy to their subordinates and to invite active participation by subordinates to the mutual advantage of all. Decentralization of managerial authority is really one of the broadest phases of participation that any company can indulge in. It is an open challenge to managers to motive them to higher standards of performance, and it encourages them to extend the same principle to their subordinates.

The degree of participation in any company will thus hinge on top management's orientation towards the whole concept of authority. Participation tends to be higher and more active when the formal structure is decentralized, with the reverse being true when the structure is centralized. Chris Argyris has a penetrating analysis of this point in his article, and he makes some salient observations concerning the formal structure and the degree of participation.

PARTICIPATION AND UNIONISM

All of us are aware of the tremendous importance of labor unions in today's economy. There is no doubt that a large number of workers identify themselves principally with their union and not their company. Their major efforts are directed towards enhancing the status of their local and its membership, and towards increased participation in union affairs.

Progressive labor leadership during the past twenty-five years has fostered a growing amount of participation on the part of members. Workers are encouraged to hold office in the local and to participate in all types of union activities. Because the union provides many benefits for its members and does all in its power to protect their rights and welfare, workers soon begin to sense that they are a part of something, that through their union they are given more say-so over the factors influencing their behavior on the job. In short, through the outlet for participation that the union provides, some workers completely shift their allegiance from their company to their union.

Most modern-day unions realize that in the main their success depends upon the success of the companies they have organized. Therefore, they actively strive to participate more in certain managerial activities. Although the subject of union inroads into management prerogatives is always a hotly debated one and one with extensive ramifications, it nevertheless cannot be denied that in many firms unions now participate rather freely in such activities as time and motion study for determining job content and for setting production standards, job evaluation for determining wage rates, and the handling of grievances. In addition, they exert profound influences on personnel activities, such as hiring, layoffs, promotions, transfers, and so on. All of this is achieved by union policies aimed at increasing the amount of union participation in the affairs of the company.

Union leaders, however, frequently look with disfavor upon management's attempts to secure more worker participation. They fear that such attempts will shift worker loyalty from the union to the company. Hence, union leaders often oppose such efforts, claiming they are paternalistic or anti-union in nature. Management's job, therefore, frequently becomes one of convincing union officials that worker participation on behalf of the company will benefit the union as well as the organization. Clearly, mature attitudes are required on the part of both sides to implement successfully this kind of participation.

It is necessary to realize that unions, at least at the rank-and-file level, do sometimes complicate the problem of participation. On the one hand, they tend to offer an outlet for a person's basic need to participate, and in so doing they attract loyalty to the union rather than to the company. On the other hand, they may deliberately oppose management attempts to solicit more worker participation. In many instances, management invites such actions because of its own resistant attitude towards unionism, although this is slowly but surely becoming a thing of the past.

BENEFITS OF PARTICIPATION

The role of participation in working organizations has become increasingly important over the past few decades. During this time period, the theory underlying participation and its many benefits has been transformed into actual practice, and it has been proven rather conclusively that participation will work and will result in advantages to both employers and employees.

One of the major results of participation is that it aids in making people more mature and responsible individuals, both on and off the job. By being allowed to express himself in his work, rather than being absorbed into a complex system of procedures and systems, the individual assumes a feeling of dignity and status. If he knows he can express his opinions and ideas, a personal sense of gratification and involvement takes place within him and tends to manifest itself in his personality.

Participation also leads to increased understanding throughout the organization. People learn that others have problems besides themselves. If the workers are invited to share in these problems and to work towards common solutions, a greater degree of organizational balance occurs because of decreased misunderstanding and individual and group conflict. This also holds true when a union is involved. Mutual interest is brought to the forefront. The future holds great promise for peaceful and beneficial labor relations if both parties will lean towards increased participation.

Individual creativity and response to job challenges are also enhanced by participation. If given the opportunity to question and suggest instead of always having to follow a rigid set of instructions, an employee's natural ingenuity and ability are allowed expression. Hence, he is given the opportunity to grow and to develop himself. In discussing the advantages of participation and training in his article, Jennings shows that the two must go together to obtain the best results for purposes of development.

Studies further show participation to be a leading factor in getting people to accept changes. People who are consulted about changes, who are allowed to participate in decisions about the changes, are normally people who best adjust to such decisions. So it can be seen that participation along these lines greatly facilitates individual adjustment and satisfaction.

Although there are many other advantages to be realized from participation, they are far too numerous to be covered here. But it should be emphasized how tremendously important this subject is to today's managers. Many possibilities lie ahead for utilizing participation in management. It remains to be seen just how far companies are willing to go. Obviously there are limits here, but it is up to the individual concern to adapt to these.

PARTICIPATION AND ROLE BEHAVIOR

The concept of role behavior is best defined as a set of expectations as to how an individual *should* behave in a given situation. All of us assume different roles at different times—as Kahn points out in his article—and our role posture will depend upon our perception of what types of differing behaviors are called for in given situations. Our level in the organization, our status and authority, as well as the status, level and authority of those we interact with, all influence our role behavior. Most of us are called upon to assume roles such as father, husband, wife, mother, subordinate, friend, etc., and because of these multiple role demands, we develop *response sets* to accommodate each role.

At work, role behavior is heavily influenced by the various formal and informal groups an individual belongs to—either due to choice or requirement. Groups and individual members exert pressures on other members to direct the behavior of the latter, since this insures compliance with group norms and standards. Hence, group members behave in a predictable fashion which is comforting and safe to the group as a whole. Note that we all have an image of how we are expected to react in certain situations, largely geared to obtaining the favor of our peers. Behavior regulated by peer authority is perhaps the most powerful motivator in any organized culture or society, including the working organization.

Kahn points out that individuals often experience *role conflict*. Such conflict occurs when our personal expectations relative to a particular role conflict or differ with the expectations of other individuals or groups. The internal pressures created by these conflicts can frequently be quite severe, especially if we perceive such conflict as threatening to our health or career.

To accommodate these conflicts, selected responses are developed. For example, one can reject the demands of others or at last array them in order of perceived importance; rationalization, where established customs or roles are rigidly followed with no deviation, is another type of reaction; excessive formality and resorting to custom is another response—the "colder" we can get toward others means less involvement and hence conflict. We can also deceive, stall, vascillate, escape, or become psychologically sick to escape severe role conflicts. So there is a choice of responses to role conflicts, with the severity of the conflict along with its very nature essentially determining the type of response selected.

Participative management, like McGregor's Theory Y discussed in Article 20, greatly aids individuals in responding in a healthy fashion to role conflict. Not only does participation and involvement assist in making people comfortable in their various roles, it also helps to prevent role conflict generated by feelings of excessive dependency on authoritarian managers or feelings of uncertainty caused by being "left out" or uninformed. Participation thus acts as a "mental stabilizer" for many persons in the working organization, thereby reducing interpersonal conflicts and enhancing individual and group adjustment to an uncertain environment.

34. PARTICIPATION BY SUBORDINATES IN THE MANAGERIAL DECISION-MAKING PROCESS *

R. Tannenbaum and F. Massarik

I. Introduction

The role of "participation" by individuals or groups in American culture in general and in industrial organizations specifically has been treated by many writers. Its implications for political theory as well as for a theory of human relations in formal organizations are numerous. However, in spite of this academic and extra-academic interest, a clear-cut, operational definition of the concept, or a precise set of hypotheses regarding its dynamics, has not been developed. While to do so will be the object of this paper, the treatment will not be completely operational. The development of appropriate methods of measurement is conceived as a next step that should follow the preliminary one of conceptual clarification undertaken in this paper.

A review of the literature indicates that three major approaches have been taken in dealing with "participation":

(1) *The Experiential Approach.* This approach is exemplified by writers who in the course of their experience in enterprising work have obtained a "feel" for the role of participation in the decision-making process and have put down their experiences in article or book form.[1] Writings such as these provide a set of insights and hunches whose verification in any systematic fashion has not been attempted. The actual referents from which these formulations are derived often are single sets of observations in a single or in a few enterprises—observations generally made in an uncontrolled fashion.

The experiential approach, operating outside the bounds of scientific method, nonetheless adds to scientific knowledge indirectly by providing the raw material from which hypotheses may be moulded. The precise structure of these hypotheses is not stated neatly by the experiential writers, but rather remains to be formulated.

---

* From the *Canadian Journal of Economics and Political Science*, Vol. 16, No. 3 (August, 1950), pp. 408-418. Reprinted with permission.

[1] For example: H. H. Carey, "Consultative Supervision and Management" (*Personnel*, Mar., 1942); Alexander R. Heron, *Why Men Work* (Palo Alto, 1948); Eric A. Nicol, "Management through Consultative Supervision" (*Personnel Journal*, Nov. 1948); James C. Worthy, "Changing Concepts of the Personnel Function" (*Personnel*, Nov., 1948).

(2) *The Conceptual, Non-Experimental Approach.* **This** approach characterizes the writings of authors who are, essentially, academicians with strong theoretical backgrounds. It is typified by writings that deal with "conditions," "functions," and other abstractions, generally of a socio-psychological nature, that attempt to explain the dynamics of participation.[2] The conceptual, non-experimental approach at its best is the process of theory or hypothesis formulation. Ideally it lays the groundwork for actual testing and experimental work, but much of this type of technical literature so far published on participation lacks the clarity of conceptual definition necessary to make it useful as a basis for experimental work.

(3) *The Experimental Approach.* This approach is found in the writings of authors who have seen fit to apply experimental techniques either to especially constructed social situations involving participation, or else in natural settings in which participational activities prevail.[3] With adequate controls and with a meaningful theoretical structure within which individual findings may be placed, this approach is doubtless the most fruitful. Ideally it indicates what will happen under specified sets of conditions and with what degree of probability. Unfortunately, up to now experimental work on the dynamics of participation in the decision-making process has been sporadic.[4]

The present paper is of the conceptual, non-experimental type. Participation in the decision-making process is conceived here as an instrument that may be used by the formal leadership of an enterprise in the pursuit of its goals. No attempt will be made to examine it from an ethical standpoint or in terms of its consistency within the frame of a democratic society, although it is by no means assumed that such considerations are less important than the ones set forward here.

II. DEFINITION OF PARTICIPATION

It is essential, in dealing with participation, to make clear the meaning which is to be attached to the concept. One must specify both who the participators are and in what they are participating.

---

[2] For example: Douglas McGregor, "Conditions for Effective Leadership in the Industrial Situation" (*Journal of Consulting Psychology*, vol. VIII, Mar.-Apr., 1944); Gordon W. Allport, "The Psychology of Participation" (*Psychological Review*, May, 1945).

[3] For the concept of the "natural experiment," see F. Stuart Chapin, *Experimental Designs in Sociological Research* (New York, 1947), and Ernest Greenwood, *Experimental Sociology* (New York, 1945).

[4] For a good summary of relevant experimental work, see Ronald Lippitt, "A Program of Experimentation on Group Functioning and Productivity" (in *Current Trends in Social Psychology*, Pittsburgh, 1948).

Too frequently in the available literature on the subject the reader must determine these matters for himself since no explicit statements bearing on them are made by the writers.

As already indicated, this paper is primarily concerned with participation as a managerial device. Attention is therefore focused on the subordinates of managers in enterprises as the participators. It is important to note that these subordinates may be either non-managers or managers.[5] If they are managers, they are subordinates of superior managers in the formal organization of the enterprise in addition to having subordinates who are responsible to them.

Because of space limitations, consideration of the participation of individuals as union members in specific activities of an enterprise is excluded from the scope of this paper. Suffice it to say here that in those cases where the participation of union members is direct and personal, the benefits to be derived by the enterprise are similar to those derived from participation within the superior-subordinate relationship. However, in those cases (which are the greatest in number) where the participation of the union member is indirect and impersonal, it is doubtful if such is the result. It is our conclusion that most of the statements which follow are relevant to the former cases.[6]

What then is the meaning of participation, and with what type of participation by subordinates are we here concerned? An individual participates in something when he takes a part or share in that thing. Since taking a part or sharing is always involved, participation takes place in a social context. Managerial subordinates in formal enterprises are responsible to their superiors for the performance of designated tasks. In such performance, they are participating in the production of the good or service of the enterprise. They also participate (share), through the receipt of wages or salaries, in the distribution of the total revenue received by the enterprise. These types of participation are common to all enterprises. But there is another type of participation which is much less frequently encountered, although its use as a managerial device has, of recent years, grown rapidly in importance. This type involves participation by subordinates with their superiors in the managerial decision-making process.

---

[5] For definitions of these terms as used here, see Robert Tannenbaum, "The Manager Concept: A Rational Synthesis" (*Journal of Business*, Oct., 1949).

[6] In connexion with this discussion, it should be noted that when participation takes place within the superior-subordinate relationship, managers have primary control over the nature of the activity; when it takes place as part of the manager-union relationship, they may or may not, depending upon the relative power of the two parties.

Decisions are made by managers in order to organize, direct, or control responsible subordinates to the end that all service contributions be co-ordinated in the attainment of an enterprise purpose.[7] Since managers are those who accomplish results through subordinates, the latter are always directly and intimately affected by managerial decisions and therefore may have a considerable interest in them. Because of this possible interest, subordinates may have a strong desire, particularly in a nation with deeply-ingrained democratic traditions, to participate in the determination of matters affecting them. It is of importance, therefore, to consider the form which such participation might assume.

Decision-making involves a conscious choice or selection of one behaviour alternative from among a group of two or more behaviour alternatives.[8] Three steps are involved in the decision-making process. First, an individual must become aware of as many as possible of those behaviour alternatives which are relevant to the decision to be made. Secondly, he must define each of these alternatives, a definition which involves a determination of as many as possible of the consequences related to each alternative under consideration. Thirdly, the individual must exercise a choice between the alternatives, that is, make a decision.

In enterprises, managerial subordinates, as subordinates, can participate in the first two steps of the managerial decision-making process. They cannot participate in the third step. The actual choice between relevant alternatives must be made or accepted by the manager who is responsible to his superior for the decision.[9] However, subordinates can provide and discuss with their manager information with respect both to relevant alternatives and to the consequences attendant upon specific alternatives. In so doing they are participating in the managerial decision-making process.[10]

---

[7] See Tannenbaum, "The Manager Concept: A Rational Synthesis."

[8] This discussion of the decision-making process is based upon Robert Tannenbaum, "Managerial Decision-Making" (*Journal of Business*, Jan., 1950).

[9] In a democratic group, the choice can be made through a vote participated in by the rank and file. But, in such a case, the leader is organizationally responsible to the rank and file, and the members of the rank and file are not properly, in so far as the decision is concerned, subordinates of the leader.

Members of a democratic group, making the final choice in matters directly affecting them, may be more highly motivated as a result thereof than managerial subordinates who are granted the right to participate only in the first two steps of the managerial decision-making process. For evidence of the motivational effects of group decision, see Kurt Lewin, "Group Decision and Social Change" (in T. M. Newcomb and E. L. Hartley (eds.), *Readings in Social Psychology*, New York, 1947).

[10] It is this type of participation that most writers, who deal with human relations in enterprises, have in mind when they use the concept. The following examples illustrate this contention: "One of the most important conditions of the

The participation with which we are here concerned may take place in two different ways. First, it may involve interaction solely between a subordinate and his manager.[11] This would be the case where a worker originates a suggestion which he transmits to his boss. Secondly, it may involve interaction between a group of subordinates and their manager. This would be the case where a manager calls his subordinates together to discuss a common problem or to formulate a recommendation.[12]

III. Possible Advantages of Participation as a Managerial Device

It becomes useful to inquire why managers might find it advantageous to use this device. In other words, what are the possible benefits which might accrue to an enterprise whose managers made it possible for subordinates to participate in the decision-making process? In providing an answer to this question, it is first necessary to indicate the criterion which would guide the managerial choice relating to the use of participation.

A manager of an enterprise (profit or nonprofit) who behaves rationally will attempt to make a selection from among alternatives related to any problem which will maximize results (the degree of attainment of a given end) at a given cost or which will attain given

---

subordinate's growth and development centers around his opportunities to express his ideas and to contribute his suggestions before his superiors take action on matters which involve him. Through participation of this kind he becomes more and more aware of his superiors' problems, and he obtains genuine satisfaction in knowing that his opinions and ideas are given consideration in the search for solutions" (D. McGregor, "Conditions for Effective Leadership in the Industrial Situation," p. 60) ; "I am not suggesting that we take over intact the apparatus of the democratic state. Business cannot be run by the ballot box. . . . We must develop other inventions, adapted to the special circumstances of business, which will give employees at all levels of our organizations a greater sense of personal participation and 'belonging' " (J. Worthy, "Changing Concepts of the Personnel Function," p. 175) ; "Action initiated by the responsible head to bring his subordinates into the picture on matters of mutual concern is not a sharing of prerogatives of authority. Rather, it is an extension of the opportunity for participation in the development of points of view and the assembly of facts upon which decisions are made" (H. Carey, "Consultative Supervision and Management," p. 288).

[11] The concept of interaction as used here is not restricted to direct person-to-person, two-way communication (as in the process of superior-subordinate discussion), but encompasses more indirect forms (such as, for example, written communication) as well.

[12] It may be observed that participation in the latter way, where there is communication between participators and where the act of participation is carried out through the medium of the group (as in cases of "group decision"), may often yield the more useful results. The level of derivable benefits may be higher than if participation had proceeded through channels in which there had been no inter-participator communication. Some factors important in this context are the following: (a) the feeling of "group belongingness" obtained by means of "action together" and (b) the role of norms, set as a result of group discussion, toward which behaviour will tend to gravitate.

results at the lowest cost.[13] This is the criterion of rationality. Guided by this criterion, rational managers will find it advantageous to use participation whenever such use will lead to increased results at a given cost or to the attainment of given results at a lower cost.

There are many advantages which *may* stem from the use of participation as a managerial device. The following are the principal ones:

(1) A higher rate of output and increased quality of products (including reduced spoilage and wastage) as a result of greater personal effort and attention on the part of subordinates.[14]

(2) A reduction in turnover, absenteeism, and tardiness.

(3) A reduction in the number of grievances and more peaceful manager-subordinate and manager-union relations.

(4) A greater readiness to accept change.[15] When changes are arbitrarily introduced from above without explanation, subordinates tend to feel insecure and to take countermeasures aimed at a sabotage of the innovations. But when they have participated in the process leading to the decision, they have had an opportunity to be heard. They know what to expect and why, and they may desire the change. Blind resistance tends to become intelligent adaptation as insecurity is replaced by security.

(5) Greater ease in the management of subordinates.[16] Fewer managers may be necessary, the need for close supervision may be reduced, and less disciplinary action may be called for. Subordinates who have participated in the process leading toward a determination of matters directly affecting them may have a greater sense of responsibility with respect to the performance of their assigned tasks and may be more willing to accept the authority of their superiors.

---

[13] The term *cost* is here used in its highly precise form to refer to whatever must be given or sacrificed to attain an end. See "Price," *Webster's Dictionary of Synonyms*. The term *end* is broadly conceived to embrace whatever factors (monetary or nonmonetary) the managers themselves define as the formal ends of the enterprise.

[14] For examples, see Lippitt, "A Program of Experimentation on Group Functioning and Productivity"; John R. P. French, Jr., Arthur Kornhauser, and Alfred Marrow, "Conflict and Cooperation in Industry" (*Journal of Social Issues*, Fed., 1946); *Productivity, Supervision and Morale* (Survey Research Center Study no. 6, Ann Arbor, 1948).

[15] See, for example, Alex Bavelas, "Some Problems of Organizational Change" (*Journal of Social Issues*, Summer, 1948); Elliott Jacques, "Interpretive Group Discussion as a Method of Facilitating Social Change" (*Human Relations*, Aug., 1948); Lewin, "Group Decision and Social Change."

[16] See, for example, L. P. Bradford and R. Lippitt, "Building a Democratic Work Group" (*Personnel*, Nov., 1945); O. H. Mowrer, "Authoritarianism vs. 'Self-Government' in the Management of Children's Aggressive (Anti-Social) Reactions as a Preparation for Citizenship in a Democracy" (*Journal of Social Psychology*, Feb., 1939, pp. 121-6).

All managers possess a given amount of formal authority delegated to them by their superiors. But formal authority is not necessarily the equivalent of effective authority. The real source of the authority possessed by an individual lies in the acceptance of its exercise by those who are subject to it. It is the subordinates of an individual who determine the authority which he may wield. Formal authority is, in effect, nominal authority. It becomes real only when it is accepted. Thus, to be effective, formal authority must coincide with authority determined by its acceptance. The latter defines the useful limits of the former.[17] The use of participation as a managerial device may result in a widening of these limits, reducing the amount of resistance to the exercise of formal authority and increasing the positive responses of subordinates to managerial directives.

(6) The improved quality of managerial decisions. It is seldom if ever possible for managers to have knowledge of *all* alternatives and *all* consequences related to the decisions which they must make. Because of the existence of barriers to the upward flow of information in most enterprises, much valuable information possessed by subordinates never reaches their managers. Participation tends to break down the barriers, making the information available to managers. To the extent that such information alters the decisions which managers make, the quality of their decisions may thereby be improved.

These, then, are the principal advantages which *may* stem from the use of participation as a managerial device.[18] The conditions under which it *will* accomplish them—under which participation will lead to motivation—is the concern of the section which follows.

IV. The Psychological Conditions of Effective Participation

All managers of an enterprise are faced with the problem of eliciting service contributions from their subordinates at a high level of quality and intensity. These service contributions are essential if the formal goals of the enterprise are to be attained. What induces subordinates to contribute their services? What motivates them?

A motivated individual is one who is striving to achieve a goal; his activity is goal-oriented.[19] But it should be stressed that motivation is only *potential* motion towards a goal. Whether or not the goal

---

[17] This concept of effective authority is expanded upon in Tannenbaum, "Managerial Decision-Making."

[18] These advantages will henceforth be referred to as enterprise advantages.

[19] A goal is defined as a result which, when achieved, has the power to reduce the tension of the organism that has caused the organism to seek it.

is reached depends not only upon the strength of the force in the direction of the goal, but also upon all other forces (both driving and restraining) in the given situation.[20] To illustrate, a person may be motivated to produce 200 units of an item per day, but the restraining force in the form of machine failure or a quarrel with the foreman may lead him to attain an output of only 150 units.

In enterprises, the goals towards which individuals strive may be of two kinds. They may be the formal goals of the enterprise, or they may be other goals which are complementary to the formal goals. The latter is the typical case. Individuals may strive for monetary reward, prestige, power, security, and the like; or they may strive for certain psychological gratifications through the very act of doing the job (that is, they work because they like their work). The primary reason why they contribute their services is to attain these latter goals. In attaining these desired goals, they make possible the attainment of the formal goals of the enterprise which to them are simply means to their own ends. In this sense, the desired goals and the formal goals are complementary.

In the former case, the goals desired by the individual and the formal goals are the same. The individual contributes his services primarily because such contribution makes possible the attainment of the formal goals of the enterprise which coincide with his own personal goals. To the extent that this coincidence of goals exists, the necessity for managers to provide complementary goals for subordinates is thereby lessened, and related costs are reduced. It is suggested that participation tends to bring about a coincidence of formal and personal goals.[21] It may be that through participation, the subordinate who formerly was moved to contribute his services only because he sought, for example, security and financial rewards, now comes to be moved additionally because he recognizes that the

---

[20] Thus, motion in the direction of goals may be achieved not only by adding forces in the goal-direction, but also by reducing forces impeding such motion. See K. Lewin, "Frontiers in Group Dynamics" (*Human Relations*, vol. I, no. 1, 1947, pp. 26-7).

[21] It must be noted that participation as used in this context is only one device which may lead to additional motivation by bringing about a coincidence of formal and personal goals. For example, some other devices that under certain conditions may result in motivational increases and their derivative benefits to the enterprise are permitting personal discretion to the person to be motivated and stimulation of a sense of pride of workmanship. In the former context, managers in all enterprises must always decide the amount of discretion to permit to subordinates. Many considerations naturally underlie this decision. For present purposes, it is important to emphasize that in many circumstances, the granting of considerable discretion may lead to substantial increases in motivation. Several devices may be used concurrently, and the dynamics of the devices themselves are interrelated. For example, use of discretion may bring about an enhanced pride-of-workmanship feeling.

success of the enterprise in turn will enhance his own ability to satisfy his needs.[22]

Whether one conceives of participation as involving separate subordinates with their superiors or subordinates-in-groups with their superiors, in the final analysis one must not lose sight of the fact that the subordinate is a unique human being with a given personality. This implies that whether or not participation will bring forth the restructuring of his goal pattern (incorporating the formal goals within the scope of the personal goals) will depend upon a set of dynamic psychological conditions, the primary ones of which are outlined below:

(1) The subordinate must be capable of becoming psychologically involved in the participational activities. He must be free from "blockages" which may prevent him from re-arranging his particular goal pattern in the light of new experience. He must possess some minimum amount of intelligence so that he may grasp the meaning and implications of the thing being considered. He must be in touch with reality. If he responds to a dream world, any "real" developments, such as opportunities to take part in certain decision-making processes, may not penetrate without gross distortion and as a result miss their point.

(2) The subordinate must favour participational activity. In other words, the person who believes that "the boss knows best" and that the decision-making process is none of his business is not likely to become strongly motivated if given an opportunity to participate. It is apparent that for personality types shaped intensely by an authoritarian system, opportunities for participation may be regarded as signs of weakness and leadership incompetence and on that basis may be rejected unequivocally.[28]

(3) The subordinate must see the relevance to his personal life pattern of the thing being considered. When he realizes that through participation he may affect the course of his future in such a fashion as to increase its positive goal elements and to diminish the negative ones, he will become motivated. For example, a person who can see the relationship between "putting his two bits" into a discussion of a new way of using a stitching machine and the fact that this may mean greater job security and increased pay for himself may be motivated.

---

[22] It must be recognized that typically goal configurations, rather than single goals, act as motivating agents.

[28] For example, see A. H. Maslow, "The Authoritarian Character Structure" (in P. L. Harriman (ed.), *Twentieth Century Psychology*, New York, 1946). For more detailed treatments see the major works of Erich Fromm and Abram Kardiner.

(4) The subordinate must be able to express himself to his own satisfaction with respect to the thing being considered. He must be psychologically able to communicate; and, further, he must feel that he is making some sort of contribution. Of course, if he cannot communicate (owing to mental blocks, fear of being conspicuous, etc.), by definition he is not participating. If he does not feel that he is contributing, he may, instead of becoming motivated, come to feel inadequate and frustrated. This presupposes that not only is he articulate, but that he has a certain fund of knowledge on which to draw. Participation may fail if it involves considering matters that are quite outside the scope of experience of the participators.

All of the above conditions must be satisfied to some minimum extent. Beyond this requirement, however, the conditions may be mutually compensating, and a relatively low degree of one (although necessarily above the minimum) may be offset somewhat by an extremely high degree of another. For example, if a subordinate is unusually anxious to take part in participational activity (perhaps for reasons of prestige desires), he may come to be quite involved in the process of restructuring his goal pattern so that it will include some of the formal goals, even though he is not always certain as to whether or not he is really contributing anything worthwhile. Further, the relationships specified by the conditions are essentially dynamic. Opportunities for participation, reluctantly used at first, ultimately may lead to a change of mind and to their enthusiastic acceptance.[24]

It is apparent that individual differences are highly important in considering the effectiveness of participation as a motivational device; however, the "amount of participation opportunities" made possible by the managers is also a variable quantity. Thus, it is necessary to enquire what the limits to opportunities to participate are in terms of maximum results.

Common sense experience indicates that when some subordinates are given too many opportunities for participation, or too much leeway in participating, they may tend to flounder; they may find themselves unable to assimilate effectively the range of "thinking

---

[24] It should be stressed that "life spaces" of individuals (that is, their conceptions of themselves in relation to the totality of a physical and psychological environment) and their readiness for action in the light of these conceptions are never static. Constant change and "restructuring" take place, making for an essentially dynamic patterning of behaviour. For alternative definitions of the concept "life space" see Robert W. Leeper, *Lewin's Topological and Vector Psychology* (Eugene, 1943), p. 210.

opportunities" with which they are faced.[25] On the other hand, if they are given little or no opportunity to take part in the decision-making process, by definition they will not come to be motivated by participational activity. For each individual, an amount of participation opportunities lying somewhere between these two extremes will result in a maximum amount of motivation. A hypothesis stemming from this formulation is that for effective operation of participation as a motivational device in a group situation, the members of the group must respond similarly to given amounts of participation, for wide divergences of response may bring forth social tensions and lack of team work within the group.

Of course, many factors act together to motivate an individual. Therefore, the usefulness of the conceptualization advanced depends upon the possibility of breaking down the total of motivational forces into those owing to participation and those owing to other factors. Experimental control methods, matching of cases, and similar devices may have to be utilized to make such an analysis possible. Whether or not the increment of motivation owing to participation is worthwhile depends to an important extent upon the level of intensity of motivation that prevailed previous to introduction of the device of participation. No doubt, there are upper limits to intensity of motivation, and, if motivation has been strong all along, the effect of participation may not be very great.

V. EXTRA-PARTICIPATIONAL CONDITIONS FOR EFFECTIVE PARTICIPATION

Beyond the factors governing the relationship between participation and possible resultant motivation, certain conditions "outside" the individual must be considered by the managers in deciding whether or not this particular device is applicable.[26] It would be possible to distinguish a great number of such outside conditions that may determine whether or not the use of participation is feasible in a given situation. Those here indicated are suggestive rather than fully definitive. All are viewed with this question in mind: "Granting that participation may have certain beneficial effects, is it useful in a given instance if the ends of the enterprise are to be achieved?"

---

[25] For the belief that "thinking" as a solution for the industrial problem of motivation is usable more effectively on the supervisory level, but less applicable on the "lower levels" of the organizational hierarchy, see Willard Tomlison, "Review of A. R. Heron, *Why Men Work*" (*Personnel Journal*, July-Aug., 1948, p. 122).

[26] For analytical purposes, this article differentiates between conditions regarding the dynamics of participation as a psychological process and all conditions outside this psychological participation-to-motivation link. The latter category of conditions is treated under the present heading.

To answer this question affirmatively, the following conditions must be met:

(1) *Time Availability.* The final decision must not be of a too urgent nature.[27] If it is necessary to arrive at some sort of emergency decision rapidly, it is obvious that even though participation in the decision-making process may have a beneficial effect in some areas, slowness of decision may result in thwarting other goals of the enterprise or even may threaten the existence of the enterprise. Military decisions frequently are of this type.

(2) *Rational Economics.* The cost of participation in the decision-making process must not be so high that it will outweigh any positive values directly brought about by it. If it should require outlays which could be used more fruitfully in alternative activities (for example, buying more productive though expensive equipment), then investment in it would be ill-advised.

(3) *Intra-Plant Strategy.*

(a) *Subordinate Security.* Giving the subordinates an opportunity to participate in the decision-making process must not bring with it any awareness on their part of unavoidable catastrophic events. For example, a subordinate who is made aware in the participation process that he will lose his job *regardless* of any decisions towards which he might contribute may experience a drop in motivation. Furthermore, to make it possible for the subordinate to be willing to participate, he must be given the feeling that no matter what he says or thinks his status or role in the plant setting will not be affected adversely. This point has been made effectively in the available literature.[28]

(b) *Manager-Subordinate Stability.* Giving subordinates an opportunity to participate in the decision-making process must not threaten seriously to undermine the formal authority of the managers of the enterprise. For example, in some cases managers may have good reasons to assume that participation may lead non-managers to doubt the competence of the formal leadership, or that serious crises would result were it to develop that the subordinates were right while the final managerial decision turned out to be in disagreement with them and incorrect.

(4) *Inter-Plant Strategy.* Providing opportunities for participation must not open channels of communication to competing enter-

---

[27] See Chester I. Barnard, *Organization and Management* (Cambridge, 1948), p. 48.

[28] See McGregor, "Conditions for Effective Leadership in the Industrial Situation," *passim.*

prises. "Leaks" of information to a competitor from subordinates who have participated in a given decision-making process must be avoided if participation is to be applicable.

(5) *Provision for Communication Channels.* For participation to be effective, channels must be provided through which the employee may take part in the decision-making process. These channels must be available continuously and their use must be convenient and practicable.[29]

(6) *Education for Participation.* For participation to be effective, efforts must be made to educate subordinates regarding its function and purpose in the over-all functioning of the enterprise.[30]

It must be stressed that the conditions stipulated in this section are dynamic in their own right and may be affected by the very process of participation as well as by other factors.

VI. EFFECTS OF PARTICIPATION AS A FUNCTION OF TIME

An area of research that still remains relatively unexplored is that relating to the variation of the effects of participation with time. Some experimental studies have examined these effects in terms of increased productivity over a period of several weeks or months and found no appreciable reductions in productivity with time; while other evidence indicates that in some cases participation may have a sort of "shock" effect, leading to a surge of interest and increased motivation, with a subsequent decline.[31] Inadequate attention seems to have been given to this rather crucial question, and the present writers know of no studies that have traced the effects of participation (or other motivational devices) over periods as long as a year. However, on *a priori* grounds, and on the basis of experiential evidence, it would seem that, after an initial spurt, a plateau of beneficial effects will be attained, which finally will dissolve into a decline, unless additional managerial devices are skillfully employed.

---

[29] For a rigorous mathematical treatment of channels of communication within groups see Alex Bavelas, "A Mathematical Model for Group Structures" (*Applied Anthropology*, Summer, 1948, pp. 16 ff.).

[30] See French, Kornhauser, and Marrow, "Conflict and Co-operation in Industry," p. 30.

[31] For evidence of no decline in the motivational effect of certain participational procedures in an industrial re-training situation after a relatively brief time period subsequent to initiation of participation had elapsed, see, for example, L. Coch and J. R. P. French, "Overcoming Resistance to Change" (*Human Relations*, vol. I, no. 4, pp. 522-3). Also Lewin, "Group Decision and Social Change," pp. 338 and 343. For the hypothesis that under certain conditions decline may occur with time, see Heron, *Why Men Work*, p. 180.

QUESTIONS

1. Historically, what have been the three approaches for dealing with the problem of participation?
2. How do these authors define participation?
3. What advantages do they claim participation offers as a managerial device?
4. List and explain the psychological conditions that are needed to secure effective participation.
5. How does time influence the overall effectiveness and values of participative management?

35. ORGANIZATIONAL LEADERSHIP AND PARTICIPATIVE MANAGEMENT *

Chris Argyris

IMPORTANCE OF PARTICIPATION

"Participative management" and "democratic leadership" are phrases that are currently in the limelight in most management circles. These phrases are taken to mean that the subordinates should be given an opportunity to participate in the various decisions that are made in their organization which affect them directly or indirectly. Many executives, consultants, and research scientists, including the author,[1] have written and continue to write about the advantages of participative management. These people encourage supervisors and executives to increase the employees' participation in various organizational activities, especially in the decision-making process. They point out that, among other things, studies show that participative management tends to (1) increase the degree of "we" feeling or cohesiveness that participants have with their organization; (2) provide the participants with an over-all organizational point of view instead of the traditionally more narrow departmental point of view; (3) decrease the amount of conflict, hostility, and cutthroat competition among the participants; (4) increase the individuals' understanding of each other which leads to increased tolerance and patience toward others; (5) increase the individual's free expression of his personality, which results in an employee who sticks with the organization because he (i.e., his personality) needs the gratifying experiences he finds while working there; and (6) develop a "work climate," as a result of the other tendencies, in which the subordinates find opportunity to be more creative and to come up with ideas beneficial to the organization.

Although these trends are admittedly desirable, many supervisors and executives ask, "Exactly how far can this notion of participation and democracy be carried out?" Lately we have been asking ourselves the same question. Although we cannot answer it completely within the space of this paper, we would like to present for the reader's consideration some preliminary thoughts on the matter.

* From the *Journal of Business*, Vol. 28, No. 1 (January, 1955), pp. 1-7. Reprinted with permission.

[1] Argyris, "Techniques in Member Centered Training," *Personnel*, XXVIII, No. 3 (November, 1951), pp. 236-46.

Factors Influencing the Successful Introduction of Participative Management In An Organization

Much attention has been given and continues to be given to (1) the executives' feelings and attitudes about participative management; (2) the small informal groupings within the organization; and (3) the personnel policies of the organization. The assumption is that these are the three crucial factors in making participative management work.

We agree that these three factors are crucial, but we would like to add another. It seems to us that the kind of organizational structure within which these factors operate is also crucial. It is this factor that we propose to examine further.

How may we characterize the nature of most modern industrial and business organizations? One way to answer this question is to note the underlying rules or principles used by administrators to create and administer these organizations.

Simon defines some of the more common principles of administration upon which organizations are based as:

> 1. Administrative efficiency is increased by a specialization of the task among the group. [Specialization.]
> 2. Administrative efficiency is increased by arranging the members of the group in a determinate hierarchy of authority. [Unity of Command.]
> 3. Administrative efficiency is increased by limiting the span of control at any point in the hierarchy to a small number. [Span of Control.] [2]

These principles serve as the basis for the definition of organizational structure. They point out the kind of organization within which we usually try to introduce participative management programs. The question arises, "What problems can we predict will tend to arise when we try to introduce participative management to such an organization?"

In order to answer this question, we find it necessary first to re-examine and perhaps to redefine exactly what we mean by "organization."

A Concept of Organization

We may begin by defining an organization as an aggregate of parts (e.g., individuals, departments) integrated into an organized "whole." [3]

---

[2] Herbert A. Simon, *Administrative Behavior* (New York: Macmillan Co., 1947), pp. 20-21.

[3] More specifically, an organization may be defined as (1) any aggregate of parts (2) in a hierarchical order (3) co-existing (4) and interrelated in such a

How do these parts (e.g., individuals) become integrated into an organized whole? Research at the Yale Labor and Management Center indicates that the following *organizational processes* must be performed if an aggregate of individuals is to become an organization:

1. A *Work-flow Process* to define the behavior sequence that the parts of the organization must accomplish to achieve the objective (e.g., in a shoe factory a series of behavior sequences must be set up which people must perform in order to produce shoes)
2. A *Reward and Penalty Process* to induce people to do the work the organization assigns to them (in other words, the Reward and Penalty Process "taps" human motivation by rewarding or penalizing according to the acceptability of the actions performed)
3. An *Authority Process* to direct the employees in order that the organizational requirements be met
4. A *Perpetuation Process* to maintain and replenish the basic resources of organization (men, materials, and ideas)
5. An *Identification Process* to select and define clearly understood emotionally toned symbols, concepts, or other such aspects which will help individual employees identify with the organization as a whole, which in turn automatically helps to point out the uniqueness of the organization in the larger environment in which it is imbedded
6. A *Communication Process* to provide media and paths for communication

In other words, according to this scheme, we assume that an organization cannot exist unless someone performs at least these essential (but not sufficient) processes. We may now begin to understand how the principles of specialization and unity of command affect the possibilities of successfully initiating "participative management" in organizations.

Let us assume that we have a plant all set up to manufacture shoes. We have purchased the plant, the equipment, and the materials necessary to produce our product. We now need only "labor" to make the shoes. We hire these employees, and, if we administer our organization according to the modern management principle of task specialization, we will assign them to the specific task (or set of tasks) of making shoes. In terms of our outline this means that we assign them to tasks in the work-flow process.

But, according to our definition of organization above, these employees cannot be welded into an organization because they lack

---

unique manner (5) that the parts are able to maintain themselves only through this unique interrelatedness; (6) and simultaneously these parts work together in order to achieve the purpose which the organization is intended to achieve. (7) And to achieve Nos. 5 and 6 by adapting, within the limits, to any external influences, thereby (8) maintaining the characteristic interrelated state of these parts (i.e., maintaining organization).

the remainder of the organizational processes (e.g., authority, reward and penalty, etc.). In order to provide these processes and thus create an organization out of this aggregate of people, we create a new job containing the missing processes. We give the person who takes this job control over the authority, reward and penalty, perpetuation, and other processes. We call this person the "organizational leader." Now, the employees who are making the shoes can be welded into an organized unit. But, to do so, they must by definition become dependent upon the organizational leader for the missing processes of organization. They must turn to him for their authority, reward and penalties, perpetuation, etc. Thus the principle of unity of command is now "translated" into the principle that the subordinates are to report to one leader and are to be dependent upon him for certain crucial activities.

In other words, the scheme suggests that what is customarily called "the principle of unity of command" is actually the principle of inducing the subordinates to follow the leader by making them dependent upon him and by paying them to accept this dependence. There is, therefore, a "built-in" sense of dependency of the subordinates upon the organizational leader.[4] This dependency, we suggest, is inevitable if we follow the principles of task specialization and unity of command.

Do Dependence and Participation Go Together?

The question arises, "How truly participative (i.e., how spontaneous and free) can subordinates be if they are to be dependent upon their leader?" "How much democracy can we have if the power lies in the one who leads and not in the ones who are led?" Or, if we take the leader's point of view, "How democratic can he be if his job *is* to control the processes of organization?" Unfortunately, these and other similar questions are not answered by the many interesting and provocative studies in small-group dynamics from which so much of our information about the value of participation stems. The reason is that most of the research is based upon experimentally created or actual groups whose basic purpose is *not* to give any one leader a "life-or-death grip" (to quote an employee) on the other members of the group. Leadership in these groups seems to arise at any given time from the individual's ability to fulfil the needs of the other members of the group. It does not arise because of any predeter-

---

[4] The leader is dependent upon the subordinates in terms of the work flow; he depends upon them to produce.

mined power of any one member over the other members of the group.

Although we also do not have a clear-cut answer to the question of "How much participation is possible?" there are some implications in our analysis which might be useful in eventually helping us to arrive at an answer. We discuss some of these implications below.

A BASIC CONFLICT BETWEEN ORGANIZATION DEVELOPMENT AND PERSONALITY DEVELOPMENT

If the modern management principles (e.g., unity of command, task specialization, span of control, etc.) are to obtain *ideal* expression in an organization, the management would have to assign non-supervisory employees to a job which tends to (1) permit them little control over their work-a-day world; (2) place them in a situation where their passivity rather than initiative would frequently be expected; (3) lead them to occupy a subordinate position; (4) permit them a minimum degree of fluidity (variety) and emphasize the expression of one (or perhaps a few) of the agent's relatively minor abilities; and (5) make them feel dependent upon other agents (e.g., the boss).[5]

The problems that would tend to arise if we assign people to such jobs can be seen by asking the following questions, "What sorts of personality characteristics do people in our culture tend to exhibit?" Or, to put it another way, "What needs do relatively normal adults in our culture have?" "Would these needs be able to find some such expression in a job situation as the one we describe above?"

A somewhat detailed analysis of much of the material available on the development of the human personality suggests that people in our culture (1) tend to develop from receiving and incorporating aspects of culture as an infant to controlling, using, redefining, and helping others incorporate these aspects of culture as an adult; (2) develop from a state of being passive as an infant (i.e., having other people initiate action for them) to a state of being increasingly active as an adult (i.e., they initiate action as much or more than other people toward them); (3) develop from being capable of behaving only in a few ways and in a rigid manner as an infant to being capable of behaving in many different ways and behaving in a flexible manner as an adult; (4) develop from being in a subordinate position in the family and society as an infant, to occupying a more

　　　[5] F. W. Taylor, *Scientific Management* (New York: Harper & Bros., 1947), and L. Urwick, *The Elements of Administration* (New York: Harper & Bros., 1944).

equal and/or superordinate position in the family and society as an adult; and (5) develop from a state of high dependence on others as an infant to a state of independence and finally to a state of inter-dependence in their society as an adult.[6]

If we assume, for a moment, that the people who come to work for us are relatively normal, then may we not conclude that these people will tend to desire to find work which will help them fulfil some combination of the above trends? (The exact combination naturally depends on the individual.) In order to accomplish this, an individual would require a job in which he can (1) define for himself a ratio of activity (initiation of action) to passivity where activity is greater than passivity (passivity defined as others initiating action for the individual) ; (2) define for himself a position equal and/or superordinate to the other people with whom he interacts; (3) define for himself tasks where he is able to provide expression for the many learned ways of behaving that are important to him (this includes the expression of important abilities, needs, sentiments, and personal goals) ; (4) define for himself a sense of fluidity and flexi-bility that is comparable to his personality fluidity and flexibility; (5) express feelings of independence and interdependence in rela-tion to the other people in the organization; (6) feel that he has the respect of other individuals who are important in his life; and (7) obtain from his job a degree of creature sufficiency he desires.[7]

Thus, relatively normal individuals are characterized as "having built into them (through the process of growing up) tendencies to

---

[6] Chris Argyris, *Personality Fundamentals for Administrators* (rev. ed.; New Haven: Yale Labor and Management Center, 1953).

[7] It seems necessary that we pause for a moment and make a few important comments concerning the listing just presented.

First, we want to emphasize that the exact combination of these requirements and the degree to which each one of them is to be fulfilled for any given indivi-dual can be ascertained only by analysis of that individual case. Thus, it is possible that Individual A, for example, requires primarily 1, 2, and 4, with an emphasis on 1. On the other hand, Individual B may require that all the above be fulfilled, with an emphasis on 5 and 6.

It is also conceivable that Individual C may desire 1 *not* to be active, *not* to have an equal or superordinate position; 2 *not* to desire to feel independent; 5, etc. According to our viewpoint, this adult would have to be classed as "not matured." He is still at a more childlike stage of development. Psychologists may call him "fixated" at an earlier stage of development. This individual would not require a function which permits him to accomplish the items suggested in 1-7.

The point we want to emphasize is that we are *not* eliminating individual differences, nor are we imposing our developmental scheme on everyone. This is not a "budding rosebud" theory. We are simply suggsting that a normal individual, living in and interacting with our culture, will tend to exhibit these developmental trends but in his own unique combination. If the individual does not depict any of these trends, then we would suggest that, broadly speaking, he is not mature and that he will tend to be in equilibrium in the kind of function in which a mature individual will not be in equilibrium.

be active, to be independent, to be flexible, and to express their many and varied abilities," etc. Job situations, on the other hand, are described as requiring an individual to be passive, to be dependent, and to express only one or two abilities.

The job requirements are clearly different from, and in some cases antagonistic to, the requirements of relatively normal individuals. However, they *are* substantially similar to the requirements of an infant in our culture.

Thus, we are led to conclude that it would be difficult for the organization to place relatively normal adult individuals in "ideal" job (i.e., from the organization's point of view) situations without creating difficulties. Similarly, it would be difficult for the individual to obtain ideal personality expression without blocking the efficient expression of the organizational principles.

There are a number of ways out of such a dilemma for both the employees and the management. For example, some recent research at the Yale Management and Labor Center indicates that employees may adapt to their working situation in various ways. Individuals may (1) leave the organization; (2) accept the frustration on the assumption that if they work hard they will eventually be raised to a leadership position; (3) become apathetic and not "give a damn" about their work; (4) create informal activities and informal groups to help them adapt (if the groups are found to be effective, the individuals may desire to stabilize them and make certain that these groups will always exist; this might be accomplished by the individuals bringing to bear upon the work situation power which is inherently theirs, i.e., that which comes from the political, social, and economic privileges given to all people in this country; thus, the groups may be stabilized in the form of trade-unions) ; and (5) come into the organization prepared (through culture training) to expect no high degree of personality expression; this expectation tends to act to reduce the negative effects of the actual lack of personality expression obtained on the job.

Management, on the other hand, may act to minimize the difficulties by decreasing the employees' dependence upon the organization leader.[3] This is one of the main objectives of increased employee participation in decision-making. The point we would make is simply

---

[3] Management may also decrease the negative effects of specialization through "job enlargement." In terms of our framework, this means giving employees more work-flow tasks. Our research suggests that an increase in work-flow tasks does not necessarily lead to better-adapted individuals. It is the inclusion of authority, reward and penalty, and perpetuation tasks that really counts.

that, if we are to use participation to decrease dependency, then we may also have to change the nature of our organization. Our organization is no longer being administered by the principles described above. In short, participative management implies a different set of organization principles.

If what we have said to date makes sense, then clearly there are some interesting implications for executive training. First, is there not a need for a reexamination of the basic structure of organization as defined by traditional administrative principles? Perhaps a different type of organization structure is necessary if "participative management" is really to work. Until such basic changes are made, might it not be more realistic to teach participative management principles to executives *after* they have been helped to understand the effects that this basic dependency relationship has upon the employees? We could teach them to understand the nature of a dependency relationship and point out how it conflicts with normal personality needs.[9] This would help the supervisors gain more insight into the "why" of the often-observed apathetic, disinterested behavior on the part of employees. It would help the supervisor to understand the *adaptive value* of the many informal activities that employees create but which management may dislike. For example, what would happen if the supervisor is helped to realize that apathy may be a healthy way to adapt to the type of work situation in which a person is usually placed? Would it not lead the supervisor to ask himself, "How can I minimize this dependency relationship and reduce the number of personality-blocking aspects of the organization without detracting from the efficient management of the organization?" He would do this *before* he spent hours making "morale" speeches about "everybody getting on the team."

Moreover, would not this knowledge help us to learn to set realistic limits to participative management, thereby making the supervisors more secure in its use? It seems to us that one reason many supervisors resist participative management is that they feel that there are no limits to its use. Also, would it not help to alleviate, or at least to decrease, the often-produced feelings of inadequacy and perhaps guilt that supervisors have after listening to how democratic they ought to be?

---

[9] For further discussion of these points see the author's "Executive Leadership: Developing It in Yourself and in Others," speech before the Harvard Business School Club of New York, February, 1954 (to be published as a chapter of a monograph by the McKinsey Foundation for Management Research, Inc.).

We close with this point. Let nothing in this paper be construed to mean that we are implying that modern management principles are "bad" or that apathy and indifference on the part of members of organizations are "good." We are simply trying to spell out what *is*. It seems to us, if we all (employees and executives) understand the basic difficulties inherent in organization, there should result a greater tolerance for and patience and understanding of the organization's problems, our own problems, and the problems of others.

QUESTIONS

1. Why does Argyris feel that participative management is so important?
2. What is the relationship between dependence and participation according to this article?
3. What is the conflict between organization development and personality development?
4. What remedies does Argyris suggest for the conflict between organization development and personality development?
5. Do you agree or disagree with Argyris' criticisms of management principles?

36. THE CASE FOR PARTICIPATIVE MANAGEMENT *

Keith Davis

Participation is an overworked word in business and government, but an underworked activity. The idea sounds good to most managers, but they are frequently unsure of what to do with it. Some grossly misinterpret what it is, so that when they say, "Participation is great," they are really talking about something else; others are not sure when to apply it or how far to go with it.

One reason for the slow growth of participation is that it is a difficult philosophy to understand, and even more difficult to develop in a group. Genuine social science skill is required to make participation work. Many supervisors get in over their heads in a burst of enthusiasm and, after experiencing a rebuff, tend to withdraw from further efforts at participation. It appears that improperly applied participation may be worse for productivity and morale than simply doing nothing. Ineffective attempts to secure participation may make a group feel manipulated, resentful, confused, or lacking in objectives.

In spite of the difficulty of developing participation, it does have enormous potential for raising productivity, bettering morale, and improving creative thinking. The need of people to participate is not a passing fancy. It is rooted deep in the culture of free men around the world, and it is probably a basic drive in man.[1] Because of its significance and permanence, participation is a method to which leaders need to devote long-range efforts. Means of tapping this source of creativity and of using its cohesive power for teamwork need to be developed. Participation affords a means of building some of the human values needed in a group. It can create an asset in morale so that when necessary orders are given, people will respond more cooperatively because they are participating in their group, although they did not participate in determining the instruction they have most recently received. The importance of participation has been described as follows:

> Two thousand years ago we put participation in the religion which has come to dominate the Western world. Two hundred years ago we

* From *Business Horizons*, Vol. 6, No. 3 (Fall, 1963), pp. 55-60. Reprinted with permission.

[1] Comparative studies in England and the United States suggest that participation is a basic human drive rather than a cultural acquisition. See N. R. F. Maier and L. R. Hoffman, "Group Decision in England and the United States," *Personnel Psychology*, XV (Spring, 1962), p. 86.

put this essential element in our political and social structure. We are just beginning to realize that we ought to put participation in business as well.[2]

Classical experiments

Classical experiments by Roethlisberger, Bavelas, and Coch and French confirm our belief that participation is extremely valuable. Roethlisberger and his associates originally sought to show the relationship of physical change in environment and output. In the course of their experiments, new relationships, many of them involving participation, developed between workers and supervisors, and workers and experimenters. The results convincingly showed that these social changes improved both productivity and morale. Although participation was not the whole cause of these improvements, it seemed to be a significant cause.[3]

Bavelas worked with a group of women performing a sewing operation on a group incentive basis. For his experiment, he chose a superior group whose production averaged about 74 units hourly, with a range of 70 to 78. He asked them to set their own production goal. After considerable discussion they agreed unanimously on a goal of 84 units hourly, which they exceeded within five days. A goal of 95, set at a later meeting, could not be met. The goal was then reduced to the relatively permanent level of 90 units. During the next several months, the group's output averaged about 87 units with a range of 80 to 93. The net increase after participation was about 13 units hourly.[4] Coch and French achieved similar results in experiments with sewing machine operators.[5]

The benefits of participation are evident in the experience of a large aircraft manufacturer, who employed from 5,000 to 20,000 shopworkers during the decade following World War II. The company used a safety committee system in which each department was represented by one worker. During these ten years, not one person suffered

---

[2] Ralph M. Besse, "Business Statesmanship," *Personnel Administration*, XX (January-February, 1957), 12.

[3] F. J. Roethlisberger, *Management and Morale* (Cambridge: Harvard University Press, 1941), p. 14.

[4] Norman R. F. Maier, *Psychology in Industry* (Boston: Houghton Mifflin Company, 1946), pp. 264-66. Lawrence and Smith have since repeated Bavelas' experiments with similar results. See Lois C. Lawrence and Patricia Cain Smith, "Group Decision and Employee Participation," *The Journal of Applied Psychology*, XXXIX (October, 1955), pp. 334-37.

[5] Lester Coch and John R. P. French, Jr., "Overcoming Resistance to Change," *Human Relations*, I (No. 4, 1948), 512-32, and John R. P. French, Jr. and Alvin Zander, "The Group Dynamics Approach," in Arthur Kornhauser (ed.), *Psychology of Labor-Management Relations* (Champaign, Ill.: Industrial Relations Research Association, 1949), pp. 73-75.

a disabling injury while serving as safety committeeman. This record was made despite the facts that hundreds of workers served on the committee during the decade, and accident-prone workers sometimes were appointed to the post in order to make them safety conscious. Although some committeemen probably returned to work earlier than they should have after an accident in order to preserve their record, the facts still show a significant difference between committeemen and other workers. Part of the difference was surely due to the fact that the committeemen were participating in a safety program.

Participation is especially important in encouraging people to accept change, a persistent pressure on all of us in our dynamic society. Participation is helpful both in planning and installing change, because when employees understand the objectives and content of a change, they are confident that management is not trying to "pull a fast one" on them. Participation may actually improve carefully devised management plans, because it elicits the ideas of the persons who are most thoroughly acquainted with the working effects of those plans. It may cancel a poor plan and thus save management many headaches. In any case, it broadens the outlook of those involved and helps them feel that they have an active part in what is taking place.

When a change is within management's control, such as the determination of a new work method, best results are realized when the group participates in the recognition of the need for change. Participation is less effective if it begins only after management has decided that a change is necessary.

Key ideas in participation

Participation is defined as an individual's mental and emotional involvement in a group situation that encourages him to contribute to group goals and to share responsibility for them. This definition contains three important ideas.

First, participation means mental and emotional involvement rather than mere muscular activity. The involvement of a person's *self,* rather than just his skill, is the product of his mind and his emotions. The person who participates is ego-involved instead of merely task-involved.[6] Some managers mistake task-involvement for true participation. They go through the motions of participation, but it is clear to employees that their manager is an autocrat who does not

---

[6] Gordon W. Allport, "The Psychology of Participation," *The Psychological Review,* LIII (May, 1945), 22.

really want their ideas. Employees cannot become involved in this kind of situation.

A *second* important characteristic of participation is that it motivates contribution. Individuals are given an opportunity to direct their initiative and creativity toward the objectives of the group. In this way, participation differs from consent,[7] which uses only the creativity and ideas of the leader who brings his idea to the group for their approval. Participation requires more than mere approval of something already decided. It is a two-way psychological and social relationship among people rather than a procedure imposing ideas from above.

A *third* characteristic of participation is that it encourages people to accept responsibility for an activity. Because they are self-involved in the group, they want to see it work successfully. Participation helps them become responsible citizens rather than nonresponsible automatons. As individuals begin to accept responsibility for group activities, they become interested in and receptive to teamwork, because they see in it a means of accomplishing a job for which they feel responsible. A person who is actively involved in something is naturally more committed to carrying it out. Of his own free will, he creates responsibility rather than having it forced upon him by delegation. By making himself responsible, he gains a measure of independence and dignity as an individual making his own decisions, even though these decisions are heavily influenced by his group environment.

Managers often ask, "If I share decisions with my personnel, don't I lose authority? I can't afford to give up authority because I'm responsible." This is a perfectly normal worry of an executive who is considering the values of participation for the first time, but it is hardly a justifiable worry. The participative manager still retains his authority to decide. He shares his problems with the group by means of a process that may be called social delegation. Social delegation in the human relations domain is comparable to formal delegation in the organizational domain. Neither type of delegation weakens a manager's organizational authority. No manager of the future—say twenty years hence—will object to a certain amount of social delegation through participation under normal conditions. It will be as much his stock in trade as formal delegation is today.

---

[7] Mary P. Follett, "The Psychology of Consent and Participation," in Henry C. Metcalf and L. Urwick (eds.), *Dynamic Administration: The Collected Papers of Mary Parker Follett* (New York: Harper and Brothers, 1941), pp. 210-12.

Practice limitations

These experiments (and the conclusions drawn from them) have a number of limitations that managers cannot ignore. Their success is no guarantee that all similar practices will be successful. The experiments described were performed by professional men skilled in human relations; similar efforts by ordinary supervisors undoubtedly would not produce such consistent results. The step from experimentation to practice is a long one indeed. The experiments were mostly one-shot efforts in a narrow work situation, using small groups who were doing repetitive work and undergoing changes. Participation in large work groups may be more difficult. In any case, managers should not go overboard for participation as they once did for scientific management. The latter was a worthwhile development, but managers' failure to recognize its uses and limitations in particular situations nearly ruined it.

In developing participation, we must be able to strike a precarious balance between counterfeit participation, which would arouse distrust, and excessive participation, which would consume valuable work time and destroy unified direction. Many issues are involved. Counterfeit participation may be tinsel and ribbon to make people happy, or it may be a more insidious tool handled by skilled social scientists, the engineers of consent.

Another danger of participation—as was true of scientific management—is that practitioners will get lost in the procedures of participation and overlook its philosophy. The substance of participation does not automatically flow from its procedures; there is no such mechanistic connection. Rather, when procedures are used at the right time and in the right circumstances, they enable it to develop.

Another issue concerns a person's right not to participate. There is no evidence that advanced participation is required for everybody; there is evidence that many persons do not want to be bothered with participation. Shall we force them into a mold merely because we think it is good for them? Some persons want a minimum of interaction with their supervisor and associates. The role expectation of many employees is to work for an autocratic supervisor, and consequently they produce effectively with this type of leadership. Research shows that the more authoritarian personality derives less benefit from participative methods, while the more equalitarian personality is more favorably affected.[8] Sometimes a group can be kept participat-

---

[8] Victor H. Vroom, "Some Personality Determinants of the Effects of Participation," *Journal of Abnormal and Social Psychology*, LIX (November, 1959), 322-27.

ing only by pressure from above. When that pressure is released, the group reverts to patterns of less participation.[9]

Prerequisites for participation

Finally, it should be emphasized that the success of participation is directly related to how well certain prerequisites are satisfied. Some of these conditions occur in the participants; some exist in the environment. Taken together, they mean that participation works better in some situations than others—and that in certain situations, it works not at all.[10]

The first prerequisite is that ample time must be allowed to participate before action is required. Participation may not be appropriate in emergency situations. Second, the financial cost of participation should not exceed the values, economic and otherwise, that it produces. Third, the subject of participation must be relevant to the participant's organization, something in which he is interested, or he will regard it as mere busy work. Fourth, the participant should have the abilities, intelligence, and knowledge to participate effectively.

Fifth, the participants must be able to communicate in order to be able to exchange ideas. Sixth, no one (employee or manager) should feel that his position is threatened by participation. Seventh, participation for deciding a course of action in an organization can take place only within the group's area of job freedom. Some degree of restriction on subunits is necessary in any organization in order to maintain internal stability; subunits cannot make decisions that violate company policy, collective bargaining agreements, or similar restraints.

Since participation is a deep-seated need of man, it is worth trying: (1) if the manager understands what he is doing; (2) if he has developed some social science skill; (3) if he will meet the prerequisites; (4) if he will respect the role expectations of his people; and (5) if he will begin in a small way, rather than shooting for the moon in the first few months. Managers should proceed with caution, building each improvement upon past successes—but by all means, they should proceed.

---

[9] Robert N. McMurry, "The Case for Benevolent Autocracy," *Harvard Business Review*, XXXVI (January-February, 1958), 82-90.

[10] For further explanation, see Robert Tannenbaum, Irving R. Weschler, and Fred Massarik, *Leadership and Organization: A Behavioral Science Approach* (New York: McGraw-Hill Book Company, Inc., 1961), pp. 88-100.

Questions

1. Explain how Davis justifies the importance of participation in a business firm.
2. What are some of the guidelines a manager should observe in encouraging participation on the part of his subordinates?
3. What are some of the guidelines to be observed in developing participative practices in the firm?
4. Some critics of participative management claim that such practices condone inefficiency and profit losses. Do you agree or disagree? How might participation have both effects in a firm?
5. How participative should a manager be? How does the individual manager determine this? What other factors in a situation influence the degree and amount of participation? Does one's level in an organization have an effect here?

37. GROUP PROCESSES AND ORGANIZATIONAL PERFORMANCE *

Rensis Likert

Research in organizations is yielding increasing evidence that the superior's skill in supervising his subordinates *as a group* is an important variable affecting his success: the greater his skill in using group methods of supervision, the greater are the productivity and job satisfactions of his subordinates.

Nonsupervisory employees of a public utility were asked, "Do group discussions do any good?" and could check one of the alternatives listed: "Yes, the supervisor likes to get our ideas and tries to do something about them," "No, not really, it's just talk," "No, we don't get a real hearing for our own ideas." When their answers were related to their attitudes on job-related matters, a marked relationship was found (Mann & Dent, 1954a). (Job-related attitudes include those toward the work itself, supervision, working conditions, pay, promotion, etc.) For both blue-collar and white-collar employees, those with favorable job-related attitudes were much more likely to feel that group discussions did some good, that their supervisor liked to get their ideas and tried to do something about them (Figure 1).

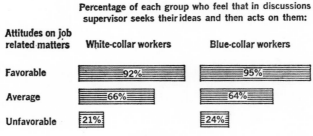

FIGURE 1

RELATION OF EMPLOYEE ATTITUDES ON JOB-RELATED MATTERS TO FEELING THAT GROUP'S DISCUSSIONS WITH SUPERVISOR ARE WORTHWHILE

The frequency of work-group meetings, as well as the attitude and behavior of the superior toward the ideas of subordinates, affects the extent to which employees feel that the supervisor is good at

* From Rensis Likert, *New Patterns in Management* (New York: McGraw-Hill Publishing Co., Inc., 1961), pp. 26-43. Used by permission.

handling people. These results are shown in Figure 2. Of those who report that the superior holds meetings frequently and that he "likes to get our ideas and tries to do something about them," 74 per cent feel that their superior is good in dealing with people. On the other hand, of those who say their boss seldom holds meetings and when he does, "it's just talk, we don't really get a hearing for our ideas," 12 per cent feel that their supervisor is good in dealing with people. Of those who say that their supervisor *never* holds meetings, 39 per cent feel that he is good in dealing with people.

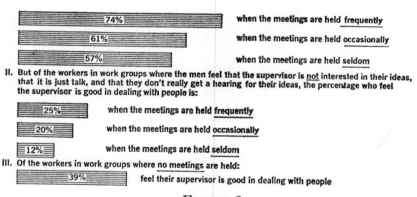

I. Of the workers in work groups where the men feel that the supervisor likes to get their ideas and tries to do something about the ideas, the percentage who feel the supervisor is good in dealing with people is:

74% — when the meetings are held frequently
61% — when the meetings are held occasionally
57% — when the meetings are held seldom

II. But of the workers in work groups where the men feel that the supervisor is not interested in their ideas, that it is just talk, and that they don't really get a hearing for their ideas, the percentage who feel the supervisor is good in dealing with people is:

25% — when the meetings are held frequently
20% — when the meetings are held occasionally
12% — when the meetings are held seldom

III. Of the workers in work groups where no meetings are held:

39% — feel their supervisor is good in dealing with people

FIGURE 2

THE PROPORTION OF WORKERS WHO FEEL THAT THEIR SUPERVISOR IS GOOD AT DEALING WITH PEOPLE AS AFFECTED BY THE FREQUENCY OF THE SUPERVISOR'S USE OF WORK-GROUP MEETINGS AND HIS USE OF IDEAS WHICH EMERGE IN THE MEETINGS

These data demonstrate that if a superior is not genuinely interested in his subordinates' ideas and prepared to act upon them, he is better off not having group meetings to discuss work problems. The data in Figure 2 are from nonsupervisory employees in a large public utility. Almost identical results have been obtained in other studies involving quite different kinds of work. Moreover, the same pattern is obtained at different hierarchical levels. Superiors at every level influence their subordinates' evaluation of them by the frequency with which they hold meetings and the extent to which they display interest in the ideas of their subordinates and make use of these ideas.

Typical of the relationships between the judged performances of a supervisor and the frequency with which he holds group meetings to discuss work-related problems are the data shown in Figure 3. Supervisors who are evaluated highly by management make much more frequent use of group meetings to deal with work-related problems than do supervisors who receive a mediocre or poor rating (Mann & Dent, 1954).

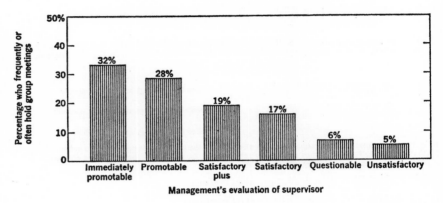

FIGURE 3

RELATIONSHIP BETWEEN MANAGEMENT'S EVALUATION OF SUPERVISOR AND FREQUENCY WITH WHICH HE HOLDS GROUP MEETINGS

Supervisors who "consider employees as individuals rather than merely persons to get the work out" and who, when dealing with problems, "identify primarily with employees or with both company and employees rather than identifying primarily with the company" develop greater pride in their work groups than supervisors who behave otherwise (Morse, 1953). A supportive attitude on the part of the superior, as well as the constructive use of group meetings, is necessary to develop group pride and loyalty.

Another important relationship is shown in Figure 4. Foremen of high-production work groups report much more frequently than do the foremen of low-production groups that their work groups perform well when the foremen are absent. High-production supervisors apparently develop within the work group the expectation, the capacity, and the goals required to function effectively whether or not the foreman is present (Institute for Social Research, 1951).

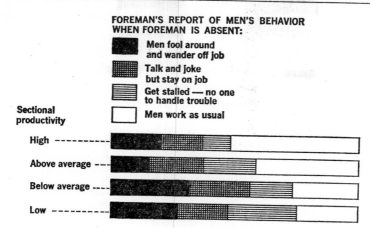

FOREMAN'S REPORT OF MEN'S BEHAVIOR
WHEN FOREMAN IS ABSENT:

- Men fool around and wander off job
- Talk and joke but stay on job
- Get stalled — no one to handle trouble
- Men work as usual

Sectional productivity

High
Above average
Below average
Low

FIGURE 4

HIGH-PRODUCTIVITY WORK GROUPS PERFORM WELL WHEN FOREMAN IS ABSENT

Group loyalty and organizational performance

In several studies involving such widely different kinds of work as clerical, manufacturing, sales, and delivery services, the loyalty of nonsupervisory employees toward their work group and pride in its ability to produce are found to have a low positive relationship with productivity (Kahn, 1956; Katz et al., 1950; Likert & Willits, 1940; Seashore, 1954). Figure 5, which presents results for clerical workers and railroad maintenance-of-way crews (Katz et al., 1950; Katz et al., 1951), illustrates the magnitude of this relationship. Work groups with greater pride in their capacity to produce or with greater loyalty and attraction to the group tend to be the groups producing at a higher level. [In India, Bose (1957) found similar results.]

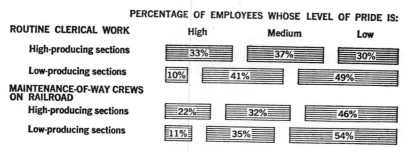

PERCENTAGE OF EMPLOYEES WHOSE LEVEL OF PRIDE IS:

ROUTINE CLERICAL WORK	High	Medium	Low
High-producing sections	33%	37%	30%
Low-producing sections	10%	41%	49%
MAINTENANCE-OF-WAY CREWS ON RAILROAD			
High-producing sections	22%	32%	46%
Low-producing sections	11%	35%	54%

FIGURE 5

RELATION OF PRIDE IN WORK GROUP TO PRODUCTIVITY

In the study of the clerical operations, the workers and supervisors who displayed pride in their work group made such comments as, "We have a good group," "We work together well," or "We help out each other." One supervisor said about her group, "They all have definite assignments and they're a nice cooperative crowd. They just jump in and do things and never bother me. They have a responsibility toward the group."

High peer-group loyalty (loyalty among the workers toward one another irrespective of their attitude toward their supervisor) is not necessarily associated with high productivity. There is substantial evidence, both from operating experience and from the more precise measurement obtained in research projects, that work groups can have goals which will influence productivity and cost either favorably or adversely. The power and tendency of work groups to restrict production have been found in many studies. One of the most important conclusions, for example, emerging from the famous Western Electric study by Mayo and his associates showed that industrial organizations almost always have an "informal organization" which consists of all or most of the subordinate members of work groups. The goals of this "informal organization" often tended to restrict production, to increase absence, and in other ways to run counter to the general objectives of the organization (Mayo, 1931; Roethlisberger & Dickson, 1939; Whitehead, 1938).

These findings have been confirmed in many studies conducted since the original Western Electric project. Studies have shown that group goals which lead to unnecessary waste and at least some restriction in output are widespread in our industrial and governmental organizations. This restriction and waste occurs among white-collar workers as well as among blue-collar workers (French & Zander, 1949). It occurs among unorganized workers, as well as organized (Mathewson, 1931). It occurs at the nonsupervisory level and at higher levels. The armed services also provide evidence of this phenomenon (Stouffer et al, 1949). Several of these studies have been summarized by such writers as Argyris (1957c), Dubin (1951), Roethlisberger (1941), Viteles (1953), and W. H. Whyte (1955).

The research findings from these studies also provide extensive evidence that productivity can be increased substantially and waste correspondingly lessened when the goals of work groups shift so as to become more consistent with the objectives of the organization. This was probably the most striking result of the original Western Electric study. When the attitudes of the girls in the first Relay Assembly

Room gradually shifted from opposition to the objectives of the company to greater acceptance of these objectives, a substantial increase in production occurred and important information about the total operation of which management had been unaware began to flow (Roethlisberger & Dickson, 1939).

Work groups which have high peer-group loyalty and common goals appear to be effective in achieving their goals. If their goals are the achievement of high productivity and low waste, these are the goals they will accomplish (Lewin, 1958). If, on the other hand, the character of their supervision causes them to reject the objectives of the organization and set goals at variance with these objectives, the goals they establish can have strikingly adverse effects upon productivity (Zaleznik, Christenson, & Roethlisberger, 1958). Analyses by Seashore (1954) provide impressive evidence of the power of the goals of cohesive groups.[1] His study showed that the greater the peer-group loyalty, the greater the influence which the goals of the group have on the performance of members of the group. Thus, in work groups with high peer-group loyalty, the variations in productivity from worker to worker are less than in work groups with low peer-group loyalty. This relationship, based on data from a company manufacturing heavy machinery, is shown in Figure 6. Moreover, as the data in the figure show, the greater the peer-group loyalty, the greater are the differences between the groups in the level of productivity. Increased peer-group loyalty evidently is associated with greater motivational pressure to produce at the level which the group feels is appropriate. (Further evidence on this point appears in the table on page 639.)

This conclusion is borne out by the results in Figure 7. In this analysis, work groups were divided into two clusters, based roughly on the extent to which the work groups accept or reject company goals. The relationship was then examined between the level of peer-group loyalty and the productivity of each of these two clusters. As was expected, the data show that among the work groups which tend to accept company goals, high peer-group loyalty is associated with higher productivity. On the other hand, among the work groups which tend to reject company goals, high peer-group loyalty is associated with lower productivity (Seashore, 1954).

---

[1] Seashore defined his measurement of group loyalty as group cohesiveness and used questions dealing with the following dimensions: whether workers feel a part of the group, want to stay in the group, stick together, help each other, and get along together. These dimensions are essentially the same as those used in the other studies and referred to here as peer-group loyalty.

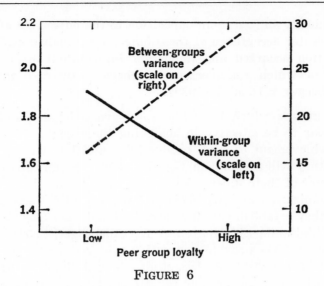

FIGURE 6

RELATIONSHIP OF PEER-GROUP LOYALTY TO VARIANCE
ON ACTUAL PRODUCTIVITY

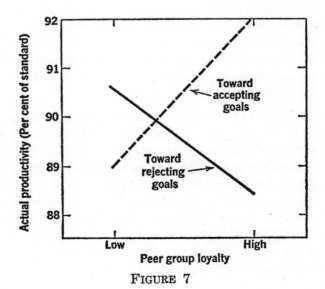

FIGURE 7

RELATIONSHIP OF PEER-GROUP LOYALTY TO PRODUC-
TIVITY WHEN MOTIVATION IS TOWARD ACCEPTING
VERSUS REJECTING COMPANY GOALS

As we observed in Figure 6, work groups with high peer-group loyalty are, on the average, somewhat more productive. This indicates that among groups with high peer-group loyalty there are more groups with high performance goals than with low. Supervisors who have the skill to build high peer-group loyalty evidently tend to have the leadership ability to create relatively high performance goals. This would suggest that there should be a fairly marked relationship between peer-group loyalty and attitudes toward the supervisor. This proves to be the case. In work groups with high peer-group loyalty, attitudes toward the supervisor are appreciably more favorable than in work groups with low peer-group loyalty ($r = +0.50$ to $+0.70$). This relationship is shown in Figure 8 (from unpublished data collected by S. E. Seashore and Basil Georgopoulos). Peer-group loyalty also has been found to have a fairly marked relationship with a combined index of attitudes toward supervision and attitudes toward the company. Thus, Seashore (1954) found that work groups with high peer-group loyalty had more favorable attitudes toward supervision and toward the company than work groups

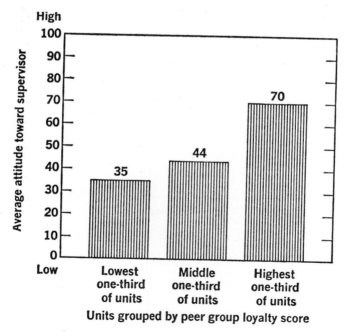

FIGURE 8

RELATION BETWEEN PEER-GROUP LOYALTY AND
ATTITUDE TOWARD SUPERVISOR

with low peer-group loyalty. The relationship he obtained is slightly less marked than that shown in Figure 8.

As might be expected from the preceding results, work groups with high peer-group loyalty tend to have more favorable attitudes toward production than do groups with low peer-group loyalty. Thus, groups with greater peer loyalty differ from groups with less peer loyalty in having higher production goals. Their opinion as to what is reasonable production is higher and is more nearly the same as that of their foreman (Katz et al., 1951; unpublished data collected by R. L. Kahn). Moreover, the groups with high peer loyalty have a more favorable attitude toward the high producer (R. Likert, 1958b; Morse, 1953).

High peer-group loyalty is associated also with less anxiety on matters related to the job (Figure 9). Evidently, when an individual is a member of a group with high peer-group loyalty, he feels that he has greater support and security and, consequently, feels less anxiety, even when restricting production, than do those persons in groups with low peer-group loyalty (Seashore, 1954).

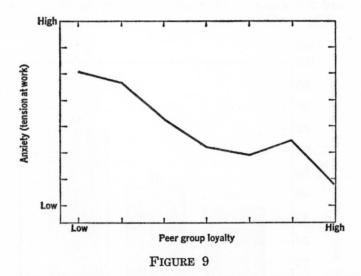

FIGURE 9

RELATIONSHIP OF PEER-GROUP LOYALTY TO FEELING
OF TENSION AT WORK

Group factors contributing to performance

Several reasons may account for the higher productivity of work groups with high peer-group pride and loyalty. One is that workers in these groups show more cooperation in getting the work done than do members of groups with low peer-group loyalty. In the high-loyalty groups, there tends to be a flow of work back and forth between the workers, depending upon the load. In groups with low peer-group loyalty, there is more feeling that each worker is on his own, that how he gets along in his work is his own responsibility.

The effect upon productivity when workers help one another is shown in Figure 10. When foremen in a company manufacturing heavy equipment were asked, "How does your section compare with other sections in the way the men help each other on the job?" the answers showed a marked relationship to the productivity of the sections. The foremen of high-production sections reported much more often than the foremen of low-production groups that their men helped one another (Katz & Kahn, 1952).

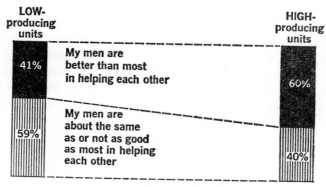

FIGURE 10

RELATIONSHIP OF GROUP SOLIDARITY TO PRODUCTIVITY (FOREMAN'S REPORT)

Workers in the high-production work groups not only have greater peer-group loyalty and help one another more, but give this help on their own initiative. The willingness of the groups with high peer-group loyalty to help one another seems to come from better interpersonal relationships developed by the foreman's effective leadership. This atmosphere seems to be fostered by leadership which uses group methods of supervision [2] and which develops in the entire group a sense of responsibility for getting the total job done.

Low levels of peer-group loyalty are found when the foreman deals with workers individually and makes individual work assignments. One supervisor of a low productive clerical group described his pattern of supervision as follows: "I apportion out the work to the

---

[2] Group methods of supervision are discussed in Chapters 8, 11, and 12.

people in my section and generally supervise the work handled. If a clerk is out, I have to make arrangements to have her work done. The work must go on even though there are absences. This involves getting work redistributed to those who are there."

In contrast to these specific individual assignments, the supervisors of groups with high productivity and high group loyalty more often create a sense of group responsibility for getting the work done. Thus, one of these supervisors reported: "We use the honor system. There are a certain number of girls and a certain amount of work comes in. We leave it up to each girl to take her share and get it done" (Katz et al., 1950).

Another factor contributing to the higher level of productivity of groups with high peer-group loyalty is their lower rate of absence from the job. As Figure 11 shows, persons in groups with high peer-group loyalty are much less likely to be absent from work than persons in groups with low peer-group loyalty. This chart is based on data from white-collar workers (Mann & Baumgartel, 1953a). Similar results were obtained for blue-collar workers. Apparently the warm, friendly reaction and security which one gets or fails to get from his work group profoundly affects his desire to be present in the group.

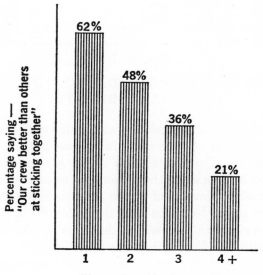

FIGURE 11

RELATION OF GROUP SOLIDARITY TO ABSENCE
(WHITE-COLLAR MEN)

As we have seen in the preceding pages, groups with high peer-group loyalty display a consistently different pattern from that shown by groups with a low degree of loyalty. In addition to the differences mentioned, the following characteristics have been found: The members of groups with greater peer loyalty are more likely to have:

1. Greater identification with their group and a greater feeling of belonging to it.
2. More friends in the group and in the company rather than outside the company.
3. Better interpersonal relations among the members of the work group.
4. A more favorable attitude toward their jobs and their company.
5. Higher production goals and more actual production with less sense of strain or pressure.

As the importance of group influences has been recognized and as more precise measurements have been obtained, there is increasing evidence which points to the power of group influences upon the functioning of organizations. In those situations where the management has recognized the power of group motivational forces and has used the kinds of leadership required to develop and focus these motivational forces on achieving the organization's objectives, the performance of the organization tends to be appreciably above the average achieved by other methods of leadership and management. Members of groups which have common goals to which they are strongly committed, high peer-group loyalty, favorable attitudes between superiors and subordinates, and a high level of skill in interaction clearly can achieve far more than the same people acting as a mere assemblage.

Those results are consistent also with the findings of other researchers. Argyris (1957c), Cartwright and Zander (1960), Viteles (1953), and W. H. Whyte (1955) have reported or summarized the results of a number of other studies consistent with the findings reported here. The recent study by Zaleznik, Christenson, and Roethlisberger (1958) adds impressive confirmation as does Marrow's report based on operating experience as well as experimental research (French et al., 1958; Marrow, 1957).

Studies in the armed services also yield evidence as to the importance of peer-group loyalty in influencing performance (Merton & Lazarsfeld, 1950; Stouffer et al., 1949). For example, an abstract [a] of Goodacre's study (1953) reports:

---

[a] *Human Organization Clearinghouse Bull.*, 1954, 3(1), 29.

. . . Men in squads making high scores on the criterion problem reported a significantly greater number of men in their squads "buddying around" together on the post after duty hours, and taking the initiative to give orders to other men during the problem, although they had no authority to do so. The men in the high scoring squads also reported fewer disagreements with the way their squad leader ran the problem, more satisfaction with the present positions held by the men in their squads, more pride in their squad, and the feeling that their squad was one to which more men would like to belong.

Similar results have been obtained in research in the Army on the importance of stable anchorage in a friendly face-to-face group as a factor influencing the capacity of the soldier to function effectively under the stress of battle conditions. Those soldiers who faced the stress of combat as members of a small, well-knit group with loyalty among the members performed better and were less likely to break down than those soldiers who lacked group support. Poor performance occurred when soldiers were sent into combat as individual replacements in an outfit new to them or when their group was not well knit because of poor leadership (A. M. Rose, 1951).

Corroborative research findings

Research and experience in other countries also provide corroborative evidence. For example, the studies being conducted by the Tavistock Institute in England on the human factors affecting the productivity of coal miners provide evidence as to the importance of the work group. With mechanization of the English coal mines came the "longwall" method of mining. This method organizes the work in such a way that the traditional face-to-face working teams of miners is completely disrupted. Instead of the usual small team of two to four men doing all the operations involved in extracting the coal, the longwall method used about 40 workmen, spread over three shifts. The work is broken down into a standard series of component operations that follow each other in rigid succession. The entire cycle is spread over three work shifts of 7½ hours each, so that a total cycle is completed only once every 24 hours. Two of the shifts, "cutting" and "ripping," generally use 10 men each, and the third shift, "filling," uses 20 men. Reorganizing the work and giving up the small face-to-face group led to serious problems of absenteeism, turnover, and sickness among miners, including psychosomatic disorders. Quite spontaneously, sporadic and rather guarded innovations in work organization modifying the "longwall" method have occurred during the past several years. Though differing from each other, these innovations have involved restoration of the face-to-face work group with responsible autonomy, greater work-group cohesiveness, and greater job satisfaction. Trist and Bamforth (1951, p. 38), in an analysis of the disappointing results obtained in England from increased mechanization of the mines, state the following conclusion with regard to the longwall method of coal getting:

> The immediate problems are to develop formal small-group organization on the filling shift and to work out an acceptable solution to the authority questions in the cutting team. But it is difficult to see how these problems can be solved effectively without restoring responsible autonomy to primary groups throughout the system and ensuring that each of these groups has a satisfying sub-whole as its work task, and some scope of flexibility in work pace.

The substantially better results obtained from the shortwall method of mining substantiates Trist and Bamforth's conclusion. As Wilson (1951) points out, the improved productivity and increased worker satisfaction come from organizing the work so that it is conducted by stable, well-knit teams.

Revans (1957) has demonstrated marked relationships between the size of an enterprise and such variables as absence, accidents, and strikes. He found that both the total size of the enterprise and the size of the work groups within the organization are related to the above variables. He has found that for coal mining, quarries, hospitals, and telephone exchanges, the larger the unit, the less favorable are the results so far as absence, sickness, accidents, and strikes are concerned. Two reports dealing with the adverse effects of increased size have been published by the Action Society Trust (1953; 1957). Other material dealing with the relation of size to the functioning of an organization appears in *Large-scale Organisation* (Milward, 1950).

Group forces are important not only in influencing the behavior of individual work groups with regard to productivity, waste, absence, and the like, they also affect the behavior of entire organizations. Georgopoulos (1957) has demonstrated that group forces in the form of group standards or norms are related to the performance of industrial organizations. Moreover, he presents evidence to show that "for the study of organizational effectiveness in large-scale organizations, the group, and not the individual performer, is the proper unit of research and analysis" (Georgopoulos, 1957, p. 150). He found that the variability between work groups was almost six times as much as the variability between workers within groups. Meltzer (1956) similarly found that for many variables related to the performance of any organization, analyses reflecting the situation for groups yield clearer and more significant differences than analyses dealing only with the measurements for individuals.

The preceding discussion demonstrates that there is a growing body of evidence indicating that significantly better results are obtained when an organization uses its manpower as members of well-knit, effectively functioning work groups with high performance goals than when its members are supervised on an individual man-to-man basis. As the data in this chapter also indicate, this pattern of organizational functioning tends, at present, to be the exception rather than the rule. The use of the coordinated efforts of well-integrated work groups to achieve organizational objectives apparently requires greater leadership skills and a different philosophy of management than that generally prevailing today. The highest-producing managers, much more than other managers, sense the power of group processes and are making greater use of them.

An experimental study

In addition to surveys comparing the behavior of high- and low-producing managers, the Institute for Social Research has conducted experiments on leadership, management, and organizational effectiveness. The experiments in industrial plants bear out the relationships between productivity and such variables as leadership principles and skills and group loyalty which have been examined in this chapter. For example, Coch and French conducted an experiment involving variations in group-participation procedure. They describe their results as follows (Coch & French, 1948, pp. 520-522):

> The first variation involved participation through representation of the workers in designing the changes to be made in the jobs. The second variation consisted of total participation by all members of the group in designing the changes. Two experimental groups received this total participation treatment. A fourth (control) group was used as a control and treated in the customary manner.
>
> The control group went through the usual factory routine when they were changed. The production department modified the job, and a new piece rate was set. A group meeting was then held in which the control group was told that the change was necessary because of competitive conditions, and that a new piece rate had been set. The new piece rate was thoroughly explained by the time study man, questions were answered, and the meeting dismissed.
>
> Experimental group 1 was changed in a different manner. Before any changes took place, a group meeting was held with all the operators to be changed. The need for the change was presented as dramatically as possible, showing two identical garments produced in the factory; one was produced in 1946 and had sold for 100 per cent more than its fellow in 1947. The group was asked to identify the cheaper one and

could not do it. This demonstration effectively shared with the group the entire problem of the necessity of cost reduction. A general agreement was reached that a savings could be effected by removing the "frills" and "fancy" work from the garment without affecting the folders' opportunity to achieve a high efficiency rating. Management then presented a plan to set the new job and piece rate:

1. Make a check study of the job as it was being done.
2. Eliminate all unnecessary work.
3. Train several operators in the correct methods.
4. Set the piece rate by time studies on these specially trained operators.
5. Explain the new job and rate to all the operators.
6. Train all operators in the new method so they can reach a high rate of production within a short time.

The group approved this plan (though no formal group decision was reached), and chose the operators to be specially trained. A sub-meeting with the "special" operators was held immediately following the meeting with the entire group. They displayed a cooperative and interested attitude and immediately presented many good suggestions. This attitude carried over into the working out of the details of the new job; and when the new job and piece rates were set, the "special" operators referred to the results as "our job," "our rate," etc. The new job and piece rates were presented at a second group meeting to all the operators involved. The "special" operators served to train the other operators on the new job.

Experimental groups 2 and 3 went through much the same kind of change meetings. The groups were smaller than experimental group 1, and a more intimate atmosphere was established. The need for a change was once again made dramatically clear; the same general plan was presented by management. However, since the groups were small, all operators were chosen as "special" operators; that is, all operators were to participate directly in the designing of the new jobs, and all operators would be studied by the time study men. It is interesting to note that in the meetings with these two groups, suggestions were immediately made in such quantity that the stenographer had great difficulty in recording them. The group approved of the plans, but again no formal group decision was reached.

The results are shown in Figure 12 and demonstrate the effectiveness of participation on production.

As a further test of these results, the group used initially as the control group was exposed to the full participative approach when it underwent another change several months after the original experiment. When treated like experimental groups 2 and 3, this group showed a productivity record identical with that shown by experimental groups 2 and 3. Figure 13 shows these curves.

In each part of the experiment data were obtained which show the force of group standards in determining the level of production. The following is also taken from Coch & French (1948, pp. 529-530):

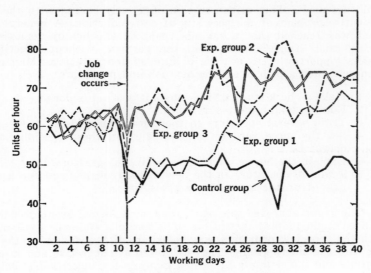

FIGURE 12

THE EFFECT OF PARTICIPATION ON PRODUCTION

(After Lester Coch and J. R. P. French, Jr., "Overcoming Resistance to Change, "*Human Relations*," 1948, I (4), 512-32. By permission of the publishers.)

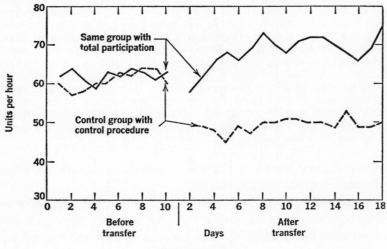

FIGURE 13

A COMPARISON OF THE EFFECT OF THE CONTROL PRO-CEDURE WITH THE TOTAL PARTICIPATION PROCEDURE ON THE SAME GROUP

(After Lester Coch and J. R. P. French, Jr., "Overcoming Resistance to Change," *Human Relations*, 1948, I (4), 512-32. By permission of the publishers.)

Probably the most important force affecting the recovery under the control procedure was a group standard, set by the group, restricting the level of production to 50 units per hour. Evidently this explicit agreement to restrict production is related to the group's rejection of the change and of the new job as arbitrary and unreasonable. Perhaps they had faint hopes of demonstrating that standard production could not be attained and thereby obtain a more favorable piece rate. In any case there was a definite group phenomenon which affected all the members of the group. . . .

An analysis was made for all groups of the individual differences within the group in levels of production. In Experiment I the 40 days before change were compared with the 30 days after change; in Experiment II the 10 days before change were compared to the 17 days after change. As a measure of variability, the standard deviation was calculated each day for each group. The average daily standard deviations before and after change were as follows:

GROUP VARIABILITY

	Before change	After change
Experiment I:		
Control group	9.8	1.9
Experimental 1	9.7	3.8
Experimental 2	10.3	2.7
Experimental 3	9.9	2.4
Experiment II:		
Control group	12.7	2.9

There is indeed a marked decrease in individual differences within the control group after their first transfer. In fact the restriction of production resulted in lower variability than in any other group. Thus, we may conclude that the group standard at 50 units per hour set up strong, group-induced forces. . . .

The table of variability also shows that the experimental treatments markedly reduced variability in the other four groups after transfer.

Coch and French found, in their different groups, changes in employee attitudes and reactions to supervision and management corresponding with the changes which occurred in productivity. For the control group they found (Coch & French, 1948, pp. 522-523):

. . . Resistance developed almost immediately after the change occurred. Marked expressions of aggression against management occurred, such as conflict with the methods engineer, expressions of hostility against the supervisor, deliberate restriction of production, and lack of cooperation with the supervisor. There were 17 per cent quits in the first 40 days. Grievances were filed about the piece rate, but when the rate was checked, it was found to be a little "loose."

For experimental group 1 they reported:

 . . . During the 14 days, the attitude was cooperative and permissive. They worked well with the methods engineer, the training staff, and the supervisor.
 . . . There was one act of aggression against the supervisor recorded in the first 40 days.

For experimental groups 2 and 3 they found:

 . . . They worked well with their supervisors and no indications of aggression were observed from these groups. There were no quits in either of these groups in the first 40 days.

These results [4] of Coch and French confirm the power of group goals. As they show, group goals can push production down or up, depending upon the level at which the group sets them. Additional evidence of the influence of the group is shown by the small deviations by members of the group from the goals set by the group. In an experimental study with small groups, Emmy Pepitone (1952) obtained results consistent with the Coch and French findings. She found that both "the quantity and quality of productivity correspond to the degree of responsibility felt to the group."

Results consistent with the experiment of Coch and French have been obtained by the Institute for Social Research in other industrial situations. Thus, Mann (1957) has demonstrated that increased use of group meetings to analyze and act on data dealing with attitudes, perceptions, communication, and motivation improved the job-related attitudes of nonsupervisory employees in a number of accounting departments. Mann has also shown that such group meetings can achieve substantial increases in productivity (unpublished). A company with several thousand employees on measured day work achieved a 12 per cent increase in productivity in one year's time. Costs have been reduced in another company (McAnly, 1956; I. A. Rose, 1956).

Experiments by others have also yielded results confirming the general pattern emerging from the research by the Institute. For example, in his experiments and research in textile mills in India, Rice (1958) has obtained substantial evidence of the better results obtained when the work is organized by teams of workers and the social organization of the mill is built on a work-group basis. Bose (1957) reports that results comparable with those obtained by Coch and French were found in an experiment of comparable design.

---

 [4] For an excellent theoretical analysis of group forces and how they function, see Lewin (1951).

QUESTIONS

1. What does Likert conclude concerning group effects on individual productivity? Loyalty?
2. What were the conclusions of the Coch and French study relative to participation and job changes?
3. What is a peer group? Do peers influence one's behavior at work? How? For better or for worse?
4. How can a manager go about aligning group goals with organizational objectives?
5. Some people suggest that small groups at work should be broken up by management and discouraged, while others maintain they should be encouraged more than they currently are. What is your viewpoint on this issue and why?

38. ROLE CONFLICT AND AMBIGUITY IN ORGANIZATIONS *

Robert L. Kahn

Our studies of role conflict and ambiguity in industry are among a number of researches which share a common and distant goal: to make understandable the effects of the contemporary environment on the person including his physical and mental health. We begin by thinking of the environment of any individual as consisting very largely of formal organizations and groups. From this point of view the life of the person can be seen as an array of roles which he plays in the particular set of organizations and groups to which he belongs. These groups and organizations, or rather the sub-parts of each which affect the person directly, together make up his objective environment. Characteristics of these organizations and groups (company, union, church, family, and others) affect the physical and emotional state of the person, and are major determinants of his behavior.

The first requirement for linking the individual and the organization is to locate the individual in the total set of ongoing relationships and behaviors comprised by the organization. The key concept for doing this is "office," by which we mean a unique point in organizational space, where space is defined in terms of a structure of inter-related offices and the pattern of activities associated with them. Associated with each office is a set of activities or potential behaviors. These activities constitute the role to be performed by any person who occupies that office. Each office in an organization is directly related to certain others, less directly to still others, and perhaps only remotely to the remaining offices included in the organization. Consider the office of press foreman in a factory manufacturing external trim parts for automobiles. The offices most directly related to that of press foreman might include general foreman and superintendent, from which press foreman's work assignments emanate and to which he turns for approval of work done. Also directly related to the office of press foreman will be the foreman of the sheet metal shop, which provides stock for the presses, the inspector who must pass or reject the completed stampings, the shipping foreman who receives and packages the stampings, and of course, the fourteen press operators for whose work press foreman is responsible. We can imagine the organizational

* From *The Personnel Administrator*, Vol. 9, No. 2 (March-April, 1964). pp. 8-13, 31. Reprinted with permission.

chart spread before us like a vast fish net, in which each knot represents an office and each string a functional relationship between offices. If we pick up the net by seizing any office, we see immediately the other offices to which it is directly attached. Thus, when we pick the office of press foreman, we find it attached directly to nineteen others —general foreman, superintendent, sheet metal foreman, inspector, shipping room foreman, and fourteen press operators. These nineteen offices make up the role set for the office of press foreman.

In similar fashion each member of an organization is directly associated with a relatively small number of others, usually the occupants of offices adjacent to his in the work flow structure. They constitute his role set and usually include his immediate supervisor (and perhaps his supervisor's direct superior), his immediate subordinates, and certain members of his own and other departments with whom he must work closely. These offices are defined into his role set by virtue of his work flow, technology, and authority structure of the organization. Also included in a person's role set may be people who are related to him in other ways—close friends, respected "identification models," and others within or outside the organization who for one reason or another are concerned with his behavior in his organization role. (Figure 1)

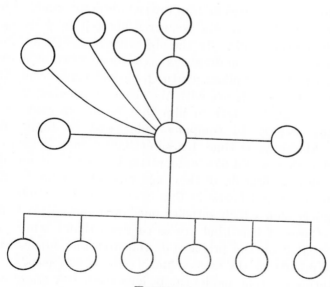

FIGURE 1

FOCAL PERSON AND ROLE SET

All members of a person's role set depend upon his performance in some fashion; they are rewarded by it, or they require it in order to perform their own tasks. Because they have a stake in his performance, they develop beliefs and attitudes about what he should and should not do as his role. These preferences, which we will refer to as role expectations, are by no means restricted to the job description as it might be given by the head of the organization or prepared by some specialist in personnel.

For each person in an organization then, there is a pattern of role expectations which exists in the minds of members of his role set, and represent standards in terms of which they evaluate his performance. The expectations do not remain in the minds of members of the role set, however. They are communicated in many ways—sometimes directly, as when a supervisor instructs a subordinate in the requirements of his job; sometimes indirectly, as when a colleague expresses admiration or disappointment in some behavior. The crucial point is that the activities which define a role consist of the expectations of members of the role set, and that these expectations are communicated or sent to the focal person (the person occupying the role being studied).

It is apparent from the approach to social role described above that various members of the role set for a given office may hold quite different role expectations toward the focal person. At any given time, they may impose pressures on him toward different kinds of behavior. To the extent that these role pressures are felt by him, he experiences psychological conflict. In the objective sense, then, role conflict may be defined as the simultaneous occurence of two or more sets of pressures such that compliance with one would make more difficult or render impossible compliance with the other. For example, a person's superior may make it clear to him that he is expected to hold his subordinates strictly to company rules and to high production schedules. At the same time, his subordinates may indicate in various ways that they would like loose, relaxed supervision, and that they will make things difficult if they are pushed too hard. The pressures from above and below in this case are incompatible, since the style of supervision which satisfies one set of pressures violates the other set. Cases of this kind are so common that a whole literature has been created on the problem of the first line supervisor as the man in the middle, or the master and victim of double-talk.

Several types of role conflict can be identified. One might be termed intra-sender conflict: different prescriptions and proscriptions from a given member of the role set may be incompatible, as for example when a supervisor requests a man to acquire material which is unavailable through normal channels and at the same time prohibits violations of normal channels.

A second type might be termed inter-sender conflict: pressures from one role sender oppose pressures from another sender. The pressures for close versus loose supervisory styles cited above constitute an example of this type of conflict.

A third type of conflict we refer to as inter-role conflict. In this case the role pressures associated with membership in one organization are in conflict with pressures which stem from membership in other groups. For example, demands on the job for overtime or take-home work may conflict with pressures from one's wife to give undivided attention to family affairs during evening hours. The conflict arises between the role of the person as worker and his role as husband and father.

All three of these types of role conflict begin in the objective environment although they will regularly result in psychological conflicts for the focal person. Other types of conflict, however, are generated directly by a combination of environmental pressures and internal forces. A major example is the conflict which may exist between the needs and values of a person and the demands of others in his role set. This fourth type of conflict we will call person-role conflict. It can occur when role requirements violate moral values—for example, when pressures on an executive to enter price fixing conspiracies are opposed by his personal code of ethics. In other cases a person's need and aspirations may lead to behaviors which are unacceptable to members of his role set; for example, an ambitious young man may be called up short by his associates for stepping on their toes while trying to advance in the organization.

All the types of role conflict discussed above have in common one major characteristic—members of a role set exerting pressure to change the behavior of a focal person. When such pressures are generated and sent, they do not enter an otherwise empty field; the focal person is already maintaining some kind of equilibrium among the disparate forces and motives which he experiences. Pressures to change, therefore, represent new and additional forces with which he must cope; by definition they threaten an existing equilibrium. Moreover, the stronger the pressures from role senders toward change in the behavior of the focal person, the greater the conflict created for him.

This approach to the understanding of behavior in organizations in general and the understanding of role conflict in particular is summarized in Figure 2 which illustrates a role episode: that is a complete cycle of role sending, response by the focal person, and the effects of that response on the role senders.

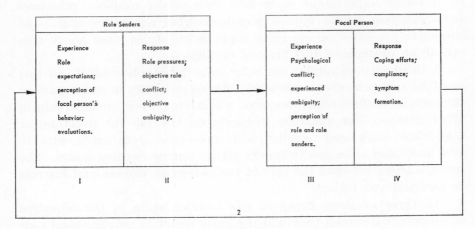

FIGURE 2

A MODEL OF THE ROLE EPISODE

The four boxes in Figure 2 represent events that constitute a role episode. The arrows connecting them imply a causal sequence. Role pressures are assumed to originate in the expectations held by members of the role set. Role senders have expectations regarding the way in which the focal role should be performed. They also have perceptions regarding the way in which the focal person is actually performing. They correlate the two, and exert pressures to make his performance congruent with their expectations. These pressures induce in the focal person an experience which has both perceptual and cognitive properties, and which leads in turn to certain adjustive (or maladjustive) responses. The responses of the focal person are typically perceived by those exerting the pressures, and their expectations are correspondingly adjusted. Thus, for both the role senders and the focal person the episode involves experience and the response to experience. Let us look in more detail at the contents of the four boxes in Figure 2 and at the relations among them.

A role episode starts with the existence of a set of role expectations held by other persons about a focal person and his behavior on the job. Speaking of the members of a person's role set as a group is a matter of convenience. In fact, each member of the role set behaves toward the focal person in ways determined by his own expectations and his own anticipations of the focal person's responses. Under certain circumstances a member of the role set, responding to his own immediate experience, expresses his expectations overtly; he attempts to influence the focal person in the direction of greater conformity with his expectations. Arrow 1 indicates that the total set of such influence attempts affects the immediate experience of the focal person in a given situation (Box 3). This experience includes for example the focal person's perception of the demands and requirements placed on him by members of his role set, and his awareness or experience of psychological conflict. The specific reactions of each focal person to a situation are immediately determined by the nature of his experience in that situation. Any person who is confronted with a situation of role conflict, however, must respond to it in some fashion. One or more members of his role set are exerting pressure on him to change his behavior, and he must cope somehow with the pressure they are exerting. Whatever pattern of response he adopts may be regarded as an attempt to attain or regain an adequately gratifying experience in the work situation. He may attempt a direct solution of the objective problem by compliance or by persuading others to modify their incompatible demands. He may attempt to avoid the sources of stress, perhaps by using defense mechanisms which distort the reality of a conflictful or ambiguous situation. There is also the possibility that coping with the pressures of the work will involve the formation of affective or physiological symptoms. Regardless of which of these, singly or in combination, the focal person uses, his behavior can be assessed in relation to the expectations of each of his role senders.

The degree to which the focal person's behavior conforms to the expectations held for him will affect the state of those expectations at the next moment. If his response is essentially a hostile counterattack, members of his role set are apt to think of him and behave toward him in ways quite different than if he were submissively compliant. If he complies partially under pressure they may increase the pressure; if he is obviously overcome with tension and anxiety, they may "lay-off." In sum, the role episode is abstracted from a process which is cyclic and ongoing; the response of the focal person to role pressure feeds back on the senders of those pressures in ways that alter or reinforce them. The next role sendings of each member of the set depend on his evaluations of the response to his last sendings, and thus a new episode begins.

In order to understand more fully the causal dynamics of such episodes and their consequences for the person's adjustment, the model must be extended to include three additional classes of variables—organizational factors, personality factors, and the character of interpersonal relations between the focal person and other members of his role set. Taken in combination, these factors represent the context within which the episode occurs. In Figure 3 the role episode is shown in the context of these three additional classes of variables. Figure 2 forms the core of Figure 3. However, the circles in Figure 3 represent not momentary events, but enduring states of the organization, the person, and the interpersonal relations between focal person and other members of his role set. An analysis of these factors makes more understandable the sequence of events in a role episode. Figure 3 provides a convenient framework within which to summarize the major research findings obtained from an intensive study of fifty-four role sets in a number of different industries, and from a national survey of approximately 1,500 households.

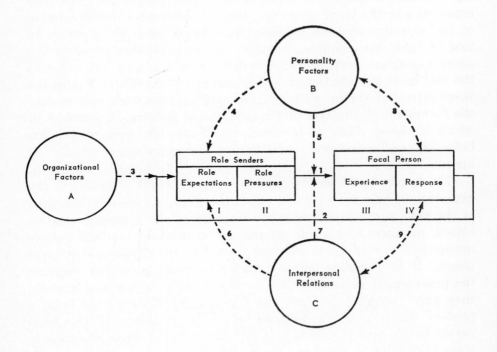

FIGURE 3

A THEORETICAL MODEL OF FACTORS INVOLVED IN ADJUST-
MENT TO ROLE CONFLICT AND AMBIGUITY

Effects of Conflict and Ambiguity

Role conflict

The experience of role conflict is common indeed in the work situation. Almost half of our respondents reported being caught "in the middle" between two conflicting persons or factions. These conflicts are usually hierarchical; 88 per cent of the people involved in them report at least one party to the conflict as being above them in the organization. Somewhat less than half report that one of the conflicting parties is outside the organization. One of the dominant forms of role conflict is overload, which can be thought of as a conflict among legitimate tasks, or a problem in the setting of priorities; almost half of all respondents reported this problem.

The intensive study, in which role senders and focal persons were interviewed independently, deals more directly with the causal sequences initiated by conditions of conflict. Measures of objective conflict, as derived from the expectations of individual role senders, are strongly associated with the subjective experience of conflict, as reported by the focal person, who is target of incompatible expectations. These, in turn, are linked to affective and behavioral responses of that person.

For the focal person, the emotional costs of role conflict include low job satisfaction, low confidence in the organization, and high scores on the multi-item index of tension. The most frequent behavioral response to role conflict is withdrawal or avoidance of those who are seen as creating the conflict. Symptomatic of this is the attempt of the conflicted person to reduce communication with his co-workers and to assert (sometimes unrealistically) that they lack power over him. Case material indicates that such withdrawal, while a mechanism of defense, is not a mechanism of solution. It appears to reduce the possibility of subsequent collaborative solutions to role conflict.

Role ambiguity

The prevalence of role ambiguity appears to be approximately comparable to that of role conflict. Four specific subjects of ambiguity are cited as disturbing and troublesome in approximately equal numbers by respondents. These include uncertainty about the way in which one's supervisor evaluates one's work, about opportunities for advancement, about scope of responsibility and about the expectations of others regarding one's performance. Each of these areas of ambiguity was mentioned by approximately one-third of the respondents. In all, about two persons out of five considered that they were given insufficient information to perform their jobs adequately.

Among the major sources of role ambiguity about which we speculated were complexity of task and technology, rapidity of organizational change, interconnectedness of organizational positions, and that managerial philosophy which advocates restriction of information on the assumption that the division of labor makes broad information unnecessary for most positions.

The individual consequences of ambiguity conditions are in general comparable to the individual effects of role conflict. These include, for ambiguity: low job satisfaction, low self-confidence, a high sense of futility, and a high score on the tension index. There is evidence, however, that the response of the person to ambiguity is highly selective. For example, ambiguity regarding the evaluations of others does not decrease the intrinsic satisfaction of the employee with the job, although it does decrease his self-confidence and weaken his positive affect for co-workers.

DETERMINANTS OF CONFLICT AND AMBIGUITY

The major organizational determinants of conflict and ambiguity include three kinds of role requirements—the requirement for crossing organizational boundaries, the requirement for producing innovative solutions to non-routine problems, and the requirement for being responsible for the work of others (Arrow 3).

Let us consider first the requirement for crossing a company boundary. Both the frequency and the importance of making contacts outside one's company are associated with the experience of role conflict. Crossing the company boundary is associated also with experienced tension, but the relationship is curvilinear: greatest tension is experienced by those who have discontinuous contacts outside the organization. We propose the hypothesis that in positions which require extra-company contacts on a continuous basis, there are special facilities or some other organizational acknowledgement of boundary difficulties which renders them less painful.

Hypothetical explanations for the stressfulness of boundary crossing are available primarily from case materials. It appears that the person who must frequently deal with people outside the company usually has limited control over these outsiders. He cannot strongly influence their demands and the resources which they supply to him. Moreover, a person in a boundary position is likely to be blamed by people in his own company for what his outside contacts do or fail to do. They in turn may blame him for shortcomings in his own company. The difficulties of living at the boundary of an organization are intensified when the boundary-dweller must coordinate his extra-organizational activities with people in other departments within the company.

In general, living "near" a departmental or other intra-organizational boundary has effects very like those just remarked for boundaries of the organization itself. Nearness to a departmental boundary and frequency of dealing across such boundaries are associated with felt conflict and with experienced tension.

Roles which demand creative problem-solving are associated with high role conflict and with tension. The occupants of such roles appear to become engaged in conflict primarily with older and often more powerful individuals in the organization, who want to maintain the status quo. Among the major role conflicts which persons in innovative jobs complain of is the conflict of priority between the non-routine activities which are at the core of the creative job and the routine activities of administration or paper work. These latter, according to the people who fill innovative positions, are unduly time-consuming, disrupt the continuity of their creative work, and are generally unpalatable.

There is considerable evidence that organizations exercise selective effort in choosing people for innovative positions. People in such positions tend to be characterized by high self-confidence, high mobility aspirations, high job-involvement, low apathy, and a tendency to rate the importance of a job extremely high compared to the importance of other areas of their lives.

Supervisory responsibility emerges as a major organizational determinant of role conflict. Either the supervision of rank and file employees or the supervision of people who are themselves supervisors appears to have substantial effects on the degree of objective conflict and the amount of experienced conflict. In combination, direct and indirect supervisory responsibility produce very substantial role conflict and tension. There is a systematic relationship also between rank and role conflict, as there is between rank and tension. The often heard assertion that the lowest levels of supervision are subjected to the greatest conflict is not borne out by these data. Rather, there is a curvilinear relationship in which the maximum of conflict and conflict experience occurs at what might be called the "upper

middle" levels of management. We interpret this in part as a consequence of the still unfulfilled mobility aspirations of middle management, in contrast to the better actualized aspirations of top management people.

INTERPERSONAL RELATIONS AND ROLE CONFLICT

The sources of pressure and conflict for a person can be expressed
rather fully in terms of his inter-personal relations with these pressure sources. The greatest pressure is directed to a person from other
people who are in the same department as he is, who are his superiors
in the hierarchy, and who are sufficiently dependent on his performance to care about his adequacy without being so completely dependent as to be inhibited in making their demands known (Arrow
6). The people who are least likely to apply such pressures are a person's peers and role senders outside his own department.

The kinds of pressure which people are prepared to apply, as
well as the degree of that pressure, vary considerably with their
formal inter-personal relationship to the potential target of their
pressures. Thus, supervisors seem to refrain from exerting coercive
power where it might impede the performance of the focal person and
perhaps reflect upon the supervisor himself. On the other hand, the
techniques used by subordinates to apply coercive power are precisely
those which threaten the efficiency of the organization. They include
the withholding of aid and information.

When a person is surrounded by others who are highly dependent
on him and who have high power over him and exert high pressure
on him, his response is typically one of apathy and withdrawal (Arrow
7). Moreover, under such circumstances, his experience of role conflict is very high and his job satisfaction correspondingly reduced.
Emotionally he experiences a sense of futility and attempts a hopeless
withdrawal from his co-workers.

There is significant evidence that close and positive interpersonal
relations between a focal person and members of his role set can
mediate substantially the effects of role conflict (Arrow 7). A given
degree of objective role conflict is experienced as less stressful in the
context of positive affective relations with others. Nevertheless, experienced conflict and ambiguity appear to cause deterioration in
interpersonal relations (Arrow 9). Thus, a consequence of role conflict is decreased trust, respect, and liking for co-workers, and in the
presence of experienced ambiguity there is a similar attempt on the
part of the focal person to weaken interpersonal relations. As with

conflict, this weakening of interpersonal relations is self-defeating, since he finds himself withdrawing in the face of ambiguity from the very persons from whom he requires information.

PERSONALITY VARIABLES IN CONFLICT AND AMBIGUITY

Several personality dimensions mediate significantly (Arrow 8) the degree to which a given intensity of objective conflict is experienced as strain by the focal person. These personality dimensions include emotional sensitivity, sociability and flexibility-rigidity. With respect to sociability, we find that the effects of objective role conflict on interpersonal bonds and on tension are more pronounced for people who are unsociable (independent). The independent person, in other words, develops social relations which, while often congenial and trusting, are easily undermined by conditions of stress. The preference of such people for autonomy becomes manifest primarily when social contacts are stressful, that is, when others are exerting strong pressures and thereby creating conflict for the persons. In similar fashion, emotional sensitivity conditions vary sharply the relationship between objective conflict and tension, with emotionally sensitive persons showing substantially higher tension scores for any given degree of objective conflict. There is also a tendency for people of different personality characteristics to be exposed by their role senders to differing degrees of objective conflict (Arrow 4). Thus, people who are relatively flexible are subjected to stronger pressures than those who have already demonstrated by their rigidity the futility of applying such pressures.

CONCLUSION

Much of the role conflict in industry takes the form of overload, especially in managerial positions. The focal person has more demands flooding in on him than he can possibly satisfy. He may try to deal with such pressures by exporting his work-induced tensions to outside groups, such as his family, but this is a form of industrial drainage which the community can ill afford. Some persons shut off communication from others in the work situation and thus reduce their own pressures—at the same time reducing the effectiveness of the organization and increasing the pressures of those people who try in vain to communicate with them.

It is not exaggeration to say that most of the responses which we have observed for coping with conflict, ambiguity, and overload are less than satisfactory for individual and for organization. It seems that more constructive resolution of pressure situations ought to be possible. For example, why should the person who experiences role conflict or ambiguity not convene the members of his role set, who have in effect created the situation which he finds stressful, so that they can make a joint attack on the problem? None of the people in the set knows the totality of the focal person's job requirements (any more than he knows theirs), but this is something he can explain to them. Each person in an organization is the ultimate expert in this single respect: He knows better than anyone else the combination of demands which are being made upon him and what their immediate sources are.

A ceremony of confrontation and joint problem-solving would seem to be a useful mode of conflict resolution. Why does it not happen? Two factors may work to prevent it. The first is subjective, a feeling that such an approach is unorthodox, unlikely to work, or even downright dangerous. The second may be inherent in the structure of hierarchical organizations.

Regarding the subjective factor, it is indeed difficult to find people who are willing and able to undertake such a confrontation of superiors, subordinates, and peers. A person may have deliberately created overload, conflict, or ambiguity in order to further his own organizational ambitions or to increase his power. More often, his feelings of insecurity and embarrassment prevent him from attempting such a group solution to his problems. Regarding the organizational factor, the risks and rewards of industrial life often cause individuals to keep their information sources private and hold as much power as possible in their own hands. Confrontation under such circumstances could be viewed as a giving away of precious power and information, or even as an admission of incompetence. More frequently, perhaps, the person in conflict feels that he lacks the power to convene the members of his role set in the first place. How many people in industry can recall taking the initiative in bringing together their subordinates, supervisors, and peers to consider the incompatibilities in their various expectations?

Nevertheless, there is in many managements a growing interest in solving the human problems of large-scale organizations, a growing realization that the solutions will involve structural changes as well as gains in interpersonal skills, and a growing willingness to innovate and evaluate in the effort to put organizations more fully into the service of human needs. These attitudes of management, in combination with research, offer new possibilities for understanding organized human behavior. We know of no goal more deserving of effort.

QUESTIONS

1. What does the concept of "role behavior" mean?
2. What are the various types of role conflict presented by Kahn? Can you think of any he may have omitted?
3. Define the following: (a) role sender, (b) role ambiguity, (c) role expectations.
4. How, in general, do the concepts presented in this article aid us in understanding what motivates individual behavior both on and off the job?
5. How do personality variables affect our role perceptions?

GENERAL QUESTIONS ON PART VII

1. Explain the major values of participative management for the following:
   a. Individual workers.
   b. Managers.
   c. The working organization as a whole.
2. Why does Argyris feel that participation is so important in a working organization?
3. How do some of the traditional concepts and principles of organization and management limit participative practices in working organizations?
4. In what way does organizational authority enter into the problem of obtaining meaningful participation?
5. How do executive and managerial attitudes influence the degree of participation in a firm?
6. Do you think informal groups affect participation in any way? How?
7. How do role relationships and expectations affect individual and group productivity? Cite studies documented in this section to support your answers.
8. How would you relate the ideas presented in this section to McGregor's article, "The Human Side of Enterprise" in Part IV?
9. List and explain some policies, procedures, and practices that managers can develop to encourage more participation by their subordinates.
10. What is meant by "group dynamics"? Why do people associate in groups and what is their impact on managers and supervisors in the work place?

PART VIII. ORGANIZATIONAL CHANGE

In order to remain stable and flexible and to insure long-run success, most organizations must operate within a dynamic environment. This means, in essence, that management must be alert to, must plan for, and must adapt itself, the company, and employees to myriad changes that are necessary for the efficient operation of a business enterprise. If this is not done—that is, if dynamism, flexibility, and adaptability do not exist—then there is great danger that complacency and stagnation will set in. The result, particularly in highly competitive industries, could well be serious damage to or even termination of the organization concerned.

WHY PEOPLE RESIST CHANGE

Because change of every conceivable type and form is highly important to the success of an organization, it is unfortunate that many people have the tendency overtly or covertly to resist it, frequently to the extent of seriously impeding or completely thwarting its effectuation. Perhaps a basic reason why this resistance occurs, whether it is manifested in the form of apathy and indifference or in the form of opposition and rebellion, is that most changes disturb the equilibrium of the situation and environment in which individuals and groups exist. To overcome this disequilibrium and to return to a state of balance requires people to go through a period of adaptation and adjustment to the change. If this inevitable process of adjustment is facilitated, especially prior to initiation of the change, so that a new state of equilibrium can be quickly achieved, then little or no resistance usually results. On the other hand, if management ignores this fundamental facet of human behavior and does nothing to help people adjust, then resistance will occur and a state of disequilibrium will continue to exist. How serious this situation will be is, of course, impossible to say, because it will depend upon the nature of the people and the change concerned.

Although disequilibrium is the result of change and the cause of resistance, it is important to recognize that the state of disequilibrium which exists is actually an imbalance in need satisfaction. The assumption here is that prior to a change the individual exists within an environment in which the satisfaction of his needs has reached a high degree of stability. When a change occurs, particularly in the absence of adjustment facilitation, there is immediately manifested a threat to motive satisfaction. In other words, there now occurs the possibility that the change may prevent or decrease need satisfaction. Whether or not the change actually has this result makes no difference at this stage. The important point is that, until proven otherwise, the person believes or assumes that this threat will materialize. As a consequence, he feels his needs are no longer satisfied to the degree that they were satisfied and a state of imbalance exists. Only when he recognizes that the change will not affect his need satisfaction, or when he adapts himself to a change that in fact does decrease or prevent the satisfaction of a need, will equilibrium return and resistance disappear. In either case, however, some degree of adjustment must occur.

Types of Changes That Create Disequilibrium

The types and kinds of changes that cause disequilibrium and resistance are legion. They range in nature from attitudinal changes, such as a supervisor changing a positive attitude toward a subordinate into a negative attitude, to fantastic technological advancements, such as a new machine that will displace twenty old machines. Because it would be impossible to consider here every conceivable form of change, we shall devote our attention only to those types of changes that are likely to occur in most organizations. No attempt will be made to rank them in order of importance, because changes affect people in different ways; consequently, a change that causes great resistance in one person may create little or no disequilibrium for another individual.

Changes in tools, machines, and equipment

Almost every organization has experienced difficulty with employees who resist the installation of new tools, machines, and equipment. Whether such changes are the result of technological advancement or managerial efficiency makes little difference—a threat to security, status, and other basic needs has occurred. Consequently, even if the change is potentially beneficial to the employee, resistance usually results.

Like all changes, those concerning the mechanisms and devices with which people work establish an element of the unknown. In the case of a new machine, for example, especially one that has the potential to displace workers, people resist its introduction because they do not know how it will affect them. Accordingly, they begin to wonder about things such as whether or not the machine will displace them, if they will have the skill required to operate it, and so on. Until these unknowns are resolved, people will assume without realizing it that their fears and suspicions will be confirmed. This is particularly true of any change in machines that actually poses a threat to job security. In fact, it could be said that resistance to automation is one of the chief areas of resistance that management is faced with today, primarily because the results of technological advancement have actually resulted in the displacement of people and the loss of jobs.

Changes in methods and procedures

It is frequently said that we are creatures of habit. Although this statement connotes a detrimental characteristic of man, it should be recognized that habit, especially in the context of a business organization, does possess several distinct advantages. Perhaps one of the most important of these concerns the fact that the way we habitually do things, assuming that these habits are correct and efficient, can lead to the development of greater proficiency in doing work. In other words, by doing the same thing over and over, we can acquire a high degree of skill in performing various aspects of our jobs.

When a change occurs in a method or a procedure that we have been habitually accustomed to using, we have the tendency to resist it because it may decrease our proficiency and hence the pride we take in our work. In addition, we sometimes feel that the change was directed at us, that is, that we were not performing the job correctly and that we have lost face because we did not perceive and effectuate the change in the first place. Although such reactions sometimes border the ridiculous, they are nevertheless very real to those who experience them and hence are powerful motivators of behavior. How many times, for example, have we heard someone say "it won't work" when we know very well that the individual concerned definitely does know it will work? Changes in methods and procedures, therefore, like all other changes, establish many unknowns that must be clarified if adjustment is to take place.

Changes in personnel

A change that frequently results in a great deal of covert resistance in many organizations occurs when a subordinate is placed under the supervision of a new superior. Usually the degree of resistance developed in such a situation is correlated with the length and the satisfaction of the previous superior-subordinate relationship. In other words, the longer and more satisfied we were with our "old boss," the more we visualize and fear the unknowns created by the appearance of a new boss, especially if he is a total stranger. Until proven otherwise, we suspect and fear the worst about his ability to perform his job and to perceive our proficiency. Most important of all, we wonder what sweeping changes he will make (as many new bosses do) and what effect they will have on us. Without being able to express what has happened to us, we have lost in one moment much of the feeling of stability we had in need satisfaction. Until we bring back into balance our desire for belonging, recognition, status, and other motivating forces, we shall continue to view the new man with suspicion. Unfortunately, the attitudes that result from these fears become the very barriers that hinder the new superior in proving his worth to his employees and in providing the means or opportunity to satiate their basic needs.

Changes in formal organization structure

The creation of a formal structure, as the section on organization pointed out, establishes lines of authority and responsibility in an organization. Along with these lines there are also created channels of communication and interpersonal relationships. When changes in this formal structure occur, unknowns about future lines of authority and relationships develop. We wonder who will be responsible for what and why, who our new boss will be, what opportunities it will take away from us or create for us, and so on. The result of these worries is that we no longer maintain equilibrium in our need satisfaction. Consequently, faced with the possibility of loss of status, prestige, belonging, recognition, and so forth, we become involved in a state of imbalance and resist the change.

Another aspect of formal structure concerns the question of who has the authority to make a change. Quite frequently employees resist changes, not because of the change *per se*, but because of the person who initiated or requested it. An example of this would be the foreman of Department B telling a worker in Department C to use a new procedure in the performance of his work. Although the new procedure may be very efficient and acceptable to the employee, he resists it because the foreman has no authority over him. The same type of reaction also occurs when changes are made by people who have the authority to make changes but whose authority is not known or accepted by the worker. This frequently happens when staff people have been delegated the authority to initiate changes. An illustration would be the industrial engineer who has been given the task of developing and installing better job methods. Because the employee tends to view his own boss as the only person who has a right to tell him what to do, he also tends to resist and reject any change proposed by the engineer.

Changes in informal organization

The informal relationships established between people in an organization become a very important part of our existence, basically because many of our primary motivational forces find their satisfaction in these relationships. Our urge to belong, for example, finds satisfaction in the many informal groups and cliques with which we associate. Our desire for recognition is satisfied by the accord given to our skills, talent, and abilities by various friends and acquaintances in the organization. Likewise, our needs for prestige, status, achievement, and many other basic sociological and psychological motives depend to a great degree on various aspects of informal organization for their satisfaction. Consequently, when management makes any change that disturbs the informal relationships established between people, there is bound to be created a state of imbalance and, hence, resistance to the change.

Of all the classes of changes that can disturb informal relationships, perhaps one of the most important for management to recognize and understand is that type of change which results in the separation of groups and individuals. Whenever people find it difficult or impossible to continue or maintain informal relationships, they find it equally difficult or impossible to maintain stability in need satisfaction. The reason for this, of course, is that the means to need satisfaction, namely, the people with whom we associate informally, no longer is present or easily accessible after the change. The result is that stability in motive satisfaction disappears and resistance sets in. It is no wonder, therefore, that people resist changes such as transferring an employee from one department to another or the simple moving of a clerk from one end of an office to the other end.

How People Resist Change

Resistance to change can take many forms. At one extreme, people suffer a temporary disequilibrium in need satisfaction, ask a few questions about the change, quickly adjust to it, and resume their previous behavior. At the other extreme, reaction can take the form of open opposition, rebellion, and even destruction. In between these extremes lie many other forms of behavior, such as apathy, indifference, and antagonism. What type of reaction occurs in a particular situation is a function of the nature of the change and the people concerned. It is especially a function of how well adjustment to the change was facilitated.

Whatever general form resistance to change may take, it is important for managers to recognize that human behavior will always be influenced by it. This means that immediately or ultimately the change will exert an impact on employee performance. Depending upon the nature of the resistance, therefore, behavior can be reflected in such things as quantity and quality of production, absenteeism, tardiness, turnover, grievances, accidents, strikes, and so on. Unfortunately, many of these concrete results of resistance are very difficult to relate to the change that caused them, not only because of physical and organizational elements, but also because they are frequently so subtly manifested by employees that it is difficult to observe and measure them in the first place. This is just another reason why management must make every effort possible to effectuate the change properly and to facilitate adjustment to it.

Facilitating Adjustment to Change

Although the following articles consider in detail methods of overcoming resistance to change, several important points deserve mention here. One of the most important of these concerns the fact that preventing and overcoming resistance demands that managers respect and understand employee reaction to change. Altogether too frequently, people in leadership positions assume that, because a change will definitely be beneficial to people, it will be acceptable to them. Actually, nothing could be farther from the truth. Consequently, whether threats to need satisfaction are real or imagined, they must always be recognized as powerful motivators of behavior. As such, some manner or form of adjustment facilitation must take place.

Another important point for managers to understand is that there is no one simple panacea for preventing or overcoming resistance to change. Although it may be possible in one situation to rely exclusively on one particular method, such as participation, for example, it is most unlikely that such a technique will be universally and solely applicable in all resistance problems. What is more likely is that the manager (the leader) must utilize many different methods, techniques, and procedures to prevent and to remedy resistance to change situations. This means that, in addition to participation, he may certainly have to counsel and train employees, particularly if a change actually results in the prevention or decrease of need satisfaction. It may also mean that if the situation warrants it, he will have to dispense with the change or completely adjust his thinking about it. Most fundamentally of all, however, it means that he must determine and communicate to his employees the things they consciously and subconsciously want and need to know to resolve the unknowns that pose the real or imagined threat to the satisfaction of their motivating forces. In other words, preventing and remedying resistance to change demands efficient leadership and the practice of human relations.

Although the literature on resistance to change is not as complete as one would like it to be, there are, nevertheless, several outstanding articles on this subject. McMurry's article, for example, contains a useful appraisal of resistance to change as a handicap to industrial progress. Zander, in his article, discusses the nature of resistance, the conditions that are associated with its development, and ways of preventing or decreasing it. Dorwin Cartwright offers an excellent statement of some principles of achieving change in people. Floyd C. Mann analyzes some of the problems of conducting research on change and shows how we can create and study it.

39. THE PROBLEM OF RESISTANCE TO CHANGE IN INDUSTRY *

Robert N. McMurry

A medium-sized Middle Western manufacturing company recently installed a new and greatly improved wage incentive plan at a cost in excess of $20,000. The work was done entirely by outside engineers. These engineers did an excellent job technically and management was satisfied; the only difficulty was that three weeks later the new plan had been completely abandoned and the investment of $20,000 had been totally lost. Why was this?

Industrial progress finds one of its greatest handicaps in the frequent resistance of both management and workers to change of any sort. This is especially marked if the change is introduced without proper advance notice and explanation to those whom it will affect. Even innovations which are obviously advantageous are often objects of attack. Where the changes threaten either the status or job security of either workers or management, their reaction is certain to be quick and violently negative. In those organizations where employee and supervisory insecurity is present, even minor revisions of policies or procedures may evoke profoundly disturbing reactions among individuals and groups. An effort is made at once either to block the introduction of the new methods or to discredit them after their installation and force their removal.

Even ordinarily honest and loyal workers and executives will sometimes lie, misrepresent, and engage in outright sabotage of the new procedures, so bitter are the antagonisms aroused. Nor are these manifestations limited to individuals. Large groups of employees may react with equal violence when their security or status is at stake. An example of this is the frequent reaction of white employees to the introduction of Negroes into the work force. The latter are a threat both to their security (the Negroes are considered as competitors in the labor market) and to their status (the whites resent being grouped with the Negroes whom they regard as of lower status). Actually the Negroes may be highly desirable as employees and may contribute to the welfare of the organization as a whole. Nevertheless, their introduction is violently resisted. While it is customary to attribute these resistances to the reluctance of

* From the *Journal of Applied Psychology*, Vol. 31, No. 6 (December, 1947), pp. 589-593. Reprinted with permission.

people to change well-established habits, it is probable that the chief causes lie far deeper.

The principal root of this hostility to anything which threatens security or status is *fear* (frequently reinforced and rationalized by accumulated resentments and rivalries). The hostility which this fear generates, in turn, leads to attacks upon the sources of the anxiety. The amazing feature of these attacks is that many of them come from employees who, because of their rank or long service, have no real ground to fear for either their status or security. Nevertheless, quite without adequate justification, many feel extremely insecure. This is because deep-seated fears exist within the individual himself. Everyone knows fear. Even the infant is prey to this emotion because it is innate, inborn. Furthermore, everyone is constantly faced by very real and tangible grounds for anxiety and insecurity. Nature is cruel. The law of the fang prevails to a greater extent than many recognize. The world at large is no place for the weakling. Even business is highly competitive. Rivalries and conflicts exist within nearly every business. Realistically regarded, life is far from a bed of roses for most people.

Hence, the real and justifiable fears which beset the average person are legion. There is always somewhere in the future the danger of economic disaster, of another depression with its threat to savings, to the home, to security. Everyone is faced with the problem of old age and its attendant likelihood of illness, suffering, and dependence. Even in youth and the prime of life, there is always the immediate possibility of illness, of accidents, and the inevitability of death. Nor are these real grounds for fear confined to the individual himself. There is also the fear of misfortune to loved ones; a fear, again, which the war years have greatly stimulated. Finally, there is almost always the more or less immediate danger to everyone of loss of his job or of being displaced or demoted, with its attendant loss of prestige, "status," and earnings.

It must be kept in mind that the average rank-and-file employee in industry today, unlike his counterpart of fifty years ago, does not even own his own tools. The only commodity he has to sell is his labor or some readily replaceable skill. He is, therefore, much more dependent economically upon his job tenure than was the case with the man who could, if necessary, set up in business for himself. In addition, the longer he has remained with a particular company, often the greater his difficulty in getting work elsewhere. This is because the bulk of the routine jobs in industry today do not require

great skill; certainly not in the sense of the old-time master craftsman. Consequently, the employee who has spent ten to twenty-five
years in a particular line of work has gained little that is saleable,
but has lost his youth, his vigor, and his adaptability to new lines
of endeavor. He has given the best years of his life and often has
little of vocational value to show for it.

It is because of this that there is such a feeling of need for some
sort of job security among most working people (whether it be
seniority or some other form of property rights in the job). For
the same reason, anything which threatens job security or hard-
won status, such as it is, is desperately feared and resented.

Unfortunately, these real and understandable grounds for fear are
not the only ones which contribute to employee insecurity. Nearly
all persons also suffer to a greater or less degree from neurotic
anxieties and fears which have no basis in reality whatever. Among
these latter are the insecurities which grow out of the passive dependent tendencies of the emotionally immature. Others grow out
of the repeated rejections to which the individual may have been
subjected during childhood or youth. Still others have their origin
in an over-strict conscience, resulting from too rigorous an up-
bringing. (Nearly everything such persons do makes them feel
guilty.) Likewise, many neurotic anxieties have their basis in buried
but powerful hostilities toward loved ones and others which produce a free-floating sense of guilt and anxiety and lead to constant
worrying.

Many of these fears, regardless of their nature, are too painful
to be faced; they cannot be lived with. Hence, they have been thrust
out of the center of the individual's consciousness; they are vaguely
present on the periphery. They are not entirely repressed; merely
out of sharp focus. Nevertheless, they continue to exist in a latent
state, their power to disturb quite undiminished. Their presence
constantly disturbs the individual's emotional equilibrium and makes
its balance a precarious one. When any new challenge to his status
or security occurs, it accentuates his existing anxieties and feelings
of insecurity. These added fears almost inevitably upset his emotional balance. His latent fears, having been reinforced, once more
threaten to become painfully conscious. This must be avoided at any
cost. Hence, he has powerful incentive to rid himself of the source
of danger to his status and security.

Fears which even trivial changes arouse are often so powerful
that they are overwhelming. The fear thus induced is so real and

poignant that it may even induce a state of actual panic. At this point, the victim ceases to be entirely rational, in spite of the fact that he may appear outwardly calm and possessed. If it appears politically expedient, he may even indicate a high degree of favor for the very changes which have excited his anxiety. Nevertheless, he will stop at nothing to save himself. (This attitude of superficial acceptance of an innovation is sometimes barefaced hypocrisy; more often the individual's fears are so acute that he cannot take an open stand against anything.)

Because of the highly emotional character of these resistances to change, a direct, logical presentation of the merits of the change is often futile. The more they are discussed, the more violent the anxieties they are likely to arouse and the greater the individual's need to discredit and eliminate them. Even worse, however, is to attempt to explain to him the *sources in himself* of his antagonisms to the projected change. This only makes him react more violently because it mobilizes fresh anxieties within him and breaks down his defenses against them. It not only forces him to face his naked fears himself, but makes him aware that others know his weaknesses. This adds to his anxieties—and to his aggressiveness.

In view of the foregoing circumstances, great caution must be exercised in making any changes in organization or methods, even those which are obviously and badly needed. It will never be possible wholly to eliminate anxieties in workers and supervisors with consequent resistances to change for its own sake and as a threat to their status or security. Hence, it is essential that any modification of product, procedures, organization, or policies which may affect status or may be interpreted as an implied threat to job security should be considered carefully before it is made. It is particularly important that its implications be considered from the standpoint of the insecurities and possible anxieties of the employees affected. It must always be kept in mind that, regardless of the facts, those who will be affected may interpret it somehow as a threat to them and respond accordingly.

Sometimes it is better, in the long run, not to make moderately needed changes because the disturbance they will occasion may be more costly in the end than will a continuance of the *status quo*. In those cases, where there is some real threat to an employee's status and security in the change, it will prove wiser and cheaper to "kick him upstairs" to some "advisory" job (thus retaining his status and job security), rather than risk the organization-wide disturbance of morale which his demotion or other "face" destroying course of action might bring with it. It is entirely possible for *one* individual, if sufficiently aroused, to disrupt the morale and smooth functioning of an entire segment of a business by pointing out that what has happened to him *could* happen to many others.

If it is finally decided that a change must be made, it is wise to move very slowly. Only one innovation should be introduced at a time; ample warning must precede it, and a full statement must be given of the reasons for it and the benefits which are expected to result from it. If this is done, there is less likelihood that the emotional equilibrium of the individual or group will be upset. Informing the employee in advance will do much to allay the fears that a sudden change might otherwise arouse. There will always be some anxiety, but this will help to minimize it.

Further to allay the fears of those affected, they should be given maximum opportunity to participate in the discussion and planning of proposed changes in advance of their introduction. They should also have some voice in deciding how and when they will be made effective. This gives them a feeling of having had at least some part in the determination of their own destinies. This tends to minimize their feelings of helplessness and consequent anxiety in the face of the changes. At the same time, it will give them a better insight into, and understanding of, the conditions calling for the innovations and the way in which they will be of personal benefit to those affected. This, in turn, will allay their anxieties and discourage the development of resistances and hostilities.

Finally, if a program calling for other than minor changes is to gain acceptance and use, it is imperative that ready outlets be provided for the expression and relief of the hostilities which will almost inevitably arise. Under the best of conditions, some of those affected will be disturbed and unhappy. Therefore, it will be necessary to provide these employees with easily accessible facilities to "talk out" their anxieties and resentments from time to time. They will not be aware that it is largely *fear* which stimulates their aggressions and needs for reassurance; all they will know is that having talked about them, they will feel better. Periodic, informal meetings between small groups of the affected employees and a representative of top management are to be recommended for this purpose. He must be patient and sympathetic and give the employees' complaints about the changes, no matter how absurd or unreasonable, a fair hearing. This thus provides a release for their accumulated tensions. Such meetings, by bringing resistances out into the open, have the advantages both of relieving the rancor of the disgruntled worker or supervisor before he has had a chance seriously to disrupt departmental morale, and of reviewing the worthwhileness of the new procedures and methods. Sometimes it will be indicated that even further changes are necessary.

The resistance of workers, supervisors, and executives to change is irritating and often frustrating. This is especially true when the improvements are designed specifically to help them and the company as a whole. However, if it is recognized that it is their basic anxieties and insecurities which underlie and stimulate their lack of cooperation, not sheer stubbornness, selfishness, and stupidity, a more understanding and sympathetic view can be taken of the problem. These resistances will probably never be totally overcome, but through the awareness of the basic fears and the application of the principles outlined above, an informed and constructive course of action can be undertaken to insure the acceptance and continued use of the new procedures and policies, even though they may incorporate a number of radical innovations.

QUESTIONS

1. Explain why people resist change.
2. Why is it difficult to overcome resistance to change?
3. What cautions must be exercised in making changes?
4. Why is it sometimes better not to make a change? Do you agree?
5. What does McMurry recommend to make changes effectively?

40. RESISTANCE TO CHANGE—
ITS ANALYSIS AND PREVENTION *

Alvin Zander

In order to derive the benefit from research in industrial relations, someone must plan a program of action to apply them. When one begins implementing, he must change the social system in some way. The creation of this change can cause the development of resistance in those influenced by the change.

First, we shall look at what resistance is; second, the conditions that appear to be associated with its development; and third, some means whereby resistance may be prevented or decreased.

Nature of resistance

Let us look at some examples of resistance growing out of administrative changes.

A large number of foremen in a company were given training in how to treat their men like human beings. They liked the course and were eager to apply their learnings on the job. The company found, however, that relatively few of the foremen are really behaving any different on the job. They know their stuff but do not use it.

In one of the paper-shuffling government agencies a new data form was developed which all admitted was briefer, more logical, and easier to use. Yet, this department found that the employees often omitted much of the data needed on this form, their speed of work decreased, and they objected to it on many insignificant grounds.

Our favorite example of resistance was furnished by a farmer in the TVA area. He assured us that he knew all about contour plowing, the rotation of crops, and the use of what he called "phosaphate" for improving the soil. He allowed as how these were good ideas, "But," he said, "I don't do it that way."

These examples have one common denominator which might serve here as a definition of resistance. They describe behavior which is intended to protect an individual from the effects of real or imagined change. This reaction might be to either real or imagined change since the resister might be reacting to things that were really not changed but he thinks were, or fears that they might be. If a person

---

* From *Advanced Management*, Vol. 15, No. 1 (January, 1950), pp. 9-11. Reprinted with permission.

believes a change has been made, or fears potential change, it makes no difference whether or not it is true in fact. He will act as though there has been a change.

How can one recognize when resistance is working? Unfortunately, there is no list of typical behavior which can be described as the symptoms of resistance, which, if present, indicate that one is dealing with this phenomenon. It is the protective function which the behavior is providing which determines whether or not a person is resisting, rather than the kind of thing he does. By the same token, all behavior which opposes change is not necessarily resistance. Some opposition to change may be perfectly logical and grounded on well-supported reasons. The behavior must be attempting to protect the person against the consequences of the change in order for it to be resistance. This may be clearer if we look at the origin of the concept.

The hostility pattern

The term and the concept we are using here has been borrowed from psychotherapy. When a therapist is attempting to change the behavior of the patient, he expects resistance from him. The therapist takes the position that the pattern of behavior used by the patient (which makes him a "sick" person) is a means to some satisfaction for him even though it also may make him ineffective or unhappy. Resistance occurs in the patient when the process of change (therapy here) comes close to being successful. When faced with the unpleasant necessity of giving up the behavior he does not like, but somehow needs, he begins to balk. He becomes silent, blushes, changes the subject, tells fibs, comes late to appointments, becomes angry with the therapist, or any of a number of similar things. The therapist watches for the context in which these signs of resistance occur since these indicate the crucial problems in the way the patient sees and deals with his world.

For the administrator, resistance may occur under fairly similar conditions. When he attempts to create a change the administrator may develop, unintentionally, many threats to the person or groups with whom he works. The behavior used by the resister may take many forms.

It may take the form of hostility either openly expressed or obliquely implied. The aggression may be directed against the change itself or against the administrator. What is done depends on how the person can safely resist without further endangering himself in that situation. Other symptoms of resistance may be sloppy effort after the change has been made, or fawning submissiveness which is a hybrid of applepolishing and apathy. It can occur by lowering the level of aspiration to an inefficient degree, discouragement, or the development of unhappy cliques and outspoken factions. It is important, however, to remind ourselves, that it is the function which such actions are performing for the person that makes them resistance rather than what they look like.

Where resistance starts

It will be helpful if we look at a few conditions conducive to resistance.

1. Resistance can be expected if the nature of the change is not made clear to the people who are going to be influenced by the change. In one of the largest government agencies, a change required one department which originally had the responsibility of processing papers involved in contacts with certain industries to share this task with another office. Announcement of the change was issued in a brief statement. The immediate reaction was violent objection, even though some of the workers privately admitted that it was a wise and necessary move. They were reacting to incomplete information. Many people fear incomplete information about changes which influence them. It is more comfortable to know exactly where one stands.

There is some evidence to support the hypothesis that those persons who dislike their jobs, will most dislike ambiguity in a proposed change. They want to know exactly what they must do in order to be sure to avoid the unpleasant aspects of their jobs. Some administrators may attach too much importance to the value of information itself. Apparently they reason that people "ought not" to resist the way they do because the administrator has told them everything he thinks is important for them to know about the impending change.

2. Different people will see different meanings in the proposed change. Some of the resistant reaction described above came about because some workers saw the change as an indication that they had been doing a poor job, others assumed it meant their office would soon be abolished, still others were troubled since they were losing some of the power they had formerly controlled. We tend to see in our world the things that we expect to see. Complete information can just as readily be distorted as incomplete information, especially so if the workers have found discomfort and threats in their past work situation.

3. Resistance can be expected when those influenced are caught in a jam between strong forces pushing them to make the change and strong forces deterring them against making the change.

4. Resistance may be expected to the degree that the persons influenced by the change have pressure put upon them to make it, and will be decreased to the degree that these same persons are able to have some "say" in the nature or direction of the change. In a garment factory a change was required. The switch meant that workers would be asked to change their jobs and, in many cases, to develop working relationships with new people. An experiment was made in which three different styles of introducing this change were tried out. One group of workers were simply informed about the change and were allowed to ask questions. They developed the most resistance as measured by turnover, absenteeism, and slowness in learning the job. Resistance was *less* in those groups who sent representatives to a meeting in which the nature of the change was discussed and all persons present made plans to carry out the change.

Resistance was *least* in the groups in which those to be affected discussed the nature of the change, laid plans for making it, and as a total group made decisions which were satisfactory to the entire group. In this latter group everyone participated. They had an opportunity to develop their own motivation instead of making the change only on the basis of orders from the boss. The fact that they were able to develop their own understanding of the need for the change and their own decisions about how to do it, reduced resistance most effectively.

5. Resistance may be expected if the change is made on personal grounds rather than impersonal requirements or sanctions. A supervisor posted the following notice:

> I have always felt that promptness is an important indicator of an employee's interest in his job. I will feel much better if you are at your desk at the proper time.

Employees responded to this notice by appointing a committee to get information which would justify their late arrival at the office. Many administrators can expect trouble in establishing a change if it is requested in terms of what "I think is necessary"; rather than making the request in the light of "our objectives," the rules, the present state of affairs, or some other impersonal requirement.

6. Resistance may be expected if the change ignores the already established institutions in the group. Every work situation develops certain customs in doing the work or in the relations among the

workers. The administrator who ignores institutionalized patterns of work and abruptly attempts to create a new state of affairs which demands that these customs be abolished without further consideration will surely run into resistance.

These are a few of the conditions in which resistance might be expected to occur. There probably are many others.

Decreasing resistance

Some procedures on the part of the administrator might be useful in preventing or decreasing the resistance which arises in a changed situation. Let us look at a major principle in preventing resistance and some of its basic implications:

Resistance will be prevented to the degree that the changer helps the changees to develop their own understanding of the need for the change, and an explicit awareness of how they feel about it, and what can be done about those feelings.

This principle implies that the administrator can use resistance as an important symptom. Specifically, he can use the nature of the resistance as an indicator of the cause of resistance. It will be most helpful to him as a symptom, if he diagnoses the causes for it when it occurs rather than inhibiting it at once. The same resistant behavior, for example, may indicate that one person feels that he has lost prestige by the change, to another it may mean that he has lost power over an area of influence which he formerly controlled, and to still another it may mean that he fears that his friends will think less well of him. An administrator must know what the resistance means in order that he may effectively lessen it by working on the causes instead of the symptom.

There has been a good deal of experience in recent years in staff meetings and in work conferences like the National Training Laboratory for Group Development with the use of a group observer. This observer gives to the group, and the leaders, information about the group and the nature of any resistance. In these cases, the data about itself is made common group property for all members to discuss and to use in planning better work relations.

This communication must go in both directions. If two-way communication is not maintained, negative attitudes created during resistance will tend to persist.

Restoring understanding

In a utility company a new office was formed with a new set of supervisors. The entire staff of supervisors called the workers together and scolded them for shortcomings in their performance. The tone used by the supervisors was so aggressive that the employees found it difficult thereafter to discuss anything with them except those topics directly related to the effectiveness of production. The workers kept themselves at a distance from the supervisors and the supervisors made no move to close the gap. The result was that distance between these two groups made it impossible for them to come to any new understanding of each other. This mounting hostility was lessened only when the personnel department advised a number of "gripe-sessions" with small groups of workers in which the two levels developed a new understanding of each other.

Another implication in the above principle is that there is value in blowing off steam. The psychologists call this a "catharsis." There is good evidence that new attitudes can be accepted by a person only if he has a chance to thoroughly air his original attitude. Resistance to accepting the rigid, and often apparently meaningless, rules of military life, showed itself in flagrant violation of the rules, often in a most aggressive manner. Punishment only increased the resistance. Relief was provided by group sessions in which men were able to thoroughly gripe. After this relief of tension, they were able to turn to a reasonable discussion about what they could do to learn to live in terms of these requirements. It is as though new air can be put in the tire only after the old air is released.

A third implication of the earlier expressed principle is that resistance may be less likely to occur if the group participates in making the decisions about how the change should be implemented, what the change should be like, how people might perform in the changed situation, or any other problems that are within their area of freedom to decide. The experiment in which three ways of introducing a change were tried out showed that the workers, who had a chance to make a group decision about the ways in which the change should be made, developed much less resistance than did those who were simply called together to be told about the change and have all of their questions answered. What is important here is that the workers feel that they have a chance to discuss the major factors involved in the change, a chance to understand the nature of the fears they have in facing this change, and a chance to plan what they will do to calm their fears.

Self-diagnosis gets action

Still another implication is that resistance will be less likely to develop if facts which point to the need for change are gathered by the persons who must make the change. A number of high level supervisors in a utility industry came to feel that the workers had many negative attitudes about their jobs which were due to poor supervisory practices. Each supervisor, quite naturally, felt that other supervisors were at fault. Top management set up a number of study groups in which the supervisors first learned how they could diagnose the causes of these negative attitudes. Each supervisor then returned to his own work place and gathered facts that would be necessary for him to analyse the causes of negative attitudes he could spot among his workers. Later the supervisors came together to report their findings. At this meeting their enthusiasm for change in their own practices was high because they had participated in gathering the facts which best described their problems. People will be more likely to act in terms of information they gather themselves than in terms of information gathered by others and delivered to them. If it is clear that a change is indicated in a given state of affairs, but the people who must abide by the change are resisting the shift, they can come to see it themselves by obtaining the facts which properly "case" the situation.

To summarize, we have said that resistance is a problem which any person who is responsible for social change must face. Even though it is strange and unexpected behavior, there are causes for the development of this phenomenon. These causes may be understood, and resistance may be prevented, if the administrator will help the changees develop their own understanding of the need for change and explicit awareness of how they feel about it, and what can be done about those feelings.

QUESTIONS

1. Describe resistance to change in terms of human behavior.
2. How can one recognize when resistance to change is working?
3. What conditions are conducive to resistance to change?
4. Discuss the ways resistance to change can be prevented or decreased.
5. What part does communication play in resistance to change?

41. ACHIEVING CHANGE IN PEOPLE: SOME APPLICATIONS OF GROUP DYNAMICS THEORY *

Dorwin Cartwright

I

We hear all around us today the assertion that the problems of the twentieth century are problems of human relations. The survival of civilization, it is said, will depend upon man's ability to create social inventions capable of harnessing, for society's constructive use, the vast physical energies now at man's disposal. Or, to put the matter more simply, we must learn how to change the way in which people behave toward one another. In broad outline, the specifications for a good society are clear, but a serious technical problem remains: How can we change people so that they neither restrict the freedom nor limit the potentialities for growth of others; so that they accept and respect people of different religion, nationality, color, or political opinion; so that nations can exist in a world without war, and so that the fruits of our technological advances can bring economic well-being and freedom from disease to all the people of the world? Although few people would disagree with these objectives when stated abstractly, when we become more specific, differences of opinion quickly arise. How is change to be produced? Who is to do it? Who is to be changed? These questions permit no ready answers.

Before we consider in detail these questions of social technology, let us clear away some semantic obstacles. The word "change" produces emotional reactions. It is not a neutral word. To many people it is threatening. It conjures up visions of a revolutionary, a dissatisfied idealist, a trouble-maker, a malcontent. Nicer words referring to the process of changing people are education, training, orientation, guidance, indoctrination, therapy. We are more ready to have others "educate" us than to have them "change" us. We, ourselves, feel less guilty in "training" others than in "changing" them. Why this emotional response? What makes the two kinds of words have such different meanings? I believe that a large part of the difference lies in the fact that the safer words (like education

* From *Human Relations*, Vol. 4, No. 4 (1951), pp. 381-392. Reprinted with permission.

or therapy) carry the implicit assurance that the only changes produced will be good ones, acceptable within a currently held value system. The cold, unmodified word "change," on the contrary, promises no respect for values; it might even tamper with values themselves. Perhaps for this very reason it will foster straight thinking if we use the word "change" and thus force ourselves to struggle directly and self-consciously with the problems of value that are involved. Words like education, training, or therapy, by the very fact that they are so disturbing, may close our eyes to the fact that they too inevitably involve values.

Another advantage of using the word "change" rather than other related words is that it does not restrict our thinking to a limited set of aspects of people that are legitimate targets of change. Anyone familiar with the history of education knows that there has been endless controversy over what it is about people that "education" properly attempts to modify. Some educators have viewed education simply as imparting knowledge, others mainly as providing skills for doing things, still others as producing healthy "attitudes," and some have aspired to instil a way of life. Or if we choose to use a word like "therapy," we can hardly claim that we refer to a more clearly defined realm of change. Furthermore, one can become inextricably entangled in distinctions and vested interests by attempting to distinguish sharply between, let us say, the domain of education and that of therapy. If we are to try to take a broader view and to develop some basic principles that promise to apply to all types of modifications in people, we had better use a word like "change" to keep our thinking general enough.

The proposal that social technology may be employed to solve the problems of society suggests that social science may be applied in ways not different from those used in the physical sciences. Does social science, in fact, have any practically useful knowledge which may be brought to bear significantly on society's most urgent problems? What scientifically based principles are there for guiding programs of social change: In this paper we shall restrict our considerations to certain parts of a relatively new branch of social science known as "group dynamics." We shall examine some of the implications for social action which stem from research in this field of scientific investigation.

What is "group dynamics"? Perhaps it will be most useful to start by looking at the derivation of the word "dynamics." It comes from a Greek word meaning force. In careful usage of the phrase, "group dynamics" refers to the forces operating in groups. The investigation of group dynamics, then, consists of a study of these forces: what gives rise to them, what conditions modify them, what consequences they have, etc. The practical application of group dynamics (or the technology of group dynamics) consists of the utilization of knowledge about these forces for the achievement of some purpose. In keeping with this definition, then, it is clear that group dynamics, as a realm of investigation, is not particularly novel, nor is it the exclusive property of any person or institution. It goes back at least to the outstanding work of men like Simmel, Freud, and Cooley.

Although interest in groups has a long and respectable history, the past fifteen years have witnessed a new flowering of activity in this field. Today, research centers in several countries are carrying out substantial programs of research designed to reveal the nature of groups and of their functioning. The phrase "group dynamics" has come into common usage during this time and intense efforts have been devoted to the development of the field, both as a branch of social science and as a form of social technology.

In this development the name of Kurt Lewin has been outstanding. As a consequence of his work in the field of individual psychology and from his analysis of the nature of the pressing problems of the contemporary world, Lewin became convinced of society's urgent need for a *scientific approach* to the understanding of the dynamics of groups. In 1945 he established the Research Center for Group Dynamics to meet this need. Since that date the Center has been devoting its efforts to improving our scientific understanding of groups through laboratory experimentation, field studies, and the use of techniques of action research. It has also attempted in various ways to help get the findings of social science more widely used by social management. Much of what I have to say in this paper is drawn from the experiences of this Center in its brief existence of a little more than five years.[1]

II

For various reasons we have found that much of our work has been devoted to an attempt to gain a better understanding of the ways in which people change their behavior or resist efforts by others to have them do so. Whether we set for ourselves the prac-

[1] D. Cartwright, *The Research Center for Group Dynamics: A Report of Five Years' Activities and a View of Future Needs* (Ann Arbor: Institute for Social Research, 1950).

tical goal of improving behavior or whether we take on the intellectual task of understanding why people do what they do, we have to investigate processes of communication, influence, social pressure—in short, problems of change.

In this work we have encountered great frustration. The problems have been most difficult to solve. Looking back over our experience, I have become convinced that no small part of the trouble has resulted from an irresistible tendency to conceive of our problems in terms of the individual. We live in an individualistic culture. We value the individual highly, and rightly so. But I am inclined to believe that our political and social concern for the individual has narrowed our thinking as social scientists so much that we have not been able to state our research problems properly. Perhaps we have taken the individual as the unit of observation and study when some larger unit would have been more appropriate. Let us look at a few examples.

Consider first some matters having to do with the mental health of an individual. We can all agree, I believe, that an important mark of a healthy personality is that the individual's self-esteem has not been undermined. But on what does self-esteem depend? From research on this problem we have discovered that, among other things, repeated experiences of failure or traumatic failures on matters of central importance serve to undermine one's self-esteem. We also know that whether a person experiences success or failure as a result of some undertaking depends upon the level of aspiration which he has set for himself. Now, if we try to discover how the level of aspiration gets set, we are immediately involved in the person's relationships to groups. The groups to which he belongs set standards for his behavior which he must accept if he is to remain in the group. If his capacities do not allow him to reach these standards, he experiences failure, he withdraws or is rejected by the group and his self-esteem suffers a shock.

Suppose, then, that we accept a task of therapy, of rebuilding his self-esteem. It would appear plausible from our analysis of the problem that we should attempt to work with variables of the same sort that produced the difficulty, that is to work with him either in the groups to which he now belongs or to introduce him into new groups which are selected for the purpose and to work upon his relationships to groups as such. From the point of view of preventive mental health, we might even attempt to train the groups in our communities—classes in schools, work groups in business, families, unions, religious and cultural groups—to make use of practices better designed to protect the self-esteem of their members.

Consider a second example. A teacher finds that in her class she has a number of trouble-makers, full of aggression. She wants to know why these children are so aggressive and what can be done about it. A foreman in a factory has the same kind of problem with some of his workers. He wants the same kind of help. The solution most tempting to both the teacher and the foreman often is to transfer the worst trouble-makers to someone else, or if facilities are available, to refer them for counselling. But is the problem really of such a nature that it can be solved by removing the trouble-maker from the situation or by working on his individual motivations and emotional life? What leads does research give us? The evidence indicates, of course, that there are many causes of aggressiveness in people, but one aspect of the problem has become increasingly clear in recent years. If we observe carefully the amount of aggressive behavior and the number of trouble-makers to be found in a large collection of groups, we find that these characteristics can vary tremendously from group to group even when the different groups are composed essentially of the same kinds of people. In the now classic experiments of Lewin, Lippitt, and White [2] on the effects of different styles of leadership, it was found that the same group of children displayed markedly different levels of aggressive behavior when under different styles of leadership. Moreover, when individual children were transferred from one group to another, their levels of aggressiveness shifted to conform to the atmosphere of the new group. Efforts to account for one child's aggressiveness under one style of leadership merely in terms of his personality traits could hardly succeed under these conditions. This is not to say that a person's behavior is entirely to be accounted for by the atmosphere and structure of the immediate group, but it is remarkable to what an extent a strong, cohesive group can control aspects of a member's behavior traditionally thought to be expressive of enduring personality trains. Recognition of this fact rephrases the problem of how to change such behavior. It directs us to a study of the sources of the influence of the group on its members.

Let us take an example from a different field. What can we learn from efforts to change people by mass media and mass persuasion?

---

[2] K. Lewin, R. Lippitt, and R. K. White, "Patterns of Aggressive Behavior in Experimentally Created 'Social Climates'," *Journal of Social Psychology*, Vol. 10 (1939), pp. 271-299.

In those rare instances when educators, propagandists, advertisers, and others who want to influence large numbers of people, have bothered to make an objective evaluation of the enduring changes produced by their efforts, they have been able to demonstrate only the most negligible effects.[3] The inefficiency of attempts to influence the public by mass media would be scandalous if there were agreement that it was important or even desirable to have such influences strongly exerted. In fact, it is no exaggeration to say that all of the research and experience of generations has not improved the efficiency of lectures or other means of mass influence to any noticeable degree. Something must be wrong with our theories of learning, motivation, and social psychology.

Within very recent years some research data have been accumulating which may give us a clue to the solution of our problem. In one series of experiments directed by Lewin, it was found that a method of group decision, in which the group as a whole made a decision to have its members change their behavior, was from two to ten times as effective in producing actual change as was a lecture presenting exhortation to change.[4] We have yet to learn precisely what produces these differences of effectiveness, but it is clear that by introducing group forces into the situation a whole new level of influence has been achieved.

The experience has been essentially the same when people have attempted to increase the productivity of individuals in work settings. Traditional conceptions of how to increase the output of workers have stressed the individual: select the right man for the job; simplify the job for him; train him in the skills required; motivate him by economic incentives; make it clear to whom he reports; keep the lines of authority and responsibility simple and straight. But even when all these conditions are fully met we are finding that productivity is far below full potential. There is even good reason to conclude that this individualistic conception of the determinants of productivity actually fosters negative consequences. The individual, now isolated and subjected to the demands of the organization through the commands of his boss, finds that he must create with his fellow employees informal groups, not shown on any table of organization, in order to protect himself from arbitrary

[3] D. Cartwright, "Some Principles of Mass Persuasion: Selected Findings of Research on the Sale of United States War Bonds," *Human Relations*, Vol. 2, No. 3 (1949), pp. 253-267.

[4] K. Lewin, *Field Theory in Social Science* (New York: Harper and Brothers, 1951), pp. 229-236.

control of his life, from the boredom produced by the endless repetition of mechanically sanitary and routine operations, and from the impoverishment of his emotional and social life brought about by the frustration of his basic needs for social interaction, participation, and acceptance in a stable group. Recent experiments have demonstrated clearly that the productivity of work groups can be greatly increased by methods of work organization and supervision which give more responsibility to work groups, which allow for fuller participation in important decisions, and which make stable groups the firm basis for support of the individual's social needs.[5] I am convinced that future research will also demonstrate that people working under such conditions become more mature and creative individuals in their homes, in community life, and as citizens.

As a final example, let us examine the experience of efforts to train people in workshops, institutes, and special training courses. Such efforts are common in various areas of social welfare, intergroup relations, political affairs, industry, and adult education generally. It is an unfortunate fact that objective evaluation of the effects of such training efforts has only rarely been undertaken, but there is evidence for those who will look that the actual change in behavior produced is most disappointing. A workshop not infrequently develops keen interest among the participants, high morale and enthusiasm, and a firm resolve on the part of many to apply all the wonderful insights back home. But what happens back home? The trainee discovers that his colleagues don't share his enthusiasm. He learns that the task of changing others' expectations and ways of doing things is discouragingly difficult. He senses, perhaps not very clearly, that it would make all the difference in the world if only there were a few other people sharing his enthusiasm and insights with whom he could plan activities, evaluate consequences of efforts, and from whom he could gain emotional and motivational support. The approach to training which conceives of its task as being merely that of changing the individual probably produces frustration, demoralization, and disillusionment in as large a measure as it accomplishes more positive results.

A few years ago the Research Center for Group Dynamics undertook to shed light on this problem by investigating the operation of a workshop for training leaders in intercultural relations.[6] In

⁵ L. Coch and J. R. P. French, Jr., "Overcoming Resistance to Change," *Human Relations*, Vol. 1, No. 4 (1948), pp. 512-532.
⁶ R. Lippitt, *Training in Community Relations* (New York: Harper and Brothers, 1949).

a project, directed by Lippitt, we set out to compare systematically the different effects of the workshop upon trainees who came as isolated individuals in contrast to those who came as teams. Since one of the problems in the field of intercultural relations is that of getting people of good will to be more active in community efforts to improve intergroup relations, one goal of the training workshop was to increase the activity of the trainees in such community affairs. We found that before the workshop there was no difference in the activity level of the people who were to be trained as isolates and of those who were to be trained as teams. Six months after the workshop, however, those who had been trained as isolates were only slightly more active than before the workshop whereas those who had been members of strong training teams were now much more active. We do not have clear evidence on the point, but we would be quite certain that the maintenance of heightened activity over a long period of time would also be much better for members of teams. For the isolates the effect of the workshop had the characteristic of a "shot in the arm" while for the team member it produced a more enduring change because the team provided continuous support and reinforcement for its members.

III

What conclusions may we draw from these examples? What principles of achieving change in people can we see emerging? To begin with the most general proposition, we may state that the behavior, attitudes, beliefs, and values of the individual are all firmly grounded in the groups to which he belongs. How aggressive or cooperative a person is, how much self-respect and self-confidence he has, how energetic and productive his work is, what he aspires to, what he believes to be true and good, whom he loves or hates, and what beliefs and prejudices he holds—all these characteristics are highly determined by the individual's group memberships. In a real sense, they are properties of groups and of the relationships between people. Whether they change or resist change will, therefore, be greatly influenced by the nature of these groups. Attempts to change them must be concerned with the dynamics of groups.

In examining more specifically how groups enter into the process of change, we find it useful to view groups in at least three different ways. In the first view, the group is seen as a source of influence over its members. Efforts to change behavior can be supported or blocked by pressures on members stemming from the group. To make constructive use of these pressures the group must be used *as a medium of change*. In the second view, the group itself becomes the *target of change*. To change the behavior of individuals it may be necessary to change the standards of the group, its style of leadership, its emotional atmosphere, or its stratification into cliques and hierarchies. Even though the goal may be to change the behavior of *individuals*, the target of change becomes the group. In the third view, it is recognized that many changes of behavior can be brought about only by the organized efforts of groups *as agents of change*. A committee to combat intolerance, a labor union, an employers association, a citizens group to increase the pay of teachers—any action group will be more or less effective depending upon the way it is organized, the satisfactions it provides to its members, the degree to which its goals are clear, and a host of other properties of the group.

An adequate social technology of change, then, requires at the very least a scientific understanding of groups viewed in each of these ways. We shall consider here only the first two aspects of the problem: the group as a medium of change and as a target of change.

The group as a medium of change

Principle No. 1. If the group is to be used effectively as a medium of change, those people who are to be changed and those who are to exert influence for change must have a strong sense of belonging to the same group.

Kurt Lewin described this principle well: "The normal gap between teacher and student, doctor and patient, social worker and public, can . . . be a real obstacle to acceptance of the advocated conduct." In other words, in spite of whatever status differences there might be between them, the teacher and the student have to feel as members of one group in matters involving their sense of values. The chances for re-education seem to be increased whenever a strong we-feeling is created.[7] Recent experiments by Preston and Heintz have demonstrated greater changes of opinions among members of discussion groups operating with participatory leadership than among those with supervisory leadership.[8] The implications

---

[7] K. Lewin, *Resolving Social Conflicts* (New York: Harper and Brothers, 1948), p. 67.
[8] M. G. Preston and R. K. Heintz, "Effects of Participatory vs. Supervisory Leadership on Group Judgment," *Journal of Abnormal and Social Psychology*, Vol. 44 (1949), pp. 345-355.

of this principle for classroom teaching are far-reaching. The same may be said of supervision in the factory, army, or hospital.

Principle No. 2. The more attractive the group is to its members the greater is the influence that the group can exert on its members.

This principle has been extensively documented by Festinger and his co-workers.[9] They have been able to show in a variety of settings that in more cohesive groups there is a greater readiness of members to attempt to influence others, a greater readiness to be influenced by others, and stronger pressures toward conformity when conformity is a relevant matter for the group. Important for the practitioner wanting to make use of this principle is, of course, the question of how to increase the attractiveness of groups. This is a question with many answers. Suffice it to say that a group is more attractive the more it satisfies the needs of its members. We have been able to demonstrate experimentally an increase in group cohesiveness by increasing the liking of members for each other as persons, by increasing the perceived importance of the group goal, and by increasing the prestige of the group among other groups. Experienced group workers could add many other ways to this list.

Principle No. 3. In attempts to change attitudes, values, or behavior the more relevant they are to the basis of attraction to the group, the greater will be the influence that the group can exert upon them.

I believe this principle gives a clue to some otherwise puzzling phenomena. How does it happen that a group, like a labor union, seems to be able to exert such strong discipline over its members in some matters (let us say in dealings with management), while it seems unable to exert nearly the same influence in other matters (let us say in political action)? If we examine why it is that members are attracted to the group, I believe we will find that a particular reason for belonging seems more related to some of the group's activities than to others. If a man joins a union mainly to keep his job and to improve his working conditions, he may be largely uninfluenced by the union's attempt to modify his attitudes toward national and international affairs. Groups differ tremendously in the range of matters that are relevant to them and hence over which they have influence. Much of the inefficiency of adult education could be reduced if more attention were paid to the need that influence attempts be appropriate to the groups in which they are made.

---

[9] L. Festinger *et al.*, *Theory and Experiment in Social Communication: Collected Papers* (Ann Arbor: Institute for Social Research, 1950).

Principle No. 4. The greater the prestige of a group member in the eyes of the other members, the greater the influence he can exert.

Polansky, Lippitt, and Redl [10] have demonstrated this principle with great care and methodological ingenuity in a series of studies in children's summer camps. From a practical point of view it must be emphasized that the things giving prestige to a member may not be those characteristics most prized by the official management of the group. The most prestige-carrying member of a Sunday School class may not possess the characteristics most similar to the minister of the church. The teacher's pet may be a poor source of influence within a class. This principle is the basis for the common observation that the official leader and the actual leader of a group are often not the same individual.

Principle No. 5. Efforts to change individuals or subparts of a group which, if successful, would have the result of making them deviate from the norms of the group will encounter strong resistance.

During the past few years a great deal of evidence has been accumulated showing the tremendous pressures which groups can exert upon members to conform to the group's norms. The price of deviation in most groups is rejection or even expulsion. If the member really wants to belong and be accepted, he cannot withstand this type of pressure. It is for this reason that efforts to change people by taking them from the group and giving them special training so often have disappointing results. This principle also accounts for the finding that people thus trained sometimes display increased tension, aggressiveness toward the group, or a tendency to form cults or cliques with others who have shared their training.

These five principles concerning the group as a medium of change would appear to have readiest application to groups created for the purpose of producing changes in people. They provide certain specifications for building effective training or therapy groups. They also point, however, to a difficulty in producing change in people in that they show how resistant an individual is to changing in any way contrary to group pressures and expectations. In order to achieve many kinds of changes in people, therefore, it is necessary to deal with the group as a target of change.

---

10 N. Polansky, R. Lippitt, and F. Redl, "An Investigation of Behavioral Contagion in Groups," *Human Relations*, Vol. 3, No. 4 (1950), pp. 319-348.

The group as a target of change

Principle No. 6. Strong pressure for changes in the group can be established by creating a shared perception by members of the need for change, thus making the source of pressure for change lie within the group.

Marrow and French [11] report a dramatic case-study which illustrates this principle quite well. A manufacturing concern had a policy against hiring women over thirty because it was believed that they were slower, more difficult to train, and more likely to be absent. The staff psychologist was able to present to management evidence that this belief was clearly unwarranted at least within their own company. The psychologist's facts, however, were rejected and ignored as a basis for action because they violated accepted beliefs. It was claimed that they went against the direct experience of the foremen. Then the psychologist hit upon a plan for achieving change which differed drastically from the usual one of argument, persuasion, and pressure. He proposed that management conduct its own analysis of the situation. With his help management collected all the facts which they believed were relevant to the problem. When the results were in they were now their own facts rather than those of some "outside" expert. Policy was immediately changed without further resistance. The important point here is that facts are not enough. The facts must be the accepted property of the group if they are to become an effective basis for change. There seems to be all the difference in the world in changes actually carried out between those cases in which a consulting firm is hired to do a study and present a report and those in which technical experts are asked to collaborate with the group in doing its own study.

Principle No. 7. Information relating to the need for change, plans for change, and consequences of change must be shared by all relevant people in the group.

Another way of stating this principle is to say that change of a group ordinarily requires the opening of communication channels. Newcomb [12] has shown how one of the first consequences of mistrust and hostility is the avoidance of communicating openly and freely about the things producing the tension. If you look closely at a pathological group (that is, one that has trouble making deci-

[11] A. J. Marrow and J. R. P. French, Jr., "Changing a Stereotype in Industry," *Journal of Social Issues*, Vol. 1, No. 3 (1945), pp. 33-37.
[12] T. M. Newcomb, "Autistic Hostility and Social Reality," *Human Relations*. Vol. 1, No. 1 (1947), pp. 69-86.

sions or effecting coordinated efforts of its members), you will certainly find strong restraints in that group against communicating vital information among its members. Until these restraints are removed there can be little hope for any real and lasting changes in the group's functioning. In passing it should be pointed out that the removal of barriers to communication will ordinarily be accompanied by a sudden increase in the communication of hostility. The group may appear to be falling apart, and it will certainly be a painful experience to many of the members. This pain and the fear that things are getting out of hand often stop the process of change once begun.

Principle No. 8. Changes in one part of a group produce strain in other related parts which can be reduced only by eliminating the change or by bringing about readjustments in the related parts.

It is a common practice to undertake improvements in group functioning by providing training programs for certain classes of people in the organization. A training program for foremen, for nurses, for teachers, or for group workers is established. If the content of the training is relevant for organizational change, it must of necessity deal with the relationships these people have with other subgroups. If nurses in a hospital change their behavior significantly, it will affect their relations both with the patients and with the doctors. It is unrealistic to assume that both these groups will remain indifferent to any significant changes in this respect. In hierarchical structures this process is most clear. Lippitt has proposed on the basis of research and experience that in such organizations attempts at change should always involve three levels, one being the major target of change and the other two being the one above and the one below.

IV

These eight principles represent a few of the basic propositions emerging from research in group dynamics. Since research is constantly going on and since it is the very nature of research to revise and reformulate our conceptions, we may be sure that these principles will have to be modified and improved as time goes by. In the meantime they may serve as guides in our endeavors to develop a scientifically based technology of social management.

In social technology, just as in physical technology, invention plays a crucial role. In both fields progress consists of the creation of new mechanisms for the accomplishment of certain goals. In both fields inventions arise in response to practical needs and are to be evaluated by how effectively they satisfy these needs. The relation of invention to scientific development is indirect but important. Inventions cannot proceed too far ahead of basic scientific development, nor should they be allowed to fall too far behind. They will be more effective the more they make good use of known principles of science, and they often make new developments in science possible. On the other hand, they are in no sense logical derivations from scientific principles.

I have taken this brief excursion into the theory of invention in order to make a final point. To many people "group dynamics" is known only for the social inventions which have developed in recent years in work with groups. Group dynamics is often thought of as certain techniques to be used with groups. Role playing, buzz groups, process observers, post-meeting reaction sheets, and feedback of group observations are devices popularly associated with the phrase "group dynamics." I trust that I have been able to show that group dynamics is more than a collection of gadgets. It certainly aspires to be a science as well as a technology.

This is not to underplay the importance of these inventions nor of the function of inventing. As inventions they are all mechanisms designed to help accomplish important goals. How effective they are will depend upon how skilfully they are used and how appropriate they are to the purposes to which they are put. Careful evaluative research must be the ultimate judge of their usefulness in comparison with alternative inventions. I believe that the principles enumerated in this paper indicate some of the specifications that social inventions in this field must meet.

QUESTIONS

1. What is "group dynamics"?
2. What, according to Cartwright, is a basic reason why we have encountered trouble in explaining resistance to change?
3. What principles of achieving change in people are emerging from the application of the group dynamics theory?
4. What influence does the group exert on the individual?
5. Are the principles of achieving change in people flexible? Why?

42. STUDYING AND CREATING CHANGE: A MEANS TO UNDERSTANDING SOCIAL ORGANIZATION *

Floyd C. Mann [1]

Social organizations are functioning entities with interdependent structures and processes. They are not fixed, static structures, but rather continuously moving patterns of relationships in a much larger field of social activity. To understand what their essential elements and dimensions are, what it is that gives an organization its unity, it is necessary to study and create social change within organizational settings.

Relatively little is known about organizational change. Social scientists stress the study of the dynamic in social systems, but few [2] accept the risks involved to gain the knowledge and skills needed to create and measure changes in functioning organizations. This is not surprising, for research within large-scale organizations is at such an early stage that the social scientist knows little about how (1) to gain access to these research sites, (2) to initiate and sustain organizational change, and (3) to measure such changes. We have only begun the systematic codification of the working knowledge and skills necessary for the researcher to get into, and maintain himself within, the social science laboratories of functioning organizations. [3] Systematic, quantitative measurement of change processes in complex organizational settings is in its infancy. Longitudinal studies are rare—social scientists seldom attempt to obtain more than a single "before" and "after" measurement and are often content to try and decipher findings from *ex post facto* study designs. The actual steps and skills necessary to initiate and sustain changes within an organization are not only relatively unknown, but there is even some suspicion that knowledge of social action and an ability to engineer change are not appropriate for the social scientist.

* From *Research in Industrial Human Relations*, ed. Arensberg *et al.* (New York: Harper & Brothers, 1957), Chapter X, pp. 146-167. Reprinted with permission.

[1] Drs. Rensis Likert, Daniel Katz, Robert Kahn, and Norman R. F. Maier have made especially helpful suggestions concerning the organization and presentation of this material. They can, of course, in no way be held responsible for the shortcomings which remain.

[2] For an account of a conspicuous exception to this, see N. C. Mare and E. Reimer, "The Experimental Manipulation of a Major Organizational Variable," in *Journal of Abnormal and Social Psychology* (1956).

[3] F. Mann and R. Lippitt, eds., "Social Relations Skills in Field Research," *Journal of Social Issues*, Vol. 8, No. 3, 1952.

While social scientists are not spending any sizable proportion of their time in learning how to change interpersonal and intergroup relations in functioning organizations, a wide variety of practitioners are. These include at the one extreme the consultants or the "operators" who take over organizations which are failing and rebuild them, and at the other extreme, the "human relations" trainers. Most of these men know very little theoretically about processes of organizational, attitudinal, and behavioral change, but they do know a great deal intuitively about the problems of changing people in an organization. This is especially true of the training men.

This suggests that there should and can be a closer working relationship between those concerned with actually *changing* organizational structure and processes and those researchers concerned with *understanding* organizational change. Social scientists have not begun to take advantage of their opportunities for learning about organizations from those in the "practicing professions"—those who are *doing*.[4] Observations and systematic measurements around the practitioner's efforts to alter systems of relationships in organizations can provide the researcher with valuable insights into the dynamics of organization. Gaps in knowledge become excruciatingly apparent; new sources of data and problems for research emerge. In turn, social scientists can contribute to practitioners by helping them assess what effect their actions as change agents have. Most practitioners—and especially those trainers who are concerned with changing the human relations skills of supervisors—have very little systematic, and no quantitative, evidence on the success of their efforts to create changes in individuals or organizations. It seems clear that there is a broad basis for cooperation here. Systematic studies of the work of those attempting to change the way things are done in an organization may contribute to our understanding of social organizations. And developments in measurement and the procedures used by researchers to understand organizations better may contribute to the working knowledge of trainers and others in the "practicing professions."

In this chapter we will focus on the description and evaluation of several different types of procedures designed to change interpersonal and intergroup relations in complex organizations. We will first look at two human relations training programs whose effects have been systematically and quantitatively studied. Then we will

[4] Donald Young, "Sociology and the Practicing Professions," *American Sociological Review*, Vol. 20 (December, 1955), pp. 641-648.

describe briefly the development and evaluation of a change procedure with which we are experimenting to increase the understanding, acceptance, and utilization of survey research findings. At the close of the chapter these two specific types of procedures for creating change in organizational settings are contrasted as a first step in identifying facets of change processes which merit greater experimentation and in providing insights into the structure and functioning of organizations.

CHANGING INTERPERSONAL RELATIONS THROUGH TRAINING SUPERVISORS

Recurrent opportunities for social scientists to study a change process within an organizational setting are provided by human relations training programs for supervisors. As change procedures, these programs are formal, rational, purposeful efforts to alter institutional behavior. In contrast to the day-to-day attempts of management to bring about change, they are bounded in time and organizational space, and are thus easily studied intensively.

Because of the several historical developments described in Chapters I, II, and XIII, management by the late forties began to be convinced that training might be useful for their supervisors, and there has since been a wholesale adoption of human relations training programs. While there was and still is a remarkable range in the content, methods, and settings of these programs, nearly all of them have centered around improving supervisory skills in dealing with people—either as individuals or in face-to-face groups. They are frequently directed at teaching the supervisor how to work with an employee as an individual, occasionally at working with employees as members of a small group, but only rarely at understanding and working within the complex social system of the large corporation or factory. Another way of saying this is that the courses have drawn heavily from psychology, to a lesser extent from social psychology, and usually not at all from sociology.

There are no commonly agreed-upon ways by which these programs can be described. The following headings are, however, useful: objectives, content, methods, setting, training leader, and training unit. For example, the objectives of these programs are usually very general and quite ambitious: "to assist supervisors in developing the skills, knowledge, and attitudes needed to carry out their supervisory responsibilities," or "to improve morale, increase production, and reduce turnover." Their contents usually include human nature, personality, motivation, attitudes, and leadership, and other information about relevant psychological principles and research findings may also be included. More often than not the methods of training are some variant of the "lecture-discussion method." The settings are frequently in a classroom away from the job. The trainers are generally staff men whom the trainee did not know before the training; the trainees, first-line supervisors or foremen meeting with other supervisors from other parts of the organization.

Few systematic, quantitative studies have been made to investigate the effectiveness of these programs.[5] This is not to say that there has been no interest in evaluation. Any review of the literature will indicate many such attempts and many testimonials about the relative advantages of different procedures of training. Mahler and Monroe[6] reported a number of "evaluative studies" after reviewing the literature and conducting a survey of 150 companies known to have training programs. While these studies almost without fail acclaim the many benefits of such training, few of them meet more than a fraction of the requirements necessary for a rigorous test of the basic underyling assumptions.

What are these assumptions? In general, they are that training supervisors in human relations will result in changes in the supervisors' attitudes and philosophy, that these changes will be reflected in their behavior toward employees on the job, that this changed behavior will be seen by the employees, and that they will in turn become more satisfied with their work situation, then more highly motivated, and, ultimately, more productive workers.

While there is a good deal of evidence that human relations training programs do meet part of these assumptions—e.g., they do appear to change the verbal veneer of supervisors—there are few scientifically rigorous, quantitative studies which have demonstrated that these changes in what supervisors *know* affect their attitudes and behavior as seen or experienced by their subordinates. Few studies show that human relations training of supervisors is related to changes in the attitudes or productivity of employees under those supervisors.

---

[5] A nonquantitative, but extraordinarily thorough and insightful study of foreman training was made by A. Zaleznik, *Foreman Training in a Growing Enterprise* (Boston: Graduate School of Business Administration, Harvard University, 1951).

[6] W. R. Mahler and W. H. Monroe, *How Industry Determines the Need for and Effectiveness of Training,* Personnel Research Section Report 929 (Washington: Department of the Army, 1952).

It is not possible to make a complete review of these studies here. A review of the findings from several recent, major evaluative studies will, however, provide a good deal of evidence concerning the effectiveness of certain types of training programs. The findings will certainly emphasize the need for more systematic, quantitative research to assess the most effective combinations of content, methods, settings, training units, and trainers.

The Canter-Tyler studies

In 1949, Canter [7] developed a human relations training course for first-line supervisors in the home offices of a large insurance company. The three objectives of the course were "(1) to establish facts and principles concerning psychological aspects of behavior and group functioning to enable supervisors to become more competent in their knowledge and understanding of human behavior; (2) to increase supervisors' capacities for observing human behavior; and (3) to present personality adjustment concepts to aid in integration of achievements made in the first two objectives." This training was designed to provide a foundation of information on which to build later through additional practice and "technique" training. Specific content was primarily psychological: human nature, personality, motivation, attitudes, leadership, and group structure. Method was lecture-discussion. The training occurred in the conference rooms of the company; Canter himself was the trainer. The trainees were eighteen supervisors whose superiors had participated in a preliminary run for executives. The course was presented in ten two-hour weekly sessions.

To determine the influence of this training, Canter employed a battery of paper-and-pencil questionnaires and tests which were given before and after training to two groups of supervisors: an experimental group of eighteen from one department who received the training, and a control group of eighteen from two other departments who did not receive training. The two groups were similar in type of work performed, age (about thirty), education (thirteen years), and proportion of men and women. While the control group had more years of service with the company (7.5 and 4.6, respectively) and higher mean scores on a mental alertness test, the statistical technique used in the final analysis did not require prematched individuals or groups.

---

[7] R. R. Canter, "A Human Relations Training Program," *Journal of Applied Psychology*, Vol. 35 (February, 1951), pp. 38-45.

Six tests, yielding a total of twelve separate scores, were used. (1) General Psychological Facts and Principles; (2) "How to Supervise"; (3) General Logical Reasoning; (4) Social Judgment Test; (5) Supervisory Questionnaire; and (6) Test for Ability to Estimate Group Opinion. The major findings were that the trained supervisors obtained mean scores on all tests better than would have been predicted on the basis of the performance of the untrained group alone. For five out of the twelve measures, the differences were statistically significant at the 5 per cent level; for two other measures, differences were significant at the 10 per cent level. Other important conclusions were that trained supervisors became more similar in abilities measured by the tests and more accurate in estimating the opinions of employees in their departments, but not their sections. It was also found that those holding highest scores initially gained the most on all measures except the Test of Ability to Estimate Group Opinion, where the opposite result was obtained.

While Canter assumed in his design that cognitive training—i.e., an ability to understand human relations concepts and principles—would have to precede any behavioral training in supervisory skills, practices, and attitudes, Tyler [8] designed a companion study to measure any changes in employee morale which might be attributed to this training. Her morale surveys indicated improvement in employee morale scores for *both* the experimental and control departments. Morale improved by an average of 11 points per section (range 2-25 points) in five of seven sections in the experimental group, and decreased slightly in two others. "In the control groups, morale increased in eight of the nine sections by an average of 14 points (range 5-32 points). The decrease in the other section was seven points. The only category which showed a somewhat consistent change among sections was 'supervision' on which scores for over half of the sections decreased." After warning the reader of the possible effect of the before-test experience, she notes: "Undoubtedly, the difference in change in morale between the control and the experimental groups is not large enough to be significant" (page 47). Canter, however, points out that in Tyler's study "morale was quite high initially, which might account for the lack of any improvement in the experimental department over the control."

The strength of the Canter-Tyler studies is that they used both *before* and *after* measures for experimental and control groups.

[8] B. B. Tyler, "A Study of Factors Contributing to Employee Morale" (Master's thesis, Ohio State University, 1949).

Canter's use of multiple criteria against which to evaluate the various sub-goals of the training program is also noteworthy. The use of Tyler's perceptual and employee morale measures in conjunction with Canter's attitudinal and cognitive measures permits an evaluation of the course's effectiveness at two levels: the supervisor's intent, and his on-the-job performance. The findings from this combination of studies make it obvious that classroom learning does not guarantee the translation of such learning into job performance. It should be remembered, however, that Canter did not set out to change supervisors' skills and practices, but only their understanding of human relations concepts and ideas.

Fleishman-Harris studies

Working with the education and training staff of a large company manufacturing trucks and farm machinery, Fleishman [9] developed a study design and a battery of research instruments for measuring the continuing effectiveness of leadership training. The general objectives of this training [10] were to change understanding, attitudes, habits, and skills of foremen by giving them solid foundation in four basic areas of industrial knowledge. These areas were personal development, human relations, economics, and company operations. The method was primarily lecture-discussion. The training staff included full-time instructors, former supervisors, and part-time university faculty. The training was given to foremen who were taken from a wide variety of operations and plants and sent to a central school in Chicago for two weeks of eight-hours-a-day intensive development.

To determine the effects of this course on foremen from one motor-truck plant who had taken this training, Fleishman employed an *ex post facto* design with four groups of about thirty each. One group had not received the training; the other three had, 2-10, 11-19, and 20-29 months earlier. The groups were alike on a number of background characteristics: age (early forties), education (eleven years), length of service (sixteen years), supervisory experience (seven years), size of work group (about twenty-eight), and supervisory experience with present work group (six years). Seven paper-and-pencil questionnaires were used to obtain opinion, expectation, and perceptual data about leadership practices from the trainees,

---

[9] Edwin A. Fleishman, "Leadership Climate, Human Relations Training, and Supervisory Behavior," *Personnel Psychology*, Vol. 6 (Summer, 1953), pp. 205-222.

[10] Charles L. Walker, Jr., "Education and Training at International Harvester," *Harvard Business Review*, Vol. 27 (September, 1949), pp. 542-558.

their superiors, and their subordinates. This battery gave Fleishman an opportunity to investigate the differences between supervisory beliefs as reported by the foreman himself and supervisory practices as reported by his employees, and to explore the interaction of training effects with the supervisor's "leadership climate." Each questionnaire contained two independent leadership dimensions which had been identified by factor analysis: "consideration"—the extent to which the supervisor was considerate of the feelings of employees; and "initiating structure"—the extent to which the supervisor defined or facilitated group interactions toward goal attainment.

The results obtained by giving attitude questionnaires to foremen on the first and last days of their training in Chicago provide evidence of how the topics stressed in this leadership training affected these two dimensions. The results obtained from these before and after measures showed a significant increase in "consideration" (.05 level) and an even more marked decrease in "initiating structure" (.01 level). The on-the-job effects of the training, however, appeared to be "minimal." "The training did not produce any kind of permanent change in either the attitudes or behavior of the trained foremen." The employees under the most recently trained foremen actually saw them as *less* considerate than the employees under the untrained foremen saw their superiors. This statistically significant finding was supported by other trends toward more structuring and less consideration by those foremen who had the training. Thus, while the human relations approach was stressed in the course and understood at least well enough to be registered as an opinion change on a paper-and-pencil questionnaire, it was not evident in what trained foremen said they did, or what their employees saw them doing in the actual work situation.

The most important variable found to affect leadership was the climate within which the foreman worked. In fact, the kind of superior under whom the foreman operated seemed "more related to the attitudes and behavior of the foremen in the plant than did the fact that they had or had not received the leadership training."

These results, showing that the training was not meeting its objective of making foremen more human-relations oriented in the plant, left two alternatives open: redesign the course, or initiate an intensive criterion study relating supervisory behavior to group effectiveness. The latter alternative was chosen, and Harris [11] de-

---

[11] E. F. Harris, "Measuring Industrial Leadership and Its Implications for Training Supervisors" (Doctoral thesis, Ohio State University, 1952).

signed a study in the same plant to investigate (1) the relationship between these two dimensions of leadership behavior and various measures of work efficiency, and (2) the effects of a training course planned as a brief refresher for the central school training in Chicago. It is the findings from this second objective in which we are primarily interested here.

The course, lasting one week, was given at a small nearby college. The effects were evaluated by field experimental design with before and after measures for experimental and control groups. Two groups of thirty-one foremen were established through matching on a number of variables, including length of time since attending the central school (almost three years), scores on before measures (including leadership climate), and other personal factors. One group was given the training. Questionnaires, similar to Fleishman's, were used to obtain information from employees and foremen about the foremen's attitudes and behavior.

Harris used several different methods of analyzing his findings. His most rigorous method indicated there were no statistically significant differences in the foremen's own leadership attitudes or the workers' descriptions of their foremen's behavior—before and after this additional refresher course. The only significant difference he found was a decrease in the degree to which the foremen in the *control* group showed structuring in their leadership behavior as described by their employees. Building on Fleishman's gradual decreases in structuring and increases in consideration the longer the foreman is back on the job, Harris suggests this finding might be interpreted to mean that the refresher course may have "tended to retard a general decrease in structuring."

Harris and Fleishman [12] in analyzing the data from both of their studies in the same plant have uncovered one finding which tends to qualify the general, completely negative conclusion of their findings regarding the effectiveness of this training. This finding concerns the stability of leadership patterns of individual foremen who did not have the training in contrast to those foremen who had the training. They find there is *less* stability in the pre-post measures for the foremen who had the training than for those foremen who did not have training. This suggests that the courses had markedly different effects on different foremen, and that "large individual

---

[12] E. F. Harris and E. A. Fleishman, "Human Relations Training and the Stability of Leadership Patterns," *Journal of Applied Psychology*, Vol. 39 (February, 1955), pp. 20-25.

shifts in scores occur in both directions." They conclude that their research findings show no significant changes in *group* means among trained foremen and that future research should be directed toward investigating personal and situational variables which interact with the effects of training.

At best, these two studies suggest that this type of training has little or no general effect on the behavior of foremen in the plant. At worst, they suggest that the unanticipated consequences of separating foremen from their work groups and making them keenly aware of their role in management more than offset the anticipated consequences of making the foremen more considerate of employees as human beings. Fleishman's finding that *leadership climate* appeared to be a better predictor than *training* of foremen's plant attitudes and behavior underscores the importance of considering the constellation of expectation patterns in which the trainee is embedded. Training which does not take the trainee's regular social environment into account will probably have little chance of modifying behavior. It may very well be that human relations training—as a procedure for initiating social change—is most successful when it is designed to *remold the whole system of role relationships of the supervisor.*[13]

The findings from these four studies suggest that trainers, researchers, and others interested in social change need to rethink what forces are necessary to create and sustain changes in the orientation and behaviors of people in complex systems of relationships. There is a good deal of evidence that management and trainees are enthusiastic about these training courses in general. Management's enthusiasm may be an index of whether the training will continue, but it does not indicate whether training is achieving changes in behavior. And while trainee satisfaction and acceptance may be important as an antecedent to learning, these factors do not indicate whether the training will produce attitudinal and, more significantly, on-the-job behavioral changes.

It should be stressed that the criterion which has been used here for measuring the effects of human relations training is not easily met. There is ample quantitative evidence in the preceding studies that supervisors' information about, and verbal understanding of, human relations principles can be increased. There is much less evi-

---

[13] For a full account of these two studies combined, see E. A. Fleishman, E. F. Harris, and H. E. Buntt, *Leadership and Supervision in Industry* (Columbus: Personnel Research Board, Ohio State University, 1955).

dence that these courses have an effect on the trainee's on-the-job behavior as seen by those working under him. And the hard fact remains that there are no quantitative studies which indicate that these courses in leadership affect workers' job satisfactions or motivations.

FEEDBACK: CHANGING PATTERNS OF RELATIONSHIPS BETWEEN SUPERIORS AND SUBORDINATES BY USING SURVEY FINDINGS

Long-range interest in the actual varying of significant variables in organizations has necessitated that members of the Human Relations Program of the Institute for Social Research, University of Michigan, not only study existing programs for training and changing people in organizations, but that we *develop* new techniques for changing relationships, and that we learn how to *measure* the effects of such changes within organizations. As a result, we have invested a good deal of professional effort in exploring the effectiveness of different procedures for changing attitudes, perceptions, and relationships among individuals in complex hierarchies without changing the personnel of the units. The latter is an important qualification, for we have found that the changes in subordinates' perceptions and attitudes which follow a change in supervisory personnel are frequently of a much larger order than those generated by training or other procedures for changing the attitudes or behavior of incumbents.

Exploratory and developmental phase

One procedure which we developed and subsequently found to be effective in changing perceptions and relationships within organizations has been called "feedback." This change process evolved over a period of years as we [14] tried to learn how to report findings from human relations research into organizations so that they would be understood and used in day-to-day operations. Work began on this process in 1948 following a company-wide study of employee and management attitudes and opinions. Over a period of two years, three different sets of data were fed back: (1) information on the attitudes and perceptions of 8,000 nonsupervisory employees toward their work, promotion opportunities, supervision, fellow employees,

---

[14] A number of people contributed to the design of this feedback process during its developmental phase. They included Sylvester Leahy, Blair Swartz, Robert Schwab, and John Sparling from the Detroit Edison Company, and Rensis Likert, Daniel Katz, Everett Riemer, Frances Fielder, and Theodore Hariton from the Survey Research Center.

etc.; (2) first- and second-line supervisor's feelings about the various aspects of their jobs and supervisory beliefs; and (3) information from intermediate and top levels of management about their supervisory philosophies, roles in policy formation, problems of organizational integration, etc. We had several aims in this exploratory phase: (1) to develop through first-hand experience an understanding of the problems of producing change; (2) to improve relationships; (3) to identify factors which affected the extent of the change; and (4) to develop working hypotheses for later, more directed research.

The process which finally appeared to maximize the acceptance and utilization of survey and research findings can be described structurally as an interlocking chain of conferences. It began with a report of the major findings of the survey to the president and his senior officers, and then progressed slowly down through the hierarchical levels along functional lines to where supervisors and their employees were discussing the data. These meetings were structured in terms of organizational "families" [15] or units—each superior and his immediate subordinates considering the survey data together. The data presented to each group were those pertaining to their own group or for those subunits for which members of the organizational unit were responsible.

Members of each group were asked to help interpret the data and then decide what further analyses of the data should be made to aid them in formulating plans for constructive administrative actions. They also planned the introduction of the findings to the next level. The meetings were typically led by the line officer responsible for the coordination of the subunits at a particular level. Usually, a member of the Survey Research Center and the company's personnel staff assisted the line officer in preparing for these meetings, but attended the meetings only as resource people who could be called upon for information about the feasibility of additional analyses.

These meetings took place in the office of the line supervisor whose organizational unit was meeting, or in the department's own small conference room. All of the survey findings relative to each group were given to the leader and the members of his organizational unit; they decided what to consider first, how fast to work through each topic, and when they had gone as far as they could and needed to involve the next echelon in the process.

---

[15] F. Mann and J. Dent, "The Supervisor: Member of Two Organizational Families," *Harvard Business Review*, Vol. 32 (November-December, 1954), pp. 103-112.

This feedback change procedure was developed in an organization where a great amount of effort had already been invested in the training of management and supervisors. During the war the company had participated in the various J-programs sponsored by the War Manpower Commission, and more important, during the several years we were experimentally developing the feedback process, Dr. Norman R. F. Maier was working with all levels of management to improve their understanding of human relations and supervision.[16] The supervisors with whom we were working to increase their understanding of their own organizational units therefore had a great deal of training in the application of psychological principles to management.

Our observations of the feedback procedure as it developed suggested that it was a powerful process for creating and supporting changes within an organization.[17] However, there was no quantitative proof of this, for our work up to this point had been exploratory and developmental.

A field experiment in accounting departments

In 1950, when eight accounting departments in this same company asked for a second attitude and opinion survey of their seventy-eight supervisors and eight hundred employees, we [18] had an opportunity to initiate the steps necessary to measure the effects of this organizational change process. The questionnaires used in this resurvey were similar to those used in 1948 and provided the basis for a new cycle of feedback conferences. The general plan for the handling of these new resurvey data was to let everyone in the departments—employees and department heads—see the over-all findings for eight accounting departments combined as soon as they were available, and then to work intensively on their use in *some* departments, but not in others until there had been a third survey.

While our objective was to test the effectiveness of the basic pattern of feedback developed during the preceding two years, we encouraged department heads and their supervisors to develop their own variations for reporting data to their units and maximizing their use in the solution of problems. After the all-department meetings

---

[16] For a thorough description of this training, see N. R. F. Maier, *Principles of Human Relations* (New York: Wiley, 1952).

[17] F. Mann and R. Likert, "The Need for Research on Communicating Research Results," *Human Organization*, Vol. 11 (Winter, 1952), pp. 15-19.

[18] F. Mann and H. Baumgartel, *Survey Feedback Experiment: An Evaluation of a Program for the Utilization of Survey Findings*, monograph in preparation, Survey Research Center, University of Michigan.

had been concluded, the chief executive of the accounting departments held a meeting with each department head in the experimental group. At this meeting, the findings for the department head's unit were thoroughly reviewed. The findings included comparisons of (1) changes in employee attitudes from 1948 to 1950, (2) attitudes in that department with those in all other departments combined, and (3) employees' perceptions of supervisory behavior with supervisory statements about their behavior. Department heads were encouraged to go ahead with feedback meetings as soon as they felt ready, tentative next steps were discussed, and assistance from the researchers and the company personnel staffs was assured. Four departments launched feedback activities which were similar to each other in purpose but somewhat different in method. The programs varied in duration (13-33 weeks), in intensity (9-65 meetings), and in the extent to which nonsupervisory employees were involved in the process. During the eighteen months that these differences were unfolding, nothing was done in two of the remaining four departments after the first all-departments meetings. This was done so they might be available as "controls." Changes in key personnel eliminated the remaining two departments from any experimental design.

A third survey of attitudes was conducted in these departments in 1952 after the natural variations in the feedback programs had run their courses. In 1950 and 1952 surveys were then used as "before" and "after" measurements, the four departmental programs as "experimental variations," with the two inactive departments as "controls."

Our findings indicate that more significant positive changes occurred in employee attitudes and perceptions in the four experimental departments than in the two control departments. This was based on two measures of change: (1) a comparison of answers to sixty-one identical questions which were asked in 1950 and 1952, and (2) of a comparison of answers to seventeen "perceived change" questions in which employees had an opportunity to indicate what types of changes had occurred since the 1950 survey. In the experimental group, a fourth of the sixty-one items showed relative mean positive changes, significant at the .05 level or better; the change for another 57 per cent of the items was also positive in direction, but not statistically significant. Major positive changes occurred in the experimental groups in how employees felt about (1) the kind of work they do (job interest, importance, and level of responsibility); (2) their supervisor (his ability to handle people, give recognition, direct their work, and represent them in handling complaints); (3) their progress in the company; and (4) their group's ability to get the job done. The seventeen perceived-change items were designed specifically to measure changes in the areas where we expected the greatest shift in perceptions. Fifteen of these showed that a significantly higher proportion of employees in the experimental than in the control departments felt that change had occurred. More employees in the experimental departments saw changes in (1) how well the supervisors in their department got along together; (2) how often their supervisors held meetings; (3) how effective these meetings were; (4) how much their supervisor understood the way employees looked at and felt about things, etc. These indicate the extent to which the feedback's effectiveness lay in increasing understanding and communication as well as changing supervisory behavior.

Comparisons of the changes among the four experimental departments showed that the three departments which had the two feedback sessions with their employees all showed positive change relative to the control departments. The change which occurred in the fourth was directionally positive, but it was not significantly different from the control departments. In general, the greatest change occurred where the survey results were discussed in both the departmental organizational units *and* the first-line organizational units. The greater the involvement of all members of the organization through their organizational families—the department heads, the first-line supervisors, *and* the employees—the greater the change.

Implications of these findings

The basic elements of this feedback process described above are not new. They involve (1) the orderly collection of information about the functioning of a system, and (2) the reporting of this information into the system for (3) its use in making further adjustments.

Work by Hall [19] and others who have had considerable practical experience with the use of information about a system for creating change show a similarity in both action steps and basic approach. This suggests there are certain psychological and sociological facts which must be taken into consideration in attempting to change

---

[19] Milton Hall, "Supervising People—Closing the Gap Between What We Think and What We Do," *Advanced Management*, Vol. 12 (September, 1947), pp. 129-135.

the attitudes and behavior of an *individual* or a *group of individuals* in an *organizational setting.*

1. Attitudes and behavior of an individual are functions of both basic personality and social role. *Change processes need to be concerned with altering both the forces within* an individual and the forces in the *organizational situation* surrounding the individual.

2. Organizations, as systems of hierarchically ordered, interlocking roles with rights and privileges, reciprocal expectations, and shared frames of reference, contain tremendous forces for stability or change in the behavior of individuals or subgroups. Change processes need to be designed to harness these forces for creating and supporting change. *As forces already in existence, they must first be made pliable, then altered or shifted, and finally made stable again to support the change.*

3. Essentially, unilateral power and authority structures underlie the hierarchical ordering of organizational roles. *Expectations of the superior are therefore more important forces for creating change in an individual than the expectations of his subordinates.* Also, those with a direct authority relationship—line superiors—have more influence than those without direct authority—staff trainers.

4. The attitudes, beliefs, and values of an individual are more firmly grounded in the groups which have continuing psychological meaning to him than in those where he has only temporary membership. The supervisor's role of interlocking the activities of two organizational units requires that he have continuing membership in two groups: (a) the organizational unit directed by his superior in which he is a subordinate along with his immediate peers; and (b) the organizational unit for which he is responsible. *Change processes designed to work with individual supervisors off the job in temporarily created training groups contain less force for initiating and reinforcing change than those which work with an individual in situ.*

5. Information about the functioning of a system may introduce a need for change. This is especially true when the new data are seen as objective and at variance with common perceptions and expectations. Change processes organized around objective, new social facts about one's own organizational situation have more force for change than those organized around general principles about human behavior. *The more meaningful and relevant the material, the greater the likelihood of change.*

6. Involvement and participation in the planning, collection, analysis, and interpretation of information initiate powerful forces for change. Own facts are better understood, more emotionally acceptable, and more likely to be utilized than those of some "outside expert." *Participation in analysis and interpretation helps by-pass those resistances which arise from proceeding too rapidly or too slowly.*

7. Objective information on direction and magnitude of change—knowledge of results—facilitates further improvement. *Change processes which furnish adequate knowledge on progress and specify criteria against which to measure improvement are apt to be more successful in creating and maintaining change than those which do not.*

Comparison of "Classroom" Human Relations Training and Organizational Feedback

This is only a partial listing of the points with which a scientifically based technology of social change in organizational settings will have to be concerned. Our conceptualization and the identification of the relevant individual and organizational variables and their interrelationship is at a primitive stage. The systematic quantitative investigation of the effectiveness of different change procedures has scarcely begun. Even at this early date, however, a comparison between the structure and process of feedback and "classroom" human relations training as two different types of change procedures may be a useful exercise. It may help identify variables or facets of change processes which merit greater experimentation and investigation both by the practitioners and by those researchers interested in organizational change. By a "classroom" human relations program we mean a training which would consist of a series of classroom-like meetings in which supervisors from many different points of the organization meet to listen to a presentation of psychological principles which a trainer from the personnel department thinks they ought to know about and be ready to use on the job after a brief discussion following the training. This kind of training experience differs from the feedback process in a number of respects. These differences are stated to keep the comparisons reasonably brief and to sharpen the contrasts.

1. What are the objectives?

"Classroom" Training—Improve supervisor-subordinate relations through changing the supervisors' understanding of human behavior, attitudes, and skills.

Organizational Feedback—Improve organizational functioning through changing understanding, attitudes, and behavior among all members of the organization.

2. What is the setting in which change is being attempted?

"Classroom" Training—Trainees are taken off the job and out of the network of interpersonal relationships in which they normally function for training in an "encapsulated" [20] classroom-like situation.

Organizational Feedback—Change is attempted as a regular part of the day's work in established organizational relationships.

3. What is the informational content?

"Classroom" Training—General psychological principles of human behavior, case materials, or data from outside the training group and

---

[20] M. Haire, "Some Problems of Industrial Training," *Journal of Social Issues*, Vol. 4, No. 3 (1948), pp. 41-47.

often the organization, only occasionally using problems from the group's own experience.

Organizational Feedback—Objective quantitative information about attitudes, beliefs, and expectations of the trainees themselves, or the subordinates in their own organization.

4. What is the method?

"Classroom" Training—Lectures, presentations, films, skits, and occasionally role-playing followed by discussion on how to apply what has been learned back on the job.

Organizational Feedback—The progressive introduction of new information about the problems within the groups for which the trainees are responsible. Group discussions of the meaning and action implications of the findings, followed by group decisions on next steps for changing or handling the situation.

5. Who are the trainees?

"Classroom" Training—First-line supervisors and foremen whose superiors may have, but more often have not, had the course.

Organizational Feedback—Everyone in the organization from the top down [21]—the president, top management, intermediate and first-line supervision, *and* employees.

6. What is the training unit?

"Classroom" Training—An aggregate or collection of individual supervisors from different departments throughout the organization. A functional conglomerate without continuing psychological meaning for the individuals. Frequently seen as a "group" simply because the individuals are in close spatial proximity to one another.

Organizational Feedback—An organizational unit whose members have an organizational function to perform and whose members (a superior and his immediate subordinates) have continuing psychological meaning perceptually and behaviorally to one another as a team or family.

7. Who is the change agent?

"Classroom" Training—An outsider—an expert, a staff man—who has no direct, continuing authority or power over the trainee and few recurrent opportunities to reinforce the training.

Organizational Feedback—The organizational unit's line supervisor, who is given some help through pre- and post-meeting coaching by the expert outsider.

8. How is the pace or rate of change set?

"Classroom" Training—The trainer sets the pace, attempting to gear the training to average trainee's ability to comprehend and assimilate the material.

Organizational Feedback—The members of the group move from one topic to another as they are ready for the next step.

---

[21] N. R. F. Maier, "A Human Relations Program for Supervision," *Industrial and Labor Relations Review*, I (April, 1948), pp. 443-464.

9. How long does the change process continue?

"Classroom" Training—A fixed number of days or weeks, seldom less than 16 or more than 80 hours.

Organizational Feedback—No fixed length of time, the change procedure usually continues over a period of months—6 to 24 months.

10. How much tension is there?

"Classroom" Training—Usually relatively little, most trainees feel they already know a good deal about human behavior and how others feel.

Organizational Feedback—Frequently considerable, as objective information and particularly the differences between supervisory beliefs and practices come into a focus so sharp that complacency is shattered and the security about what is social reality is shaken.

11. What assumptions are made about attitudes and how they are changed? [22]

"Classroom" Training—The primary assumption is that the trainee does not know certain facts, that his previous organization of relevant information will be altered when he understands the new facts. Attitudes are seen as a function of the range of information available to the trainee; they are changed by altering cognitive structure.

Organizational Feedback—Here the assumptions are that the trainee already has satisfying ways of seeing things and relating to others, that attitudes and behavior can be changed only by altering their motivational bases. Norms of psychologically relevant groups are seen as more important determinants of attitudes than cognitive processes.

12. How is effectiveness of the change measured?

"Classroom" Training—Usually by informal comments of trainees, occasionally by interviews or questionnaires with the trainees after the training.

Organizational Feedback—By changes in employees' perception of their supervisor's behavior.

The differences drawn between these two types of procedures for creating change in an organizational setting may not be as marked as presented here. Human relations training programs do vary tremendously from company to company and from time to time. There is no single pattern. Since we know little about the frequency of different species of human relations training programs, the specific mix of content, method, setting, etc., which we used as the basis of our contrast may no longer be found in organizations. Our comparison aimed to emphasize the extent to which various characteristics of change processes vary on the basic dimension of *motivation for change.*

---

[22] I. Sarnoff and D. Katz, "The Motivational Bases of Attitude Change," *Journal of Abnormal and Social Psychology*, XLIX (January, 1954), pp. 115-124.

Different contents, different methods, different settings, different training units, and different change agents contain different motivational impacts for change. What constitutes the most effective combination for changing behavior in organizations is not known. Few practitioners have really done any bold experimenting; almost none have combined measurement and experimenting to search for the most significant dimensions and variables in change processes. This is an area in which there is a great need for social experimentation and social invention.

In the social sciences, as in the physical sciences, invention plays a crucial role. Inventions in social technology—skills and processes for creating change—and innovations in measurement both contribute speedily to progress in understanding social phenomena. The responsibility of experimenting with different methods of measuring change and with new procedures for investigating the interrelationship of functioning organizational processes rests heavily with the students of social organization. The rate at which knowledge about organization is developed will probably be closely correlated to the rate at which we try new approaches to the study of problems in this area.

QUESTIONS

1. What part are social scientists playing in the process of change? What can social scientists contribute to practitioners in this area?
2. How can change be created and studied? Cite an example.
3. Explain what is meant by "feedback"? Is it a useful process for creating and supporting change? Why?
4. What psychological and sociological facts must be taken into consideration in attempting to change attitudes and behavior?
5. How does the "classroom approach" differ from organizational feedback? Which is best for creating change in an organization?

GENERAL QUESTIONS ON PART VIII

1. What effect does change have on people? Why?
2. Why is resistance to change a problem in industry?
3. Explain the difference between social and technical change. Which has the greatest influence on the human being? Why?
4. How does resistance to change differ from reaction to frustration?
5. Prepare a list of specific changes that affect people.
6. What approach would you follow when a necessary change actually results in disequilibrium in need satisfaction of employees?
7. Discuss the ways in which people resist change. Illustrate with examples from your own experience.

8. Explain how resistance to change is related to leadership and human relations.
9. How would you initiate a change? Show where your approach agrees or differs with the approaches indicated in the articles in this part.
10. Can resistance to change be prevented? Why?

PART IX.   HUMAN RELATIONS SKILLS, SENSITIVITY, AND PRODUCTIVITY

Throughout this book little attention was given to the implementatiton of human relations concepts and principles. Instead, every effort was made to provide for the reader an opportunity to study the fundamental aspects of human relations, such as leadership, motivation, communication, and so on, which are foundational to its practice. The reason for doing this is, of course, obvious: the skill with which any function of the manager's job is practiced is directly correlated with the practitioner's knowledge and understanding of that function.

FUNDAMENTAL ASPECTS OF PRACTICING HUMAN RELATIONS

Although the major purpose of this section is to discuss some of the more concrete aspects of practicing human relations and the results thereof, it is necessary first to give brief consideration to several basic points that have not been discussed in previous sections but that are equally fundamental to the practice of human relations. Perhaps the most important of these points concerns the fact that the successful practice of human relations requires the manager to know and understand the basic needs of people and to do everything in his power to arrange and construct the work environment so that employees can find the means and the opportunity to satisfy their physiological, sociological, and psychological motives. This does not imply, incidentally, that the practice of human relations is solely dependent upon motivation *per se*. On the contrary, it merely indicates that motivation is the core of influencing employee behavior. Practicing human relations successfully still requires the manager to know and understand the impact of organization and change upon people; the importance and influence of communication, counseling, and participation; and the integrating and coordinating nature of leadership. Most important of all, it requires the manager to use his knowledge of these areas to design and modify a work environment that is conducive to need satisfaction.

Another important point upon which rests the successful practice of human relations is that of empathy. Although Robert N. McMurry discusses this subject in detail in a following article, it should be mentioned here that one of the chief reasons why we fail to practice human relations successfully is because we are too easily inclined to assume we know how people think and feel about things. Studies by the score have indicated that what we think about the attitudes and needs of people is altogether too frequently in direct contrast with what people themselves actually say their thoughts and needs are. This is particularly true of the superior-subordinate relationship. Consequently, to think you know what people want or need at any point in time is indeed a dangerous assumption. The only way to practice human relations effectively, therefore, is to know what the attitudes and motives of your employees are. This means you must empathize, that is, put yourself in the shoes of your employees. From a more practical viewpoint, it means you must find out directly from your subordinates what they think and feel about the many facets of their jobs and work environment and then act accordingly.

A third basic point upon which the practice of human relations rests concerns the fact that managers, in addition to knowing and understanding the motives of their subordinates, must be definitively sensitive to their own wants and needs. As Robert Tannenbaum points out in his article, our behavior, and hence the way we practice human relations, is greatly influenced by our own needs. This means, in essence, that what we do to satisfy our own motive forces may be the type of behavior that thwarts the satisfaction of the needs of our subordinates. When this situation arises, the manager, if he wishes to motivate his people effectively, must obviously adjust his actions accordingly. Whether or not he is willing to do this depends, of course, on his ability both to restructure his needs and, when necessary, to subordinate them to the needs of his employees.

A fourth and final fundamental aspect of practicing human relations is concerned with the hierarchical nature of human needs. As the section on motivation pointed out, motivating forces are structured according to their importance to the human being. Obviously, therefore, physiological needs take precedence over all other motives. When these needs are satisfied, other forces, namely, sociological and psychological needs, take precedence. Unless the manager recognizes this, he is apt to commit the common error of assuming that employees are more interested in wages and fringe benefits than they are interested in the more subtle aspects of their working environments. Practicing human relations on this assumption means, of course, that little attention would be paid to such important forces as belonging, acceptance, and so forth, and that consequently employees would not be properly motivated.

Constructing a Proper Work Environment

It is self-evident that if employees are to behave and produce effectively, they must find while working in the organization the means to satisfy their basic needs. This means that the practice of human relations must be directed toward the construction and maintenance of a work environment that is conducive to need satisfaction. Furthermore, it means that managers are responsible for arranging and combining the factors that make up and influence the environment in which an employee works because they, more so than any other people, have control over most of these factors.

Unfortunately, the factors that make up and influence the work environment are legion. They range in nature from personal contact with human beings to inanimate and inarticulate things such as policies, procedures, equipment, and the basic duties and responsibilities inherent in jobs. Even the color of paint and the level of illumination have been proven to exert an effect on human behavior. Because it would be impossible to discuss in this text all the known factors that influence and are a part of the working environment, attention shall be given only to those factors over which managers have the most control and which are most directly related to need satisfaction.

Policy

Undoubtedly the basic starting point in the actual practice of human relations is to formulate, determine, and communicate to all personnel explicit and concise statements of human relations policy. As every student of management knows, policy is a statement of intention, a guide to action that gives course and direction to the carrying out of any function. Because the importance of human relations as a managerial function is neither greater nor less than the importance of other functions in an organization, it should also be based on a strong foundation of policy. If this is not done, the actual practice of human relations, particularly with respect to the design of procedures and other factors that influence human behavior, will be left to the whims and fancies of the managers involved. Quite frequently the result of this is complete inattention to the impact of procedures, techniques, and so forth on the human being. It should be stressed, therefore, that human relations will be practiced uniformly and successfully only when it is the avowed intention of the organization to do so. In other words, the practice of human relations is correlated with—in fact, dependent upon—the strength and the effectiveness of policy statements concerning this basic function.

Recruitment

Seldom recognized by many people is the fact that the practice of human relations commences when a prospective employee comes in contact with the organization for the first time. This indicates that recruitment, which is the function of finding candidates for employment, plays an important role in employee motivation. The nature of the advertisement that is first used to contact him, the treatment he is accorded when he applies for a job at the employment office, the physical condition of the organization—these and many other aspects of this function exert a tremendous impact on behavior. If any of these facets creates doubt about opportunity for need satisfaction, there is a good chance, especially during periods of full employment, that candidates will seek jobs elsewhere. This is why, for example, so many of the recruitment advertisements we see today stress points such as "good supervision," "challenging work," "opportunity for advancement," and so on, in addition to "good wages" and "benefits."

One of the basic reasons why effective recruitment is so important in human relations is because at this point in time the prospective employee knows little if anything about the organization; consequently, a great many unknowns about need satisfaction exist in his mind. What he "sees" in the advertisement, therefore, is basically what he "sees" in the organization. This is particularly true of the treatment he receives at the employment office. If the receptionist he meets is dour and impolite, he will frequently tend to assume that this person is representative of all the employees in the organization and that, consequently, the people he may work with will be equally discourteous. Illogical as this may be, it is a well-known aspect of human behavior.

Selection

Selection is the function of screening candidates for employment and hiring those who are best suited for the jobs to be filled. This function is an important part of the work environment, and hence of human relations, for two reasons. First of all, like recruitment, the treatment the candidate receives while being screened by interviews, tests, and physical examinations exerts a tremendous influence on his behavior. If he is treated curtly or bombarded with examinations that confuse and frighten him, there will arise within him doubt concerning many of his basic needs.

A second fundamental reason why the selection function is important to the practice of human relations is that it is the point in time when an employee is matched to a job. If care is not given to equate a person's knowledge, skill, and ability with those demanded by the job, there is danger that many motivating forces will go unsatisfied. For example, if an individual is placed on a job for which he is neither presently nor potentially qualified, he is likely to become frustrated when his behavior fails to achieve a level of performance that is necessary for pay raises, promotions, and so on. On the other hand, an individual who is placed on a job for which he is over-qualified frequently fails to achieve a sense of accomplishment and, as a consequence, finds many of his basic needs, especially psychological motives, going unsatisfied. The only solution to this important problem is to screen definitively all candidates for employment and to hire only those whose talents meet the requirements of the job. This means, of course, that managers must in the first place know what the various jobs demand of people. In other words, it means that all jobs must be analyzed and that accurate and complete job descriptions and job specifications must be written and used.

Guided adjustment to the work environment

The moment an individual becomes an employee of an organization, he faces a process of adjustment that is extremely critical to his behavior on the job. He must, for example, adjust himself to the people with whom he will work and adapt himself to myriad policies and rules. If this period of adjustment is facilitated so that he successfully conditions himself to his new work environment, there is every reason to expect that he will become a properly motivated employee. If, however, managers pay little attention to this critical aspect of employment, there is every reason to expect that the new employee will encounter many situations that are not conducive to need satisfaction.

Induction, the process of facilitating adjustment to a new work environment, therefore becomes an extremely important function of management. New employees must be properly introduced to their jobs and their fellow employees. They must be acquainted with policies and procedures that affect the work they do and the level of performance expected of them. They must be shown where their job fits into the whole and what is expected of them in terms of quantity and quality of production. They must, in effect, be given all the information they need to know and want to know to perform their jobs effectively. Unless these things are done, they will not feel that they are members of the organization and, consequently, will experience dissatisfaction in needs like acceptance and belonging. Furthermore, lacking the information they need for successful performance, they will soon discover that it is extremely difficult, if not impossible, to behave on the job in the manner necessary for need satisfaction.

Training and development

There are at least two reasons why there is no such thing as an employee, whether he be the chief executive or the janitor, who needs no training or development. In the first place, learning is a continuous process. Because training is the direction of learning, it must also be continuous, especially if we want people to learn things properly and efficiently. In the second place, within every organization there are constantly occurring situations that demand training of some type or kind. New employees must be acquainted with duties, responsibilities, and job methods. Present employees must be introduced to new techniques, processes, and equipment. Junior executives must be groomed for higher-level responsibilities. And so on.

Although training is obviously necessary for organizational efficiency, it is also equally necessary for successful human relations. There are several reasons why this is true. First of all, proper training, in conjunction with good recruitment and selection, should result in employees who are better able to perform their duties and responsibilities. This means, in essence, that people will have the ability to perform at a level necessary to obtain recognition, acceptance, achievement, status, and so forth. Secondly, proper training can facilitate goal achievement on the part of employees. Many people, for example, have the potential to work at higher levels in an organization. This potential usually results in a desire to attain these higher levels for various reasons. To achieve these responsibilities, however, requires that potential be developed by proper training and experience. In other words, potential must be converted into capability. If this is done successfully, then there is reason to expect that people will be better equipped to achieve their higher goals. If it is not done, that is, if training is not keyed to the development of potential, then employees will find it impossible to achieve the objectives they have set for themselves. The result, of course, as Part IV pointed out, will be frustration and undesirable behavior.

Employee appraisal

Most employees prefer to know where they "stand" in an organization. They want to know if they are performing at a level necessary for wage increases and promotions. They want to know their strengths and weaknesses, particularly the latter, so that they can direct their energies toward improving themselves. Most important of all, they want to know that their superiors are aware of their capabilities, potential, and performance, and that they are being measured by a consistent, uniform, and fair set of standards.

Organizations that have not established a formal employee appraisal system cannot guarantee these things to their employees. They cannot, for example, base promotions on a foundation of ability. They cannot consistently grant wage increases on a basis of merit. They cannot, in any way possible, guarantee that superiors will be aware of the true worth of their subordinates. Most important of all, they cannot practice human relations successfully. Only when managers are definitely and accurately aware of employee performance can they possibly influence the behavior of their employees in an effective manner. Until an efficient rating system is established, therefore, it can be expected that people will not be able to achieve the degree of satisfaction they desire for needs such as recognition, achievement, security, fairness, and so on.

Promotions and career mobility

Although the subject of promotions has been alluded to several times in this section, it should be pointed out again that most employees have as basic needs the opportunity for advancement and achievement for physiological, sociological, or psychological reasons. Because of this, a great deal of their behavior will be directed toward getting "ahead" in the organization. Although it has been stated that behavior of this type can be induced and facilitated by effective rating systems and training, it must be recognized that an equally important requirement is a sound systematic promotion program.

Systematic promotion refers to the fact that lines of relationship have been established between jobs. Based on accurate job descriptions and job specifications, these lines indicate which jobs lead to other responsibilities and what skills and knowledges are needed to be promoted. They in no way, it should be noted, guarantee that employees will automatically be moved in accordance with their direction. But they do point out with emphasis that management has established a promotion system based on need and ability, rather than on whim and bias. When joined with proper training and employee rating, such a system has obvious human relations implications.

With the swelling ranks of managers and administrators in the organizational society of today, career mobility and advancement opportunities within the working organization become increasingly important. Studies of managerial motivation, such as Herzberg's in Part IV, find that managers place great stress on career development and advancement. Unless management policy allows for advancement and personal growth generated by advancement, too many managers either become "shelf sitters" with arrested careers or seek opportunity with other companies. Productivity of both individual and organization will suffer in this stilted climate. Increasingly, enlightened managements are beginning to see the need for handling their managers as true professionals, therefore allowing them to "practice" their managerial skills for career enhancement as managers and not simply as technicians or paper handlers.

Employee compensation

It was pointed out earlier in this section that too many managers give too much thought and attention to the monetary aspects of the work environment. Basically, the major reason for this is failure to recognize the hierarchical nature of human needs. As a consequence, these people overemphasize the quantitative aspects of employee compensation.

Unfortunately, the number of dollars *per se* an employee receives for his services is not the only facet of compensation that is important to him. What is frequently more important is the relationship of his wage to the wage another individual receives for the same or a different job. If, for example, another employee is receiving more for the same work, and factors such as experience, length of service, and merit do not account for this difference, then imbalance in need satisfaction occurs. This same result occurs when a person on a less difficult job is paid more than an individual who is working on a more difficult job.

Another aspect of compensation that is extremely and fundamentally important to the individual concerns the relationship of his pay to his contribution on the job. If he feels, rightly or wrongly, that he is underpaid for his services, a decrease in satisfaction of needs will obviously result. The effect of this is frequently a reduction in performance.

Perhaps most important is a recognition as to *why* money does motivate people. Often, management fails to realize that money is seldom an end in itself. Since it cannot be eaten or driven or lived in, there must be more to the dollar than sheer possession. Although the strength of money motivation varies among individuals, it is for many a *symbol*—a symbol of accomplishment, of attainment. Equally important, it serves as a *substitute* for other needs perhaps frustrated in the work place. A continual badgering of management by employees for more and more salary increases should serve as a warning to the former that quite possibly other than economic needs are lacking among the dissident employees. All in all, money appears to serve as a badge for some, a replacement for others. It is also a nebulous factor that needs far more research to be understood in the motivational schema of things.

Supervision: quality and style

Although the subject of supervision was discussed in the section on leadership, because every supervisor is a leader, it must be noted here that managers are responsible for the selection of supervisory personnel. Because we know today that the major responsibility of a supervisor is to lead people, that is, to get work done through subordinates, every effort must be made to employ leaders who are skilled in motivation and other basic aspects of human relations. This means, consequently, that the age of promoting the best worker, technician, or specialist to a supervisory position has long since disappeared. The effective motivation of employee behavior requires leadership ability, not technical skill. Although technical ability may be an important requirement of some supervisory jobs, it is certainly in no way correlated with leadership skill. The selection of supervisors, that is, the hiring of people who must successfully practice human relations, must therefore be based on a sound recruitment and screening program. It must also to a great extent be based on proper training and development for effectively motivating their subordinates.

Job design and technology

It would be impossible to discuss here the nature of the various duties and responsibilities that people have in business and industry.

Yet it is extremely important for managers to recognize that the work people do greatly affects and influences employee behavior. At one extreme, for example, people can obtain a great deal of satisfaction, such as status, prestige, achievement, and so forth, in the work they do. At the other extreme, jobs can make people become bored, listless, apathetic, and indifferent. This latter point is particularly true of the thousands of routine, menial, tedious tasks that exist in many organizations today. Robert Guest's article explores this in detail.

Although it is undoubtedly impossible to design jobs that are challenging and interesting to all employees who must perform the tasks involved, there are several things managers can do to make the work more satisfying. In the first place, greater attention can be given to the selection of individuals who must work on these so-called nonchallenging jobs. This means that, in addition to considering the knowledge and skill needed for the job in question, attention must also be given to the level of mental ability and the type of personality that the job requires. By doing this, a much better matching of job and employee will occur.

Among other things managers can do to make jobs more interesting and challenging to people is to offer them opportunity for a change in their routine. For example, instead of having them do the same thing over and over, their duties and responsibilities can be rotated periodically so that, for a time at least, boredom and monotony can be alleviated. This technique is, in fact, almost a necessity for motivating junior managers who are destined for future high-level responsibilities. It is extremely difficult to keep motivated, indeed at times to keep employed, future executives who for the time being must be kept employed at tasks that do not challenge their abilities.

MANAGERIAL SENSITIVITY, HUMAN RELATIONS SKILLS, AND ORGANIZATIONAL GROWTH AND PRODUCTIVITY

The articles by Argyris and This and Lippitt stress the need for educating and training managers, who are responsible for leading others, in terms of increased self-awareness and understanding of their own behavior as well as that of others. In short, the motivations and behavior of others cannot be understood until one comprehends the reasons behind his own behavior.

This type of training in interpersonal dynamics is popularly referred to as sensitivity training. Its goal, of course, is to assist managers in understanding their impact on others, in knowing how their feelings affect their behavior towards others, and in becoming more sensitive to ways people communicate with one another—all adding up to improved interpersonal competence and organizational performance. It is carried out by essentially unstructured training groups, composed of participants who are practicing managers and who become actively involved in observing one another in somewhat stressful discussion and problem-solving situations. Open, free and frank discussion of personal motivations, attitudes, and values is encouraged in a "laboratory" type situation.

Although sensitivity training has been criticized as much as it has been praised, it has been on the rise in the past few years, with more and more managers undergoing laboratory experience. There are undoubtedly shortcomings in sensivity training; but if as a result of such training managers gain an increased awareness of self and of others, it would seem to be a useful technique for improving managerial competence.

Perhaps the crucial issue centers around the definite need for better interpersonal relationships in organizations to enhance productive work efforts. If, as much behavioral research suggests, the manager is the primary agent influencing productivity in the work place, then well-designed developmental efforts of all types would appear appropriate in assisting managers in achieving higher levels of professional competence in directing the work of others. Certainly, heightened awareness of self and sensitivity to others, whether labeled as human relations skills or not, cannot help but result in personal improvement and growth which, in turn, result in organizational growth and productivity. The ultimate aim of any such development is for both personal and organizational benefit and improvement. If individual productivity is increased, so also is organizational productivity to the mutual benefit of all concerned.

43. EMPATHY: MANAGEMENT'S GREATEST NEED *

Robert N. McMurry

From time to time George French has wondered why he is so manifestly and inescapably unpopular. He cannot understand it. He has always tried to do the right thing. In fact, he has often gone out of his way to be helpful.

As a department head with the Booth Manufacturing Company, he has regarded it as his duty to help his subordinates to improve themselves in every way. As a result he has always made it his practice periodically to counsel with them and point out their shortcomings to them. That they have not always been wholly receptive to his constructive criticisms is one of the crosses he has had to reconcile himself to bear. Nevertheless, in spite of this, he still feels it is his duty to help them in this way.

His father, whom he has always greatly admired and tried to emulate, had always told him that one of his greatest obligations in life was to help his fellow man. In consequence, he has persevered, even though his subordinates have not only frequently failed to follow his advice, but some have gone so far as to nickname him the "Broadaxe of Dept. 126."

All his life he has dedicated himself to doing his duty, however painful though it might be. Early in his life his father gave him a set of maxims which he has tried to follow faithfully, regardless of how strongly he might be tempted to swerve from the path of duty. These maxims are:

1. Always respect your superiors (they have had more experience and know their jobs or they would not be in them).

2. Always follow instructions as given (there is a good reason for every rule).

3. Always be honest and forthright in your dealings with others (while some may not like it, they will respect you for it).

4. Always put the interests of your employer before your own (this is one of the best ways to make progress on your job).

5. Always try to help others, even though they may not be appreciative of it.

* From *Advanced Management*, Vol. 18, No. 7 (July, 1953), pp. 6-11, 34. Reprinted with permission.

It has not always been easy for George to follow his father's admonitions. Some of his decisions have been hard for him to make. There was, for example, the case of old Pete Rogers. Pete had been with the company for 35 years. When it came time for him to retire, a review of his personnel file revealed that, due to a clerical error, he had never been officially listed as an employee with the insurance company which administered the retirement trust.

In consequence, technically Pete was not eligible for a pension. George had tried to explain to Pete that while it *was* unfortunate, mishaps of this character did occur and that there was nothing that he could do to help him. When Pete protested, he had even shown him the contract with the insurance company which stated explicitly the conditions under which employees were eligible for a pension, and had explained why he was ineligible. He hadn't liked to deal with such situations, but a rule is a rule.

Then there was the case of Molly Stevenson. Molly was a clerk in his department handling the first step in processing orders received from customers. With the help of the company's methods expert, he had worked out performance standards for each clerk's activities. In this way he knew exactly what each girl should be expected to produce.

Molly had originally been one of his best and most faithful performers. Her work was accurate, and she spent little time in the washroom or in idle talk with the other girls. But over a period of time, her work had begun to deteriorate both in quantity and quality. He had spoken to her about it on several occasions. Each time she had promised to improve and for a short time she had. Later, she had slipped back, each time a little further.

In the meantime, he had heard that Molly's widowed mother, of whom she was the sole support, was suffering from cancer and that Molly was attempting to care for her at night to save the cost of a nurse. He suspected that this might be the reason her work was suffering. Hence, when he next talked to Molly he had told her that she would have to find someone to care for her mother at night because it was affecting her work.

Molly burst into tears and said she would try but she didn't know whether she could because doctor bills were already taking everything she earned. He had said that he understood, but that she must remember that her work must come first if she expected to stay in his department. She promised that she would try and for a while did show some improvement.

Ultimately, however, her performance had shown a further retrogression and it had been necessary for him to call her in and release her. He had explained and she agreed that he had given her fair and ample warning. He had hated to do this, but his conscience was clear. She had been unable to meet the department's production standard; she had been warned; she had to be replaced.

Persons like George are not intentionally cruel. They are not overt sadists; they derive no immediate personal satisfaction from making others unhappy. They are, of course, pleased with the *power* they have over others. If the exercise of this power results in suffering, they may even feel a momentary pang of regret that it is they who have been chosen as the instruments through whom circumstances or a higher authority have chosen to act. Such experiences are unpleasant, they admit, but they are all part of the day's task. They constitute one of the less pleasant aspects of the supervisor's work.

In short, such persons are neither vicious nor vindictive; they are simply incapable of *empathy*, of emotional resonance, of the capacity to put themselves in the place of another and respond as he does. In simple terms, *they are completely and totally insensible to the needs or feelings of others.* They have no insight into or real interest in people.

They regard people in the same casual, detached impersonal manner that they think of inanimate objects or animals. If a pair of shoes wears out, they are discarded; if a pet develops distemper, he is destroyed; if an employee ceases to be productive, he is taken off the payroll. It is this quality of complete conscienceless unconcern for others which reaches its apex, its finest flowering, in the ruthless dictator, e.g., Stalin; in the "torpedo" (the professional killer); or in the master of a mass extermination establishment such as Buchenwald.

Most individuals who lack empathy are not inhuman in a calculated manner; they are simply persons who find it difficult or impossible to form attachments to people. They cannot make even minimal emotional investments in others. Their capacity for affection, even interest in anyone outside of themselves, is usually quite limited.

What little warmth and love they have is jealously hoarded within their own egos and is lavished almost exclusively on themselves. Such persons are frequently not unfriendly; they may even be quite affable, especially with superiors and associates. Often they are very public-spirited and generous, but always in a rather impersonal manner.

Hereditary or environmental?

No one knows precisely why some individuals have a marked capacity for empathy, some less, and some practically none at all. It is probable that constitutional (inherited) factors may have a part to play. It is more likely, however, that early environmental factors have a vital influence in determining the degree of empathy of which a person may be capable.

Where the child has been reared in a cold, loveless, rigid, and overdemanding environment or one in which he has known little emotional security (his parents may have given him material benefits but little or uncertain affection), he may have feared to invest love or even interest in others for fear that it would not be reciprocated. Living always under the threat of emotional rejection by those from whom he seeks support and love, he dares not risk permitting himself to become too closely attached to others. They might (and perhaps have done so) reject his timid advances. In such instances, it is safer to hoard one's love within oneself.

People vs. things

Under such circumstances, it is natural for an individual to turn his field of interest from people to *things*. Things are not expected to be a source of love; therefore, they cannot reject and hurt. *They are emotionally safe.* In addition, in a scientific age such as the present, things can be both fascinating and challenging. In consequence, they have tremendous appeal to many, particularly those who are especially sensitive to rejection.

Also in the American society of today, a preoccupation with *things* is highly acceptable socially. This is the "scientific age," and science, until very recently, has concentrated its activities almost exclusively on *things* rather than on people. It is not surprising, therefore, that business and industry with their emphasis on production, research, accounting, engineering, and finance have had unusual appeal to "thing-minded" persons.

Even sales work, which presumes to deal with people, has been largely mechanized through the introduction of research designed to determine the best means of exploiting the public wants and needs through advertising and other standardized marketing techniques.

In consequence, business and industry probably have a higher concentration of predominantly thing-minded persons than do many of the professions, e.g., medicine, the church, and the arts. And from a purely materialistic point of view this is probably advantageous.

A single-minded concentration on *things* by management with less regard for humanitarian considerations has probably contributed largely to the industrial development of this country. It has doubtless resulted in a vast contribution to the national product and the tremendous improvement in the American standard of living which has accompanied it. Whether this growth and increase in efficiency has also sometimes been at the cost of human well-being is a debatable question.

Certainly many of the frictions and conflicts which now plague business and industry may be attributed to the extent to which business management today is permeated with George Frenches— dynamic, efficient, loyal, and creative administrators who are also largely or totally insensitive to the needs, problems, and anxieties of the people with whom they work and whom they supervise.

The union as defender

Probably the best evidence of the acuteness of this problem is to be seen in the rapidity of the growth of the labor movement, once the social and legal shackles were removed from it. There are many conditions which influence workers' decisions to join unions. But one of the chief of these is the feeling on their part that management's points of view and attitudes lack an understanding for and appreciation of employee needs and problems. This, they recognize, is due in part to failures of intra-company communication—management is literally ignorant of much that affects its people. But even when improved communication techniques have been introduced so that management is adequately informed, it is still often reluctant to take what the employees regard as needed action. Hence, many feel that they need a union as a defense against management's ignorance, indifference, or intransigence.

It is not that most workers distrust management's basic motives: The old stereotype of the capitalist as a hard-eyed, blood-sucking leech, mercilessly exploiting the helpless proletariat, has been relegated chiefly to Communist propaganda circles. Most employees are sufficiently sophisticated to know that top and middle management is composed of hired hands whose positions are fundamentally no different from theirs, except that the pressures are greater.

What they resent is management's blithe assumption that it already knows, on an *a priori* basis, what its subordinates need and how their problems should be handled. Too many management policies reflect either a complete ignorance of what is actually transpiring at the worker level or a total disregard for employee sensibilities and needs.

Typical of this latter type of thinking was that shown by the manager of an eighty-year-old plant which was being closed because it was no longer competitive. He told his employees, many of whom had over 30 years' service, that he would give separation allowances *only to those who were too old and feeble to obtain employment elsewhere.*

This manager was not deliberately and willfully attempting to be cruel. He was simply shortsighted. By excluding all but those who were manifestly incapable of other employment, he (by profession an engineer) estimated that he could save his employers approximately $30,000.

It never occurred to him to consider what $200 or $300 would mean to an aging employee who had given the best years of his life to the company. This was because *he was completely without empathy.* He lacked entirely the capacity to put himself in his people's shoes. He was a rational automaton to whom people are merely ciphers and are to be treated as such.

It is largely because industry has more than its quota of such executives that the unions have had such a rapid growth and continue to have the support of their members. The union, after all, constitutes their sole defense against such management.

The schism in attitudes

More immediately, however, this lack of empathy by supervisors and executives at every level is productive of many misunderstandings and conflicts in the course of day-to-day operations. These arise out of what may be termed "conflicts of attitudes."

An example may be seen in the difference between management and union attitudes toward incentive compensation based upon time studies. Management considers such incentives to be quite legitimate, even somewhat generous, since they enable the employee to share in the rewards of any additional effort which he expends. The unions, on the other hand, as well as many employees, regard them as instruments for the "speed-up," the conscienceless exploitation of the worker through appeals to his avarice.

Here may be seen the same technique of management as looked at from two violently opposed points of view: Those of management and labor. The attitudes of management are enthusiastic; that of labor is bitterly in opposition. Furthermore, neither has either sympathy or understanding for the other's point of view. Nor is either desirous of learning to understand the bases for the other's attitudes. Each group is monolithic in its opposition to the viewpoint of the other.

Furthermore, this conflict is based on no coldly rational difference of interpretation of the evidence; it is highly toned emotionally. Feelings run riot on both sides. Arguments pro and con are vigorously impassioned; factual evidence gives way to elaborate rationalizations; the level of discourse ascends higher and higher on the ladder of abstraction.

As the contestants become farther and farther removed from reality in their discussions, the higher and shriller becomes the emotional tone of their arguments. Ultimately, an impasse is reached. The parties to the conflict are so far apart that there is no hope for its resolution. The outcome is an uneasy state of armed truce. The net result is that time study rates become in themselves a symbol of management-labor conflict. Obviously, this does not enhance their effectiveness as incentives. (On the average, 70% of union grievances center on time study rates.)

This illustrates the fact that a lack of sympathy for others' points of view is not confined to supervisors and company executives. It is equally common among rank-and-file workers and their union representatives. Neither they nor members of management are able successfully to place themselves in the positions of those with whom they are in disagreement or are even desirous of attempting to do so.

In short, the cause of much industrial strife is to be found less in the specific practices and policies at issue and more in the *attitudes* of their protagonists and opponents toward them. It is not *the thing in itself* which is significant but the *feelings* which are associated with it. It is they which cause and perpetuate the difficulty. Therefore, if the conflict is to be resolved, the first step is to change the parties' attitudes toward the matter at issue.

Changing antagonistic attitudes

Superficially, this appears to be easy. It would seem to be only a matter of the clarification of misunderstandings. Given all of the facts it should not appear to be difficult for both parties to see the logic of the situation and reach an agreement. This would be true if both could observe the identical facts from the same perspective, i.e., objectively and without bias. This, unfortunately, is where the difficulty arises.

No one can ever be entirely objective about anything: He is always to some degree the prisoner of his preconceptions. In short, he has an *attitude* toward every issue with which he comes into contact. Further, each attitude has some (usually considerable) emotional toning or coloring. In other words, everyone is likely to feel at least reasonably strongly on nearly every issue toward which he has a well-established attitude.

If these feelings were strictly rational, they might be amenable to influence by logic. Unfortunately, they are not. Two factors influence them. The first of these is the *displacement of affect.* By this is meant the extent to which attitudes which are generated by one set of circumstances and which may well have been appropriate and justified are shifted or "displaced" on to other quite foreign and often inappropriate objects.

A common example is the young man who (entirely unconsciously) displaces his hostilities toward his father onto his foreman. The father may have been an unconscionable autocrat, the foreman a mild, ineffective, and well-intentioned nonentity, but both are "authority figures." The young man's resentments toward authority, as embodied in his father, can easily, and frequently do, displace onto the foreman. This is not because the foreman is arbitrary or demanding. It is simply because he, like the father, symbolizes authority. (This, incidentally, explains why so many young people are drawn to Communism which purports to be dedicated to the destruction of intrenched authority.)

The second factor influencing feelings is the extent to which these attitudes are the products of deep-seated needs (many of which are not socially acceptable), hostilities, and anxieties. The high emotional toning which many of them carry likewise gives them a somewhat irrational quality. This is because their roots extend far back into the individual's infancy, and they have retained many of the prelogical characteristics of the child's thinking. They have been formed and colored by early environmental and subsequent cultural influences.

Among these influences are such factors as the individual's cultural heritage, economic level, occupational status, education, character of associates, political beliefs, and specific experiences on the job (relations with supervision, the union, etc.). Of particular significance also are the characteristics of the persons with whom he has identified himself in the course of his development. (If the ideal he strove to emulate was John D. Rockefeller, he would have radically different attitudes toward management than would be the case had John L. Lewis been his hero.)

The menace of inflexibility

Because the roots of most of everyone's attitudes are deeply buried in his past, their sources, even their very existence, are almost entirely unknown to him. Furthermore, because of their long standing they are also practically immutable. They have become firmly embedded in his personality. The holder will, in consequence, defend them literally to the death. He does not know he acquired them; he is not even too greatly concerned about their consistency or logic. He is convinced of one thing only: *What he believes is right.* Such mental sets as these are encountered frequently in the field of politics, e.g., the unreconstructed Democrat who still votes as his pappy did and whose motto is: "Right or wrong, I'll always be a Democrat." Unfortunately, such firmly held attitudes are not confined to politics; they are equally common in the field of labor-management relations.

As a result, neither workers nor their union representatives nor members of management can approach most of the issues on which conflict exists objectively and with an open mind. Each has his own particular constellation of attitudes on every topic. Furthermore, each is not only convinced that his attitudes are the only right ones, but that any opinions which differ from his are *irrevocably and indisputably wrong.* This makes agreement almost completely impossible.

Since neither party to the dispute actually has much solid, factual ground for his opinions (he is probably discussing the "interpretation" of the facts at issue), he is more likely chiefly to be expressing his *attitudes.* Hence, it is obvious that any meeting of the minds will be difficult to bring about. Not only will each party to the dispute find it difficult to place himself in the position of the other, but assuming that one or the other tries, he will still have difficulty in accepting the viewpoint of his opponent.

Thus, the major problem facing industry, if it is to enjoy labor peace and benefits of good employee morale, is a twofold one: First, it must stimulate a higher degree of empathy in its supervisors and executives to improve their immediate handling of their interpersonal relationships. Secondly, it must arouse management to a clearer awareness of the part that *its own* attitudes play in clouding and biasing its analysis of the labor relations problems with which it is faced.

Management initiative

Most important, it must recognize that *the initiative for improvement in this area must come principally from management itself,* first, because empathy is one of the prime requisites for success as a supervisor or executive and secondly, because neither the mass of the workers nor their union representatives, generally, have any reason to be aware that there may be an element of illogic in their attitudes and beliefs.

The unions, being part of a "movement," rarely question the essential rightness of their goals and the means employed to gain them. The majority of the workers and their representatives are still comfortably but implacably convinced that *their* viewpoints are invariably the only correct ones. Hence, they cannot be expected to see any need to question the soundness of their beliefs, much less take the initiative to change them in any way or to recognize that the employer's position may have any merit whatever.

Even within a presumably enlightened management group, the difficulties of stimulating a greater degree of empathy will be great. To begin with, if a supervisor's or executive's insensitivity to the feelings and needs of others is actually symptomatic of a deep-lying personality deformation, of a basic incapacity to invest affection in others, no amount of training or admonition will be of much help. Such persons must be recognized as inherently incapable of empathy. Situations such as this must be faced realistically. A George French can never be given much empathic insight.

On the other hand, if supervisors such as he are recognized as empathic cripples, their capacity for harm can be minimized. As far as possible, they can be taken out of line, administrative positions and given staff responsibilities. There they will have little contact with people, but can concentrate all of their efforts on *things* (production, engineering, accounting, etc.). If it is impossible to relieve them of administrative responsibilities, their personnel activities can be audited periodically by contacts with their subordinates (using exit interviews, follow-up interviews, counseling sessions, and periodic opinion polls) to discover, correct, and forestall their more egregious blunders in the field of human relations.

Where there *is* demonstrated capacity for empathy among them, much can be accomplished to make middle and top management aware of its nature, the need for it, and what it can accomplish in bettering human relationships. At the same time, it is essential that a recognition be given top and middle management of the magnitude of the differences which may exist between their beliefs and attitudes on various aspects of company operations and those of lower level supervision and the rank-and-file employees.

Since the nature and range of these differences are frequently unknown to both parties, it is desirable to bring them to management's attention. This will often eliminate sources of misunderstanding and friction and at the same time illustrate, often dramatically, the variety and character of existing differences in attitudes between groups.

Both of these objectives can be attained by conducting a study designed to measure objectively and quantitatively the nature and extent of empathic differences at varying levels in a business organization. Either as a part of an employee opinion poll or independent of it, a series of identical attitude questions are asked of members of top and middle management and of hourly rated employees.

Typical of such questions is the following: "Do you believe that the Taft-Hartley Law is a 'slave labor act'?" Each respondent is asked to give a categorical "yes" or "no" answer to indicate his personal opinion relative to the issue. Following this, he is asked to indicate what answer ("yes" or "no") a majority of his associates and peers will give to the same question. Next (if he is a member of top management) he is asked to state how a majority of the members of his middle management (supervisory) and hourly-rated employees will respond. Members of middle management are asked to indicate how they believe top management and the rank-and-file employees will answer, as well as to state their own opinions. The hourly-rated group is asked to report similarly on middle and top management as well as on themselves.

Assessing the differences

When these responses are tallied it becomes possible to measure the extent to which:

1. Absolute differences in attitude toward each issue exist among the three groups.

2. Members of each group understand (are empathic to) the attitudes of:

a. Their own (their peer) group.

b. Groups ranking above and below them in the organization.[1]

[1] For a discussion of the problem and the potentialities of this technique, see H. A. Rammers, "A Quantitative Index of Social-Psychological Empathy," *American Journal of Orthopsychiatry*, 520, 1950, pp. 161-5, and A. M. Anikeeff, "Reciprocal Empathy: Mutual Understanding Among Conflict Groups," *Purdue University Studies of Higher Education*, 77, 1951, pp. 1-48.

It is often a shock to members of the various groups, particularly those in top management, to discover the magnitude of existing differences in attitudes at the various levels. They are frequently even more seriously disturbed to learn the degree of their own errors in estimating the attitudes of the members of other groups. Findings of this character, as indicated, present graphically and dramatically the range of the differences in opinion existing among employees of different levels in the enterprise and the frequent lack of insight into the attitudes of others by various management and worker groups. These findings can then serve as a basis both for training top and middle management in the nature and importance of empathy and for highlighting significant differences in attitudes among employee groups. Once these distinctions have been established, management can take constructive steps to discover the reasons for them and to minimize their effects.

Empathy is a critical factor in a wide variety of activities. The physician with a fine "beside manner" is merely an individual with a strong inherent "feel" for his patients' needs, problems, and anxieties. He senses them largely by intuition, but, as a result, is able to respond to them with keener insight and hence greater effectiveness than does his colleague to whom his patients' complaints represent merely a formal catalogue of symptoms.

Most truly successful salesmen are empathic to a high degree. While they are rarely aware of the part empathy plays in their effectiveness, its contribution is a major one. It enables them intuitively to sense the prospects' true (as distinct from *stated*) needs. They then direct their sales presentations to showing how their products satisfy these more basic needs. In short, they have a resonance, a sensitivity, to the prospects' emotional as well as rational needs and respond predominantly to the former.

They then use logical appeals only to *rationalize* (justify on logical grounds) the use of their products to gratify needs which are never even made articulate but which the salesman can sense empathically. Such persons are invariably more successful than those who, being incapable of empathy, must rely wholly on purely logical appeals directed at obvious needs.

Element of leadership

All really successful leaders, including every dictator, have great empathic sensitivity. The essence of leadership of the masses is the development of an intuitive awareness of what they need and want.

As most groups of this type are notoriously inarticulate, the leader must sense their needs instinctively, i.e., by empathy. He does this by placing himself in their positions and thinking what he himself would want under those conditions.

Knowing their needs, he can then chart a course designed to give them what they want and also justify his program. He may claim authorship for his plan himself, but the true roots of the appeal of his program are to be found in his *empathic awareness of what the group wants*. He insures that his followers will respond to his commands because in so doing, *they are actually only doing what he has sensed they have wanted to do anyway.*

This was the secret of Hitler's power over the German masses: Being of lower middle class background himself, he knew what they needed and wanted. He simply promised that if they followed him they would have what they wanted. The secret of his success lay in the fact that he was *emotionally in tune* with his followers. In consequence, whatever he demanded of them was what they desired to do anyway, regardless of its illogic, its nature, or its consequences.

Because of the tremendous power of this intuitive type of leadership and the great, albeit ordinarily unrecognized, cost of the failure of management and supervision to see others' problems from their points of view, the need for empathy must be of constant concern to management at all levels. Top management must look at itself objectively and appraise its own capacity for empathy.

In evaluating the competence of members of middle management, the ability to understand and respond to the needs and problems of others must be given a weight equal to that given to technical skills and productivity. Great reluctance must be shown to promote anyone to an administrative or supervisory position who has demonstrated an appreciable incapacity for empathy. Regardless of his other qualifications, if he is an empathic cripple, he will experience difficulty in handling people. He can never be truly effective as a leader without some ability to sense his subordinates' needs and problems. He can function only as a dictator in a completely regimented, authoritarian autocracy.

But as all totalitarian regimes have discovered to their sorrow, slave labor is rarely efficient and productive. *Participation* by subordinates is vital if their creativity and effort is to be maximized. But participation is impossible in an autocracy, particularly where the supervisor is incapable of empathy. If participation is to be encouraged, the leader must be capable of establishing and maintaining rapport with his subordinates. This he cannot do if he has no capacity for empathy. Therefore, empathic sensitivity is vital to effective leadership at all levels. Without it, no supervisor or executive can get the most from his people.

Even more vital is the role of empathy in resolving the conflicts which arise from differences in *attitudes* toward specific issues on company practices. If management representatives are incapable of empathy, it will be natural for them to assume that there is no question concerning the essential rightness of *their* positions on every issue. In short, they will be completely intolerant of the opinions and positions of their subordinates and the latters' union representatives.

Because a lack of empathy for management's viewpoint is also to be expected on the part of these employee and union groups, the result can rarely be other than a continuing and bitter deadlock. Often the consequences of such conflicts are both costly and distressing, taking as they do the form of slowdowns, work stoppages, limitations of output, theft, insubordination, abuse of equipment, and generally substandard morale.

A reasonable approach

Granting that management personnel has at least some empathic sensitivity, its reaction to a conflict situation will be to attempt to be reasonable. When confronted with a conflict of attitudes as in the case of time studied incentive rates or promotions on merit rather than on seniority, it will not immediately adopt a two-valued orientation, i.e., assume that everything is absolutely right or absolutely wrong and that it has a monopoly on being in the right. It will grant that not everything is completely black or white; there may be some grays. It will further admit that it may be at least partly in the wrong. Most important, it will seek to ascertain not only what the employees and their union representatives believe and want, *but why they have these particular opinions and make these demands.*

Furthermore, its approach to such conflicts will not be doctrinaire. It will honestly seek the truth; it will not be looking solely for substantiation of its firmly held convictions. Such management really wants to learn the facts, even though they may perhaps be personally embarrassing and may pose difficult problems. In short, this type of top management may discover that its people actually have compelling and valid reasons for their beliefs and for making their demands. It can also discover that many of its own cherished opinions are not only incorrect, but are positively harmful.

It's up to management

The key to the resolution of these attitudinal conflicts lies, therefore, in the ability and willingness of those who determine company policy to try objectively and without passion to see both sides of the problems which face them. And, as already indicated, the *initiative must come from management.* Only management is in a position to correct many of the conditions which create or exacerbate employee ill-will and feed the fires of their hostility toward itself and what it stands for.

This, in turn, presupposes that relatively clear channels of communication exist between top company executives and the workers. The most empathic executive in the world is not going to be able to put himself in his subordinates' places if he is unable adequately to communicate with them. While it is customary to think of the chain of command, the hierarchy of supervision, extending from president to laborer, as offering a clear channel of communication, a little reflection will indicate that this is rarely the case.

There are too many barriers to communication and sources of distortion in such a hierarchy. (The chief of these is the desire of each of those in each echelon to impress *his* superiors with the superlative quality of *his* performance. Hence, nothing is permitted to come to his superior's attention which might raise embarrassing questions about *his* competence.) Therefore, the line organization must be supplemented as a dependable channel of communication.

Likewise, for a number of reasons, the union hierarchy rarely provides a clear channel of management-employee communication. To begin with, the union is rarely an impartial, disinterested agency. Many of the issues in a conflict situation are ones toward which it is vehemently partisan. Furthermore, many unions themselves are rife with factionalism and internecine strife. Precisely what will be communicated will depend greatly upon which faction is in power. These internal difficulties, therefore, seriously affect a union's value as a dependable medium of management-worker communication.

"Talking it out"

If management is to obtain a comprehensive and valid picture of its employees' opinions and attitudes and their sources, it must provide facilities for them to talk them out freely, at length, and without reservation. This generally excludes counseling conferences with supervision (relatively few foremen, department heads, and even executives have the skill, time, patience, and empathic sensitivity to make such contacts successfully).

Only persons who have demonstrated a high degree of empathy and who have been trained in the use of the unstructured, open end or nondirective interview can be used. Interviews of this type should be conducted with all employees (including supervisors) at regular intervals. All new employees should be interviewed a few weeks after starting on the job; older employees should have a counseling interview at least once each year, and all employees on leaving should be given an exit interview.

Ideally, an opinion poll should be conducted biennially to provide a static cross-section of employee and supervisory attitudes as a control on the findings of the less formalized procedures. From these several sources, data can be assembled and collated which will provide management with a detailed, explicit, and fluid picture of precisely what each employee wants and believes, and why he wants and believes what he does.

"Do unto others . . ."

If, on the basis of the information obtained in this manner, management will then take the initiative in trying to see its people's problems *from their perspective*, it may discover that there is merit in many of their beliefs and demands. It may likewise learn that many of their complaints are justified.

Of the greatest significance, however, it will find it easier to resolve many management-worker conflicts of interest and attitude, some of which at first seem quite irreconcilable. It will not always be easy for management to accept others' (particularly the unions') points of view; and efforts in this direction may well be looked upon with suspicion by many in business—if for no other reason than that an approach of this nature is a distinct novelty in most companies.

It will be charged that this is a "soft," "appeasing," way to handle these problems. (It is *not*, because seeing the other person's side does not necessarily imply weakness—it does not preclude disciplining.) Most significant, where an open-minded, albeit firm, atittude toward employee problems has been tried, the results have almost invariably been good. In nearly every instance where an enterprise has been consistently free from labor trouble, it has had top management which has applied this philosophy.

And why should the results not be good? The principle on which this method is based is at least 2,000 years old. It is simply the application in modern industry of the Golden Rule, "Do unto others as ye would have others do unto you."

QUESTIONS

1. Explain what is meant by empathy.
2. What misunderstandings and conflicts arise because of lack of empathy?
3. Why must the initiative for improvement in labor-management relations come principally from management itself? Do you agree?
4. How is empathy related to leadership and communication?
5. What must management do to obtain a valid picture of employee opinions and attitudes?

44. DEALING WITH OURSELVES BEFORE DEALING WITH OTHERS *

Robert Tannenbaum

Frequently when we talk to executives about the problems they face in dealing with other people, these leaders will point the finger at some one else. A usual comment after a session such as this is: "You know, this is most helpful but my boss should have been here." Frequently, too, executives will ask how to deal with a particular person whom they describe, but rarely do they talk about themselves. Nevertheless, the place to begin human relations is at home—that is, with ourselves.

Analogy from the craftsman

In the area of interpersonal relations, an analogy can be drawn from the craftsman on the job. When the craftsman works at his machine, he has to ask himself three questions: What do I use this instrument for? How do I use this instrument? What is the result of using this instrument? In interpersonal relations, the instrument is ourselves, and we have to ask the same questions.

As for the first question, some executives might say: "Well, I am responsible for attaining certain organizational objectives. Therefore I use myself for whatever influence potential I have for bringing about organizational goals." Other executives might say: "We have so many *wiggits* to turn out per hour. I use myself in relation to my subordinates or in relation to the line in order to get this organizational goal accomplished."

Still others might give this answer. "I use myself to help other people realize their own potential as fully as possible." And some individuals who particularly like to work in a group participatory way might say they use themselves to facilitate the attainment of the group goal.

But let's not be too hasty here. As we watch many executives at work, we find in reality they often consciously think they are using themselves to attain the kind of objectives mentioned but in fact are trying to attain unconscious personal goals. Here are a few instances.

Often we, as executives, get up to a certain point in the organization. We attain a certain title, and this title becomes a source of

---

* From *Office Executive*, Vol. 32, No. 8 (August, 1957), pp. 29-30, 35. Reprinted with permission.

security that helps us to block off many threats or potential threats that might come our way in our relations with subordinates. We use our status to block communications upward, for often our subordinates, particularly those who are on the make, have ideas that may be better than ours.

If a subordinate passes an idea up the line, he may in a sense show us up in a bad light. He makes us feel uncomfortable. We feel his hot breath on our neck. We are afraid he will take our job over. Therefore we try to make it difficult for him to really communicate his ideas upward. Or, we use our status to put him in his place.

For example, suppose a subordinate offers a criticism about something we have just done. We turn to him, using our status, and say: "Look, Joe, I have been through the ropes. I know this work a lot better than you do. It seems to me I should be calling the shots here."

Probably, consciously, we would justify talking to him this way because, after all, our time is important. Of course, we know the real answer for our response, but we do use rationalization of this kind. The reality may well be that we use our status to put Joe in his place or to frighten him.

Dependency relationship

Consider another instance. We managers give a great deal of lip service daily to the importance of developing our subordinates— really helping them to grow. Yet, most of us tend to keep people in the dependency relationship with respect to us. We are careful about giving individuals wide latitude and freedom in which they will have the opportunity to grow and develop. We are even cautious about giving them an opportunity to make mistakes as a basis for learning.

Having people look up to us satisfies our ego. We prefer individuals who turn to us for the answers, individuals who can't make a move until we call the shots for them. To play the role of the puppet-man, keeping the employee at the end of the dangling strings so that he moves only when we make the appropriate gesture, gives our egos satisfaction.

Our rationalization here is that we have to direct the fellow closely because he just does not know how to work. Or, he has not had sufficient experience. Or, "I know more than he does about what he is doing. And because I know more, I am watching him closely, directing him rather sharply to further organizational objectives." Often we are afraid to look at our own real motivations.

Typically when we behave in this way we are meeting primarily our own needs—needs for security; needs for status; needs for comfort in the work situation. Such behavior on our part represents our own immaturity, our own inability to be actually big in a psychological sense in relation to those with whom we deal.

Hence, when we ask how we use ourselves as an instrument, we have to look behind or deeply beneath the usual rationalization we come up with. We have to ask ourselves: "Am I really meeting my own needs when I behave the way I do?"

A great temptation

Consider the second question—How do I use this instrument that is myself? A great temptation here is to ask for a few do's and don't's to use as the *open sesame* in interpersonal relations. But the reality of success in interpersonal relations is by no means this simple. Dealing effectively with other people depends upon not only what we are but also upon the nature of the people with whom we are dealing and the situation. Different kinds of behavior are called for in different situations.

Effectiveness in interpersonal relations depends on two essential qualities—*social sensitivity* and *behavioral flexibility. Social sensitivity* means the ability to accurately understand another individual. People differ from each other rather markedly in this ability. Some persons are much more accurate in their perception of other people. Most of us have real blind spots when we look at other individuals. We tend to see only what we want to see or have to see in order to feel comfortable in our relations with another person.

Frequently, for example, time and method study men, accountants, production managers and marketing specialists see individuals through a lens or filter that distorts the reality that is there. They see only what they want to see or have to see to feel comfortable.

Behavioral flexibility means the ability to behave appropriately in the light of the understanding of the other person. While some individuals are socially sensitive, they have little behavioral flexibility, and the reverse is true.

What differentiates people who are low in behavioral flexibility and social sensitivity from those who are high in these qualities? The person who is relatively mature emotionally, the person who has worked through many personality problems, is the individual who tends to be high in both traits. On the other hand, the person who is relatively immature emotionally is the individual who is lacking in high performance in these two traits. Persons wishing to develop greater social sensitivity must become aware of the need they are serving when they distort the mechanism they set up; otherwise they will continue to see things inaccurately.

For instance, in a recent executive training period one of the participants gave a lengthy discussion on the "listening technique." He suggested to the group that a good idea would be for the members to each listen to one of their employees for one week and then report on the experience at the next meeting. The idea was accepted, and the man who made the recommendation was the first to give a report.

"You know," he said, "I learned a lot about myself when I tried this experiment with the employee. I found as I tried to listen that I was extremely uncomfortable. As I look back at this discomfort, I realize that when I gave the other person an opportunity to do the talking, I was no longer in the position of control. The other person was determining what was being said. I discovered when I hit these periods of silence that I couldn't wait them out. I couldn't stand it. I had to start talking."

Unconstructive situation

This executive hit on two areas that got in his way from the standpoint of behaving in a new manner. First was his need to control people; second, which he did not understand at the time, was his discomfort in what might be called an unconstructive situation. The situation was not carefully defined. Nothing is as unconstructive as a period of silence.

We find in training sessions, for instance, that if we do not follow an agenda, if we as trainers don't tell our trainees what to do, a certain number of us feel uncomfortable because the meeting lacks structure. In other words, the executive who finds silence uncomfortable has unresolved personality problems within himself. These problems get in the way of his being more effective when he tries to listen. Hence, for such an executive to behave more effectively and flexibly, he would have to take care of the unresolved problems.

Consider next the third question. What is the result of the use of this instrument, ourselves? Few individuals really know what their impact is on other individuals—how other people see them, respond to them or feel about them.

One time, for example, in a training activity with eight top men, I interviewed each one individually. At the end of each interview I asked this question: "How do you think the other seven fellows in this group see you?" If you were in this particular spot in your own organization and knew that I would be talking with the other seven men about how they really saw you, what would your answer be? If your answer is a question mark, as in the case with many persons, the situation is serious.

For years as office managers, you have been talking about the importance of all types of managerial controls as far as office procedures are concerned. You have argued that statistical and accounting controls are essential if you are to run a business effectively. You set your goals or standards, and you need a quick report on the accounting, statistical and other operating data so that you can quickly check performance against goals.

People who work with guided missiles know these missiles have to have a control device or feed-back that will detect deviation of the missile from the target. Yet, in our interpersonal relations, we rarely, if ever, have any control mechanism or feed-back. A feed-back mechanism could let us know how other people see us. It could be a means of telling us whether we are on the target or not.

Why don't we find out exactly how other people feel about us? Perhaps finding out would make us too uncomfortable. Maybe intellectually we would like to know but emotionally we don't want to. The idea makes us shudder.

We go around like ostriches

Hence we go around like ostriches, believing what we really want to believe of ourselves rather than believing what reality would tell us. Our inability to get feed-back on our impact on other people stems from our own inability to permit other people to call the shots as they see them.

How, then, can we improve this instrument, ourselves? More and more training classes are being designed to help executives gain the kind of increased insights into themselves to help them become more effective along the lines previously mentioned. The American Management Association, for instance, has set up special training programs for executives. In addition, the National Training Laboratory is available at Bethel, Maine, and many other training laboratories in group development have been set up. The University of California at Los Angeles has a special program called "Sensitivity Training for Management."

However, special programs are not the only types of activity that can be used as a means for improving oneself in greater emotional maturity. The listening skill referred to is a key in self-development. This skill has many other beneficial outcomes. We can't really understand ourselves better unless we get the feed-back that we need from other people—the people with whom we interact. If we never give these individuals an opportunity to tell us what they think, we deny ourselves much useful information needed in our own personal growth and development.

The direction each of us needs to grow is in the direction of real listening skill—the ability to develop an atmosphere around ourselves, an atmosphere of security, lack of threat, of acceptance and warmth that makes it possible for other people to feel comfortable and free of negative reaction.

Listening isn't easy. It can not be accomplished by turning the right knob. The ability to listen takes time to acquire but pays off when developed.

QUESTIONS

1. What are the essential qualities for effectiveness in interpersonal relations?
2. Why do people who have social sensitivity lack behavioral flexibility?
3. Why do many executives keep employees in a dependency relationship?
4. What part does emotion play in social sensitivity and behavioral flexibility?
5. What does Tannenbaum recommend we do to improve our social sensitivity and behavioral flexibility?

45. AN EXPERIMENT IN MANAGEMENT: PUTTING THEORY Y TO THE TEST *

Arthur H. Kuriloff

For some time now, Douglas McGregor, Professor of Industrial Management at M.I.T., has been insisting that most organizations today are managed on principles that run counter to what we now know about human behavior. There's no doubt that McGregor's views, which he explained at length in his book, *The Human Side of Enterprise,* published by McGraw-Hill in 1960, have created considerable stir among serious students of management. But whether they have had any real impact on the way our business organizations are actually run is, of course, quite another question, and a pertinent one.

My guess is, though, that many practicing managers who haven't yet got around to reading McGregor's book, much less acting upon it, are at least aware that it discusses two sharply divergent concepts of management, which McGregor calls Theory X and Theory Y. Theory X is the conventional approach to management, which, McGregor says, is based on hidebound traditional assumptions about human behavior.

This author's Theory Y, by contrast, derives from the findings of modern behavioral science research—in other words, it is based on how people actually do behave in the work situation, not on how managers think they will or should behave. If companies want to get the best out of their people, McGregor asserts, they should operate in accordance with the principles of Theory Y, *not* Theory X.

Now one of the difficulties of McGregor's position is that Theory X, whatever its shortcomings, manifestly works up to a point. Obviously, if it did not, business would be at a complete standstill, a state of affairs we have hardly reached yet. Theory Y, on the other hand, is still little more than a theory—and a theory, moreover, that turns most of our time-honored ideas about the management of people inside out. It may indeed conceptualize a far more effective way of managing than Theory X—but where's the proof?

For all I know, there are many organizations that are now quietly experimenting with Theory Y, but if so, they are not talking about it. Shortly after McGregor's book appeared, though, my company, Non-Linear Systems, Inc., decided to make the switch. In this article I

* From *Personnel*, Vol. 40, No. 6 (November-December, 1963), pp. 8-17. Copyright 1963 by the American Management Association. Reprinted with permission of the American Management Association.

shall describe how we went about converting Theory Y into practice and what results we have achieved. Before doing so, however, perhaps it would be advisable for me to place both Theory X and Theory Y in their conceptual framework, so that we can more clearly see their differences.

As I have said, Theory X management, the conventional approach, springs from certain assumptions about human behavior in the work situation—assumptions that are frozen in our culture. According to McGregor, these assumptions are:

1. Human beings are inherently lazy and will shun work if they can.
2. People must be directed, controlled, and motivated by fear of punishment or deprivation to impel them to work as the company requires.
3. The average human being prefers to be directed, wishes to avoid responsibility, has relatively little ambition, and wants security above all.

These negative assumptions underlie the philosophy of the assembly line and the robotization of human existence—an evolution clearly foreseen by Thoreau over a century ago. Even then, Thoreau pointed out, most men led "lives of quiet desperation." We have gone much further along the road to depersonalization since Thoreau's day, and the quiet desperation we now see so clearly all around us is surely due in great part to the assembly line, to the mechanization of *people* as well as of processes.

The organizational structure that develops from the assumptions of Theory X is the customary pyramid—multilayered, complex. As we all know, it is clogged with communication blocks and distortions as orders and information limp up and down the organizational ladder.

If we were to invert the pyramid and balance it on its point, we would have a condition of instability not uncommon in reality. Moving through the layers to the apex, we pass through sections of decreasing area, with the managers at each level feeling with increasing intensity the pressures in supporting the organization above them. If we were further to imagine the individual managers loosely linked together by elastic bands across and between tiers, we would find them in violent random motion, like the dance of Brownian particles. The frenetic movements of the dance are aimed at keeping the organization from toppling and falling apart with a crash.

This, then, is the traditional organization, based, as I have said, on no more than time-honored beliefs about human behavior. Now let's take a look at the assumptions of Theory Y, which, as I have also stressed, derive from the facts of life that have been uncovered by objective behavioral research. According to McGregor, these assumptions (which are constantly being reinforced by new data as psychological and motivational research accumulates) are:

1. The expenditure of physical and mental effort in work is as natural as play or rest.
2. External control and the threat of punishment are not the only means of inducing people to work toward organizational goals. Man will exercise self-direction and self-control in the service of objectives to which he is committed.
3. Commitment to objectives is a function of the rewards associated with their achievement.
4. The average human being learns, under proper conditions, not only to accept but also to seek responsibility.
5. The capacity for exercising a relatively high degree of imagination, ingenuity, and creativity in solving organizational problems is widely, not narrowly, distributed in the population.
6. Under the conditions of modern industrial life, the intellectual potentialities of the average human being are only partially utilized.

The psychological foundations on which these assumptions rest include the well-known formulation of human needs developed by A. H. Maslow of Brandeis University. According to Maslow, man is a creature of ever-expanding wants. Once his basic needs have been satisfied, others take their place. Thus, man's needs may be ordered in a hierarchy, starting with his basic biological requirements and proceeding through a series of levels, each more intangible than the preceding one. To satisfy his needs, man expends energy; but once a need has been fairly well fulfilled, it no longer acts as a motivating force and man's efforts are then directed toward satisfying the need of the next level in the hierarchy. In this hierarchy of needs, Maslow has identified five levels:

1. *Physiological needs.* These are the needs for food, water, air, shelter, rest, exercise, and others required to satisfy the biological demands of the human organism.
2. *Safety needs.* These are needs to be free from fear of deprivation, danger, and threat, on the job and off.
3. *Social needs.* These are the needs people have for gregariousness and social interaction. Men like to group together for many purposes of life. They need to associate, to belong, to accept and be accepted, to love and to be loved.
4. *Ego needs.* These are the needs for reputation, self-respect, and self-esteem. Men need to feel competent and knowledgeable. They need respect, recognition, and status.
5. *Self-actualization needs.* The needs for the realization of individual potential, the liberation of creative talents, the widest possible use of abilities and aptitudes—in short, for personal fulfillment.

It should be noted, however, that these needs overlap and are interdependent. A higher, less tangible need emerges before the lower one is fully satisfied. Thus, Maslow has estimated that, in our society, the average citizen is about 85 per cent satisfied in his physiological needs, 70 per cent in his safety needs, 50 per cent in his social needs, and 40 per cent in his ego needs, but only 10 per cent in his self-actualization needs.

Since we live in an economy where the basic human needs are reasonably well taken care of, more and more people today tend to be motivated by the intangible rewards offered by the higher levels in the needs hierarchy. It is these motivating forces that Theory Y management proposes to tap. In other words, Theory Y management aims at integrating individual goals with those of the organization—at making the job the principal means through which each employee can enlarge his competence, self-control, and sense of accomplishment. In such an atmosphere, Theory Y holds, employees are likely to identify with the goals of the organization because the organization identifies with their goals. In effect, the organization is propelled by the motivation of its various members, whose individual contributions combine to achieve the over-all goals of the enterprise.

This self-propelled, self-disciplining kind of organization is what we have been aiming for in our experiment in management at Non-Linear Systems. Our company develops and sells precision electronic instruments and we have been in business for 11 years. When we started our experiment three years ago, we had a work force of about 225 employees. Today we have 350.

We began by adopting a horizontal form of organization. We have an executive council of eight members, which establishes basic strategy and initiates action toward its accomplishment. This council is headed by our president. Working with him are seven vice presidents. Each council member is responsible for one of the eight areas of operation identified by Drucker as fundamental to the attainment of goals in any business: innovation, market standing, profitability, productivity, physical and financial resources, manager performance and development, worker attitude and performance, and public responsibility.

Horizontal responsibility

Each vice president is responsible for the functioning of his area of operations throughout the organization. Thus, our vice president for productivity works to improve output per unit in every phase of the company's operations, whether it be the number of hours required to assemble an instrument, the streamlining of paper work, the elimination of waste motions in shipping, or determining the optimum number of personnel in a department or group. Similarly, the vice president for manager performance and development is concerned with training employees to understand company objectives, establishing courses for improving skills at all levels, developing improved hiring techniques, assessing performance throughout the company and, in general, making sure that there is a continual reservoir of knowledgeable and skilled people to assume the posts of increasing responsibility that open up as the company grows.

The executive council divorces itself from day-to-day tactical activities. These are the duties of some 30 department managers. All the departments are on a single level, just below the executive council. The department managers report to the executive council as a whole and not to individual members, and so executive-manager relationships follow functional lines. Any department head may seek out the member of the executive council who is concerned with the area central to the problem in question. Since areas often overlap and cannot be sharply delineated, members of the council often act by mutual consent; frequently they substitute for one another. Over the past three years our managers and indeed, most of our employees, have learned where to go for counsel. They are not at all perturbed at finding themselves talking to two or three vice presidents either singly or at the same time, to cover all areas involved in the problem. Implicit in this conduct of the company's affairs is an atmosphere of mutual trust and acceptance.

Emphasis on teaching

In accordance with the Theory Y philosophy we regard management as basically an affair of teaching and training, not one of directing and controlling. We do control, of course, but we control the process, not the people. To understand how we are trying to achieve this kind of control we might look at our company in terms of Theory Y and Maslow's formulation of human needs.

Physiological needs in our society can be taken care of by money. Hence we decided to pay a minimum salary at least sufficient to provide for food, shelter, and the other physical necessities and leave a little over, if possible. At the beginning of 1961, therefore, we established a minimum wage of $100 a week.[1] Simultaneously, we did away with time clocks. Time clocks are an offense to human dignity and imply mistrust of people. We also abandoned the practice of docking employees when they are out ill. Nevertheless, our absentee rate for

---

[1] This rate is approximately 60 cents more, on an equivalent hourly basis, or $24 per week, than comparable rates paid in the community.

the past year has been 2.8 per cent less than half the prevailing rate in similar businesses in our community.

To provide for safety needs we strive for an unconstraint coupled with a consistent managerial approach. Our objective is to achieve a calm, unharried atmosphere that induces rational, creative behavior throughout our operations. We try, as a company, to maintain steady employment. When sales are low, we stockpile finished products; when orders come pouring in, we do not hire at an accelerated pace. We prefer to ask our customers to bear with us for a little longer delivery than usual. In this way we avoid those cyclical hiring and firing peaks that cause employees to feel insecure and uncertain about their jobs. We have made this policy widely known throughout the company. We believe that it is well understood and has effectively contributed toward satisfying our employees' safety needs.

For the fulfillment of social needs we use the small group approach wherever we can. Gregariousness, affiliation, belonging—all these needs are served in the group. The individual members exchange information and gossip; they help and teach each other. Hence, we have discarded our assembly lines and reorganized the people who had been manning them into a number of seven-man teams. This we did in 1960, heading each team with a competent technician, whom we called Assistant Assembly Manager. Under his tutelage, the groups were asked to build complete instruments. This they have since learned to do and do well.

Self-paced teams

Today these teams complete instruments from kits of parts, electronic components, and hardware. They insert components on the printed circuit boards, solder and fabricate wiring harnesses. They bolt the hardware together. They complete the subassemblies, testing as they go. They run-in and calibrate finished instruments. There is no formal planning. By mutual agreement the team members decide who will do what and in what sequence. They pace themselves at their own rhythm. They know each other's strengths and generally do a far better job of planning than if directed by some external authority. As a result productivity in man-hours per instrument has steadily improved. Today it is 30 per cent better than at any period in the company's history.

The group method, we have found, is an ideal way also to provide for the ego needs. Within the group a man is recognized for his excellences. He attains status by virtue of his demonstrated abilities. Since everyone has skills of one kind or another, each member of the group is deferred to in the area of his special competence. He is given the chance to achieve and to be acknowledged for his achievement. No one is pushed around. Each man can speak up and be listened to. He develops pride in his product and the company as he perfects his skills.

In these small groups we very often see one member teaching another some special technique or skill. This appears to us the highest accolade one can give—to defer to the expertise of another. The result has been a noticeable improvement in the quality of our products, which has steadily decreased the number of complaints from the field. These are now 70 per cent fewer than they were three years ago.

When it comes to satisfying the highest area of human needs, self-actualization, we are dealing with the factor that holds the greatest potential for organizational growth and improvement. As I have said, we believe that the prime job of management is teaching and training, and so we endeavor to release dormant creativity by encouraging employees to improve their skills. We regularly conduct numerous classes and training groups. These cover a variety of subjects and are held both on and off company time.

Almost all our training courses are completely voluntary. Some are led by trainers from within the company, some by specialists brought in from outside: Sometimes we have a senior engineer teaching a class of young engineers logic circuitry theory at night, an electronic technician teaching basic electricity to a group of men and women assemblers during the lunch period, and another group learning the elements of selling from an outside consultant in the morning.

Our training goes on at many levels. We have a number of small groups taking management training on a continuing basis. Some of these are "family" groups, some "cousins," and some "strangers" groups; that is to say, some groups are all from one department, some are made up of people holding the same positions but coming from different departments, while others are made up of people from a variety of departments and job levels. The training, though, is the same for all—the fundamentals of Theory Y management.

On the lookout for talent

Inherent in our management approach is a restless and never-ceasing search for talent. We continually assess performance. We do not use a formal procedure—evaluation in our book is a subjective process performed by our managers at all levels. In this process, we have come to rely heavily on insight and feeling. Not that we disparage objective testing—we employ an outside testing service, for example, to help us compile an inventory of employee aptitudes. However, in the final say, we have learned to trust our own observations and judgments.

We often move employees from one position to another in order to better match aptitudes and talents to job requirements. People may themselves request transfers to other kinds of work. We also dip into our reservoir of trained personnel when promotions open up. Of the 16 assistant managers in our instrument assembly department two years ago, not one remains in his original post. All have been moved up to more responsible positions calling for greater skills or more specialized knowledge.

From start to finish

We also try to arrange work so employees can obtain "closure," that is, the completion of a whole job. Seeing the whole job is a fundamental element of Theory Y. In the assembly line approach of Theory X, by contrast, all the worker can see is the minute segment that's in front of him. A complete job is likely to engage a variety of aptitudes and skills. By providing closure—engaging the whole man, as it were, in the job—self-actualization becomes a vital motivating force. In this fashion we strive to create an operating climate that is conducive to commitment to work. The satisfaction of doing a whole job and a genuine commitment to work tend to produce a healthier employee—therefore a healthier organization.

To illustrate these ideas more specifically, let's take a look at a typical operation—our materials department. This department is responsible for all our purchasing. It is headed by a department manager and is subdivided into three groups, which act in parallel. Each group is headed by an assistant department manager. Working with him are an administrative assistant, a stockroom clerk, and a receiving inspection technician.

Since our executive council sets a limit on the total amount of dollars that can be tied up in the stockroom, the groups have to plan very carefully to insure that their purchases keep within the prescribed bounds. They must be alert to our constantly changing product mix and take particular account of long-lead procurement items. To guide their planning they receive data from the weekly meetings of the managers of our production departments and the distribution department. The latter is in daily touch with our marketing offices around the country, and so provides vital information on sales and sales prospects. The information given to managers of the materials department enables them to assess current and prospective changes in our product mix. They adjust their purchasing schedules accordingly, taking calculated risks where their judgment so dictates.

We buy about 2,500 different items. Each materials group buys about one-third of this number. Their planning task is therefore a formidable one and requires continuous attention to avoid critical shortages. The groups buy parts, components, and raw stock. They inspect the incoming materials to make sure that what they have bought is up to specification. They stock these materials. They assemble individual kits of the parts, components, and hardware required for the manufacture of each instrument, and they deliver these kits on demand to the instrument assembly department. Finally, in the act that provides closure to their part of the company's operations, they write the checks to pay for what they have bought.

The structure of our organization is such as to encourage meetings of many kinds for the exchange of information. Since there is only a limited chain of command, we get along with very few formal memos. Employees are advised to seek whatever information they need from those best able to give it. In fact, we have thrown out the classic injunction, "Write it, don't say it," and substituted, "Say it, don't write it," in its stead. As a result, we have no need for the informal organization that arises *sub rosa* in the conventionally run company and usually gets things done regardless of how the organization chart indicates they should be done.

By "saying it" instead of "writing it" we have opened up numerous channels of communication instead of confining ourselves to one medium in which many people have limited capability anyway. When people talk face-to-face, their understanding is almost invariably improved—tone, inflection, facial expression, and all such nuances reinforce the message that is being transmitted. Above all, there is a fair guarantee that the message has actually been received. In this way we aim at minimizing error.

Fallibility expected

Error, however, does creep in, as it does in any organization composed of human beings. The Theory Y philosophy accepts human error so long as it is within reasonable bounds. Growth, creativity, and productivity must involve mistakes from time to time and their correction. In most companies, memos are frequently written as a protection against error. We believe that where there is mutual trust there is no need for protective paper. Mutual trust is mutually reinforcing. We still have a great distance to go, but I believe we have made notable progress in improving openness and trust throughout the organization since our experiment in management began three years ago.

I realize that what I have written here may sound somewhat pious. Nevertheless, Theory Y suggests, to our minds, a return to the rugged, inner-directed qualities that drove our forefathers to hew civilization out of the wilderness. The calculated democratization of our enterprise represents, we think, an organic situation in which individual growth is encouraged and stimulated and in turn contributes to the continued growth of the enterprise as a whole.

At all events, in these past three years we have witnessed significant improvements in our capabilities. We have multiplied our product line fourfold, with no more than minor dips in our steadily improving productive effectiveness. We have probed and tested new ways of doing things. It's true that we have made mistakes along the way, but we have corrected them. We expect to make mistakes and correct them in the future. But at this point we feel that we are well launched on an exciting experiment that ultimately will not only pay off in larger profits for the company but will also contribute in some small measure toward the betterment of our industrial society.

QUESTIONS

1. What does Kuriloff mean by "closure"? What effect does this have on employee productivity?
2. What role does the group play in the Non-Linear motivational system?
3. What does Kuriloff mean by "mutual trust"? How does this relate to Theory Y?
4. What would you say are the prime advantages accruing to Non-Linear because of the implementation of Theory Y?
5. What connection do you see between Tannenbaum's previous article and Non-Linear's managerial system?

46. T-GROUPS FOR ORGANIZATIONAL EFFECTIVENESS *

Chris Argyris

❧ *What causes dynamic, flexible, and enthusiastically committed executive teams to become sluggish and inflexible as time goes by? Why do they no longer enjoy the intrinsic challenge of their work, but become motivated largely by wages and executive bonus plans?*

❧ *Why do executives become conformists as a company becomes older and bigger? Why do they resist saying what they truly believe —even when it is in the best interests of the company?*

❧ *How is it possible to develop a top-management team that is constantly innovating and taking risks?*

❧ *Is it inevitable that we get things done only when we create crises, check details, arouse fears, and penalize and reward in ways that inadvertently create "heroes" and "bums" among our executive group?*

Ask managers why such problems as these exist and their answers typically will be abstract and fatalistic:

— "It's inevitable in a big business."
— "Because of human nature."
— "I'll be damned if I know, but every firm has these problems."
— "They are part of the bone and fabric of the company."

Statements like these *are* true. Such problems *are* ingrained into corporate life. But in recent years there has evolved a new way of helping executives develop new inner resources which enable them to mitigate these organizational ills. I am referring to *laboratory education*—or "sensitivity training" as it is sometimes called. Particularly in the form of "T-groups," it has rapidly become one of the most controversial educational experiences now available to management. Yet, as I will advocate in this article, if laboratory education is conducted competently, and if the right people attend, it can be a very powerful educational experience.

How does laboratory education remedy the problems I have mentioned? By striving to expose and modify certain values held by typical executives, values which, unless modified and added to, serve

* From *Harvard Business Review*, Vol. 42, No. 3 (March-April, 1964), pp. 60-73. Reprinted with permission.

Exhibit I
THE PYRAMIDAL VALUES

There are certain values about effective human relationships that are inherent in the pyramidal structure of the business organization and which successful executives (understandably) seem to hold. Values are learned commands which, once internalized, coerce human behavior in specific directions. This is

"Have you ever been in a meeting when the disagreement got quite personal?"

why an appreciation of these values is basic in understanding behavior.

What are these "pyramidal" values? I would explain them this way.

1. The important human relationships —the crucial ones—are those which are related to achieving the organization's objective, i.e., getting the job done, as for example:

"We are here to manufacture shoes, that is our business, those are the important human relationships; if you have anything that can influence those human relationships, fine."

2. Effectiveness in human relationships increases as behavior becomes more rational, logical, and clearly communicated; but effectiveness decreases as behavior becomes more emotional. Let me illustrate by citing a typical conversation:

"Have you ever been in a meeting where there is a lot of disagreement?"
"All the time."
"Well, yes I have, but not very often."
"What would you do if you were the leader of this group?"
"I would say, 'Gentlemen, let's get back to the fact,' or I would say, 'Gentlemen, let's keep personalities out of this.' If it really got bad, I would wish it were five o'clock so I could call it off, and then I would talk to the men individually."

3. Human relationships are most effectively motivated by carefully defined direction, authority, and control, as well as appropriate rewards and penalties that emphasize rational behavior and achievement of the objective.

If these are the values held by most executives, what are the consequences? To the extent that executives believe in these organizational values, the following changes have been found to happen.

(1) There is a *decrease* in receiving and giving information about executives' interpersonal impact on each other. Their interpersonal difficulties tend to be either suppressed or disguised and brought up as rational, technical, intellectual problems. As a result, they may find it difficult to develop competence in dealing with feelings and interpersonal relations. There is a corresponding decrease in their ability to own up to or be responsible for their ideas, feelings, and values. Similarly there is a dropping off of experimentation and risk-taking with new ideas and values.

(2) Along with the decrease in owning,* openness, risk-taking, there is an *increase* in the denial of feelings, in closeness to new ideas, and in need for stability (i.e., "don't rock the boat"). As a result, executives tend to find themselves in situations where they are not adequately aware of the human problems, where they do not solve them in such a way that they remain solved without deteriorating the problem-solving process. Thus, if we define interpersonal competence as (a) being aware of human problems, (b) solving them in such a way that they remain solved, without deteriorating the problem-solving process, these values serve to decrease interpersonal competence.

(3) As the executives' interpersonal competence decreases, conformity, mistrust, and dependence, especially on those who are in power, increase. Decision making becomes *less effective*, because people withhold many of their ideas, especially those that are innovative and risky, and organizational defenses (such as management by crisis, management by detail, and through fear) *increase*. So do such "protective" activities as "JIC" files (just in case the president asks), "information" meetings (to find out what the opposition is planning), and executive politicking.

* Defined in text, page 760.

If this analysis is valid, then we must alter executives' values if we are to make the system more effective. The question arises as to what changes can and *should* be made in these values.

But since executives are far from unknowledgeable, why have they clung to these pyramidal values? First, because they are *not necessarily wrong*. Indeed, they are a necessary part of effective human relationships. The difficulty is that alone they are not enough. By themselves they tend to lead to the above consequence. What is needed is an additional set of values for the executives to hold. Specifically there are three.

1. The important human relationships are not only those related to achieving the organization's objectives but those related to maintaining the organization's internal system and adapting to the environment, as well.

2. Human relationships increase in effectiveness as *all* the relevant behavior (rational and interpersonal) becomes conscious, discussable, and controllable. (The rationality of feelings is as crucial as that of the mind.)

3. In addition to direction, controls, and rewards and penalties, human relationships are most effectively influenced through authentic relationships, internal commitment, psychological success, and the process of confirmation. (These terms are clarified in the body of the article.)

to impair interpersonal effectiveness. As Exhibit I explains, these values are ingrained in the pyramidal structure of the business enterprise. The exhibit summarizes several basic causes of management ineffectiveness as isolated by three studies: (1) in a large corporate division—30,000 employees, grossing $500 million per year; (2) a medium-size company—5,000 employees, grossing in excess of $50 million per year; and (3) a small company—300 employees. The results of these studies are reported in detail elsewhere.[1]

CHANGE THROUGH EDUCATION

But how does one change an executive's values? One way is by a process of re-education. First there is an unfreezing of the old values, next the development of the new values, and finally a freezing of the new ones.

In order to begin the unfreezing process, the executives must experience the true ineffectiveness of the old values. This means they must have a "gut" experience of how incomplete the old values are. One way to achieve this is to give them a task to accomplish in situations where their power, control, and organizational influences are

[1] Chris Argyris, *Interpersonal Competence and Organizational Effectiveness* (Homewood, Illinois: Richard D. Irwin, Inc., 1962); *Understanding Organizational Behavior* (Homewood, Illinois: The Dorsey Press, Inc., 1960); and *Explorations in Human Competence* (manuscript, Department of Industrial Administration, Yale University, New Haven, 1964).

minimized. The ineffectiveness of the old values, if our analysis is correct, should then become apparent.

A second requirement of re-education arises from the fact that the overwhelming number of educational processes available (e.g., lecture, group discussion, and the like) are based on the pyramidal values. Each lecture or seminar at a university has clearly defined objectives and is hopefully staffed by a rational, articulate teacher who is capable of controlling, directing, and appropriately rewarding and penalizing the students. But, as I have just suggested, these represent some of the basic causes of the problems under study. The educator is in a bind. If he teaches by the traditional methods, he is utilizing the very values that he is holding up to be incomplete and ineffective.

To make matters more difficult, if the re-educational process is to be effective, it is necessary to create a *culture* in which the new values can be learned, practiced, and protected until the executives feel confident in using them. Such a culture would be one which is composed of people striving to develop authentic relationships and psychological success. Briefly, *authentic relationships* exist when an individual can behave in such a way as to increase his self-awareness and esteem and, at the same time, provide an opportunity for others to do the same. *Psychological success* is the experience of realistically challenging situations that tax one's capacities. Both are key components of executive competence.

The creation of a re-educational process where the unfreezing of the old values, relearning of the new values, and refreezing of the new values under primary control of the students, embedded in a culture that is rarely found in our society, is an extremely difficult task. Yet an approach to fulfilling these requirements is offered by laboratory education.

Probably because of its novelty, laboratory education has become one of the most talked about, experimented with, lauded, and questioned educational experiences for top executives. The interest of top executives has been so great that the National Training Laboratories (a nonprofit educational organization which administers most of the laboratories) has had to increase the program manyfold in the past ten years.[2]

Any educational experience that is as novel as laboratory education is destined to be controversial. And this is good because reasoned

---

[2] For information regarding the training laboratories that are available, one may write to Dr. Leland P. Bradford, National Training Laboratories, National Education Association, 1201 16th Street, Northwest, Washington 6, D. C.

controversy can be the basis for corrections, refinements, and expansions of the process. Research (unfortunately not enough) is being conducted under the auspices of the National Training Laboratories and at various universities such as the University of California, Case Institute of Technology, Columbia, George Washington, Harvard, M.I.T., Michigan, Texas, and Yale, to name a few.

Aims of program

The first step in a laboratory program is to help the executives teach themselves as much about their behavior as possible. To do so they create their own laboratory in which to experiment. This is why the educational process has been called "laboratory education." The strategy of an experiment begins with a dilemma. A dilemma occurs when, for a given situation, there is no sound basis for selecting among alternatives, or there is no satisfactory alternative to select, or when habitual actions are no longer effective.

What do people do when confronted with a dilemma? Their immediate reaction is to try out older methods of behaving with which they are secure, or else to seek guidance from an "expert." In this way, the anxiety so invariably associated with not knowing what to do can be avoided. In the laboratory, then, the anticipated first reactions by participants to a dilemma are to try traditional ways of responding.

Only when conventional or traditional ways of dealing with a dilemma have been tried—unsuccessfully—are conditions ripe for inventive action. Now people are ready to think, to shed old notions because they have not worked, to experiment, and to explore new ways of reacting to see if they will work. The period when old behavior is being abandoned and when new behavior has yet to be invented to replace it is an "unfrozen" period, at times having some of the aspects of a crisis. It is surrounded by uncertainty and confusion.[3]

Fullest learning from the dilemma-invention situation occurs when two additional types of action are taken:

1. One is feedback, the process by which members acquaint one another with their own characteristic ways of feeling and reacting in a dilemma-invention situation. Feedback aids in evaluating the consequences of actions that have been taken as a result of the dilemma situation. By "effective" feedback I mean the kind of feedback which minimizes the probability of the receiver or sender becoming defensive and maximizes his opportunity to "own" values, feelings,

---

[3] See Robert K. Blake and Jane S. Mouton, *The Managerial Grid* (Houston, Texas: Gulf Publishing Co., 1963).

and attitudes. By "own" I mean being aware of and accepting responsibility for one's behavior.

2. The final step in the dilemma-invention cycle is generalizing about the total sequence to get a comprehensive picture of the "common case." When this is done, people are searching to see to what extent behavior observed under laboratory conditions fits outside situations. If generalization is not attempted, the richness of dilemma-invention learning is "lost."

T for training

The core of most laboratories is the T (for training) group.[4] This is most difficult to describe in a few words. Basically it is a group experience designed to provide maximum possible opportunity for the individuals to expose their behavior, give and receive feedback, experiment with new behavior, and develop everlasting awareness and acceptance of self and others. The T-group, when effective, also provides individuals with the opportunity to learn the nature of effective group functioning. They are able to learn how to develop a group that achieves specific goals with minimum possible human cost.

The T-group becomes a learning experience that most closely approximates the values of the laboratory regarding the use of leadership, rewards, penalties, and information in the development of effective groups. It is in the T-group that one learns how to diagnose his own behavior, to develop effective leadership behavior and norms for decision making that truly protect the "wild duck."

Role of educator

In these groups, some of the learning comes from the educator, but most of it from the members interacting with each other. The "ground rules" the group establishes for feedback are important. With the help of the educator, the group usually comes to see the difference between providing help and attempting to control or punish a member; between analyzing and interpreting a member's adjustment (which is not helpful) and informing him of the impact it has on others. Typically, certain features of everyday group activity are blurred or removed. The educator, for example, does not provide the leadership which a group of "students" would normally expect. This produces a kind of "power vacuum" and a great deal of behavior which, in time, becomes the basis of learning.

---

[4] For a detailed summary of research related to laboratory education, see Dorothy Stock, "A Summary of Research on Training Groups," in Leland Bradford, Kenneth Benne, and Jack Gibb (eds.), *T-Group Theory and Laboratory Method; Innovation in Education* (New York: John Wiley & Sons, Inc., 1964).

There is no agenda, except as the group provides it. There are no norms of group operation (such as *Robert's Rules of Order*) except as the group decides to adopt them. For some time the experience is confusing, tension-laden, frustrating for most participants. But these conditions have been found to be conducive to learning. Naturally, some individuals learn a great deal, while others resist the whole process. It is rare, however, for an individual to end a two-week experience feeling that he has learned nothing.

Usually the T-group begins with the educator making explicit that it is designed to help human beings to—

> . . . explore their values and their impact on others,
> . . . determine if they wish to modify their old values and develop new ones,
> . . . develop awareness of how groups can inhibit as well as facilitate human growth and decision making.

Thus a T-group does not begin without an objective, as far as the educator is concerned. It has a purpose, and this purpose, for the educator, is emotionally and intellectually clear.

However, the educator realizes that the purpose is, at the moment, only intellectually clear to the members. Thus, to begin, the educator will probably state that he has no specific goals in mind for the group. Moreover, he offers no specific agenda, no regulations, no rules, and so on. The group is created so its members can determine their own leadership, goals, and rules.

There is very little that is nondirective about a T-group educator's role. He is highly concerned with growth, and he acts in ways that he hopes will enhance development. He is nondirective, however, in the sense that he does not require others to accept these conditions. As one member of the T-group, he will strive sincerely and openly to help establish a culture that can lead to increased authentic relationships and interpersonal competence.

However, he realizes that he can push those in the group just so far. If he goes too far, he will fall into the trap of masterminding their education. This is a trap in which group members might like to see him fall, since it would decrease their uncomfortableness and place him in a social system similar (in values) to their own. In other words, his silence, the lack of predefined objectives, leadership, agenda, rules, and so on, are not designed to be malicious or hurt people. True, these experiences may hurt somewhat, but the hypothesis is that the pain is "in the service of growth."

At this point, let me assume that you are a member of such a **T-group, so that I can tell you what you are likely to experience.**

Action & reaction

At the outset you are likely to expect that the educator will lead you. This expectation is understandable for several reasons:

1. An educator in our culture tends to do precisely this.
2. Because of the newness of the situation, the members may also fear that they are not competent to deal with it effectively. They naturally turn to the educator for assistance. It is common in our culture that when one member of a group has more information than the others as to how to cope with the new, difficult situation, he is expected by the others, *if he cares for them*, to help them cope with the new situation. For example, if I am in a cave with ten other people who are lost and I know how to get out, it would be from their viewpoint the height of noncaring for me to fail to help them get out.
3. Finally, the members may turn to the educator because they have not as yet developed much trust for each other.

The educator may believe it is helpful, during the early stages of a T-group, to tell you that he understands why you feel dependent on him. But he will also add that he believes that learning can take place more effectively if you first develop an increasing sense of trust of one another and a feeling that you can learn from one another.

In my case, when I act as the educator for a T-group, I freely admit that silence is not typical of me and that I need to talk, to be active, to participate. In fact, I may even feel a mild hostility if I am in a situation in which I cannot participate in the way that I desire. Thus, anything you (members) can do to help me "unfreeze" by decreasing your dependence on me would be deeply appreciated. I add that I realize that this is not easy and that I will do my share.

Typically, the members begin to realize that the educator supports those individuals who show early signs of attempting to learn. This is especially true for those who show signs of being open, experimentally minded, and willing to take risks by exposing their behavior. How are these qualities recognized?

There are several cues that are helpful. First, there is the individual who is not highly upset by the initial ambiguity of the situation and who is ready to begin to learn. One sign of such an individual is one who can be open about the confusion that he is experiencing. He is able to own up to his feelings of being confused, without becoming hostile toward the educator or the others. Such an individual is willing to look at his and others' behavior under stress, diagnose it, and attempt to learn from it. Some of these individuals even raise questions about other members' insistence that the educator should get them out of the ambiguous situation.

Some members, on the other hand, react by insisting that the educator has created the ambiguity just to be hostile. You will find that the educator will encourage them to express their concern and hostility as well as help them to see the impact that this behavior (i.e., hostility) is having on him. There are two reasons for the educator's intervention: (1) to reinforce (with feelings) the fact that he is not callous about their feelings and that he is not consciously attempting to be hostile; and (2) to unfreeze others to explore their hostility toward him or toward each other. Such explorations can provide rich data for the group to diagnose and from which to learn.

Problem of mimicking

As the group continues, some members begin to realize that the educator's behavior now may serve for what it is. That is, it may be as valid a model as the educator can manifest of how he would attempt (a) to help create an effective group, and (b) to integrate himself into that group so that he becomes as fully functioning a member as possible. The model is his; he admits owning it, but he is *not* attempting to "sell" it to others or in any way to coerce them to own it.

You may wonder if viewing the educator as a source of "model behavior" would not lead you simply to *mimic* him. (In the technical literature this is discussed as "identification with the leader," or "leader modeling behavior.") Although this may be the case, we should not forget that as you begin to "unfreeze" your previous values and behavior, you will find yourself in the situation of throwing away the old and having nothing new that is concrete and workable. This tends to create states of vacillation, confusion, anxiety, ambivalence, and so on.[5] These states in turn may induce you to "hang on" to the old with even greater tenacity. To begin to substitute the new behavior for the old, you will feel a need to see (1) that you can carry out the new behavior effectively and (2) that the new behavior leads to the desired results.[6]

Under these conditions the members usually try out any bit of behavior that represents the "new." Experimentation not only is sanctioned; it is rewarded. One relatively safe way to experiment is to "try out the educator's behavior." It is at this point that the individual is mimicking. And he should feel free to mimic and *to talk about the mimicking and explore it openly*. Mimicking is helpful if you are aware of and accept the fact that you do not *own* the behavior, for the behavior with which you are experimenting is the

---

[5] Roger Barker, Beatrice A. Wright, and Mollie R. Gonick, "Adjustment to Physical Handicap and Illness," *Social Science Research Council Bulletin 55*, 1946, pp 19-54.

[6] Ronald Lippitt, Jeanne Watson, and Bruce Westley, *The Dynamics of Planned Change* (New York: Harcourt, Brace & World, Inc., 1958).

educator's. If the educator is not anxious about the mimicking, the member may begin safely to explore the limits of the new behavior. He may also begin to see whether or not the educator's behavior is, for him, realistic.

Individual vs. group

At the outset the educator tends to provide that assistance which is designed to help the members to—

> . . . become aware of their present (usually) low potential for establishing authentic relationships,
> . . . become more skillful in providing and receiving nonevaluative descriptive feedback,
> . . . minimize their own and others' defensiveness,
> . . . become increasingly able to experience and own up to their feelings.

Although interpersonal assistance is crucial, it is also important that the T-group not be limited to such interventions. After the members receive adequate feedback from one another as to their inability to create authentic relationships, they will tend to want to become more effective in their interpersonal relationships. It is at this point that they will need to learn that group structure and dynamics deeply influence the probability of increasing the authenticity of their interpersonal relations. For example:

> As soon as the members realize that they must become more open with those feelings that typically they have learned to hide, they will need to establish group norms to sanction the expression of these feelings. Also, if members find it difficult in the group to express their important feelings, this difficulty will tend to be compounded if they feel they must "rush" their contribution and "say something quick," lest someone else take over the communication channels. Ways must be developed by which members are able to use their share of the communication channels. Also, group norms are required that sanction silence and thought, so that members do not feel coerced to say something, before they have thought it through, out of fear that they will not have an opportunity to say anything later.

An example of the interrelationship between interpersonal and group factors may be seen in the problems of developing leadership in a group. One of the recurring problems in the early stages of a T-group is the apparent need on the part of members to appoint a leader or a chairman. Typically, this need is rationalized as a group need because "without an appointed leader a group cannot be effective." For example, one member said, "Look, I think the first thing we need is to elect a leader. Without a leader we are going to get nowhere fast." Another added, "Brother, you are right. Without leadership, there is chaos. People hate to take responsibility and without a leader they will goof off."

There are several ways that your group might consider for coping with this problem, each of which provides important but different kinds of learning:

1. One approach is to see this as a group problem. How does leadership arise and remain helpful in a group? This level of learning is important and needs to be achieved.

2. Another possibility is for the group members to explore the underlying assumptions expressed by those individuals who want to appoint leaders. For example, in the case illustrated above, both men began to realize that they were assuming that people "need" appointed leadership because, if left alone, they will not tend to accept responsibility. This implies a lack of confidence in and trust of people. It also implies mistrust of the people around the table. These men were suggesting that without an appointed leader the group will flounder and become chaotic. Someone then took the initiative and suggested that their comments implied a lack of trust of the people around the table. Another individual suggested that another dimension of mistrust might also be operating. He was concerned how he would decide if he could trust the man who might be appointed as the leader. The discussion that followed illustrated to the group the double direction of the problem of trust. Not only do superiors have feelings of mistrust of subordinates, but the latter may also mistrust the former.

   One of the defendants of the need for leadership then said, "Look, Mr. B. over there has been trying to say something for half an hour, and hasn't succeeded. If we had a leader, or if he himself were appointed leader temporarily, then he might get his point of view across." Several agreed with the observation. However, two added some further insightful comments. One said, "If we give Mr. B. authority, he will never have to develop his internal strength so that he can get his point across without power behind him." "Moreover," the other added, "if he does get appointed leader, the group will never have to face the problem of how it can help to create the conditions for Mr. B. to express his point of view." Thus we see that attempting to cope with the basic problems of group membership can lead to an exploration of problems of group membership as well as requirements of effectively functioning groups.

   The question of trust, therefore, is a central problem in a T-group, indeed, as it is in any group organization. If this can be resolved, then the group has taken an important step in developing authentic relationships. As the degree of trust increases, "functional leadership" will tend to arise spontaneously because individuals in a climate of mutual trust will tend to delegate leadership to those who are most competent for the subject being discussed. In doing so, they also learn an important lesson about effective leadership.

3. Another kind of learning that usually develops clearly is that the group will not tend to become an effective task-oriented unit without having established effective means to diagnose problems, make decisions, and so on. It is as the group becomes a decision-making unit that the members can "test" the strength and depth of their learning. The pressure and stress of decision making can help to show

the degree to which authenticity is apparent rather than real. It can also provide opportunity for further learning, because the members will tend to experience new aspects of themselves as they attempt to solve problems and make decisions.

FURTHER COMPONENTS

Laboratory education has other components. I have focused in detail on T-groups because of their central role. This by no means describes the total laboratory experience. For example, laboratory education is helpful in diagnosing one's organizational problems.

Diagnosing problems

When a laboratory program is composed of a group of executives who work in the same firm, the organizational diagnostic experiences are very important. Each executive is asked to come to the laboratory with any agenda or topic that is important to him and to the organization. During the laboratory, he is asked to lead the group in a discussion of the topic. The discussion is taped and observed by the staff (with the knowledge of the members).

WHO LEARNS FROM T-GROUP EXPERIENCES?

People who learn in T-groups seem to possess at least three attributes:

1. A relatively strong ego that is not overwhelmed by internal conflicts.
2. Defenses which are sufficiently low to allow the individual to hear what others say to him (accurately and with minimal threat to his self), without the aid of a professional scanning and filtering system (that is, the therapist, the educator).
3. The ability to communicate thoughts and feelings with minimal distortion. In other words, the operational criterion of minimal threat is that the individual does not tend to distort greatly what he or others say, nor does he tend to condemn others or himself.

This last criterion can be used in helping to select individuals for the T-group experience. *If the individual must distort or condemn himself or others to the point that he is unable to do anything but to continue to distort the feedback that he gives and receives, then he ought not to be admitted to a T-group.*

To put this another way, T-groups, compared to therapy groups, assume a higher degree of health—not illness—that is, a higher degree of self-awareness and acceptance. This is an important point. *Individuals should not be sent to the laboratory if they are highly defensive.* Rather, the relatively healthy individuals capable of learning from others to enhance their degree of effectiveness are the kinds of individuals to be selected to attend.

Once the discussion is completed, the group members listen to themselves on the tape. They analyze the interpersonal and group dynamics that occurred in the making of the decision and study how these factors influenced their decision making. Usually, they hear how they cut each other off, did not listen, manipulated, pressured, created win-lose alternatives, and so on.

Such an analysis typically leads the executives to ask such questions as: Why do we do this to each other? What do we wish to do about it, if anything?

On the basis of my experience, executives become highly involved in answering these questions. Few hold back from citing interpersonal and organizational reasons why they feel they have to behave as they do. Most deplore the fact that time must be wasted and much energy utilized in this "windmilling" behavior. It is quite frequent for someone to ask, "But if we don't like this, why don't we do something about it?"

Under these conditions, the things learned in the laboratory are intimately interrelated with the everyday "real" problems of the organization. Where this has occurred, the members do not return to the organization with the same degree of bewilderment that executives show who have gone to laboratories full of strangers. In the latter case, it is quite common for the executive to be puzzled as to how he will use what he has learned about human competence when he returns home.[7]

Consultation groups

Another learning experience frequently used is to break down the participants into groups of four. Sessions are held where each individual has the opportunity both to act as a consultant giving help and as an individual receiving help. The nature of help is usually related to increasing self-awareness and self-acceptance with the view of enhancing interpersonal competence.

Lectures

As I pointed out above, research information and theories designed to help organizational learning are presented in lectures— typically at a time when it is most clearly related to the learnings that the participants are experiencing in a laboratory.

---

[7] For an example, see Argyris, *Interpersonal Competence and Organizational Effectiveness, op. cit.,* Chapter 9.

Role-playing of "real" situations

As a result of the discussions at the laboratory program, many data are collected illustrating situations in which poor communications exist, objectives are not being achieved as intended, and so on. It is possible in a laboratory to role-play many of these situations, to diagnose them, to obtain new insights regarding the difficulties, as well as to develop more effective action possibilities. These can be role-played by asking the executives to play their back-home role. For other problems, however, important learnings are gained by asking the superiors to take the subordinates' role.

Developing and testing recommendations

In most organizations, executives acknowledge that there are long-range problems that plague an organization, but that they do not have time to analyze them thoroughly in the back-home situation (for example, effectiveness of decentralization). In a laboratory, however, time is available for them to discuss these problems thoroughly. More important, as a result of their laboratory learnings and with the assistance of the educators, they could develop new action recommendations. They could diagnose their effectiveness as a group in developing these recommendations—have they really changed; have they really enhanced their effectiveness?

Intergroup problems

On of the central problems of organizations is the intergroup rivalries that exist among departments. If there is time in a laboratory, this topic should be dealt with. Again, it is best introduced by creating the situation where the executives compete against one another in groups under "win-lose" conditions (i.e., where only one can win and someone must lose).

CORRECTING MISUNDERSTANDINGS

Any educational activity that is as new and controversial as laboratory education is bound to have misconceptions and misunderstandings built around it. Therefore, I should like to attempt briefly to correct a few of the more commonly heard misunderstandings about laboratory education.

(1) *Laboratory methods in general, and T-groups in particular, are not a set of hidden, manipulative processes by which individuals*

can be "brainwashed" into thinking, believing, and feeling the way someone might want them to without realizing what is happening to them.

Central to a laboratory is openness and flexibility in the educational process. It is open in that it is continually described and discussed with the participants as well as constantly open to modification by them.

Along with the de-emphasis of rigidity and emphasis on flexibility, the emphasis is on teaching that kind of knowledge and helping the participants develop those kinds of skills which increase the strength and competence to question, to examine, and to modify. The objectives of a laboratory are to help an individual learn to be able to reject that which he deeply believes is inimical to his self-esteem and to his growth—and this would include, if necessary, the rejection of the laboratory experience.

(2) *A laboratory is not an educational process guided by a staff leader who is covertly in control and by some magic hides this fact from the participants.*

A laboratory means that people come together and create a setting where (as in the case in any laboratory) they generate their own data for learning. This means that they are in control and that any behavior in the laboratory, including the staff member's, is fair game for analysis.

I should like to suggest the hypothesis that if anything is a threat to the participants, it is not the so-called covert control. The experience becomes painful when the participants begin to realize the scope and depth to which the staff is ready "to turn things over to them." Initially this is seen by many participants as the staff abdicating leadership. Those who truly learn come to realize that in doing this the staff is expressing, in a most genuine way, their faith in the potentiality of the participants to develop increasing competence in controlling more of their learning. As this awareness increases, the participants usually begin to see that their cry of "abdication of leadership" is more of a camouflage that hides from them how little they trusted each other and themselves and how overprotected they were in the past from being made to assume some responsibility for their learning.

(3) *The objective of laboratory education is not to suppress conflict and to get everyone to like one another.*

The idea that this is the objective is so patently untrue that I am beginning to wonder if those who use it do not betray their own anxiety more than they describe what goes on in a laboratory. There is no other educational process that I am aware of in which conflict is generated, respected, and cherished. Here conflict, hostility, and frustration become motivations for growth as well as food for learning. It is with these kinds of experiences that participants learn to take risks—the kinds of risks that can lead to an increase in self-esteem. As these experiences are "worked through" and the learnings internalized, participants soon begin to experience a deeper sense of self-awareness and acceptance. These, in turn, lead to an increased awareness and acceptance of others.

And this does *not* necessarily mean liking people. Self-acceptance means that individuals are aware of themselves and care so much about themselves that they open themselves to receiving and giving information (sometimes painful) about their impact on others and others' impact on them, so that they can grow and become more competent.

(4) *Laboratory education does not attempt to teach people to be callous, disrespectful of society, and to dislike those who live a less open life.*

If one truly begins to accept himself, he will be less inclined to condemn nongenuineness in others, but to see it for what it is, a way of coping with a nongenuine world by a person who is (understandably) a nongenuine individual.

(5) *Laboratory education is neither psycho-analysis nor intensive group therapy.*

During the past several years I have been meeting with a group of psychiatrists and clinical psychologists who are trying to differentiate between group therapy and everything else. One problem we discovered is that therapists define therapy as any change. The difficulty with this definition is that it means any change is therapy.

We have concluded that it may be best to conceive of a continuation of "more" or "less" therapy. The more the group deals with unconscious motivations, uses clinical constructs, focuses on "personal past history," and is guided in these activities by the leader, the more it is therapy. Therapy is usually characterized by high proportions of these activities because the individuals who are participating are so conflicted or defensive that they are not able to learn from each other without these activities.

In my view, a T-group is—or should be—a group that contains individuals whose internal conflicts are low enough to learn by:

1. Dealing with "here and now" behavior (what is going on in the room).
2. Using relatively nonclinical concepts and nonclinical theory.
3. Focusing on relatively conscious (or at most preconscious) material.
4. Being guided increasingly less by the leader and increasingly more by each other.
5. Accomplishing this in a relatively (to therapy) short time (at the moment, no more than three weeks).

This does not mean that T-groups do not, at times, get into deeper and less conscious problems. They do; and, again, they vary primarily with the staff member's biases. Usually most educators warn the group members against striving to become "two bit" psychologists.

(6) *Laboratory education does not have to be dangerous, but it must focus on feelings.*

Interpersonal problems and personal feelings exist at all levels of the organization, serving to inhibit and decrease the effectiveness of the system. Does it seem to be logical (in fact, moral) for a company to say that it is not going to focus on something that people are already experiencing and feeling? The truth is that people *do* focus on interpersonal problems every hour of the day. They simply do not do it openly.

Now for the argument that the laboratory program can hurt people and is, therefore, dangerous. The facts of life are that people are being hurt every day. I do not know of any laboratory program that did, or could, create for people as much tension as they are experiencing in their everyday work relationships.

It is true that laboratory education does require people to take risks. But does anyone know of any learning that truly leads to growth which does not involve some pain and cost? The value of laboratory education is that it keeps out the people who want to learn "cheaply" and it provides the others with control over how much they wish to learn and what they want to pay for it.

(7) *The objective of laboratory education is to develop effective reality-centered leaders.*

Some people have expressed concern that if an executive goes through such a learning experience, he might somehow become a weak leader. Much depends on how one defines strong leadership. If strong leadership means unilateral domination and directiveness, then the individual will tend to become "weaker." But why is such leadership strong? Indeed, as I have suggested, it may be weak. Also it tends to develop subordinates who conform, fear to take risks, and are not open, and an organization that becomes increasingly rigid and has less vitality.[8]

Nor can one use the argument that directive leadership has worked and that is why it should remain. There are data to suggest that directive leadership can help an organization under certain conditions (e.g., for routine decisions and under extreme emergencies). But these conditions are limited. If directive leadership is effective beyond these relatively narrow conditions, it may be because of a self-fulfilling prophecy. Directive leadership creates dependence, submissiveness, and conformity. Under these conditions subordinates will tend to be afraid to use their initiative. Consequently, the superior will tend to fill in the vacuum with directive leadership. We now have a closed cycle.

The fact is that directive leaders who learn at a laboratory do not tend to throw away their directive skills. Rather, they seem to use directive leadership where and when it is appropriate. It cannot be emphasized too strongly that there is nothing in laboratory education which requires an individual to throw away a particular leadership pattern. The most laboratory education can do is help the individual see certain unintended consequences and costs of his leadership, and help him to develop other leadership styles *if* he wishes.

(8) *Change is not guaranteed as a result of attendance.*

Sometimes I hear it said that laboratory education is not worthwhile, because some individuals who have attended do not change, or if they do change, it is only for a relatively short period of time.

Let me acknowledge that there is an immense gap in our knowledge about the effectiveness of a laboratory. Much research needs to be done before we know exactly what the payoff is in laboratory education. However, there are a few statements that can be made partially on the basis of research and experience and partially on the basis of theory.

One of the crucial learnings of a laboratory is related to the development of openness and trust in human relationships. These factors are not generated easily in a group. It takes much effort and risk. Those who develop trust in a group learn something very important about it. Trust cannot be issued, inspired, delegated, and transferred. It is an interpersonal factor which has to be *earned* in each relationship. This is what makes trust difficult to develop and precious to have.

---

[8] *Ibid.*

Thus, it does not make very much sense to expect that suddenly an individual will act as if he can trust and can be trusted in a setting where this was never true. One executive was needled by the corporate president, who observed that he had not seen any change in the former's behavior. The executive responded: "What makes you think I feel free to change my behavior in front of you?"

This remark points up the possibility that if there is not any observable change, it could mean that the individual has not learned much. But it could also mean that he has learned a great deal, *including* the fact that he ought not to behave differently when he returns. For, it must be emphasized, laboratory education is only a partial attack on the problem of organizational effectiveness. If the changes are to become permanent, one must also change the nature of the organizational structure, managerial controls, incentive systems, reward and penalty systems, and job designs.[9]

IMPACT ON ORGANIZATION

The impact of laboratory education on the effectiveness of an organization is extremely difficult to isolate and measure.[10] Organizations are so complex, and their activities influenced by so many factors, that it is difficult to be precise in specifying the causes of the impact.

In one study that I conducted of the 20 top executives of a large corporate division, I did find a significant shift on the part of the experimental group toward a set of values that encouraged the executives to handle feelings and emotions, deal with problems of group maintenance, and develop greater feelings of responsibility on the part of their subordinates for the effectiveness of the organization. This shift is quantified in Exhibit II.

As the exhibit shows, the impact of laboratory education continued at a high level for a period in excess of six months. However, during the tenth month a fade-out began to appear. *This was studied and data were obtained to suggest that the executives had not lost their capacity to behave in a more open and trustful manner, but*

[9] For a more theoretical discussion of this matter, see Chris Argyris, *Integrating the Individual and the Organization* (New York: John Wiley & Sons, Inc., 1964).

[10] Robert K. Blake and Jane S. Mouton, "Toward Achieving Organization Excellence," in Warren Bennis (ed.), *Organizational Change* (New York: John Wiley & Sons, Inc., 1964). As this article went to press, I read an excellent manuscript of a speech evaluating the effectiveness of laboratory education, "The Effect of Laboratory Education Upon Individual Behavior," given by Douglas R. Bunker before the Industrial Relations Research Association in Boston on December 28, 1963.

Exhibit II

BEFORE AND AFTER VALUES OF 11 EXECUTIVES WHO EXPERIENCED LABORATORY EDUCATION

In an administrative situation, whenever possible . . .	Before T-group	Six months after
1a. The leader should translate interpersonal problems into rational intellective ones	100%	10%
1b. The leader should deal with the interpersonal problems	0	81
2a. The leader should stop emotional disagreement by redefining the rational purpose of the meeting	90	10
2b. The leader should bring out emotional disagreements and help them to be understood and resolved	6	81
3a. When strong emotions erupt, the leader should require himself and others to leave them alone and not deal with them	100	18
3b. When strong emotions erupt, the leader should require himself and offer others the opportunity to deal with them	0	82
4a. If it becomes necessary to deal with feelings, the leader should do it even if he feels he is not the best qualified	100	9
4b. The leader should encourage the most competent members	0	90
5a. The leader is completely responsible for keeping the group "on the track" during a meeting	100	0
5b. The group members as well as the leader are responsible for keeping the group "on the track"	0	100

they had to suppress some of this learning because the corporate president and the other divisional presidents, who were not participants in the laboratory, did not understand them.

This finding points up two important problems. Change is not going to be effective and permanent *until the total organization* accepts the new values. Also, effective change does *not* mean that the executives must lose their capacity to behave according to the pyramidal values. They do so whenever it is necessary. However, now they have an additional way to behave, and they use it whenever possible. They report that irrespective of the problem of acceptance by others, they find the pyramidal values are effective when they are dealing primarily with *routine, programmed* decisions. The new values and manner of leadership seem to be best suited for decisions that are *unprogrammed, innovative,* and require high commitment.

It is important to emphasize that laboratory education does *not* tell anyone what type of leadership to select. It does not urge him always to be more "democratic" or "collaborative." A successful laboratory helps the executives realize the unintended costs of the "old," develop "new" leadership behavior and philosophies, and become competent in utilizing whatever leadership style is appropriate in a given situation. A laboratory helps an individual increase his repertory of leadership skills and his freedom to choose how he will behave. If it coerces the executive, it is for him to become more *reality-centered.*

Another way of describing the impact of a laboratory program of an organization is for me to offer you excerpts from a tape of a meeting where the executives discussed the difficulties as well as successes that they were having 30 days after the program. The first part of the tape contains a discussion of examples of concrete changes which the members felt were a result of the laboratory. Here is a sample of the changes reported:

1. Executives reported the development of a new program for certain pricing policies that could not be agreed upon before, and laid part of the success to their new ability to sense feelings.
2. One executive stated, "We are consciously trying to change our memos. For example, we found a way to decrease the 'win-lose' feelings and 'rivalries.' "
3. The personnel director reported a distinct improvement in the sensitivity of the line managers to the importance of personnel problems, which before the laboratory seemed to have a second-class status. He said he was especially pleased with the line executives' new awareness of the complexity of personnel problems and their willingness to spend more time on solving them.

The rest of the tape is excerpted and presented in Exhibit III.

Conclusion

While I do not hold up laboratory education as a panacea to remedy all organizational problems, I do feel that six conclusions can fairly be drawn:

1. Laboratory education is a very promising educational process. Experience to date suggests that it can help some organizations to *begin* to overcome some of their problems.
2. Laboratory education is *not* a panacea, nor is it a process that can help every organization. Furthermore, it must be followed by changes

Exhibit III

DISCUSSION OF ATTITUDE CHANGES BY T-GROUP MEMBERS

The excerpt presented here mirrors the tone of the entire meeting. I have not purposely selected only that section in which the men praised the laboratory. If the men had criticized the laboratory, such criticism would have been included. As you may see, the researcher actually pushed the group for more negative comments.

Except for minor editing, these are direct quotes:

No. 4 [after reporting that his superior, a member of the experimental group, had made a decision which should have been left to him]: I was really fuming. I was angry as hell. I walked into his office and I said to myself, "No matter what the hell happens, I'm going to tell him that he cannot do that any more." Well, I told him so. I was quite emotional. You know it floored me. He looked at me and said, "You're right; I made a mistake, and I won't do that again." Well I just don't think he would have done that before.

No. 7: The most important factor in motivating people is not what you say or do; it's giving a person the opportunity to express his views and the feeling that one is seriously interested in his views. I do much less selling but it sure takes longer.

No. 2: I've had a problem. I now have a greater need for feedback than before, and I find it difficult to get. The discussion on internal commitment made much sense to me, and I try to see if I can create conditions for it.

The thing that bothers me is that I try to handle it correctly, but I don't get feedback or cues as to how well I'm doing, as I used to at the lab. The meeting is over, and you don't know whether you've scored or not. So after each meeting I've got 10 question marks. The things that before were never questions are now question marks. You don't get feedback. You ask for something and they respond, "I know what you're trying to do." They think I've got something up my sleeve. All I want is to get feedback. It was obvious to me they were all waiting for me to make the decision. But I wanted them to make it. This was their baby, and I wanted them to make it. Two days later they made it. Fine, in this case I got feedback. The point was that their decision was a severe reversal, and I realize it was difficult for them to make. But they made it. Before, I simply would have pointed out the facts, and they would have "agreed" with the reversal, but down deep inside they would have felt that they could have continued on. As it is now, it's their decision. I think they now have a greater sense of internal commitment. People are now freer to disagree.

No. 11: My list of decisions to be made is longer. I am hoping that they will make some decisions. I now know how much they wait for me.

No. 11 [after telling how he wrote a note which in effect damned No. 2 and maintained his own correctness, then reread it and realized how defensive he was]: Before I wouldn't have even seen this.

No. 2: One of our most difficult jobs will be to write our feelings and to write in such a way that others can express their feelings.

No. 3: I have some difficulties in evaluating this program. What have we gotten out of this? What are we able to verbalize about what we got out of this? Do others of you have difficulty in verbalizing?

No. 2: I have the same difficulty. I have been totally ineffective describing the experience.

No. 8: Each time I try I give a different answer.

No. 1: I don't have too much difficulty. One thing that I am certain of is that I see people more as total human beings. I see aspects of them that I had never seen before.

No. 9: I'm frustrated because I now realize the importance of face-to-face communication. I'm so far from the general managers that it is not so hot. Has anyone tried to write memos that really get feelings brought out?

I find myself questioning much more than I ever did before. I have a more questioning attitude. I take into account more factors.

No. 4: We've been talking about things as if we've slowed down a bit. We haven't. For example, remember you [No. 1] and I had a problem? I'm sure Arden House was very helpful. If I hadn't been there, my reaction to you would have been different. I would have fought you for hours.

No. 1: I know we can talk to each other more clearly. It's not a conscious way. It's spontaneous.

No. 3: I have to agree we can make some decisions much faster. For example, with No. 2 I simply used to shut up. But now I can be more open. Before the laboratory, if I had an intuitive feeling that something

EXHIBIT III

DISCUSSION OF ATTITUDE CHANGES
BY T-GROUP MEMBERS (Cont.)

was wrong, but I wasn't sure, I'd keep quiet until things got so bad that then I'd have a case to go to the boss. Now I feel freer to talk about it sooner and with No. 2.

I now feel that we are going to say exactly how we feel to anyone. You [the president], for example, don't have to worry, and, therefore, question, probe, and draw us out.

PRESIDENT: Yes, and today I found No. 1, who told me that he simply would not agree with me. And I said to myself, "God bless you. He really is open now."

No. 1: I agree. I would not have expressed this feeling before being in this group. It's obvious that one should but I didn't.

[No. 2 and No. 1 show real insight into how they are being manipulated by people outside and above the group. They are much more aware of the manipulative process. "This kind of manipulation is dynamic. It burns me up."]

No. 1: Yes, it's really horrible to see it and not be able to do anything about it.

No. 7: In this case it seems to me you've got to really hit hard, because you're dealing with an untrained man [laughter] . . . . I think I now have a new understanding of decision making. I am now more keenly aware of the importance of getting a consensus so that the *implementation* is effective. I am not trying to say that I do this in every meeting. But I do strive more to give opportunity for consensus.

No. 1: One of the problems that I feel is that the "initiated" get confused so they don't play the game correctly. Sometimes I feel walked upon, so I get sore. This is difficult. [Many others expressed agreement.]

No. 6: Does it help to say, "I trust you?" I think it does.

No. 11: For example, No. 2, you went to a meeting where you admitted you had made a mistake. Boy, you should have heard the reaction. Boy, Mr. —— admitted a mistake. Well, wonderful; it helped to get these guys to really feel motivated to get the job done.

No. 9: Yes, I heard that many took on a deeper feeling of responsibility to get the program on the right track.

No. 7: I'd like to come back to what No. 6 said. I used to say to people that I trusted them, that I was honest, and so on. But now I wonder if people really believe me, or if they don't begin to think if I'm not covering that I'm not honest.

No. 3: Another example which I am now

aware of is the typical way we write memos. We start off: "I have confidence in your judgment to handle this question," and so on. Few more paragraphs. Then fifth paragraph reads: "Please confirm by return mail exactly what you have done and what controls have been set up."

No. 2: I agree. We do an awful lot to control people. Although I think that we're trying.

[No. 7 gave examples of how he stopped making a few phone calls to exert pressure. Others agreed.]

THE RESEARCHER: Aren't there negative comments?

No. 11: We have one man who has chosen not to be here. I wonder why?

No. 3: Well, really, to me that is a sign of health in the group. He feels he would still be accepted even if he didn't come. It certainly would be easy for him to come and just sit here.

No. 1: Yes, he wouldn't go to the trouble of avoiding a meeting that you didn't think was important.

No. 3: The only negative that I can think is: "What can you tell me that actually increases effectiveness?" I am not sure, but I must agree that there is a whale of a different climate.

No. 7: Well, I'd like to develop a list of things that we feel we have gotten out of this program so far. How do others of you feel? [All agreed, "Let's try."]

[ALL GROUP MEMBERS reporting they reached the following conclusions]:

(a) All of us begin to see ourselves as others see us . . . a real plus.

(b) A degree of greater confidence in oneself in meetings and in interviews. Beginning to be more comfortable with self.

(c) Greater confidence in associates. We feel more secure that you're telling what you think. . . . Greater feeling of freedom of expression to say what you really think.

(d) Individuals have a greater understanding and appreciation of viewpoint of associates.

(e) Greater appreciation of the opposite viewpoint.

(f) An awareness of what we do and others do that inhibits discussion.

(g) More effective use of our resources . . . getting more from them, and they feel this . . . patient to listen more.

(h) Meetings do not take longer and implementation is more effective. Internal commitment is greater.

(i) We have had a great realization that

Exhibit III

DISCUSSION OF ATTITUDE CHANGES
BY T-GROUP MEMBERS (Cont.)

being only task-oriented, we will not get the best results. We must not forget worrying about the organization and the people. (j) We get more irritated to infringement of our jobs and unique contributions. (k) Fewer homemade crises.

No. 6: One of the difficult thinks about the list is that when you look at it, you wake up to the fact that you haven't really been using these principles. When you tell someone else who doesn't realize the gap between knowing something and actually doing it, he doesn't realize.

No. 7: But I think I really did learn and do care. Now when I think what I used to do, because that was the way. Today I realize that I could have had three times as much if I had known what I know now."

in the organization, its policies, managerial controls, and even technology. Not all organizations can profit from it; nor do all organizations need similar amounts of it. All these factors should be carefully explored before becoming involved.

3. Not all laboratory programs are alike. Some focus more on interpersonal learning, some on intellectual problem solving, some on small groups, some on intergroups, and some on varying combinations of all of these. Again a careful diagnosis can help one to choose the right combination for the organization, as well as the appropriate educators. Nor are all laboratory programs equally effective. The competence of the educators can vary tremendously, as well as the receptivity of those who attend. The best thing to do is to attempt to attend a laboratory program conducted by competent professionals.

4. Openness, trust, commitment, and risk-taking grow only where the climate is supportive. A one-shot program, even at its best, can only begin the process of unfreezing the executive system. For optimum results, repeat or "booster" programs will be necessary.

5. Although I personally believe that a laboratory program with the "natural" or actual working groups has the greatest probable payoff, it also has the greatest risk. However, one does not have to begin the process this way. There are many different ways to "seed" an organization, hoping to develop increasing trust and risk-taking. The way that will be most effective can best be ascertained by appropriate study of the executive system.

6. Finally, if you ever talk to an individual who has had a successful experience in a laboratory, you may wonder why he seems to have difficulty in describing the experience. I know I still have difficulty describing this type of education to a person who is a stranger to it.

I am beginning to realize that one reason for the difficulty in communication is that the meaningfulness of a laboratory experience varies enormously with each person. Some learn much; some learn little. I find that my learning has varied with the success of the laboratory. Some can hardly wait until it is over; others wish that it would never end. Anyone who understands a laboratory realizes that all these feelings can be real and valid. Consequently, to attempt to describe a laboratory (especially a T-group) to an individual who has never experienced one is difficult because he may be one of those persons who would not have enjoyed the process at all. Therefore, an enthusiastic description may sound hollow.

Another reason why it is difficult to communicate is that the same words can have different meanings to different people. Thus one of the learnings consistently reported by people who have completed a laboratory is that the trust, openness, leveling, risk-taking (and others) take on a new meaning—a meaning that they had not appreciated before the laboratory. This makes it difficult for a person who found laboratory education meaningful to describe it to another. He may want very much to communicate the new meanings of trust, risk-taking, and so on, but he knows, from his own skepticism before the laboratory, that this is a difficult undertaking and that it is not likely to succeed.

The point to all this is that the results of laboratory education are always individualistic; they reflect the individual and the organization. The best way to learn about it is to experience it for one's self.

QUESTIONS

1. What values does Argyris hold as being crucial to effective human relationships and the attainment of organizational objectives?
2. What does Argyris mean by executive reeducation? Why do successful executives need to be reeducated?
3. Define: (a) laboratory training, (b) T-groups, (c) authentic relationships, and (d) values. Now, what is the relationship between these terms?
4. What does "laboratory education" *not* consist of? What, then, does it consist of?
5. Of what value is laboratory education to (a) participating executives, (b) business firms, and (c) the subordinates of participating executives?

47. MANAGERIAL GUIDELINES TO SENSITIVITY TRAINING *

Leslie This and Gordon L. Lippitt

Some strong opinions have been expressed pro and con about sensitivity training by leaders in the field of management. Dr. Douglas McGregor [1] says this kind of training can ". . . bring about significant improvements in the skills of social interaction," while Dr. George S. Odiorne [2] indicates that he feels that many human relations laboratories have become ". . . perverted into psychological nudist camps which end up mainly as self flagellation societies."

While much has been written about sensitivity training, most of the literature is either technical or descriptive of personal experience. Neither approach is helpful to the training director or manager who wants to answer the pragmatic question, "Is this kind of training desirable in my organization and related to my organization's problems, needs, and objectives?"

When trying to get an answer to this kind of question, the organizational decision-maker usually consults someone who has been through a program. Almost inevitably he is told, "Oh, I couldn't begin to tell you about it—you just have to experience it." This is not helpful for effective decision-making. The manager then turns to a professional person who usually doesn't distinguish between the direct work-related benefits and the more complex areas of personality integration, social responsibility, self-fulfillment, and other person-oriented values of such training.

This article is an attempt to help the organizational leaders answer the question, "Is sensitivity training desirable for my organization?" We have divided the material into major areas of consideration or questions [3] that have frequently been asked about this kind of training.

* From *Training Directors Journal*, Vol. 17, No. 4 (April, 1963), pp. 3-13. Reprinted with permission.

[1] Douglas McGregor, "The Human Side of Enterprise," p. 221, McGraw-Hill, 1960.

[2] George S. Odiorne, "Managerial Narcissism—The Great Self Development Binge," *Management of Personnel Quarterly*, Vol. I, Issue 3 (Spring, 1962); Bureau of Industrial Relations; Graduate School of Business, University of Michigan.

[3] The authors wish to acknowledge the contribution of Mr. Rowland Geddie of the Atlanta ASTD chapter who organized a January 1963 chapter meeting on Sensitivity Training which raised some of these questions with Dr. Lippitt.

WHAT IS "SENSITIVITY TRAINING"?

The expression "Sensitivity Training" is an inadequate phrase that is popularly used in describing a particular theory and method utilized in human relations training. This kind of training usually includes the methods of unstructured group learning, individual feedback, skill practice, and information sessions. The theory behind such methods is based on a laboratory concept of learning which believes that individuals can best learn inter-personal and group skills through actual experience which is analyzed for the benefit of the learner.

The words "sensitivity training" were first applied to this kind of learning in connection with the three-week Human Relations Laboratories, sponsored by the National Training Laboratories at Bethel, Maine. Since those early years beginning in 1947, this training has spread to many University-sponsored laboratories, in-house organization programs, and the development of consultant service to provide this kind of training to particular clients.

HOW IS THIS TRAINING ACCOMPLISHED?

One of the assumptions underlying sensitivity training is that the man best learns these kinds of insights by self-discovery.[4] It does little good to be "spoken to," or to read, many of these kinds of learnings. The training, then, must provide the kind of setting and methods that will best enable men to discover these insights and knowledges. These methods have been found most helpful:

1. Sensitivity training groups

Participants meet in groups of 12-15 with a professional trainer. They have no formal agenda or prior-determined leader. Normally the groups meet once a day for two hours, but may meet twice a day for approximately two-hour sessions.

Participants struggle with making decisions about how to spend the time profitably and how to provide structure and leadership. They have time to "thresh out" their struggles and examine their group life. As they do, they begin to get insights into the forces that are at work—things like the leadership struggle, group structure, group objectives, accommodating individual objectives to group objectives, group standards to guide their conduct, what improves and lessens

---

[4] Malcolm E. Knowles, "The Leader Looks At Self Development," *Looking into Leadership* (Monographs: Leadership Resources, Inc., 1961).

the group's appeal to them, how decisions will be made, how to handle the participation of members, how one's behavior is influencing this group, and how the behavior of other members is influencing one's behavior.

As the group pauses to study parts of their group life that has interest for them, the trainer helps them to understand the forces at work at that moment. From time to time an individual member may want to test out with others the effect his behavior is having on them—how they see him—and may ask for reactions and information (feedback)—and the members try to help him see himself as they see him in the life of the group.

2. Information sessions

Usually the problems with which the learning groups and individuals are concerned about, at any given time in the training, can be fairly well predicted. Presentations are made, drawing on research and experiences, to further explain the forces or factors involved with a particular area of interest. Usually the design of the program is such that it is flexible and may be modified to meet the needs and interests of the participants. Real life experiences need to be compared and generalized from the findings of other experiences and research.

3. Skill practice sessions

As a man gets knowledge about what may be, for him, a better way to perform as a manager, he wants to practice trying out the new way. Skill exercise periods are provided to let the participants try out new ways of behaving, or to test out ways that have been suggested in the presentation or by the groups. Here he has little at stake since he knows he is in a training setting and encouraged to experiment with new ways of behaving. If it seems to him to be better than his old pattern, the chances are enhanced that he will try it out in his job when he returns home.

These are the main methods employed. Other action learning methods are also utilized—skill practice, case studies, informal group discussion, film, gaming and coaching teams. All of these methods are utilized as appropriate to a particular program to provide the maximum opportunity for participants to learn.

Why Does the Training Seem So Mysterious?

It isn't so seen by those who know what the training is designed to accomplish. However, as we indicated earlier, the learnings about oneself are so highly personal that it is difficult to share them with another person in a meaningful way. How would a superior react if you told him, "I learned that people mistake my seriousness for aggressiveness, and I'm going to try to do something about it"? It is in this area that it is difficult to explain one's learning.

Perhaps it is a reflection of our culture and the need for this training that we find it difficult to share one's own feelings, emotions, and behavior. This is the nature of the sensitivity group experience.

There is no excuse whatever for there being any misunderstanding about the content of the information sessions or the skill practice sessions. These you can listen to, talk about, read and perform. These activities form an important part of the actual content. Because the learnings of a personal nature are so vivid and meaningful, in comparison to the substantive learnings, it is understandable that the total training experience tends to be seen as that component of the learning activity in which trainees gained their most meaningful insights.

Contributions to Organization Goals

Sensitivity training means many things to many people. However, it seems to us that it serves three basic organizational concerns:

I. A manager works in a complex organizational system

Organizations are more than the physical "things" that go on its inventory lists. It is not possible to think of an organization without thinking of people—their functions and inter-relationships. If people are removed from an organization, you are left with a catalogue of items occupying space—little more than a poorly utilized warehouse.

It is people that have organizational objectives—that need a division of labor—that do the work—or give the service—that need meetings—need directives—need policies—need methods for delegating work—need controls—need to know how to get the most from other people.

Too little is really known about the human dynamics of organizations. One of the objectives of sensitivity training is to help the participant to see "organizations" not as the eye sees the buildings—

but the informal, unseen, or unnoticed functions, elements, characteristics, forms, authority, tradition and interpersonal processes at work. The premise is that the more he understands the nature of the human encounter in the organization, the better equipped he will be to utilize, release, and control the organization for the attainment of organizational objectives.

2. Organizations accomplish their work through the motivations of people

Most managers know their technical specialty quite well, and usually are quite well informed about the functions in their jobs such as planning, reporting, controlling, etc.

What they are less knowledgeable about is how to get the maximum efficiency and productivity from people. Down through history one of the precepts noted by successful leaders has been "Know thyself." Whether a manager recognizes it or not, his behavior, posture, gestures, tone of voice, ways of reacting to people and situations, silence—these and many other personal factors influence greatly how other people react to him and the jobs he asks them to do.

It would follow that the more a man understands himself, and how his behavior, consciously or unconsciously, will affect others—the more effective he can be in his relationships with other human beings. The objective is not to become an amateur psychiatrist, but to be more sensitive to the influence his behavior has on others, and vice versa.

Such sensitivity is not designed to make a person "thin-skinned," but more aware of his surroundings. The human organism has the "radar" of its many senses which frequently are dormant or undeveloped. It is in the sharpening of these senses that sensitivity training can assist.

3. A manager works frequently in groups

The life of today's manager is spent in settings with two or more persons in an organizational work unit, conferences, institutes, planning groups, task forces and similar groupings. Many of the factors at work in individual-to-individual contexts are also at work within groups. However, as every manager knows, when a number of individuals are brought into a group setting, additional factors and forces are manifested. Many of us have commented, "How can people, who individually are such fine persons, behave so ineffectively when I call them together to work on a task?"

There is a body of knowledge about the factors at work when people work in groups, and the more a manager understands these factors, the more effectively he can work with people in work groups. Dr. Rensis Likert has recently summarized much of the research in this area, and its implications for managers and organizations, in his book "Patterns of Management." [5] The research on morale and productivity indicate that people potentially meet their needs and accomplish work effectively in the face-to-face work unit of the organization.

These three areas, then, are the major areas of learning that sensitivity training explores. Since much of what is learned is peculiar to the individual in attendance, it is difficult to list what specific learning or insights each participant will discover. To know oneself better is a different experience for each of us, and that is why a personal insight for one person is not an insight to another. This in part explains why participants find it so difficult to agree on what they learned at a human relations laboratory experience.

People develop their skill and awareness through various learning experiences. An experience which will further interpersonal competence will need to provide the following conditions for learning. [6]

1. The recognition on the part of the trainee of a need for improving his own human relations skills.
2. An opportunity for a trainee to interact in a learning situation so that actual behavior may serve as the curriculum.
3. A supportive and helpful climate for learning created by the total experience.
4. An opportunity for the trainees to give "feedback" on the effect of their behavior in both structured and unstructured learning experiences.
5. A basic knowledge of individual, group, and organizational behavior to give guidance to the learner.
6. A chance to practice new skills of relating in person-to-person and person-to-group situations.
7. An opportunity to relate his learning to back-on-the-job situations.

These conditions for learning are essential elements in what has been referred to as the "laboratory" approach to human relations training.

KINDS OF ORGANIZATIONAL PROBLEMS IT CAN AFFECT

We will immediately make two assumptions: 1, that training can affect some organizational problems; and, 2, that individuals and groups may be considered organizational problems.

[5] Rensis Likert, "Patterns of Management," McGraw-Hill, 1962.
[6] A more complete discussion of the conditions for laboratory learning may

There are some organizational problems which are not the primary province of any kind of training. If the organizational product or service is not needed, wanted, or of a deliberate inferior quality—training isn't the answer. If the market falls out from under a product because of technological or international factors, training is out of its field in attempting to solve such a problem. There are some organizational matters that are the main province of other facets of organizational problem solving. Sometimes organizations mistakenly see training as the answer to all their problems. Organizational effectiveness, in all its aspects, can never be equated with training or the lack of training.

If, however, a manager suspects that some of the organization's effectiveness is being disturbed or affected by some of the following kinds of problems, he may well consider sensitivity training:

1. An otherwise effective manager whose attitudes, skills, relationships with his work force, relationships with other persons and sub-units, effectiveness in meetings, ability to diagnose personal relationship problems in their embryonic stage, are seen as inadequate.
2. Where the basic face-to-face units of the organization do not seem to be achieving a level of morale and productivity that is in keeping with their abilities.
3. Where the organization is concerned with public relations and its managerial staff have enough contacts with outside groups that the totality of these contacts can materially affect the organization's image.
4. Where it is important for communication to flow as uninhibitedly as possible between peers, between subordinate and superior, and between work units even though they appear as separate prongs on the organizational chart.
5. Where there is good reason to believe that managers in the organization are, by organizational practice or climate, discouraged from being inventive, creative, and exercising or receiving appropriate responsibility, delegation of authority, and exercising initiative in meeting operational problems.
6. Where the organization gets its work done in large measure through the use of group meetings, conferences, and informal group activities.

What Must Exist Before Sensitivity Training?

The training should be consistent with the organizational objectives, goals, and processes of decision-making.[7] There must be an understanding, beginning at top management and permeating down

---

be found in Leland P. Bradford, "The Teaching-Learning Transaction," *Adult Education*, Spring, 1958 and also in Selected Readings Series No. 3 "Forces In Learning," National Training Laboratories, National Education Association, 1961.
    [7] Jarold Niven and Allen Zoll, "A Survey of Sensitivity Training for Industrial Managers," Boeing Airplane Co., Seattle, Washington.

through the levels to be trained, of the purpose of the training and acceptance and support of the training objectives. The training program should be designed to help solve one or more identified management problems, and tailored to fit the particular organization needs. The program and design should be carefully worked out and planned. It is usually helpful if some of top management have had a personal experience with this kind of training.

The training should be seen as voluntary, and an employee should be permitted to decline to undertake the training without punishment or embarrassment. There should also exist an organizational understanding and climate that will enable a participant to "try out" and practice his learnings in the organizational setting.

A qualified staff should be utilized for such training. The staff should include social scientists with experience in this kind of training, but they should be provided ample opportunity to become familiar with the organization and to be accepted by the management of the organization. Such training should also have a well designed evaluation plan to measure the effectiveness of the training.

Lately, we think the organization must see the training as a part of the organizational life and be committed to provide follow-up and supplementary training opportunities to reinforce the process that has been begun.

Some of the Issues About Various Approaches

This kind of training has developed a number of approaches in its application.

1. Length of training

Some training programs last three weeks—others for as short a period as two days. Some organizations have a series of two-day sessions at intervals over a period of several months. There is some disagreement as to what is the desired length, or whether a continuous program is better.

There can be little assurance as to how much more learning takes place in a week's program versus a three-week's program—or a three-day program vs. a one-week program. Probably common sense is the best guide. One can expect that more can be learned in one week than in three days. Rarely has this kind of training been undertaken without having at least twelve hours of group learning time plus the other aspects of the program.

In the shorter programs the organization would need to identify what kind of skills, insights, and knowledges are most important to focus on, and to design the training program for intensive concentration in these pre-determined areas. Generally, most organizations seem to find an experience of at least one week's duration most desirable. This is particularly true if one is focusing on personal insight. It takes time to create a group atmosphere, and individual readiness, that will permit constructive and direct feedback of a helpful nature to trainees.

2. Heterogenous or family groups

Opinions differ as to whether it is better to train men in programs made up from different organizations, within one industry or business, within one department in an organization, along peer lines, or vertically from several levels. There are advantages and disadvantages to each. Generally speaking, the advantage of "family" training is that all members of a work group, or related work groups, get the same kind of training at one time and get to know each other quite well.[8] They can also use the learning process in their day by day work to solve operating problems.

One of the major disadvantages of family groupings is that participants can never completely forget the setting and work relationships and the inter-actions among participants may be less intense and direct. It has been proven valuable in heterogeneous training to send a team of persons from an organization to increase impact back in the organization. Which pattern one chooses would depend upon the length of the program, the experience of the persons to be trained, the objectives of the program for the organization.

The authors have conducted sensitivity training using both approaches with governmental, community, and industrial organizations, and found real impact for organizational change to be possible in either approach.

3. Use of trainer or instruments in the unstructured group phase of the learning

Some experimentation has been done recently with so-called instrumental groups.[9] The instruments consist of both individual and group

---

[8] One example of the "family" approach to training is reported in *Interpersonal Competence and Organizational Effectiveness*, by C. Argyris, Dorsey-Irwin Press, 1962.

[9] R. Blake and J. Mouton, "The Instrumented Training Laboratory," in *Issues In Human Relations Training*, National Training Laboratories, National Education Association, Washington, D. C., 1962.

administered questionnaires in which reactions can be coded, analyzed, and then "fed back" to the participants. A trainer does not sit with the basic training group, but does assist in the design of the training activity and provides materials to help the groups analyze their behavior as they work together. The trainer may also lead data summarizing sessions or presentations as well as assist the group with practice exercises.

The results of these programs do indicate that learning does take place under such circumstances. A group, through the use of well developed data collection instruments, can feed back data to itself for effective learning.

Many of the specialists in this field feel that the trainer should be present to help with inter-personal feedback and group analysis as well as to prevent attempts at ill-advised therapy by trainees of each other.

It is also felt by some that such training can best utilize a professional at all times during the training. The experience to date would indicate the value in using both the trainer and effective data collection instruments for maximizing the learning.

4. Use of outside vs. inside organization trainers

Some managers ask the question: "Can't my training director do this kind of training?"

Perhaps he can if he has had extensive training.[10] Certainly he can probably handle some of the elements, with proper knowledge and experience, like information presentations and skill exercises. However, the sensitivity training group experience and the integration of all the elements of the training program into a meaningful experience require a great deal of specialized knowledge, skill, and experience.

These can be learned by many training directors, but the expenditure in time, effort, and money is considerable. There is frequently the additional problem of the training director being handicapped by operating within the organization and not being seen as a resource in this kind of developmental process. Many organizations feel it is best to go outside the organization for professional guidance in this field of training. The training director's job has so many responsibilities that frequently he can not become an expert in this or other highly specialized areas of training if he is to most importantly serve as a consultant to management on how training can help management solve its problems.

---

[10] Gordon L. Lippitt and Leslie E. This, "Is Training a Profession?", *The Journal of the ASTD*, April, 1960.

WHAT ORGANIZATIONS SHOULD NOT USE SENSITIVITY TRAINING?

Sensitivity training may have little to offer where the *management of the organization—*

1. Is highly directive and intends to remain that way.
2. Is not concerned with public relations, even though publics are a major factor in its operations.
3. Is not concerned about the needs of employees being met or becoming compatible and closely related to the organization's needs.
4. Is predicated on the assumption that men are motivated solely, or mainly, by money, promotional opportunity, threats and rewards.
5. Believes that training is only for those in positions subordinate to them and is either anti-training or luke-warm to training.
6. Sees the organization as composed of tight sub-units that have their own job to do and what happens elsewhere in the organization is none of their business.
7. Operates on a "hard-nosed" basis and is solely production-centered regardless of the means employed.

One of the dangers in setting down a list such as the above is that most organizations will deny they have any of the attributes or characteristics so listed. These are not set down here in a judgmental way—they may be perfectly valid for that organization. Just because these characteristics aren't popular today doesn't necessarily mean they have nothing to recommend them. We are only suggesting that given a number of these characteristics, and intending to continue to operate in this way, an organization would not find sensitivity training of sufficient benefit to warrant the investment of the required time and money. Other approaches to organizational change would need to precede the adoption of sensitivity training as a part of the development programs of this organization.

WHAT IS MANAGEMENT'S ROLE?

Management must see the training as compatible with organizational objectives, understand the training objectives, and help managers see that management "buys" the philosophy of participative way of working with staff. Management should publicly endorse the program by its own way of behaving (men supervise as they are supervised—not as they are taught to supervise), be willing to finance the program adequately, and provide conditions that will allow men to put their learnings into operational practice.

What Are The Risks?

There is always the risk that here and there an individual may be upset by the experience. A not too well integrated person may be threatened by self-knowledge. It is not demonstrated that the experience will really do more than precipitate a personal situation that existed previously.

There is the further risk that some managers exposed to this training may reach wrong conclusions about principles and ways of operating and be less effective than before. This is usually the result of the wrong application of a principle, or the misunderstanding of a learning. Specialists in laboratory training do not advocate that all decisions should be group decisions or that everyone in an organization needs to like each other, but a few participants in this type of training may draw inappropriate conclusions which is a possible consequence of any form of educational endeavor.

There is always the risk of seeing the training as a panacea for too many organizational ills. It does not guarantee results. It promises only more knowledgeable personal performance. It can not substitute for a better product or service; or for organizational imperfections in financing, advertising, production, etc.

Where Do I Start?

You begin by discussions with your top staff. Are the learnings that can be enhanced by sensitivity training seen as bearing on the problems of your organization? Enough to want you to do something about them? If not, you turn to some other approach.

If it all still makes sense to you and is seen as desirable, you find a reputable university or outside professional training organization that has knowledgeable resource persons to help you look specifically at your problem and the impact this kind of training can have on them.

Constantly you keep testing the applicability of this kind of training in your organization for your kind of problems, the staff you possess, and with the other priorities facing you. And then, as with all decision making, if this course of action still seems to make good sense, you initiate the first action steps to implement it.

To summarize, if an organization wants its managers to know organization structure and dynamics, to know themselves better so that they can conduct themselves more effectively as they work with other individuals, and to know the forces and factors at work when people work in groups so they can become more effective—sensitivity training is probably a desirable part of your training program. If these concerns, or objectives, are not seen as desirable, needed, or important, an organization should not consider sensitivity training.

QUESTIONS

1. What does sensitivity training consist of according to these authors?
2. In what ways does this article complement the previous one by Argyris? In what ways does it tend to disagree with some of the points made by Argyris?
3. What types of problems can best be accommodated by sensitivity training?
4. What are family groups?
5. When should organizations not use sensitivity training?

48. BETTER UTILIZATION OF SKILLS THROUGH JOB DESIGN *

Robert H. Guest

More than 15 years ago the Chairman of the Board of a large American corporation was walking through a department in one of his many plants. He paused momentarily at a drill machine. He watched the worker take a part out of the bin, place it on the machine, press a pedal to drill the part, release the pedal, and lay the part into another bin where it was carried away for inspection. He began to chat with the operator and then posed a question: "If you were the head of this company (the girl didn't know who he was) and if you knew as much about *this* job as you do, what would you do to make it a better job?" The operator made it clear that she thought the job dull and monotonous, that she was only there for the pay, and that, in her opinion, there were a lot of things that could be done that would make the job not only more interesting but more efficient. She thought that with very little extra training she could learn not only how to operate the machine but to set up her own machine (a task which the setup men performed), keep track of the inventory of different types of parts (a task of the stock men), and do her own inspection of the parts, (a job which the inspectors were doing).

This incident set in motion a chain of events which was to have a profound effect on this worker's job, on others in the department, and on many routinized manufacturing operations throughout the company. Indeed, the actions which this high official took, based in part on this chance discussion, were to lead to the birth of the concept which was later named "job enlargement" by my colleague, Charles Walker.

The original publicity later led other companies to begin new experiments in the area of job design, an area which had been traditionally considered the exclusive domain of the time and motion engineer. As I will hasten to point out later, these experiments never took on the proportion of a great movement. They did, however, have the effect of causing a number of observers and practitioners to question seriously the traditional assumptions about job design.

Concern about the nature of work itself and its effects on human beings is as old as the industrial revolution itself. Particularly with

* From *Management of Personnel Quarterly*, Vol. 3, No. 3 (Fall, 1964), pp. 3-11. Reprinted with permission.

the accelerated trend toward mass production in the early part of this century, a trend which had parallel effects on clerical operations, many persons were beginning to question not only the morality of stripping work of any intrinsic interests but also its consequences on efficiency as well. The primary principle of mass production was specialization. The concept of specialization was the target of this condemnation. The personal target usually singled out was Frederic W. Taylor, father of scientific management. Walker and I were but two of the many critics. After acknowledging the many obvious contributions of Taylorism, work measurement and mass production, we asked the following questions:

> If a man spends at least a third of his life in direct contact with a mass production environment, why shouldn't we consider as important (to him and to society) the hours of living time he spends inside the factory—as important and valuable, for example, as the product he produces which is consumed outside the factory? We talk of a high standard of living, but frequently mean a high standard of consumption. Man consumes in his leisure, but fulfills himself not only in his leisure but in his work. Is our mass production work environment making such fulfillment possible?

This condemnation of ours includes the vast army of clericals and has strong moralistic overtones. But the research and practical experience in business behind these questions prompted us to ask some rather pragmatic questions as well with respect to a worker's productivity and the quality of his output.

Peter Drucker argued that using workers (and this could include clerical workers) as a single-purpose machine tool was not only inefficient engineering, but a waste of human resources. As he put it:

> The principle of specialization is productive and efficient, but it is very dubious, indeed, whether we yet know how to apply it except to machinery. There is the first question of whether "specialization" is, as understood and practiced today, a socially and individually satisfying way of using human energy in production—a major question of the social order of industrial society.[1]

THE MARCH TOWARDS OVER-SPECIALIZATION

No one questioned the obvious advantages of specialization as such. No organization could possibly function without it. It was over-specialization that people questioned. Many thought that over-specialization was based on a much-too-narrow concept of what really

---

[1] Peter F. Drucker, *The New Society* (New York: Harper and Brothers, 1950), p. 171.

motivates people to put out their best effort. Application of the concept to the extremes of cold engineering logic tended to force those running large-scale organizations to organize human effort in purely mechanistic terms, just the same way the engineer tends to design a machine. And, as I have already suggested, there were even technical people who, themselves, were questioning the efficiency of overspecialization. People were beginning to ask, "Are there any alternatives?" "Are there not limits to which jobs can be fractionated?" "Apart from the primary and measurable advantages stemming from breaking work down into its simplest constituent motions, are there not long-term effects which interfere not only with the work-flow processes themselves but with the motivation of people who maintain the work flow?" Professor Louis E. Davis of the University of California, an industrial engineer whose inquiring mind brought him face to face with problems of motivation, began to look into these questions. He saw that the traditional concepts for the design of jobs were predicated primarily on technical imperatives. He called the traditional industrial engineering approach process-centered. The prevailing practice in designing the content of jobs relied primarily on the criterion of minimizing immediate costs as measured by minimum unit operation time.[2] This criterion demanded that:

1. Skills be specialized.
2. Skill requirements be minimized.
3. Learning time be minimized.
4. Work loads be equalized with each operator having a full and measurable work load.
5. Work conform to the layout of equipment or facilities as they exist.
6. Worker's satisfaction be provided for (more or less as an afterthought).

In combining individual tasks in the specific jobs:

1. Limit the number and variety of tasks in a job.
2. Make the job as repetitive as possible.
3. Minimize training time.[3]

The criterion of minimizing immediate costs as measured by minimum unit operation time had been carefully worked out over the years out of rational and empirical experience, especially following the profound influence of Taylor, Gantt and Gilbreth. They were rational and measurable and, if one could accept the assumptions on which they were based, practical. Davis, an engineer, had technical grounds for frontal assault on these assumptions.

---

[2] L. E. Davis, "Job Design and Productivity," *Personnel*, March, 1957.
[3] *Ibid.*, p. 420.

EMPLOYER CONCERN OVER JOB EFFICIENCY

Concern about job efficiency and employee motivation was not merely an academic question. James C. Worthy of Sears, Roebuck, and Company, having conducted research among more than 100,000 employees, probing into employee satisfactions and organizational effectiveness, found:

> The evidence of studies conducted in our own company strongly supports (the) conclusion (that) where jobs are broken down too finely, we are more likely to have low output and low morale. From the standpoint of the individual employee, it tends to destroy the meaning of the job. The worker cannot see the total process; he sees only the small and uninteresting part to which he and his fellows are assigned. In a real sense the job loses its meaning to the worker—meaning, that is, in all terms except the pay envelope.[4]

Worthy's observation closely paralleled the findings of the assembly line studies as conducted at the Yale Technology Project. The single most important factor of job dissatisfaction did not have to do with general working conditions, pay, human relationships with fellow workers and with supervision, but rather with the nature of the job itself, what men did with hand muscle, minute by minute throughout the work day. In spite of our warnings, neither the management nor the higher union officials in the automobile industry wholly recognized the importance of this simple fact. The costly strikes in 1961 following the signing of the general contracts were, in large measure, an unorganized spontaneous expression of the bitterness men held toward the immediate job. Here is just a fleeting quote of what one of the more than 400 workers we interviewed said about his job:

> It's easy for them time-study fellows to come down there with a stop watch to figure out just how much you can do in a minute and 52 seconds. There are some things they can see and record with their stop watch. But they can't clock how a man feels from one day to the next. Those guys ought to work on the line for a few weeks, and maybe they'll feel some of the things they never pick up on that stop watch.
> I like a job where you feel you are accomplishing something and doing it right. When everything is laid out for you and the parts are all alike, there is not much you feel you can accomplish. And the big thing is that steady push of the conveyor—a gigantic machine which I can't control.

The studies that we conducted on assembly lines perhaps represent the extreme form of work fractionalization and specialization, but other studies carried similar overtones.

---

[4] James C. Worthy, "Organization Structure and Employee Morale," *American Sociological Review*, Vol. 15, No. 2 (April. 1950), p. 169.

It is a curious fact that while those responsible for managing and effectively utilizing human resources have been keenly aware of work problems such as economic incentives, working conditions, employee-supervisory relations, and many other facets of employment, there has been little concentration on the effects of the immediate job on morale and productivity.

The design of jobs, to repeat, has been left to those trained in the observable measurement of work and the specialist in methods procedures with the payoff criteria being the quantity of work performed in a measurable but limited unit of time. I say it is curious because there is a wealth of empirical, experimental evidence demonstrating that the nature of the content of the job is a source of deep dissatisfaction among employees engaged in repetitive work.

Several years ago a compilation was made of 16 of the more important studies in employee attitudes.[5] These studies were based on a sample of more than 11,000 employees. Sixteen discrete factors in employee attitudes were listed including such items as wages, working conditions, supervision, hours of work, benefits, security, and opportunity for advancement.

Of the 16 factors those which pertained to the interest in the job itself and its intrinsic aspects were second only to security as the most important factors in attitudes. They outranked such items as opportunity for advancement, supervision, wages, social aspects of the job, working conditions, hours, and benefits. This same compilation of studies also made the observation that "Intrinsic aspects of the job are generally more important to office workers such as clerical and sales personnel than to factory workers." [6]

Most of what I have said so far has begged the question, "What do you do about it?" Before giving a few illustrations of what in fact has been done, I would just like to point out why it has been difficult to face up to the action question. The chief difficulty has not been specialization of jobs at lower levels, but specialization of managerial functions. An enlightened approach to job design in the direction of job enlargement requires the combined skills of persons in different functional areas of management. Historically these skills have developed from separate streams and never brought in confluence. Here are four historical developments to consider:

1. To repeat what was said earlier, the whole area of job design has been dominated (and I don't say this invidiously, necessarily) by the

[5] Frederic Herzberg, Bernard Mausner, Richard O. Peterson, and Dora F. Capwell, *Job Attitudes: Review of Research and Opinion*, Psychological Service of Pittsburgh, Pittsburgh, Pennsylvania, pp. 44-46, 1957.

[6] *Ibid.*, p. 72.

Taylor tradition of scientific management, the rise of industrial engineering as a profession, and the proliferation of such groups in industry and public institutions as methods specialists, those concerned with the establishment and measurement of work standards and incentives, and those persons with a particular interest in work simplification.

2. Another stream of activity historically has come through the introduction of concepts of human engineering. This managerial function has been concerned primarily with the design of equipment and machines so that they can be operated most efficiently with human hands.

3. From an entirely different dimension has come the rise of psychology in its application and concern with the proper selection and placement of employees. The contributions of the psychologists are obvious. But in all of the work of applied psychology the technology of the job itself has been assumed to be a "given"—something not in the psychologist's realm to alter.

4. From a slightly different dimension there is the influence of the famous Hawthorne experiment and the proliferation of ideas and practices stressing the importance of the human relations approach to work and to the motivation of employees. The human group became the center of focus as a prime determinant of job satisfaction, morale, and productivity. The power of the primary group to generate unusual effort or to engage in the worst kind of goldbricking was recognized. This interest in human relations, of course, gave rise to supervisory training programs in human relations, and these programs have become part of the fabric of management.

The human relations efforts, the influence of psychology, time study and those focusing on one slice of the total work pie concentrated on questions of motivation and/or productivity, yet in most instances these interests were not blended together to assess and to take action on the total costs of over-specialized work content.

The blame, as I indicated, is in the nature of organization itself. Rarely is there a functional group or a single individual in the organization whose job it is to focus on the nature of work utilizing the combined skills of engineers and methods specialists and the skills of those concerned with psychological personnel, and human relations problems.

Key Challenges: Focus on Job Design

The key challenge, it would seem, is finding organizational mechanisms for bringing the separate skills to focus on job design. Or put it in another context. Ways need to be found which will obtain the satisfaction of the employees' needs and at the same time satisfy the productive requirements of the organization. In business, and perhaps to a lesser extent in government, many have claimed that these two needs or requirements are antithetical. The best that can be expected, it is said, is some kind of an accommodation of personal needs and production requirements. A few voices in the wilderness have claimed that a sound theory of job design properly applied means neither compromise nor accommodation.[7]

Richard Marks, the first to attempt a successful controlled experiment using an integrative concept, began by observing that jobs have five interrelated components:

1. Work content—the assigned tasks which grow from the needs of the technical process, e.g., typing, drafting, machining, assembling, and inspecting.

2. Methods content—manner in which work activities or tasks are to be performed. Methods content, usually referred to as methods design, ranges from the specification of motion elements to the manner in which the employee participates in the planning stages of the technical process.

3. Structural content—the organizational setting in which the assigned tasks are carried out. This would include, for example, the makeup of the work group, its size, the division of labor as required by the work flow, the position of the job in the formal hierarchy, the span of control of supervision, and spacial layout.

4. Personal content—the physical and psychological requirements placed upon the employee by various aspects of the job. (Degree of fatigue, physical exertion, and mental attention)

5. Reward content—tangible and intangible compensation available to the employee for his part in assisting the organization in attaining its goals, e.g., monetary compensation, or the rewards or frustrations evolving from the other components of the job.[8]

The design of the job involves not only being perceptive about each of these five components but understanding the interrelationship of one to another. This understanding permits one to consider ways of enlarging the total job content.

Observations, Studies and Experiments

With this introduction as a framework, let us turn to the few actual observations, studies, and experiments which demonstrate the potential of the integrated approach for enriching or enlarging the character of routinized work. Let it be clear from the outset that we are dealing with spotty evidence of successful experiments. There is no formalized movement, organization, or society promoting the

---

[7] Richard Marks, "Man, His Work, and the Organization." A Paper presented before the Congress of the International Association of Applied Psychology, Rome, Italy, April, 1958.

[8] *Ibid.*, p. 7.

thesis of job enlargement. And there is a very scanty body of literature. There are no rule books or manuals.

Caveats

The evidence I intend to present can serve only as a stimulus for
"thinking around" the problem. I am personally convinced that there
are many thousands of lower-level jobs which do not lend themselves
to job enlargement. There are many individuals, fewer than is popularly supposed, who would not respond to added job scope. Finally,
there are thousands of routinized operations which are one step away
from being automated. The sooner they are, the better, technological
unemployment notwithstanding. With all these disclaimers I am convinced that we can utilize our resources at the work level far better
than we do.

Enlargement in a factory job

The first known successful application of integrated job design
principles was referred to in my opening remarks concerning the
drill press operator. Her job was changed to include setup of operation,
the performance of the job and the inspection of the work. Combining
the discrete operations into one total operation by an operator was
expanded to cover several hundred operators in the manufacturing
plant. In the machining operations, for example, the enlarged job
called for the operator to read blueprints, to do routine machine
maintenance, to sharpen his own tools, to have a knowledge of how
deviations from tolerances will effect the part in subsequent operations, and to make a complete check of the finished part after the
operation is performed. Six years following the initiation of the
program the company reported continued reduction in losses from
defects and from scrap. Less idle time, both for machines and
operators, resulted. "It has been found that the operators can set up
and check with a greater economy in time if they perform these
duties themselves rather than calling over setup men and inspectors
to do the job for them. The cost of setting up and inspecting has been
reduced 95 percent." [9] Interviews with the workers involved clearly
indicated that they much preferred the enlarged job to the former
highly repetitive single operation job. Today, the concept of job
enlargement has been adopted as standard practice.

---

[9] Charles R. Walker, "The Problem of the Repetitive Job," *Harvard Business
Review*, Vol. 28, No. 3 (May 1950).

White collar job enlargement—application clerks

Another example comes from observations I made in an insurance company.[10]

In three areas of its operations the company reversed the time-honored principle of breaking jobs down into their simple logical elements and assigning jobs to a fraction of the whole.

In the underwriting department the head of the methods group was being called repeatedly into the department because of the high error ratio, high turnover, and generally poor morale. Over a 20-month period in one group of four jobs, 32 people had been hired and quit.

Although the operation involved large volumes of work, it was not complicated. But the work flow was a mess to say the least. It was thought best to apply good sound methods procedures and to assign girls to individual jobs, each working on a fraction of the underwriting clerical procedure of application setting up, application control, and application suspense. Still, no perceptible change.

Perhaps something was wrong with supervision, it was thought; but nothing showed up after careful examination. With the high turnover they felt that their placement policy was not right. Consideration was given to choosing girls for this work on the basis of psychological aptitudes. Then the head of the methods department, having heard of the job design experiment I referred to earlier, decided to try an experiment.

Each of four girls was given the title of Application Control Clerk. Each was made responsible for the entire policy application control procedures . . . from the point of incoming mail reception to final mailing with the exception of one process involving approving the application by the professional underwriter. Each girl was also made responsible for a group of applications broken down in alphabetical sequence of names, rather than numbers.

I talked at length with the supervisor in charge. Her enthusiasm was obvious. She admitted that, at first, the idea sounded impractical.

> I wasn't too happy about the change, although we all knew something had to be done. With a turnover of twelve girls for four jobs, the supervisor was spending at least a half a day just training people. A girl would be here a couple of weeks and leave; then we would have to begin all over.
>
> When the change was made, the girls, at first, thought they couldn't do half of the work. Gradually it built up. It took six months to perfect the system. After a while, not only did they find they could handle the work load, but there was even some idle time, so a

---

[10] R. H. Guest, "Job Enlargement—A Revolution in Job Design." *Personnel Administration*, Vol. 20, No. 2 (March-April 1957).

filing operation was added. They also actually came to do some of the routine correspondence work and made contacts with the field agents to check on applications details. In three years in my particular section I have had only one girl leave. She got married. We have kept track of the accuracy picture. We used to have as high as 50 to 60 percent errors. And working the way we did, you could never pin the errors down. Now, with one girl handling all phases of the application, we know precisely who is responsible.

As a matter of fact, our error rate is less than one percent, and as a supervisor I am much freer to carry out planning functions, make outside contacts, and run statistical surveys. I have also been able to make up a complete procedure manual in detail. When a girl is absent, I have complete flexibility because any one of the others can step in on the job. We don't have any bottlenecks trying to break someone in on a single operation. Each girl knows all of the operations.

Not only was I able to talk to the supervisors but also with a number of girls involved and as one of the girls commented, "I wouldn't go back to the old system for anything."

The same job enlargement principle was applied to other sections of the company and with considerable success. I was amazed at the scope of the job for many of the girls. In what was called the debit policy department, for example, I observed five girls, each of whom was performing all of the following functions:

1. Sorting and distributing incoming mail.
2. Matching and attaching various papers.
3. Ordering name-file search.
4. Setting up application files.
5. Maintaining suspense files and follow-up.
6. Numbering and photo-copying.
7. Calculating premiums.
8. Coding for punch-card accounting.
9. Checking and binding, then mailing the policy.

According to all of the methods principles I had ever read, such a broad combination of operations vested in one person was inefficient, if not impossible.

For some of the more complicated jobs, management acknowledged that jobs were reclassified upward by one class group, but, according to the manager, the unit costs have not increased.

"In other sections that have been reorganized there has been a reduction in unit costs with an increase in volume with no increase in personnel. Turnover is obviously lower," the manager reported.

The manager also observed the other cost savings:

1. Better coverage during periods of sickness and vacation.
2. Fewer bottlenecks (in other words, work does not all pile up on the desk of an absent clerk).

3. Pinpointing of errors.
4. Greater flexibility in periods of fluctuating business.
5. Increased understanding of overall operations and the way segments of the operation fit into the total process.
6. Less monotony and greater interest in the jobs reported by the operators.

Incidentally, in time, many of these clerical operations were later programmed for the computer. It was reported to me that the planning process was considerably facilitated because it was easier to find out about the sequence of operations under the new job design program they had adopted.

Detroit Edison billing clerks

The next study I would like to report took place in a large segment of the Detroit Edison Company a few years back. Here was a company, J. Douglas Elliot reports, that had more than a million customers in the Detroit area.[11] In its Customer's Billing Department more than 30,000 accounts per day were handled. "In addition to billing accounts, over 2,000 customers' service orders are processed each day for setting up, closing, or correcting existing customer records."

Using a punch-card system of billing, "Billing records flow from operation to operation, gradually accumulating billing information, much as a product flows down an assembly line in a factory."

In describing one segment of the operation, Elliott pointed out as follows:

> We have three machine work groups. (These machines were used to make checks on the billings.)
> The work flows from machine to machine within and between these groups in a traditional production-line fashion. As a result, we had many specialized machine jobs within each of the work groups. Such a high degree of specialization began to take its toll in low employee morale and in lack of flexibility of operations. So we established one machine-job classification in each work group, requiring each operator to perform any job in the group. These operators are now assigned by their supervisor to any task necessary to produce an even flow of work when disrupted by absences, machine breakdown, and the like. In fact, formal "assignment" to tasks by the supervisor is not always necessary, as the employees know themselves where they are needed the most.
> In one of the machine groups, among other things, we prepare statements for customers whose bills are past due. While these statements are run on tabulating machines, it is necessary to type a good portion of them. We have needed three typists to keep up with the

---

[11] J. Douglas Elliot, "Increasing Office Productivity Through Job Enlargement." *Office Management Series*, No. 134, American Management Association, 1953.

machine. The typists were typing practically all day long, and one of the rotating machine operators was operating the machine at all times. The typists were also supposed to help the operator to run the machines, but there was a tendency not to do so, particularly because there was a full-time operator assigned to the machine. The supervisor in charge of the group thought it would be better, job enlargementwise, to replace one of his machine operators with a typist. It would then be the full responsibility of the four typists to work as a unit and to run their own printing machine. . . .

This gave the typists more variety and better understanding of their operation, and it gave the supervisor much more flexibility. Previously there was a certain proportion of lost time on the part of the machine operator and the three typists who were waiting for each other's work. This time is no longer wasted.[12]

According to Elliot this recombination of jobs was carried out in many areas of the large Billing Department very successfully. The job enlargement concept was expanded to include not only the intrinsic work of individual operators, but to whole groups of operators. As he describes it,

We had one work group which maintained the tabulating cards in which were punched the names and addresses of all of our customers. This was a voluminous file containing over 1,700,000 tabulating cards. It was the duty of the people in this group to assign account numbers to new customers by making reference to the file, as well as the many other tasks normally performed in relation to maintaining such a file. We had another group which set up the name and address cards and other billing records from service orders received from customers. This group consisted primarily of a battery of key-punch operators and a battery of checkers. This group and the file group work closely together.

We decided to assign the activities of these specialized groups to two new identical work groups, each of which would be responsible for all the functions performed by both the old groups. In other words, one group would be responsible for the keypunching, checking, and maintenance of the name and address cards for about one-half of our customers, and the other group would have the same responsibilities for the other half. The old groups were nearly the same size, having about 17 employees each. All the employees were divided evenly between the two new groups except for two employees who were assigned to a third group.

Before the change was made, one group in particular was consistently behind schedule. People in this group were being pushed all the time and were working overtime a great deal. There seemed to be a greater number of discrepancies than there should have been. We had reached the point where it was quite obvious that additional help was needed.

Immediately after the change, the two supervisors discovered that much duplication had existed in the two former groups. They had been making certain checks on each other's work and performing many other operations made necessary by the constant flow of work between the

12 *Ibid.*, p. 7.

two groups. This was no longer necessary because each group was fully responsible for the operations within its sphere of activities. With the discontinuance of these fringe jobs, the work groups were practically on schedule within a week after the change was made.[13]

Elliott then goes on to point out that in many examples of job enlargement higher job classifications were required. But the costs were offset in many other economies. He pointed out that overtime was running well under half of what it was the previous year and that the total volume of work of the two groups had increased five percent. Absentees dropped between 10 and 15 percent.

Elliott summed up the experience this way:

> There is an upward movement of job value which results in some higher pay rates to compensate employees for their broadened duties. Overall costs are reduced and productivity is increased owing to such factors as increased job interest on the part of the employee, greater flexibility of workers, elimination of needless operations, less wasted time, and reduced work force. Employees are capable of assuming broader responsibilities and like it.

Elliott then went on to make the important observation that the changes were not arbitrarily dictated and that there was a small percentage of workers who did not want to assume the enlarged responsibility or who were not capable of adjusting to the new enlarged job. In no instances was this forced on the employees as individuals or as a group.

Many of them had a "say" in the planning process. I would make the observation, in passing, that the chances for a successful program in job redesign are remote if it is arbitrarily forced on the employees. The word participation may be overworked but the fact of participation is still imperative.

Controlled experiment in job enlargement

The final example I would like to give is in the form of a controlled experiment in job enlargement rather than an observed case.[14] It was conducted by Richard Marks. The purpose of the study was to investigate how productivity could be improved by changing the intrinsic content of the jobs. The hypothesis was that higher productivity and greater quality performance could be achieved by (1) increasing the number of tasks in a job and (2) combining tasks that (a) have a

---

[13] *Ibid.*, p. 10.
[14] "An Investigation of Modifications of Job Design in an Industrial Situation and Their Effects on Some Measures of Economic Productivity," Ph.D. dissertation, University of California, 1954. This study was under the direction of Drs. R. R. Canter and Louis E. Davis.

similar technological content and skill demands, (b) are sequentially related in the technical process, (c) include final activities in the process or sub-process, (d) increase worker responsibility by enlarging the area of decision making concerning the job and, (e) increase the opportunity for the worker to perceive how his contribution is related to the completion of the work process.

> The experimental setting was a manufacturing department of a unionized company on the West Coast. The department had been the subject of detailed engineering study for some years, and its activities were organized according to the latest engineering practices. A similar department in the same company was used as a control group to permit monitoring of plant-wide changes which might affect employee attitude and performance.
>
> At the start of the experiment, the product, a hospital appliance, was being made on an assembly line at which 29 of the department's 35 members worked, the rest of the workers being engaged in supplying the line and inspecting the product. The 29 line workers were unskilled women with an average of 4½ years experience on line.
>
> Each job on the line consisted of performing one of nine operations (these had similar skill requirements and technological content) as well as inspection in the form of rejecting defective parts. The operations were spaced at stations along the conveyor line, and the women rotated between hard and easy stations every two hours. Since the conveyor line set the pace, the workers were not responsible for the rate of output and job rotation, in effect, eliminating any individual responsibility for the quality of output.[15]

There were four phases to the experiment. The first phase was described as the line job design. This was the original assembly-line job used as a reference base.

In the second phase the conveyor was eliminated but individual operations remained the same. That is, each girl worked on one of nine phases of the total assembly. Each worked at separate benches and the material was brought to each, then transferred to the next bench for the next operation.

The third phase was known as individual Job Design No. 1. Here, each of the workers performed all of nine operations at her own separate station, controlled the sequence of assembly, procured supplies, and inspected her own products. In the final phase (Job Design No. 2) the job content was the same as before but the workers were located in the main production area. The first phase study lasted 26 days under the regular old line job design. The next phase of the group job design lasted four days. The next phase lasted six days, and the final phase lasted up to the 83rd day. When the second experimental phase was put into effect, productivity took a big drop, from a

---

[15] Louis E. Davis, "Job Design and Productivity: A New Approach," *Personnel*, March, 1957.

norm of 100 to one of slightly below 90. Obviously the moving conveyor was more efficient. In the next period under the individual job design where each of the workers performed what was formerly all nine operations the productivity began to increase but was still somewhat below 100 percent.

In the last phase, when each of the operators was performing all nine operations but now in the general production area, the rate of increase continued. Each successive day it continued so that after only six days the group as a whole averaged a fraction of a percent higher than 100 percent. Some individual performances were lower, but the interesting thing was that some individual performances were as much as 30 to 40 percent higher. For the balance of the observed period productivity maintained itself close to and above the 100 norm.

On the fact of it the experiment did not prove out the hypothesis that productivity under conditions of individual job design was superior to the assembly operations in which each girl worked on one ninth of the total operation.

But the experiment was eminently successful if we look at total costs and cost reduction. The most remarkable result of the experiment was that there was an almost immediate 75 percent *decrease* in the number of rejects caused by faulty workmanship. This low incidence of rejects was maintained throughout the entire study.

I would now like to quote and paraphrase some of the observations which the original experimenter, Dr. Marks, made. The desire to want to maintain a higher level of quality came from a new reward and punishment system which the new design almost automatically introduced.[16] Here are some of the workers speaking:

> You are more careful because you are most closely involved if a reject appears.
> It is your own work; the rejects come back at you. (When only one of the nine operations was performed under the old system, they can't blame anybody.)
> Table method (individual job design) produces better work—you put your heart and soul into it. I preferred this method. You are more careful about everything, more conscientious in the long run because the work is strictly your own.[17]

In the final interview among several interviews held in sequence the following kinds of comments were made:

> I was trying hard (while learning to work on the line), I couldn't catch on. I used to get bawled out.

---

[16] Marks, *op. cit.*, p. 29.
[17] *Ibid.*, p. 31.

> I was nervous on the line when I first started. They (the girls) would keep up, and you couldn't, and it upset you. I was frightened. I couldn't keep up.

Dr. Marks goes on to observe:

> The individual job design brought an elimination of the conveyor line "pressure," and it emphasized individual recognition, for passing both good and defective assemblies. As a result, a potential learning situation was created and the reaction of the employees was quite evident. The employees participating in the individual job design became most interested in any defects found by the inspector as she visited their work stations to inspect the finished units. In fact, in the early stages of experience on the group and individual job designs, the workers "ganged up" on the inspector in a friendly fashion.
>
> The women placed emphasis on the fact that they were dealing with a whole component of the product rather than isolated parts. As one of them said, I have learned how important quality is because I had a hand in finishing them. I was concerned with the quality of the set as a whole.[18]

Dr. Marks, in this experiment, also pointed out the cost benefits that accrued. He observed that because smaller and fewer samples had to be taken over time, this reduced the amount of quality control inspection. He observed that there was less rework necessary on rejected lots. In-process inspection operations were, of course, eliminated because each operator inspected her own total product.

Marks also noted the same benefits which I referred to earlier in the insurance study and which Mr. Elliott referred to in the Detroit Edison study, namely,

1. The absence of one operator did not threaten all operations as it did formerly on the assembly line. Before, it was imperative that all stations be manned all the time while the line was running.
2. Under the individual job design program it was much easier to run small lots of certain orders than it was on the assembly line. Or to put it more accurately, it was not necessary to build up large inventories as it was under the assembly-line process.
3. The assembly line or conveyor system was frequently subject to mechanical failures. Under the new system this was no longer a problem.
4. Under the assembly-line system the speed of the line had to be geared to the pace of the slowest worker. Under the new system there was no limitation on the pace that the worker could work.

Dr. Marks sums up his experiment with observations that could apply to the other studies reported here. He says:

> The findings reported here clearly confirm what many have suspected, that there is a point of diminishing returns to specialization.

---

[18] *Ibid.*, p. 35.

Hence, delegation of responsibility, even on the production floor, can be beneficial to the organization in terms of productivity, improved quality of the product and increased flexibility of manufacturing, and at the same time, it can also be beneficial to the individual.

It therefore appears desirable and perhaps essential for those who design jobs, e.g., industrial engineers and foremen, to cooperate with the personnel selection staff and even conduct in-plant experiments of the type described in this report. When more experience is gained in the area of job design, it is likely that management would find it advantageous to develop specialists who would supervise the combined job design *and* personnel selection functions.

The mating of production engineering, work analysis, and the behavioral sciences in the area of job design appears to have promise.[19]

This plea may seem like an extremely difficult challenge. Even if one undertakes even the most modest experiment, how can these skills of the industrial engineer, systems expert, psychologist, and the "human relationist" be combined into one person? The answer, of course, is that no one possesses all of these skills in professional depth. But it is this observer's conviction that any intelligent manager who seeks out the advice of the specialists can take some simple and effective steps in the direction of improved job design.

PREREQUISITES TO SUCCESS

There are three essential requirements for success:

1. The people involved—hourly workers or clericals—must have a substantial voice in the planning process.
2. If the general system of operations is functioning poorly, if the work flow is subject to constant breakdown, if management is operating on a day-to-day emergency basis—putting out fires—then attempts for job enlargement might only lead to the "enlargement" of confusion. A reasonably good understanding and control over the total in-put out-put process is essential.
3. Management's basic attitudes toward those at the lowest levels of organization must include a healthy respect for the needs and the intelligence of the average person at these levels. If management really believes that the average person is capable of responding to greater job responsibility, it need have no worries as to what the response, in fact, will be. If management thinks only in terms of manipulation or if management thinks primarily in terms of controlling the shirkers and goldbrickers, then it can expect only second-rate effort from the great majority of those who want to do a good day's work.

Job enlargement, in short, not only involves the redesign of the immediate job at the worker-clerical level. It requires an enlargement of a sense of respect by those who manage. In our complex,

---

[19] *Ibid.*, p. 19.

impersonal, bureaucratic organizations, this respect for the individual can be lost all too quickly. Without this respect we can never expect to make full use of our human resources.

QUESTIONS

1. Explain in some detail what is meant by the concept of "job enlargement."
2. What is the effect of excessive job specialization on employee morale and productivity?
3. Contrast the basic scientific management approach to job design with that of job enlargement.
4. What conditions must be present in the work place for job enlargement to be successful?
5. How do the ideas in this article compare to those of Kuriloff?

GENERAL QUESTIONS ON PART IX

1. What does the successful application of human relations principles require of managers and executives?
2. What is the relationship of managerial sensitivity to the needs of others and to productive performance in the work place?
3. List some of the major factors that influence productivity in the working organization.
4. Can all managers be expected to apply human relations concepts in a highly successful fashion? What personal and organizational obstacles can exist here?
5. Explain how managerial functions such as planning, organizing, leading, and controlling are related to the practice of human relations.
6. Cite several examples of poor human relationships in some of the organizations to which you belong. What would you do to improve these situations?
7. How can sensitivity training be useful in helping managers improve their relationships with superiors and subordinates?
8. What are some of the problems involved in sensitivity training?
9. How important is job design in influencing personal motivation, loyalty, and productivity for both managers and nonmanagerial employees?
10. Summarize some of the advantages to working organizations of people-oriented management as opposed to traditional scientific management as illustrated by the many studies cited in this part.

PART X. HUMAN RELATIONS IN PERSPECTIVE

Today, the dynamics of American industrial progress are unchallenged throughout the world. Since the Civil War, the tremendous versatility of both men and production processes in adapting to technological changes ceases to be nothing short of unquestioned brilliance. These changing years have also brought forth successive generations of businessmen with differing philosophies of management and human relations.

As one looks back over the years, several distinguishable phases of the human relations movement in industry stand out. The first decade of the twentieth century, for example, showed management in somewhat of a pioneering stage, primarily concerned with developing systems and procedures for improving overall corporate efficiency and with little attention paid to the human relations aspects of running a business. Principal concentration here focused on matters of finance and investment, and paternalism and "welfare management" were the approaches to personnel problems.

Next, industry entered into what can be termed the "engineering stage." Specialization became the vogue, and small distinction was made between men and machines. Technical innovations were rampant between World Wars I and II. Management concerned itself with costs, with production processes, and with product development. Once again, it was the human side of the enterprise that suffered. However, some progressive companies were beginning to establish personnel departments for dealing with certain aspects of employee relations. Research efforts also were directed along these lines.

But it really was not until the middle 1940's that the human relations movement blossomed out into full force. Paced by the emergence of the personnel function as a major aspect of company organization, this human relations movement has been gaining impetus for the past fifteen to twenty years. We are now beginning to recognize the vital importance of the behavioral sciences and their relation to the business environment. Study after study has delved into worker motivation, human behavior, group dynamics, and so on. Furthermore, increasing numbers of managements have expressed

confidence in this human relations movement and the many benefits
it has to offer.

THE CONTROVERSY OVER HUMAN RELATIONS IN INDUSTRY

Benefits notwithstanding, some prominent writers and scholars
have been rather critically attacking many human relations teachings
and principles. These criticisms are diverse and range from one extreme to the other. Some claim, for example, that there is today a
great overemphasis on the human relations aspects of work. The
overtone of this criticism seems to be that industry has been invaded
by the "happiness boys," bringing with them a bag of Freudian tools
for achieving their ends. These people further claim that current
emphasis on human relations training, especially at the college level,
is virtually a waste of time; that only mature, seasoned executives
can benefit by formal training as such. In retrospect, these critics
present many salient and provocative points, orienting their arguments
against group dependency and manipulation, meanwhile stressing the
need for strengthening and encouraging individual development and
self-reliance.

Other critics contend that overdependency on human relations
techniques breeds mass conformity within an organization, thereby
stifling the initiative of creative individuals. They also state that
most human relations practices are basically "manipulative" in nature,
apparently assuming that people respond to this manipulation without
realizing that they are responding to it. Others hold that the majority
of human relations principles are not, and never will be, exact in
nature; therefore, they feel that we should not rely on them to any
great extent.

We could write extensively on these many criticisms of the human
relations movement, but space limits us along these lines. Perhaps
it is wisest to state, therefore, that anyone in any way connected with
the teaching or the application of human relations principles fully
admits the many shortcomings and inconsistencies along these lines.
But this does not decry or in any way inhibit the tremendous advances
that have been made in this area. Certainly, a great deal of effort
has yet to come forth. Some of our ideas do rest on shaky underpin-
nings; perhaps in some organizations human relations techniques are
utilized to produce mass conformity. But in the final analysis, these
are all questions that must be decided and that involve judgments
that must be made by individuals directly concerned. It is easy to
sit back and criticize but still another thing to stand up and try to

improve. This is the task now facing us—to strive constantly to improve our human weaknesses concerning human understanding.

THE EMERGING DISCIPLINE

Part 1 made explicit the point that we are using the term "human relations" as a focal point for explaining and discussing a new discipline that is slowly but surely beginning to take form. It is not our contention that such a discipline exists today in the sense that recognition is given to social sciences like economics, psychology, sociology, and so on. However, we do wish to emphasize that the application of these behavioral sciences to the business world has resulted in an increasing amount of both theory and empirical evidence regarding the behavior of industrial man.

As these social and behavioral sciences have developed, their sphere of interest has been greatly broadened. As a result, their penetration into corporations, small and large companies, governmental agencies and bureaus, service organizations, labor unions, and other organizations where human beings interact and whose efforts are directed and controlled by others is being crystallized into definite principles and concepts having a wide range of applicability. Experiments under controlled conditions with real-life working groups are conducted continuously to test the workability and the pragmatic aspects of principles and theories concerning human behavior. The march towards accumulating knowledge about man and his work moves relentlessly forward, never ceasing to uncover new information vital to industrial progress and productivity.

Part I also dealt in some detail with the interdisciplinary nature of management. It was explained there that the subject of human motivation is indeed a highly complex one. Furthermore, it was emphasized that a proper understanding of human motivation necessitates a drawing together of all the behavioral sciences. We labeled this as the interdisciplinary approach to the process of management. It is paramount that the student now recognize that a successful understanding and practice of human relations in the workplace is dependent upon the degree to which managers and leaders are able to draw together and apply the principles of these distinct, yet related, behavioral sciences.

It is now the goal of many researchers and academicians to help the manager in his task of better understanding of human behavior with all of its ramifications. Countless numbers of research efforts

are continuously being directed along these lines. Many of our universities and foundations are sponsoring research within the industrial environment, constantly trying to test the hypotheses and the
principles of the recognized behavioral sciences. Clearly, this is no
simple task; numerous problems confront such efforts. For example,
it is not always easy to convince business firms of the worthwhileness
and values to be derived from participating in studies of this kind.
They are expensive and time consuming, and in all truthfulness their
results do not always pay off in monetary terms. Then too, when
dealing with the human variable, it is not always possible to prove
conclusively our assumptions concerning behavior. Frequently, we
must generalize and recognize that prediction—as far as human
behavior is involved—is not completely reliable.

But in the final analysis, while this emerging discipline of human
relations can offer great aid to the businessman, it cannot replace the
human judgment that each and every manager must bring to his job.
By combining this judgment, however, with the valuable knowledge
that is offered by the behavioral sciences, vast gains are to be reaped
by both the manager and the worker. The latter will attain greater
job satisfaction and a more complete integration with his work, while
the former will find his own effectiveness in his work enhanced
appreciably.

The authors also recognize, and fully admit, that as of this writing many challenges remain for developing awareness and appreciation on the part of many for this new, formalized field of human
relations. But the rapid strides made along these lines since the conclusion of World War II, and the ever-growing complexities and
problems that continue to arise, make it mandatory that businessmen
and leaders of business accord human relations the proper emphasis
it deserves. Industrial progress of the future will ultimately depend
upon how far industry is willing to go in establishing a community
of mutual responsibility between the highest paid executive and the
lowest paid production worker. One of the principal objectives of
this human relations movement must be this needed integration.

The Broadening Scope of the Human Relations Movement

In addition to the fact that human relations is emerging as a
discipline per se, it should also be noted that it is broadening considerably in scope. Whereas in the past attention had been focused
primarily on the individual, small groups, and the superior-subordinate
relationship, the boundaries of the movement have now expanded to

the point where the totality of man's behavior—and the consequences of that behavior—lie within its domain. In a sense this is nothing new, for the intent of the discipline has always been to explain and understand the behavior of industrial man. The point we wish to emphasize here, however, is that the frontiers of the discipline now include a concerted effort to explore and integrate myriad complex subjects—such as organization theory, particularly with respect to organizational adaptability and the relationship of organization structure to human behavior; decision-making theory; managerial behavior, not only with respect to the manager's function of getting work done through others but also in terms of why and how he behaves as he does, the ethical and moral aspects of his behavior, and how his behavior affects the organization in particular and society in general; and many, many others. We have made an attempt to include as much of the newer research and thinking as the space limitations of this edition would permit. We recognize, however, that the volatile and dynamic state of the field make it impossible to investigate all of its empirical and theoretical facets at this time. Further exploration and integration, therefore, must be left to the initiative and inquisitiveness of the reader.

THE HUMAN RELATIONS MOVEMENT: SOME BASIC ASSUMPTIONS

Underlying the human relations movements are some critically important assumptions. One must recognize (1) that a business enterprise is primarily an organization of people; (2) that these people must be *motivated* to perform at peak efficiency; (3) that the objectives of workers and the objectives of the enterprise are not always the same and, indeed, are sometimes directly opposing; and (4) that business policies and procedures designed for achieving objectives have certain effects on people, and that these effects are not always those desired by the policymakers.

Human relations theory and principles, therefore, have developed in part to aid the integration of people with organizations. This body of knowledge attempts to understand human behavior in the workplace and to channel such behavior towards desirable ends, desirable in the sense that both the managed and the manager can realize goal and need satisfaction.

Furthermore, properly understood principles of human behavior can greatly enhance managerial effectiveness. The professional manager of today must assemble vast amounts of knowledge about people. **why they are what they are,** why they react like they do, to what environment forces they best respond, and so forth. This is no simple task. It demands a tremendous amount of time and effort. And even more basic, it demands a complete and unrelenting appreciation on the part of the manager for his fellow man and for the fact that theirs is a mutual endeavor. Consequently, the application of tested and proven human relations principles can and will bring about greater human understanding, provided that the above conditions are present. People can be motivated to higher and higher performance, human understanding can be broadened, and basic needs can be fulfilled if only both parties—the manager and the worker—will assume more responsibility in their roles as industrial citizens. Much yet remains to be accomplished. However, the road has been smoothed out by the accumulation of a large body of knowledge devoted to man and his work. A great deal of this knowledge has been assembled in the pages of this book for the interested student to read, ponder, and disseminate. And further progress in the management of men will depend heavily on the inquiring mind, on those who are willing to question and to change. Herein lies the great challenge to our industrial future—to find new and better ways to effect a common ground where men at all levels can understand and be understood.

In the following articles the reader will find some excellent analyses of various aspects of the nature and scope of the human relations movement. Donald Schoen, for example, sets forth many tangible benefits that can be realized by business executives with a proper orientation towards human relations. Robert Freedman, Jr. examines what he believes is a conflict between the businessman's role as an administrator of society's human resources and his moral and ethical goals and suggests a direction that a resolution of this conflict could take. Keith Davis, in an article relating management power to social responsibilities, argues that this power will be eroded by society and government if socio-human responsibilities of the manager are not exercised with regard for human values. Chris Argyris, basing his comments upon research results, hypothesizes about trends that he predicts will occur in human relations policies and practices. And lastly, George S. Odiorne, in a penetrating review of changes in management methods, discusses the style of management that he predicts will become the model of this decade.

49. HUMAN RELATIONS: BOON OR BOGLE? *

Donald R. Schoen

Have business and business education gone overboard in their current interest in "human relations"? Is an interest in human relations to be equated with tender-mindedness, sentimentality, and an unrealistic desire to make everyone happy? Does the concept of "human relations skill" imply cynical manipulation of other people, undue invasions of other people's privacy, an anti-intellectual and amoral concern with the emotional aspects of human behavior? Would we all be better off if we cast aside these newfangled notions of "communication," "participation," "listening," "group dynamics," and "development of social skills" and returned to the fundamental emphasis on "the home," "the church," "the lessons of experience," "self-discipline," and "individual initiative and responsibility" of an earlier day?

Questions like these are being raised with increasing frequency. For example:

Professor Malcolm P. McNair, in "Thinking Ahead: What Price Human Relations?" is skeptical about human relations training for younger men and believes that the very concept of "human relations skill" is a dangerous one.[1]

Fortune Editor William H. Whyte, Jr., has written a best-selling book, *The Organization Man*, which argues that our present-day acceptance of "the social ethic" has disturbing implications for the future of our society.[2]

Dr. Erich Fromm, the distinguished psychoanalyst, in an article, "Man Is Not A Thing," sees human relations leading to a distortion of the basic concepts and practice of democracy.[3]

Peter F. Drucker, in *The Practice of Management*, argues that the insights of human relations have been essentially negative and discusses the inadequacies of the human relations approach for the job of managing an organization.[4]

What are we to conclude from the arguments of such responsible critics? Does it follow that the field of human relations is outliving its usefulness; that the interests, points of view, findings, and teach-

* From the *Harvard Business Review*, Vol. 35, No. 6 (November-December, 1957), pp. 41-47. Reprinted with permission.
[1] *Harvard Business Review* (March-April, 1957), p. 15.
[2] New York, Simon & Schuster, Inc., 1956.
[3] *The Saturday Review* (March 16, 1957), pp. 9-11.
[4] New York, Harper & Brothers, 1954.

ings of human relations specialists are at odds with the practical realities of effective business leadership; that the human relations approach is in conflict with our basic democratic ideals and our concepts of personal morality; that it is a mistake to try to teach executives and would-be executives human relations skills?

Drawing on my own experience—both practical and theoretical, in business and in education—I would like to try to put some of these issues in perspective. Let me tip my hand: my personal conviction is that the field of human relations has important relevance to executive action and business leadership, *provided* one recognizes that leadership, management, and business action involve more than just human relations. I find it hard to see where human relations and generally accepted moral and ethical codes are in conflict, *provided* one specifies what one means by human relations and does not ascribe to human relations itself a body of moral doctrine. I feel that human relations can and should be taught, *provided* one has a realistic understanding of how slow and difficult any real learning must be, and does not assume that human relations has a corner on wisdom.

While I am very definitely *pro* human relations, I am also *pro* "tough-mindedness," "making practical decisions," "self-discipline," "profit consciousness," "high standards of performance," "individual initiative," "creative imagination," "hiring able men," "firing misfits," and, above all, "getting results." What is more, I do not see any conflict between one and the other.

CENTRAL CONCEPTS

Probably one of the important sources of difficulty in talking about human relations is that the term now means so many different things to so many different people that one person's brand of human relations may differ in many respects from another's.

What I refer to here as human relations has its roots in the work done by Elton Mayo, Fritz Roethlisberger, and L. J. Henderson at Harvard University in the 1920's and 1930's. As conceived by this group, human relations is a field of research, teaching, and practice, just as is the field of medicine. While the professors at Harvard did not pretend to be businessmen, or even men of action, they felt that they and the businessman had a kindred interest and a kindred approach. Both theorist and practitioner were interested in the process of getting cooperative action in organized human activity.

Out of careful study of what goes on in actual, concrete situations where organized groups of poeple are trying to achieve a common goal, the human relations specialists felt they could identify *some* of the crucial determinants of effective collaboration, *some* of the reasons why attempts of people to work together end in chaos, confusion, unnecessary friction, and *some* of the roots of many of the disturbing and disruptive aspects of our modern industrial society.

Today interest in research, teaching, and practice in human relations has spread far beyond Harvard. Throughout the United States and the rest of the world, many other research workers, teachers, and people in business have picked up the threads of the work of the Mayo group.[5] While many of these people claim to have gone beyond the concepts and approaches of the original work in human relations, few deny their heritage from the Mayo group.

Executive effectiveness

There are two aspects of the original work in human relations which I think are at its core, so far as businessmen are concerned.

First, there is insistence that the traditional way organizational leaders have viewed their jobs, especially in industry, leaves out some of the major dimensions of the process of collaboration or cooperation. This does not mean that economic forces, technology, and logical action designed to achieve efficiency have little to do with shaping the destiny of an organization. Managers must of course plan, make decisions, apply analytical judgments, worry about costs, productivity, profits, competitive trends, and so forth, and typically are well aware of this fact. How well these jobs are done is what fundamentally determines whether or not a business is able to survive in a competitive economy.

At the same time, however, whether the process of cooperation itself is effective, whether individuals willingly and wholeheartedly work toward the common purposes of a group effort without loss of self-esteem and without giving up their individual identity and personal integrity, depends on much that the traditional ways of thinking about organizations will not explain.

To understand organizational behavior one must recognize that it is a product of human sentiments, nonlogical (but not necessarily illogical) behavior, personal hopes and aspirations, customs, traditions, and so forth. This is more than simply saying that the idiosyncrasies of individual human beings affect how they behave on the job. It is a contention of human relations that it is useful to view

---

[5] For a brief statement of current developments in human relations research, see William Foote Whyte, "Human Relations Theory—A Progress Report." *Harvard Business Review* (September-October, 1956), p. 125.

organizational effort *as a social or sociological process,* and that it is useful to view a group as having an organic structure of its own if one wants to understand why it behaves as it does.

The second fundamental tenet of human relations thinking is the conviction that both men of action and people interested in research in group behavior need to have a different method for observing, understanding, or working with the social process than is applicable to observing, understanding, and working with the technical, economic, or logical aspects of organization. This method the human relations people label "clinical," because it is analogous to the doctor's diagnosis of what happens in the human organism.

The clinical method helps the research student to obtain knowledge about group behavior, to develop simple generalizations to explain what happens, and to identify the kind of behavior which facilitates effective action. The clinical method helps the man of action become more effective. The specialists in human relations believe that if a person in a responsible position is able to supplement his ability to respond logically to the technical, economic, and purposive aspects of leadership with a clinical orientation toward the social process, certain results will occur:

> (1) Within the group of which he is a part, cooperative action will be made easier, understanding between people will be improved, unnecessary conflict will be minimized, and useless frustration will be reduced. These of course are all relative matters; they are not keys to Utopia.
>
> (2) The individuals within the group will be better able to serve the group's purposes without losing their personal identity, with a minimum of conflict between their own individual aspirations, goals, needs, or beliefs and the demands of the group itself. The hoped-for result is not conformity, but individual integrity—not happiness, but the right to work out one's own salvation.

These, I believe, are the essential elements of human relations: an insistence on the necessity for viewing concrete organizational situations not only in technical and economic but also in social terms, a conviction that you can understand the social process of group behavior only if you are committed to relating yourself to it with a clinical viewpoint, a fundamental belief that the person charged with the responsibility of getting action in group situations both facilitates cooperation and helps people maintain their own integrity if he is able to orient himself clinically to such situations.

Central to such a set of tenets, therefore, is the concept of a clinical orientation. Before we can ask, "Is all this valid, relevant, useful for the business leader?" we must explore further what is meant by the term "clinical."

CLINICAL APPROACH

Now, since what we will be talking about is a total, integrated, organic way of thinking, feeling, responding, and behaving, any attempts to describe or explain it, to reduce it to words, must of necessity be incomplete or fragmentary. Who is to say what makes up a doctor's skill? It is far easier to point to such an approach in concrete situations than to describe it. The danger in trying to reduce the concept of a clinical approach to words is that it is not something that can be inspected with a collection of "go-no go" gauges.

Despite the risks of oversimplification, however, I suggest that a leader has learned to approach concrete situations clinically if:

—*An underlying element of his approach to other people is an attempt to understand them, which involves a high degree of acceptance of people as they are.* This is a cornerstone of human relations in practice. It implies respect, tolerance, acceptance of human frailty, and recognition of the uniqueness of each human personality. Implied also is an ability to understand how other individuals see, feel, and think about themselves and their environment.

While I have said—and believe—that it is a mistake to view human relations as a code of ethics or series of moral absolutes, I do not believe it is possible for a person to respond clinically to concrete situations if he is incapable of accepting this one basic premise of our generally accepted traditions of civilization, morality, and religion.

This does not mean, however, that it is necessary for a leader to condone irresponsible action, sloppy performance, or self-indulgent laziness. It is entirely possible for a good Marine sergeant to understand his recruits while a psychiatrist probing the innermost aspects of a patient's personality may not be capable of a clinical orientation if his actions are not based on respect.

—*He has an awareness of and sensitivity to differences between his outlook and another man's, coupled with an ability to maintain his own individual point of view in the face of such differences.* This is in a sense a corollary of the first point. A clinically oriented person takes it for granted that his values, aims, aspirations, and reactions are in some measure unique and does not expect other people to be exactly like himself. The sales manager who thinks all research scientists are simply "queer," the successful businessman who thinks all those who make less money than he does are therefore less able, the Republican who thinks all Democrats are stupid, the Anglo-Saxon Protestant who has no use for any Irish Catholics—these are all examples of the absence of a clinical orientation.

—He has an ability to respond to and understand not only the logical content of what other people say but also the feelings and sentiments implied in their words and their behavior. This particular aspect of the clinical approach and human relations, first articulated by the authors of the well-known study at Western Electric,[6] is the best known and most widely criticized.

Professor McNair in his recent HBR article points out that "sometimes people damn well mean what they are saying and will rightly regard anything less than a man-to-man recognition of that fact as derogatory to their dignity."[7] This is without a doubt true. At the same time, the emphasis on "listening" and on "reflecting feeling" has been put up by some human relations experts as an absolute precept: "The administrator must first and above all listen to other people." This is clearly nonsense.

But the fact remains that if you believe it appropriate to achieve some understanding or communication with a person who is angry, disturbed, or upset, an ability to go beyond the words he is using, to understand how he feels about something, will help you to get different results than if you simply respond to the logical content of his expression.

We do, after all, live in a world where it sometimes is necessary to try to understand or communicate with people who are not behaving as our own logic tells us they should. Sometimes it is desirable to understand why this is so. Sometimes it is useful to know that when a supervisor is criticizing the way another department is run, he is really asking for approval of what he himself is doing; or that when a group of people complain about the light in their office or the ventilation or the crowded facilities, they are prompted to do so by sentiments having more to do with pride than comfort.

The clinically oriented person is *able* to understand other people's feelings. Whether or not it is appropriate for him to manifest that understanding is an entirely different matter.

—He has some awareness of himself and of the impact of his behavior on other people. The qualifying word "some" is important, for this is a matter of degree, as are all aspects of the clinical orientation. Complete self-understanding is impossible. Undue preoccupation with self-analysis is unhealthy, as many critics of human relations have pointed out.

---

[6] See Elton Mayo, *The Social Problems of an Industrial Civilization* (Boston Division of Research, Harvard Business School, 1945), and F. J. Roethlisberger and W. J. Dickson, *Management and the Worker* (Cambridge, Harvard University Press, 1939).

[7] Malcolm P. McNair, *op. cit.*, p. 28.

The executive who recognizes, however, that his own tensions may communicate themselves to his subordinates has a way of dealing with this problem. But the executive whose aggression, energy, and brilliance lead his subordinates to lean on him and who does not see that his own behavior has something to do with why "it's hard to delegate responsibility" may never understand what goes on around him. The one has self-awareness; the other has not.

Generally speaking, a distinguishing characteristic of the clinically oriented person is an intuitive understanding of himself and the way he acts which squares roughly with the way he looks to others.

—*He has an effective way of understanding the nature of the social structure or social system of which he is a part.* He has a feeling for the basic elements of social organization which human relations experts have identified: informal organization, status relationships, traditions or customs, and so forth.

It is beyond the scope of this article to try to explain in detail the concept of "social system," [8] or even to prove that organizations do in fact manifest regularities, uniformities, and characteristic ways of behaving which are a function of their prevailing social systems. At the same time, it is probably generally recognized that most companies have their office grapevines; that employees may establish "norms" limiting their output which have nothing to do with any rational concept of efficiency; that the factory worker will readily accept membership in a union while his blood brother making less pay in a white-collar job will have nothing to do with a union; that even though the president of a company boasts about his "open-door policy," few of the rank and file will visit him uninvited.

The point is not that any of these things are desirable or undesirable, but that they are part of the fabric of organizational behavior, factors which help to determine how effectively an organization will function. The clinically oriented person has some way of understanding this.

—*He is realistic about the existence of a hierarchy of authority, responsibility, status, and position in his particular organization and is alert to the way this hierarchy affects people's behavior, his own included.* That hierarchies do exist, that rank has its privileges, that people ordinarily do not act with their bosses the way they act with their equals, is probably generally accepted. Authority, rank, and status are special aspects of the basic concept of social struc-

---

[8] For a fuller discussion of this point, see Fritz Roethlisberger, *Management and Morale* (Cambridge: Harvard University Press, 1941), especially Chapter IV, "The Social Structure of Industry."

ture. But just how far relationships to persons of authority affect people's behavior is perhaps less well understood than the fact that the relationships do exist.

—*In taking action in an organizational situation, he is instinctively able to predict (within limits) how the organization will respond.* Again the qualifying "within limits" should be stressed. Human beings are not machines, and individual and organizational behavior is far too complex for anyone to be omniscient about it. What is important is that the clinically oriented person characteristically asks himself, "If I do this, what *will* happen?" instead of saying, "Since I believe that such and such *should* happen, other people *ought* to see it the same way and respond accordingly."

—*In taking action, he makes intuitive, judicious use of those generalizations about social phenomena which he has constructed and tested by his own experience, and at the same time he continually watches for the unique elements in every concrete situation.* It is axiomatic that experience is the best teacher, whether for the doctor, the scientist, the skilled mechanic, or the executive. What is not so well understood is that one important aspect of learning from experience is the assimilation of generalizations about the world around us. At a simple level, this is obvious: the child who avoids the stove after having been burned has learned, "If I put my hands on the fire, it will hurt."

One of the contributions of human relations research has been to point up some of the regularities in the way people respond to social situations, from one organization to the next, from one point in time to another. Without uniformities in human behavior, learning from experience would be impossible, and the idea of organization itself would be nonexistent.

The classic study at the Western Electric plant highlighted the fact that people respond in the form of higher productivity to a simple overt recognition of their importance. Since then a variety of experience has made it clear that people who are allowed to participate in the making of decisions will ordinarily be more effective in carrying out such decisions.

I also believe it is valid—despite the fuss and fury that surrounds this point—that on many occasions it is possible to understand another person's actions or statements by interpreting his behavior in a social context, by listening for what he feels rather than for the explicit meaning of his words. Once you have discovered for yourself the validity of some of these generalizations, in practice you do not need to start completely fresh in approaching **every** situation.

Again though, the qualifier "completely" is as important as the point itself. In some situations, stressing a recognition of people's importance may lead to less rather than to more productivity. If the fire chief allows participation in decision making, the house may burn down. Sometimes talking out in anger may lead to better communication than will listening.

TANGIBLE RESULTS

We come now to another question: Does the clinical approach, as just described, actually help an executive to develop cooperative action in a group while making it possible for the individual members of the group to maintain their personal integrity?

It would appear at first that all we need do to prove or disprove the basic propositions of human relations is test them. In an age where scientific inquiry is dominant, the accepted way to verify a basic hypothesis or assumption is to test it. In fact, over the last quarter of a century or so, much of the research work in human relations has been directed toward trying to demonstrate that a clinical orientation facilitates cooperative action and that the absence of such an approach leads to difficulty.

Nevertheless, it is not my purpose here either to try to review the results of such research or to prove the basic assumptions on which human relations rests. I believe that accepting these assumptions is as much an act of faith as an act of rational judgment. The world is too complicated a place, and human relations much too new (compare its 25 years as a field of systematic study with medicine's 2,500), to prove the implications of a clinical orientation in the same way that we can demonstrate the laws of gravity.

Once one has observed or taken part in situations where key participants have been able to bring to bear what I would describe as a clinical orientation, however, one is inclined to attribute what happens in part to the presence of such a point of view. What cannot be proved can often be illustrated. For this purpose let us take a few kinds of problems that must be faced in many business organizations. How does the kind of orientation I have been describing facilitate effective action in such situations?

Union negotiations

In labor problems disagreement, rather than agreement, is ordinarily the starting point. If the problem of reconciling this disagreement is treated simply as a conflict over dollars and cents or over basic management and union principles, the job of getting a contract is likely to be far more difficult, unproductive, and perhaps costly than if the negotiators recognize that bargaining is also a social process. The men at the machine do have different aims, aspirations, and sentiments from those of the management members or even the union brass. These often influence what happens just as much as differences over whether the contract should include a nickel or a dime per hour increase, or when seniority should prevail.

The management (or union) negotiator who starts with a recognition of this fact is more likely to keep the ball rolling than is the one who does not.

Interdepartmental disputes

It has surprised me on several occasions to find how much similarity there appears to be in widely differing organizations as to where points of friction occur among departments. Design engineers are often more likely to disagree with production superintendents than with other design engineers. A foreman is likely to find that his fellow foremen are extremely cooperative but that people in sales are usually very unreasonable. The sales manager cannot understand why he gets along so well with customers but has trouble with the controller.

In these situations, a problem may become insoluble if it is not understood. Here the clinical orientation on the part of one or more of the parties becomes a priceless ingredient in obtaining effective action.

Management meetings

There are probably few organizations in which the management has not wondered if too much time was being spent in meetings. Nonetheless, calling a group of people together to solve a problem or make a decision is one of the commonest activities in American business. No amount of awareness of social processes can make geniuses out of dullards. Yet it seems to me clear that the group that is fortunate in having a leader or participants who are alert to some of the dynamics of the group process, as well as the substance of what is being discussed, typically make more progress.

Reorganization

Someone has said that a tendency to change the organization structure is a peculiarly American characteristic. Be that as it may, it is frequently necessary for managers to reassign responsibilities, to bring in new people, to fire key subordinates, and to abolish groups performing a particular function.

Here, again, it seems to me that an ability to understand and predict what such steps will mean to an organization, and to sense when and how they can be handled with a minimum of disruption, involves a clinical orientation. And the gain in this case, as in the others just mentioned, is not only effective action. Personal integrity and independence, rather than conformity, should increase if the approach of responsible leaders is clinical. For the person who is concerned with understanding others and accepts differences as part of the scheme of things includes in his point of view a desire and willingness to respect and encourage others' attempts to be themselves.

The problem of conformity in an age of mass media, large organizations, and the common man cannot be assessed or dismissed lightly, but to ascribe to human relations the source of the problem seems by definition contradictory.

Aid to Leadership

Even if all that I have argued so far is true and the clinical approach is agreed to be valid, whether it is possible, appropriate, and desirable for the business executive remains to be shown. We may grant that such an orientation does facilitate cooperation, but is it the right approach for one who is or aspires to be a leader? This is a question which apparently has troubled some of the people who have been critical of the whole development called human relations.

It seems to me that the answer rests largely on what we mean by human relations. My understanding of human relations, spelled out earlier in this article, makes it hard for me to see why there need be any question of its relevance, appropriateness, and usefulness to executive action. But let me set some limits:

> Human relations and its point of view are *not* concerned with making everyone happy or sugar-coating harsh reality.
> Human relations, or the clinical orientation, is *not* and should not be equated in toto with the job of management or executive leadership.

So much, it seems to me, is obvious; but perhaps at times the more enthusiastic proponents of human relations in industry have tended to blur things. Running an industrial enterprise, or managing a part of it, requires a capacity to size up competitive trends, to understand the dynamics of cost and profit, to conceptualize a series of programs and objectives, to keep up with the technology of an industry, and to cope with a host of other things with which human relations as such is not directly concerned. Decisions, actions, plans, and day-to-day activities of businessmen must be carried out with reference to these things, as well as to the human aspects of cooperation.

If a person does not have the basic personal characteristics which make him an executive or potential executive, no amount of concern with human relations per se will make him one. Personal integrity, energy, intellectual capacity, moral courage, strength of purpose, and imagination, to mention a few, are the basic qualities of which successful organization effort is made. It is a mistake, as I see it, either to oppose these qualities to human relations or to ignore their importance. Many of them, however, coincide with the qualities demanded by the clinical approach.

The question of what makes a successful leader is probably an unanswerable one, if we are seeking to define one single road to glory. Being able to orient oneself clinically to social phenomena is probably *not* a necessary skill of *every* sucessful leader. Many people who possess an ability to facilitate cooperative effort in others lack other skills which are required for particular management jobs. It does seem to me, however, that every organization can increase its effectiveness if someone in a key position understands and has assimilated the characteristic approach to group activity I have attempted to describe. This may not be the top man, but a key subordinate.

I believe it is amply clear that the fundamental assumptions of human relations are valid and there is nothing inherent in human relations which conflicts with other management functions. Should we not continue our attempts, through research and teaching, to widen our understanding of human relations in American business?

QUESTIONS

1. Explain what Schoen means by his suggested clinical approach to human relations at work.
2. What are the central concepts of human relations that he presents?
3. What does Schoen claim executive effectiveness to rest upon?
4. Summarize Schoen's conclusions. Do you agree with them? Why?
5. How does his clinical approach aid the leadership function?

50. THE CHALLENGE OF BUSINESS ETHICS *

Robert Freedman, Jr.

Judging by the outflow of articles, books, and speeches by business-men and business writers on the subject of business morality, it ap-pears certain that there is a growing concern for the moral responsi-bilities which the power and prestige of today's businessmen demand.

In all of the books and articles the refrain is the same—the busi-nessman should accept responsibilities beyond that of profit maximiz-ing. He should be a statesman, concerning himself with the problems of the nation and, indeed, the entire world. He should make decisions on behalf of employees, customers, and stockholders which are judicious and right. Finally, he should cleanse himself of narrow self-interest and devote his energy to the improvement of the individuals with whom he comes into contact.[1]

The contention of this writer is that this is a dead-end approach to the problem of business morality. For many reasons, to be spelled out below, the kind of uneasy compromise which the businessman is being asked to make between his role as administrator of society's physical and human resources and his humanistic goals can never be satisfactory. The businessman must live in an imperfect world and make choices, none of which can be ultimately satisfying. This essay seeks to illuminate the conflict between the businessman's role and his moral goals and to suggest the direction which a resolution of this conflict could take.

The view of social responsibility sketched out above is, according to business writers, a radical departure from the ideology inherent in the economic model of Adam Smith and his followers which, along with Social Darwinism, formed the attitudes of nineteenth century businessmen.[2] It is my contention that, while this claim is to some extent true, the new morality is essentially a continuation and a refurbishing of the nineteenth century doctrine of trusteeship which demands an attitude of noblesse oblige on the part of the wealthy and powerful.[3]

---

* From *Atlanta Economic Review*, May, 1962, p. 7-12. Reprinted with permission.

[1] Some books are: B. M. Selekman, *A Moral Philosophy for Management* (New York: McGraw-Hill, 1955); Dan H. Fenn, Jr., *Management's Mission in a New Society* (New York: McGraw-Hill, 1959); Sylvia and Benjamin Selek-man, *Power and Morality in a Business Society* (New York: McGraw-Hill, 1956).

[2] W. G. Sumner, *The Challenge of Facts, and Other Essays*, ed., A. G. Keller (New Haven: Yale Press, 1914).

[3] Andrew Carnegie, "Wealth," *North American Review*, June, 1889.

The nineteenth century world was a simpler one of owner-operated firms in a society whose main problem was widespread poverty and whose economic goal, accordingly, was maximum production. Businessmen, in this world dominated by ideology derived from Adam Smith and Charles Darwin, had to be ruthlessly competitive. This meant that they saw their roles primarily as administrators of resources and, in general, left social questions to religionists (such as bearers of the Social Gospel) and philanthropists. The imperatives of the economic system did not permit the businessman to concern himself with larger moral issues. He did tend to invoke the Puritan doctrine of hard work and thrift as a goad to himself and his workers, to accept Social Darwinism to justify ruthless competition, and to appeal to Adam Smith (really the Manchester School) to legitimize laissez faire. His rule was to "buy cheap and sell dear." By and large, the ethics of the businessman were subordinated to the necessity to survive.

Moral Concern

A result of affluent corporate society

A few of the larger business firms and more successful business magnates such as Andrew Carnegie were freed by their monopolistic position to concern themselves with the moral implications of their position. The nineteenth century doctrine of trusteeship grew from the firm conviction that God or nature had not only provided the businessman with success and wealth but had made him responsible for the administration of this wealth in the interests of those less fortunate.[4] The marriage of Social Darwinism and the Protestant Ethic produced in certain affluent nineteenth century businessmen attitudes quite similar to those now widely held by twentieth century businessmen, if the literature to which I have earlier alluded accurately reflects the modern climate of opinion. The connection between the nineteenth and twentieth century business ideology is this: the widespread affluence of modern corporate society protected by large size from the immediate pressures of the market has made it possible for a large number of business executives to be concerned not simply with the profits of their firms, but the morality of their actions. What is new is not the doctrine of trusteeship, which was held by

---

[4] This is different from A. Smith's total conception in *A Theory of Moral Sentiments* and *The Wealth of Nations*. In *A Theory of Moral Sentiments* the doctrine of trusteeship is suggested by man's inherent "fellow feeling," but in the more famous work fellow feeling is strongly supported by the dispersion of power through competition.

certain affluent nineteenth century Puritan businessmen such as Daniel
Drew, Rockefeller, and Henry Ford, but the degree to which it is now
spread throughout our society.

Today, big business, because of the general affluence of our society
and the size of the economic unit, has surpluses to distribute. The
question which businessmen are asking themselves is, "How shall
these surpluses be distributed?" What the businessman seeks to find
out is what constitutes moral action under conditions of affluence.

I have no quarrel with this question. The world is certainly better
because corporations now attempt to treat generously and humanely
employees and executives on all levels who have lost their usefulness
by keeping them on salary by various featherbedding devices. Also,
there seems to be a clear social gain as business firms continually
increase their contributions to worthy charities such as universities,[5]
the Community Chest, and so forth. Class conflict is reduced to the
extent that businessmen believe that wages should be "fair" rather
than competitive; profits should be "reasonable" rather than ex-
orbitant; and prices should be noninflationary. International relations
can be served (and also the long-run interests of the firm) when business firms can be successfully reminded of their moral obligation to
pursue the goals of American foreign policy while conducting business abroad.

A departure from the traditional mandate of business

But what proponents of this view of business morality have never
adequately shown, and I doubt that such a demonstration is possible,
is that the businessman, whose clear mandate (derived from the intellectual tradition of Adam Smith and his successors) is to allocate
society's scarce resources in accordance with individual and social
demand, has either a moral right or obligation to take upon himself
the righting of social wrongs according to his own view of this matter
or as a special agent of society.

My reasons for holding this view are these: In the first place, the
theory which justifies private property and free enterprise, limits the
role of the businessman to that of allocator of physical and human
resources. The businessman receives his income from providing these
services to society. In a highly competitive economy, he simply reacts

---

[5] For a particular business firm to contribute to a particular university or
group of universities may not be economically rational even though it appears
to be an investment in human capital. The reason is that the "return" to the
firm cannot be calculated and, given the diffuse consequences of education, is
probably less than the outlay.

to or anticipates successfully the desires of consumers. Where competition is perfect, there is no corporate economic surplus for social purposes. If wages are "too low," it is because of low worker productivity, poor organization on the part of the worker, poor management, or small demand for the product. If wages in a particular industry cannot adequately meet some "basic" standard of income, it is the obligation of society through the tax system or other devices to redistribute income in socially desirable ways. It is neither the prerogative nor the responsibility of the businessman to decide these issues in his corporate role. *Since, in the theory of free enterprise, the individual businessman does not create social problems, he, in his role as businessman, is not responsible for their solution.*

Inherent problems

Criteria for judgment? It may be objected that whatever may be said of the origin of surpluses, they do exist and the businessman must distribute them in some way. I agree. But it remains true, nevertheless, that the fact that the businessman *must* act does not make any specific action morally defensible. The most important reason for saying this is that *the businessman has no generally acceptable criteria for judging the relative worth of different individuals or different groups.* Since there is no way in which the businessman can be moral with respect to the nation, world, employees, stockholders, and the public at the same time, he must make choices based on some criteria and according to some hierarchy of values. For this decision, only his intuition, prejudices, or class attitudes are available.[6]

The morality of power itself? Another point, which is not often considered in the writings on this subject, relates to the morality of power itself. By what right do some men order the lives of others— even for good? What right has the soap manufacturer to use the profits earned in selling soap to influence social life according to his personal outlook? The problem of the right to the use of power is either evaded or ignored by business writers. Even those whom I shall presently refer to as conservative critics—nonbusiness leaders such as theologians and economists who generally accept the business civilization as it is but opt for marginal improvement—generally would reduce the abuse of power rather than challenge the businessman's right to power.

---

[6] Two interesting collections of essays, one edited by H. F. Merrill, called *The Responsibilities of Business Leadership,* and another by T. V. Houser, *Business and Human Values,* exhort the businessman to be responsible in all areas of social life. Unfortunately there is no hint as to what responsibility consists of, and there is no suggestion for determining a priority system of values between the various claimants.

The morality of business itself? Finally, a standpoint which is entirely overlooked in the discussion of business morality is that of the morality of the system taken as a whole. Can any business system be moral? The businessman in dealing with problems of moral action, usually takes the business system as given and never raises the question of whether an individual can act morally in a system which itself may be inherently immoral.

Before businessmen can begin to deal adequately with the problem of business morality they must delve into the questions raised above. The literature on business morality, for the most part, shows no insight into these issues.

The Literature on Business Morality

In the literature on business morality, the businessman is exhorted to act morally for three general reasons, the lesser of which concerns the matter of prudence. It is sometimes argued that the misuse of power could lead to the loss of the free enterprise system, to socialism or other forms of governmental intervention.[7] Sometimes the misuse of business power is decried in terms of America's world position.[8] Our prestige as a good society is at stake.

But the most important concern is the purely moral one. Business power is to be used wisely for its own sake, as a matter of commitment to moral responsibility. A larger number of articles appearing in *Fortune, Harvard Business Review, Rotarian, Dun's Review, Nation's Business,* and *America* exhort businessmen to act morally. But rarely do writers deal with the basic issues raised above. The clear implication of the literature is that the businessman can become morally responsible simply by the process of self-examination and character training. Most of these writers appear to be unaware of the fact that the businessman's capacity for autonomous action is limited by the requirements of maintaining a profitable concern. The businessman is by no means free to do what is "right." Failure to understand that there may be a conflict of what is "right" and what is "necessary" leads many of these writers to the view that outside social checks on the businessman are unnecessary. For implicit in the argument is that once the businessman sees the true meaning of morality, he will reform himself.[9]

[7] For example: C. B. Randall, "Free Enterprise is Not a Hunting License," *Atlantic Monthly*, March, 1952; W. K. Jackson, "Citizen Heal Thyself," *Nation's Business*, December, 1946.

[8] For example: B. M. Selekman, "Cynicism and Managerial Morality," *Harvard Business Review*, September, 1958.

[9] See "The Moral History of U.S. Business," *Fortune*, December, 1949; "The

Conservative critics

It is only this last aspect of the problem of business power that is widely criticized outside of business circles by conservative critics. Conservative critics limit their concern to the reduction of the degree of arbitrary power rather than the morality of power itself. What conservative critics find wrong with concentrated power is that it might be misused.

Most academic economists are conservative critics who derive their critical view of the economic order from the politico-economic model of perfect competition inherited from Adam Smith and his followers. Adam Smith's model of perfect competition solves the twin problems of optimum resource allocation and arbitrary power by the device of removing the power of decision from the businessman. The businessman simply reacts to prices and costs provided impersonally by the market. In Adam Smith's monopoly-free model, the businessman is provided no leeway for autonomous action.

Reduce, not remove, business power. Conservative critics are, above all, "realists" who, recognizing that perfect competition cannot and perhaps ought not be achieved, compromise the issue of business power by advocating policies to reduce rather than eliminate it. Antitrust prosecution and governmental regulation are the basic policies of this group. Most economists recognize and defend the fact that such policies fail to eliminate business power. They would prefer to leave some power in the hands of large firms in the interests of "progress," which Schumpeter assures them requires some degree of monopoly. J. K. Galbraith [10] solves the problem of excessive power by elaborating a theory of "countervailing power" which also limits power without eliminating it. This doctrine of checks and balances starts with the assumption that there is a tendency to monopoly in modern large-scale society. Galbraith declares as virtually a natural law that "original" power begets countervailing power. The existence of power itself brings about its own check.

Whatever the device, economists seem generally satisfied to deal with only one aspect of the moral problem—the problem of the excessive concentration of power.[11] The only argument between economists and businessmen is that businessmen believe that they don't

---

Transformation of American Capitalism," *Fortune*, February, 1951; Frederick Meyers, "Dual Standards for Corruption," *The Nation*, March 1, 1958; Bernard DeVoto, "Why Professors Are Suspicious of Business," *Fortune*, April, 1951; W. A. Orton, "Business and Ethics," *Fortune*, October, 1948; L. Finkelstein, "Businessmen's Moral Failure," *Fortune*, September, 1958.

[10] J. K. Galbraith, *American Capitalism* (New York: Houghton Mifflin Co., 1952).

[11] Of the economists, Sylvia and Benjamin Selekman are the only ones in

require checks to power and the economists believe that they do. But conservative programs leave economic surpluses in the hands of business firms, unlike Adam Smith's perfectly competitive order, which does not. Thus the modern economist is content to leave this surplus for distribution by the businessman so long as these surpluses are not used to the detriment of other groups such as consumers and laborers.

Even modern Protestant theologians are content with the conservative formula. In the entire series of books sponsored by the Federal Council of Churches of Christ in America (now merged with the National Council of Churches of Christ in America) nothing is added to the criticism of the conservative economists. Howard Bowen, an economist rather than a theologian, has written the most complete statement of position in the entire series of books.[12]

Control through law and organized groups. Bowen notes that since individuals cannot be trusted to have selfless motives, social control through law is justified. He also recommends the countervailing power of unions and cooperative organizations. As religiously oriented people do, he tries to place the burden of morality upon the businessman by stipulating the following responsibilities: the businessman should recognize the dignity of the worker and should show compassion toward him. He should deal justly with customers, suppliers, and everyone else with whom he deals. He should not discriminate on the basis of race and color; he should provide opportunity for the self-development of the young, provide safer and healthier working conditions, pay just wages, and recognize human need as one of the criteria for compensation.

This position, although it compromises the issue of power, takes him somewhat further than Galbraith. It leaves unsolved the question of priorities among recipients, leaves unanswered the question of the right of the businessman to make decisions as to the comparative values of different persons, and leaves entirely alone the question of the morality of the business system as a whole.

Even one of America's most perceptive theologians, Reinhold Niebuhr, has little to add. His pessimistic view of human nature leads him away from radical or utopian solutions. The best that he can suggest is that men of affairs turn to religion, affirm the law of

the literature reviewed who see that the problem of power goes beyond that of market power. Sylvia and Benjamin Selekman, *Power and Morality in a Business Society* (New York: McGraw-Hill, 1956).

[12] H. R. Bowen, *Social Responsibilities of the Businessman* (New York: Harper, 1955). Other books not cited elsewhere in this series have such titles as A. D. Ward, *Goals of Economic Life;* K. Boulding, *The Organizational Revolution;* J. C. Bennett, *et al., Christian Values and Economic Life.*

love, become aware of the persistent dangers of self-love, and develop a sense of responsibility toward others. Niebuhr, the realist, then goes on to suggest that power be reduced by creation of a system of balance and equilibria of power.[13]

Thus, the real distinction between conservative critics and the businessman is simply that the conservative critics doubt that the individual businessman by soul-searching can be depended upon to act with moral restraint. They compromise the *in principle* problem of the right of the businessman to exert social power beyond that which is mandated by his social role as an administrator of society's resources, and then evade the other moral issues.

THE CONFLICT: BUSINESS SYSTEM VS. MORALITY

Ever since the Industrial Revolution there has been a drumfire of radical criticism of the business system. Socialists, Christian Socialists, Christian Democrats, medievalists, humanitarians, humanists, radical agrarians, and others have always made the argument that the business system is immoral in principle. It is neither possible nor necessary in this short space to develop the arguments of all of these groups in detail. Essential characteristics bind the arguments together.

A society which puts material things ahead of spiritual values, a society which treats individuals as if they were commodities on the market, a society which places the individual on the level above that of the group, a society which builds greed and avarice into its social system, which coops men up in factories, which fights wars for profit, which substitutes competition for brotherhood is, according to this criticism, clearly undesirable.[14] In the business literature reviewed, virtually no one deals with the morality of the system as a whole.

Protestant theologians do, of course, see the conflict between acquisitive and Christian values; but with Reinhold Niebuhr, they tend to despair, accepting this as the only world they are likely to be able to get, denying the optimistic view that man can create the Kingdom of Heaven on earth, being grateful for small reforms.

---

[13] In J. M. Hughley, *Trends in Protestant Idealism* (New York: Columbia University Press, 1948), p. 151.
[14] Although much of this criticism has been voiced since the inception of the industrial revolution, not all of it represents criticism relevant for modern capitalism. Some of it is romantically nostalgic for a long-lost primitive idea. Some is simply anti-industrial. But the point is that they ask a basic question, "Is this a good society?" Business writers invariably assume the basic morality of the industrial system itself.

In the modern idiom Frank Knight, the great economist-philoso-pher, has provided the most incisive, devastating, and relevant evalua-tion of the morality of the business system to be found anywhere.[15]

Whose wants are to be satisfied?

In his classic article Knight argues that the only legitimate func-tion of the system of free enterprise is to satisfy consumer wants. However, such a view leaves unanswered certain important and sticky questions related to values. *Whose* wants are to be satisfied is a ques-tion of prime importance in judging the morality of the system. The question of whose wants are to be satisfied is related to the entire question of distribution of income, which is in turn related to the great issues of social justice. Why should the highest income go to the economically productive? Why not to the most virtuous, the most needy, and so forth? The economy may require as an operating principle a close connection between work and rewards. But this is a prudential rather than a moral argument.

Which wants are to be satisfied?

Second, the question of *which* wants are to be satisfied has been raised by Knight. Our economy satisfies whatever wants individuals in our society prefer, with certain exceptions such as habit-forming drugs. But this does not mean that simply because the wants we have are not damaging, they are desirable. Articles of conspicuous consumption, for example, may not be destructive of the character of the user, but they may bring about envy in others.

How are wants created?

A third point is that the economic system is the *creator of wants,* although it is supposed to be simply the satisfier of wants. It creates wants both in the sense of *goods* and in the sense of *activity,* which helps mold human personality. By producing and distributing the goods which some people want, the system helps to create a desire for emulation on the part of others. Whether emulation is a desirable human characteristic may be debated.

As an activity, Knight shows that the business system creates the kind of personality necessary for business success. In the era of laissez

[15] Frank Knight, "The Ethics of Competition," *Quarterly Journal of Eco-nomics,* 1923, pp. 579-624. This is a basic article, echoes of which can be found in W. H. White, *The Organization Man;* David Reisman's writings; and most all sophisticated social criticism today.

faire the inner-directed, frugal, work-oriented, self-centered, money-oriented, shrewd are more likely to succeed. In the milder climate of today's world, William Whyte tells us that the other-directed, security-minded, adaptable, gregarious conformist is best suited to business success. In either event, the issue is raised by Knight as to whether the personality types created by the economic system are ethically desirable.

Is business a game?

Finally, although he goes much further than this, Knight evaluates business as a *competitive game*. Knight says "the good man has given way to the good sport." And what is the good sport? A man who plays the game and accepts its outcome. Whether the game is ethically defensible or whether the contest is in some sense noble is not to be questioned.

Knight's position raises basic issues. Economic life cannot be separated from social life, and to some extent the kind of a man you are depends upon the kind of thing that you do. There are moral consequences to work as well as to other human activities. Ultimately, according to Knight, the businessman must face up to the fact that the economic system has its own logic. The businessman who wishes to be a moral being is faced by the dilemma of having to participate in an economic order whose morality is itself in doubt.

In Summary

This article has sketched out with extreme brevity the wide areas which have been left untouched by the businessman in his search for moral standards in his role as a businessman. I contend that the businessman has not begun to understand the complexity of the problem which faces him and, until he does, can make no certain progress in his quest. The largest obstacle to progress is, I believe, that he does not understand that the problem of doing right cannot merge from introspection and developing the habits of "right thinking." He must understand first that moral action is always restrained and conditioned by the environment in which the individual acts. Thus the businessman qua businessman should realize that there is often no escape from compromising what is right and what is necessary. In the end the business role demands that the businessman protect his business and encourage its growth. Attempts to compromise may only lead him away from his prime responsibility as allocator of society's resources toward the custodianship of social power which, I have argued, is not within the businessman's province or capacity.

The psychological burden of social power and responsibility is, I am sure, the force which compels the businessman to go beyond this role and seek to legitimize through good works the power he exerts. Were he divested of this power, the burden would disappear. He needs to understand that it is society's job to ensure social justice, not his.

Society, as a practical matter, means government. But to substitute government ownership or regulation of business or private is to change the cast of characters who are burdened with moral problems of power. Therefore the solution is not found in governmentalizing society.

To prevent the exercise of power of man over man, each individual must be provided with adequate and roughly equal power. No man should depend on the good will of another for his protection. The difficulty with any kind of paternalism—business or governmental—is not only that it depends on the moral sense of the powerful (which may be faulty), but that it degrades the recipient. Business ethics as evidenced by what businessmen and their spokesmen write and say seems to suggest that, as a solution to the problem of power, businessmen become more paternalistic. This point of view ought to be rejected out of hand.

However, any imaginable society is likely to contain hierarchies of responsibility and therefore have a tendency toward differential power. It is therefore concluded that it is the *moral* responsibility of the businessman to demand no more than that power which is clearly relevant to his role as businessman, to reject the paternalistic solution, and to welcome social checks in the form of countervailing power as one device to prevent the misuse of power to which most human beings are prone. In the policy sense this "solution" is quite conservative. It simply suggests that marginal rather than radical change in the social structure be made. It appeals to policies such as countervailing power. It is conservative partly because there is much of value to conserve and partly because radical social change is often more damaging than the evil it intends to correct.

In another sense it is conservative because it does not attempt to deal with the more general and difficult issues raised by those who deny that any business (or even industrial) system can be moral. This writer tends to the view implicit in the position of conservative theologians that while a business society cannot maximize the moral life, it can at least minimize the immorality of arbitrary power.

In an ideological sense this solution is radical. It affirms that the businessman face up to the necessity for conducting himself by one set of rules in his capacity as businessman and by another in his capacity as citizen.

This essay has argued that the businessman with moral concerns should not attempt to bridge the gap by refusing to fulfill his commitment as businessman. To commit himself to be a businessman is to agree to follow rules which may conflict with one's social sense. If an individual cannot accept the commitment to act as a businessman, he should seek a more congenial career.

It may be that it is psychologically unsatisfactory, if not impossible, for thoughtful people to be five-day sinners and two-day saints. However, so long as it remains true that the mandates of the business system are often in conflict with the moral imperatives of the Judeo-Christian tradition, and so long as the business system is thought to be the best realistic alternative, the businessman has no option but to follow the rules of his occupation. In his role as citizen, the morally responsible individual should direct himself to the improvement of the general climate of social life.

When the businessman learns to give up the personal quest for standards of moral action in his role as businessman and permit society its proper role in this area, he may then be freed to go about the task which justifies his control of society's resources—the creation of wealth.

QUESTIONS

1. Explain the relationship between business ethics and human relations.
2. What does Freedman mean by the "traditional mandate of business"?
3. What, according to Freedman, is the conflict between the business system and morality? Why does the conflict arise? Do you agree that it exists? Why?
4. What is Freedman's general conclusion? Do you agree? Why?
5. Based on your experience, how have managers approached the question of business ethics?

51. CAN BUSINESS AFFORD ıO IGNORE SOCIAL RESPONSIBILITIES? *

Keith Davis

Few persons would deny that there are significant changes taking place in social, political, economic, and other aspects of modern culture. Some of these changes businessmen may want and others they may dislike, but in either instance the changes do exist and must be faced. As our culture changes, it is appropriate—even mandatory—that businessmen re-examine their role and the functions of business in society. One area undergoing extensive re-examination is the responsibility businessmen have to society in making business decisions. These are the questions that are being asked:

Why do businessmen have social responsibilities, if in fact they do? How does a businessman know in what directions his social responsibilities lie?

If businessmen fail to accept social responsibilities incumbent upon them, what consequences may be expected?

It is my purpose in this article to discuss these questions in a very fundamental way. Without looking at specific company practices and without insisting upon a particular program of action, I wish to discuss three basic ideas which must underlie all of our thinking about social responsibility, regardless of what choices we eventually make. The first two ideas are constant and enduring, no matter what social changes occur. The third is more directly related to social changes today, but I believe it is just as fundamental as the others.

Social responsibility is a nebulous idea and, hence, is defined in various ways. It is used here within a management context to refer to *businessmen's decisions and actions taken for reasons at least partially beyond the firm's direct economic or technical interest.*[1] Thus, social responsibility has two rather different faces. On the one hand, businessmen recognize that since they are managing an economic unit in society, they have a broad obligation to the community with regard

---

* Reprinted from the *California Management Review*, Volume II, No. 3, Spring, 1960. Copyright 1960 by The Regents of the University of California.

[1] Some socially responsible business decisions by a long, complicated process of reasoning can be "justified" as having a good chance of bringing long-run economic gain to the firm and thus paying it back for its socially responsible outlook. This long-run economic gain is often merely rationalization of decisions made for non-economic reasons, and in any case the connection is so problematical that some social responsibility is bound to be present also. An example is a decision to retain a very old employee even though his productivity is low.

to economic developments affecting the public welfare (such as full employment, inflation, and maintenance of competition). A quite different type of social responsibility is, on the other hand, a business-man's obligation to nurture and develop human values (such as morale, cooperation, motivation, and self-realization in work). These human values cannot be measured on an economic value scale. Accordingly, the term "social responsibility" refers to both socio-economic and socio-human obligations to others. Popular usage often omits or underplays the socio-human side, but I shall suggest later in this article that it deserves more emphasis.

Note that the importance of social responsibility in this context derives from the fact that it affects a businessman's decisions and consequently his actions toward others. Social responsibility has ap-plied in any situation if it *influences* a businessman's decision even partially. It is not necessary that a decision be based wholly on one's attitude of social responsibility in order to qualify. For example, when a businessman decides to raise or lower prices, he is normally making an economic decision; but if the management of a leading automobile firm decided not to raise prices because of possible effects on inflation, social responsibility would be involved. As a matter of fact, *rarely* would social responsibility be the exclusive reason for a decision.

While it is true that only businessmen (rather than businesses *per se*) make socially responsible decisions, they decide in terms of the ob-jectives and policies of their business institution, which over a period of time acquires social power in its own right. Thus each business institution and the entire business system eventually come to stand for certain socially responsible beliefs and actions. But in the last analysis it is always the businessman who makes the decision. The business institution can only give him a cultural framework, policy guidance, and a special interest.

Responsibility goes with power

Most persons agree that businessmen today have considerable social power. Their counsel is sought by government and community. What they say and do influences their community. This type of in-fluence is *social power*. It comes to businessmen because they are leaders, are intelligent men of affairs, and speak for the important institution we call business. They speak for free enterprise, for or against right-to-work policies, for or against their local school bond election, and so on, *in their roles as businessmen*. When they speak and act as citizens only, and those involved recognize this fact, then whatever social power businessmen possess is that of a citizen and is beyond the bounds of this discussion. In practice, however, it is often difficult to distinguish between these two roles, thereby further complicating the situation.

To the extent that businessmen or any other group have social power, the lessons of history suggest that their social responsibility should be equated with it. Stated in the form of a general relationship, it can be said that *social responsibilities of businessmen need to be commensurate with their social power.* Though this idea is deceptively simple on its face, it is in reality rather complicated and is often overlooked by discussants of social responsibility. On the one hand, it is argued that business is business and anything which smacks of social responsibility is out of bounds (i.e., keep the power but accept no responsibility). On the other, some would have business assume responsibilities as sort of a social godfather, looking after widows, orphans, water conservation, or any other social need, simply because business has large economic resources. Both positions are equally false.

The idea that responsibility and power go hand in hand appears to be as old as civilization itself. Wherever one looks in ancient and medieval history—Palestine, Rome, Britain—men were concerned with balancing power and responsibility. Men, being something less than perfect, have often failed to achieve this balance, but they have generally sought it as a necessary antecedent to justice. This idea appears to have its origins in logic. It is essentially a matter of balancing one side of an equation with the other.

The idea of co-equal power and responsibility is no stranger to business either. For example, one of the tenets of scientific management is that authority and responsibility should be balanced in such a way that each employee and manager is made responsible to the extent of his authority, and vice versa.[2] Although this tenet refers to relationships *within* the firm, it seems that it would apply as well to the larger society outside the firm. As a matter of fact, businessmen have been one of the strongest proponents of co-equal social power and responsibility, particularly in their references to labor unions.

Based upon the evidence, it appears that both business leaders and the public accept the idea of co-equal power and responsibility. Although businessmen accept the logic of this idea, their problem is learning to respect and apply it when making decisions. Granted that

---

[2] Harold Koontz and Cyril O'Donnell, *Principles of Management* (New York: McGraw-Hill Book Company, Second Edition, 1959), p. 95.

there are no pat answers, they still need some guides, else each shall take off in a different direction. At this point, the idea already stated continues to offer help. If "social responsibilities of businessmen need to be commensurate with their social power," then, in a general way, *in the specific operating areas* where there is power, responsibility should also reside. Let us take an example:

> Company "A" is the only major employer in a small town. It is considering moving its entire plant out of the area. Company "B" is considering moving its plant of the same size out of a large city where it is one of many employers. It would seem that, other things being equal, Company "A" should give more weight to social responsibilities to the community when considering its move.

Even accepting the greater responsibility of Company "A," and some would not go this far, we still do not know how much greater nor in what way Company "A" should let its decision be amended, if at all. Thus the principle of co-equal power and responsibility can at best serve only as a rough guide, but a real one. For example:

> Do businessmen by their industrial engineering decisions have the power to affect worker's feeling of accomplishment and self-fulfillment on the job? If so, there is roughly a co-equal responsibility.
> Do businessmen have power as businessmen to influence unemployment? To the extent that is so, is there not also social responsibility?
> Do businessmen have power to determine the honesty of advertising? To the degree that they do, is there also social responsibility?

One matter of significance is that the conditions causing power are both internal and external to the firm. In the example of advertising honesty, power is derived primarily internally from the authority structure of the firm and management's knowledge of product characteristics. In the case of Company "A" described earlier, much of its social power is derived from the external fact that it is the only employer in a small town. Each case is situational, requiring reappraisal of power-responsibility relationships each time a major decision is made.

There are, of course, other viewpoints concerning the extent of business social responsibility, and most of them offer a much easier path for businessmen than the one I have been describing. Levitt, in a powerful attack on social responsibility of businessmen, points out that if business assumes a large measure of social responsibility for employee welfare it will lead to a sort of neo-feudalism with all its paternalistic and autocratic ills. The result would be socially less desirable than in the days before businessmen were concerned with social responsibility.[3] Selekman, in an important new analysis, suggests that attention to social responsibility will undermine the main objective of all business, which is to provide economic goods and services to society.[4] A collapse of business' basic economic objectives would indeed be a catastrophe. Certainly the primary economic objectives of business must come first, else business will lose its reason for existence. Selekman's solution is a form of constitutionalism in which the responsibility of the business, other than its economic goals, is to administer its affairs with justice according to a constitutional framework mutually established by all groups involved. These criticisms and others raise questions about putting much social responsibility into business' kit of tools, a fact which leads directly to the second fundamental point of this discussion.

Less responsibility leads to less power

Certainly, if social responsibilities could be avoided or kept to insignificant size in the total scheme of business, a weighty, difficult burden would be raised from businessmen's shoulders. Business progress would be a primrose path compared to the path of thorns which responsibilities entail. But what are the consequences of responsibility avoidance? If power and responsibility are to be relatively equal, *then the avoidance of social responsibility leads to gradual erosion of social power.* To the extent that businessmen do not accept social-responsibility opportunities as they arise, other groups will step in to assume these responsibilities. Historically, government and labor have been most active in the role of diluting business power, and probably they will continue to be the principal challenging groups.[5] I am not proposing that this *should* happen, but on basis of the evidence it appears that this will tend to happen to the extent that businessmen do not keep their social responsibilities approximately equal with their social power. In this same vein Howard R. Bowen, in his study of business social responsibilities, concluded, "And it is becoming increasingly obvious that a freedom of choice and delegation of power such as businessmen exercise would

---

[3] Theodore Levitt, "The Danger of Social Responsibility," *Harvard Business Review*, September-October, 1958, pp. 41-50.

[4] Benjamin M. Selekman, *A Moral Philosophy for Business* (New York: McGraw-Hill Book Company, 1959), especially chapter 27.

[5] For government's role, see George A. Steiner, *Government's Role in Economic Life* (New York: McGraw-Hill Book Company, 1953) and Wayne L. McNaughton and Joseph Lazar, *Industrial Relations and The Government* (New York: McGraw-Hill Book Company, 1954). For labor's role, see Neil W. Chamberlain, *Collective Bargaining* (New York: McGraw-Hill Book Company, 1951) and John A. Fitch, *Social Responsibilities of Organized Labor* (New York: Harper and Brothers, 1957).

hardly be permitted to continue without some assumption of social responsibility." [6]

Admiral Ben Moreell, Chairman of the Board, Jones and Laughlin Steel Corporation, put this idea more dramatically:

> I am convinced that unless we do [accept social responsibilities], the vacuum created by our unwillingness will be filled by those who would take us down the road to complete statism and inevitable moral and social collapse.[7]

History supports these viewpoints. Under the protection of common law, employers during the nineteenth century gave minor attention to worker safety. Early in the twentieth century, in the face of pressure from safety and workmen's compensation laws, employers genuinely accepted responsibility for safety. Since then there have been very few restrictions on business power in this area, because business in general has been acting responsibly. At the opposite extreme, business in the first quarter of this century remained callous about technological and market layoff. As a result, business lost some of its power to government, which administers unemployment compensation, and to unions, which restrict it by means of tight seniority clauses, supplemental unemployment benefits (SUB), and other means. *Now business finds itself in the position of paying unemployment costs it originally denied responsibility for, but having less control than when it did not pay!*

A current problem of social responsibility is gainful employment for older workers. The plight of workers in the over-45 age bracket is well known. In spite of public pronouncements of interest in them and in spite of their general employability, many of them find job opportunities quite limited or even nonexistent. I have said elsewhere that "unless management . . . makes reasonable provision for employing older persons out of work, laws will be passed prohibiting employment discrimination against older workers." [8] Just as a glacier grinds slowly along, the responsibility-power equation gradually, but surely, finds its balance.

In line with the foregoing analysis, Levitt's proposal of "business for business' sake" loses some of its glamor, because it means substantial loss of business power. Historian Arnold J. Toynbee predicts this result when he speaks of business managers being part "of a new

---

[6] Howard R. Bowen, *Social Responsibilities of the Businessman* (New York: Harper and Brothers, 1953), p. 4.
[7] Admiral Ben Moreell, "The Role of American Business in Social Progress" (Indianapolis: Indiana State Chamber of Commerce, 1956), p. 20.
[8] Keith Davis, *Human Relations in Business* (New York: McGraw-Hill Book Company, 1957), p. 415.

world civil service," not necessarily working for government, but working under such stability and elaborate rules both from within and without that they form a relatively powerless bureaucracy similar to the civil service.[9]

It is unlikely that businessmen will concede their social power so easily, and I for one do not want them to do so. Businessmen are our most capable core of organization builders and innovators. We need them. In spite of pessimistic views, businessmen during the next fifty years probably will have substantial freedom of choice regarding what social responsibilities they will take and how far they will go. As current holders of social power, they can act responsibly to hold this power if they wish to do so. If their philosophy is positive (i.e., *for* something, rather than against almost any change) they can take the initiative as instruments of social change related to business. They will then be managers in the true sense of shaping the future, rather than plaintive victims of a more restrictive environment. The choice *is* theirs.

Non-economic values in business

Early in this discussion I distinguished two types of social responsibilities. One was socio-economic responsibility for general economic welfare. The other was socio-human and referred to responsibility for preserving and developing human values. Let us now further discuss this distinction as it relates to a third idea underlying the entire problem of social responsibility.

There is general consensus that the "economic man" is dead if, indeed, he ever did exist. Men at work, as customers, and as citizens of a plant community do expect more than straight economic considerations in dealing with business. Since man is more than an economic automaton computing market values, what will be the role of business in serving his other needs? My third basic idea is that *continued vitality of business depends upon its vigorous acceptance of socio-human responsibilities along with socio-economic responsibilities.* A number of people accept the general idea of social responsibility, but they argue that business is wholly an economic institution and, therefore, its responsibilities are limited only to economic aspects of general public welfare. Following this line of reasoning, businessmen might be concerned with economic costs of unemployment, but not with the loss of human dignity and the social disorganization that

---

[9] Arnold J. Toynbee, "Thinking Ahead," *Harvard Business Review,* September-October, 1958, p. 168.

accompany it. They would be concerned with making work productive in order to better serve society's economic needs but not with making it meaningful in a way that provided worker fulfillment.

The idea of confining social responsibility within economic limits fails on several counts. In the first place, it is hardly possible to separate economic aspects of life from its other values. Business deals with a *whole* man in a *whole* social structure, and all aspects of this situation are interrelated. It is agreed that the economic functions of business are primary and the non-economic are secondary, but the non-economic do exist. Second, even if economic aspects of life could be wholly separated out, the general public does not seem to want business confined only to economics. They also have human expectations of business. Third, businessmen currently have socio-human power; hence, if they ignore responsibility in this area, they will be inviting further loss of power. On three counts, then, it appears unwise to equate social responsibility with economic public welfare.

As a matter of fact, it is not a question of "Will these non-economic values be admitted to the decision matrix?" but "To what extent will they be admitted?" Regardless of professions to the contrary, businessmen today are influenced by other than technical-economic values when making decisions. Businessmen are human like all the rest of us. They do have emotions and social value judgments. It is foolish to contend that they, like a machine and unlike other human beings, respond only to economic and technical data.

Businessmen in making decisions typically apply three separate value systems, along with overriding ethical-moral considerations. These are:

> Technical—Based upon physical facts and scientific logic.
> Economic—Based upon market values determined by consumers.
> Human—Based upon social-psychological needs other than economic consumption needs. This value system often goes by the term "human relations."

In many business decisions all three of these value systems exert some weight upon the final decision. Because man is human this aspect of his life cannot be ignored by any institution that deals with him.

But there are dangers in generalizations which are too sweeping, such as, "Business is responsible for human values in general." What is needed is a concept which marks business as an instrument *for specific human goals* (along with technical-economic ones) in the life of man and his society—something which gives direction and hope to the climb of mankind from the depths of the Stone Age to the great potential which his Creator has given him. This kind of concept does not come easily but it must come eventually. By giving people motivation, social goals, and work fulfillment, business might over the long pull be termed a "movement" in the same way that history refers to the labor movement.

Certainly some major efforts at being explicit have been made recently. Theodore V. Houser, writing from the point of view of big business, stated five specific areas of social responsibility, ranging from employees to government.[10] Selekman's idea of constitutional justice was discussed earlier.[11] Crawford Greenewalt emphasized the importance of individual creativity and stated, "The important thing is that we bring into play the full potential of all men whatever their station."[12] And there are many others. For my own use I have summed these ideas into a single manageable phrase, as follows: *To fulfill the human dignity, creativity, and potential of free men.*[13] This can be businessmen's long-run guide to socially responsible action in each situation they face. The term "fulfill" is used because business cannot award goals such as human dignity. It can only develop the proper climate for their growth. The term "man" is used because unless *man* is free, men cannot be free. Other institutions and groups will also be interested in this goal. Businessmen are not wholly responsible here, but only partially so, approximately to the extent of their social power.

An important choice ahead

The subject of social responsibility places business at an important cross-roads in its history. Which way it will go is not known, but in any event social responsibility will tend to equate with social power, which means that avoidance of responsibilities as they develop will lead to loss of business power. Some hard thinking is needed so that the right course can be charted. This is not the time for pat slogans, clichés, and wheezes. Clearly, economic functions of business are primary, but this does not negate the existence of non-economic functions and responsibilities. The price of social freedom is its responsible exercise.

Because society is changing, evidence suggests that the continued vigor of business depends upon its forthright acceptance of further

[10] Houser (see note 2), p. 2.
[11] Selekman (see note 2), p. 7.
[12] Greenewalt (see note 2), p. 2.
[13] One analyst has put this point even more strongly: "The making of goods is incidental and subordinate to the making of men." Raphael Demos, "Business and the Good Society," in Edward C. Bursk (ed.), *Business and Religion* (New York: Harper and Brothers, 1959), p. 190.

socio-human responsibilities. In spite of protestations of impending corporate feudalism and dilution of economic objectives, the trend in this direction is already apparent. Some of the more fruitful avenues of interest are: making work meaningful, developing persons to their fullest potential, preservation of creativity and freedom, and fulfillment of human dignity.

In summary, the *first* social responsibility of businessmen is to find workable solutions regarding the nature and extent of their own social responsibilities.

We can be confident that modern business leadership does have the capacity to deal with questions of social responsibility. Although the next fifty years will bring major social change, business should perform effectively in this instability because it is geared for change. Typically, during the last century it has had an unstable economic environment; yet it has learned to live and prosper therein. It can do the same during a period of social re-evaluation by developing flexible responses to the needs of society. But if it does not do so, it will use up its capital in human and spiritual values, which is a sure way to go socially bankrupt.

QUESTIONS

1. Define "social responsibility" and explain its relationship to human relations.
2. Distinguish between socio-economic responsibility and socio-human responsibility.
3. Upon what, according to Davis, does the continued vitality of business depend? Do you agree? Why?
4. Compare Davis's views with those of Freedman. What differences exist?
5. Explain what Davis means by the "first social responsibility of businessmen." Do you agree? Why?

52. HUMAN RELATIONS: A LOOK INTO THE FUTURE *

Chris Argyris

For anyone to make predictions about trends in human relations policies and practices is extremely difficult. For a researcher to make them based upon research results may be considered dangerous if not presumptuous. However, I have been asked to try, and try I will. Please keep in mind that what follows is, most of the time, *one* researcher's opinions, expectations, and hopes, and, at other times, his guesses into the future. Because of the limitation of time, I will state my views in terms of predictions that I *hypothesize* will tend to occur. The validation of these hypotheses is another matter.

I predict company human relations policies will shift:

I. From: The policy that requires people always to be friendly and like one another.
To: The policy that permits freedom for people to dislike as well as to be friendly.

Some reasons for this change are:

1. It is unrealistic to expect all people to like one another; it is inhuman to require it; it may be harmful to the individual and the company to enforce it.

2. The ability to express one's honest hostilities need not stifle cooperative effort. In fact, if done effectively, it can enhance such effort. In also can unleash much energy being used up when people attempt to withhold their feelings.

II. From: The policy that individuals are conceived as the most important part of an organization.
To: The more realistic policy that individuals are but one part of the organization whose importance varies under different conditions.

Some reasons for this change:

1. Employees who are self-responsible are not fooled by talk of their "importance," especially when they experience the tensions and

* From *Management Record*, Vol. 2, No. 3 (March, 1959), pp. 82-84. Reprinted with permission of author and publisher.

frustrations inherent in production bogies, budgets, etc. (and I am not saying this is bad). Many of them are self-responsible and willing to accept the need for the organizational requirements made upon them.

2. At best employees view these policies as "unreal whims of management," who "might feel guilty about being the boss." At worst, as conscious manipulations that betray management's basic (but perhaps unknowing) lack of confidence in the individual.

III. From: The policy that people (especially executives) should become so close to the organization that they are inseparable and indistinguishable from it.
To: The policy that people should give of themselves without giving up themselves.

Some reasons for this change:

1. An "overflowing" executive will tend to breed a sick organization.

2. He will also tend to distort reality in order not to see the impact of his leadership upon the organization and, ironically, upon himself.

IV. From: The policy that maximum communication among individuals is necessary.
To: The policy that optimum communication is most effective.

Reason for this change:
Managements who are anxious about communications at times clog up the channels with much noise; other times they forget to listen; and still other times they may communicate information that either baffles the employees or makes them defensive. One sign of trust in a human relationship is appropriate silence.

V. From: The policy that an effective organization is one with high production, low turnover, low absenteeism, and low grievance rates.
To: The policy that emphasizes the total health of an organization.

Some reasons for this change:
1. Research suggests that the traditional objectives of profit can be achieved by employees who are apathetic, indifferent to the company and alienated from their management and from each other.

2. This could lead to an organization becoming increasingly rigid and defensive. This rigidity can lead to the inability of the participants to see the necessity and high cost of change and maintaining organizational growth.[1]

VI. From: The belief that superiors can develop subordinates to be more skillful in interpersonal competence and diagnosing accurately administrative situations.
To: The belief that no one can develop anyone else except himself. The door to development is locked from the inside.

Some reasons for this change:

1. Much of what goes by the name of development is developing people in the image of a select group of executives. The danger is clear: today's managerial skills of success may pave the way for tomorrow's failure.

2. The criterion, if a superior has truly developed his subordinates, is not necessarily how many of his subordinates have succeeded. The criterion should be how many of his subordinates have gone on to develop their subordinates.

3. The responsibility of management is not to develop people. It is to develop the climate and the opportunities for self-development.

VII. From: The objective of executive development programs to change the executive's behavior.
To: The objective of helping the executive become aware of himself and become more tolerant, accepting of himself and therefore of others.

Some reasons for this change:

1. Changing behavior implies to the individual that his present behavior is wrong. Such implications, if the executive is healthy, tend to create defensiveness and resistance. Moreover, who knows what is the correct leadership behavior?

2. Research increasingly suggests that no one leadership pattern is best for all administrative situations. Effective executive leadership may require a number of different kinds of leadership patterns, each to be used in specific types of situations. I believe management

[1] Chris Argyris, "The Organization: What Makes It Healthy?" *Harvard Business Review*, November-December, 1958.

is going away from "democratic" or "autocratic" leadership toward a concept of "reality-centered" leadership.[2]

3. It may be condemnable and not laudable that people in three, thirteen or thirty-six weeks can be influenced to change their basic values and behavior that have taken a lifetime to develop.

4. Human wisdom, understanding and tolerance begin with oneself. If the individual can truly (emotionally) begin to care for himself, he will begin to care for others.

An individual who cares for himself will tend (a) to have a high sense of inner worth, (b) to decrease his defensiveness, (c) to increase his own internal freedom and creativity and (d) to permit others to achieve the same if they so desire.

> **VIII. From: The objective of executive development programs that teach an executive how he ought to behave or how he ought to think.**
> **To: The objective of helping the executive learn how to learn.**

Reason for this change:

Development and change will be a main characteristic of management in the next twenty years. Teaching the executive what he ought to read, how he ought to behave and think emphasizes *end results*. These end results may not apply when the executive is given the opportunity to use this knowledge. Emphasizing the *processes* of how to learn, how to diagnose administrative situations, how to learn from experience—these are timeless wisdoms.

The former approach emphasizes developing *learned* men. The latter emphasizes developing *learning* men.

> **IX. From: The belief that human relations problems are caused primarily by poor organizational planning, poor budgets, incentive systems, etc.**
> **To: The awareness that effective organizational planning, budgets, incentive systems, etc. also can cause human problems.**

Some reasons for this change:

1. Research suggests that the very nature of organization and managerial controls, if used correctly, can cause employees to feel

---

[2] Chris Argyris, *Personality and Organization* (New York: Harper & Brothers, 1957).

dependent, subordinate, submissive, and to use relatively few of their adult abilities.

2. Employees, who are relatively healthy, may adapt by absenteeism, turnover, apathy, indifference, and unionization.

3. Not as often seen, and therefore worth emphasizing, is the trend, on the part of employees, of increasingly viewing wages as compensation for *dissatisfaction* and not necessarily as a reward for past performance, or as a motivation for future performance.

The economic man may exist. If so, this may be one of the deepest human problems our society will face in the future.

Closing comments

Management philosophy initially developed from an emphasis on scientific management and organization to an emphasis on people and human relationships. The future, I predict, will see an increasing emphasis that neither approach by itself is adequate.

Effective management may require the "right" combination of both approaches. What combination? How much emphasis on the company demands? How much on the individual needs? Fundamentally, these questions cannot be answered without much research to tell us what is the precise impact of each and a realistic philosophy of management to provide the manager with a set of basic values from which to make his choice.[3]

I predict increasing research that will focus on the requirements for an effective or healthy organization. This implies that what is needed is a philosophy of management that views the individual and the organization not only as interrelated but actually *interpenetrating* one another. A philosophy of management where not only do the individual and the organization have a right to health, but where it is acknowledged that their health can only come from this dynamic process of man interpenetrating the organization and the organization interpenetrating man.

QUESTIONS

1. Why does Argyris predict that company human relations policies will shift?
2. Explain what Argyris means by the "total health" of an organization.
3. Define "reality-centered" leadership.
4. Do you agree with Argyris's predictions? Why or why not?
5. Discuss the meaning of the statement: What is needed is a philosophy of management that views the individual and the organization not only as interrelated but actually interpenetrating one another."

---

[3] Argyris, *op. cit.*

53. A MANAGEMENT STYLE CHANGE FOR THE SIXTIES *

George S. Odiorne

Changes in style, including automobiles, women's dresses, and even architecture are commonplace to most of us. What's less obvious but nonetheless true is the fact that styles of *management* also change. Less often then the annual model change in cars, such changes in management methods seem to come out of pressures from the changing economic environment in which management is practiced. An analysis of management style changes provides a guide to action for the manager who wants to be more effective himself and who wants to get more mileage during the coming decade out of the investment he has made in managers and key people. Let's look at the style changes in the recent past to see what clues they give us for predicting the model of manager we'll see in the sixties.

Without going back any further than most middle-aged managers can recall from personal experience, the management styles which we've lived through fall into these distinct patterns:

1. The hard-nosed manager of the nineteen twenties and thirties,
2. The human relator of the nineteen forties and early fifties,
3. The management-by-pressure type of the mid and late fifties,
4. The new "manager of situations" which is emerging for the sixties and will become (I predict) the model of manager of this decade.

Let's look at each of these in turn, not simply to resurrect the past but to single out some useful guides to making our managers attuned to the new management model of the sixties, and get more mileage from our present key people.

The hard nose: management model of the 1920's and 1930's

One of the commonest articles of faith of one kind of old fashioned manager is the belief that "people don't want to work like they did when I started working." This is partly true, and reflects some of the rigorous and often harsh standards which managers applied in directing the work force during the twenties and thirties. The labor climate then was one of an unskilled work force, mainly unorganized, comprised in large part of immigrants or first generation people who accepted strict control—in fact expected it. During the thirties this

* From *Michigan Business Review*, Vol. 12, No. 5 (November, 1962), pp. 1-5. Reprinted with permission.

philosophy continued unabated with the support of labor surpluses which made it easier to replace key people from the pool of unemployed people outside the plant gate. Many foremen, supervisors, and company presidents found it possible to manage in ways that gave little recourse to the workers for anything that seemed unduly strict, unfair, or downright tough. Hiring by the method that Tom Spates of General Foods described as "crooking his finger at the applicant" was easy to apply. Once on the job, the rigor and discipline was firmly enforced, and the manager was most successful if he was tough. Human relations, motivation, and similar techniques of management weren't needed in such a climate, and since they weren't needed, weren't used. Fear of getting fired was an important ingredient in getting people to follow orders, and discipline was based upon a desire to hold one's job.

About the time of World War II the style which worked during the thirties ended, and a new style of management came into being.

The human relator: model manager of the forties

As the crowd outside the plant gate and employment office shrank under the high employment demands of the early war-time forties, the kind of management practices used inside the shop and office changed too. More fawning upon employees, more benefits and privileges, and widespread attempts to make people *happy* came into favor with management. Experiments of the social scientists in the Hawthorne works of the Western Electric Company during the early thirties had resulted in a great wave of social scientists entering industry to develop a theory of management by human relations. It suited the times perfectly, with pressing shortages of help, and expansion of firms for war and expanded civilian production. "Make your employees contented," one such study said, "and they will remain on their jobs, and be productive."

This psychology of contentment—called "cow sociology" by Daniel Bell—brought to the fore the kind of manager who was adept at pleasing people, keeping morale high, and understanding human behavior in order to achieve this euphoric state in which happy employees would—it is said—become productive employees. Training courses sprang up by the score, emphasizing the ways in which managers could produce happiness in the shop.

This continued until the late forties, when a new style change became necessary. This wasn't brought about by any new breakthroughs in social science. It resulted from rising inflation which began to press harder and harder upon top management and the economy generally. Some companies discovered that not all contented employees were productive, and that happiness and fawning weren't necessarily equated with producing a good product and selling it at a low cost.

Claude Swank, Vice President of Manufacturing of Johnson and Johnson in 1951 told a reporter that "We've got to find some pegs to hang this human relations business onto so it will produce more, not just make people contented." During the first years of the fifties annual reports began to state more and more that sales volume was going up, while profits were going down. A management style change was obviously indicated, and actually occurred.

Management by pressure: style for the fifties

This pressure for cost reduction was recognized in the late forties by some companies, such as autos, chemicals, rubber, and others, and by the end of the Korean War was in full swing. The "cost price squeeze" brought about some new styles in management, most of which resulted in a *management by pressure* in which the management from top down exerted heavy pressure on the points where costs were getting out of line. The Hard Line in labor relations, the expansion of industrial engineering departments, the improvement of systems and procedures, the introduction of the computer to cut office and paper work costs, resulted in promoting a more action-oriented kind of manager who could "make things happen." Management expert Peter Drucker suggested in 1954 that *management by objective* —making managers responsible for results rather than fitting them into human relations patterns—would be the way of management in the future. He also added that in practice it was more realistic to note that the prevailing method of managing was to exert fearful pressure upon organization for results, and went on to suggest that this kind of pressure probably wouldn't achieve as good results as a sounder more rational kind of management by results.

The manager of the fifties became a kind of pressure expert, serving, as David Moore of Michigan State put it, as a kind of "giant thermostat" who turned the heat off and on for the people below him. Management controls became a kind of thumbscrew which told the top fellow where to twist hardest for greatest effect. The willingness to fire people who hadn't produced once again became acceptable. The fellow who could take it and respond with good results moved up quickly. Yet, it wasn't exactly a return to the hard-nose days of the thirties, because there were still shortages of help in many areas, and despite some dips in the cycle of 1953 and 1958, good men in many key areas,—especially the high talent professionals—were sufficiently scarce that they required delicate handling or they'd pack their papers and depart. The trick then became one of exerting pressure through the human relations methods we'd learned during the forties to keep people on the payroll, and still working harder than before. An all-out attack on the "age of the great goof-off" as ad-man Charles Brower dubbed it, was in full swing. In this climate, the new model of management for the sixties was developed.

The manager of situations: manager for the sixties

There's some concrete evidence that the manager of the sixties will be different from most of these models of the past. He'll be more of a manager of situations than any of his counterparts—or than he himself was in the past. Getting managers to adapt their style to this new model may be the key to getting maximum mileage out of key personnel during the sixties.

What, then, does the top manager do to fit his management team into the new situation? Basically there are two things required:

1. Get a firm grip on what it means to "manage by situation"; and
2. Make some changes in present ways of management development to gear management practices to the new demands.

Who is the manager of situations?

There are six things about the manager of situations which distinguishes him from the pressure artist, the human relator, or the hard-nose of the past. Briefly they are:

1. *He's judged by what his followers do.* The leader is a person who has followers. This logically leads us to conclude that the quality of a manager is directly related to the quality of followers he has behind him, and his own results are essentially those of his followers. He'll be confronted with more complex technical and commercial problems, won't be able to do it all himself even if he wanted to, and will become more dependent upon good men working for him. Thus, if he's built an organization of pipsqueaks, as management development expert Jim Hayes puts it, "he's nothing more than chief pipsqueak." On the other hand, if he's pulled together a team of tigers working for him, he's head tiger.

2. *There's no "executive personality."* The old game of seeking a pattern of personality traits that always describes the executive is

getting rather outworn as we enter the sixties. More firms are realizing that there's no point in trying to inculcate certain traits (such as initiative, loyalty, judgment) when we have learned that there is no single trait—nor set of them—that always is present in successful executives and absent in unsuccessful ones. Appraisal systems and personality testing which aims at whittling away objectionable knobs on a man's personality, or grafting new ones onto his basic personality, not only won't work; they can't produce managers who can adapt to their environment and control it.

3. *The good manager makes things happen.* Nicholas Murray Butler, former president of Columbia University, once said that there were three kinds of people: those who make things happen; those who watch what goes on; and those who don't know what happened. The manager of situations knows what is happening, and he's also making things happen. He decides that sales should increase, products should be developed, costs should be cut, or quality improved, and he puts in the brains, the drive, and the leadership to make it happen.

4. *He's more of a generalist than in the past.* A manager of situations is more of a generalist than ever before, because he knows that he's going to face problems that go beyond any specialty. He's more apt to be a generally adaptable, facile, and flexible person than any specialist could possibly be. Because he manages situations, he's more of an expert in analyzing situations, classifying problems, seeing causes, and identifying proper courses of action for others (who are specialists) than he is in being an expert on everything in his organization. He's more apt to be a creative thinker in unforeseen situations than an expert in familiar problems and areas of activity. In a world that's changing because of competition, costs, changing social structure, and a shrinking world he's more apt to be what Rensis Likert of Michigan calls a "change agent" than a technical overseer.

5. *He works more through organization than personal effort.* Despite the dangers of conformity and stifled initiative which large organizations have inherent in their structure, the use of management teams, task forces, and sound organization will increase in the sixties. The very numbers of people involved, the specialization in some areas, and the rise of pressure groups for special interest will take greater organizational skills for the manager of the situation than personal actions to get things done. He'll delegate more, but the vital point is that after delegating details he'll spend more time in

studying and organizing the situation than he could if he attended to too many lesser facets of the job himself.

6. *He's results- and responsibility-oriented.* The manager of situations emerges as the leader because he's got his eyes fixed squarely on *results* and *responsibilities*. These dual goals can't be split into distinct parts without some adverse effects either. Take the most common results which are sought from the typical manager—*profits* and *growth*. These aren't ends to be accomplished without full regard for the responsibilities of the manager in terms of doing it by the right *means*. He can't extract profits and growth from his business through unethical conduct, through being a bad citizen of his community and country, and without meeting the ordinary standards of fair play and good citizenship.

Here was one of the flaws of the management-by-pressure style of leadership. It hammered the unfortunate manager for results without especially concerning itself with how he got them. Occasionally he found that the pressure for results forced him into some paths that inevitably reacted on him. The difference here is that the responsibilities of a manager entail doing things within a value system. The manager of a steel mill in the Urals or a steel mill in the midwestern United States have different responsibilities to the society in which they work. Tonnage alone doesn't measure their comparative worth. The tonnage is needed in either case, everyone agrees. The basic difference between the two systems is *how* it was done.

How to grow managers of situations

Breeding new managers—or altering the behavior of old ones— who will hold down the heavy management positions during the sixties and beyond will take some education. It's already under way, and we can draw on the tested methods used by companies which have bred the new kind of manager out of the experienced manager of the past. Here are some ways it is done.

1. *Better selection of managers.* During the coming decades more attention will be paid to picking able men. If a manager is judged by his follower's abilities, then picking sound performers is a vital skill of management. This is based simply on judging future performance on what his record shows—and doing some projecting on educated guesses. Testing will probably increase, but along some drastically different lines than we've sometimes seen in the past. It

will merely be one of several kinds of evaluative information used in identifying potential management ability.

2. *A big switch in appraisal systems.* The old system of sitting down annually and ticking off a score from a check list of personality traits like "initiative—drive—ingenuity" etc., is due for a trip to the laundry. Appraisals in the future will stress what the man *did* and *how* he did it rather than the state of his libido and how he reacted to the obstetrician.

3. *Emphasis upon situational thinking in training.* Executive training and development will tack even further away from the old lecture—textbook style and move more toward cases, in-basket, simulation games, and role-playing to give the man the feel of countless kinds of situations. The goal here will not be to teach specific techniques, but to help him develop skill at decision making, problem solving, and situational leadership.

4. *More behavioral science—less human relations.* The old sentimental style of human relations training which was generally soft and sentimental is being supplanted by a more sophisticated, scientific, and sometimes quantitative approach to interpersonal relations. This situational manager will be trained to be more sophisticated in understanding people as individuals and in groups than any manager we've seen. The recent trend in the collegiate business schools toward more behavioral science and quantitative methods will begin to be felt in middle management ranks during the decade. More companies will be doing retread jobs on their obsolete managers to sharpen their skill, protect the substantial investment already poured into the existing group, and relate the past to the future.

5. *Increased investment in human capital.* During the sixties we'll see larger investment in "human capital," as economist Theodore Schultz calls it. Already economists have discovered the leverage which comes from this kind of investment compared with investment in conventional hardware kinds of capital. This will be the age of the high talent man, the vital few. Vice President Watters of General Foods told a University of Michigan audience that we'll see more management for the "classes, not the masses" with the decline of the unskilled worker, and rise of the trained man. This emphasis, especially in developing managers who are generalists, make things happen, and who are results- and responsibility-oriented will be the moving force behind the new management style dictated by the economic climate of the sixties.

QUESTIONS

1. Briefly discuss the basic differences between the following styles of management:
   a. Hard-nosed.
   b. Human relator.
   c. Management by pressure.
2. What does Odiorne mean by "manager of situations"? Is this the same as situational leadership? Explain.
3. What characteristics distinguish the manager of situations from other types of managers?
4. Can the manager of situations be bred? How?
5. Do you agree with Odiorne's conclusion? Why?

GENERAL QUESTIONS ON PART X

1. What were some of the historical landmarks in the growth of human relations in industry?
2. List and evaluate the criticisms of human relations principles and practices. Do you agree with these criticisms?
3. How does the practice of human relations relate itself to executive success?
4. What do you think the future is for industrial human relations?
5. Why do you think the human relations movement has become so important in today's economy?
6. What attitudes toward human relations should an executive adopt?
7. Why is human relations considered an emerging discipline?
8. Define the scope of the human relations movement. List the subjects that you believe lie within the boundaries of the movement.
9. Do you feel that human relations will ever become an exact science? Why or why not?
10. What is your conclusion about the trend of the human relations movement during the next ten years. State your reasons for your conclusion.

SELECTED BIBLIOGRAPHY

Part I. Human Relations and Administration: An Overview

Anshen, M. L., and G. L. Bach. *Management and Corporations, 1985.* New York: McGraw-Hill Book Co., Inc., 1960.

Berle, A. A., and G. C. Means, *Power Without Property.* New York: Harcourt, Brace and Co., 1959.

Cyert, R. M., and J. G. March. *A Behavioral Theory of the Firm.* Englewood Cliffs, New Jersey: Prentice-Hall, Inc., 1963.

Davis, K. *Human Relations at Work.* New York: McGraw-Hill Book Co., Inc., 1961.

Drucker, P. F. *The Practice of Management.* New York: Harper and Bros., Inc., 1954.

————. *Managing for Results.* New York: Harper and Row, 1963.

Dubin, Robert. *Human Relations in Administration,* 2nd ed. Englewood Cliffs, New Jersey: Prentice-Hall, Inc., 1961.

Forrester, J. W. *Industrial Dynamics.* New York: John Wiley and Sons, Inc., 1961.

Gardner, B. B., and D. G. Moore. *Human Relations in Business,* 4th ed. Homewood, Illinois: Richard D. Irwin, Inc., 1964.

Gross, B. M. *The Managing of Organizations,* Vols. 1 & 2. New York: The Free Press of Glencoe, 1964.

Katz, D., and R. L. Kahn. *The Social Psychology of Organizations.* New York: John Wiley and Sons, Inc., 1966.

Latham, J. L. *Human Relations in Business.* Columbus, Ohio: Charles E. Merrill Books, Inc., 1964.

Saltonstall, R. *Human Relations in Administration.* New York: McGraw-Hill Book Co., Inc., 1959.

Scott, W. G. *Human Relations in Management.* Homewood, Illinois: Richard D. Irwin, Inc., 1962.

Thompson, J. D. *Approaches to Organizational Design.* Pittsburgh: University of Pittsburgh Press, 1966.

Part II. The Manager: Background, Personality, and Role

Blake, R. R., and J. S. Mouton. *The Managerial Grid.* Houston: Gulf Publishing Co., 1965.

Collins, O. F., D. G. Moore, and D. B. Unwalla. *The Enterprising Man.* East Lansing, Michigan: Bureau of Economic and Business Research, Michigan State University, 1964.

Dalton, M. *Men Who Manage.* New York: John Wiley & Sons, Inc., 1959.

Dill, W. R., T. L. Hilton, and W. R. Reitman. *The New Managers.* Englewood Cliffs, New Jersey: Prentice-Hall, Inc., 1962.

Dommermuth, W. P. *The Road to the Top.* Austin, Texas: Bureau of Business Research, The University of Texas, 1965.

Eliott, O. *Men at the Top.* New York: Harper & Bros., Inc., 1959.

Ewing, D. W. *The Managerial Mind.* New York: The Crowell-Collier Publishing Co., 1964.

Flory, C. D. (ed.). *Managers for Tomorrow.* New York: The New American Library, 1965.

Granick, D. *The European Executive*. Garden City, New Jersey: Doubleday & Co., Inc., 1962.

Harrell, W. T. *Managers' Performance and Personality*. Cincinnati: South-Western Publishing Co., Inc., 1961.

Jennings, E. E. *The Executive*. New York: Harper and Row, Publishers, 1962.

_____. *The Executive in Crisis*. East Lansing, Michigan: Bureau of Business and Economic Research, Michigan State University, 1965.

Lawrence, P. R., *et al. Organizational Behavior and Administration*, 2nd ed. Homewood, Illinois: Richard D. Irwin, Inc., 1965.

Lewis, R., and R. Steward. *The Managers*. New York: The New American Library, 1961.

Livingston, R. T., and W. W. Waite. *The Manager's Job*. New York: Columbia University Press, 1960.

Newcomer, M. *The Big Business Executive*. New York: Columbia University Press, 1955.

Packard, U. *The Pyramid Climbers*. New York: McGraw-Hill Book Co., Inc., 1964.

Piotrowski, Z. A., and M. R. Rock. *The Perceptanalytic Executive Scale*. New York: Grune and Stratton, Inc., 1963.

Sayles, L. *Managerial Behavior*. New York: McGraw-Hill Book Co., Inc., 1964.

Scientific American. *The Big Business Executive*, 1965.

Warner, W. L., *et al. The American Federal Executive*. New Haven, Conn.: Yale University Press, 1963.

Warner, W. L., and J. C. Abegglen. *Big Business Leaders in America*. New York: Harper & Bros., Inc., 1955.

Part III. Leadership

Batten, J. *Tough-Minded Management*. New York: American Management Association, 1963.

Bellows, R. *Creative Leadership*. Englewood Cliffs, New Jersey: Prentice-Hall, Inc., 1959.

Browne, C. G., and T. S. Cohn. *The Study of Leadership*. Danville, Illinois: The Interstate Printers and Publishers, Inc., 1958.

Davis, K. *Human Relations at Work*, 2nd ed. New York: McGraw-Hill Book Co., Inc., 1962.

Golembiewski, R. T. *Men, Management and Morality*. New York: McGraw-Hill Book Co., Inc., 1966.

Hardwick, C. T., and B. F. Landuyt. *Administrative Strategy*. Cincinnati: South-Western Publishing Company, Inc., 1966.

Jennings, E. E. *An Anatomy of Leadership*. New York: Harper and Brothers, Publishers, 1960.

_____. *The Executive*. New York: Harper and Row, Publishers, 1962.

Petrullo, L., and B. M. Bass. *Leadership and Interpersonal Behavior*. New York: Holt, Rinehart and Winston, Inc., 1961.

Porter, D. H., and P. B. Applewhite. *Studies in Organizational Behavior and Management*. Scranton: International Textbook Co., 1964.

Simon, H. *Administrative Behavior*, 2nd ed. New York: The Macmillan Company, 1965.

Tannenbaum, R., I. R. Weschler, and F. Massarik. *Leadership and Organization: A Behavioral Science Approach*. New York: McGraw-Hill Book Co., Inc., 1961.

Part IV. Motivation and Behavior

Argyris, C. *Understanding Organizational Behavior*. Homewood, Illinois: The Dorsey Press, 1960.

Bass, B. M. *Organizational Psychology*. Boston: Allyn and Bacon, Inc., 1965.

Berelson, B., and G. A. Steiner. *Human Behavior: An Inventory of Scientific Findings*. New York: Harcourt, Brace and World, Inc., 1964.

Costello, T. W., and S. S. Zalkind. *Psychology in Administration*. Englewood Cliffs, New Jersey: Prentice-Hall, Inc., 1963.

Fisk, G. (ed.). *The Frontiers of Management Psychology*. New York: Harper and Row, Publishers, 1964.

Gellerman, S. W. *Motivation and Productivity*. New York: American Management Association, 1963.

Golembiewski, R. *Behavior and Organization*. Chicago: Rand McNally and Company, 1962.

Haire, M. *Psychology in Management*, 2nd ed. New York: McGraw-Hill Book Co., Inc., 1964.

Herzberg, F., B. Mausner, and B. Snyderman. *The Motivation to Work*. New York: John Wiley and Sons, Inc., 1959.

Krech, D., R. S. Crutchfield, and E. L. Ballachey. *Individual in Society*. New York: McGraw-Hill Book Co., Inc., 1962.

Leavitt, H. *Managerial Psychology*, 2nd ed. Chicago: The University of Chicago Press, 1964.

Lindzey, G., and C. S. Hall. *Theories of Personality*. New York: John Wiley and Sons, Inc., 1965.

Maslow, A. *Motivation and Personality*. New York: Harper & Brothers, Publishers, 1954.

McGregor, D. *The Human Side of Enterprise*. New York: McGraw-Hill Book Co., Inc., 1960.

Patten, A. *Men, Money and Motivation*. New York: McGraw-Hill Book Co., Inc., 1961.

Vroom, V. *Work and Motivation*. New York: John Wiley & Sons, Inc., 1964.

Whyte, W. F. *Men at Work*. Homewood, Illinois: R. D. Irwin, Inc., 1961.

Zaleznik, A., and D. Morment. *The Dynamics of Interpersonal Behavior*. New York: John Wiley and Sons, Inc., 1964.

Part V. Organization Structure and Dynamics

Argyris, C. *Personality and Organization*. New York: Harper & Bros., 1957.

Blau, P. M., and W. R. Scott. *Formal Organizations*. San Francisco: Chandler Publishing Company, 1962.

Caplow, T. *Principles of Organization*. New York: Harcourt, Brace & World, Inc., 1964.

Cooper, W. W., H. J. Leavitt, and M. W. Shelly. *New Perspectives in Organization Research*. New York: John Wiley & Sons, Inc., 1964.

Cyert, R. M., and J. G. March. *A Behavioral Theory of the Firm*. Englewood Cliffs, New Jersey: Prentice-Hall, Inc., 1963.

Etzioni, A. *Complex Organizations*. New York: Holt, Rinehart and Winston, Inc., 1961.

————. *Modern Organizations*. Englewood Cliffs, New Jersey: Prentice-Hall, Inc., 1964.

Gross, E. *Industry and Social Life*. Dubuque, Iowa: Wm. C. Brown Company, 1965.

Haire, M. *Modern Organization Theory*. New York: John Wiley and Sons, Inc., 1959.

Katz, D., and R. L. Kahn. *The Social Psychology of Organizations*. New York: John Wiley and Sons, Inc., 1966.

Leavitt, H. J. (ed.). *The Social Science of Organizations*. Englewood Cliffs, New Jersey: Prentice-Hall, Inc., 1963.

Likert, R. *New Patterns in Management*. New York: McGraw-Hill Book Co., Inc., 1961.

Litterer, J. *Organizations: Structure and Behavior*. New York: John Wiley and Sons, Inc., 1963.
_____. *The Analysis of Organizations*. New York: John Wiley and Sons, Inc., 1965.
March, J. G., and H. A. Simon. *Organizations*. New York: John Wiley and Sons, Inc., 1958.
Pfiffner, J. M., and F. P. Sherwood. *Administrative Organization*. Englewood Cliffs, New Jersey: Prentice-Hall, Inc., 1960.
Rubenstein, A. H., and C. J. Haberstroh. *Some Theories of Organization*, Rev. ed. Homewood, Illinois: The Dorsey Press, Inc. and Richard D. Irwin, Inc., 1966.
Thompson, J. D. (ed.). *Approaches to Organizational Design*. Pittsburgh: University of Pittsburgh Press, 1966.
Thompson, V. A. *Modern Organization*. New York: Alfred A. Knopf, 1961.

Part VI. Communication

Chase, S. *Roads to Agreement*. New York: Harper and Row, 1951.
Dooher, M. J. (ed.). *Effective Communication on the Job*. New York: American Management Association, 1956.
Haney, W. V. *Communication: Patterns and Incidents*. Homewood, Illinois: Richard D. Irwin, Inc., 1960.
Hayakawa, S. I. *Language in Thought and Action*. New York: Harcourt, Brace and Company, 1949.
_____. *The Use and Misuse of Language*. Greenwich, Conn.: Fawcett Publications, Inc., 1962.
Lee, I. J. *Customs and Crisis in Communication*. New York: Harper and Bros., Publishers, 1954.
Lee, I. J., and L. L. Lee. *Handling Barriers in Communication*. New York: Harper and Brothers, 1957.
Nichols, R. G., and L. A. Stevens. *Are You Listening?* New York: McGraw-Hill Book Co., 1957.
Redfield, C. E. *Communication in Management*. Chicago: The University of Chicago Press, 1953.
Rogers, C. R. *Client-Centered Therapy*. Boston: Houghton Mifflin Company, 1951.
_____. *Counseling and Psychotherapy*. Boston: Houghton Mifflin Company, 1942.
Thayer, L. O. *Administrative Communication*. Homewood, Illinois: Richard D. Irwin, Inc., 1961.
Zelko, H. P., and F. E. X. Dance. *Business and Professional Speech Communication*. New York: Holt, Rinehart and Winston, Inc., 1965.

Part VII. Participation and Group Dynamics

Barnes, L. B. *Organizational Systems and Engineering Groups*. Boston: Division of Research, Harvard University, 1960.
Blake, R. R., H. A. Shepard, and J. S. Mouton. *Managing Intergroup Conflict in Industry*. Houston: Gulf Publishing Company, 1964.
Bonner, H. *Group Dynamics*. New York: The Ronald Press Company, 1959.
Cartwright, D., and A. Zander. *Group Dynamics: Research and Theory*, 2nd ed. Evanston, Illinois: Row, Peterson and Company, 1960.
Collins, B. E., and H. Guetzkow. *A Social Psychology of Group Processes for Decision Making*. New York: John Wiley and Sons, Inc., 1964.
Gordon, T. *Group-Centered Leadership*. Boston: Houghton Mifflin Company, 1955.
Grew, M. C. *Group Life*. New York: Philosophical Library, 1950.
Hare, A. P., *et al*. *Small Groups*. New York: Alfred A. Knopf, 1955.

Kahn, R. L., *et al. Organizational Stress: Studies in Role Conflict and Ambiguity.* New York: John Wiley and Sons, Inc., 1964.

Kemp, C. G. *Perspectives on the Group Process.* Boston: Houghton Mifflin Company, 1964.

Sayles, L. R. *Behavior of Industrial Work Groups.* New York: John Wiley and Sons, Inc., 1958.

Seashore, S. E. *Group Cohesiveness in the Industrial Work Group.* Ann Arbor: University of Michigan, 1955.

Thelen, H. A. *Dynamics of Groups at Work.* Chicago: The University of Chicago Press, 1954.

Thibaut, J. W., and H. H. Kelley. *The Social Psychology of Groups.* New York: John Wiley and Sons, Inc., 1959.

Vroom, V. H. *Some Personality Determinants of the Effects of Participation.* Englewood Cliffs, New Jersey: Prentice-Hall, Inc., 1960.

Part VIII. Organizational Change

Adams, L. P., and R. L. Aronson. *Workers and Industrial Change.* Ithaca, N. Y.: Cornell University Press, 1957.

Argyris, C. *Organization and Innovation.* Homewood, Illinois: Richard D. Irwin, Inc. and The Dorsey Press, 1965.

Bennis, W. G., *et al. The Planning of Change.* New York: Holt, Rinehart and Winston, Inc., 1962.

————. *Interpersonal Dynamics.* New York: Holt, Rinehart and Winston, Inc., 1964.

Ginsberg, E., *et al. Effecting Change in Large Organizations.* New York: Columbia University Press, 1957.

Guest, R. H. *Organizational Change: The Effect of Successful Leadership.* Homewood, Illinois: The Dorsey Press and Richard D. Irwin, Inc., 1962.

Ronken, H. O., and P. R. Lawrence. *Administering Changes: A Case Study of Human Relations in a Factory.* Boston: Harvard University Press, 1952.

Schein, E. H., and W. G. Bennis. *Personal and Organizational Change Through Group Methods.* New York: John Wiley and Sons, Inc., 1965.

Siegel, S., and L. E. Fouraker. *Bargaining and Group Decision Making.* New York: McGraw-Hill Book Co., Inc., 1960.

Part IX. Human Relations Skills, Sensitivity, and Productivity

Argyris, C. *Interpersonal Competence and Organizational Effectiveness.* Homewood, Illinois: Richard D. Irwin, Inc., 1962.

————. *Integrating the Individual and the Organization.* New York: John Wiley and Sons, Inc., 1965.

Bradford, L. P., J. R. Gibb, and K. D. Benne. *T-Group Theory and Laboratory Method.* New York: John Wiley and Sons, Inc., 1964.

Herzberg, F. *Work and the Nature of Man.* Cleveland: The World Publishing Company, 1966.

Knudson, H. R. *Human Elements of Administration.* New York: Holt, Rinehart and Winston, Inc., 1963.

Maslow, A. H. *Eupsychian Management: A Journal.* Homewood, Illinois: Richard D. Irwin, Inc. and The Dorsey Press, 1965.

Massarik, F., and P. Ratoosh. *Mathematical Explanations in Behavioral Science.* Homewood, Illinois: R. D. Irwin and The Dorsey Press, 1965.

Morrow, A. J. *Behind the Executive Mask.* New York: American Management Association, 1965.

Purcell, T. V. *The Worker Speaks His Mind.* Cambridge, Mass.: Harvard University Press, 1953.

_____. *Blue Collar Man: Patterns of Dual Allegiance in Industry*. Cambridge, Mass.: Harvard University Press, 1960.

Sayles, L., and G. Strauss. *Human Behavior in Organizations*. Englewood Cliffs, New Jersey: Prentice-Hall, Inc., 1966.

Stagner, R., and H. Rosen. *Psychology of Union-Management Relations*. Belmont, California: Wadsworth Publishing Co., Inc., 1965.

Steiner, G. A. (ed.). *The Creative Organization*. Chicago: University of Chicago Press, 1965.

Tannenbaum. A. S. *Social Psychology of the Work Organization*. Belmont, California: Wadsworth Publishing Co., Inc., 1966.

Zaleznik, A., C. R. Christensen, and F. J. Roethlisberger. *The Motivation, Productivity, and Satisfaction of Workers*. Boston: Harvard University Graduate School of Business, 1958.

Part X. Human Relations in Perspective

Daiute, R. J. *Scientific Management and Human Relations*. New York: Holt, Rinehart and Winston, Inc., 1964.

Davis, K., and R. L. Blomstrom. *Business and Its Environment*. New York: McGraw-Hill Book Co., Inc., 1966.

Ells, R. *The Government of Corporations*. New York: The Free Press of Glencoe, 1964.

Johnson, H. *Business Ethics*, 2nd ed. New York: Pitman Publishing Company, 1961.

Kerr, C., et al. *Industrialism and Industrial Man*. Cambridge, Mass.: Harvard University Press, 1964.

Mason, E. S. *The Corporation in Modern Society*. Cambridge, Mass.: Harvard University Press, 1964.

McGuire, J. *Business and Society*. New York: McGraw-Hill Book Co., Inc., 1963.

Moore, W. E. *The Conduct of the Corporation*. New York: Random House, Inc., 1962.

Sayles, L. R. *Individualism and Big Business*. New York: McGraw-Hill Book Co., Inc., 1963.

Schlender, W. E., W. G. Scott, and A. C. Filley. (eds.). *Management in Perspective: Selected Readings*. Boston: Houghton Mifflin Company, 1965.

Simon, H. *Models of Man*. New York: John Wiley & Sons, Inc., 1957.

Stagner, R. *The Psychology of Industrial Conflict*. New York: John Wiley and Sons, Inc., 1956.

Strother, G. B. (ed.). *Social Science Approaches to Business Behavior*. Homewood, Illinois: The Dorsey Press, Inc. and Richard D. Irwin, Inc., 1962.

Warner, W. T. *The Corporation in the Emergent American Society*. New York: Harper & Brothers, Publishers, 1962.

Wirtenberger, H. J. *Morality and Business*. Chicago: Loyola University Press, 1962.

INDEX

Contributing Authors

Argyris, Chris, 24, 26-27, 31-32, 40, 44, 78-81, 94-97, 296, 428-429, 443, 478-479, 482-483, 485, 587, 606, 611, 626, 633, 720, 755, 757, 767, 773, 788, 816, 851, 853-855

Barrett, Dermot, 519, 572
Bavelas, Alex, 78, 247, 281, 315, 519, 572, 597, 604, 616
Bernthal, Wilmar F., 7, 74
Brown, Wilfred, 416, 488, 499

Cartwright, Dorwin, 39, 272, 274, 304, 306, 308, 311, 318, 633, 662, 676, 678, 681
Carzo, Rocco, Jr., 416, 441
Clark, James V., 84, 332, 375, 384-385

Davis, Keith, 11, 31, 44, 48-49, 421, 423, 425, 615, 816, 841, 845
Doty, Roy A., 105, 163, 306

Freedman, Robert, Jr., 816, 829

Ghiselli, Edwin E., 105-106, 132, 139-141, 150-151, 190, 228
Gibb, Jack R., 519-520, 760
Golembiewski, Robert T., 247, 267, 277, 279
Guest, Robert H., 79, 382, 720, 793, 801

Haire, Mason, 10, 24, 26, 29, 32, 34, 80, 84-85, 106, 133, 151, 190, 218, 428-429, 433, 439, 446, 477, 706
Henry, W. E., 105, 180, 218, 220, 223-224, 227, 306
Herzberg, Frederick, 36, 39, 332, 375-376, 396, 398-400, 402, 797
Higham, T. M., 530, 537
Huttner, L., 105, 153

Jennings, Eugene E., 81, 110, 215, 221, 247, 249, 589

Kahn, Robert L., 96, 274, 278, 308, 315-317, 379, 459, 462, 466-467, 590, 625, 630-631, 642, 690
Knowles, William H., 7, 9, 31-32, 34
Kuriloff, Arthur H., 745

Leavitt, Harold J., 7, 13, 24, 96, 577
Levy, S., 105, 153
Likert, Rensis, 79, 96, 136, 316-317, 319, 332, 366, 416, 446, 452, 456, 458-459, 462, 479, 481, 483-484, 486-487, 584, 622, 625, 630, 690, 700, 702, 785
Lippitt, Gordon, 720, 780, 789
Livingstone, John L., 416, 476

McFarland, Dalton E., 7, 84
McGregor, Douglas M., 79, 331, 356, 376, 378, 446, 482, 591, 593, 596, 603, 745, 747, 780
McMurry, Robert N., 81, 177, 620, 662-663, 722
Mann, Floyd C., 53, 313, 316-317, 466, 622, 624, 632, 640, 662, 690, 701-702
Maslow, A. H., 331-333, 335, 341-343, 352, 375-376, 378, 380, 395, 486, 531-532, 600, 747
Massarik, Fred, 78, 295, 592, 620
Moore, David G., 7, 59, 220, 421, 424, 858

Nichols, Ralph G., 519, 543

Odiorne, George S., 780, 816, 856

Porter, Lyman W., 106, 133, 139, 151, 190, 225, 228

Rosen, E., 153, 219, 228

Schmidt, Warren H., 49, 248, 289, 301, 321
Schoen, Donald R., 816-817
Scott, William G., 7-8, 40, 415, 417
Spotts, James V., 248, 303
Stieglitz, Harold, 519, 563
Stopol, M., 105, 153

Tannenbaum, Robert, 42, 44, 78, 248, 289, 295, 321, 592, 594-595, 598, 620, 739
This, Leslie, 720, 780, 789
Wald, Robert M., 105, 163, 306
Warner, W. Lloyd, 102-103, 111-112, 119, 220, 224, 229-230, 238

Zander, Alvin, 39, 272, 274, 304, 306, 308, 311, 318, 616, 626, 633, 662, 669

Subject

A

Abegglen, J. C., 112, 119, 220, 224, 230, 238
Adams, Stuart, 278, 385
Adams-Lepley Personal Audit, 174
Adler, Alfred, 334, 343
administration, action-influence ideas in, 28-29; action rules in, 27; categories of recent theoretical developments in, 24-29; internal communica-tion rules in, 27; the jumping-off place in organizational thinking, 25; a normative-analytic model in, 27-28; observation rules in, 27; recent descriptive models in, 25-27
Adorno, T. W., 38, 81
Allen, Louis A., 419, 424
Allport, Gordon W., 539, 593, 617
Andrews, Kenneth R., 45, 53
Anikeeff, A. M., 732
Anthony, E. J., 36, 44, 46, 48, 51-52, 55